Philip D. Hill

STUDIES

IN THE

BOOK OF DANIEL

VOLUME I

BY

ROBERT DICK WILSON, Ph.D., D.D.

WM. H. GREEN PROFESSOR OF SEMITIC LANGUAGES AND
OLD TESTAMENT CRITICISM
PRINCETON THEOLOGICAL SEMINARY

BAKER BOOK HOUSE
Grand Rapids, Michigan

Reprinted 1972
by Baker Book House Company
from the original edition
copyrighted 1917
by Robert Dick Wilson

ISBN: 0-8010-9530-1

PHOTOLITHOPRINTED BY CUSHING - MALLOY, INC.
ANN ARBOR, MICHIGAN, UNITED STATES OF AMERICA
1972

INTRODUCTION

THIS volume is concerned especially with the objections made to the historical statements contained in the book of Daniel, and treats incidentally of chronological, geographical, and philosophical questions. In a second volume, it is my intention to discuss the objections made against the book on the ground of philological assumptions based on the nature of the Hebrew and Aramaic in which it is written. In a third volume, I shall discuss Daniel's relation to the canon of the Old Testament as determining the date of the book, and in connection with this the silence of Ecclesiasticus with reference to Daniel, the alleged absence of an observable influence of Daniel upon post-captivity literature, and the whole matter of apocalyptic literature, especially in its relation to predictive prophecy.

The *method* pursued is to give first of all a discussion of some of the principles involved in the objections considered in the pages following; then, to state the objections with the assumptions on which they are based; next, to give the reasons why these assumptions are adjudged to be false; and, lastly, to sum up in a few words the conclusions to be derived from the discussion. As to the details of my method, it will be observed that I have sought in the case of every objection to confront it with documentary evidence designed to show that the assumptions underlying the objection are contrary to fact. When no direct evidence is procurable either in favor of or against an objection, I have endeavored to show by analogy, or the production of similar instances, that the events or statements recorded in Daniel are possible; and that the objections to these events, or statements, cannot be proved by mere assertion unsupported by testimony.

In the first chapter, *the inadequacy of the argument* from silence to prove that the books of the Old Testament contain misrepresentations, is shown by giving a résumé of the historical documents of the Hebrews, Assyrians, Babylonians, Egyptians, and others, in their relations to one another. A careful reading of this summary of the known evidence ought to convince all unbiased judges that an argument from the silence of one document as to events which are recorded in another, is usually devoid of validity. In many cases, it will be seen that for long periods of time there are no extra-biblical documents whatever; in other cases, there is, for long periods of time, no evidence either biblical or extra-biblical. Again, often when documents of the same time are found, they treat of subjects entirely alien to the subjects treated of in the other, and hence have no bearing on the case. Or, even when they treat of the same subjects, the narrators look at them from a different point of view and one will be intentionally silent where the other enlarges upon the topic.

Chapter two discusses the objections made by Dean Farrar to the very existence of Daniel on the ground that his *name* even is *not mentioned* on the monuments of his time. Here I show, first, that it is not to be expected that the Jewish name of Daniel would ever have been used in Babylonian documents, inasmuch as Nebuchadnezzar changed it to Belteshazzar on his arrival in Babylon; secondly, that the name Belshazzar, under which form the name Belteshazzar might be written in Babylonian, does occur on the Babylonian tablets as the name of several individuals and that one of these may have been the Daniel of our book; thirdly, that it is difficult to make any possible identification of Daniel, owing to the fact that his ancestors are not mentioned in the Bible; fourthly, that even if his ancestors were known, he could not be identified from the monuments, because on them the father or grandfather is never mentioned in the case of slaves, or even of foreigners, except in the case of kings and their children; and lastly, that it is unreasonable to expect to find the name of Daniel upon the monuments, first, because the names of slaves are rarely mentioned; secondly, because the names of slaves are never found as witnesses, and those of foreigners but rarely; thirdly, because the annals and display and building inscriptions of the kings never mention the names of anybody except occasionally the names of the kings they conquer, of an occasional general, and of the members of their own families. In fact, no better illustration than this of Dean Farrar can be found of the fact that a man, however brilliant as a preacher and as a writer and however accomplished as a classical scholar, is but a blind leader of the blind when he attempts to speak upon such complicated matters as those which are involved in an introduction to the book of Daniel, without having first mastered the languages and the literature of Babylon and Persia.

Chapter three treats of the *silence of the other biblical documents and of the monuments* as to an expedition of Nebuchadnezzar, said by Daniel to have been made against Jerusalem in the third year of Jehoiakim. It

will be noted that in this particular case of the alleged
silence of other sources, there is a tacit overlooking of
the testimony to this expedition afforded by the fragments of Berosus, who states that Nebuchadnezzar was
in Palestine at the time when his father Nabopolassar
died, which according to the Babylonian system of
reckoning the years of a king would have been the
third year of Jehoiakim. It will be noted, further, that
the critics in their allegations of error against the author
of Daniel have failed to consider the whole matter of the
different ways of reckoning the regnal years of a king,
and the different times at which, among different nations, the year was supposed to begin. This frequently
renders it very difficult to determine the corresponding
months and years of a king's reign in the different
countries, and should make us slow in asserting that
the third year of a king in one document might not
be the same as the fourth year in another. Again,
I show in this chapter that Jeremiah and the books
of Kings and Chronicles do not purport to give us
a complete history of the times of Nebuchadnezzar,
and that, hence, it is not fair to say that an event which
is mentioned in Daniel cannot be true because it is
not mentioned in these other writings; and, further,
that the monuments of Nebuchadnezzar say nothing
definite about his military expeditions, except about
one to Egypt in his thirty-seventh year, although they
do show conclusively that he was king of Syria and
many other countries, whose kings are said to do his
bidding. Lastly, it is shown that in the fragments of his
history of Babylon, Berosus supports the statement of
Daniel, that Nebuchadnezzar made an expedition to
Palestine before he was crowned king of Babylon, and
carried away spoils from Judea which were placed in his

temple at Babylon, and that there is no statement
made in Daniel about this expedition which is in any
way controverted by any other direct testimony.

Chapter four answers a further question connected
with the expedition of Nebuchadnezzar against Jerusalem in the third year of Jehoiakim, arising from the
charge that the author of Daniel made *false interpretations* of the sources known to him.   An exami-
nation of the alleged sources of Daniel's information
showed that he does not contradict these sources nor
make erroneous interpretation of them; but that, on
the contrary, it is the critics who, on the ground of
their own implications and conjectures and sometimes
of their crass ignorance of geography and of the historical situation, have really manufactured or imagined a case against Daniel. No more astonishing
example of the fabrication of evidence can be found
in the history of criticism than the use which is made of
the statements of the Old Testament with regard to
Carchemish, in order to show that Nebuchadnezzar
cannot have moved against Jerusalem as long as this
fortress was in the hands of the Egyptians.   The critics
of Daniel have assumed not merely that the Egyptians
had Carchemish in their possession, but also that it
lay on the way from Jerusalem to Babylon, so as to cut
off, if in an enemy's hands, a possible retreat of Nebuchadnezzar from Palestine to Babylon.   A knowledge
of the position of Carchemish and of the lines of traffic
from Damascus to the Euphrates should have precluded
them from statements so unscientific from a geographical and military point of view.

Chapter five investigates the *use of the word for king*,
especially in the Semitic languages.   This discussion
shows that Nebuchadnezzar may have been called king

before his father's death; and will serve also as an introduction to the discussion of the kingship of Belshazzar and that of Darius the Mede, in that it illustrates that there might be two kings of the same place at the same time.

Chapter six considers the objections made to the book of Daniel on the ground of what it says in regard to *Belshazzar.* Here, it is shown that Belshazzar, the son of Nabunaid, may, according to the usage of those times, have been also the son of Nebuchadnezzar; that there is good reason to suppose that he was king of the Chaldeans before he became king of Babylon; that he may have been king of Babylon long enough to justify the writer of Daniel in speaking of his first year as king of that city; that the fact that he is not called king elsewhere by his contemporaries is simply an argument from silence, paralleled by other instances; and that neither the biblical sources outside of Daniel, nor the monuments, say that any man other than Belshazzar was last *de facto* king of the city of Babylon. In short, it is shown that the evidence fails to substantiate the assertion that the statements of Daniel in regard to Belshazzar are false.

Chapters seven to thirteen treat of all the questions that have been raised concerning *Darius the Mede* and the Median Empire, showing that if we identify Darius with the Gubaru of the inscriptions, there is no objective reason for denying the truth of the biblical statements with regard to him. It is shown, that Darius may have been the name of a Mede; that he may have been the son of a man called Xerxes (*i. e.*, Ahasuerus) of the seed of the Medes; that he may have reigned at the same time as Cyrus and as sub-king under him; that he could have appointed one hundred and twenty satraps over his kingdom, even though it was restricted to Chaldea and Babylonia alone; that he may have had a den of lions, containing lions sufficient to have devoured the conspirators against Daniel and their families; that he could not have been a reflection of Darius Hystaspis, or of any one, or all, of the Persian kings of the name Darius; in short, that, granting that Darius the Mede had two names (for which supposition there is abundant evidence from the analogy of other kings), there is no ground for impugning the veracity of the account of Darius the Mede as given in the book of Daniel.

To particularize, it is shown, in chapter seven, that it is pure *conjecture* to suppose that the author of Daniel thought *that Darius* the Mede *preceded Cyrus* the Persian as king of Babylon, or that Cyrus succeeded to the empire of Babylon on the death of the Median Darius; further, it is shown, that Darius the Mede may have had a *second name*, Gubaru (Gobryas), and that he probably received the government of Chaldea and Babylon from Cyrus.

Chapter eight treats of the statements of Daniel with regard to the part taken by the Medes and Persians respectively in the *conquest of Babylon*, and shows that they are in harmony with the monumental evidence.

Chapter nine discusses the allegation that the author of Daniel was *deficient in knowledge* and confused in thought in the statements which he makes with regard to the Persian empire, especially with regard to the names and number of its kings, the absolute rulership of Darius the Mede, and the division and number of its satrapies.

Chapter ten answers the assumption that Darius the Mede has been *confused with Darius Hystaspis*, because each of them is said to have organized his kingdom into satrapies. It is shown that the satrapies varied so in extent, that there may easily have been one hundred and twenty of them in the dominions over which Darius the Mede was made king; and that Darius Hystaspis did not originate the government by satraps, since the Assyrian monarchs, especially Sargon the Second, had organized their possessions in the same manner.

Chapters eleven and twelve treat of the assumption that Darius the Mede is a *reflection of Darius Hystaspis*. By a careful comparison of what Daniel says about Darius the Mede with what is known from all sources about Darius Hystaspis, the evidence is given to show that, whatever else Darius the Mede may have been, he cannot have been a reflection of Darius Hystaspis. In chapter eleven are discussed the names and families of the two kings, showing that in these particulars Darius the Mede cannot have been the reflection of Darius the Persian.

Chapter twelve shows how *the two kings differ* in the age and manner of their becoming king, in the names and extent of the kingdoms over which they ruled, in their relation to other kings, in their methods of government, and in their personal characteristics.

Chapter thirteen treats of the *alleged confusion* by the author of Daniel of Xerxes and Darius Hystaspis, and of his further alleged confusion of this alleged confused Xerxes-Darius with Darius Codomannus. It treats, further, of the alleged belief of the author, that there was a triumphant repulse by Alexander the Great of an attack on Greece by this confused Xerxes-Darius-Hystaspis-Codomannus.

Chapter fourteen gives the latest evidence to show

that *Susa* in the time of Daniel's vision was in all probability a province of the Babylonian empire.

Chapter fifteen gives the latest evidence from the monuments and from medical science tending to confirm the historicity of all the statements made in Daniel about the fact, the character, and the duration, of the *madness of Nebuchadnezzar*.

Chapter sixteen discusses the theory that the edicts of the king are impossible. I here show that those *edicts cannot be* called either morally, legally, physically, or historically *impossible*. That they are not *morally* impossible is shown from analogy by the edicts of the Roman emperors, and by the tenet of the Roman hierarchy that the church may justly inflict on heretics the penalty of death; and, also, by a study of the character of Nebuchadnezzar as revealed in his monuments, and of Darius the Mede as revealed in Daniel, in comparison with such tyrants as Henry VIII of England, Philip II of Spain, and Louis XIV of France. That they are not *legally* impossible is shown by a review of what is known of the laws of ancient Babylon and Persia. That the execution of these decrees was not *physically* impossible is shown by numerous examples of similar cases given in the histories of Assyria and Babylonia. Many examples prove the commonness of burning in the fire as a method of punishment. The possibility of the destruction of the one hundred and twenty satraps and their families by lions is shown from the fact that the monuments of the kings of Assyria say that they had menageries containing "all the animals of the mountains and of the plains," including elephants, panthers, and lions. Further, it is shown that lions at that time were the pest of the Euphrates Valley, hundreds of them being killed in a

single hunting expedition, and that in one case mentioned by Ashurnasirapal, king of Assyria, fifty young
lions were captured alive and shut up by him in the city
of Calach. Finally, the assertion that there is an *historical* impossibility involved in the decrees recorded in
Daniel is shown to be the baseless fabric of the critics'
imagination, inasmuch as of the many decrees which
the monarchs of Babylon and Persia must have made,
only one or two have come down to us. The opinion of
certain men to-day that these decrees could not have
been made, must yield to the positive evidence. To
deny the historical possibility of the decrees is a pure
case of *opinion versus evidence*.

Chapters seventeen and eighteen discuss the possibility
of the use of *the word "Chaldean"* in the sixth century B.C.
to denote the wise men, or a part of the wise men of
Babylon, and the relation in which Daniel stood to the
wise men. The evidence gathered together in these
chapters shows that there is no sufficient reason for
denying that the word "Chaldean" to denote a class
of Babylonian wise men may have been employed as
early as 600 B.C.; nor for denying that a strict Jew may
have been a member of the class of Babylonian wise
men to which Daniel is said to have belonged. The use
of the words for *wise* in all the Semitic languages proves,
that the term is always used in an honorable sense, and
that it is a groundless supposition of the critics that any
blame was ever attached by the writers of the Old Testament, or by the Jewish scribes, to any class of real wise
men to whatever nation they may have belonged.

Hoping that this volume may confirm the faith of any
wavering ones in the historicity of a book which was so
highly prized and so often quoted by our Lord and his
apostles, and that it may show particularly to men who

have a due regard for the laws of evidence, how flimsy are the grounds on which some would reject the testimony and impugn the veracity of the writer of Daniel, I send it forth upon its mission in the world. If it shall have served no other purpose, it has at least accomplished this:—it has convinced the writer that the methods pursued by many so-called higher critics are illogical, irrational, and *unscientific*. They are illogical because they beg the question at issue. They are irrational because they assume that historic facts are self-evident, and that they can set limits to the possible. They are unscientific because they base their conclusions on incomplete inductions and on a practical claim of omniscience.

Before closing my introduction, a few words ought to be said about the sources from which I have derived my evidence. Generally, it will be observed that I have appealed to the standard editions of texts in the original languages in which they are written. When there exist good translations as in the case of some of the classical historians, I have made free use of these translations, always, however, after comparison with the original texts. In the case of others, I have secured as good versions as possible, my son, Philip Howard Wilson, A.B. (died June 27, 1913), honor man in classics of the class of 1911 at Princeton University, being responsible for many of the translations from the classical writers whose works have not yet been rendered into English.

In the case of Assyrian and Babylonian documents, I have made use, where possible, of the *Keilinschriftliche Bibliothek* (denoted by *K. B.*), translating from the German version, revised in the light of the transliterated Assyrio-Babylonian text. In doubtful and important connections I have consulted the original texts, so far as they are published. This method has been pursued, also, with all other original documents; that is, I have used the best version available, but always in comparison with the original texts.

My hearty thanks are due to the Rev. Prof. Jesse L. Cotton, D.D., of Louisville, to the Rev. Oswald T. Allis, Ph.D., of Princeton, and to the Rev. J. B. Willson, M.A., B.D., for the invaluable assistance which they have given me in the preparation of this volume.

R. D. W.

Princeton, N. J.,
    April, 1917.

CONTENTS

	PAGE
INTRODUCTION	III

CHAPTER

I.—THE ARGUMENT FROM SILENCE . .	I
II.—WAS DANIEL AN HISTORICAL CHARACTER?	24
III.—JEHOIAKIM'S THIRD YEAR AND THE ARGUMENT FROM SILENCE . .	43
IV.—NEBUCHADNEZZAR'S EXPEDITION AGAINST JERUSALEM	60
V.—THE USE OF THE WORD "KING" . .	83
VI.—BELSHAZZAR	96
VII.—DARIUS THE MEDE	128
VIII.—THE MEDES AND THE CONQUEST OF BABYLON	145
IX.—DARIUS THE MEDE AND THE KINGS OF PERSIA	160
EXCURSUS ON WORDS FOR LAND AND PEOPLE	186
X.—DARIUS THE MEDE NOT A CONFUSION WITH DARIUS HYSTASPIS . .	200
XI.—DARIUS THE MEDE NOT A REFLECTION OF DARIUS HYSTASPIS . .	221

Contents

CHAPTER   PAGE

XII.—DARIUS THE MEDE NOT A REFLECTION (*Continued*) 238

XIII.—OTHER ALLEGED CONFUSIONS OF KINGS 264

XIV.—SUSA 276

XV. NEBUCHADNEZZAR'S MADNESS . . 283

XVI.—WERE THE EDICTS OF THE KINGS POSSIBLE? 296

XVII.—THE CHALDEANS 319

EXCURSUS ON THE CHALDEANS . . 341

XVIII.—DANIEL AND THE WISE MEN . . 367

STUDIES IN
THE BOOK OF DANIEL

CHAPTER I

THE ARGUMENT FROM SILENCE

I SHALL begin the consideration of the historicity of Daniel and of the book of Daniel with a discussion of the argument from silence, not merely because of its intrinsic importance, but because of its bearing upon many of the objections made against the existence of Daniel himself and against the authenticity and genuineness of the book which bears his name. Before considering these objections, it may be well to state explicitly what is meant in this connection by an argument from silence. When the argument from silence is invoked against a statement of a record of any kind, it is implied that the statement is probably not true because there is no evidence to be gathered from other sources of information in support or confirmation of it. It is a purely negative argument. For example, our Lord is said to have accompanied his parents to a feast at Jerusalem in his twelfth year and to have been present at several feasts in the same place during the years of his ministry. Nothing is said in the gospel records about his attendance at the feasts during the period intervening between his twelfth year and the beginning of his Judean ministry. It would be an argument from silence to maintain that Jesus was never at a feast at Jerusalem during this long period of his life, inasmuch as no mention of his having been there is to be found either in the gospels, or in any other credible document. But the argument is clearly inconclusive and unsatisfactory, because it may be used as well to show the probability that he was there at many, or all, of the feasts of the intervening years,—that it was his habit to attend the feasts. Certainly, the fact that his presence at a feast in his twelfth year is mentioned in but one of the gospels does not render that statement improbable. Nor does the fact that his attendance at certain other feasts during the years of his ministry is stated in but one of the four gospels render such an attendance improbable. The commands laid upon the Israelites to go up three times a year to the feasts, the rigid observance of these commands by other Israelites of that period, and the well-known obedience of our Lord to the injunctions of the law, would make it probable that he observed the feasts. The fact that he is said to have been present at several of them would imply that he probably was present at more. But the mere failure of more than one of the sources, or even of all of them put together, to mention his attendance at a given feast during the whole period from his twelfth year onward, cannot be regarded as proof of his absence from it.

The failure, therefore, of any given authority to mention an event recorded in another, or the fact that a given event is recorded in only one authority, while others pass it by in silence, does not prove that the

event did not occur. Most events of antiquity of which
we have any knowledge are mentioned in but one
contemporary source of information. For most of the
history of Cyrus, Cambyses, Smerdis, Darius, and
Xerxes, we are absolutely dependent for our information upon Herodotus, often at best a second-hand and
unreliable source. For Artaxerxes I, Darius II, and the
first part of the reign of Artaxerxes II, we have the
fragments of Ctesias, the partial accounts of Xenophon,
and allusions and short references in Thucydides and a
few other writers. For the history of Assyria and
Babylonia, and for that of Syria, Phenicia, and Egypt
before 500 B.C., we have no historian, strictly so-called,
either native or foreign, who was contemporaneous with
the events which transpired. For the history of the
Hittites and for that of Elam, Lydia, Media, and Persia,
we have no native historians, of any age, whether contemporaneous or not. For the history of all of these
countries from 500 B.C. to 300 B.C., we are limited as to
contemporaneous historians to the Greeks, especially
to Herodotus, Ctesias, Thucydides, and Xenophon.
About 300 B.C., a native Egyptian, Manetho by name,
wrote in Greek what purported to be a history of Egypt
from the earliest times, which, he asserted, he had derived from the records of the Egyptians. About the
same time, also in Greek, Berosus wrote a history of the
Babylonians; Menander, a history of Tyre; and Nicolaus, a history of Damascus. Unfortunately, fragments
only of these historians have been preserved to us,
mostly excerpts found in Josephus and Eusebius.

But while, strictly speaking, we have no histories
from any of the nations who came into contact with the
ancient Israelites, we have from some of them a large
number of documents affording us for certain periods

the sources, or materials, from which to construct a more or less continuous history, and to obtain for certain epochs and individuals a more or less satisfactory knowledge of their civilization and especially of their political conditions and relations. The relative and even the absolute chronology of the times in which the Israelites flourished is becoming clearer and more definite. The geographical terminology and limitations are becoming known. The laws, manners, customs, science, art, and religion are becoming revealed. Some kings of Assyria, such as the Tiglath-Pilesers, the Shalmanesers, Ashurnaṣirpal, Sargon, Sennacherib, Esarhaddon, and Ashurbanipal have left us annals which supply the place of histories and cause these kings to stand out before us as real characters. Hammurabi, Merodach-Baladan, Nebuchadnezzar, and Nabunaid, kings of Babylon, have left us inscriptions from which we can in a measure construct their biographies. The inscriptions of Nabunaid, Cyrus, and Darius Hystaspis enable us, also, to supplement what the Greek historians and the biblical writers have to say about the early days of Persia; while the Egyptian and Phenician records, though not as satisfactory, give us at least a chronological background and check for much of the history. The records of the Hittites, Lydians, and Elamites, also, are being resurrected in part from the graves of oblivion, and even the Arabian deserts are yielding up their long-buried secrets.

But when all these discoveries are taken into consideration, they present at best but a very imperfect view of the general or particular history of the nations of antiquity, that preceded the empires of Greece and Rome. It is impossible as yet to write a continuous history of any one of them. The records are so incomplete and sporadic that they fail frequently to give us information where we most desire to have it. Moreover, when we compare the records of one country with those of another, we find that most frequently those of a given country fail to mention matters which are found recorded at length in the documents of another. Most of them abstain from mentioning occurrences derogatory to the dignity of their kings or to the honor of their country. It is often only from silence or inference that we can supply the gaps, which indicate defeat in the midst of victory, or periods of decay lying between periods of comparative prosperity. The silence of one record, therefore, is no disproof of the accuracy or truthfulness of another. It does not even show that the writer of the record was not cognizant of the event. It is simply and absolutely no evidence at all.

In order to show the futility of the argument from silence when adduced against the trustworthiness of an event, or the existence of a person, mentioned in the Old Testament records, and as a special introduction to the discussion of the following chapters which are chiefly concerned with proving the veracity of the statements of the book of Daniel with regard to historical matters, I shall now proceed to give a series of parallels illustrating the fact of the silence of certain documents with reference to the statements made in others.

I.   In the *Scriptures themselves* many examples can be cited of the silence of one book with regard to an event which is mentioned in another. For example, in Isaiah xx, 1, Sargon is called king of Assyria, although he is not mentioned elsewhere even by name. In view of the fact that Sargon was one of the greatest of the kings of Assyria; that according to the monuments it was he,

or his general, who actually captured the city of
Samaria, which Shalmaneser, his immediate predecessor,
had besieged; and that he reigned from 722 B.C., the
year of Samaria's fall, till 705 B.C., *i. e.*, through a large
part of Hezekiah's reign, this silence of the Scriptures
with regard to him is a noteworthy fact, especially
since, according to his own inscriptions, Sargon fought
with Gaza, Ashdod, Samaria, Damascus, Egypt,
and other powers in the immediate neighborhood of
Jerusalem.

Again, it is said in Ezra iv, 10, that the great and
noble Asnapper brought various peoples over and settled them in Samaria.   Whoever this Asnapper may
have been, he is not mentioned elsewhere in the Scriptures, unless he be the same as "Esarhaddon, king of
Assyria" who, according to Ezra iv, 2, had brought the
inhabitants of Samaria thither.   But if Asnapper be
Esarhaddon, this transaction of his, so great in its
bearing on the history of the Jews, is not mentioned
elsewhere in the Scriptures.   Esarhaddon, it is true, is
named in 2 Kings xix, 37 and in the parallel passage, Is.
xxxvii, 38, as the son and successor of Sennacherib, and
is referred to in 2 Chron. xxxiii, 11–13 as the "king of
Assyria" who captured and carried captive to Babylon
and afterwards released Manasseh, king of Judah; but
nothing is said in any of these books, or elsewhere, of a
settlement of nations made by him, or by anyone under
him, in Samaria, or in any other place.   If the importa-
tion described in 2 Kings xvii, 24–41 refers to this
event, it is remarkable that out of the five names of the
peoples imported, as given in Kings, only one, that of
Babylon, should be given in the list of names found in
Ezra iv, 9, 10.   If, however, as is more probable,
Asnapper be Ashurbanipal, the successor of Esar-

haddon, this transaction of his is mentioned nowhere else, either in the Scriptures or in the monuments.

II. Parallels are numerous, also, where the *Scriptures* are silent as to events or persons that are mentioned on the *Monuments*. For example, Shalmaneser III of Assyria (860–825 B.C.) mentions a campaign against the king of Damascus and his allies, among whom was Ahab of Israel, who contributed 2000 chariots and 10,000 warriors to the army of Hadadezer, king of Damascus.[1] The Scriptures do not mention this event in the career of Ahab, nor Shalmaneser's five later campaigns against Damascus and her allies in 849, 848, 845, 842 (?), and 839 B.C.[2]

Shalmaneser claims also that in his eighteenth year, 842 B.C., he received the tribute of Jehu, son of Omri.[3] No mention of this is found in the Scriptures. Again, Sargon says that he subdued the land of Judah[4] although there is no mention in the Scriptures of this conquest and only one mention of his name, to wit, in Isaiah xx, 1.

III. Further, the *Scriptures* in general are silent as to the *history* of the great world monarchies, and also of the smaller kingdoms, in the midst of which the Israelites were placed.

For example, of the history of Egypt from Solomon's time down to the time of Alexander, only a very few persons and events are named in the Scriptures.[5]

---

[1] *Monolith Inscription*, KB i, 172.

[2] Winckler's *History of Babylonia and Assyria*, pp. 220, 221.

[3] III R 5, No. 6;. KB i, 140, 150. [4] KB ii, 36.

[5] (1) *Solomon* married the daughter of Pharaoh, king of Egypt,[1] for whom he built a special house outside of the city of David,[2] and for whom he received as dower the city of Gezer.[3] Solomon had commer-

---

[1] 1 Kings iii, 1. [2] 1 Kings vii, 8; 2 Chron. viii, 11.
[3] 1 Kings ix, 16.

8   The Book of Daniel

IV. The instances, also, are numerous where the Scriptures mention *events* and *persons* that are not mentioned on the monuments.[1]

Among *persons* we need only name Abraham, Lot, Isaac, Ishmael, Jacob, Esau, Joseph, Moses, Aaron, all the judges, and their antagonists; all the prophets; Saul, David, Solomon, and, in fact, all the kings of both Israel and Judah, except Azariah, Ahaz, Hezekiah, and

cial dealings with Egypt, especially in horses.[1] The king of Egypt received Hadad, the Edomite of the king's seed in Edom, gave him houses and lands, and for a wife the sister of Tahpanes, his queen; and a son of Hadad, Genubath by name, the issue of this marriage, was among the king of Egypt's sons in the house of Pharaoh.[2] Jeroboam, the son of Nebat, having fled from the wrath of Solomon, was received by Shishak, the then king of Egypt, and remained in Egypt until the death of Solomon.[3]

(2) In the reign of *Rehoboam*, we are told that Jeroboam returned out of Egypt to Shechem at the summons of the people[4]; and that Shishak, in Rehoboam's fifth year, came up against Jerusalem and took away all the king's treasures,[5] and captured all his fenced cities,[6] and made his people servants of the king of Egypt.[7]

(3) In the reign of *Asa*, Zerah the Cushite, came against Judah and was defeated at Mareshah.[8]

(4) *Hoshea*, king of Israel, conspired against Shalmaneser, king of Assyria, and sent messengers to So, king of Egypt.[9]

(5) The Rabshakeh of Sennacherib, king of Assyria, accused *Hezekiah* of trusting for help to the king of Egypt. Sennacherib heard that Tirhakeh, king of Ethiopia, had come out against him.[10]

(6) Thebes (*No*) was captured and her inhabitants carried away into captivity.[11]

(7) In *Josiah's* days, Pharaoh-Necho, king of Egypt, came up against the king of Assyria to the river Euphrates; and king Josiah went against him and met him at Megiddo.[12]

[1] Rawlinson's *Bampton Lectures* for 1859.

[1] 1 Kings x, 28, 29; 2 Chron. i, 16, 17; ix, 28.
[2] 1 Kings xi, 14–22.
[3] 1 Kings xi, 26, 40.
[4] 1 Kings xii, 2–20
[5] 1 Kings xiv, 25, 26; 2 Chron. xii, 9.
[6] 2 Chron. xii, 4.
[7] 2 Chron. xii, 8.
[8] 2 Chron. xiv, 9–15.
[9] 2 Kings xvii, 1–4.
[10] 2 Kings xviii, 19–21; xix, 9, 10.
[11] Nahum iii, 8–10.
[12] 2 Kings xxiii, 27–34.

Manasseh, of the kingdom of Judah, and Omri, Ahab, Jehu, Menahem, Pekah, and Hoshea, of the kingdom of Israel. Nor do we find on the monuments the names of Zerubbabel, Daniel, Esther, Mordecai, Ezra, or Nehemiah, nor of any of the high priests from Aaron down to Jaddua, except of Johanan, the predecessor of the last named.[1] Nor do we find in any hitherto discovered monuments the names of Jabin, king of Hazor, of Barak and Eglon, kings of Moab, of Cushan-Rishathaim, king of Aram-Naharaim, nor of Nahash, Hanun, and Baalis, kings of the Ammonites.

Among *events* not mentioned except in the Scriptures, are the sojourn in Egypt, the plagues, the exodus, the wanderings, the conquest, the wars of the Judges and of David and Solomon, the expedition of Zerah, king of Ethiopia (Cush), the wars of Israel and Judah with each other and with the immediately surrounding tribes and cities (except what is recorded on the Moabite stone), the whole story of the relations between

---

(8) Nebuchadnezzar defeated Necho's army at Carchemish in the fourth year of *Jehoiakim.*[1]

(9) Pharaoh-*Hophra* was to be delivered into the hands of his enemies.[2]

(10) Pharaoh-*Hophra's* army caused the raising for a short time of Nebuchadnezzar's siege of Jerusalem[3]; but the Egyptians were soon compelled to return to Egypt.[4]

(11) After the fall of Jerusalem, *Johanan*, the son of Kareah and all the captains of the forces of the Jews and all the people, men and women and children, and the king's daughters, and Jeremiah the prophet, and his scribe Baruch, went down to Egypt to the city of Tahpanhes.[5]

(12) *Jeremiah* prophesied at Tahpanhes, that Nebuchadnezzar would set his throne upon the stones that he had hidden at that place[6]; and that the men of Judah who had come down to Egypt should be consumed there.[7]

[1] Sachau *Aramäische Papyrus*, p. 5.

---

[1] Jer. xlvi, 2.   [2] Jer. xliv, 30.   [3] Jer. xxxvii, 5.   [4] *Id.*, v. 7.
[5] Jer. xliii, 5-7.   [6] *Id.*, v. 10.   [7] Jer. xliv, 27.

Judah and Babylon from Merodach-Baladan down to Cyrus, and, also, of those between the Jews and the Persians in general, and in particular, except the information supplied by the lately discovered Egyptian papyri.

V. There are numerous decades and even centuries of *Israelitish history* as to which there is a universal silence in the *Scriptures*. For example, nothing is stated as to the history of the people during their long sojourn in Egypt, except a long account of why they went there and another of why and how they came out. Thirty-eight years of their sojourn in the wilderness are relieved by scarcely a notice of events. The same is true of numerous decades in the time of the judges, and of long periods of time in the history of nearly all the great kings of Israel and Judah. The forty-seven chapters of the books of Kings contain all that is said of the history of Israel from the accession of Solomon to the destruction of Jerusalem! Seven verses only are devoted to the events of the reign of Jeroboam II, who was the greatest king of the Northern Kingdom and ruled forty years; and a like number to those of Azariah, king of Judah, who reigned for fifty-two years! Eighteen verses only are given to the fifty-five years of Manasseh, most of them taken up with a description of his idolatry and of the punishment certain to follow.[1]

VI. There are numerous decades and centuries of *Israelitish history*, as to which there is absolute silence on the *Monuments*.

For example, on the Egyptian monuments, there is but one reference to Israel down to the time of Shishak, that is, in the song of triumph of Merenptah, in which

[1] 2 Kings xxi, 1-18.

he says: "The people of Israel is laid waste, their crops are not."[1] These two monarchs, are separated, according to Petrie, by a period of 250 years. After Shishak, there is no reference on the Egyptian monuments to any relations between Egypt and either Israel or Judah.

The first mention of the Israelites on the Assyrian monuments is that by Shalmaneser III in the narrative of his campaign made in 854 B.C.[2] Twelve years later, he received the tribute of Jehu the son of Omri. Then, there is silence for about forty years, till Adad-Nirari mentions "the land of Omri."[3] The next notice is more than sixty years later in the records of Tiglath-Pileser IV, who mentions Jauhazi of the land of Judah as among his tributaries,[4] and says that he ruled over all lands from the rising of the sun to the land of Egypt.[5] He received, also, the tribute of Menahem of the city of Samaria,[6] and speaks, on a fragment, of the land of Beth-Omri, all of whose inhabitants, together with their possessions, he carried away to Assyria, having killed Pekah their king and set up Hoshea in his place.[7] Shalmaneser IV, the king who besieged Samaria, reigned for five years (727–722 B.C.), but has left to us but one inscription.[8] Sargon,[9] tells of his subjugating Judah[10]; and that he besieged and took Samaria, adding,[11] that he carried 27,290 men away into captivity with 50 chariots,

---

[1] Petrie, *History of Egypt*, iii, 114.

[2] Pinches, *The Old Testament in the Light of the Historical Records of Babylonia and Assyria*, pp. 329–332.

[3] *Stone Inscription of Calah*, 12.   [4] *Nimrud*, 61.

[5] *Id.*, 3, 4.   [6] *Annals*, 50.   [7] KB ii, 31, 32.

[8] This is on a lion's weight, and gives nothing but the words, "Palace of Shalmaneser, king of Assyria; two minas of the king" (KB ii, 32).

[9] *Nimrud Inscription.*   [10] *Annals.*   [11] *Display Inscription*, 24.

leaving the remainder in possession of their goods,
but appointing over them his own officials and imposing
on them the tribute which they had formerly paid.
He adds, that he plundered the whole land of Bit-Omri[1];
that he conquered Samaria and the whole land of
Bit-Omri,[2] and finally,[3] that he carried away captive
and settled in the city of Samaria the people of Tamud,
Ibadidi, Marsimani, Haiapa, and the distant Arbai,
who inhabited the wilderness, who knew neither scholar
nor scribe, and who had never before brought tribute to
any king.

The references to Judah and its affairs by Sennacherib
are numerous[4]; but from his death in 680 B.C. to the fall
of Nineveh about 606 B.C., the only mention of Judah
is found in the parallel lists of Esarhaddon and Ashurbanipal, where Manasseh is called by the former, "King
of the city of Judah," and by the latter, "King of the land
of Judah."[5] Esarhaddon informs us, indeed, that he was
king of the kings of Egypt, of Patros, and of Ethiopia,[6]
and of all the kings of the land of the Hittites, including
Manasseh king of Judah.[7] Ashurbanipal, son of Esarhaddon, says, also, that his father entered Egypt and
overthrew Tirhakeh, king of Ethiopia, and destroyed his
army, conquering both Egypt and Ethiopia and taking
countless prisoners, changing the names of their cities,
and giving them new names, entrusting his servants with
the government and imposing tribute upon them.[8] He
names, moreover, their kings and the cities they ruled
over,[9] and tells of his conquest of Tyre.[10] He mentions,
further, Psammetichus, king of Egypt, his revolt and

[1] Hall XIV.   [2] Pavement Inscription, IV.
[3] Annals, 94–97.   [4] KAT, 285–332.
[5] KAT, 354–357, and KB ii, 49, 131, and 239.
[6] KAT, 336, and KB ii, 151.   [7] KB ii, 149.
[8] KAT, 338, and KB ii, 159–169.   [9] *Id.*, 161–163.   [10] *Id.*, 169–171.

his overthrow;[1] and his wars with the grandsons of Merodach-Baladan, king of the Chaldeans;[2] and with the kings of the Arabians, Edom, Ammon, Moab, and Nabatea.[3] Yet, except the mention of Manasseh as being among the twenty-two vassals of the land of the Hittites, no notice of Judah is found on the Assyrian monuments after about 685 B. C.; that is, after the reigns of Hezekiah and Sennacherib.

On the Babylonian documents, neither Israel, nor Judah, nor anyone nor anything connected with either, is ever mentioned; though we know from one fragment of an historical inscription of Nebuchadnezzar that he invaded Egypt.[4] Nabunaid, also, speaks of the kings of Phenicia[5] and of the tribute of the kings of the land of Amurru;[6] and says that he mustered the scattered peoples (*ummania rapshati*) from Gaza on the frontier of Egypt by the Upper Sea to beyond the Euphrates as far as the Lower Sea.

VII. There are numerous decades, or longer periods, during the history of Israel, which are practically *a blank* as far as the outside world is concerned, the most that is known concerning foreign nations being the occasional mention of the name of a king. The contemporaneous, or synchronous, history of these kings is consequently frequently impossible to establish; and even their order and the length of their reigns, we are often unable to determine.

For example, in the history of Egypt from about 1200 B. C. during the reign of the ten kings from Rameses III to Rameses XII inclusive, the succession "has long been doubtful and is not yet certain"; and

---

[1] *Id.*, 177.　　[2] *Id.*, 211–213.　　[3] *Id.*, 215–229.　　[4] KB iii, ii, 140.
[5] Nabunaid-Cyrus *Chronicle*, Col. ii, 3.
[6] *i. e.*, Phenicia-Palestine, Cyrus *Cylinder*, 29, 30.

even after the time of the Ramessids but little is known of the history of Egypt down to the time of the Persian conquest.[1]

Similarly, to cite a few instances from the history of Babylon and Assyria, for the interval—more than half a millennium—between the end of the First or Hammurabi Dynasty and the time of Nebuchadnezzar I; for the period—about two hundred years—between Tiglath-Pileser I and Ashurnaṣirpal II and for the much shorter interval—about twenty years—between the death of Ashurbanipal and the fall of Nineveh the historical information is very meager. Even regarding the Neo-baby-lonian period we know comparatively little. There are only a few historical inscriptions and the numerous building inscriptions and contract tablets do not supply their deficiencies to any marked degree.

[1] Petrie, *History of Egypt*, iii, 137. Of these kings, Mr. Petrie says as follows: "Of Rameses V, the stele of Silsileh is the only serious monument of the reign and that contains nothing but beautiful phrases" (*id.*, 171); of Rameses VI, "There is not a single dated monument of this reign, and no building, but only steles, statues, and small objects, to preserve the name" (*id.*, 173); of Rameses VII, "No dates exist, the works and objects are all unimportant" (*id.*, 177); of Rameses VIII, "The stele of Hora, an official of Busiris, is the only monument of this reign to reward the search" (*id.*, 177); of Ramees IX, "This king is only known by a vase and a scarab" (*id.*, 177); of Rameses X, "with the exception of an inquiry into the thefts from the tomb of Amenhotep I, we know nothing of the history of this reign" (*id.*, 183); of Rameses XI, there is nothing but a "list of documents about the necropolis robberies" (*id.*, 185); of Rameses XII, "there is no more to be said about this reign than about the other obscure reigns before it" (*id.*, 187).

Again, of the reign of Men-kheper, from 1074 to 1025 B. C., he says, "There are but poor remains of this long reign" (*id.*, 211); of the next ruler, "There is nothing to show that this prince reigned" (*id.*, 214). The documents of Pasebkhanu, 1006–952 B. C., give merely his cartouche and call him a son of Pinezem (*id.*, 219). There is but one important document from the reign of Nesibadadu, 1102–1076 B. C. (*id.*, 220). Of Pasebkhanu I, 1076–1035 B. C., we know that he refounded a temple at Tanis and surrounded it with a mighty wall and that he built a

As to the documents from Tyre, Sidon, Moab, and other sources, they are so few, short, and fragmentary, that it would be utterly impossible to relate them in any way with the general history of the ancient world, or to one another, were it not for the annals of the Israelites, and of the Assyrio-Babylonians. The almost entire absence of documents from Persian sources must also be noticed here. Strictly speaking, with the exception of the Nabunaid-Cyrus *Chronicle* and the Cyrus *Cylinder*, which are both written in Babylonian alone, the polylingual *Behistun Inscriptions* of Darius Hystaspis are the only historical documents from the Persians; and from the Medes not one document has survived. Some historical information, it is true, may be gathered from miscellaneous inscriptions of the Persian kings, Darius Hystaspis, Xerxes, and the

---

temple at Gizeh (*id.*, 221–233); of his successor, Neferkara,. 1035–1031 B. C., we have nothing except the mention of his name in Manetho (*id.*, 223); of the next king, Amenemapt, 1031–1022 B.C., we know only that he continued to build the temple at Gizeh (*id.*, 223); of the next king, Siamen, 1022–996 B.C., we know nothing of importance, except that he built a temple at Tanis (*id.*, 224, 225); of the next, Hez-haq-ra, 987–952 B.C., scarcely anything is known (*id.*, 225). Of the kings of the twenty-second dynasty, "very little is known about the reign of Uasarkon I, 930–894 B. C. (*id.*, 240); Takerat I, 901–876 B. C., was formerly not even recognized as king (*id.*, 244); of Takerat II, 856–831 B. C., no historical facts are recorded (*id.*, 254); of Shishak IV, 782–742 B.C., "nothing whatever is known" (*id.*, 259).

In the twenty-third dynasty, there were two Pedu-basts who reigned between 755 and 736 B. C.; but "we can only infer which is the earlier of these" (*id.*, 262). Of the other kings of this dynasty, scarcely the names even are known (*id.*, 263–265).

Of the twenty-fourth dynasty, nothing is known of Kashta, 725–715 B. C., (*id.*, 280); of Shabataka, 707–693 B. C., "not a single fact of history is recorded" (*id.*, 287); of the remaining kings very little is known, except about Tirhakeh, 701–667 B. C. (*id.*, 290–311).

Of the twenty-fifth dynasty, from the first reign, that of Tafnekht II about 749–721 B. C., we have only two steles (*id.*, 314); of Tafnekht II (Uahab-ra), scarcely anything is known (*id.*, 317, 318).

three Artaxerxeses, and from their coins and the ruins
of their buildings; but in general it may be said that
from the time of the Behistun inscription (*cir.* 515
B.C.) to the destruction of the Persian empire by
Alexander of Macedon we are dependent for our information as to the history of Persia upon external
sources, such as the Hebrew and Greek historians, the
Babylonian tablets, and the Aramaic papyri.

VIII. There are numerous cases in which events
which are mentioned in the *documents* of one country
are entirely *wanting* in those of another. For example, the Tel-el-Amarna letters give us much information about the relations existing between Egypt on
the one hand and Assyria and Babylon on the other;
but the scanty Assyrian and Babylonian documents
of that time are devoid of any reference to Egypt.
After the time of Amenophis IV, however, the
Egyptians make no explicit reference whatever to
either Assyria or Babylon. Ashurbanipal gives lengthy
accounts of his campaigns, and of that of his father,
against Egypt, giving us the names of the kings and
governors of Egypt; but the Egyptian records are silent as to the Assyrian invasions and dominations, unless
indeed there be an allusion to them in the inscriptions of
Mentemhet, "a prince of the Theban principality,"
from the time of Taharka, where he speaks of the whole
land as having been overturned as a divine chastise-
ment.[1] Of the Babylonian invasion of Egypt, the
Egyptians have left no record. In fact, outside the
Scriptures, the only reference to it is in the fragment
of Nebuchadnezzar found near the Suez Canal and
written in Babylonian.

[1] Breasted, *Ancient Records of Egypt*, vol. iv, p. 461; Petrie, *History
of Egypt*, iii, 305.

IX.   There are numerous cases, also, where certain *events* of a man's life are mentioned in one of his documents and entirely *passed over* in others, which might have been expected to mention them.

For example, a recently published inscription of Sennacherib,[1] contains an account of two great expeditions of the Assyrians against Cilicia in the time of Sennacherib, of which the latter has said nothing in his numerous inscriptions previously published.   So in the case of Nebuchadnezzar, his conquest of Egypt is mentioned only in the fragment found in Egypt; but even the name of Egypt is absent from his other records.   Again, in the three accounts on the Babylonian monuments of the war between Cyrus and Astyages, the Cyrus *Cylinder* says simply, "the land of the Kuti, the totality of the host of the Manda he (Merodach) caused to bow at my [Cyrus'] feet"; the *Chronicle* says that the latter's troops revolted against him and that he was taken and delivered up to Cyrus; the *Abu-Habba* inscription says that "Cyrus the king of Anzan, his insignificant (small) vassal, scattered with his few troops the widespread armies of the Manda, and that Astyages their king was seized by Cyrus and brought as prisoner to his land."   He adds, also, that it was in the third year, presumably of Nabunaid, that the event happened.   In like manner, Nabunaid's dream about the destruction of the Umman-Manda is mentioned only in the Abu-Habba inscription, though others of his dreams (for he was a great dreamer) are mentioned elsewhere.

X.   There are cases, also, where the silence of an author with regard to the *method* of his procedure in drawing up a document has *misled* us into a *false*

---

[1] CT xxvi. London, 1909.

interpretation of it.   Perhaps the best exemplification of this is to be found in the brilliant study of Sargon by Dr. A. T. Olmstead,[1] in which the author shows that many misapprehensions and misinterpretations of the campaigns of Sargon have arisen from a failure to understand that some of Sargon's inscriptions are chronological, some geographical, some logical, and some a mixture of two or all of these.

XI.   There are many nations and persons, whose *names merely* are known, but over whose history the pall of a universal silence has fallen, as far as *native records* are concerned.   The most notable examples of this kind from antiquity are the Medes and the Carthaginians.   With the exception of a few votive and many almost identical mortuary inscriptions, the sources of information which we have with regard to the city of Dido must be found in the works of her enemies.   If only we could find the memoirs of Hannibal!   With regard to the Medes, we have absolutely no original information, since Weissbach has very conclusively shown[2] that the third language of the inscriptions of the Persian kings is not the language of the Medes. In view of this, what an astounding statement is that which was made in Dean Farrar's *Daniel*, that Daniel could not have existed, inasmuch as his name does not appear on the Median monuments!   Other examples of nations of antiquity about which we know nothing from native records are the Trojans, the Scythians, the Cimmerians, and the Gauls.

There are many other *nations* known to have

---

[1] In his introduction to the work entitled: *Western Asia in the Days of Sargon of Assyria;* (New York, 1908).

[2] In his introduction to *Die achämeniden Inschriften zweiter Art.* and in *Die altpersischen Keilinschriften*, p. xxxi.

flourished about which we know nothing from any source, except their names.   For example, in Herodotus' list of the nations subject to Darius Hystaspis,[1] the Milyens, the Hygennians, the Pantimathians, the Aparytæ, the Paricanians, and the Pausicæ are absolutely unknown except by name.   Many other cases can readily be gathered from the great work of Herodotus. So, also, in the inscriptions of the Assyrian kings, numerous examples of nations conquered by them, are found as to which we know nothing except the names. In view of the general trustworthiness of their information where it can be tested by other testimony, as in the case of the Hittites and Elamites and Israelites and Babylonians and Egyptians, no one could reasonably doubt that what they say as to their conquest of these otherwise unknown nations is true.

XII.   Again, there are many persons said to have been *men of eminence* in their day, who are *merely mentioned* by name and title, or position, about whom we know absolutely nothing further.   In Herodotus there are scores of such men, as for example in the catalogue of the generals and admirals of Xerxes.   In the inscriptions of Darius Hystaspis, in the contract and historical documents of Assyria and Babylon, in the royal lists of Egypt, and in the synchronous and eponym tablets of Assyria and Babylon, there are the names of hundreds more of such men.

XIII.   There are thousands, perhaps we might better say tens of thousands, of *eminent men*, whose names even are *never mentioned* on any document, but who we know must have *existed*.   Take Egypt, for example.   Every once in a while a new mummy, or monument, or papy-

[1] Bk. III, 89–97.

rus is discovered, which reveals to us the name and deeds of some hitherto unknown individual, who in his day loomed up large in the view of his contemporaries. Not to mention others, we might speak of Mentemhet from the reign of Taharka, Ibe from the reign of Psamtik I, Nesuhor from the reign of Apries, and Pefnefdineit from the reign of Amasis. All of these were distinguished as priest, steward, general, or physician; and the inscriptions of these which have come to light enable us to get a comparatively fair view of their life and character. But during the long period of the Egyptian dynasties, how many thousands of others equally eminent in every walk of life must have flourished, though their very names have passed into oblivion!

A frequently recurring phrase on the Assyrian monuments, after a record of a conquest of numerous countries and kings, is: "I set my officers over them as governors, or deputies." But the names of these high officials are not given. It may be truly said, that one would never expect to find the name of an Assyrian governor (*qipu*, *shaknu*, or *bel pihati*) on a royal inscription. Tiglath-Pileser I says that he conquered sixty kings of the Nairi-land; but only one is mentioned by name.[1]

Of all the sub-kings, governors, deputies, and generals who must have served under the dominion of the Chaldean kings of Babylon from 625 to 538 B. C., the Babylonian historical and building inscriptions mention none by name except Nabunaid II and Belshazzar, the sons of Nabunaid I. On the contract tablets from that period, we find the names of only fourteen *asharidus*, twenty *qipus*, and four *bel pihatis*. No *shaknus* are mentioned. In the inscriptions from Persian times

---

[1] Lotz, *Die Inschriften Tiglath–Pileser's* I. (Col. iv, 43–v, 32.)

we find the names of no sub-kings, of only two satraps, of three *pihatis*, of three *bel pihatis*, of twelve *asharidus*, of twenty-one *qipus*, and of no *shaknus*. In Herodotus, whose history of Persia extends from 555 B. C. to 480 B. C., we find the names of three or more sub-kings and of about a dozen archons and hyparchons.[1] With the exception of a score or so of judges, scarcely any civil officers are mentioned among the thousands of names collected by Tallquist.[2] With the exception of those mentioned in the Behistun inscriptions, very few generals are named in the Persian or Babylonian documents; though the frequent mention of them in Herodotus and in other Greek historians would teach us that there must have been hundreds of them from 625 B. C. to 330 B. C.

XIV. Lastly, it must be remembered, that, when all has been said, we have discovered but a very limited proportion of the ancient documents which once existed. This is true as to both public and private documents. For example, of the kings of Persia, we have no public documents of Cambyses, Smerdis, Darius II, Xerxes II, Sogdianus, Arses, and Darius III, and only one each of Artaxerxes I and III, two, possibly, of Cyrus, and two of Artaxerxes II, six of Xerxes I, and about a dozen all told of Darius Hystaspis. Of private documents from the time of the Persian kings we have few after the time of Artaxerxes II, and the ones we have are nearly all from Babylonia. There are at most two in Babylonian from the time of Artaxerxes II, who reigned from 404 to 359 B. C.[3]

---

[1] The word satrap does not occur in Herodotus, although he twice uses the term "satrapy."

[2] *Neubabylonisches Namenbuch.*

[3] Tablet 86 of the Morgan collection, part I, is from the fifth month

The places also where the records of Babylon and Persia have been found are comparatively few in number compared with the numerous places where they must have existed; and in these places, but a very few of the whole number that once existed have come down to us. Thus, there were doubtless many banking firms, like the *Murashu* and the *Egibi* houses at Babylon and many storehouses for contracts; but most of the contracts known have come from a few localities. Aramaic papyri were probably composed in a score of other Jewish colonies, but unfortunately only the one great find of Elephantine has thus far been made. The letters to Amenophis III and IV found at Tel-el-Amarna were most likely not the only ones ever sent by the vassals of the Egyptian kings to their sovereign lords. The reports to Assyrian kings thus far discovered are doubtless but a small part of those which must have been sent to Nineveh during the 500 years from Tiglath-Pileser I to Ashurbanipal.

CONCLUSION

In concluding these general remarks upon the so-called argument from silence, and having in view our almost absolute lack of first-class evidence bearing upon the historicity of the statements made in the Old Testament in general and of Daniel in particular, we refuse to accept as true the indiscriminate charges and multitudinous specifications entirely unsupported

---

of the 41st year of Artaxerxes. Since Artaxerxes I reigned less than 41 years and Artaxerxes II about 46 years, this tablet must be from the reign of the latter. Some of the astronomical tablets mention Artaxerxes II and one at least Artaxerxes III. See Kugler: *Sternkunde und Sterndienst in Babel*, i, 70–82.

by evidence which are often made against the truthfulness of the Old Testament writings. A man is
presumed to be innocent until he is proven guilty. A
book, or document, is supposed to be true until it is
proven false. And as to particular objections made
against the historicity of a person or event mentioned
in the book of Daniel on the ground that other authorities fail to notice them, would it not be well for us to
possess our souls in patience, until such charges are
supported by some direct evidence bearing upon the
case? Why not give Daniel the benefit of the doubt,
if doubt there be?

CHAPTER II

WAS DANIEL AN HISTORICAL CHARACTER?

THERE will be discussed in this chapter the definite claim of the late Dean Farrar that such a man as Daniel could not have existed because his name even has not been found as yet upon the documents dating from the sixth century B.C. It will be shown, that it is not certain that Daniel, under his new Babylonian name given him by Ashpenaz, the prince of the eunuchs of Nebuchadnezzar,[1] is not mentioned upon the records of Babylon; and, also, that even if it be not mentioned, this affords no presumption against the existence of Daniel, inasmuch as the kinds of records that have come down to us could not have been expected to mention his name. To be sure, by a lucky chance, or a special providence, his name might have been recorded in one of the documents thus far discovered; but these documents being such as they are, it would be most extraordinary if it had been recorded there. Moreover, unless some new kind of document should be discovered, or unless the library containing the contract tablets of the bank, or office, at which Daniel transacted business, should be unearthed, it is hopeless to expect that his name will ever be found on any document yet to be discovered.

[1] Dan. i, 7.

To be sure, we might have found, or may still find, a letter to him or from him; but the chance of ever finding such a letter is extremely small. As to the decrees, especially those of Nebuchadnezzar in chapter four and of Darius in chapter six, which purport to have been written, and to have been written most probably in different languages, we might naturally suppose that one or more of them would be discovered. But when we recall the fact that these at best would be but a few out of thousands of the decrees of the kings of Babylon and that not one of their decrees has thus far been unearthed, it is scarcely reasonable, to say the least, to expect that these particular decrees which are mentioned in Daniel should ever be found. To hope for the discovery of an historical document recording Daniel's name is groundless in view of the character and paucity of those we already possess. No public records of the kings would be likely to record the name of a servant, and we have no evidence that any private histories were ever written among the Babylonians or Persians. Our only reasonable expectation would seem to be that some future find may disclose to us a literary work, like the Achikar papyrus, which may contain some allusion to the events of Daniel's life, or even make mention of his name. But at present, we can deal only with the records that are known; and to these let us now address ourselves, citing first the objection of Dean Farrar and then proceeding to the assumptions involved in this objection and to a discussion of the evidence in favor of these assumptions, and closing with a few words summing up the conclusions to be derived from the evidence.

Objection Stated

"It is natural that we should turn to the monuments and inscriptions of the Babylonian, Persian, and Median empires to see if any mention can be found of so prominent a ruler. But hitherto neither his name has been discovered, nor the faintest trace of his existence."[1]

Assumptions Involved

It is assumed in this objection, (1) that the absence of the name of Daniel from the inscriptions of the period in which he is presumed to have lived would prove that he did not exist at that time, and (2) that inasmuch as we have not found on the monuments hitherto published "the faintest trace of his existence," he did not in fact exist.

Answer to Objections

These charges will have weight only with those who have never investigated the subject-matter and especially the proper names of the documents of that period. But, inasmuch as this absence of Daniel's name from all documents outside the Scriptures seems to have impressed Dean Farrar as a strong reason for denying his existence, we shall proceed to discuss the whole matter at some length. Let it be said, then, that this argument is fallacious because of the character of the documents to which Dean Farrar has turned for traces of Daniel's existence. These documents extend from the time of Nabopolassar, the father of Nebuchad-nezzar, down to and including the time of Darius

[1] See *The Expositor's Bible, The Book of Daniel*, p. 5.

Hystaspis, thus covering the whole period during which Daniel is said to have lived. They may be divided into (1) contract tablets, (2) building inscriptions, (3) historical inscriptions, and (4) miscellaneous documents.

1. We place the *contract tablets* first, because they are the most numerous, because they have the largest number of proper names of persons upon them, and because these names have been almost all published and classified in a form easily accessible, by Prof. Knut L. Tallquist,[1] who has collated 3504 tablets, containing about 3000 names connoting about 12,000 persons. Among these we might have found the name of Daniel. But we do not find it there. When we examine these names a little more closely, however, the surprise and doubts engendered by this failure to find his name are dissipated. The name of Daniel, it is true, does not appear on these tablets; but neither can we be certain that the name of any other Hebrew is found there. *Certain*, we say; for it is probable that we do find several Hebrew names upon them, and it is possible that a number of persons denoted by Babylonian names may have been Hebrews. Several initial difficulties confront us in our endeavor to identify and establish the existence of the names of Jews on the documents of this period. The first is that most of the *forms* and *roots* of Hebrew names were common to the Jews along with the Moabites, Ammonites, Edomites, Phenicians, or Arameans, so that it is exceedingly difficult to affirm with confidence, that a given name, without a clearly defining context, is the name of a Jew. The second is, that the way of writing the Hebrew names for God

[1] *Neubabylonisches Namenbuch zu den Geschäftsurkunden aus der Zeit des Šamašsumukin bis Xerxes.*

in the Babylonian texts is not clear. The third is, that it seems certain that many of the Jews and people of other nations who came to Babylon to settle, or were brought there as slaves, adopted, or were called by, native Babylonian names, thus destroying the trace of their race and nationality contained in their original native names. The fourth is, that in the case of the Jews, and of those who might have had the same names as Jews, the gentilic title (which is found a number of times with the names of Persians, Egyptians, and others) has never yet been found upon the Babylonian tablets. The fifth is that a different nomenclature was commonly employed for denoting slaves from that which was used for freemen.[1]

For these reasons, we may be pardoned for being exceedingly sceptical as to the possibility of the identification of the Jewish personal names of the Babylonian tablets from Nabopolassar to Darius Hystaspis inclusive; that is, during all the period in which Daniel is said to have lived. A few men, mostly slaves, like the frequently occurring Bazuzu, may have been Jews; but they may just as well have been Arabs or Arameans.[2]

---

[1] The freeman is X, the son of Y, the son of Z; the slave is merely X, —his parentage is never given. The reason for this being that the slave had no legal standing. He was the son of nobody and his children, in like manner, were the children of a nobody, since he could not be the founder of a family (*mar banu*)

[2] *E. g.*, Aqabi-ili (Nk. 393:4), Bariki-ili (Nk. 346:5, 408:2), Samaki-ili (Nk. 138:12), Adi-ili (Nk. 70:1, 7), Yadi-ili (Nk. 70:13), Idda son of Iddia a slave (Nk. 31:11), Aqabuya (Nd., 542:2), Hashda son of Ibna (Nd. 997:3), Samaku Cyr. 379:5, may just as well have been Arameans as Hebrews. Addu-natannu (Nd. 201:9) is a good Aramaic word. Shalti-ili is called an Arab slave (Nbp. 19:20). Padi might be Hebrew, but may, also, be Phenician. It was the name of a king of Ekron in Sennacherib's time and is found a number of times in the Assyrian

The fact, then, that the name Daniel has not been found on the Babylonian tablets of the sixth century B. C. does not prove that he did not live at Babylon at that time, any more than the fact that the names of other Jews are not found there proves that there were no Jews at Babylon. And yet this is the very time of the captivity! Surely, no one is going to deny that the Jews were taken to Babylon at all!

But even if the name were found, this would not prove that the man so named was a Jew. For the name Daniel has been discovered on both the Nabatean and Palmyrene documents as a name in use among these peoples.[1] Besides, the Babylonian name Dannuilu, which occurs on a tablet from the eighth year of Darius Hystaspis, as the father of a witness called Zeri, may be the same name as the Hebrew name Daniel.[2]

But in order to prove that a Daniel mentioned on a tablet was the Daniel of our book, the official position of the man would have to be given in a way which is not common on the tablets. The mere name would not be enough. We would require a description of the person named. But such descriptions are not ordinarily given in the Babylonian documents except in a very general way. As stated above, the name of the father may be mentioned, and sometimes that of the grandfather.

---

records of the seventh century B. C. (Johns, *Assyrian Deeds, etc.*, iii, 238). Basia (Nk. 31:13), and Busasa (Cyr. 135: 9), have a good Syriac root and good Syriac forms, whereas the root is wanting in Hebrew. Dadia may be Phenician and is found in Assyrian as early as the seventh century B. C. (Johns, *Ass. Deeds*, iii, 526.) Barikiya the son of Akka (Cyr. 59: 8) looks like a good Hebrew name.

[1] See de Vogüé, *Syrie Centrale*, p. 62; Lidzbarski, *Nordsemitische Inschriften*, p. 256.

[2] Strass. *Inschriften von Darius*, 236, 10.

But as we know nothing of either the father or of the family of Daniel the prophet, such a description on an inscription would not help to identify him.   His calling, indeed, might have been given.   For, frequently a man is called a *shangu* (priest), or a *shangu* of a certain god, or a smith or a secretary, or a measurer of corn, etc. But these descriptions are comparatively uncommon, and are especially unusual in describing the higher officials of the state.[1]

Inasmuch, however, as the name of Daniel is said to have been changed by Nebuchadnezzar, it may well be asked, whether his new Babylonian name does not occur in the documents of this time.   But, here also, we have a great initial difficulty to overcome, in the fact that the authorities are not agreed as to what is the Babylonian equivalent of Belteshazzar.   The Greek version and Josephus confounded the name with Belshazzar, giving Baltassar for both.   Schrader took the name to be compounded of Balatsu-usur (protect his life), the name of the god being omitted.   Sayce takes it to be for Belit-sharru-usur (Oh Bilat, protect the king), claiming that, as it is written in Daniel, it is a "compound which has no sense and would be impossible in the Babylonian language."[2]   I would suggest as a third view, that we read Bel-lit-shar-usur, "Bel, protect the hostage of the king."   The evidence[3] of

---

[1] We meet, however, such descriptions as "major-domo (*rab biti*) of Belshazzar" (Nd. 270:3), "overseer of the sons of the king" (Nd. 245:3), and *qipu*, "mayor" or "officer" (Nd. 33:5 *et passim*).

[2] *Higher Criticism and the Monuments*, p. 532.

[3] I take this to be Bel-lit-shar-usur "Bel protect the hostage of the king." For the omission of the *r* and the writing of the last two parts of the name "shazzar," compare the name Belshazzar (see Schrader KAT 433). It will be seen, that the last two syllables in the names Belshazzar and Belteshazzar are written in the same way in Babylonian

the manner of transliterating Babylonian names in Aramaic is conclusive in showing that Bel-lit-shar-usur would be written with but one *l*, as we find it in the book of Daniel. This interpretation of the name avoids the necessity of supposing that in Aramaic teth has been substituted for tau, as the meaning suggested by Prof. Sayce demands;—a change, moreover, which is not supported by the transliterations of the Aramaic names of the bi-lingual inscriptions nor by the papyri. We admit, that an exception might have occurred here; but, in view of the common usage, the burden of proof rests with the asserter of the change.[1]

The view suggested by me harmonizes with the statement of the author of Daniel that Nebuchadnezzar called him after the name of his god; and also with the statements of the first chapter of Daniel, which plainly imply that "certain of the children of Israel,

---

and in Aramaic and Hebrew. As to the writing "Belit" for "Bellit" numerous parallels may be found on the Babylonian inscriptions with Aramaic dockets, or indorsements. Thus Ashurraham is written in Aramaic with only one *r* (CIS ii, 43); Bana-neshaya, with only one *n* (Clay, *Aramaic Endorsements*, 40); Sulummadu, with only one *m* (*Cun. Texts of the U. of P.*, viii, Part I, p. 15): Pani-Nabu-temu, with only one *n* (CIS ii, 62); Sar-rapid, with only one *r* (CIS ii, 81); Mar-shaggil-lumar, with only one *g* and one *l* (*id.*, 61); Bit-el-edil-ilani, with only one *il* (*id.*, 54); Ishtar-dur-kali, with *dr* written once but to be read apparently *tar-dur* (*id.*, 23); Nabu-takkil-ilani, with only one *il* (*id.*, 58). So in Syriac *kaukab-Bel* is written with one *b*. *Spiciligium Syriacum*, 15.

[1] For example, the Babylonian Beltu is always rendered in Syrian by Blty (*Spiciligium Syriacum*, 13, 14, 15.9, *et al.*), the *t* of Ahe-utir (Clay, *Aram. Indorsements*, 2), and Pihat-ah-iddina (*id.*, 80), has been correctly transliterated in the Aramaic indorsements by the letter Tau; whereas, in Bel-etir (Clay, *Aram. Ind.*, 30, 34, 41, 36 [?]), Shita (*id.*, 4), Shamash-uballit (BE, viii, ii, 68), and Pani-Nabu-temu (CIS ii, 62) the *t* is in all cases accurately transliterated in Aramaic with a Teth.

even the seed royal, and of the nobles" were taken to Babylon as hostages for the good behavior of the king and people of Judah. The taking of hostages in this manner had been a custom of the kings of Assyria and Babylonia.[1]

No valid objection can be raised against this interpretation of the meaning and of the method of writing this new name which was given by Nebuchadnezzar to Daniel. The interpretation here suggested fits in ex-

---

[1] Thus Sargon took the son of Daiakku the deputy (*Shaknu*) of Man as a hostage (*liṭu*). Later, he took one out of every three (?) of the chiefs (*nasikati*) of Gambuli as a hostage; and later still, he took hostages from the chiefs of Zami, Aburi, Nahani, and Ibuli *et al.*[1] These hostages, if youths, were brought up in the king's palace and were sometimes made kings of the subject nations. Thus Sennacherib set up as king of Shumer and Accad "Belibni a Chaldean of Babylonian origin who like a little dog had grown up in his palace."[2] Jahimilki, son of Baal, king of Tyre, was brought as a servant to Ashurbanipal[3] and afterwards was graciously given back to his father.[4] The sons of Jakinlu, king of Arwad, were brought to the same king of Assyria; one of them, Azibaal by name, was sent back to be king in his father's place, while the rest, nine in number, were clothed in rich garments, gifted with golden rings for their fingers, and caused to sit before the king.[5] The kings of Egypt were brought alive to Ashurbanipal; he showed grace to Necho, clothed him in royal apparel and a golden band, as became a king, put on his fingers golden rings, and girded him with an iron sword, adorned with gold, and with the name of Ashurbanipal upon it; gave him chariots and horses and made him king in Sais, at the same time that he set up Necho's son Nabu-shezi-banni as ruler over Athribis.[6]

It is probable that the kings of Babylon followed the example of the Assyrian kings. Thus, the members of the royal family of Judah were carried by Nebuchadnezzar to Babylon and brought up in the royal palace. The names of some of these, at least, were changed, as had been that of the son of Necho, king of Egypt, by Ashurbanipal. Daniel we are told, received the name of Belteshazzar.

---

[1] *Annals of Sargon*, 76, 262–270.
[2] Bellini *Cylinder* A, 13; KB ii, 115.
[3] KB ii, 169.   [4] *Id.*, 171.   [5] *Id.*, 173.   [6] *Id.*, 167.

actly with the position of Daniel and with his relation to the king of Babylon as a hostage for the king of Judah at the time when it was given.

Having thus determined the meaning and writing of the name, let us proceed to the main question, as to whether such a name has been found on the records of that period. But, here, at the very outset, we must inquire what name we should expect to look for in the inscriptions. One would naturally suppose that we should look only for the name *Bel-lit-shar-uṣur;* and that, if we did not find this name written in full, we should conclude, that the Babylonian designation of Daniel did not occur in these documents. But no! This is not the case. For, Dr. Tallquist has very clearly shown that in ordinary usage the native Babylonians were in the habit of abbreviating their very lengthy names. He shows, first, that the first term in a name of four words may be omitted, as *Ina-eshi-eṭir* for *Nergal-ina-eshi-eṭir;* secondly, that the two first may be omitted, as *Bel-atkal* for *Ana-amat-Bel-atkal;* thirdly, that the second may be omitted, as *Minu-Bel-daianu* for *Minu-ana-Bel-daianu;* fourthly, that the second and third may be omitted, as *Shamash-eṭir* for *Shamash-ina-eshi-eṭir.* The first of these methods of abbreviation would allow us to read for *Bel-lit-shar-uṣur, Liṭa-shar-uṣur;* the second, *Shar-uṣur;* the third, *Bel-shar-uṣur;* and the fourth, *Bel-uṣur.* The first of these has not been found. The second is found possibly in an uncertain reading of document 168 of John's *Assyrian Deeds and Documents,* the same name as the Sharezer of 2 Kings xix, 37, one of the sons of Sennacherib by whom the king was assassinated.[1] The fourth

---

[1] In Abydenus the successor of Sennacherib is called Nergilus. Putting

3

is rare, but is paralleled by Nabu-uṣur, which occurs as the name of nearly one hundred persons mentioned on Tallquist's tablets.[1] The third, Bel-shar-uṣur, coincides exactly with the name Belshazzar, the son of king Nabunaid, and is the only one of the four that is found on the tablets from which Dr. Tallquist has collected his chief list of names. Of all the Belshazzars mentioned in these lists, two or three only might possibly refer to Daniel. One of these is found on a tablet from the fourth year of Cyrus.[2] Here it is said that some *minas* of silver were to be delivered into the hands of Belshazzar the prince, or first officer, *asharidu*, of the king. On another tablet from the eighth year of the same king[3] there is mention of "Belshazzar, the man who was over the house of the king." In the second year of Darius Hystaspis, another tablet mentions a governor,[4] called Belshazzar. If we suppose that Daniel was the Belshazzar, the prince of the king, who is mentioned in the fourth year of Cyrus (535 B. C.), he would, when thus mentioned, have been only 85 years of age, if we suppose that his age when he was carried as hostage to Babylon was fifteen, or thereabout. Judging from the longevity of officials in the Orient to-day, he may have been the *major domo* of the eighth year of Cyrus, or even the governor of the

---

the two names together we would have Nergalsharezer, the first part of the name being preserved by Abydenus and the second part by the writer of Kings.[1]

[1] *Neubabylonisches Namenbuch*, p. 151.
[2] Strass. *Cyr.* 178, line 3.
[3] *Id.*, 312, line 5.
[4] *Amel piḥati*, Strassmaier, Darius 42, 3.

---

[1] KAT 330, and Eusebius, *Chron.*, ed. Schoene, i, 35.

second year of Darius Hystaspis. In the latter case, he would have been active at about 100 years of age. This is not so incredible as some would have us believe. In the preface to his great Arabic-English Lexicon, Edward William Lane mentions a number of native Arabic lexicographers from whom he derived the material for his dictionary. One of these, named Abu-Zeyd, lived to be 93; another, El-Asmafie, to be 92 or 93; another, Abu-Obajdih, to be about 98; and another, Abu-Amr Esh-Aheybanu, to be at least 110. Mr. James Creelman,[1] describing a visit to Jerusalem and other places in the Turkish empire, says that several of the heads of the great religious communities of that empire had then reached the age of nearly a hundred years, but that they were still enjoying the exercise of their high duties in apparently undiminished vigor of intellect and in certainly undisputed authority.[2]

Further, a presupposition in favor of believing that the Babylonians wrote the Babylonian name of Daniel in the same way that they wrote the name of Belshazzar, the son of the king, is to be derived from the fact that the Greek of the Septuagint version and of Jose-

[1] *Pearson's Magazine*, Sept.–Nov.,1909.

[2] The author of this chapter is especially sceptical upon this argument based upon the impossibility of Daniel's having come to Babylon in the year of the beginning of the reign of Nebuchadnezzar and yet having been alive and flourishing in the reign of Darius Hystaspis. For the sake of the bearing upon the case in discussion, he may be pardoned for saying that his great-grandmother Graham, *née* McCreery, died at the age of 99; a great grand-uncle, Thomas Dick, at the age of 101, two great-uncles, John Dick, and Robert at 92 and 94 respectively; and his great-grandfather, Joseph Wilson, at 105. This last mentioned the writer himself has seen, when he was more than 100 years old. He was active in brain and body till the last, was never ill in his life, and simply went to sleep at last one night and never waked. A simple life, lived in the fear of God, is conducive to longevity; and so may it have been with Daniel.

phus transliterated both the names in the same way in Greek; that is, by Baltasar.[1]

As we have shown, then, that a Belshazzar, who may have been the Daniel of our book, was an "*asharidu* of the king" in the fourth year of Cyrus, it may be well to ask, before we leave this inquiry, what is the meaning and use of the term *asharidu*. Delitzsch[2] defines it as "the first, the noblest, the first in rank";[3] and Muss-Arnolt,[4] as "supreme, leader, prince, first in place." It is used as an epithet of many gods. Thus, we find "Sin the first son (*asharidu*) of Bel," Shamash, Ninib, and Marduk are each called the *asharidu* of the gods. Nergal is called the *asharidu*. It is used, especially of the first-born son of the king, as "Nebuchadnezzar, the son (*asharidu*) of Nabopolassar," "Antiochus, the son (*asharidu*) of Seleucus." Kings, also, used the title of themselves; thus Ashurnasir-abal says, "I am the *asharidu*"; Sennacherib says that he is the "*asharidu* of all kings." It is used, finally, of the nobles of the land. In the tablets, which Tallquist has used, it is employed for a small number of persons only, so that Daniel may well have borne the title in his position as third ruler in the kingdom.[5]

---

[1] This Baltasar is a correct transliteration of Belshazzar into Greek through the ordinary Aramaic of northern pre-Christian Syria. Compare, for example, Iltehiri for Ilshahri, and Iltammesh for Ilshamesh. (BE X, pp. xiii, xiv.)

[2] *Assyr. Handwörterbuch.*

[3] *Der erste, der vornehmste, der an Rang hochstehende.* See HWB *in loc.*

[4] *Dictionary of the Assyrian Language.*

[5] The following are the names and dates of the *asharidus* mentioned by Tallquist, the tablets being numbered after Strassmaier.

From the reign of Nebuchadnezzar.

Nabu-ushezib Nk. 22:9;	Ubar Nk. 175:13;
Mar-Bel-atkal Nk. 40:2;	Nazia Nk. 365:12, 369:6;
Shamash-kin-ahu-Nk. 131:23;	Nabu-shar-usur Nk. 394:3.

2. Having examined the contract tablets we now turn to the so-called *building inscriptions*. Might we not expect to find the name of Daniel, or Belteshazzar, upon these? Let us look at them and see. All of the building inscriptions of the Chaldean kings have been translated by Dr. Stephen Langdon.[1] In his inscriptions, Nabopolassar mentions beside himself, no one but Nebuchadnezzar, his first born son, and Nabu-shum-lishir, the latter's twin brother, and these but once each.[2] Nebuchadnezzar, in his 27 inscriptions, gives us the names of none of his contemporaries, the only names save his own which occur being those of his father Nabopolassar and his remote ancestor Naramsin, the latter mentioned only once.[3] He speaks of kings and governors (*pihati*) once, and once of the princes (*sagganake*) of the land of the Hittites,[4] and once of "the kings of the remote regions which are by the Upper

---

From the reign of Nergal-shar-usur (Neriglissar):
Nabu-sabit-kati   Ng. 7:8, 58:6.
      From the reign of Nabunaid:
Bel-ahe-iddin Nd. 260: 3, 282:2 (?),
   517:3 (?) (-Ngl. 44:2;)   Itti-sharri-balatu Nd. 573:10;
Innia Nd. 261:3 (?)   Liburu Nd. 578:10;
Ardi-ta-? aala Nd. 282:23;   Addu Nd. 782:5.
      From the reign of Cyrus:
Bel-shar-usur Cyr. 188:3;   Sikkabul Cyr. 243;
Rihitum Cyr. 204:6;   Sin-bel-usur Cyr. 270:4.
      From the reign of Cambyses:
Ardi-ahe-shu Cam. 79:4;   Nabu-miti-uballit Cam. 368:10;
Terik-sharrutsu Cam. 93:7;   Nabu-bullitanni Cam. (407:14,
Nabu-dini-bullit Cam. 368:3;   408:12).
      From the reign of Darius Hystaspis:
Iddiranu Dar. 366:17.
   [1] *Building Inscriptions of the Neo-Babylonian Empire.*
   [2] *Inscription* i, Col. ii, 70, and iii, 5.
   [3] *Id.*, ii, 26.   [4] *Id.*, xvii, Col. iii, 10.

Sea and the kings of the remote regions which are by
the Lower Sea."[1]   Neriglissar in his two inscriptions
mentions no one but himself and his father Bel-
shum-ishkun, the latter but twice.[2]   Nabunaid, in the
seven inscriptions, with their parallels, given in Langdon's work mentions none but names of kings.[3]

In fact, the only names coming within the period we
are discussing are names of men of royal blood such as
Nebuchadnezzar, his twin brother, Shamash-shum-ukin,
and their father Nabopolassar; Nabunaid, his father
Nabu-balaṭsu-iḳbi and Nabunaid's son Belshazzar;
and Cyrus and his opponent Astyages.

The Persian building inscriptions of Darius Hystaspis bear no names of persons except those of Darius
and his father Hystaspis the Achæmenid.[4]

[1] Langdon, op. cit., xvii, Col. ii, 25–29.

[2] Id., I, Col. i, 14, and II, Col. i, 11.

[3] To wit: In the great inscription from Ur, Nebuchadnezzar and his
father Nabopolassar (Col. i, 50, ii, 40, 41, 53), Burnaburiash (Col. i, 55,
57), Sargon and Naram-Sin his son (Col. ii, 29), Kurigalzu (Col. i, 32),
Shagashaltiash (Col. iii, 44) and Belshazzar his first born son (Col. ii, 26,
iii, 59).   In the parallel passage, he names also Hammurabi (Col. ii,
20, Col. iii, 2, 28).   In the small inscription from Ur, he mentions Ur-Uk
(Col. i, 8, 12, 15, 22), Dungi his son (Col. i, 10, 13, 17, 22), and "Belshazzar, his (own) first born son, the offspring of his heart" (Col. ii, 24–
26).   In the great Cylinder from Abu-Habba, he names his own father
Nabu-balaṭsu-iḳbi the wise prince (rubu imgu), Cyrus, king of Anshan,
his (Astyages') little servant (Col. i, 29), Astyages king of the Umman-
manda (Col. i, 32), Ashurbanipal and his father Esarhaddon (Col. i,
47, 48), Shalmanassar and his father Ashur-naṣir-abal (Col. ii, 3, 4),
Nebuchadnezzar (Col. ii, 49), Naram-Sin, the son of Sargon (Col. ii,
57, 64, iii, 8), Shagashaltiburiash (Col. iii, 28, 31), and Kudur-Bel
(Col. iii, 29, 31).   In the Cylinder inscription, he mentions his own
father, Nabu-balaṭsu-iḳbi (Col. i, 16), and Naram-Sin (Col. i, 31).
Finally, on three sample bricks, there appear the names of Nabunaid
and of his father Nabu-balaṭsu-iḳbi.   It will be observed, that all
the names mentioned are the names of kings, and mostly of kings who
had lived long before Nabunaid.

[4] Spiegel, Die altpersischen Keilinschriften, H, I, B, L, X.

3. Of *historical inscriptions* from this period, we have first the fragments of one describing Nebuchadnezzar's expedition to Egypt in his 37th year. On this he mentions, beside himself, Amasis king of Egypt, and perhaps Pittacus the tyrant of Mitylene.[1]

In the Cyrus *Cylinder*, we find the names of Nabunaid, and those of Teispis, the great grandfather of Cyrus, of Cyrus his grandfather, of Cambyses his father and of Cambyses his son. In the Nabunaid-Cyrus *Chronicle*, we find the names of Astyages, Nabunaid, Cyrus, Cambyses his son, Ugbaru (Gubaru ?) and Nabu-mah (?)-rib-ahu.

On the Behistun inscription of Darius Hystaspis, there are found beside the frequent occurrence of the name of Darius, the names of Cyrus, Cambyses, and the two Smerdises; the names of Achæmenes, Teispes, Ariaramnes, Arsames, and Hystaspis, the ancestors of Darius; the names of the associates of Darius in the insurrection against Smerdis the Magian, Intaphernes the son of Vayaspara, Otanes the son of Thukhra, Gobryas the son of Mardonius, Hydarnes the son of Bagabigna, Bagabukhasha the son of Daduhya, and Ardamanish the son of Vahauka; the names of the rebels who rebelled against Darius, Gomates (Smerdis), Athrina the son of Upadarma, Nadintu-Bel and Arakhu who called themselves by the name of Nebuchadnezzar and claimed to be sons of Nabunaid, Martiya son of Cicikhrish who said he was Ummanish, Fravartish who said he was Khshathrita of the family of Uvakhshatara (Cyaxares), Citrantakhma who claimed to be of the

---

[1] The syllable *Am* is wanting in Amasis and only *ku* remains to indicate Pittacus. Whether Mitylene is the correct rendering of Butuyaman is questionable. See Zehnpfund-Langdon, *Die neubabylonischen Königsinschriften*, p. 206.

family of Uvakhshatara, Frada, and Vahyasdata who claimed to be Bardiya (Smerdis) the son of Cyrus; the names of certain generals who led the forces of Darius against the rebels, Hydarnes, Dadarshish the Armenian, Dadarshish the Persian, Vaumisa, Takhmaspada, Hystaspis (the father of Darius), Artavardiya, Vivana, and Vaidafra; and in the small inscription K, the name of Skunka, the Saka. On his other historical inscriptions, Darius mentions no one but himself and his father Hystaspis the Achæmenid.

4. Taking up the miscellaneous inscriptions, we shall look first at the one lately published by M. Pognon in his Semitic inscriptions from Syria, etc.[1] We find there the names of Ashurbanipal and Ashur-edil-ilani, kings of Assyria; of Nebuchadnezzar, Neriglissar, and Nabunaid, kings of Babylon, and of Nabunaid the son of the last named, "the offspring of his heart and the beloved of his mother."

From the times of Darius Hystaspis, we have the Suez boundary stones, several mortuary inscriptions from Naksh-i-Rustem, and some coins. These mention beside Darius himself, the name of Hystaspis the Achæmenid, his father, and the name of the bearer of his bow, Gobryas, and that of his bridle-holder and companion, Aspaçana.

It will be noticed, that in all these last three kinds of inscriptions are to be found few names beside those of kings, and the fathers and sons of kings. Most of the inscriptions contain only the name of the royal author and generally that of his father. Sometimes, distant ancestors or predecessors are named. Outside the inscriptions of Darius Hystaspis, we find altogether only the name of Ugbaru (Gubaru?) the governor of

[1] *Inscriptions sémitiques de la Syrie.*

Gutium, possibly that of Pittacus tyrant of Mitylene, and that of Nabu-mah (?)-rib-ahu.[1] In Darius' inscriptions, also, it will be noticed that aside from ancestors, kings, and pretenders, and their fathers, or ancestors, he mentions none but a few of his generals, his six fellow-conspirators and their fathers, his bearer of the bow and his bridle-holder. No civil officers are mentioned, unless we put in this category, Vivana, the satrap of Arachosia, and Dadarshish, the satrap of Bactria, who are named, also, among his generals and because they were generals.

Conclusion

Inasmuch, then, as these inscriptions mention no one filling any of the positions, or performing any of the functions, or doing any of the deeds, which the book of Daniel ascribes to its hero Belteshazzar; how can anyone expect to find in them any mention of Daniel, in either its Hebrew or its Babylonian form? And is it fair, in view of what the monuments of all kinds make known to us, to use the fact that they do not mention Daniel at all, as an argument against his existence?

What about the numerous governors, judges, generals, priests, wise men, writers, sculptors, architects, and all kinds of famous men, who must have lived during that long period? Who planned and supervised the building of the magnificent canals, and walls, and palaces, and temples of Babylon? Who led the armies, and held in subjection and governed the provinces, and adjudged cases in the high courts of justice, and sat in the king's council? Who were the mothers and wives

---

[1] A person whose name cannot be further defined, since the Nabunaid-Cyrus *Chronicle* is broken both before and after the name.

and queenly daughters of the monarchs, who sat upon the thrones of those mighty empires? Had the kings no friends, no favorites, no adulatory poets or historians, no servile prophets, no sycophantic priests, no obsequious courtiers, who were deemed worthy to have their names inscribed upon these memorials of royal pride and victory; that we should expect to find there the name of Daniel, a Hebrew captive, a citizen of an annihilated city, a member of a despised and conquered nation, a stranger living on the bounty of the king, an alien, a slave, whose very education was the gift of his master and his elevation dependent on his grace? Let him believe who can. As for me, were the documents multiplied tenfold, I would not expect to find in them any reference to this humble subject of imperious kings.

CHAPTER III

IT has been shown in the first chapter that the records preserved to us from the nations of antiquity that were contemporaneous with the Israelites during the whole period in which the Old Testament books were written are few, partial, biased, and lacunose. We have shown, also, that the Hebrew documents themselves do not present us with a full or continuous account of the history of the Israelitish people. The silence, therefore, of these documents with regard to an event or person is no sufficient evidence that the person did not live, or that a given event did not occur. In the present chapter this conclusion will be illustrated by a consideration of the objection made to the expedition of Nebuchadnezzar against Jerusalem in the third year of Jehoiakim on the ground that the records contemporary with Daniel do not mention it.

OBJECTION STATED

Concerning the statement of Dan. i, 1, that Daniel "was brought to the court of Nebuchadnezzar in the third year of Jehoiakim," De Wette-Schrader says:

It is clearly false, because according to Jer. xxv, 1, xlvi, 2, the fourth year of Jehoiakim is the first of Nebuchad-

nezzar; and according to Jer. xxv, 9, and also according to
xxxvi, 9, the Chaldeans had not yet come to Jerusalem in
the fifth year of Jehoiakim.   Besides the captivity under
Zedekiah, history knows of no other than that under Jeho-
achin in the eighth year of Nebuchadnezzar.[1]   Chronicles
alone[2] tells of a captivity of Jehoiakim.   This last place
the composer probably used and got his date from 2 Kings
xxiv, 1.[3]

Professor Prince says:

It is known from Jer. 25, 1, and 36, 9, 29, that Nebuchadnezzar did not begin his reign in Babylon until the
fourth year of Jehoiakim in Judah, and that the Babylonians in the ninth month of the fifth year of Jehoiakim had
not yet come to Jerusalem, which was taken in July, 586
B. C.   The origin of the error has been traced to a false
combination of 2 Ch. 36, 6 ff., and 2 K. 24, 1.[4]

Mr. A. R. Bevan says:

The statement in v. 1 that Nebuchadnezzar besieged
Jerusalem in the third year of Jehoiakim seems to be due to
a combination of 2 K. 24, 1, 2, with 2 Ch. 36, 6.   In Kings,
the "three years" are not, of course, the first three years of
Jehoiakim's reign, nor is there any mention of a siege.   The
idea that Jerusalem was captured under Jehoiakim appears
first in Chronicles, but no date is given.   The author of
Daniel follows the account in Chronicles, at the same time
assuming that the "three years" in Kings date from the
beginning of Jehoiakim's reign, and that "the bands of the
Chaldeans" were a regular army commanded by Nebuchadnezzar.[5]

[1] 2 Kings, xxiv, 12 ff.   According to Jer. lii, 28, in the seventh year
of Nebuchadnezzar.
[2] 2 Chron. xxxvi, 6 f.   [4] *Commentary on Daniel*, p. 18
[3] *Einleitung*, 8th ed., p. 486.   [5] *The Book of Daniel*, p. 57.

Dr. Driver says:

That Nebuchadnezzar besieged Jerusalem, and carried away some of the sacred vessels in "the *third* year of Jehoiakim" (Dan. i, 1 f.), though it cannot, strictly speaking, be disproved, is highly improbable; not only is the book of Kings silent, but Jeremiah *in the following year* (c. 25, &c., see v. 1) speaks of the Chaldeans in a manner which appears distinctly to imply that their arms had not yet been seen in Judah.[1]

Assumption Involved

The main assumption in all of these objections is that the silence of the book of Kings and other sources with regard to an expedition of Nebuchadnezzar against Jerusalem in Jehoiakim's third year renders improbable the statement of Daniel that such an expedition did occur.

Answers to the Assumption

An attempt will now be made to show that this silence does not render such an expedition improbable. Having in the first chapter discussed this kind of argument in general, I shall confine myself in this chapter to a consideration of the argument from silence in so far merely as it affects the particular statements of Dan. i, 1.

I. First of all, let us gather all the evidence that contemporary documents afford concerning the life of Jehoiakim, beginning with the *Book of Kings*. All that this book has to say on this subject will be found in 2 Kings xxiii, 36, 37, and xxiv, 1–7, which the American Standard Version renders as follows:

[1] LOT p. 498.

XXIII, 36. Jehoiakim was twenty and five years old
when he began to reign; and he reigned eleven years in
Jerusalem: and his mother's name was Zebidah the daughter of Pedaiah Rumah. (37) And he did that which was
evil in the sight of Jehovah, according to all that his fathers
had done.

XXIV, 1. In his days Nebuchadnezzar, King of Babylon, came up, and Jehoiakim became his servant three years;
then he turned and rebelled against him. (2) And Jehovah sent against him bands of the Chaldeans, and bands of
the Syrians, and bands of the Moabites, and bands of the
children of Ammon, and sent them against Judah to destroy
it, according to the word of Jehovah, which he spake by his
servants the prophets. (3) Surely at the commandment of
Jehovah came this upon Judah, to remove them out of his
sight, for the sins of Manasseh, according to all that he did,
(4) and also for the innocent blood that he shed; for he
filled Jerusalem with innocent blood: and Jehovah would
not pardon. (5) Now the rest of the acts of Jehoiakim, and
all that he did, are they not written in the book of the chronicles of the kings of Judah? (6) So Jehoiakim slept with his
fathers; and Jehoiachin his son reigned in his stead. (7) And
the king of Egypt came not again any more out of his land;
for the king of Babylon had taken, from the brook of Egypt
to the river Euphrates, all that pertained to the king of Egypt.

It will be noted that Jehoiakim reigned eleven years.
Since, according to Jer. xxv, 1, the first year of
Nebuchadnezzar corresponded to the fourth year of
Jehoiakim, they must have reigned eight years contemporaneously. Yet all that the book of Kings has to
say in regard to the relations between Babylon, Egypt,
and Jerusalem during these eight years is:

First, that in Jehoiakim's days Nebuchadnezzar the
king of Babylon came up against Jerusalem, and that
Jehoiakim served him three years.

Secondly, that then Jehoiakim rebelled again against him.

Thirdly, that the king of Egypt did not come again out of his land, because the king of Babylon had taken all that belonged to him from the brook (*wady*) of Egypt to the river Euphrates.

It will be noted, further, that the book of Kings does not say in what year Nebuchadnezzar came up. The only notes of time are, that he came up in Jehoiakim's days, and that Jehoiakim served him three years. Unless it can be shown that the phrase "King of Babylon" cannot be used proleptically, or that Nebuchadnezzar cannot have been called king before his father's death,[1] he may have come during Jehoiakim's reign at any time not earlier than the latter's third year. If Jehoiakim's rebellion was in his own eleventh year, this would leave time for the three years of service immediately before he rebelled, that is, from the eighth to the eleventh year of Jehoiakim's reign.

It will be noted, also, that Nebuchadnezzar may have come up against Judah and Jerusalem, during the period between the fall of Nineveh and the death of Jehoiakim, a number of times every year, for aught we know to the contrary. Frequent expeditions across the Euphrates were customary on the part of the kings of the Assyrians, who immediately preceded the Babylonians in the government of Syria and Palestine. Thus, Shalmaneser III says that he crossed the Euphrates twenty-two times in the first twenty-two years of his reign.[2] Is there any reason for supposing that what had been done by this king of Assyria

---

[1] For a discussion of these questions, see Chapter V.
[2] *Obelisk Inscription of Nimrud* 27, 33, 37, 45, 57, 85, 87, 89, 91, 96, 97, 99, 100, 102, 104

may not have been done, also, by the king of Babylon? What was possible for one was possible, also, for the other. Shalmaneser speaks of crossing the Amanus mountains seven times and of coming against the cities of Kati of Kana (Cilicia) four times.[1] Why may Nebuchadnezzar not have crossed Lebanon and have come against Judah in like manner, and any number of times that seemed best to him, for the accomplishment of his aims of conquest? It will not be sufficient to say in answer to this, that these campaigns could not have taken place, inasmuch as no mention of them is made on the monuments of Nebuchadnezzar; because we have no inscriptions of his that record his campaigns. We know from his building inscriptions and from the fragments of his one historical inscription that the lands to the west of the Euphrates were subject to him, and that he invaded Egypt once, at least. We are told in the writings of Berosus, Megasthenes, and Abydenus that he ruled over Egypt, Syria, Phenicia, Arabia, and Judea, and other Mediterranean lands. We are told in the Scriptures outside of Daniel that he was in possession of Syria and conquered Judea and was to be given Tyre and Sidon and Egypt. How many years and how many expeditions it took to make these conquests, we are not informed; but all authorities combine in pointing to the beginning of his reign and the years immediately preceding this, as a time of great and almost continuous activity in warlike enterprises. Consequently it is not a sufficient proof of his having made no expeditions against Judah before the fourth year of Jehoiakim to say that the Scriptures outside of Daniel do not mention such an expedition. This will appear from the following sections:

[1] *Id.*, 132, 135.

II. For all that Jeremiah, the prophet, has to say about the reign of Jehoiakim is as follows. In ch. xxv, 1–3, he says that the word of the Lord came to him:

In the fourth year of Jehoiakim the son of Josiah king of Judah, that was the first year of Nebuchadnezzar, king of Babylon. The which Jeremiah the prophet spake unto all the people of Judah, and to all the inhabitants of Jerusalem, saying, From the thirteenth year of Josiah the son of Amon king of Judah, even unto this day, that is the three and twentieth year, the word of the Lord hath come unto me, and I have spoken unto you, rising early and speaking; but ye have not hearkened.

In xxv, 8, 9, he adds:

Therefore thus saith the Lord of hosts; Because ye have not heard my words, Behold, I will send and take all the families of the north, saith the Lord, and Nebuchadnezzar the king of Babylon, my servant, and will bring them against this land, and against the inhabitants thereof, and against all these nations round about, and will utterly destroy them, and make them an astonishment, and an hissing, and perpetual desolations.

In xxvi, 1, and xxvii, 1, it is said that the word of the Lord came unto Jeremiah in the *beginning of the reign* of Jehoiakim, probably meaning his first or accession's year.   In the former, the prophet says that if they will not hearken unto Jehovah, He will make the temple like Shiloh and the city a curse to all the nations of the earth; in the latter, he says that all nations shall serve Nebuchadnezzar.   In xxxv, 1, he tells of a prophecy unto the house of the Rechabites, who came to him in the days of Jehoiakim, and explained

4

their presence in Jerusalem by saying (v. 11): "it came to pass, when Nebuchadnezzar king of Babylon came up into the land, that we said, Come, and let us go to Jerusalem for fear of the army of the Chaldeans, and for fear of the army of the Syrians; so we dwell at Jerusalem."

In chapters xxxvi, xlv, and xlvi, we have prophecies from the fourth year of Jehoiakim and in xxxvi, 9, from his fifth year. In xxxvi, 1–8, he speaks of a roll which he gave to Baruch to be read by him in the house of the Lord. In xxxvi, 9, he says that Baruch read the roll, apparently a second time, in the ninth month of the fifth year; and in the 29th and 30th verses, we learn that there were written in the roll the words: "The king of Babylon shall certainly come and destroy this land . . . and Jehoiakim shall have none to sit upon the throne of David; and his dead body shall be cast out in the day to the heat, and in the night to the frost." After the roll had been burned by Jehoiakim, we are told that another roll was written containing the same words, and also "there were added besides unto them many like words" (v. 32). Chapter xlv is a prophecy to and concerning Baruch which is said to have been written in the fourth year of Jehoiakim.

In xlvi, 1, 2, is recorded the "word of the Lord which came to Jeremiah the prophet against the Gentiles; Against Egypt, against the army of Pharaoh-Necho king of Egypt, which was by the river Euphrates in Carchemish, which Nebuchadnezzar king of Babylon smote in the fourth year of Jehoiakim." In this chapter it says that the Egyptians shall stumble and fall toward the north by ('al) the river Euphrates (v. 6); for the Lord God of hosts hath a sacrifice in the north country by ('el) the river Euphrates (v. 10); and that Egypt and all

her helpers shall be delivered into the hand of Nebuchadnezzar (v. 26).[1]

From these passages we learn:

1. That the book of Jeremiah does not pretend to
give us a history of the events of the time of Jehoiakim.
The prophecies of the 26th and 27th chapters are from
the beginning of his reign; those of the 25th, 36th, 45th,
and 46th are from his fourth year, except a part of the
36th, which is from his fifth year; and the prophecy
concerning the Rechabites in the 35th chapter is said to
be from "the days of Jehoiakim." Moreover, we are
expressly told in xxxvi, 32, that many words like to
those which have been preserved to us were added unto
them by Baruch. We have, therefore, in the book as it
stands, only selections and fragments of the records of
Jeremiah.

2. That even of the few records of the reign
of Jehoiakim preserved in the passage above mentioned, but a small number refer directly to inter-
national events. Thus, chapter xxxv concerns the Rechabites and chapter xlv, Baruch the scribe of Jeremiah;
chapter xxxvi gives an account of the roll that was written by Baruch and burned by the king; chapters xxv,
xxvi, and xxvii, are directed against Judah, and the nations round about, and especially against Jerusalem and
the temple, naming Nebuchadnezzar as God's servant
and instrument in the punishment of the nations and
the destruction of Jerusalem and the temple; chapter
xlvi alone is concerned exclusively with foreign affairs,
viz. with Egypt and Babylon.

3. That Jeremiah mentions specifically no expedition of Nebuchadnezzar against Judah or Jerusalem
in the days of Jehoiakim.

---

[1] See, also, i, 3; xxii, 18, 19.

4. But he implies in a number of places that such expeditions had been made. For,

(1) Jehoiakim had been made king by Pharaoh-Necho. When Necho was defeated and his power destroyed at Carchemish in the fourth year of Jehoiakim, Jerusalem would inevitably fall under the domination of Nebuchadnezzar.

(2) Jeremiah says that the Rechabites came and settled in Jerusalem for fear of the army of the Chaldeans, when Nebuchadnezzar king of Babylon came into the land.

(3) Jeremiah says that Nebuchadnezzar should certainly come and destroy the land and that the dead body of Jehoiakim should be cast out, apparently by the Chaldeans.

5. The only dates given are "The days of Jehoiakim" (xxxv, 1), "the fourth year of Jehoiakim" (xxxvi, 1; xxv, 1; xlvi, 2), and "the fifth year of Jehoiakim" (xxxvi, 9); the fourth year of Jehoiakim is synchronized with the first year of Nebuchadnezzar (xxv, 1); and it is stated that Jeremiah prophesied for 23 years from the 13th year of Josiah to the 4th year of Jehoiakim.

III. The book of Chronicles says with regard to the reign of Jehoiakim:

The king of Egypt made Eliakim his brother king over Judah and Jerusalem, and turned his name to Jehoiakim. And Necho took Jehoahaz his brother, and carried him to Egypt. Jehoiakim was twenty and five years old when he began to reign, and he reigned eleven years in Jerusalem; and he did that which was evil in the sight of the Lord his God. Against him came up Nebuchadnezzar King of Babylon, and bound him in fetters, to carry him to Babylon. Nebuchadnezzar also carried off the vessels of the house of the Lord to Babylon, and put them in his temple at Babylon,

Now the rest of the acts of Jehoiakim, and his abominations which he did, and that which was found in him, behold, they are written in the book of the kings of Israel and Judah. (2 Chron. xxxvi, 4–8.)

It will be noted that here it is expressly stated:

1. That Nebuchadnezzar did come up to Jerusalem in the days of Jehoiakim.

2. That he bound Jehoiakim in chains to carry him to Babylon.

3. That Nebuchadnezzar at this time carried some of the vessels of the house of Jehovah to Babylon and put them in the temple at Babylon.

IV. Neither Ezekiel, nor any other Old Testament book except Jeremiah, Kings, Chronicles, and Daniel, mentions Jehoiakim.

V. Outside the Scriptures, the testimony of the monuments bearing upon this time is as follows:

1. The monuments of Egypt which mention Necho's operations in Syria consist merely of the fragments of a stele bearing his name in hieroglyphic. This stele was found at Sidon.[1]

2. The records of Nebuchadnezzar contain nothing bearing directly upon the subject of his warlike expeditions, except the fragment found in Egypt referring to an Egyptian campaign in his 37th year.[2] The contract tablets are absolutely silent upon the political actions of his reign. As to the building inscriptions we might infer[3] that at the time when these buildings were erected,

---

[1] Breasted's *History of Egypt*, p. 405, and PSBA xvi, 91.

[2] Zehnpfund–Langdon, *Die Neo-Babylonischen Köningsinschriften*, p. 207. English original p. 182.

[3] This inference is to be made from his mention of the cedar beams with which he rebuilt Borsippa (Langdon, I, Col. ii, 2) such as Ezida (XI, Col. i, 21, and especially VII, Col. i, 25), and other of his works (*id.* V,

he held dominion over Syria, including as far as Mt. Lebanon at least.

VI.   Lastly, I shall quote what the profane historians say about these times.

1.   Josephus, in his *Antiquities*, XI, vi, 1–3, says:

In the fourth year of the reign of Jehoiakim, one whose name was Nebuchadnezzar took the government over the Babylonians, who at the same time went up with a great army to the city Carchemish, which was at Euphrates, upon a resolution he had taken to fight with Necho, king of Egypt, under whom all Syria then was.   And when Necho understood the intention of the king of Babylon, and that this expedition was made against him, he did not despise his attempt, but made haste with a great band of men to Euphrates to defend himself against Nebuchadnezzar; and when they had joined battle, he was beaten, and lost many ten thousands in the battle.   So the king of Babylon passed over Euphrates, and took all Syria, as far as Pelusium, excepting Judea.   But when Nebuchadnezzar had already reigned four years, which was the eighth of Jehoiakim's government over the Hebrews, the king of Babylon made an expedition with mighty forces against the Jews, and required tribute of Jehoiakim, and threatened, on his refusal, to make war against him.   He was frightened at his threatening, and bought his peace with money, and brought the tribute he was ordered to bring for three years.   2.   But on the third year, upon hearing that the king of the Babylonians made an expedition against the Egyptians, he did not pay his

---

Col. i, 22); his reference to the temple roofs(IX, Col. ii, 19), and his royal palace for which he brought "great cedars from Lebanon" (IX, Col. iii, 26); the great cedar beams of Emahtila (XIII, Col. i, 41, 42) of Ekua and other temples and shrines (*id.*XV, Col. iii, 27, 41, 51, Col. vi, 2, 4, and Col. viii, 3, Col. ix, 3, 10 *et al.*, XVI, Col. i, 20), and especially from XVII, Col. iii, where he speaks of summoning the princes of the land of the Hittites beyond the Euphrates westward over whom he exercised lordship. (XVII, Col. iii, 8–22.)

tribute. . . . 3. Now a little time afterwards, the king of
Babylon made an expedition against Jehoiakim, whom he
received into the city and then out of fear of the foregoing
predictions of this prophet [*i. e.*, of Jeremiah], as supposing
that he should suffer nothing that was terrible, because he
neither shut the gates, nor fought against him; yet when he
was come into the city, he did not observe the covenant he
had made; but he slew such as were in the flower of their
age, and such as were of the greatest dignity, together with
their king Jehoiakim, whom he commanded to be thrown
before the walls, without any burial; and made his son
Jehoiachin king of the country and of the city: he also
took the principal persons in dignity for captives, three
thousand in number, and led them away to Babylon; among
whom was the prophet Ezekiel, who was then but young.
And this was the end of king Jehoiakim, when he had lived
thirty-six years, and of them reigned eleven.

Further, in his work against Apion, i, 19, Josephus
says that Berosus in his History comes at length to
"Nabolassar [Nabopolassar], who was king of Babylon
and of the Chaldeans," and that Berosus in relating
the acts of this king "describes to us how he sent his son
Nabuchodonosor against Egypt, and against our land,
with a great army, upon his being informed that they
had revolted from him; and how by that means, he
subdued them all."

From these accounts of Josephus, we learn:

(1) That Nebuchadnezzar, before he became king,
was sent by his father on an expedition against Egypt
and Palestine.

(2) That Nebuchadnezzar took the government over
the Babylonians in the fourth year of Jehoiakim.

(3) That Nebuchadnezzar defeated Necho at Carchemish.

(4) That Nebuchadnezzar conquered Syria as far as Pelusium, excepting Judea, immediately after the battle of Carchemish.

(5) But that he did not make an expedition against Jerusalem till the eighth year of Jehoiakim, which was his own fourth year.

(6) That Jehoiakim paid tribute for three years.

(7) That Jerusalem was taken in the eleventh year of Jehoiakim; at which time Jehoiakim himself was killed and his body thrown before the wall without any burial.

2. In addition to the above, Berosus has the following to say about Nebuchadnezzar, to wit:

His father having perceived that the Egyptians and others had revolted, sent his son Nabuchodonosor with a great army against Egypt and against the land of Judea, who overpowered them and set fire to the temple which was in Jerusalem; and having entirely removed all the people who were in the country settled them at Babylon. It came to pass also that the city was in a state of desolation for a space of 70 years, until Cyrus king of the Persians. And he [*i. e.*, Berosus] says, that the Babylonians ruled over Egypt, Syria, Phenicia, and Arabia, and surpassed in deeds all who had been kings before him over the Chaldeans and Babylonians.[1]

Further, he says:

When Nabopolassar his [Nebuchadnezzar's] father, heard that the satrap who had been stationed in Egypt and in the plains of Cœle-Syria and Phenicia had revolted, not being able longer to endure the evil, having entrusted to his son Nebuchadnezzar, who was then in full manhood, some parts of the army, he sent him against him [*i. e.*, Nabopo-

[1] Josephus, *Contra Apion*, i, 19.

lassar sent Nebuchadnezzar against the satrap who had revolted]. And Nebuchadnezzar having joined battle with the rebel overpowered him and made the country a province under his dominion. And it happened that at this time his father Nabopolassar was seized with a lingering ailment and died in the city of the Babylonians after he had been king 29 years. Nebuchadnezzar having learned, shortly after, of the death of his father, after he had set in order the affairs in Egypt and the rest of the countries and had committed to some of his friends the captives of the Jews and Phenicians and Syrians and of the nations belonging to Egypt to bring into Babylonia with the bulk [lit. heavy part] of the army and the remainder of the spoils; he himself with a very few attendants hastened through the desert to Babylon, where he found that the affairs had been managed by Chaldeans and the kingdom watched over by the best one of them, so that he became lord of the whole of the government of his father, and he gave orders to appoint settlements for the captives in the fittest places of Babylonia, while he himself from the spoils of the war adorned the temple of Bel and other temples in a lavish manner.[1]

He then describes the walls and palaces, adding:

In these royal palaces he built lofty stone substructures and made the prospect as like to a mountain as possible by planting trees of all sorts and by making what is called a paradise; because his queen, who had been brought up in Media, desired a mountainous situation.[2]

3. Eusebius says that Abydenus in his history of the Assyrians has preserved the following fragment of Megasthenes, a Greek historian who lived about 300 B. C., and was a trusty ambassador of Seleucus Nicator[3]:

[1] *Cont. Ap.*, i, 19.   [2] *Id.*, i, 20.
[3] Abydenus himself died in 268 B. C., having written, among other works, a history of Assyria. He is said to have been a pupil of Berosus

"Nebuchadnezzar, having become more powerful than Hercules, invaded Libya and Iberia, and when he had rendered them tributary, he extended his conquests over the inhabitants of the shores upon the right of the sea."[1] These statements of Abydenus, taken from Megasthenes, are so indefinite as to be worthless as testimony in regard to the matter under discussion.

4. No other sources make any mention of the deeds of Jehoiakim, or of any other events recorded in the Scriptures as having occurred in his days.

CONCLUSION

Summing up the testimony, we find:

1. That Kings, Chronicles, Berosus, Josephus, and Daniel all affirm that Nebuchadnezzar did come up against Jerusalem in the days of Jehoiakim.

2. That Chronicles, Daniel, Berosus, and Josephus unite in saying that Nebuchadnezzar carried many captives from Judea to Babylon in the reign of Jehoiakim.

3. That Berosus supports the statement of Daniel with regard to the carrying away of some of the vessels of the house of the Lord by saying that Nebuchadnezzar brought spoils from Judea which were put in the temple of Nebuchadnezzar in Babylon.

4. That Berosus supports Daniel in declaring an expedition against Jerusalem to have occurred before the death of Nabopolassar.

5. That since Nabopolassar died while Nebuchadnezzar was in the midst of his expedition against Jerusalem, Nebuchadnezzar may have been king *de jure* before he came up against Jerusalem; for it would take

---

[1] Eusebius, *Prep. Evan.*, lib. x.

the news of the death of Nabopolassar several weeks to reach Jerusalem, and in those weeks there would have been abundance of time for Nebuchadnezzar to have captured Jerusalem, especially if Jehoiakim surrendered at this time without fighting or after a brief siege, as Josephus says that he did in his eleventh year.[1]

6. That the book of Jeremiah is silent with regard to all of these events. It does not say that Nebuchadnezzar did not come up to Jerusalem in the reign of Jehoiakim. It simply says nothing about it. Why it says nothing about it we do not know. The expedition or expeditions may have been mentioned in "the many like words" recorded by Baruch (Jer. xxxvi, 32), which have not been preserved for us.

7. That, finally, the statement of Daniel i, 1–3, that Nebuchadnezzar came up against Jerusalem in the third year of Jehoiakim and carried captive to Babylon certain of the nobility, and some of the vessels of the house of the Lord, stands absolutely unimpugned by any testimony to be produced from any reliable source of information.

[1] Jos., *Ant.*, X, vi, 3. Josephus says that Jehoiakim received Nebuchadnezzar into the city out of fear of a prediction of Jeremiah "supposing that he should suffer nothing that was terrible, because he neither shut the gate, nor fought against him."

CHAPTER IV

NEBUCHADNEZZAR'S EXPEDITION AGAINST JERUSALEM

AFTER having declared that the author of Daniel is wrong in placing the first expedition of Nebuchadnezzar against Jerusalem in the third year of Jehoiakim, because our other sources of information are silent with regard to such an expedition, the critics turn around and say that the author of Daniel was acquainted with the same sources as we are, and yet deliberately made this false statement because of his erroneous interpretations and combinations of these sources. He had before him the books of Kings, Chronicles, and Jeremiah, in the same form, as far as they refer to Nebuchadnezzar's relations to Jehoiakim and Jerusalem, that we have them; and yet, according to the critics, contrary to these sources, he incorrectly puts the third year of Jehoiakim as the year of Nebuchadnezzar's first expedition against Jerusalem, combines the statements of Kings and Chronicles in an erroneous manner, and is apparently ignorant enough of military strategy, and of the geography of Western Asia, to suppose that Nebuchadnezzar could make an expedition into Palestine, while Carchemish, as Jeremiah possibly implies, was in the hands of the Egyptians.

This is a plausible argument, and a very ingenious one. It assumes that the author of Daniel was acquainted with the canonical books of Jeremiah, Kings, and Chronicles,[1] and that these books, as far as they affect this subject, had the same text that we now find in them; and on the basis of this assumption asserts that he was either not honest enough or not intelligent enough to use his sources of information correctly.   To be more explicit, this argument assumes that the pseudo-Daniel had before him Jeremiah xxv, in which the latter is said to speak "of the Chaldeans in a manner which appears distinctly to imply that their arms had not yet been seen in Judah" before the fourth year of Jehoiakim; nevertheless he was either not bright enough or not open-minded enough to see this distinct implication, but must forsooth say that Nebuchadnezzar had been in Palestine in the third year of Jehoiakim. Again, this pseudo-Daniel had before him Jeremiah xlvi, 2, in which the defeat of the army of Pharaoh-Necho in the fourth year of Jehoiakim is mentioned,— a defeat before which, say the critics, there could be no question of Nebuchadnezzar's invading Palestine; and yet, he wilfully says that Nebuchadnezzar did invade Palestine in the third year of this same Jehoiakim. He had before him 2 Chron. xxxvi, 5, which implies that Nebuchadnezzar carried Jehoiakim and a part of the vessels of the house of the Lord to Babylon in the eleventh year of Jehoiakim's reign, and yet he states that this seizure of these vessels of the house of

[1] Of course, from the point of view of those who believe that Daniel was written in the sixth century B. C., it is impossible that Daniel could have been acquainted with either Kings or Chronicles in their present form; though he may have known their sources.   The phrase "in the books," occurring in chapter ix, 2, would seem to imply that he had read the work of Jeremiah.   If Daniel is authentic, his account of the events of the reign of Nebuchadnezzar must be accepted as genuine and original, and as of equal authority and trustworthiness with the records of Jeremiah, Kings, and Chronicles.

the Lord was in Jehoiakim's third year; because, forsooth, he had read in the book of Kings that Jehoiakim
had served Nebuchadnezzar three years before he rebelled against him.

Can anyone really suppose that the author of
Daniel, provided he had no other data than those
provided by the other biblical books, can have been
so dull as not to know that Jehoiakim, a king enthroned by Pharaoh-Necho (2 Kings xxiii, 34), can
not have served Nebuchadnezzar for *three* years
before the latter made his first expedition against
Jerusalem, inasmuch as it is plainly stated by Jeremiah
(xxv, 1) and implied in 2 Kings xxv, 8, that the first
year of Nebuchadnezzar was the fourth year of Jehoiakim? Yet the critics do make this supposition. They
do suppose that the author of Daniel, having before
him, as they say, the books of Kings, Chronicles, and
Jeremiah, did nevertheless contradict all these earlier
accounts, did fail to perceive their distinct implications,
and did make improbable and even absurd statements
as to the events already recorded in their, to him, well-
known sources. Lest injustice should seem to be done
to these critics of the authenticity of Daniel, their
objections will now be cited *verbatim et seriatim;* and
their assumptions will be discussed in the hope of showing that there is not one of them that has a real foundation of fact.

OBJECTIONS STATED

Canon Driver says:

That Nebuchadnezzar besieged Jerusalem and carried
away captive some of the sacred vessels in the *third* year
of Jehoiakim (Dan. i, 1 f.) though it cannot, strictly speak-

ing, be disproved, is highly improbable, because, Jeremiah *in the following year* (c. 25 &c.; see v. 1) speaks of the Chaldeans in a manner which appears distinctly to imply that their arms had not yet been seen in Judah.[1]

Prof. Cornill says:

Daniel's fixing the carrying away into captivity in the third year of Jehoiakim (Dan. i, 1) contradicts all contemporaneous accounts and can only be explained as due to a combination of 2 Chron. xxxvi, 6, 7, with an erroneous interpretation of 2 Kings xxiv, 1.[2]

Prof. Bevan says:

It was not till after the defeat of the Egyptian army at Carchemish on the Euphrates in the fourth year of Jehoiakim (Jer. xlvi, 2) that there could be any question of Nebuchadnezzar's invading Palestine, where for some years the Egyptians had enjoyed undisputed supremacy.[3]

Assumptions Involved

Combining these statements, we find that the carrying away into captivity (especially "of some of the vessels of the house of the Lord") in the third year of Jehoiakim is assumed to have been highly improbable:

I. Because Daniel speaks of Nebuchadnezzar as going up against Jerusalem in Jehoiakim's third year and Jeremiah implies that he did not go up before the fourth year of Jehoiakim.

II. Because of the manner in which Jeremiah in the following year speaks of the Chaldeans.

III. Because of the erroneous interpretation on the

[1] LOT p. 408.
[2] *Introduction to the Canonical Books of the Old Testament*, p. 384.
[3] *The book of Daniel*, p. 16.

part of the writer of Daniel of 2 Kings xxiv, 1, combined with 2 Chron. xxxvi, 6, 7.

IV.   Because Nebuchadnezzar is said in Jeremiah xlvi, 2, to have defeated the Egyptians at Carchemish in the fourth year of Jehoiakim; and it is not until after this battle "that there could be any question of Nebuchadnezzar's invading Palestine."

V.   Because "the Egyptians had enjoyed undisputed supremacy" in Palestine for some years before the battle of Carchemish.

VI.   Because it contradicts all contemporaneous accounts.

Before entering upon the discussion of these assumptions, it may be best to state and consider what is actually said in Daniel about what Nebuchadnezzar effected by this expedition.   The writer of Daniel says (Dan. i, 2) that the king of Babylon carried part of the vessels of the house of God into the land of Shinar to the house of his god and (Dan. i, 3, 4) that certain of the children of Israel, even of the king's seed, and of the princes, were taken to the king's palace to be taught the learning and tongue of the Chaldeans.   It is possible, also, that the writer means that Jehoiakim was taken to Babylon.   In this case, there are three points to be considered; first, is it likely that Jehoiakim was taken to Babylon in his third year; secondly, is it likely that some of the vessels of the house of the Lord were taken to Babylon at this time; and thirdly, is it likely that some of the nobility and of the royal family of Judah were taken to reside in the king's palace, and that while there they were treated as the king's protégés?

As to the first of these points, it is clear that the kings of Jehoiakim's time were in the habit of carrying off the kings of Judah into captivity.   In 2 Kings xxiii,

33, 34, it is said that Pharaoh-Necho put Jehoahaz, king of Judah, in bonds at Riblah and afterwards carried him away and that he came to Egypt and died there. In 2 Chron. xxxvi, 6, we read that Nebuchadnezzar bound Jehoiakim in fetters to carry him to Babylon. In 2 Chron. xxxvi, 10, it is said, that Nebuchadnezzar sent and brought Jehoiachin to Babylon. According to 2 Kings xxiv, 12, this was in the eighth year of Nebuchadnezzar's reign (597–8 B. C.). In this captivity Jehoiachin was kept for thirty-seven years until Evil-Merodach released him on the twenty-seventh day of the twelfth month of the year that he began to reign, that is, in the spring of 561 B. C.[1] In 2 Kings xxv, 7, we see that Zedekiah was bound with fetters of brass and carried by Nebuchadnezzar to Babylon. In Jeremiah lii, 11, we learn that he put him in prison, also, and kept him there till the day of his death. In 2 Chron. xxxiii, 11, 13, it is said that the king of Assyria (probably Esarhaddon) took Manasseh, king of Judah, and bound him with fetters and carried him to Babylon; where Manasseh prayed unto the Lord, who brought him again to Jerusalem into his kingdom.

Of course, it will be objected, that if Daniel is correct in his date, it is scarcely probable that Jehoiakim was taken to Babylon in his third year and restored and that he was taken captive to Babylon again in his eleventh year. This improbability, however, is more than offset by the certainty that Zedekiah was twice, at least, in Babylon. For in Jer. li, 59, we learn that in his *fourth* year he went to Babylon, doubtless at the behest of Nebuchadnezzar, his overlord; whereas, in his eleventh year, he was taken thither a second

[1] 2 Kings xxv, 2 f.

5

time, after he had been captured while endeavoring to escape after the fall of Jerusalem.

As to the second point, that some of the vessels of the house of the Lord were taken to Babylon in the third year of Jehoiakim, there is no good reason for doubting the statement of Daniel. To be sure, Jeremiah enumerates a large number of vessels of the house of the Lord that were carried away at the final capture of Jerusalem[1]; but according to 2 Chron. xxxvi, Nebuchadnezzar is said to have carried away vessels of the house of the Lord to Babylon at three different times, once in the eleventh year of Jehoiakim (v. 7), once a few months later when he carried away Jehoiachin (v. 10), and finally at the time of the destruction of Jerusalem (v. 18). Moreover, the writer of 2 Kings says (xxiv, 13) that the king of Babylon, at the time of Jehoiachin's captivity, cut in pieces all the vessels of gold which Solomon had made in the temple of the Lord. All of these statements are easily reconcilable, if we suppose that Nebuchadnezzar at four different times carried away part of the vessels, the last part being carried away at the time of the final capture of Jerusalem in Zedekiah's eleventh year.

As to the third of these points, that some of the nobility and of the royal family of Judah were taken to reside in the king's palace and that while there they were treated as the king's protégés we have an abundance of analogies from ancient records to prove that this may well have been true in Jehoiakim's third year, as the writer of Daniel declares.

Thus, in the Scriptures themselves, it is said in 2 Kings xxiv, 14, 15, that Nebuchadnezzar carried away to Babylon not merely Jehoiachin and his wives, but his

[1] Lii, 17–23; cf. 2 Kings xxv, 13–17.

officers (*sarisim*) and princes (*sarim*) and the mighty of the land. In like manner, in Dan. i, 1–3, it is implied that Jehoiakim was carried to Babylon along with some of the princes (here called *partumim*) and of the king's seed.

This custom was common, also, among the Assyrian kings. Thus, Tiglath-Pileser I took as hostages from Shadianteru, king of Urartinash, his sons and family.[1] Asurnaṣirabal and Shalmaneser III, also, continued the custom.[2] Shalusunu of Harruna and his sons were pardoned by Shalmaneser III, and sent back to their land. Esarhaddon granted favor to Laili, king of Jadi, and offered him friendship, gave him back his goods and the land of Bazi.[3] Ashurbanipal showed favor to Necho, king of Memphis, made treaties (*ade*) with him, clothed him with particolored garments and a golden band, put rings of gold on his fingers, and gave him an iron sword adorned with gold with the king's name upon it, presented him with wagons and horses, and established him and his son Nabushezibanni in the sovereignty of Sais.[4]

So among the Persian kings may be noted the treatment of Astyages, Crœsus, and Nabunaid by Cyrus; of Antiochus son of Miltiades and of Democedes the Crotonan physician, by Darius; and of Themistocles and Alcibiades by later kings.

Having thus reviewed what Daniel himself has to say with regard to what Nebuchadnezzar carried away captive in the third year of Jehoiakim and shown that what he says harmonizes with what we know from the documentary evidence provided by the monuments,

[1] KB i, 20. See also pages 22, 32, 34, 36.
[2] KB i, pp. 72, 88, 104, 106, 112, 144, 148.   [3] *Id.*, ii, 132.
[4] KB ii, 167. See also pp. 170, 172, 178, 184, 190, 208, 222.

we are now prepared to consider the assumptions mentioned above.

I. It is said, that Daniel seems to confound the third year of Jehoiakim with the fourth year spoken of by Jeremiah in chapter xxv, 1.

In this objection, it is assumed, that the fourth year of Jehoiakim of which Jeremiah speaks must be different from the third year of which Daniel speaks. In view of the testimony of the Babylonian and Egyptian monuments, it is impossible longer to uphold this assumption. Among the Babylonians in the time of Nebuchadnezzar, the remainder of the last year of a king was not called the "first year" of his successor, but "the year of the beginning of his reign." The *first year* began on the first of Nisan following the death of his predecessor. For example, the last dated tablet of Nebuchadnezzar to which I have had access, is dated in the forty-third year, fourth month, twenty-seventh day. The earliest from the reign of Evil-Merodach is dated in the sixth month, the fourth day of *the year of the beginning of the reign* of Evil-Merodach.[1] The next earliest is dated on the 26th day of the second month[2] and there is one from the 22nd day of the third month of the same year.[3] It is therefore evident that the forty-third year of Nebuchadnezzar is the same as *the year of the beginning of the reign* of Evil-Merodach; and the latter's first year is what would be called by many his second year.

The Egyptians, however, pursued a different method of reckoning. "The years of the kings' reigns in the twenty-sixth dynasty (of Egypt) began on New Year's day"; for "it is evident that the fraction of [Psamtik

[1] See for this usage in the Scriptures, 2 K. xxv, 27.
[2] VSD vi, 55.
[3] *Id.*, vi, 56.

the First's] incomplete (55th) year was, after his death, included in the first year of his successor, Necho."[1] As Petrie remarks, "The absence of odd months and days from the lengths of the reign shows that the dates are in fixed months of the year, and that the years were counted from New Year's day."[2] To quote Wilcken,[3] a king's " second year began with the first New Year's day which he passed on the throne, so that the last broken year of his predecessor was counted as his first."

Owing to these two methods of reckoning, it is obvious that the third year of a king according to the Babylonian calendar would be his fourth according to the Egyptian. Among the Hebrews, it is generally agreed, that the Egyptian method of reckoning the years of a king was employed.[4]

II. The expedition of Nebuchadnezzar in the third year of Jehoiakim is said to be improbable, because "of the way in which Jeremiah in the following year speaks of the Chaldeans." Dr. Driver, in this statement, refers to the 25th chapter of Jeremiah, especially to the first verse. The American Revision gives the chapter as follows:[5]

(1) The word that came to Jeremiah concerning all the people of Judah, in the fourth year of Jehoiakim the son of Josiah, king of Judah (the same was the first year of Nebuchadnezzar king of Babylon), (2) which Jeremiah the prophet spake unto all the people of Judah, and to all the inhabitants of Jerusalem, saying: (3) From the thirteenth year of Josiah the son of Amon, king of Judah, even unto

[1] Breasted, *History of Egypt*, vol. iv, sec. 975.
[2] *History of Egypt*, iii, 339.   [3] *Greichische Ostraka*, i, 783.
[4] Reginald Stuart Poole in Smith's *Dictionary of the Bible*, i, 439.
[5] We cite as far as the end of verse 33.

this day, these three and twenty years, the word of Jehovah hath come unto me, and I have spoken unto you, rising up early and speaking; but ye have not hearkened. (4) And Jehovah hath sent unto you all his servants the prophets, rising up early and sending them (but ye have not hearkened, nor inclined your ear to hear), (5) saying, Return ye now every one from his evil way, and from the evil of your doings, and dwell in the land that Jehovah hath given unto you and to your fathers, from of old and even for evermore; (6) and go not after other gods to serve them and to worship them, and provoke me not to anger with the work of your hands; and I will do you no hurt. (7) Yet ye have not hearkened unto me, saith Jehovah; that ye may provoke me to anger with the work of your hands to your own hurt. (8) Therefore thus saith Jehovah of hosts: Because ye have not heard my words, (9) behold, I will send and take all the families of the north, saith Jehovah, and I will send unto Nebuchadnezzar the king of Babylon, my servant, and will bring them against this land, and against the inhabitants thereof, and against all these nations round about; and I will utterly destroy them, and make them an astonishment, and a hissing, and perpetual desolations. (10) Moreover I will take from them the voice of mirth and the voice of gladness, the voice of the bridegroom and the voice of the bride, the sound of the millstones, and the light of the lamp. (11) And this whole land shall be a desolation, and as astonishment; and these nations shall serve the king of Babylon seventy years.

(12) And it shall come to pass, when seventy years are accomplished, that I will punish the king of Babylon, and that nation, saith Jehovah, for their iniquity, and the land of the Chaldeans; and I will make it desolate forever. (13) And I will bring upon that land all my words which I have pronounced against it, even all 'that is written in this book, which Jeremiah hath prophesied against all the nations. (14) For many nations and great kings shall make bondmen of them, even of them; and I will recompense

them according to their deeds, and according to the work of their hands.

(15) For thus saith Jehovah, the God of Israel, unto me: Take this cup of the wine of wrath at my hand, and cause all the nations, to whom I send thee, to drink it. (16) And they shall drink, and reel to and fro, and be mad, because of the sword that I will send among them. (17) Then took I the cup at Jehovah's hand and made all the nations to drink, unto whom Jehovah had sent me: (18) to wit, Jerusalem, and the cities of Judah, and the kings thereof, and the princes thereof, to make them a desolation, an astonishment, a hissing, and a curse as it is this day; (19) Pharaoh king of Egypt, and his servants, and his princes, and all his people; (20) and all the mingled people, and all the kings of the land of Uz, and all the kings of the land of the Philistines, and Ashkelon, and Gaza, and Ekron, and the remnant of Ashdod; (21) Edom, and Moab, and the children of Ammon; (22) and all the kings of Tyre, and all the kings of Sidon, and the kings of the isle which is beyond the sea; (23) Dedan, and Tema, and Buz, and all that have the corners of their hair cut off; (24) and all the kings of Arabia, and all the kings of the mingled people that dwell in the wilderness; (25) and all the kings of Zimri, and all the kings of Elam, and all the kings of the Medes; (26) and all the kings of the north, far and near, one with another; and all the kingdoms of the world, which are upon the face of the earth: and the king of Sheshach shall drink after them.

(27) And thou shalt say unto them, Thus saith Jehovah of Hosts, the God of Israel: Drink ye, and be drunken, and spew, and fall, and rise no more, because of the sword which I will send among you. (28) And it shall be, if they refuse to take the cup at thy hand to drink, then shalt thou say unto them, Thus saith Jehovah of Hosts: Ye shall surely drink. (29) For, lo, I begin to work evil at the city which is called by my name; and should ye be utterly unpunished? Ye shall not be unpunished; for I will call

for the sword upon all the inhabitants of the earth, saith Jehovah of Hosts.

(30) Therefore prophesy thou against them all these words, and say unto them, Jehovah will roar from on high, and utter his voice from his holy habitation; he will mightily roar against his fold; he will give a shout, as they that tread the grapes, against all the inhabitants of the earth.   (31) A noise shall come even to the end of the earth; for Jehovah hath a controversy with the nations; he will enter into judgment with all flesh: as for the wicked, he will give them to the sword, saith Jehovah.

(32) Thus saith Jehovah of Hosts, Behold, evil shall go forth from nation to nation, and a great tempest shall be raised up from the uttermost parts of the earth.   (33) And the slain of Jehovah shall be at that day from one end of the earth even unto the other end of the earth; they shall not be lamented, neither gathered, nor buried; they shall be dung upon the face of the ground.

It will be noted by the reader:

First, that nothing is said here about the *third* year of Jehoiakim.

Secondly, that nothing is said about an expedition in the fourth year.

Thirdly, that it is said simply, that the word of the Lord came unto Jeremiah in the fourth year.

Fourthly, that the prophecy refers to events still future with reference to the fourth year of Jehoiakim. See verses 9–33.

Fifthly, that the phrase in the eighteenth verse, "as it is this day," implies that Judah had been already conquered and devastated.

Lastly, that the failure to mention Nebuchadnezzar's expedition in the third year, or his overlordship in the fourth year, is no more striking than his failure to mention Necho. The failure to mention Necho is especially noteworthy, if he were still overlord of Judah when this prophecy was made.

III. The statement that there was an expedition in the third year of Jehoiakim is said to arise from an erroneous interpretation on the part of the writer of Daniel of 2 Kings xxiv, 1, combined with 2 Chron. xxxvi, 6, 7. The verse from Kings reads as follows:

In his days Nebuchadnezzar king of Babylon came up, and Jehoiakim became his servant three years: then he turned and rebelled against him [*i. e.*, rebelled *again* against him]. (2 Kings xxiv, 1.)

The verses from Chronicles read thus:

(6) Against him came up Nebuchadnezzar king of Babylon, and bound him in fetters, to carry him to Babylon. (7) Nebuchadnezzar also carried off the vessels of the house of Jehovah to Babylon, and put them in his temple at Babylon. (2 Chron. xxxvi, 6, 7.)

Comparing these verses with Daniel i, 1, it will be remarked:

First, that neither Kings nor Chronicles says one word about the year of the expedition, nor

Secondly, whether Nebuchadnezzar came up once, or twice, or several times,

Thirdly, that Daniel does not say anything about the putting of Jehoiakim in chains, nor

Fourthly, about the carrying of Jehoiakim to Babylon, but

Fifthly, that both Daniel and Chronicles do state that Nebuchadnezzar brought a part of the vessels of the house of the Lord to Babylon. These statements harmonize perfectly with each other, and, also, with

2 Kings xxv, 13-17, which mentions in detail the vessels, pillars, etc., of the house of the Lord which were carried to Babylon at the time of the final capture of Jerusalem.

Sixthly, there is no reason, therefore, for supposing that the writer of Daniel got his information from either Kings or Chronicles, much less that he made an "erroneous interpretation" of them. The statements of the three books are entirely harmonious. There is absolutely no error in Daniel's narrative, so far as can be seen from a comparison of his account with the accounts in Kings and Chronicles. On this matter, the average reader is just as well able to judge as the most learned professor in Christendom. There is here no dispute about texts or versions. The learned counsel for the prosecution asserts that the writer of Daniel got his information from Kings and Chronicles, and that he did not know enough to take it straight, and presumes that the ignorant jury, his credulous readers, will not be able to perceive that his assertion is not proof!

IV. It is said to be improbable that Nebuchadnezzar advanced upon Jerusalem in the third year of Jehoiakim, because in Jeremiah xlvi, 2, he is said to have captured Carchemish in the fourth year of Jehoiakim. This statement is based on the assumption that Nebuchadnezzar would scarcely have dared to advance on Jerusalem, leaving a strong garrison of Egyptians entrenched in his rear and at such a strategic point as Carchemish, which commanded the Euphrates and the great routes of possible retreat from Palestine by way of Palmyra and by way of the Orontes valley.

This argument involves several assumptions:

It is an assumption to say that Pharaoh-Necho ever conquered Carchemish. In 2 Kings xxiii, 29, it is said that Pharaoh-Necho went up against the king of Assyria to the river Euphrates; and that King Josiah went against him and was slain by him at Megiddo. In 2 Chron. xxxv, 20, it is said that "Necho king of Egypt went up to fight against Carchemish by Euphrates: and Josiah went out against him" "in the valley of Megiddo" (xxxv. 22), and in the battle, Josiah was so wounded that he died shortly after in Jerusalem (xxxv, 23, 24). We are not informed whether Necho reached Carchemish in this campaign, much less that he captured it. Our only evidence on the subject is that he went as far as Riblah in the land of Hamath,[1] which was in the valley of the Orontes on the way to the Euphrates on whose left bank Carchemish was situated. Notice, it is not affirmed that he did not reach the Euphrates, nor that he did not capture Carchemish; but merely that no texts that we have assert that he did, or to be more precise, that he reached it *in this campaign*. We are informed merely that he set out for the Euphrates and Carchemish; but Josiah interfered with his plans, and we are left to conjecture as to whether he proceeded farther than Riblah. Remember, that no contemporaneous source outside the Scripture says anything about an expedition of Necho against Assyria, nor of his ever having come to Carchemish.

But are we not told in Jeremiah xlvi, 2, "concerning the army of Pharaoh-Necho king of Egypt, which was by the river Euphrates in Carchemish, which Nebuchadnezzar king of Babylon smote in the fourth year of Jehoiakim"? True. But the assumption here is,

[1] 2 Kings xxiii, 33.

that because the army was there in the fourth year of Jehoiakim, it must have arrived there in or before his third year, when Daniel says that Nebuchadnezzar came to Jerusalem. Notice, it is not affirmed that Necho, or his army at least, did not reach the Euphrates, or that it did not capture Carchemish, in the first year, or in the second year, or in the third year of Jehoiakim, but simply, that it is an assumption, an inference, that he did. There is no direct evidence, no explicit statement, of any contemporaneous author, that Necho himself ever saw the Euphrates; nor that his army ever occupied Carchemish.

But does it not say that Necho "went up against the king of Assyria to the river Euphrates"? To be sure; but even Von Lengerke admits that the Hebrew verb must be taken here as meaning "started to go up."[1] If, however, this be not admitted, then the sentence which follows[2] can only be interpreted as meaning, that Josiah came out to meet Necho on his way back from Carchemish on the Euphrates; or the verb would have to be rendered by a pluperfect, which possibility, all critics would instantly reject.

Again, someone may say, does not the text of Jeremiah xlvi, 2, clearly state, that Nebuchadnezzar smote the army of Pharaoh-Necho by the river Euphrates *in* Carchemish? Yes. The English authorized version says so.[3] But the Hebrew may just as well be rendered

---

[1] *Das Buch Daniel*, p. 14.

[2] Introduced as it is in Hebrew by Wau converso-consecutive.

[3] Jeremiah xlvi, 1, 2, reads as follows: "The word of the Lord which came to Jeremiah the prophet against the Gentiles; against Egypt, against the army of Pharaoh-Necho king of Egypt, which was by [Heb. *'al*] the river Euphrates, in [Heb. *b'*] Carchemish, which Nebuchadnezzar king of Babylon smote in the fourth year of Jehoiakim the son of Josiah king of Judah.

at or *by* Carchemish; in which case, it is equally probable that the Egyptians were attacked while besieging the city, as while defending it. Granting, however, that the Egyptians had possession of Carchemish at the time of the battle, it does not follow that they had possession of it since the first year of Jehoiakim. It is certainly possible, that they may have captured it, or that it may have voluntarily thrown open its gates to them, between the time when Nebuchadnezzar besieged Jerusalem in the third year of Jehoiakim and the time when the battle was fought in his fourth year. The tablets show that Nabopolassar was still reigning in the second month of his twenty-first year and that Nebuchadnezzar was certainly king in the fourth month of the same year. The last tablet from the reign of Nabopolassar thus far published is dated in the 2d month of the last year of his reign. The first of Nebuchadnezzar is dated on the 14th day of the 4th month of the same year. When Nebuchadnezzar had been called back so suddenly to Babylon by the death of his father, what more likely than that Necho should have seized upon this opportunity to overrun the whole country as far as the Euphrates and that Carchemish should have surrendered to him? At least, no one can deny that this may have happened. More arduous and lengthy campaigns have been made hundreds of times. A few weeks are all that would be necessary to march from Pelusium, or Gaza, to Carchemish.

Finally, however, even granting that Pharaoh-Necho or his army reached the Euphrates in the first year of Jehoiakim, and that Carchemish was captured, or occupied peaceably, by the Egyptians before the third year of Jehoiakim, what follows? That Nebuchadnezzar did not besiege Jerusalem in the third year of

Jehoiakim, because he would not have dared, forsooth, to leave a hostile fortress in his rear? Certainly not. Such things are occurring all the time in modern warfare and have occurred in countless campaigns since the beginning of human history. Witness in our lifetime Strassbourg and Port Arthur and Adrianople and Antwerp. Witness Genoa and other Italian fortresses during Napoleon's campaigns in Italy. Witness Scipio's carrying the war into Africa, while Hannibal was still within striking distance of Rome. Witness Nebuchadnezzar's own campaign against Jerusalem, while Tyre was still unconquered in his rear. It is perfectly obvious that if Nebuchadnezzar could conquer Palestine and Syria, it would be only a question of time when Carchemish and all the other cities held by Egyptian garrisons must fall, as Danzig fell, and had to fall, when Napoleon could not make head against the allied troops and come to its relief. For it is not likely—at least we have no evidence—that either Babylon, or the line of Nebuchadnezzar's communication with Babylon, was in any danger, or can have been in any danger from the armies of Egypt then present in Syria. For a hundred years, the Egyptians had met the Assyrian armies on many a field and had been repeatedly defeated, and the land of Egypt had many times been conquered by her more warlike foes. Nebuchadnezzar's armies were composed largely of the same materials as those of his predecessors of Nineveh, and succeeded to their renown and military superiority. He may well have risked much in his consciousness of strength. It must be remembered also that Carchemish was not on the most direct line of communication between Jerusalem and Babylon. The route from Jerusalem to Babylon by way of Damascus and

Palmyra crossed the Euphrates about 250 miles below Carchemish, at a place called Thapsacus where there is a shallow ford often only eighteen inches deep. Here is where the ten thousand crossed. Here is where Alexander crossed (Arr., iii, 7). As long as the Babylonians held control of this ford and of Palmyra and Damascus, their line of communication with Palestine through the desert would be safe. Necho's only possible plans must have been either to fight and conquer Nebuchadnezzar himself in Palestine; or to break his line of communication at Damascus by an army acting from Hamath or Tyre, or at Thapsacus by an army acting from Carchemish. In either of these cases, the triumph of the Egyptians must at best have been but temporary, unless they had been powerful enough to overcome Nebuchadnezzar's army, and the army of his father Nabopolassar, in the field.

V. It is asserted, that the Egyptians had enjoyed undisputed supremacy in Palestine for some years before the battle of Carchemish.

The purpose of this assertion is to show that the statement of Daniel i, 1, that Nebuchadnezzar besieged Jerusalem in the third year of Jehoiakim is false, inasmuch as the battle of Carchemish was in the fourth year of the latter. No proofs are given in support of this assertion; and we claim, that it is a pure assumption based upon insufficient evidence, and a begging of the whole question at issue.

For, in the first place, the records of Egypt give us no ground for such a statement. Prof. Breasted,[1] gives us only two Egyptian documents bearing on the reign of Necho, neither of which so much as mentions Palestine. The Babylonian documents give us no informa-

[1] *Ancient Records of Egypt*, vol. iv, pages 498, 499.

tion upon the subject.   The only authorities regarding
the Palestinian expeditions and relations of Necho given
by Prof. Petrie in his *History of Egypt* are Herodotus
and the Bible and the fragment of an Egyptian monument found at Sidon.[1]   All that Herodotus has to say
upon Necho's connection with Palestine is as follows:
"Necho having come to an engagement with the Syrians
on land at Magdolus, conquered them, and after the
battle took Cadytis, which is a large city in Syria.
Afterward, having reigned sixteen years in all, he died
and left the kingdom to his son Psammis."[2]

The biblical sources of information upon this matter
are extremely meager.   Jeremiah mentions Necho but
once—namely, in xlvi, 2, which reads in the *American
Standard Edition;* "Of Egypt: concerning the army of
Pharaoh-Necho king of Egypt, which was by the river
Euphrates in [Heb. *b'*] Carchemish, which Nebuchadnezzar king of Babylon smote in the fourth year of
Jehoiakim the son of Josiah king of Judah." It is
possible, also that Jeremiah refers to the period before Jehoiakim's fourth year in xlvii, 1, which reads:
"The word of Jehovah that came to Jeremiah the prophet concerning the Philistines, before that Pharaoh
smote Gaza." The Egyptian fragment from Sidon
proves merely that Necho at some time in his reign
held possession of that city.

It seems clear then that we are fully justified in asserting, that there is no sufficient reason for assuming that
there is anything improbable in the statements
of the book of Daniel about the campaigns of Nebuchadnezzar against Jerusalem in the third year of
Jehoiakim.

VI. It is said by the critics that the carrying

[1] See vol. iii, 336.   [2] Bk. II, 159.

away of Judah into captivity in the third year of Jehoiakim is highly improbable because "it contradicts all contemporaneous accounts."

Inasmuch as there are no contemporaneous documents known, which say one word about the movements of either Nebuchadnezzar, or Jehoiakim, in the *third* year of the latter king, we may safely rule this objection out of court. It cannot be too strongly emphasized that whatever his creed, or learning, or critical acumen, or insight, the *ipse dixits*, the mere assertions, of any man with regard to the movements of the kings of the time of Nebuchadnezzar, are worthy of absolutely no consideration whatsoever, insofar as they are unsupported by evidence. What any man thinks about the matter is opinion, not evidence. Necho, king of Egypt, and all the records of Egypt are silent about the third year of Jehoiakim. Nabopolassar and Nebuchadnezzar, kings of Babylon, and the Babylonian documents of a private as well as of a public character, are silent about it. The biblical books of Kings, Chronicles, Jeremiah and Ezekiel, are silent with regard to it. Berosus, the Babylonian historian, and Josephus, the Jewish historian, who claim to have had access to contemporaneous documents, support the statement that Nebuchadnezzar had made an expedition across the Euphrates a short time before his father Nabopolassar died; that is, either in the third or fourth year of Jehoiakim. The writer of Dan. i, 1, declares that Nebuchadnezzar did make an expedition against Jerusalem in the third year of Jehoiakim. As to this point, the writer of the book of Daniel, at whatever time it was written, would probably know more than we do to-day; for *we know nothing*. No evidence proves nothing. This attack on the veracity of the writer of the book of Daniel

6

should be ruled out until some evidence is forthcoming to show that he did not come up against Jerusalem during this third year of Jehoiakim.

Conclusion

So that, in concluding the discussion of the objections to Daniel on the ground of the date given in chapter i, 1, let us say that to harmonize perfectly the apparent anachronisms of Daniel i, 1, and Jeremiah xxv, 1, we have only to suppose that Jeremiah writing in Palestine used the manner of reckoning common in that country, and that Daniel writing in Babylon used the method there employed; or to assume that there were two distinct expeditions, one in the 3rd and one in the 4th year of Jehoiakim.

CHAPTER V

THE USE OF THE WORD "KING"

LET me but define the terms and I shall win in almost any argument. Let me use my terms in one sense while my opponent uses the same terms in another sense, and we shall probably never agree. The importance of closely defining the use of terms and using these terms in the sense defined is commonly recognized in the spheres of philosophy, theology, grammar, law, mathematics, in every department of natural science and in every kind of rational discussion. Is man immortal? That depends on how you define immortality. Certainly, his material body is not. Are there three persons in the Trinity? That depends on your definition of person. Is a corporation, an animal, or a plant, a person? That again depends on a definition.

But the definition of a term in its present uses may differ from the definition of the term in its former, or original use. Thus the word *person* originally meant "a mask for actors." Later, it meant a "part acted on the stage." Then we have its theological, legal, grammatical, and biological uses, all strictly defined. Last of all, there are its common uses to denote an individual human being, or even "the body of a human being, or its characteristic appearance or condition."

From the present uses of the word person in English, we learn: First, that it is never used in the sense of its

Latin etymon; secondly, that in the sense of "a part acted on the stage," it has become obsolete; and thirdly, that it has several different uses in common speech and at least four different connotations in as many different sciences. It may be remarked, further, that in no other language, ancient or modern, do we find the word used in just these senses, nor any other single word exactly corresponding to it. To confirm this statement, it is only necessary to turn up an English-Latin, English-French, English-German, or English-what-you-will dictionary.

It will thus be seen that before making assertions based upon the meanings of the word person in an English work that has been translated from some foreign tongue, it would be best to look up the uses of the term in the original, in order to see if the word there found connotes exactly what person connotes in English. The question of primary importance here is, whether the word translated by person meant the same in the original language that person means in ours. And to find this out, it is not enough to know merely the meaning of the word person in English at the time that the translation was made; but, also, the meaning of the corresponding word in the original document at the time when it was written. If, at the time when the translation is made, there is not in the language into which the translation is made, a word corresponding exactly to the meaning of the original, one of three things must be done: either a new word must be coined, or a new meaning must be given to an old word, or the word of the original must be adopted into the translation.

Many of the ambiguities of the Scriptures arise from this almost insurmountable difficulty in making

a correct translation from the original text. To coin
new words, or to take over a word from the original,
is often to make the version unintelligible to the ordinary reader for whom the version is primarily prepared;
while, to use an old word in a new meaning is to lay the
reader open to a misunderstanding of the true sense of a
passage. This is the fundamental reason why all appeals in matters of biblical doctrine should be made to
the original languages of the Scripture. This is the
true and sufficient reason why all discussion among
scholars as to the meaning of disputed passages should
be based upon the *ipsissima verba*. This is a firm and
ever existing ground for the insistence of the church,
that her teachers shall be thoroughly conversant with
the original languages of the Word of God. Translations must err, because no given language has terms
for expressing thought which exactly correspond to the
terminology of another.

The above discussion will make plain to the lay
mind, why it has been thought necessary to devote a
large part of this volume to a consideration of the
connotations of terms. It is because in the sphere of
history as well as in that of theology, philosophy, and
science, the divergencies of our authorities have arisen
largely from difficulties and ambiguities arising from,
and inherent in, the very nature of language, and
especially from the inadequacy of one language to express
with exactness the ideas involved in the vocables
of another. This is a sufficient reason for devoting so
much effort to the elucidation of the terms on whose
correct definition depends in large measure the issue
of the matters in debate.

The first words to be considered are the words
for "king," because these words constitute the sub-

stance of many of the objections against the historicity of the book of Daniel. What is the meaning of the word "king"? Can Nebuchadnezzar have been called "king of Babylon" before the decease of his father Nabopolassar, king of Babylon? May Darius have been king at the same time that Cyrus was king? What is the meaning of the word "kingdom"? May Nabunaid, Belshazzar, and Cyrus, may Darius the Mede and Cyrus, the Persian, have had " the kingdom" at the same time? Upon our answer to these questions will depend largely our attitude to the question of the historicity of the book of Daniel.

That I may not seem to be beating a man of straw, I shall now revert in the discussion of this matter to my ordinary method of procedure, stating and discussing the various objections, and assumptions involved in them, in so far as they are connected with the definition of the words for king, deferring the discussion of the words for kingdom to the second volume which will be concerned solely with the language of Daniel. First of all I shall consider the case of Nebuchadnezzar.

OBJECTION STATED

Prof. Bertholdt makes the following objection to the possibility of Nebuchadnezzar's having been called king as early as the third year of Jehoiakim, that is, a year before the death of his father Nabopolassar:

Jeremiah xxv, (1) says, that Nebuchadnezzar ascended the throne in Babylon in the fourth year of Jehoiakim. How then is it possible, that according to the composer of this biographical sketch of Daniel, the *King* Nebuchadnezzar could already in the third year of Jehoiakim have besieged and taken Jerusalem?[1]

[1] Bertholdt's *Daniel*, p. 169.

That is, Nebuchadnezzar could not have been called "king of Babylon" in describing what he did in the third year of Jehoiakim, since he did not as a matter of fact become king until the latter's fourth year. Hence, only someone ignorant of this fact could possibly have written Daniel i, 1. As a man carried away by Nebuchadnezzar and living at Nebuchadnezzar's court cannot have been ignorant of such a simple matter, the mis-statement cannot possibly have been penned by the Daniel of tradition or by a contemporary of his, unless, forsooth, he had wished to misrepresent the facts.

ASSUMPTIONS INVOLVED

It will be noted, that this objection is valid only when we make one or more of the following assumptions in regard to the use of the word "king":

1. That one cannot truthfully refer to a man as king, unless he was reigning at the time referred to.

2. That a man related to a king may not have been called king for the sake of distinction or honor.

3. That the word for king as used by Daniel must have had the same meaning, the same connotation that we would assign to it to-day.

ANSWER TO THE OBJECTION

All of the assumptions just stated must be shown to be true, before we will admit that it is a valid objection to the book of Daniel that the author calls Nebuchadnezzar the king of Babylon before the decease of his father Nabopolassar. If, however, any one of these assumptions be false, the critics must admit that Nebuchadnezzar may have been called king before he actually ascended the throne, either proleptically, or for distinction or honor, or in some sense different from that in which he was king after the decease of his father.

Accordingly, we shall attempt to show the invalidity of these assumptions, following the order given above.

I. (1) First, then, it is assumed, that it is a mistake of Daniel to have called Nebuchadnezzar "king of Babylon" when referring to an act which he performed before he had actually become king. We might dismiss the objection as puerile, were it not apparently made in all seriousness. Taking the matter up seriously, then, let us ask the question what would an author of the Book of Daniel writing in 535 B. C., or thereabout, have desired his readers to understand with regard to the man who in the third year of Jehoiakim led the expedition against Jerusalem. Obviously, only so much as he deemed necessary to the reader's understanding of the story of Daniel and his three companions, which it was his purpose to relate. He attains this end by telling us that this man besieged Jerusalem and secured, perhaps in order to insure his departure without capturing the city, a number of captives of the better sort, probably as hostages; and, as a ransom, a part of the vessels of the house of the Lord. Captives and vessels were both brought to Babylon, the former to serve as eunuchs in the palace, the latter to be used in the service of the gods.

Notice, that all of these preliminary statements are necessary to an understanding of the story that follows. They introduce us to the *dramatis personæ* of the story. Now, it is certain, that the tale of *dramatis personæ* would not be complete if the author omitted the name of the hero or villain, who was none other than Nebu-

chadnezzar, the King of Babylon. It is not Nebuchadnezzar, the man, nor the general, nor the son of the
king of Babylon, nor the crown prince, that is the
principal personage of the book, but Nebuchadnezzar
the king, the king of great Babylon which he boasted
to have built,—the king, proud, haughty, defiant, putting his claims before those of God and oppressing
his true worshipers. Now, the writer might have
said, to be sure, that in the third year of Jehoiakim,
Nebuchadnezzar, while acting as general for his father
Nabopolassar, came up against Jerusalem and besieged
it and was given hostages and a ransom to induce him to
depart without capturing the city; that he did thus
depart, having been informed about that time that his
father was dead and that he had in consequence become
king of Babylon *de jure;* that he returned to Babylon
to assert his claims to be king *de facto*, bringing, or
causing to be brought with him the hostages and vessels
he had taken; and that he, as king, put the hostages in
his palace and the vessels in his temple. This would
have been explicit and detailed as to the acts of Nebuchadnezzar; but will anyone say that it is more illumin-
ating as to *who he was?* Writing seventy years after
the expedition recorded in Daniel i, 1, and twenty-five
years after the death of the general in command of the
expedition, the author would naturally suppose that his
readers would know whom he meant when he calls him
Nebuchadnezzar, the king of Babylon. Just as, to
quote Sir Robert Anderson,[1] the newspapers at the
time of the unveiling of the statue of Queen Victoria
at Kensington Gardens, spoke of the Queen's having
once lived in Kensington Palace; whereas she lived
there only before she became Queen. So we have lives

[1] *Daniel in the Critics Den*, p. 20.

of the Emperor Augustus, or of the Empress Catherine of Russia, or of President Grant, beginning in each case with an account of what they were and of what they did before they attained the highest titles by which they are now known.

(2) It is assumed, that the phrase "king of X" can be used only of a man who was *de facto* king, when some deed said to have been done by him or to him was accomplished. But who can see any impropriety in the phrase "Jesse begat David the king" in Matthew i, 6? Everyone knows it means "David who afterwards became king." Or who would pronounce it a mistake in 2 Kings xxv, 27, when it is said that Evil-Merodach "did lift up the head of Jehoiachin king of Judah"? Obviously, it means "Jehoiachin who thirty-seven years before had been king of Judah." So, if the writer of the book of Daniel composed his book about 535 B. C., he may very well have called Nebuchadnezzar "king of Babylon" when referring to a time before he had become king, meaning "that Nebuchadnezzar who some time after became king of Babylon," or "whom you, my readers, know as having been king of Babylon."

II. It is assumed that the phrase may not have been used simply for the sake of distinction or honor. But (1) as a title of distinction the phrase "the king" is used in Matthew i, 6, to distinguish the particular David meant. In Daniel i, 2, Jehoiakim is called "king of Judah" to show clearly the particular Jehoiakim that was meant. So, also, Nebuchadnezzar is called, or may be called "king of Babylon" in Daniel i, 1, to distinguish him from any other possible Nebuchadnezzar. In the second century B. C. everyone in Palestine may well have known but one Nebuchadnezzar and the title would scarcely have been necessary. But at Babylon in the sixth century B. C., there may have been many Nebuchadnezzars. Certainly, in the seventh century there were two Nebuchadnezzars.[1] Besides, a son of Nabunaid was almost certainly so called; for if not, why did the two usurpers, the rebels against Darius Hystaspis mentioned on the Behistun Inscription, assume that name?[2]

(2) The word "king" may have been used to denote the son of the king. It is so used in the Arabic of the Arabian Nights in the story of Taj-el-Molouk, where the prince is twice called "a king, the son of a king," although his father Suleiman was still reigning.[3] In like manner "queen" is frequently used to denote the unmarried daughter of a king, although she was not reigning; just as in England they would say "the Princess Victoria."[4] Antiochus Soter, calls himself "king of the lands," Seleucus his son "king" and Stratonike his wife "queen."[5] In Greek, also, the word for king is used of the son of the king or of anyone sharing in the government.[6]

(3) The word "king" may also have been used to denote the father of a king, although this father may never have actually reigned. How else can we account for the fact, that Nergal-shar-uṣur on the Cylinder inscription at Cambridge calls his father Bel-shum-ishkun "king of Babylon,"[7] whereas on the Ripley

---

[1] Johns, *Assyrian Deeds and Documents*, iii, 230.

[2] There are several tablets from Babylon assigned to Nebuchadnezzar III who claimed to be the son of Nabunaid. See Peiser in KB iv, 298–303.   [3] Lane, ii, 336.

[4] Compare the use of "queen" in the Arabian Nights stories of Badoura and Marouf, Lane, ii, 542.

[5] Weissbach, *Die Keilinschriften der Achæmeniden*, p. 135.

[6] *Od.*, iii, 394; viii, 290; Xen., *Œc.*, iv, 16.   [7] KB iii, 72.

Cylinder, he calls his father simply "the wise prince, the perfect lord, *guardian* (keeper) of the guards, or watch towers, of E-sag-il and Babylon."[1] Of course, Bel-shum-ishkun may have been a sub-king of Babylon under Nebuchadnezzar, or Evil-Merodach, or even under his own son Nergal-shar-uṣur. Or the title "king" applied to him may have been simply an honorific title of respect. In either case, it illustrates the fact that the title "king" was not confined to the reigning monarch, to the king of kings; and thus, the use of the title as applied to Nebuchadnezzar in Daniel i, 1, to Belshazzar in Daniel vii, 1, and to Darius in Daniel ix, 1, is fully justified by analogy.

It is possible, too, that Darius in the Behistun Inscription uses the word king in this broader sense of his father Hystaspis, and of other ancestors (Col. i, 8); for in the other places where Hystaspis is mentioned he is called simply the father of Darius, [2]—or merely Hystaspis without any further designation.[3] Moreover, Herodotus speaks of Hystaspis as having been in the time of Smerdis the Magian simply the *hyparch,* or governor, of Persia.[4]

III. Finally, it may be remarked that the Hebrew *melek* and the Aramaic *malka,* the words uniformly translated by "king" in the English versions, by *rex* in the Latin Vulgate, by *basileus* in Greek, and by corresponding words in the modern European versions of the Scriptures, are almost certain to be misunderstood by us, because of the arbitrary manner in which we have fixed their connotation. When we think of a king, there comes up before us the image of King

---

[1] KB, iii, ii, 76, Col. i, l. 11–13. "*Rubu emga idlum gitmalum naṣir maṣṣartim E-sag-il u Babili.*" [2] So i, 2, 4; ii, 93 et al.
[3] So ii, 94; iii, 2, 3, 4, 7 et al. [4] Book III, 70

Edward, or King Alfred, of Henry the Fourth, or Louis XIV of France, of Alexander of Macedon, or Rameses king of the Egyptians. Or we think of the king of Greece, or Denmark, or Portugal, in modern times, or of the kings of Israel, Judah, and Moab in ancient times. That is, we think of a ruler of an independent people, or country. Where we have subject peoples, or subordinate countries, we usually call the supreme ruler emperor. Or we call him Kaiser as in Germany, the kings of Saxony, Bavaria, and Württemberg being second in authority to him. Sometimes the same man is emperor and king at the same time, as in the cases of George V, king of England and emperor of India; or William II, king of Prussia and German Kaiser. As emperor of India, King George has many subject and allied rajahs or kings, of whom he may be called the king of kings, or the lord paramount. As German Kaiser, William II has associated with him kings, grand dukes, dukes, princes, and lesser potentates.

Now, among the ancient Greeks and Romans, and among most of the Semitic races, there was in each case but a single term which might be employed indiscriminately to denote the *ruler* of a city, of a kingdom, or of an empire. In Greek the word *basileus* was employed to denote the ruler of a city such as the kings of Sparta, Argos, and other cities; of countries, great or small, such as Macedon, and Cilicia, and Lydia, and Media, and Egypt; or of the great empires of Esarhaddon, Nebuchadnezzar, Cyrus, Darius, and Alexander. Thus Adrastus was king of the city of Sicyon;[1] Syennesis was king of the subject-state of Cilicia,[2] and Darius was the king of the empire of Persia.[3] In Latin, Rom-

---

[1] Herod., v, 67.   [2] Xen., *Anab.*, i, 2.   [3] *Id.*, i, 1.

ulus was king (*rex*) of the city of Rome;[1] Herod was subject-king of Judea;[2] and Pacorus was king of the independent empire of Persia.[3] In Hebrew, the word *melek* was used to denote the ruler of a city, as in Joshua xii, 9–24, where thirty-one kings of cities are mentioned; or of a small country, such as the kings of Aram, Judah, and Israel; or of the kings of kings, such as Esarhaddon, Nebuchadnezzar, Cyrus, and Darius. In Arabic, a *malik*, or king, ruled over a single city,[4] or over a province, or over an empire.[5]

In Aramaic, the *malka* ruled over a city,[6] or a small country, as the kings of Samal[7] or a subject nation, as the king of Urha;[8] or an empire, as the rulers of the Greek Empire and of Persia.[9] Finally, in Assyrian, the word for king was used to denote the kings of cities, as "Luli king of the city of Sidon";[10] the kings of subject provinces, as in the long list of subject kings, governors, and prefects, of the land of Egypt in the Rassam Cylinder of Ashurbanipal;[11] and the king of kings, as in the oft-recurring phrase "so and so, king of nations, king of Assyria, etc."

From the above, it will be seen that a "king" might

---

[1] Livy, Bk. I.   [2] Tacitus, *History*, v, 9.   [3] *Id.*

[4] *E. g.*, there was a king of the city of Balsora while Haroun Al Rashid was sultan of Bagdad.   See the Arabian Nights in Lane's translation, i, 254.   Compare also the story of the Second Royal Mendicant, *id.*, i, 73, and the story of Marouf, *id.*, ii, 537.

[5] For examples of the last two uses see Ibn Hisham's *Life of Muhammed*, vol. ii, p. 971, where the Kaiser at Constantinople is called King of the Romans, and the Mukaukas king of Alexandria (*i. e.*, Egypt), the latter being a province of the Græco-Roman empire.

[6] Aramaic Targum and Syriac versions of Joshua xii.

[7] *Sendshirli Inscriptions.*   [8] Addai the Apostle.

[9] *Joshua the Stylite, passim*, and the *Egyptian Papyri.*

[10] KB ii, 90.   [11] *Id.* ii, 160–162.

rule over any extent of territory from a single city to an empire.

CONCLUSION

The above discussion has, we think, made it clear that a man who was not actually reigning at the time to which some event in his life is afterwards referred might rightly be called king by a writer who was describing that event after the man had really been clothed with the royal dignity. It has shown, also, that a man who was never king in the sense of having himself reigned *de facto*, or *de jure*, might be called king by way of distinction or honor, because he was in some way related to the reigning king. Lastly, it has shown that the word used for king by the ancient writers is to be defined not by the modern *usus loquendi*, nor by the conception which one may have formed from present-day usage, but in harmony with the manner in which the word was employed in antiquity and in the particular language to which the term, by us translated "king," belonged. Judged by these three rules there is no good reason why the author of Daniel may not properly and justly have called Nebuchadnezzar "the king of Babylon," when referring to an event in his life that happened before he had actually ascended the throne of his father.

CHAPTER VI

BELSHAZZAR

ONE of the commonest tricks of argument is the one which is called the begging of the question at issue. This is usually done by an abrupt categorical statement that a thing is so, as if it admitted of no contradiction and required no proof. It is frequently employed in political and religious controversy. "He casteth out devils by Beelzebub the prince of the devils," is a good example of this kind of fallacy. The Jewish enemies of Jesus simply assumed the whole question at issue without giving evidence to support their assumption. Their statement was at best their opinion. They had no evidence to support it.

Another example of this kind of fallacy is the assertion of Wellhausen in his *History of Israel*, p. 387, that כבש [*kāvash*] and רדה [*rādā*] are Aramaisms.[1]

[1] Whereas *kavash* is found in all branches of the Semitic family of languages and in all stages of Hebrew literature: and *rādā* in the sense of *"rule"* is found in Hebrew of all ages and in Babylonian as early as Hammurabi, but not in Syriac nor in any other Aramaic dialect except Mandaic and in the translations of, and comments on, the original Hebrew *rādā* as found in Gen. i, 26, 28; Ps. cx, 2, and Lev. xxvi, 17. See M. Jastrow, *A Dictionary of the Targumim, etc.*, p. 1451b; Lewy, *Chaldäisches Wörterbuch* I, 352a, II 408b; Delitzsch, *Assyrisches Wörterbuch*, p. 314, 613; Lane, *Arabic-English Lexicon*, 2588; Brederik, *Konkordanz zum Targum Oukelos*, 110, 183; Norberg, *Lexidion Cod. Nas.; Harper, Code of Hammurabi*, and the Hebrew concordances and dictionaries.

Closely allied to this fallacy is that involved in an assertion implying that there is plenty of evidence at hand to prove your side of a question, if you only cared to produce it. Thus when the Jews brought Jesus before Pilate, he asked them, "What accusation bring ye against this man?" Their answer was: "If he was not a malefactor, we would not have delivered him up unto you." Having no evidence that would convict him before a Roman judge, they were condemning him by innuendo, by the mere assertion of his guilt; while at the same time they were implying that they had such an abundance of proof, and that the proof was so well known by all, that it was not reasonable in Pilate even to demand that they specify the charge against him. Whereas the fact was that they could not formulate and substantiate an accusation that would compass the purpose which they desired.

A still more insidious fallacy is that which seeks to gain the point at issue by obscuring the real point of the question. Thus, when Jesus was brought before Pilate the second time, the Jews made the accusation that Jesus perverted the nation by saying that he was "Christ a king." But when Pilate asked Jesus if he was then "the king of the Jews," he answered, "My kingdom is not of this world," etc. And Pilate gave judgment: "I find no fault in this man." Pilate was sharp enough to see that a man whose kingdom was not of this world, whose servants would not fight, and whose mission it was to bear witness to the truth, might be called a "king" without endangering the Roman state. The charge was false, because he had not claimed to be a king in the sense implied in the accusation. There was abundance of evidence to prove that he had claimed to be a king. Jesus admitted that he had said he was a

7

king. He denied, however, that he had meant that he was a king in the sense implied in the accusation against him. Pilate admitted the justice of his denial, and Jesus was declared not guilty of the charge of unfriendliness to Cæsar. For there are kings and kings.

A fourth fallacy, lies in the assumption that a statement is false because there is no convincing evidence that it is true. Thus Hitzig, writing in 1863[1] maintained that stringed instruments could not have been used by Deborah. So, also, Herodotus[2] thought that the report of the Phenician mariners whom Pharaoh-Necho had sent to sail around Africa, starting from the Red Sea and returning by the Straits of Gibraltar, was false, because they said that they "had the sun on their right hand" as they sailed around. So, Ewald thought that the records of Ezra and Chronicles were false because they use the title "king of Persia" of the Achaemenid kings before the Persian empire had passed away; whereas to-day we know nineteen different extra-biblical authors from the Achaemenid period who in twenty separate works give thirty-eight instances of the use of this title.[3]

In the objections made to the biblical accounts of Belshazzar, are to be found examples of all these kinds of fallacy. Of the first one the statements that "Nabunaid was the last king of Babylon" and that Belshazzar "was not styled king by his contemporaries." Of the second, that to represent Belshazzar as the king under whom Babylon was captured and as

---

[1] *Die Psalmm*, p. xiii. [2] Bk. IV, 42.

[3] See articles by the author on Royal Titles in Antiquity in *The Princeton Theological Review*, 1904–5, a contribution on the Titles of the Persian Kings in the *Festschrift Eduard Sachau*, Berlin, 1915, and an article in the PTR for January, 1917, on *The Title "King of Persia" in the Old Testament*.

having been "a son of Nebuchadnezzar," contradicts all the other assured witnesses of the Old Testament. Of the third, that "Belshazzar never became king in his father's place." Of the fourth, that Belshazzar was never king of Babylon at all.

It is my purpose in this chapter to make it clear that there are no tenable objections to the statements of the book of Daniel, that Belshazzar was a king, that he was king of Babylon and of the Chaldeans, that he was king for three years, that he was the last king of Babylon before the Persian domination, and that he was a son of Nebuchadnezzar. This latter will involve a full discussion of the possible uses of the words "son" and "father," and of the possibility of the existence of two kings of a country at the same time, of the different ideas connoted by the phrase "king of Babylon," of the difference between the phrases "king of Babylon" and "king of the Chaldeans," and of the twofold datings of reigns.

Proceeding in the usual order we will state first the objection to Daniel's statements with regard to Belshazzar and the assumptions involved in them. They are as follows:

OBJECTIONS STATED

1. "To represent that the king in whose reign Babylon was captured and the Chaldean empire destroyed was named Belshazzar and that he was a son of Nebuchadnezzar (Ch. V), is to contradict all the other assured witnesses of the Old Testament."[1]

2. "Belshazzar is represented as 'king of Babylon.'" "In point of fact Nabunaid was the last king of Babylon."

[1] Cornill, *Introduction to the Canonical Books of the Old Testament*, p. 384.

"Belshazzar may have distinguished himself, perhaps more than his father Nabunaid (Nabonidus), at the time when Babylon passed into the power of the Persians; and hence, in the recollections of a later age he may have been pictured as its last king; but he was not styled 'king' by his contemporaries (*cf.* Schrader on Dan. v, 1, 2)."[1]

3. "Belshazzar never became king in his father's place."[2]

Assumptions Involved

These objections resolve themselves into four assumptions: first, that the Scriptures mention elsewhere the king under whom Babylon fell; second, that Nabunaid was the last king of Babylon; third, that Belshazzar was never king of Babylon in his father's place; and fourth, that he was not called "king" by his contemporaries.

Answer to Assumptions

I. As the Scriptures nowhere else mention the name of the king who ruled over Babylon when the city was captured by the Medes and Persians, Cornill's objection, as stated, is absolutely without foundation in fact. If he means that the Scriptures elsewhere call a son of Nebuchadnezzar by the name Evil-Merodach, it does not follow from this that Nebuchadnezzar may not have had another son called Belshazzar.[3] We know from the Babylonian documents that he had at least three sons beside Evil-Merodach.[4] Why may he not have had a fifth?

---

[1] Driver, LOT, pp. 498, 499.
[2] Sayce, *Higher Criticism and the Monuments*, p. 125.
[3] See on the word "son" below, p. 117.
[4] To wit: Marduk-nadin-ahe, Nk. 382.5, Musheshib-Marduk, Nk. 381.2 (?), and Marduk-shum-usur, Nk. 372.2, 393.2.

II. It must be admitted that Nabunaid was the last *de jure* king of the Babylonian *empire* whose capital was the city of Babylon; but this does not prove that he was the last *de facto* king of the Babylonians in the city or citadel of Babylon, nor even the last *de jure* king of the same. To prove, however, that the author of the book of Daniel is wrong in calling Belshazzar the last Chaldean king of Babylon, it must be shown that no one of that name, nor with that title, can have ruled in the city of Babylon during or after the downfall of Nabunaid.

A. As to the name and titles of Belshazzar, the monuments of the Babylonians tell us as follows:

1. That there was a Bel-shar-uṣur. [1]
2. That he was the son of Nabunaid. [2]
3. That he was "the first born son" of Nabunaid, the "son of the king" *par excellence*. [3] Nabunaid expressly calls Belshazzar his first born son (*maru reshtu*) [4] just as Nebuchadnezzar calls himself the *maru reshtu* of Nabopolassar. [5]
4. That he commanded the armies of the king of Babylon in the province of Accad, certainly from the 7th to the 12th year of Nabunaid and, for all that we

---

[1] In Nabunaid's prayer to Sin, the moon god, we learn that his first born son was Bel-shar-usur. (KB iii, ii, 96.)

[2] On certain tablets from the city of Babylon, a "Bel-shar-uṣur the son of the king" is mentioned. These tablets are found in Strassmaier's edition of the inscriptions of Nabunaid numbered as follows: 50, 1; 13, year 1, month 12, day 26: 184, 1; 4, year 5, month 1, day 25; 270, lines 4, 6, 9, 21, year 7, month 11, day 9; 581, lines e, 3, 8, year 11, month ?, day 20; 688, line 3, year 12, month 12b, day 27.

[3] In other places Belshazzar is apparently called simply the "son of the king," *e.g.*, *Inscriptions of Nabonidus*, 581. 4, 331. 4, 387, 401, 50. 6. In numbers 50 and 581, it will be seen that the "son of the king" must be Belshazzar, since he is expressly so called in these tablets; see note 2 above. [4] VAB, IV, 246. 26, 252. 24. [5] *Id.*, 72, 41.

know to the contrary, during the whole reign of Nabunaid;[1] and that in certain kingly functions he is associated with his father as early as the 12th year of
the reign of Nabunaid.[2]

5. That between the 16th day of the 4th month of
the 17th year of Nabunaid and the 11th day of the 8th
month, the son of the king was in command of the
Babylonians in the citadel of Babylon and was the *de
facto* king of Babylon, inasmuch as Nabunaid had been
captured.[3]

[1] In the Nabunaid-Cyrus *Chronicle, Obv.*, ii, 5, it is said that in the
7th year of king Nabunaid "the son of the king with his princes and
troops was in the land of Accad." A like statement is made for the
9th, 10th, and 11th years, *id.*, 10, 19, 23.

[2] In the tablet published by Pinches in the *Expository Times* for 1915,
an oath was sworn in the name of Belshazzar along with his father.
Oaths were never sworn by the names of any men except kings. This
tablet is from the 12th year of Nabunaid. The tablet reads as follows: "Ishi-Amurru, son of Nuranu, has sworn by Bel, Nebo, the lady
of Erech, and Nana, the oath of Nabonidus, king of Babylon, and
Belshazzar, the king's son, that, on the 7th day of the month Adar of
the twelfth year of Nabonadus, king of Babylon, I will go to Erech
etc."
As Dr. Pinches remarks: "The importance of this inscription is that
it places Belshazzar practically on the same plane as Nabonidus,
his father, five years before the latter's deposition, and the bearing of
this will not be overlooked. Officially, Belshazzar had not been recognized as king, as this would have necessitated his father's abdication,
but it seems clear that he was in some way associated with him on the
throne, otherwise his name would hardly have been introduced into
the oath with which the inscription begins. We now see that not only
for the Hebrews, but also for the Babylonians, Belshazzar held a practically royal position. The conjecture as to Daniel's being made the
third ruler in the kingdom because Nabonidus and Belshazzar were the
first and second is thus confirmed, and the mention of Belshazzar's third
year in Dan. viii, 1 is explained." (See, also, the original text and translation of this tablet in an article by Dr. Pinches in PSBA for Jan.,
1916, pp. 27–29.)

[3] In the Nabunaid-Cyrus *Chronicle Rev.* A. 15–22, it is said that
Ugbaru (Gobryas) governor (*pihu*) of the land of Gutium and the troops

6. That if we accept the most probable rendering of the signs in the Nabunaid-Cyrus *Chronicle*, ii, 23, this son of the king was killed on the night when the citadel of Babylon was taken by the troops of Cyrus under Gobryas.

From these statements of the monuments, it is clear that there was a Bel-shar-uṣur, the first-born son of Nabunaid, who almost certainly commanded the armies of Babylon for many years and was in command of the citadel of Babylon and hence *de facto* king for four months after the capture of his father Nabunaid, and that the same *de facto* king was probably the son of the king, who was slain by Gobryas on the night that the citadel was taken. That he might properly have been called *king* has been shown above.[1]

B. Here, several further questions must be discussed.

1. Was the Bel-shar-uṣur of the inscriptions the same as the Belshazzar of Daniel? We need not pause to discuss this. For it is admitted by all that despite the difference in spelling the same person is referred to in both.[2]

2. Is the *spelling* בֵּלְשַׁאצַּר Belshaṣṣar an indication of a date as early as the 6th century, or of a date as late as the 2nd century B.C.? There are four points to be considered here.

(1) The vowels. As the vowel signs were not added to the Hebrew consonants till some centuries after Christ, and as no vowels for the proper names in Daniel

---

of Cyrus entered Babylon without a battle. Afterwards Nabunaid, having been shut up, was taken in Babylon. Cyrus entered Babylon on the 3rd day of the 8th month and Gobryas was made governor of it on the 11th of the same month.

[1] Chapter V.   [2] KAT, 2nd edition, p. 433; 3rd edition, p. 396.

can be traced farther back than the LXX version, no argument as to date can be based on the disagreement of the vowels in the name Belshazzar with the vowels of the name as found in Babylonian.　One point only is to be noted, namely that it was not customary to denote the first syllable (*u*) of *uṣur* in the Aramaic transliteration.[1]

(2) The double ṣ (Eng. *z*).　This goes back only as far as the *pointings* of the earliest Hebrew manuscripts, the Greek versions and Josephus writing but one letter for the two indicated by the present Massoretic text.

(3) Bl is the common Aramaic and Hebrew transliteration of the Babylonian Bel.[2]

(4) The transliteration of the *sh* by *sh*, instead of *s* (*samekh*) causes some difficulty.　While *shar* is commonly rendered in Aramaic by *sar*[3], as also, at times, in the Old Testament Hebrew; yet [4] *sometimes* we find Assyrian *shar* represented in Hebrew by *shar*.[5]

(5) The dropping or assimilation of the *r* from the end of *shar*.　The only example of this assimilation to be found in the inscriptions is on a seal from the seventh century B. C.[6] where the name Sassar-il probably stands for Sar-sare-il.　In Daniel we have the same assimilation also in the name Belteshazzar, if we take the last two syllables as standing for *shar-uṣur*.　The only probable example in late Aramaic is *Bazira*, "seed," for

[1] See examples in CIS ii–i, 38.6, 50 *et al.*

[2] *E.g.*, CIS ii, 16, 29, 30, 34, 35, 36, 40, 41, 44, 46; Is. xi, xlvi. 1; Jer. 1, 2, 5, 1, 1, 44; 2 Kings, 20, 12.

[3] *E.g.*, CIS i, 10, 29, 38, 22, 82, 88, 81, 21, 39.

[4] *E.g.*, in Sargon for Sharrukin.

[5] *E.g.*, in the Aramaic Sharkin = Ass. Sharrukin, CIS ii, i, 32, and in the O. T. Hebrew in Sharezer, Is. lvii, 38, 2 Ki. xix, 37, Zech. vii, 2, and in Nergal-shar-ezer, Jer. xxxix, 3, 13.

[6] CIS ii, i, 82.

barzar'a, though even this is doubtful.[1] So that there is no evidence to show that it was usual at any time in the history of the Aramaic language, nor indeed of any of the Semitic languages, for any of them to assimilate or drop an *r*. Admitting then that an *r* has been dropped, or assimilated, in the *shar* of Belshazzar, what follows as to the time when it was dropped, or assimilated? Nothing, of course. And so, the charge that Belshazzar is a late form because of the assimilated *r* and that hence the book is late falls to the ground.[2]

But even if it could be shown that the spelling was late, that would not prove that the book was late; *e.g.* American editions of English authors drop *u* from col-

---

[1] See Nöldeke, *Mand. Gram.*, p. 55; and *Neu-Syrische Gram.*, p. 53. The Babylonian-Aramaic *'ama* is probably derived from the Babylonian *amu* and not from *'amar*. See Dalman, *Gram des. jüd. pal. Aram.*, p. 101. Compare also Phenician בשם for Heb. ברשים Lidzbarski, *Nord-semit. Epigraphie*, p. 246, and Madassuma for Madarsuma. Schrö-der, *Die phönizische Sprache*, pp. 99 and 105.

[2] As to the spelling of foreign proper names by contemporaries, we would like also to say a word in this connection. We have no right to demand in this respect from the biblical writers, what we do not demand from ourselves, or from others, in the way of accuracy. We say Emperor William; the Germans say Kaiser Wilhelm. The Persians said Khshayarsha; the Hebrews, Ahashwerosh; the Greeks, Xerxes; the Egyptians, Khshyarsha; the Susians, Ikshersha, or Iksherishsha; while the Babylonians spelled it in at least twenty-three different ways, the most common of which was Ak-shi-ia-ar-shi.

The contemporaries of Darius the son of Hystaspis spelled his name as follows: the Greeks, Dareios; the Persians, Darayavaush; the Susi-ans, Tariyamaush; the Hebrews, Dareyawesh; and the Egyptians, Babylonians and Arameans in at least three different ways. See Sachau's *Aram. Papyrus* for their spellings in Egypto-Aramaic. The Peshitto gives a fourth spelling in use among the Syrian Arameans. For the many spellings in Babylonian, see Tallquist's *Namenbuch* and Clay's *Murashu Tablets*, from time of Darius II, and the author's articles on the "Titles of the Kings in Antiquity" in the *Presbyterian and Reformed Review* for 1904–5, and on the "Titles of the Persian Kings" in the *Fest-schrift Eduard Sachau*, Berlin, 1915, pp. 179–207.

our and like words, even though the English editions have it.

III. It is said, further, that Belshazzar never became king in his father's place. This is one of those ambiguous statements worthy of the oracle of Delphi. Daniel does not say that Belshazzar ever became king in his father's place, or in the same sense that his father had been king, nor over the same dominion. It simply says that he was "king of the Chaldeans" and "king of Babylon." This last phrase is used of him only once and then his first year only is mentioned. I repeat, that the book of Daniel speaks only of the first year of Belshazzar *as king of Babylon:* to wit, in the first verse of chapter seven. In chapter viii, 1 it speaks simply of the third year of the reign of Belshazzar the king, without defining over what or whom he reigned. In chapter v, 30, he is called the Chaldean king, and in verse 18 the son of Nebuchadnezzar. These statements can all be easily reconciled with the monuments by saying that Belshazzar, who, according to Daniel ix, 1, had at least for three years been king of the Chaldeans, was for at least a year or part of a year, in some sense or another, the king of Babylon. There are the following matters involved in this assertion:

1. The different ideas connoted by the word "king."
2. The possibility of there being two kings of the same country at one and the same time.
3. The different ideas connoted by the phrase "king of Babylon."
4. The difference between "king of Babylon" and "king of the Chaldeans."
5. The twofold datings of reigns.
6. The possibility of a man's having two fathers.

1. The different ideas connoted by the word "king," have already been sufficiently discussed in Chapter V.

2. On the possibility of there being two kings over the same country at the same time, we can confidently affirm that this was often the case. It may be alleged in favor of this proposition, that (1) for prudential reasons, such as for settling the succession, sons were sometimes crowned during the lifetime of their father. For example, Solomon was proclaimed king while his father David was still alive.[1] Esarhaddon had his two sons Ashurbanipal and Shamash-shum-ukin crowned respectively as kings of Assyria and Babylon before he died in 668 B. C.[2] The Persian kings also appointed a successor before they started on any expedition, (Herodotus, vii, 2). In accordance with this custom Darius Hystaspis appointed Xerxes to be king over the Persians before he prepared to march against Greece.[3] Later still the Greek Seleucid kings followed this custom; for Antiochus calls his son Seleucus king while he himself was still reigning.[4]

(2) Sometimes, the reigning monarch made his son, or some other person, king of a part of his dominion. Thus, Pharaoh-Necho made Eliakim king of Judah, changing his name to Jehoiakim;[5] and Nebuchadnezzar made Mattaniah king, changing his name to Zedekiah.[6] So, also, in 702 B.C., Sennacherib placed Bel-ibni, a scion of a noble family of Babylon who had grown up at the court of Nineveh, upon the throne of Babylon as a sub-king; and in 699 he enthroned his own son Ashur-nadin-shum in Babylon, still under subordination to

[1] 1 Kings i, 39, 43, 46, 51, 53.
[2] Winckler's *History of Babylon and Assyria*, p. 272.   [3] Her. vii, 4.
[4] Weissbach, *Die Keilinschriften der Achämeniden*, p. 145.
[5] 2 Kings xxiii, 34.   [6] 2 Kings xxiv, 17.

himself as overlord.[1]   Later, he seems to have made
his son Esarhaddon governor (Aramaic, *king*) of Babylon.[2]   In 668 B.C., Esarhaddon proclaimed his younger
son Shamash-shum-ukin king of Babylon under the overlordship of Ashurbanipal king of Assyria.[3]   He also
appointed at one time 20 sub-kings in Egypt.[4]   When
Cyrus conquered Nabunaid and Belshazzar, he seems
to have made his older son Cambyses king of Babylon,
while he, himself, took the title of king of lands.[5]

(3)   Jeremiah speaks of the "*kings* of the Medes."
This would imply that when Jeremiah wrote, there
were more kings of Media than one.   That this implication of Jeremiah is correct is supported by the fact
stated by Cyrus on the Cylinder Inscription and by
Darius on the Behistun Inscription and elsewhere, that
the father and grandfather and great-grandfather of
Cyrus, and Teispes the common ancestor of Cyrus
and Darius, were kings of Anshan (or Persia?), while
that country was still subject to the Median hegemony.
It agrees, also, with the usual system of government in
vogue in Western Asia, and, in a measure, in Egypt
also (compare Tel-el-Amarna Letters), up to the
time of Darius Hystaspis, and even in part in the Persian empire during and after his time;[6] as, also, with the
system of government employed in later times by the
Arsacid kings[7] down to the time of Ardashir, the first
of the Sassanid dynasty of Persia.[8]

---

[1] Winckler, *op. cit.*, pp. 118, 119.   [2] Winckler, *id.*, 122.

[3] *Id.*, 124.   [4] KB ii, 162.   [5] See KB iii–ii, 134.

[6] See the catalogue of Xerxes' forces which marched against Greece,
in Herodotus, vii, 61–99.

[7] The common title of the Arsacids was "king of kings." See the
author's article in PTR for Jan., 1917.

[8] According to Jacob of Sarug, "king of kings" was a title, also, of
the ancient kings of India. See Schröter, in *ZDMG* vol. xxv, 353.

That the Persian empire in the time of Cyrus, also, had more kings than one is supported by what Daniel says about Darius the Mede. Darius the Mede is not called in Daniel either king of Persia, or king of Media, or king of Medo-Persia; but simply "the Mede" (vi, 1; xi, 1); or "the son of Xerxes of the seed of Media who had been made king over the kingdom of the Chaldeans."[1] If Darius the Mede is the same as Ugbaru (Gubaru, Gobryas) the Pihat of Gutium, then he was made for a time the Pihat of the city of Babylon also. If Darius the Mede was not the same as Gobryas the Pihat of Gutium, then Daniel vi, 1, ix, 1, xi, 1, must be taken along with v, 30, as meaning that Darius received the *de jure* kingdom of Belshazzar the Chaldean, that is, the kingdom of Chaldea. In this latter case, Gobryas will have succeeded Belshazzar as Pihat of the city of Babylon and Darius the Mede will have succeeded Belshazzar as king of Chaldea, both of them being under the suzerainty of Cyrus king of Persia and of the lands. This interpretation agrees with Daniel vi, 29, where it is said that Daniel prospered in the reign of Darius and in the reign of Cyrus the Persian. It agrees, also, with the statement of chapter vi, verses 9, 13, 16, that Darius the Mede was ruling according to the laws of Media and Persia.

Further, Darius the Persian,[2] speaks of his father Hystaspis as having been a king. Inasmuch as Hystaspis can only have been a sub-king under Cyrus, this implies that the policy of Cyrus permitted of the reigning of kings under himself as king of kings. Moreover, Herodotus says that Hystaspis was hyparch, *i. e.*, satrap, of Persia under Smerdis, whereas Darius calls Hystaspis king. Again, Cyrus, according to

[1] IX, 1.   [2] *Behistun Inscription*, Col. i, line 8.

Ctesias, made his son Tanyoxarus independent sovereign of a portion of his dominion at the same time that he constituted the elder brother Cambyses his successor in the empire,[1] just as Esarhaddon established Ashurbanipal, his eldest son, as king of Assyria and Shamash-shum-ukin, a younger son, as king of Babylon. Nabunaid probably pursued this same policy; for according to one interpretation of the inscriptions of Eshki-Harran,[2] his son Nabunaid II called, like his father, "king of Babylon," was ruling as king of Harran in northern Mesopotamia under the overlordship of Nabunaid I at Babylon.[3] It is probable, also, that the "son of the king" who is mentioned in the *Chronicle* as having been in command of the army in Accad was Belshazzar, and that he had been made king of the Chaldeans with his capital at Ur.[4]

(4) Finally, that Belshazzar was in some sense looked upon and treated as a king as early as the twelfth year of Nabunaid, is evident from the tablet already cited on which a man called Iši-Amurru, son of Nuranu, is said to have "sworn by Bel, Nabu, the Lady of Erech, and Nana, the oath of Nabunaid, king of Babylon, and of Belshazzar, the king's son." That Belshazzar is here treated as a king is shown, as has been pointed out, by the fact that oaths were never sworn by the name

---

[1] Blakesly, Herodotus, ii, 430.

[2] H. Pognon, *Inscriptions Sémitiques de la Syrie*, etc., Paris, 1907.

[3] It is probable, or at least possible, that this is the king referred to in the Nabunaid-Cyrus *Chronicle* as having been conquered and killed in the 9th year of Nabunaid I (KB iii, ii, 130.)

[4] Compare Tiele, *Geschichte*, p. 463. The interpretation of the Eshki-Harran inscription given by Zehnpfund would of course modify these relations. If the high-priest of Harran be the same as Nabu-balatsu-ikbi the father of Nabunaid, it was the father who reigned at Harran while the son was king of Babylon.

of any men, except those of royal rank. It is especially noteworthy in this connection that in four, or five, cases, the names of *two* kings are found in the same oath.[1]

This new tablet removes the last reasonable objection that could be made to the right of the author of Daniel to call Belshazzar king. It will also allow of his having been king for at least five years. For this tablet dates from the 12th year of Nabunaid, whereas he was not dethroned till his 17th year.[2]

(5) We know that Nabunaid, like the other kings of the great empires of Assyria and Babylon, had many rulers, called kings, subservient to him.

[1] 1. In KU 248, the oath is "by (Šamaš), Marduk, Sumulael, and Sabium." Sumulael and Sabium were father and son.

2. In KU 380, the oath is "by Šamaš and Immerum, by Marduk and Sumulael." Immerum and Sumulael were contemporaries.

3. On a tablet published by Langdon in PSBA xxxiii, 192, we read: "By Nannar and Manana, by Zamama and Yapium they swore." According to Prof. Johns, this oath shows that Manana had probably associated Yapium with him on the throne, just as Sabium associated his son Apil-Sin with himself for at least his last year.[1]

4. In KU 420, an oath "by Marduk and Sin-Muballit, by Anum-bel-tabi (?) and his wife (?)," occurs. In this case, Ranke thinks that Anum-bel-Tabi is the name of a king of Assyria. (*Early Babylonian Personal Names, S. E. D.* iii.) If "his wife" is a correct reading, this is the only case where a woman is mentioned in an oath. If she were queen of Assyria, the rule that none but royal persons are named in oaths would still hold good.

[2] For authorities on the oath among the Babylonians and Assyrians the reader is referred to *Hammurabi's Gesetz* by Kohler, Peiser, and Ungnad (KU); also, to *Assyrische Rechtsurkunden* by Kohler and Ungnad; to *Babylonisches Rechtsleben* by Kohler and Peiser; to *Hundert ausgewählte Rechtsurkunden* by Kohler and Ungnad; to *Babylonische Verträge* by Peiser; to articles by Langdon and Johns in PSBA for 1911; to *Notes* by Thureau-Dangin in the *Revue d'Assyriologie* for 1911, and especially to an article by Prof. S. A. B. Mercer in AJSLL vol. xxix.

[1] PSBA xxxiii, 99.

For example, in the great cylinder from Abu-Habba,
Col. i, 38–43, he says that he mustered the kings,
princes, and governors, from Gaza on the border of
Egypt to the Upper Sea beyond the Euphrates to the
building of Ehullul the house of Sin.[1] So, Cyrus,
also, says on his cylinder, line 28, that the totality of
the kings of the whole world from the Upper Sea to the
Lower Sea, (and) all the kings of Amurri brought their
tribute to him at Babylon. In his prism inscription,
Col. v, 12–27, Esarhaddon gives his orders to 12 kings
of Palestine and Syria, and to 10 kings of Cyprus, all
of whom and their allies he mentions by name. In
another place, he calls himself king of the kings of
Egypt.[2] The names of these kings, 20 in number, and
their cities, are given by Ashurbanipal on the Rassam
Cylinder, Col. i, 90–109. Similar facts may be gathered in scores from the Assyrian inscriptions.

3. Can there have been more than one man called
"king of Babylon" at one time?

It is certain that Cyrus and Cambyses were both
called kings of Babylon in contract tablets of the same
month and year.[3] The inscription from Eshki-
Harran published by M. Pognon shows that Nabunaid
I and his son Nabunaid II were both called "king of
Babylon" on the same inscription. Inasmuch as the
Aramaic and Hebrew of Daniel know no words for
ruler save king, ruler, lord, and prince,[4] it is obvious
that Gobryas (Gubaru) the *pihatu*, or governor, of
Babylon, mentioned in the Nabunaid-Cyrus *Chronicle*,
Reverse 20, must have been denoted in Aramaic in his
official capacity by one of these words. The word

[1] KB ii, ii, 99.   [2] KB ii, 150; I R., 48, No. 5.
[3] Tiele, *Geschichte*, pp. 483, 484.
[4] *Melek, shallit* or *shilton, rab* and *sar*.

rab, "lord," is never used as mayor, or governor, of a city or province in the Bible in either Hebrew or Aramaic. *Shallit* is thus used in Hebrew only of Joseph, in Gen. xlii, 6, and of a ruler in general, in Ecc. x, 5; in Aramaic only in Daniel ii, 15, of Arioch, the chief (*rab*) of the executioners of the king, and in Daniel v, 29, and ii, 10.[1] *Shilton* is used in the Bible only in the Aramaic of Daniel iii, 2, 3, as a general term for all "the rulers of the provinces." *Sar*[2] is never used anywhere in any Aramaic dialect. *Melek* (king) is used over 5000 times in biblical Hebrew, always in the sense of the chief man of a city, province, kingdom, or empire. In biblical Aramaic, it is used nearly 200 times, and it is the only appropriate Aramaic word found in Daniel for the chief ruler of a city, province, kingdom, or empire, except perhaps the *shilton* of iii, 2 and 3. So, that if Belshazzar was not a king of the empire or kingdom of Babylon, but only ruler of a province, or city, the writer of Daniel was limited in the pure Hebrew to a choice of terms wherewith properly to designate him to *sar* and *melek*. He chose *melek*, perhaps because it was more definite and unambiguous. In Aramaic, the writer was limited to *malka* and *shilton*, and he chose the more common term.[3]

[1] In ii, 10 and v, 29, it is probably a verbal adjective.

[2] In Biblical Hebrew, it is used about 400 times, usually of the captain of an army, or of a part of an army, or in the sense of our word prince; a few times in the sense of the head man of a city, as in Jud. ix, 30; 1 Kings xxii, 26–2; Chron. xviii, 25; 2 Kings xxiii, 8; 2 Chron. xxxiv, 8; twice certainly in the sense of governor, as in Esther viii, 9; ix, 3; and a few times in the sense of king, as in Daniel viii, 25; x, 13; x, 20 *bis;* Hos. viii, 10 (?).

[3] The Egyptian papyri show that he might, also, have used *mâr*, a title which was given to the governors of Egypt under the Persians. See Sachau, *Aram. Papyrus*, p. 286.

8

4. Is there any difference between the terms "king of Babylon" and "king of the Chaldeans" or "Chaldean king"?

The importance of this question lies in the fact that only the first year of Belshazzar as king of Babylon is mentioned (vii, 1), whereas his third year as king is spoken of in chapter viii, 1. Now, if we suppose that Belshazzar is the "son of the king" mentioned in the Nabunaid-Cyrus *Chronicle* as having been killed at the storming of the citadel of Babylon by Gobryas, he can have been *de facto* king of that part of Babylon for only about four months. This would be enough, however, to justify the writer of Daniel in speaking of his first year as king of Babylon. But how then can this writer speak of his third year as king? Evidently, he must refer to his having been king in some sense before that time. In Daniel v, 29, he is called the "Chaldean king" or "king of the Chaldeans"; and we have only to suppose that Nabunaid I had made Belshazzar king of the Chaldeans in the southern part of his dominions, just as he had probably made Nabunaid II king in the northern part of his dominions around Harran, in order to reconcile the statements of Daniel with the inscriptions. I have already said that Professor Tiele, in his history of Babylonia, puts forth the view that Belshazzar was probably reigning at Ur in southern Babylonia, when his father Nabunaid I wrote the hymns to Sin in which Belshazzar's name is mentioned. The reader must remember, that the Chaldeans and Babylonians were not originally the same people; but that the Chaldeans had again and again conquered Babylon, and in the reign of Nabopolassar the father of Nebuchadnezzar the Great had established their dominion over it. Nabunaid I, however, seems to have been a Babylonian who superseded the Chaldean house of Nebuchadnezzar.[1] In what relation he stood to Nebuchadnezzar we have no means of determining. In what manner Belshazzar may have been called Nebuchadnezzar's son, we shall discuss below. It is sufficient for our present purpose to state that, it is probable that, for some reason or another, Belshazzar was made king of the Chaldeans, and that it was in this capacity that the writer referred to his third year. This reference to the different datings of his reign raises the next question.

5. Could the years of a king's reigning be dated in more ways than one? We have already discussed above the different ways of dating the beginning of a king's reign over a given country. Here we shall discuss different datings of his reign over *different* countries.

It will be known to the readers of British history, that James the VI of Scotland became king of England after the death of Elizabeth in 1603. But he had been crowned king of Scotland on July 29, 1567. His mother, Queen Mary, did not leave Scotland till May 16, 1568, and was not executed till Feb. 8, 1587. Here, then, are four dates, from any one of which the years of James' reign may have been dated. From July 29, 1567, he was in a sense *de jure* and *de facto* king of Scotland. In 1603, he became king of England. The historians and archives of England speak of his years as king of England; the historians and archives of Scotland, of his years as king of Scotland. The same historian might speak of either one or the other reign and date accordingly. In the dates from the 22nd dynasty of Egyptian kings, a double system is the common one. "Manetho's defective statements" with regard to the length of the

---

[1] Winckler: *History of Babylonia and Assyria*, p. 324.

reigns of the kings of this dynasty may arise from the
fact that he may refer to the length of the reigns "after
the death of the predecessor, while the regnal years on
monuments count from the beginning of a co-regency."[1]
Thus Shabaka is entitled king of Egypt as early as
725 B.C., though his accession to the throne must have
been about 715 B.C.,[2] and Taharka was already in
701 B.C. king of Cush, although he did not become
sole king till 693 B.C.[3] So, Tiglath-Pileser III was for
17 years king of Assyria, but died in his second year
as king of Babylon.[4] Ashurbanipal was king of Assyria
for 43 years, and probably king of Babylon under
the name of Kandalanu for 17 years.[5] Moreover,
Pognon argues with great plausibility, that Nabunaid
was king of Babylon for 17 years, but of Harran for
only nine.[6]

Now, the writer of Daniel was confronted by the same
situation, certainly with regard to one king, and most
probably with regard to at least three kings. The one
king is Cyrus. At first, he was king only of the city
or country of Anshan, a part of Elam. Here he began
to reign about 556 B.C. Later, about 549 B.C., he
became king of Media, after conquering Astyages and
his capital, Ekbatana. Three years later, in 546 B.C.,
he is first called king of Persia. Then, in 538 B.C., he
became king of Babylon. When Daniel speaks of his
first year, in chapter i, verse 21, he is evidently speaking of his first year as king of Babylon. When he
speaks of his third year, in chapter x, 1, he says "the
third year of Cyrus king of Persia"; so that the two

[1] Petrie, *History of Egypt*, iii, 227.   [2] *Id.*, 282.
[3] *Id.*, 296.   [4] KB ii, 277, and i, 215.
[5] Winckler, *Hist. of Bab. and Ass.*, 237–242.
[6] *Inscriptions Sémitiques de la Syric*, p. 9 foll.

statements are perfectly consistent. So, also, when
Daniel speaks in chapter viii, 1, of the third year of
Belshazzar the king, he may mean the third of his reign
as king of Chaldea; and when he speaks of his first year,
in vii, 1, he most probably means the first year as
king of Babylon.

6. The possibility of a man's having two fathers is
involved in the assumption made by the critics, that
Belshazzar cannot have been called by Daniel the son
of the Chaldean Nebuchadnezzar, and at the same
time have been the son of the Babylonian Nabunaid I.

A large part of the difficulty and confusion in the
discussion of this subject has arisen from a failure to
consider first of all what the orientals connoted by the
terms father and son. Prof. W. Robertson Smith
has discussed the terms at length as to their use in
Arabic, in his work *Kinship and Marriage in Early
Arabia.*[1] The conclusions there reached are that a man
might have four or even five fathers. These may be
called (1) procreator, (2) possessor, or "the man in
whose house one is born," (3) the foster father, or "the
one who raises, or nurtures him," (4) the protector, or
adoptive father, (5) a man who adopts one after he has
already been adopted once. To these might be added
the use of father (6) to denote a stepfather,[2] who is not
a foster or adoptive father, and (7) as a title of respect, or politeness, or endearment.[3] So, also, son was
used in ancient documents (1) to denote succession in
office, as Jehu is called the son of Omri;[4] or (2) for mem-

---

[1] Pp. 44–46, 110–114. [2] *Murabbî.*
[3] See in *Story of Badoura*, Lane's *Arabian Nights*, p. 308; and also,
in Babylonian, as in the inscription of Eshki-Harran, published by
M. Pognon in his *Inscriptions Sémitiques de la Syrie*, Paris, 1907–8.
[4] KAT, 2nd edition, 189, 22.

bers of a corporation, as the son of a prophet is used in
the Scriptures,[1] or the son of a scribe in Assyrian;[2] or
(3) for remote descendant, as son of Adam in the Arabian Nights,[3] or son of David, and son of Abraham in
the New Testament;[4] or (4) for grandson, as frequently
in the Scriptures; or (5) for members of a race, or tribe,
as sons of the Achæans,[5] or sons of Ammon;[6] or (6) to
denote a patronymic, as *sons of Babylon*, in Sargon's
inscriptions,[7] for Babylonians; or (7) to denote character, as "sons of thunder," "son of his father the
devil," "sons of God"; or (8) to denote one in a subordinate position, as a slave;[8] or (9) as a title of affec-
tion or respect;[9] or (10) stepson[10] or (11) "the son of the
bed of the man in whose house one is born";[11] or (12)
adopted son. So among the Arabs, see W. R. Smith, *id.*;
and among the Babylonians.[12]

It is evident, then, that Nebuchadnezzar may have
been called the father of Belshazzar, just because he
was his predecessor on the throne of Babylon, in the
same sense as Omri was the father of Jehu who destroyed the house of Omri, or as Naram-Sin more than
a thousand years before Nebuchadnezzar is, in one of
his inscriptions, called by the latter his "old father."[13]
Or, Nebuchadnezzar may have been the grandfather
or even the great-grandfather, of Belshazzar. When
Nebuchadnezzar made his first recorded expedition

---

[1] 1 Kings xx, 35 *et al.*
[2] Sargon: *Annals*, 378, 382, 466; Pr. 31, 109, 152 *et al.*
[3] Lane, ii, 196.   [4] Lk. xviii, 38; xix, 9.   [5] Iliad, i, 116.
[6] Num. xxi, 24.   [7] *Annals*, 296 *et al.*
[8] Johns, *Assyrian Deeds and Documents*, iii, 413, 475.
[9] So in the *Arabian Nights*, Lane, pp. 304 and 308, in the *Story of the Princess Badoura*.   [10] Arabic, *rabib*.   [11] W. R. Smith, *op cit.*
[12] Cook's *Laws of Moses and the Code of Hammurabi*, p. 131, *seq.*
[13] *Abam labiru*, Langdon, p. 69, ii, 27.

across the Euphrates in 605 B.C., he can scarcely have
been under 20. If he were 25 at that time, he would
have died at about 69 years of age, old enough to have
had a great-grandson of 15 years when Nabunaid
became king in 555 B.C., and 32 years old in 538
B.C. Or, since Nebuchadnezzar died in 561 B.C., a son
of his might easily have been flourishing in 538 B.C.
As to the relation between Belshazzar and the two
kings Nebuchadnezzar and Nabunaid, he may well
have been the son of both. First, he may have been
the procreated son of Nebuchadnezzar and the stepson
of Nabunaid, because the latter married Belshazzar's
mother after the death of Nebuchadnezzar. It was
the custom of succeeding kings to marry the wives of
their predecessors. Thus Smerdis the Magian married
the wives of his deceased predecessor Cambyses and
Darius Hystaspis married Atossa, the daughter of
Cyrus, and Phædyma, the daughter of Otanes,[1] both
of whom had been the wives of his two predecessors.
In this case, Belshazzar may have been the own son of
Nebuchadnezzar, and the foster son of Nabunaid. Or,
Nabunaid may have been merely the stepfather of Belshazzar. The queen of Daniel v, 10, may have been the
mother of Belshazzar (though she is not called this),
and still have been a young woman when the glory of
the Chaldee's excellency passed into the hands of the
conquering Medo-Persian army under Gobryas and
Cyrus. Or, Belshazzar may have been the own son of
Nebuchadnezzar and the adopted son of Nabunaid.
This would account for the fact that Berosus, according to Josephus,[2] calls Nabunaid a Babylonian, whereas
Belshazzar is called by Daniel a Chaldean. What could
have been better policy on the part of the Babylonian

[1] Herodotus, iii, 68, 88.　　　[2] *Cont. Apion*, i, 20.

Nabunaid than to attempt to unite the conquered
Babylonians and the Chaldean conquerors by adopting
as his own successor the son, or grandson, of Nebuchadnezzar, the greatest of all the Chaldean kings?
According to the code of Hammurabi, 186, 190, 193, a
man might in this way have two fathers. This was the
law, also, in the time of Nabunaid.[1]

A natural question arises here, namely, how could
Belshazzar be called by Nabunaid, not merely the
"son of the king," but "Belshazzar the first-born
son"[2] and "Belshazzar the first-born son, the offspring of my heart,"[3] if he were not the born son of
Nabunaid? Fortunately, this question is answered in
Meissner's *Altbabylonisches Privatrecht*, 98, where we
learn that an adopted son could be called, not merely
"the son," but "the eldest son" of his adopted parents.[4]

In the inscription of Eshki-Harran the high priest
calls Nabunaid his "son, the offspring of his heart";
although we know that Nabunaid was the son of Nabu-

---

[1] See Strassmaier : *Inscriptions of Nabunaid*, No. 380, and KB iv, 238,
and the able discussion in Cook's *Laws of Moses and the Code of
Hammurabi*, p. 131 *seq.* Thus, in Peiser's *Babylonian Contracts*
(*Babylonische Verträge*), xxxi, 14–17, Iddina-Nabu, the son of (*apilshu*)
Nabubanzir gives corn, etc., to his father (*abishu*) Gimillu. In number
xxxviii, 7, of the same work it is said, that Gimillu had taken Iddina-
Nabu to sonship (*ana marratu*) and Iddina-Nabu as adopted son gets
the inheritance of Gimillu (*id.*, cxxx, 5, 6). In No. 43 of Schorr's treatise (*Altbabylonische Rechtsurkunden*) Belishunu, the priestess of Shamash, and daughter of Nakarum, is adopted by Eli-eriza, the priestess of
Shamash, and daughter of Shamash-ilum, and calls Eli-eriza her mother.
So, in No. 30, 12, of the same, Shataya is called the mother of Amat-
Mamu, daughter of Sha-ilushu; but in 1, 27, Shamuhtum, also, is called
her mother (*i. e.*, own mother). So that it is clear that a child, according to Babylonian law, could have two fathers or two mothers.

[2] "*Die Grosse Inschrift von Ur*," KB iii, ii, 83, 89 (*mar rish-tu-u*).

[3] "*Die Kleine Inschrift von Ur*," KB *id.*, 97.

[4] See, also, Johns' *Babylonian and Assyrian Laws*, p. 156.

balaṭsu-iḳbi.[1] It will be seen that this law answers
the objection that might be raised, arising from the fact
that, on the Behistun Inscription, the rebels against
Darius, Nadintu-bel and Arachu, both assumed the
name of "Nebuchadnezzar the son of Nabunaid."[2]
There may have been an own son of Nabunaid with the
name of Nebuchadnezzar, and another son of the name
of Nabunaid, and yet his adopted son might be called
the first-born son and be the heir-apparent.[3]

Or Belshazzar may have been the adopted son of
Nebuchadnezzar and the own son of Nabunaid. An
adopted son might call his adopted father, "father."
Or, Nebuchadnezzar may have been the grandfather
and Nabunaid, also, the grandfather of Belshazzar.[4]
Or, finally, it is possible that Nabunaid was a lineal
descendant of Nebuchadnezzar. For the father of the
former was Nabu-balaṭsu-iḳbi, "the wise prince," and if
we take this Nabu-balaṭsu-iḳbi to be the son of the
Amelu mentioned in the tablet from the reign of Nabunaid (495, 24), and take this Amelu to be the same as
Amel-Marduk the son and successor of Nebuchadnez-

[1] See the great cylinder of Abu-Habba, i, 6.
[2] See Bezold's *Achämenideninschriften*, i, 77–90, and i, 77–89.
[3] See Johns' *Babylonian and Assyrian Laws*, p. 156.

In addition to the above places, which are given in Schrader's *Keil-schriftliche Bibliothek*, Belshazzar is called "the son of the king" in Clay's *Miscellaneous Inscriptions of the Yale Babylonian Collection*, No. 39 *bis*, and in the *Inschriften von Nabonidus* by Strassmaier, No. 581, line 4, and 1043, line 4; and "Belshazzar the son of the king" in the same book, No. 184, and No. 581, lines 2, 3, and No. 688, line 3, and No. 270, lines 4, 6, 9, and 21; also, "Belshazzar" alone, on No. 581, line 9. Tablets 184, 581, and 688 are referred to and translated in *Records of the Past*, New Series, vol. iii, 124–127.

[4] Sir Robert Anderson quotes from the *Transactions of the Victoria Institute* (vol. xviii, p. 99) as follows: "In a table of Babylonian kings, mention is made of a daughter of Nebuchadnezzar, who married the father of Nabunaid."

zar, then Nabunaid would be the great-grandson of
Nebuchadnezzar, and Belshazzar, son of Nabunaid,
would be the great-great-grandson of Nebuchadnezzar
in the direct male line.

IV.   Lastly, it is assumed that Belshazzar "was not
styled 'king' by his contemporaries," and that therefore he cannot have been a king at all, much less a king
of Babylon.   Professor Driver cites as his authority
for this statement a comment of the late Prof. Eberhard
Schrader of Berlin.   With regard to this statement of
Professor Schrader, that Belshazzar was not styled
"king" by his contemporaries, it is true that we have
documents from every year of the time during which
events described in the book of Daniel are said to have
transpired, and that not one of these documents styles
Belshazzar "king."   They support, however, the statements of Daniel in that they give us independent evidence that there was a Belshazzar; that this Belshazzar
was a son of Nabunaid, king of Babylon, and hence
might be justly called in some sense the son of Nebuchadnezzar; and that, if he were, as he most probably
was, the son of the king (Nabunaid) mentioned in the
Cyrus-Nabunaid *Cylinder*, he may have given a feast
to a thousand of his lords (Dan. v, 1), inasmuch as this
son of the king is said on the same cylinder to have been
accompanied by his lords;[1] and that Belshazzar most
probably is treated as the heir-apparent in being given
command of his father's armies, as Nebuchadnezzar had
been by his father, and in being mentioned on the Abu-
Habba *Cylinder* in conjunction with his father, just as
Cambyses is mentioned along with Cyrus on the Cyrus
Cylinder and elsewhere, and Seleukus along with his
father Antiochus on the latter's *Clay-cylinder* inscrip-

---

[1] *Rabrevin* in Daniel, *rabute* on the cylinder.

tion.[1] Certain contract tablets show, also, that Belshazzar the son of the king was a man of varied business interests.

But in no one of them is he styled "king."

From this fact it has been concluded that he was not a king.

But this conclusion is a *non sequitur*, as we shall now attempt to prove.

Before discussing the testimony of the extra-biblical documents, I shall quote the passages of the book of Daniel which mention Belshazzar. There are, first, the fifth chapter, where we find him referred to as Belshazzar the king (v. 1), king Belshazzar (v. 9), the king (v. 2, 3, 5, 6, 7, 8, 10, 13, 17, 18), Belshazzar (v. 2, 22, 29), and "Belshazzar the king of the Chaldeans" (or "the Chaldean king") (v. 30); secondly, the seventh chapter, verse 1, where we have the phrase "the first year of Belshazzar king of Babylon," and the eighth chapter, verse 1, where we have the heading, "In the third year of the reign of king Belshazzar."

There is no doubt, then, that in the book of Daniel Belshazzar is called a "king."

But how is it with the contemporaneous records?

First, let us summon the biblical witnesses. There are none to be found. There is no book of the Bible, aside from Daniel, that can testify with reference to Belshazzar, because not one of them has anything to say relevant to this period in which Belshazzar lived. The last notice of the books of Kings concerns Evil-Merodach, the immediate successor of Nebuchadnezzar, and he died in 558 B.C. The books of Chronicles say nothing about the times of Belshazzar except what is found in the last four verses; but here we find no reference to

[1] Weissbach, *Die Keilinschriften der Achämeniden*, p. 133.

Babylon, nor to any of its kings, but only to Persia and to Cyrus king of Persia, in connection with his decree for the return of God's people to Jerusalem. The book of Ezra begins with this decree, and mentions Nebuchadnezzar alone of all the kings of Babylon. The Psalms are silent with regard to the history of Babylon at this time as far as it concerns the kings, or the names of the kings. The only one of the prophets that might possibly have given us any testimony is Isaiah; but he again is silent, never mentioning any king of Babylon except Merodach-Baladan, who reigned in the latter part of the eighth century B.C.

So that, having no testimony at all to give it would have been utterly impossible for the biblical witnesses to have styled Belshazzar "king." Speaking more strictly, there are outside of Daniel no biblical witnesses to Belshazzar.

Secondly, let us examine the extra-biblical testimony. This consists of contract tablets, letters, hymns and incantations, and building and historical inscriptions.

(1) The contract tablets that mention Belshazzar are dated from the first to the twelfth year of the reign of Nabunaid. They all call Belshazzar "the son of the king," but never style him "king." We have no evidence in Daniel that Belshazzar was a king of any kind for more than three years, or king of Babylon for more than a year, or part of a year. Since Daniel says that he was slain when Babylon was captured in the 17th year of Nabunaid, it is evident that there is no necessary discrepancy between the tablets and Daniel's narrative. When the contracts were made, he was properly styled "the son of the king." When Daniel mentions him he had become a king, first of the Chaldeans

and next of Babylon. As Prof. Clay says,[1] "the fact
that Belshazzar . . . was peculiarly identified with his
father Nabonidus in his reign is illustrated by No. 39 of
the Yale collection. This tablet reads as follows: In the
month Tebet, day 15th, year 7th, of Nabunaid, king of
Babylon, Shumukin says as follows: The great star
Venus, the star Kiskaski, Sin and Shamash, in my
dream I saw, and for the favor of Nabunaid, king of
Babylon, my Lord, and for the favor of Belshazzar, son
of the king, my Lord, may my ear hearken to them.
On the 17th day of Tebet, the 7th year of Nabunaid,
king of Babylon, Shumukin says as follows: 'The great
star I saw, and for the favor of Nabunaid, king of Babylon, my Lord, and for the favor of Belshazzar, the son
of the king, my Lord, may my ear hearken.'"

Here, Belshazzar is evidently in some official position,
which entitles him to be associated with his father
in an unusual and striking manner, that is similar to the way in which Cyrus and Cambyses, and
later Antiochus and Seleucus, are associated on the
inscriptions. The only difference is, that Belshazzar
is not called king, whereas Cambyses and Seleucus are
so called. In the tablet published by Mr. Pinches in
the PSBA for January, 1916, an oath is taken in the
names of Nabunaid and Belshazzar conjointly. All the
evidence (and there is much of it) goes to show that
only the names of gods and kings were used in oaths, the
single exception being that of the city of Sippar.[2]

(2) Among the letters from the time of Nabunaid,
one was written by Belshazzar himself. In it he calls
himself simply Bel-shar-u [sur].[3]

---

[1] *Miscellaneous Inscriptions from the Yale Babylonian Collection*, pp.
55-57.   [2] See pp. 110, 111.
[3] *Mittheilungen der vorderasiatischen Gesellschaft*, xii, 15.

(3) The hymns and incantations that may possibly have been written in the reign of Nabunaid *never* mention the names of kings or of any other persons. Hence they could not be expected to have styled Belshazzar king.

(4) In the building inscriptions, Belshazzar is mentioned only in Col. ii, lines 24, 25, of the cylinders found in the corners of the *zikkurat* at Ur, where he is called "the first-born son, the darling of the heart" of Nabunaid.[1]

(5) Of the two historical inscriptions which cover any portion of the reign of Nabunaid, or Cyrus, the *Chronicle* states that a son of Nabunaid was in command of the army in Accad from the 7th to the 12th year of the king. This son was probably Belshazzar. No reason is known why he is not mentioned by name. The Cyrus *Cylinder* says that a son (?) of the king was killed at the capture of the citadel of Babylon by Gobryas. This son is not named in the inscription, nor is he given a title; but Daniel apparently calls him Belshazzar and says that he was in command of the Chaldean forces and entitles him "king." Cyrus would naturally refer to him merely as a son of the king, not having admitted his claim to be the *de jure* or *de facto* successor of his father Nabunaid.

CONCLUSION

The evidence given above shows that the author of Daniel does not contradict any "other assured witnes es of the Old Testament," when he represents Belshazzar as the king of Babylon under whom the citadel was taken. All that the book of Daniel necessarily implies when it says that Belshazzar was king of Babylon is

[1] Zehnpfund-Langdon, *Babylonische Königsinschriften*, p. 253.

that he was *de facto* king of the city after Nabunaid was taken prisoner. The evidence shows, also, that Belshazzar may have been called king of Babylon without ever having become king in his father's place over the empire of Babylonia; for in the last four months before the citadel was taken and after his father had surrendered, he was the only king whom the last defenders of Babylon could have acknowledged. His first year as king of Babylon is all that the book of Daniel mentions. He may have been king of the Chaldeans, or Chaldean king, for many years before, through the capture of his father Nabunaid by the Persians, he became king of Babylon.

Thus "the recollections of a late age," as they are presented in Daniel, will agree exactly with what the monuments tell us about the situation at the time when Babylon was taken by the Medes and Persians. Further, it has been shown by the evidence that a son of a king might be called a king; that Belshazzar may have been king at the same time that his father was; that there may have been two persons called king of Babylon at the same time; that a man might have been king of the Chaldeans, or king both of Babylon and of the Chaldeans; and that the years of the reign of a monarch might be dated in one way for his rule over one country, or people, and in another way for his rule over a second country, or people. Lastly, it has been shown that Belshazzar may legally have had two fathers; and that hence it is no objection to the accuracy of Daniel that he is called by him the son of Nebuchadnezzar, while the monuments call him the son of Nabunaid.

In short, the evidence fails to show that any of the above-named assumptions of the critics with regard to him are true.

CHAPTER VII

WHEN one asserts that the author of Daniel has "confused" events or persons, it is not enough for him to affirm that the author was thus confused. This confusion is a matter of evidence. With all due deference to the *opinion* of other scholars, I am firmly convinced that no man to-day has sufficient evidence to prove that the author of Daniel was confused. There are no records to substantiate the assertions of confusion. Neither is it clear to the critics nor can they make it clear to others, that the author of Daniel either did not understand the facts with regard to Darius the Mede, nor clearly express himself about them.

In this and the following chapters, it is my intention, then, to review the objections to the book of Daniel on the ground of what it says with regard to Darius the Mede and with regard to what it is asserted to say, or imply, with respect to the kingdom and people of the Medes. In this present chapter, the attempt will be made to show that the book of Daniel does not assert that Darius the Mede ever reigned over Babylon as an independent sovereign, and that Darius the Mede was probably the same as Gobryas the sub-king of Babylon, appointed by his overlord Cyrus. In connection with these questions will be considered the methods of dating documents used among the ancients in and about Baby-

lon, and the lack of all extra-biblical records referring to
his reign, his office, age, name, race, and official acts.

OBJECTIONS STATED

Among other objections it is asserted, that "the
author of Daniel had an entirely false idea regarding
the fall of Babylon under the Semitic dynasty. He
evidently thought that Darius the Mede preceded
Cyrus the Persian."[1] The author of Daniel "makes a
Median ruler receive Babylon after the overthrow of
the native dynasty, and then mentions later the historical Cyrus. We may suppose that the biblical writer
believed that Cyrus succeeded to the empire of Babylon
on the death of the Median Darius."[2]

ASSUMPTIONS INVOLVED

There are in these statements three assumptions: (1)
that the biblical writer believed that Cyrus succeeded
to the empire of Babylon on the death of the Median
Darius; (2) that he makes a Median ruler receive the
empire of Babylon after the overthrow of the native
dynasty; (3) that the author of Daniel mentions Cyrus
as if he were later than Darius the Mede.

ANSWER TO ASSUMPTIONS

I. Professor Prince bases the first of these statements upon Daniel vi, 29, which reads: "Daniel prospered in the kingdom of Darius and in the kingdom
of Cyrus king of Persia." It is admitted that this
might mean that Cyrus was the successor of Darius

[1] Prince, *Commentary on Daniel*, p. 127.   [2] *Id.*, p. 54.

9

the Mede. It can be shown, however, that it may
equally well mean that the two kings reigned   contemporaneously and that the one may have been subordinate and subject to the other. In support of this
statement the following evidence is advanced.

Systems of double dating were common in antiquity
as they still are in many parts of the world. The
thanksgiving proclamations of our presidents bear the
double dates of the year of the republic and of the year
of the Lord. The diplomas of our colleges bear the
double date of the year from the founding of the college
and the year of the Lord. So among the Assyrians we
find that the contract tablets were dated at times from
the year of the king and from the *limmu* (or archon, or
mayor) of the city of Nineveh. Bezold refers to more
than forty of the double-dated tablets.[1]

In the Babylonian documents from the time of the
Arsacid, or Parthian, kings, we find a regular system
of dual dates, one taken from the Arsacid era beginning
248 B.C., and the other from the Seleucid or Greek era
beginning 312 B.C.[2]

Among the Phenicians, also, we find double or even

---

[1] See his *Catalogue of the Cuneiform Tablets*, etc., p. 2005. Thus
we have a tablet dated "the 8th of Airu in the *limmu* of Manzarni
the governor (*am. pihat*) of the land of Kulbania in the year 22
of Sennacherib king of Assyria" (KB iv, 120). Another from "the
1st of Airu, the 23d year of Sennacherib, king of Assyria, the *limmu* of
Mannuki-Ramman deputy (*shakin*) of the city of Supiti" (*id.*, 122).
Another from "the 27th of the month Ab in the *limmu* of the *turtan* of
the city of Kumuh in the reign (*tarsi*) of Ashurbanipal king of Assyria"
(*id.*, 134). Another "in the 3rd year of Shalmanasharid, king of
Assyria, when Illuiada' was deputy (*shakin*) of Durilu" (*id.*, 158).

[2] Thus, to give two examples out of many, "in the year 130 [of the era]
of king Arsaces, which is the same as the year 194 [of the era of the
Greeks]." See ZA xv, 193. So, also, "in the year 145 of Arsaces,
king of kings, which is the same as the year 209" (*id.*). See, also,
numerous examples in Clay's *Morgan Collection*, Part II.

triple dates at times. Thus on a statue from Larnax Lapethos (Narnaka) there is an inscription which contains the date: "on the new moon of Zebah-shishshim, which is in the 11th year of the lord of kings Ptolemy, son of the lord of kings Ptolemy, which is the 33rd year of the people of Lapethos, while the priest to the lord of kings was 'Abd-'Ashtart, son of Ger-'ashtart governor (*rab*) of the land."[1]

So, among the Nabateans we find an inscription from Damascus having the double date "in the month Iyar, in the year 405 by the reckoning of the Romans [Greeks], which is the 24th year of king Rabel."[2] Compare, also, the double date in the inscription from Wady-Mukattib:[3] "The year 106 equivalent to the year of the three Cæsars."[4]

Among the Palmyrenes, we find the following quadruple dating to a decree of council:

In the month Nisan, the 18th day of the year 448, during the presidency of Bonne son of Bonne, son of Hairan, and the secretaryship of Alexander, son of Alexander, son of Philopater, secretary of the council and People, while the archons were Maliku, son of 'Olai, son of Mokimu, and Zebida, son of Nesa.[5]

Among the Syrians of Edessa, a double or triple dating seems to have been the rule. Thus we find the following dates: "In the year 513, in the kingdom of Septimus Severus, Emperor of Rome, and in the kingdom of Abgar the king, son of Ma'nu the king, in the month Tishri the second";[6] and "in the year 1514 of

---

[1] Cooke, *North Semitic Inscriptions*, p. 82; see, also, the same, p. 78, and Luke iii, 1 f., for other examples. [2] Cooke, *id.*, 249.

[3] Euting, 457. [4] *Id.*, 261. [5] *Id.*, 320.

[6] Assemani, B. O., i, 390.

the Greeks and the year 559 of the Arabs, while Unk Khan, that is, John the Christian king, was king over the people," etc.[1]

So, also, in the introduction to the *History of Addai the Apostle* in Syriac, we find the following date: "In the year 343 of the kingdom of the Greeks, in the kingdom of our Lord, Tiberius Cæsar, the Roman, and in the kingdom of Abgar, the king, the son of Ma'nu, the king, in the month Tisri, the first, on the 12th day." But Tiberius and Abgar were contemporaneous and the latter subject to the former.

But we have equally sure evidence not so far afield in the tablets from the reigns of Cyrus and Cambyses; to wit, in Strassmaier's tablets of Cyrus, No. 16, the subscription reads: "In the tenth day of the month Siman of the first year of Cyrus, king of lands, Cambyses [being] king of Babylon."[2]

In tablet No. 81 of Cambyses, we read "Babylon, Kislev 25, year one of Kambushiya, king of Babylon, in his day and that of Kurash, his father, king of lands." Compare tablet 46: "Babylon, Duzu 25, year one of Kambushiya, king of Babylon, when (*enuma*) Kurashu, his father, [was] king of lands." Much like this is tablet 108 of VASD vi: "Babylon, the 19th day of Ab in the year one of Cambyses king of Babylon when (*enushu*) Cyrus was king of lands." In tablet 425, both Cyrus and Cambyses are called "king of Babylon, king of lands," but the tablet is unfortunately so broken as to render the connection illegible. In No. 426, "Kambushiya king of Babylon" is twice preceded by the phrase "king of lands," but unfortunately again, the name of the king is illegible. Still, it could scarcely have been any other than Cyrus. On tablet 42 occurs:

---

[1] Assemani, B. O., iii, 2, 495.   [2] See the last clause on reverse.

"Babylon, Duzu 9, year one, of Kambushiya, king of Babylon, son of Kurash, king of lands."

It will be seen from these documents, that Cyrus and Cambyses were both given the title of king simultaneously, and this in the first year of Cyrus and again in the first year of Cambyses. It is to be presumed that Cambyses enjoyed his office and title as king of Babylon all the time that his father was king of the lands. But when did he become king of Babylon? The earliest tablet that mentions him under this title is the one given above which dates from the tenth day of the third month of the first year of Cyrus. How long before this he might have claimed the title is not certain; but in view of the fact that on the fourth of Nisan of the same year he is said in the *Annals* of Nabunaid[1] to have grasped the hand of Nebo, and since this ceremony was performed by the ruler at the new year's festival,[2] we can fairly conclude that Cambyses was in some sense king of Babylon from the fourth of Nisan of the year one of Cyrus.[3]

Having thus shown that there might be two kings of Babylon at the same time, we have only to show that Darius the Mede was the same as Gobryas in order to reconcile completely the statement of Daniel vi, 29, and the disclosures of the monuments. For we have seen above that Gobryas was Cyrus' governor (*amel pihate-shu*) of Babylon as early at least as the 3rd day of the 8th month of Cyrus' accession year.[4] He was in command on the 11th of the same month, when Belshazzar was

---

[1] KB iii, ii, 135.   [2] See Muss-Arnolt's *Dict.*, p. 861.

[3] Especially may we so conclude in agreement with Winckler's statement on page xxxvi of his *Inscriptions of Sargon* that a king submitted to this ceremony in order to be rightly proclaimed as king of Babylon.   [4] Nabunaid-Cyrus *Chron.*, KB iii, ii, 135.

slain. It is most probable—there is nothing, at least, against the supposition—that he remained in command and at the head of the government, until Cambyses was installed as king of Babylon on the 4th of Nisan of the following year. The only question here, then, is: what would be the title in Hebrew and Aramaic of Gobryas as *amel pihate* of Babylon? In answer, we can only say that *malka* or *melek* (or *sar*) would be the only suitable words; and that Gobyras could rightly be called by this title as long as he was *amel pihate* of the city or province of Babylon, *i. e.*, from the 3rd day of the 8th month of Cyrus' accession year to the 3rd of Nisan of his first year.

In favor of Darius, the Mede, having been sub-king rather than the king of kings we notice the fact that, in Daniel vi, 1, it is said that Darius the Mede received the kingdom;[1] and in Daniel ix, 1, it is said that he "was made king (*homlak*) over the kingdom of the Chaldeans." How well this harmonizes with the statement of the Nabunaid-Cyrus *Chronicle*, where Gobryas is called Cyrus' governor! How well it suits the other statements of Daniel that he succeeded "the Chaldean king," "Belshazzar the king of Babylon"! Notice that not one word is said in any book of the Bible about Darius the Mede having been king of Persia, nor even of Media.

But it is said, that no contracts are dated from the reigns of Belshazzar and Darius the Mede. We should rather say, that none dated from their reigns have as yet been found. But this is no conclusive argument. For, notice, that out of the ten years of the contemporaneous reigns of Cyrus and Cambyses, only

---

[1] See Pinches, *The Old Testament in the Light of the Historical Records of Assyria and Babylonia*, p. 419.

five tablets containing the dates with the names and
titles of both kings in an unbroken and absolutely
trustworthy text have been found, one from the first
year, so-called, of Cyrus, and two from the first year,
so-called, of Cambyses. How could we expect to find
one from the four-month reigns of Belshazzar and of
Darius the Mede? As a matter of fact, Strassmaier
gives but twelve tablets from the end of the 4th month
of the 17th year of Nabunaid when Nabunaid was
captured, until the 11th of the 8th month, when Belshazzar was slain; and all of these are dated with the
name of Nabunaid, except one bearing the name of "Cyrus king of Babylon and of the lands," and dated the
7th (or perhaps better the 4th) month of the accession
year. Only one tablet bearing the name of Nabunaid
has been found dated after that fatal night on the
eleventh of the eighth month. It bears date "the
9th month [day not given] of the 17th year of Nabunaid king of Babylon."[1]

From the time when Gobryas was made governor of
Babylon, until the 4th of Nisan of the ensuing year,
we have beside this one tablet of Nabunaid, eight
tablets dated with the name of Cyrus. All of these,
with perhaps one exception (that of tablet 3, where
the inscription is injured), have the title "king of
lands" alone, thus suggesting that someone else was
during this time king of Babylon. Besides, at no time,
except during the co-regnancy of Cyrus and Cambyses,
have we as yet found any evidence that the name of the
governor (or sub-king) of Babylon, as well as, or instead
of, that of the king of kings, was ever placed upon the
contract tablets of Babylon.

Under the Persian kings, there were many governors

[1] Strassmaier, *Ins. von Nab.*, No. 1055.

of Babylon, such as Zopyrus, mentioned in Herodotus,[1] but not one Babylonian record bears the name of any one of them, at least in his official capacity.

In this connection, it might be said, that Nirgal-sharuṣur calls his father Nabu-balaṭsu-iḳbi king of Babylon; and yet we have no documents from the father's reign; and that a Nabunaid, probably the future king of that name, is once called "son of the king of the city." Furthermore, there are many kings of Babylon mentioned in the Assyrian monuments from whose reigns we have no records of any kind. Again, from the times of the last three kings of Assyria, Ashur-etil-ilani, Sin-shar-ishkun, and Sin-shum-lishir, only six or seven tablets and a few other records have come down to us. From the reigns of Xerxes the Second, Sogdianus, Arses, and Darius the Third, we have no Babylonian records as yet published. From the long reign of Artaxerxes II there are only three contract tablets thus far published.[2] Of the time from the accession of Alexander to the end of the Arsacids, a period of about 300 years, we have all told but a few score records of all kinds.

But it might be said that not merely have we no records coming from his reign, but also that the contemporaneous documents never even so much as refer to Darius. This will not be true, if we identify him with Gobryas, for he is named three times in the Cyrus *Chronicle*.[3]

---

[1] Bk. III, 160.

[2] The astronomical tables published by Kugler in his *Sternkunde und Sterndienst in Babel*, pp. 76 and 80, must be added to these. The table on page 80 mentions Artaxerxes III also.

[3] A tablet bearing the name of Gobryas was published by Dr. Pinches in the *Expository Times* for April, 1915. It reads in part as follows: "At

Finally, it is admitted by all that Gobryas was governor, or viceroy (*malka* in Aramaic), over Babylon for a period after its conquest by Cyrus. Yet we have no contract, nor other document, dated from his reign. If then it were a valid argument against the *de facto* rule of Darius the Mede (over Babylon) to say that no records dated from his reign existed, so also would it be against the rule of Gobryas.

As to the *age* of Darius the Mede, when he became

---

the end of the month Chisleu, 4th year of Cambyses, king of Babylon and the lands, Ardia, son of Nabu-bani-ahi, descendant of Remut-Ea, the man who is over the date-offerings of Ishtar of Erech, will take five talents of early fruit, and deliver them in the palace of the king, which is situated above E-anna, to Nabu-aha-iddina, the king's captain (lord of E-anna's contribution). If he does not bring (the amount), he will commit a sin against Gobryas, governor of Babylon (*hitu ša Gubaru, awel pihati Babili, inamdin*)."

Dr. Pinches well remarks that a failure to keep the contract will be a sin against Gobryas, the governor, and not against Cambyses; and that Gobryas was governor of Babylon as late as the 4th year of Cambyses, that is, thirteen years after his conquest of that city for Cyrus, though he may not have been governor during all of the intervening time. Dr. Pinches meets Tiele's objection to the appointment by Cyrus of a Mede as governor of Babylon by saying that the Babylonian *Chronicle* distinctly says that Gobryas before his conquest of Babylon was governor of Gutium, a part of ancient Media. It might be added to this, that other Medes are known to have been appointed to high commands; for Harpagus, the greatest of the generals of Cyrus, was a Mede; and Takmaspada and Datis, two of the most distinguished generals of Darius Hystaspis, were also Medes.

The close commercial relationship existing between Babylon and Media in the time of Cyrus, while Gubaru was governor of Babylon, is shown by the fact that in the 6th year of Cyrus a contract drawn up at Durgaraš, a city on the banks of the Euphrates a short distance above Sippar, calls for the payment of interest at Ecbatana, the capital of Media (see Strass., *Cyrus*, 227).

That Gubaru, governor of Ecbatana and Babylon, may have been governor of Syria also, is shown by a tablet from the 3rd year of Darius I, according to which Ushtanni was governor (*pihat*) of Babylon and of Syria (*ebir nari*) at the same time (see Strass., *Darius*, 82).

king, we know nothing absolutely explicit, except the
statement of Daniel v, 31, that he was at that time
about sixty-two years of age. With this accord
the statements of Xenophon with regard to Gobryas,
that when he went over to Cyrus, he had a marriageable
daughter;[1] and that some time before this, his grown
son had been killed by the king of Assyria (*i. e.*, Babylon).[2]

But someone will say, how do you explain the fact
that Daniel gives the name Darius to a man whom the
other documents call Gobryas? Many kings in ancient,
as well as modern, times had two or more names; especially a pre-regnal and a regnal name. The Rameses II,
king of Egypt, seems to be the same as the Sesostris of
the Greeks.[3] So Solomon is the same as Jedidiah and
Uzziah the same as Azariah. But coming nearer to the
time of Cyrus, we find that Cyrus himself according to
Strabo was called Agradetes before he became king, and
Herodotus says that his first name was not Cyrus.[4]
Josephus says that Artaxerxes was called Cyrus before
he became king.[5] Darius Nothus and Artaxerxes III
were both called Ochus before they became kings;[6] and
the last Darius, Codomannus.[7] Why may not the
name Darius have been assumed first of all by Gobryas
the Mede, when he became king of Babylon? When
Tiglath-Pileser was proclaimed king of Babylon, and

[1] *Cyropædia*, iv, vi, 10.   [2] *Id.*, iv, vi, 2–7.
[3] On the Egyptian documents, Sesostris is found perhaps but twice,
and then with different spellings, (*Setesn* and *Sesetsn*) among the almost
innumerable titles and monuments of this king. (Brugsch and Bouriant,
Le Livre des Rois, and the author's articles on *Royal Titles in Antiquity* in PTR for 1904–5.) Prof. Sethe regards this title as belonging
to Usertesen.
[4] I, 113.   [5] *Antiq.*; xi, vi, 1.   [6] Ctesias, sec. 49.
[7] Diodorus Siculus, xxii, 5, 7.

the other Assyrian kings who adopted a policy similar to his, they often ruled as kings in Babylon under names different from those which they had as kings of Assyria. Thus Tiglath-Pileser IV of Assyria was Pul in Babylon.[1] Shalmaneser III, king of Assyria, was Ululai king of Babylon; and Ashurbanipal king of Assyria was possibly Kandalanu king of Babylon.

If we could only be sure as to the meaning of the word Darius, we might understand better why the name was given, or assumed, as a royal or princely appellation. The first part of the name may be the same as the New Persian *darâ*, "king." Or the name may be derived from the Old Persian verb *dar*, "*to hold*," and may mean simply "holder of the scepter." According to Spiegel,[2] Bartholomæ,[3] and Tolman,[4] it comes from *dar*, "*to hold*," and a hypothetical *vahu* (Sansc., *vasu*), "good wealth"; hence "possessor of wealth." The title in either case would be appropriate to Gobryas as sub-king of Babylon, and also to the royal son of Hystaspis, who was by birth a king, second in rank and race to Cyrus alone.[5]

Or, Darius may be the Persian equivalent, or translation, of the Assyrian Gubaru. Herodotus says that it means ἑρξείης "*coercitor*," a sense to be derived from the Persian *dar* "*wehren*" or "*zwingen*." This derivation would favor the opinion that Gubaru in the sense of *Gewaltthäter* was a translation of Darius. An indication that favors their equivalence is to be found in the fact that the daughter of Gobryas, according to Xeno-

---

[1] Winckler, *History of Babylonia and Assyria*, p. 115, and Johns in PSBA for 1916.

[2] *Die Altpersischen Keilinschriften*, p. 81.

[3] *Altiranisches Wörterbuch*, 738.

[4] *Ancient Persian Lexicon*, pp. 83 and 107.

[5] Behistun Inscription, lines 2 and 3.

phon,[1] married Hystaspis, and that the son of Hystaspis was called Darius. This name is not met with among the royal descendants of Achæmenes before this time. If Darius Hystaspis was not called after an ancestor on his father's side, what more natural than that he should have been named after his maternal grandfather? While saying this, I am aware that there are difficulties connected with believing that the daughter of Gobryas could have been the mother of Darius Hystaspis; difficulties arising, however, from our ignorance of the time when Hystaspis married this wife, and from our ignorance of the age of Darius Hystaspis when he became king of Persia. For the marriage of Hystaspis and for the age of Darius when he became king, we have to depend upon the Greek historians; and the Greek historians give discrepant statements. Assuming, however, that Gobryas' daughter was Darius Hystaspis' mother, it would afford a ground for assuming that Gobryas was either the equivalent of Darius, or that Gobryas bore the name of Darius also. For it was customary to transmit names of fathers to their grandsons; e. g., the grandfather of Cyrus was Cyrus, and both the father and the son of Cyrus were named Cambyses.[2] So Artaxerxes the Second was the son of Darius the son of Artaxerxes the First and Darius the Second was the great-grandson of Darius Hystaspis.[3]

Among the Achæmenidæ we have the names of five Dariuses, three of whom were kings, two kings named Xerxes, and three named Artaxerxes. Of the Seleucids, who succeeded them, there were seventeen who bore the name of Antiochus. All of the Arsacids,

---

[1] *Cyropædia*, viii, iv, 25.   [2] Cyrus *Cylinder*, lines 20, 21.
[3] Inscription of Artaxerxes Mnemon in Bezold, *Achämenideninschriften*, No. xvii, and Weissbach, *Die Keilinschriften der Achämeniden*.

the successors of the Seleucids, took the regnal name of
Arsaces. Of the twenty-nine kings of Edessa, ten were
named Abgar and ten Ma'nu.[1]

While such examples do not prove that Gobryas was
also named Darius, they do afford a presumption in
favor of the probability that he was; and in view of the
other indications in its favor, they should deter anyone
from asserting that Gobryas and Darius the Mede were
not the same.

But was Gobryas a Mede? He is called[2] the *"amel
pihat mati Gutium,"* *i. e.*, the governor of the land of
Gutium. Now, according to the Cyrus *Cylinder* (line
13), Cyrus conquered Gutium (Ḳuti) the totality of the
host of the Manda (*umman-Manda*). If Manda and
Madai are the same, Gobryas their governor would probably be a Mede. Moreover, Gutium which certainly lay
at the foot of the pass that led from Nineveh to Ecbatana, the capital of the Medes, must have been looked
upon by the dwellers in Babylon as embracing Media
also, since in the Nabunaid-Cyrus *Chronicle, Obv.,*
B. 2, Ecbatana is called the capital of Astyages, the
king of Gutium. So that it would be quibbling to
deny that Gobryas might justly have been called a
Mede.

There remains one point to be explained. Darius
the Mede is said to have placed over the kingdom one
hundred and twenty satraps, who should be in all the
kingdom.[3] This accords with the statement of the
Annals of Nabunaid, that Gobryas appointed *pihati*
in Babylon. Notice that neither in the Bible, nor on
the monuments, is anything said about the appointment
of satraps in *Persia*, but in *Babylon* or *Chaldea*. Now,

---

[1] *The Doctrine of Addai*, by Phillips, note on p. 1.
[2] *Annals* of Nabunaid, Column iii, line 15.   [3] Dan. vi, 1.

since, in the first verse of Esther, it is said that in the time of Xerxes there were an hundred and twenty-seven provinces of the *Persian* empire, it has been assumed that in Daniel, there is a confusing of the Dariuses, and that this confusion is an evidence of late origin for the book.

But notice, first, that nothing is said in Daniel about "provinces"; and that even if there were, the word used in Esther for province, מדינה, is a difficult one to define closely.   It may mean "province" or "satrapy," as in Esther i, 1.   It may also mean "city," as commonly in Syriac and Arabic, and probably in Daniel iii, 1, 2, and 1 Kings xx, 14.   In the latter place, it is said that Ahab gathered two hundred and thirty-two sons of the princes of the provinces.[1] It would be impossible to suppose that these *provinces* were of large extent.   Would not "judicial district," or *"Gerichtsbezirk"* of whatever size, express the original meaning of *Medina?*

Again, the word *satrap* is ambiguous.[2] Taking Haug's derivation as the correct one, it meant originally simply "land protector."   As to the character of the duties, and especially as to the extent of the land ruled over, the word itself gives us no clue.   Besides, the writer of Daniel applies the term to the officers of Nebuchadnezzar,[3] so that, in his view at least, the term cannot have meant merely governor of a Persian satrapy.   Moreover, according to Xenophon's *Cyropædia*, Cyrus appointed at first only six satraps; and these were sent to rule over only a small part of his dominions.[4]   Darius Hystaspis says, in the Behistun Inscrip-

---

[1] *Naaray saray ham'deenoth.*
[2] For a full discussion of the term *satrap*, see Chap IX, iii, 2, (2).
[3] Dan. iii, 2, 3, 27.   [4] Bk. VIII, 6.

tion, that twenty-three countries were subject to him, and he mentions the names of the "lands."[1]

In the *Naqs-i-Rustam* inscription of the same Darius thirty-two different provinces are mentioned. In Strassmaier's *Darius*, 82, Ushtanni is called governor of Babylon and Syria (*ebir nari*) and in his inscription on *Cyrus*, 227, the interest of a sum of gold borrowed in the land of Ailtamma Durgash is said to have been payable in Ecbatana.[2] Now, Gobryas was governor of Gutium (which at this time included Ecbatana) when he conquered Babylon. When he became governor of Babylonia, his dominion would extend over all the country from the mountains of Media to the deserts of Arabia. If, like Ushtanni, he was satrap of Syria also, his government could extend to the Mediterranean. How many satraps, or *pihati*, he would find necessary to help govern such a territory at such a time of conquest, we might safely leave to his judgment of the circumstances.[3]

CONCLUSION

From the above evidence it is clear that the author of Daniel does not state, nor even intimate, that Cyrus succeeded Darius the Mede in the *empire* of Babylon. On the contrary, he indicates that Darius the Mede received from Cyrus his overlord the kingdom of Bel-

---

[1] Bezold's, *Achämenideninschriften*, p. 33, lines 4-7.

[2] The document is dated the 16th Airu, 6th year of Cyrus, king of Babylon, king of lands.

[3] Furthermore, if this extensive rule belonged to Gobryas, who can say that one of the *pihatis* was not a man named Darius, and that this Darius was not the *malka* of the city or province of Babylon?

Finally, in this connection, it may be remarked that the verb which is employed in the *Annals* of Nabunaid, in the phrase "Gobryas his [*i. e.,* Cyrus'] *pihatu* appointed *pihatis*," is of the same root as that

shazzar the Chaldean, which at best constituted but a small portion of the empire of the Persians. The monumental evidence shows the possibility of 120 satraps being installed in the province of Babylonia, alone. This evidence shows, also, that dual datings were common among the ancient nations, and that hence Cyrus and Darius the Mede may have been reigning at the same time, one as overlord and the other as sub-king, or viceroy. It is pure conjecture to suppose that the author of Daniel "evidently thought that Darius the Mede preceded Cyrus the Persian," or that he "believed that Cyrus succeeded to the empire of Babylon on the death of the Median Darius," rather than on its conquest from Nabunaid and Belshazzar.

---

employed of Ahab in 2 Kings xx, 15 where he is said to have mustered (*paqad*) the young men of the princes of the provinces. The same verb and form were employed by Darius Hystaspis in the Babylonian recension of the *Naqs-i-Rustam* inscription, line 22, where he says "Ahuramazda appointed me to be king over them."[1]

[1] *Anaku ina muhhishina ana sharruti iptek idanni.*

CHAPTER VIII

ONE of the worst errors of the modern critics is their supposing that one can posit the sources from which a writer who lived two thousand or more years ago *must* have derived his information. The complacence and self-assurance with which a knowledge of such sources is assumed might be dismissed with a smile, were it not that these suppositions are often put forward as arguments to prove a proposition. It seems marvelous that anyone to-day should fail to recognize that the ancient writers of history, whether sacred or profane, had access to many documentary sources that have long since ceased to exist. Many of these writers claim that they used such sources. Thus, in the introduction to his *Expedition of Alexander*, Arrian says that he made use of the works of Ptolemy, the first king of Egypt, and of Aristobulus, both of whom accompanied Alexander on his campaigns, and also of many others whose names he does not mention. Josephus, in his treatise *Contra Apion*, gives the names of about forty historians of different nations from whom he culled his statements; and he asserts again and again that a large part of the material used by him had been derived either by himself or by his authorities directly from written official records possessed by the Egyptians, Babylonians, Tyrians, and Jews. Polybius gives the names of more than twenty historians from whom he derived his facts. Pliny the younger, in the first book of his Natural History, gives the names of the sources of each book that follows. For the fifth book, which contains his account of Palestine, he mentions the names of sixty historians and others from whom he derived his information; and for the whole thirty-seven books he names hundreds of authorities. It is noteworthy, also, that neither of the historians named as the sources of Arrian is mentioned by either Josephus, Polybius, or Pliny; and that each of the three last named gives among his sources the names of some who were not apparently used by the others. Further, it will be noted that many of the authorities used by Polybius, Josephus, and Pliny, for their information about Persia, Egypt, Syria, and Palestine, are historians who lived and wrote long before the second century B. C., and hence were very near to the time of the events they narrate. Furthermore, both Polybius and Josephus affirm that they themselves had access to and frequently consulted official records that had been preserved to their time; and Josephus reiterates the fact that his chief authorities made use of the archives of the respective countries whose histories they had written. Thus of Manetho he says that "he was a man who was by birth an Egyptian, yet had made himself master of the Greek learning, as is very evident; for he wrote the history of his own country in the Greek tongue, by translating it, as he says himself, out of the sacred records."[1] Of Dius, he says that he was "one that is believed to have written the Phenician History after an accurate manner," and of Menander the Ephesian, that he "wrote

[1] *Cont. Ap.*, i, 14.

the acts that were done by the Greeks and Barbarians under every one of the Syrian kings; and had taken much pains to learn their history out of their own records."[1] Of Berosus, he says that "he was by birth a Chaldean, well known to the learned, on account of his publication among the Greeks of the Chaldean books of astronomy and philosophy. This Berosus, therefore, following the most ancient records of the nations, gives us a history."[2] Moreover, many other eminent authors who wrote in the Greek language were known to Josephus, such as Ephorus (400 to 330 B. C.), Theopompus (380 to 330 (?) B. C.), Hecatæus (6th–5th cent. B. C.), Herodotus (464 to 424 B. C.), and Thucydides (471–400 B. C.). A certain Castor, also, is named by him as one of his authorities, a man so utterly unknown to the classical writers that his name even is not given in Liddell and Scott's Greek Dictionary, in the Encyclopedia Britannica, nor in the classical dictionaries.

From all this, it will be perfectly evident that all educated men living in and before the second century B. C. must have had access to so much information with regard to the number and history of the Babylonian and Persian kings, as to render it highly improbable that any writer of the second century B. C. could have been as ignorant of the history of Persia as certain critics represent the writer of Daniel to have been. Besides, if he himself had been as ignorant of the facts about which he wrote as the critics represent him to have been, how could he have palmed off his work on the Jews of that period as genuine and authentic? According to the critics themselves, it was the time of the two Ben-Siras, and of the authors of Tobit, Judith, First

---

[1] *Cont. Ap.*, i, 17.   [2] *Cont. Ap.*, i, 19.

Maccabees, the Letter of Aristeas, and many other literary compositions, so that in such an atmosphere, it is
not likely that an author of the ability of the writer
of the Book of Daniel could have had no knowledge of
the history of Persia, except what he learned from the
Jewish Scriptures; and it is especially unlikely that
the Jews of that time would have failed to recognize the
alleged historical inaccuracies of the book, did they
exist; and to reject it as they did reject Tobit, Judith,
and other works.

But after having made this great and yet absolutely
unprovable assumption that it can now be known what
sources of information a writer of the second century
B. C. may have had before him, the critics go a step
farther and assert that the author of Daniel can have
had but a "dim consciousness" of the events of the
sixth century B. C., of which he on his part assumes to
speak.   Now, whatever opinion one may have with regard to the writer of the book of Daniel, it seems certain
that the very last impression one could derive from
the book itself would be that the writer himself felt
that he had a dim and uncertain knowledge of the events
which he narrates.   Few writers are more vivid, more
circumstantial, or more given to detail.   Few writings
bear on their face clearer indication of being the narration of an eye-witness.   No document, whether a fictitious or a real story could more manifestly purport
to contain the actual words and deeds of the chief
actor around whom the plot centered.   The writer
was certainly not oppressed with the sense of having
but a dim consciousness of the things of which he
writes.   Perhaps, after all, it is we to-day who have the
dim consciousness of the times and events and persons
that he describes so graphically,—a dim consciousness,

a very limited and uncertain knowledge, of what transpired at the time when the sun of Babylon's glory rose in splendor under Nebuchadnezzar, or when it set amid the shame and confusion of Nabunaid and his first-born son. Until this dimness be dispelled and this darkness enlightened by documentary evidence we shall be compelled to believe the writer of Daniel most probably knew more about the subject than any one of us to-day with the evidence at our disposal can ever possibly know. In view of the fact that the works of Herodotus, Ctesias, Berosus, Menander, and many others which treated of the affairs of Assyria, Babylonia, and Persia, may have been known to a writer of the second century B. C., how can any man have the assurance to assert that the author of Daniel must have believed that the Medes without the assistance of the Persians must have captured Babylon? How can anyone know that he derived his information as to the capture of Babylon from the slender hints of Isaiah xiii and xxi and Jeremiah li alone, that the author of Daniel possessed but a dim consciousness of the fact that the Persian empire had grown out of the Median kingdom, or that a Darius really did capture Babylon? In the name of scholarship and for the sake of truth and righteousness, it is time to call a halt on all those who presume to a knowledge which they do not possess, in order to cast reproach upon an ancient writer, as to whose sources of information and knowledge of the facts they must be ignorant and whose statements they cannot possibly fully understand, nor successfully contradict.

It need hardly be stated that the foregoing paragraphs are concerned primarily with the defense of the historicity, rather than of the early date of Daniel. The reader, however, will recognize that in the subject discussed in this chapter, the *historicity* is the principal point of attack, and not the date. For if the author of Daniel is incorrect in what he says about the relations of the Medes to the conquest of Babylon it makes no material difference when his account of it was written, —whether in the sixth or in the second century B. C. But if the work is correct historically, the way is then open to discuss the date of the composition. If it can be shown that there is no sufficient reason for denying the correctness of its historical statements, those who believe in the possibility of miracles and predictive prophecy will be free to accept the early date of its composition. If on the other hand it can be shown that the book is wrong in its statements regarding ordinary historical events, there will be no solid ground upon which to base a defense of its miracles and predictions, nor of its authenticity and early date. The historical statements may be true without being authentic. They cannot be authentic unless they are trustworthy.

In this chapter, then, the discussion will be confined to the objections to the historicity of Daniel based upon what he is assumed to say about the connection of the Medes with the conquest of Babylon.

OBJECTION STATED

That the Medes must have captured Babylon is derived from Isa. xiii, 17, xxi, 2, and Jer. li, 11, 28, in connection with which the author possessed a dim consciousness of the fact that the Persian empire had grown out of the Median kingdom and that once *a* Darius really did capture Babylon.[1]

[1] Cornill, pp. 384, 385.

This sentence is a possible, or even probable, explanation of how a writer of the second century B.C. might have said that Babylon was taken by the Medes. But as regards the book of Daniel, there are four assumptions in it.

Assumptions Involved

It is assumed first, that Daniel says specifically that the Medes, apart from the Persians, conquered Babylon; secondly, that he derived this information from certain passages in Isaiah and Jeremiah; that, thirdly, the author had a dim consciousness of the fact that the Persian empire had grown out of the Median kingdom; and fourthly, that the writer of Daniel had as the ground of his statements with regard to Darius nothing more substantial to build on than a dim consciousness that once *a* Darius really did capture Babylon.

Answer to Assumptions

1. With regard to the first of these assumptions, there can be no doubt that the writer of Daniel might justly have said that Babylon was taken by the Medes, inasmuch as Gobryas, governor of Gutium (which, as will be shown below, was in part, at least, coextensive with Media), was the general who while commanding an army under Cyrus took Babylon for him. But as a matter of fact Daniel says nothing of the kind. He says simply that after the death of Belshazzar the Chaldean king, Darius the Mede, received his kingdom;[1] and again that Darius was made king over the realm of the Chaldeans.[2] But on the other

[1] Chapter v, 31.   [2] IX, 1.

hand Daniel does not say that the Persians under Cyrus took Babylon without the assistance of the Medes. The truth is, it was the Medes *and* Persians who conquered Babylon. If it be granted, as Professor Sayce, followed by Winckler, has contended that Astyages was not a Mede but a Scythian; then, Cyrus the Persian, and Harpagus the Mede, rebelled against the domination of the alien Scythian, and Cyrus became king of the united peoples, the Medes and Persians, from that time on one and inseparable. This view harmonizes with the facts recorded on the monuments and with the statements of the Scriptures and of the classical writers. [1]

[1] There is abundant evidence from the monuments to show that Gutium was in part at least coextensive with Media. For example, the Nabunaid-Cyrus *Chronicle* states expressly that Gubaru, the governor of Gutium, captured the citadel of Babylon. According to Winckler, in his *History of Babylonia and Assyria* (p. 48), Gutium was north of Anzan and Susa, and corresponded substantially to Armenia south of Lake Van, though in his *Untersuchungen*,[1] he says it was the country between the Euphrates and Tigris.[2] Again he renders it by "North Countries." In fact, throughout all the changes of population, the part of the world north of Assyria was known to the inhabitants of Babylon and Assyria as Gutium. In the time of Naram-Sin, the king of Gutium made a dedicatory offering in Babylonia which contains an inscription written, like those of Naram-Sin, in Babylonian. Ashurbanipal, in his *Annals* (Col. iii, 103), speaks of the kings of the land of Guti. Gubaru, governor of Gutium, may justly have been called governor of the Medes, or king of Guti in the sense employed by Ashurbanipal.

A strong argument in favor of Gutium's having been regarded by the Babylonians as embracing Media is that Media is never mentioned on the Babylonian monuments before the time of Xerxes, that Gutium designates the region of Media in the only original Babylonian document mentioning that part of the world; and that on the other hand, Gutium is not mentioned on the Behistun Inscription, but Mada denotes the region denoted earlier by the Babylonian word Gutium. A modern illustration of different names for the same country is Germany, Alle-

[1] Page 131.   [2] *History of Babylonia and Assyria*, page 124.

Inasmuch, then, as Herodotus[1] makes Astyages to have been king of Media and his capital city to have been Ecbatana and the revolted troops to have been Medes; and as the inscriptions make him to have been king of Guti, or Gutium, the revolted troops to have been the host of Manda, his capital city to have been Ecbatana, and Gobryas to have been the successor of Astyages in the government of Gutium, though as subordinate to Cyrus the conqueror of Astyages; and finally, inasmuch as this Gobryas the successor of Astyages king of Media, or of the host of the Manda, is said in the Nabunaid-Cyrus *Chronicle* to have captured Babylon for Cyrus; it is not far fetched to suppose that Gobryas may have been called by his subjects, at least in the Aramean tongue, the king of the Medes, and that his soldiers, his subjects, and himself, may have been called in the same tongue *Medes*.

---

magne, Deutschland; an ancient, Hellas, Græcia, land of the Javanites. A more ancient still is Elam, which appears in other languages under the names of Uwaga, Hatamtup, and Susiana. Again, it seems clear from the references to the destruction of Astyages by Cyrus, which we find in the Babylonian documents, that Gutium and Media were the same country in the estimation of the writers of those documents. Thus, in the Cyrus' Clay Cylinder, 13, it is said that "Marduk caused the land of Kuti (Guti) the totality of the host of the Manda, to bow at the feet of Cyrus." In the Abu Habba Cylinder, we are informed that Astyages the king of the host of Manda, together with his land and the kings his helpers, were no more, because the host had been scattered by the small army of Cyrus king of Anzan, the little vassal of Astyages; and that the latter had been captured and taken prisoner to the former's land.[2] In the Nabunaid-Cyrus *Chronicle* it is said that the troops revolted against Astyages and that he was captured and delivered into the hands of Cyrus, who advanced to Ecbatana the capital city, where he took silver, gold, and other spoils and carried them to the land of Anshan. Later in the same, it is said that Gobryas was the governor of Gutium or Kuti.

---

[1] Bk. I, 107-130.   [2] Col. i, 11-38.

It must be remembered here that the little we know about the Medes and Persians shows that there was a close relationship existing between them. According to the biblical and Greek records, they were substantially one people in race and language. On the Behistun Inscription, Darius treats the Medes and no others as the equals of the Persians. Thus in sections i, 10, 11, he speaks of Persia and Media and the other provinces. In section ix, 13, he says, "there was no one, neither Persian nor Mede nor anyone from our family, who would have wrested the kingdom from Smerdis the Magian till I came." The seat of Smerdis' kingdom was at "Sikayanvatish in the province of Nisaya in Media." Again, in section i, 14, Darius says, "I placed the people in this place, Persia, Media, and the other provinces." Again, in ii, 14, he sends a Persian and a Median army under the command of Takhmaspada, a Median, against an uprising in Sagartia. Again, in iii, 6, he sends out the Persian and the Median army against an uprising in Persia itself. In iii, 14, he sends an army against Babylon under command of a Median, Vindafra by name.

In the Babylonian contract tablets of the reign of Xerxes, we find Media mentioned along with Persia in the titles of a number of the inscriptions. For example, in the *Acts of the 8th Congress of Orientalists*, Strassmaier has given a number of contracts from the time of Xerxes. In No. 19, the subscription reads, "Xerxes, king of Persia and Media"; and in No. 20, "Xerxes, king of Persia and of the land of the Medes." So also, in vol. iv, No. 193 and No. 194, of the inscriptions published by the *Vorderasiatische Gesellschaft* of Berlin, we find "Xerxes, (king) of Persia and Media, king (?)

of Babylon (?) and of the lands."[1] Evetts, No. 3, reads: "Xerxes, king of the land of Persia and of the land of the Medes." In the *Morgan Collection*, vol. i, 85, we read: "Xerxes, king of the city of Persia (and) of the city of Media," city being used for country.[2]

In the Greek writers of the fifth century B. C. the ordinary designation for the people and kings was Mede, not Persian.[3]

2. The second assumption is that the author of Daniel derived most of his information about the conquest of Babylon by the Medes from certain passages in Isaiah and Jeremiah. These passages read as follows:

"Behold I shall stir up the Medes against them, which shall not regard silver" (Is. xiii, 17). "Go up, O Elam, besiege, O Media, according to the sighing thereof have I made thee to cease" (Is. xxi, 2). "Make bright the arrows, gather the shields Jehovah hath stirred up the spirit of the Medes. For his device is against Babylon to destroy it" (Jer. li, 11). "Prepare the nations against her, the kingdoms of Ararat, Minni, and Ashkenaz. . . . Prepare against her the nations with the kings of the Medes, the captains thereof and the rulers thereof . . . for every purpose of Jehovah shall be fulfilled against Babylon" (Jer. li, 28, 30).

It will be noted (1) that the nations mentioned in these prophecies are Elam, Media, Ararat (*i. e.*, Armenia), Minni, and Ashkenaz; of which all except

---

[1] So also in Evetts, No. 4, and VSD 118 and VI, 181.

[2] See the author's article on the "Titles of the Kings of Persia" in the *Festschrift Eduard Sachau*, Berlin, 1915.

[3] See, for example, Herodotus and Thucydides, in numerous places, and the writer's articles on the "Titles of Kings in Antiquity," in the *Pres. and Ref. Review* for 1904–5.

the last are frequently named on the monuments from the time of Shalmanezer III to that of Ashurbanipal inclusive.[1]

Of these countries Daniel mentions Elam as a province of Belshazzar (viii, 2), and speaks several times of the Medes and of Darius the Mede; but he never speaks of the land, kingdom, or kings of the Medes, nor of their captains and rulers. Neither does he mention Minni, Ararat, or Ashkenaz. On the other hand, he refers to Persia, Javan, Chaldea, Shushan, Ulai, and the plain of Dura, which are not mentioned in the passages of Isaiah and Jeremiah cited by Prof.

[1] Elam is mentioned frequently in the inscriptions from the time of Isaiah (e. g., by Sargon, KB ii, 40; by Sennacherib, KB 102, 104, 106; by Esarhaddon, KB 128, 144; by Ashurbanipal, KB ii, 180–214 passim). Jeremiah speaks of the kings of Elam (xxv, 25), and of the impending destruction of its king and princes (xlix, 35–39). Nebuchadnezzar does not mention it. Nabunaid refers once to the fruit of the land of Elam; and once to Ishtar the mistress of Elam who dwells in Susa (Zehnpfund-Langdon, *Neubabylonische Königsinschriften*, p. 276, iii, 41, and 292, iii, 15). Darius Hystaspis put down a rebellion in it, which occurred shortly after his accession (Beh. Insc. § 16), and it is frequently mentioned by the Persian kings as a province of their empire.

Media is frequently named on the Assyrian inscriptions from Shalmanezer III onward (KB i, 142, 180, ii, 7, 18, 128, 132, 146). It occurs many times in the Behistun Inscription in the Babylonian recension as well as in Persian and Susian. It is found also on some Babylonian tablets from the first years of Xerxes. Commonly elsewhere on the Babylonian documents, Gutium is used to denote what the Assyrians call Media (e. g., on stele Nab.-Con. iv, 21, and Cyr.-Cyl., 13 and 31). A third designation for the country is "the land of Ecbatana" (Nab.-Cyr. Chronicle, B. 3, 4, and Strass. Cyr., 60, 16).

Ararat as the name of Armenia is common in Assyrian and Babylonian from Shalmanezer's time to that of Darius Hystaspis (KB i, 144, 164, ii, 6, 18, 146; Behistun, §§ 26, 52). Minni occurs in Assyrian from the time of Shalmanezer to Ashurbanipal (KB i, 146, 178, ii, 128, 178).

If Ashkenaz be the same as Asquzai, it is mentioned twice in the inscriptions of Esarhaddon (KB ii, 146. See Jeremias, *The Old Testament in the Light of the Ancient East*, i, 283, and Knudtzon, *Assyrische Gebete an den Sonnengott*, Nos. 23–35).

Cornill.   In view of these facts, how can it be said that Daniel derived his information as to the conquest of Babylon from these sources?

3.   The third assumption admits that the author of Daniel knew that the Persian empire had grown out of the Median kingdom.   But Prof. Cornill asserts that this knowledge was a "dim consciousness."   As to what he means by this phrase he does not enlighten us, nor does he give any examples, nor any proof of it. If he means that the author of Daniel says little explicit about the relations existing between Media and Persia, it will be admitted.   Daniel, indeed, speaks of the laws of the Medes and Persians,[1] and says that Belshazzar's kingdom was divided and given to the Medes and Persians,[2] and interprets the two horns of the ram that was seen in his vision as denoting the kings of Media and Persia, both horns springing from the same head, but the Persian being later and higher than the Median.[3]   He says also that Daniel prospered in the reign of Darius and in the reign of Cyrus the Persian[4]; and speaks of the first year of Cyrus the king[5] and of the third year of Cyrus, king of Persia,[6] of the first year of Darius the Mede,[7] and of the first year of Darius the son of Xerxes of the seed of the Medes, who had been made king over the realm of the Chaldeans.[8] He says, further, that this Darius the Mede received the Chaldean Kingdom, when he was about sixty-two years of age,[9] and that he organized this kingdom for governmental purposes.[10]   Finally, he speaks of a "prince of Persia"[11] and of "kings of Persia."[12]

But all this does not imply that he had a dim con-

---

[1] VI, 8, 12, 15.   [2] V, 28.   [3] VIII, 3, 20.   [4] VI, 29.
[5] I, 21.   [6] X, 1.   [7] XI, 1.   [8] IX, 1.
[9] VI, 1.   [10] VI, 2-4.   [11] X, 13, 20.   [12] X, 13, xi, 20.

sciousness that the Persian empire had grown out of the Median kingdom—a subject which he does not propose to state or discuss—but rather an exact knowledge of the fact that the kingdom of Darius the Mede had been established on the ruins of the kingdom of the Chaldeans which had been conquered from Belshazzar. For notice (1) that the author of Daniel does not call anyone "king of Media" or "king of the Medes"; (2) that he always puts the Medes before the Persians, as if he knew that the Median hegemony had preceded the Persian; (3) that Darius the Mede is said to have received the kingdom of Belshazzar the Chaldean; (4) that he makes Cyrus the Persian to be the real successor to the power of Nebuchadnezzar, king of Babylon (i, 1, 18, 21, vi, 29); (5) that he does not purport to discuss the origin of the kingdom of Persia, nor its relation to Media; (6) that he gives the years of the reigns of Belshazzar, Darius, and Cyrus, and other items of information, which attest the honesty of his intentions and challenge the denial of his veracity; and (7) that no evidence has been produced by Prof. Cornill to show that he was either dishonest in his intentions, or unveracious in his statements.

4. The fourth assumption of Professor Cornill is that the writer of Daniel had nothing but a dim consciousness that once a Darius really did conquer Babylon. In the following chapters it will be shown that this assumption is a pure assertion without any proof and incapable of proof.

CONCLUSION

The above discussion has shown that the book of Daniel does not state that the Medes conquered Babylon apart from the Persians; nor that the Persians conquered Babylon without the assistance of the Medes. Hence, there is no cause for assuming that the writer had nothing but a dim consciousness that once *a* Darius did conquer Babylon, inasmuch as the statements of the book are in absolute harmony with the facts made known from other sources.

CHAPTER IX

DARIUS THE MEDE AND THE KINGS OF PERSIA

In this and the following chapters, will be considered a number of objections against the book of Daniel on the allegation that it is clear that the author was deficient in knowledge or confused in thought. I shall endeavor to show that these objections are based, not upon what the author really says, but upon false interpretations of what he says. These false interpretations arise partly from wrong definitions of terms, partly from a misinterpretation of the meaning of the author's statements, and partly from the pure creative imagination of the objectors. To the first of these belong the objections which are based upon wrong definitions of such words as satrap, peoples, nations, and tongues; to the second, the assumptions as to the number of the kings of Persia that were known to the author of Daniel, and that are mentioned in the Old Testament; to the third, the assertions that Darius the Mede was a reflection into the past of Darius Hystaspis, that the author confused Darius Hystaspis with Xerxes, and with Darius Codomannus and that he states that Alexander the Great repulsed an attack upon Greece made by the last king of Persia.

OBJECTIONS STATED

When we find him (*i.e.*, Daniel) attributing to the Persian empire a total of only four kings (Dan. xi, 2; comp., also, vii, 6), this clearly arises from the fact that by accident the names of only four Persian kings are mentioned in the O. T.; when we find that he makes the fourth of these exceedingly rich, provoke a mighty war against Greece, and in a triumphant repulse of this attack by the Greek king Alexander the Great to be defeated and dethroned—it is clear that the author has confused Xerxes and Darius Hystaspis by making them one and the same person, and mistaken the latter for Darius Codomannus.[1]

In 6:1, the temptation to suspect a confusion (of Darius the Mede) with Darius Hystaspes—who actually organized the Persian empire into "satrapies" though much fewer than 120—is strong.   Tradition, it can hardly be doubted, has here confused persons and events in reality distinct.[2]

"Darius the Mede" must be a reflection into the past of Darius Hystaspes, father—not son—of Xerxes, who had to reconquer Babylon in B. C. 521 and again in 515, and who established the system of satrapies, combined, not impossibly, with indistinct recollections of Gubaru (or Ugbaru), who first occupied Babylon in Cyrus' behalf, and who, in appointing governors there, appears to have acted as Cyrus' deputy.[3]

Dr. Driver further cites Prof. Sayce's *Higher Criticism and the Monuments*, pp. 524–537, as showing "that the representations in the book of Daniel are inconsistent with the testimony of the inscriptions," and "that the aim of the author was not to write history, in the proper sense of the word, but to construct, upon a historical basis, though regardless of the facts as they actually occurred, edifying religious narratives (or '*Haggadah*')."

[1] Cornill, *Introduction to the Canonical Books of the Old Testament*, pp. 385, 386.   [2] Behrmanns, *Daniel*, p. xix.
[3] Driver, *Lit. of the O. T.*, p. 500.

11

Assumptions Involved

There are here the following assumptions:

I.　That the author states that the Persian empire had a totality of only four kings.

II.　That only four Persian kings are mentioned in the Old Testament.[1]

III.　That Darius the Mede is represented as absolute ruler of the Persian empire and as having divided it into 120 satrapies.[2]

IV.　That the author of Daniel supposed Xerxes the Great to be the father and not the son of Darius Hystaspis.[3]

V.　That the author of Daniel confused Darius the Mede with Darius Hystaspis.[4]

VI.　That Darius the Mede must have been a reflection into the past of Darius Hystaspis.[5]

VII.　That the author confused Darius Hystaspis and Xerxes by making them one and the same person.[6]

VIII.　That he mistakes Darius Hystaspis for Darius Codomannus.[7]

IX.　That the author states that the attack of the fourth king of Persia on Greece was repulsed by Alexander the Great.[8]

Answer to the Assumptions

I.　The author does not say that the Persian empire had only four kings.　Daniel xi, 2, which Prof. Cornill cites to show this, reads as follows: "And now will I show thee the truth.　Behold, there shall stand up yet three kings in Persia; and the fourth shall be far richer

---

[1] See p. 165.　[2] See p. 172.　[3] See p. 199.　[4] See p. 200.
[5] See p. 221.　[6] See p. 264.　[7] See p. 272.　[8] See p. 274.

than they all: and when he is waxed strong through his riches, he shall stir up all against the realm of Greece." Daniel vii, 6, with which Prof. Cornill compares xi, 2, reads: "After this I beheld, and, lo, another, like a leopard, which had upon its back four wings of a bird; the beast had also four heads; and the dominion was given to it."

I.   It is obvious that before this second verse can even be considered in this connection, it must be clearly shown that it really refers to the Persian empire at all.   But this cannot be clearly shown.   It will only be regarded as referring to the Persian empire by those who believe that the third kingdom of Daniel's prophecies is the Persian, rather than the Grecian.   But this itself is an assumption, which, while it may be accepted by some, cannot be proven.   There are in our opinion stronger reasons for holding that the leopard (or panther) of the verse cited refers to Alexander the Great than to the Persian empire.   The lion of verse 4 would then be the Babylonian empire; the bear, the Persian; and the leopard, the Macedonian.   Certainly, if we accept the view that Darius the Mede reigned contemporaneously with Cyrus the Persian as a sub-king under him, there seems to be no reason for speaking of a separate Median empire as set forth in any of the visions of Daniel.   If such a separate Median kingdom be ruled out, the leopard must refer to Alexander's rapid conquests.   The number four, used with reference to the wings and heads of the beast, cannot be pressed further than the figure of the vision allows.   Daniel himself merely makes them a part of the wings of the flying and devouring leopard, to which dominion was given.

If this interpretation of vii, 6, be admitted, it is obvi-

ous that it cannot be brought in to show Daniel's opinion as to the number of the Persian kings. But, even if
Dan. vii, 6 did refer to the Persian empire, the four
wings and four heads cannot possibly be used to show
that Daniel believed that the empire of the Persians had
only four kings. We repeat, these four wings and four
heads most naturally refer to the rapidity of the movements and to the voracity of the beast. The assumption that they refer to four kings (an assumption which
is not the obvious nor the most natural interpretation),
and the further assumption that the leopard refers to
the Persian empire, cannot be used to support the
assumption that the author of Daniel "attributes to the
Persian empire a total of only four kings."

2. As to Daniel xi, 2, it is certain that if the writer
saw his vision in the first year of Darius the Mede, who
was a sub-king, or contemporary of Cyrus, king of Persia, and there were still to be three kings of Persia and
the fourth was to stir up all against Greece, that the
three kings would be in the order of their reigns Cambyses, the Pseudo-Smerdis, and Darius Hystaspis. The
fourth king would be either Darius Hystaspis, or his
son and successor Xerxes. It would be the former if we
begin to count with Cyrus as first; and Xerxes, if we
count Cambyses as first. It seems, then, that the most
likely interpretation would make Darius Hystaspis to be
the fourth king. This would agree best with the history
of the Persian expedition against Greece as recorded in
Herodotus,[1] where it is stated positively that it was
Darius who was the instigator of the first war against
Greece which culminated at Marathon; and that he
prepared before his death for the second expedition,
which was repulsed at Salamis and Platæa, Xerxes

[1] Bk. VI.

himself being disinclined to the war.[1] To represent
Darius Hystaspis as the arranger of these expeditions
against Greece, harmonizes with the alleged motive of
Alexander's subsequent expedition against Persia. For
Quintus Curtius,[2] says that the cause of his attack on
Persia was said by Alexander in a letter to Darius III
to be that Darius I had devastated the Ionian colonies of
the Greeks, had crossed the sea with a great army and
borne arms against Macedonia and Greece, and that
Xerxes had come again with a force of cruel barbarians
to fight against them. Arrian, also, in his history of
the expedition of Alexander[3] gives a letter to Darius
Codomannus in which Alexander says that the cause
of his expedition against the Persians was to take vengeance on them because their "ancestors having come
into Macedonia and the rest of Greece had entreated
them evilly." If Alexander could thus connect his
expedition in B. C. 332 with the expeditions of Darius
and Xerxes of 490–480 B. C., and rightly so, why may
not the prophet in vision have seen them in this close
connection? At any rate, the placing of the counter
movements of the two empires in juxtaposition, whether
by prediction or *post eventum*, would not prove that the
author of Daniel was ignorant of the other kings of
Persia, any more than it would prove that Alexander
himself, or his historians, Curtius and Arrian, were thus
ignorant. No one that knew the history of the Persian
expeditions against Greece could well avoid placing
them in contrast with the Greek expedition against
Persia.

II.   Prof. Cornill states that only four Persian kings

[1] *Id.*, Bk. VII, 5.
[2] *Life and Exploits of Alexander the Great*, Bk. IV, § 2.
[3] Bk. II, § 14.

are mentioned in the Old Testament and implies that
the author of Daniel supposed from this that Persia
had had only four kings.[1]

But it is impossible to prove that only four Persian
kings are mentioned in the Old Testament. It must be
admitted that only four different *names* of Persian
kings are found there. But since there were certainly
three kings of Persia who bore the name of Darius, let
alone others of the name who were not kings, such as
Darius the son of Xerxes mentioned in Ctesias,[2] it will
have to be shown that the author of Daniel was ignorant of more than one Darius, before Prof. Cornill's
contention can be admitted. The sangfroid with
which this can be asserted without any proof to establish the assertion is astonishing, to say the least. Of
course, we admit that such ignorance on the part of
the author of Daniel is possible, but affirm that it is
very far from probable, and most certainly far removed from such a degree of certainty as would
enable any cautious historian to calmly state it as a
fact, without even so much as a qualifying particle.
If, as Prof. Cornill believes, we know nothing about the
author of the book of Daniel, except that we are compelled "to recognize in Daniel the work of a pious Jew,
loyal to the law, of the time of Antiochus Epiphanes,
who was animated with the desire to encourage and support his persecuted and suffering comrades in the faith
by the promise that the kingdom of heaven had nearly
arrived,"[3] how can he be so certain as to his ignorance of either Jewish or profane history? The author,
whoever he was, whenever he wrote, must have
had some means of information as to the history

[1] See p.160.   [2] *Exc. Pers.*, § 20.
[3] *Introduction to the Canonical Books of the Old Testament*, page 388.

of Babylon and Persia other than that to be derived
from Jeremiah and Ezekiel, and Nehemiah-Ezra, or
any other known book or writer of the Jews who lived
before 165 B. C.; else, how could he have known there
was a Belshazzar at all, especially since his name even
is not found in Herodotus, Xenophon, Ctesias, Berosus,
or any other known writer sacred or profane? As to
Nebuchadnezzar, also, if the author got his information
from Jeremiah, how can he have said that he made a
campaign against Jerusalem in the 3rd year of Jehoiakim, if, as some critics contend, Jeremiah states, or
implies, that his first expedition against that city was in
Jehoiakim's 4th year? And if Jeremiah and Ezekiel
were the sources of his information, what becomes of the
argument against the early date of Daniel, based upon
his manner of spelling the name Nebuchadnezzar?[1]
The early Greek writers, so far as they are known to us,
cannot have been the source of his knowledge; for they
do not even so much as mention the name of Nebuchadnezzar.

As to his knowledge of Darius the Mede, moreover,
the author cannot have derived his information from
the Jewish writings, nor from the profane, so far as we
know; for there is not one of them who mentions such
a man, at least under the name of Darius, and with
the appellative "the Mede." If writings existed in
the time of Antiochus Epiphanes, which described the
times from Nabopolassar to Cyrus, then they must
either have mentioned Darius the Mede, or not. If
they did mention him, the author of Daniel would on
this supposition and to this extent be confirmed as to

---

[1] Nebuchadnezzar may be the Aramaic translation of the Babylonian
Nebuchadrezzar. *Kudur* in the sense of worshiper is the same in
meaning as the Aramaic *kedin* or *kedan.*

his statements with reference to him. If they did not mention him, then how can this author have supposed that he might console the Jews of his time with an easily exposed fiction about an imaginary king? The fortunate escape from deadly perils of a Don Cæsar, a David Balfour, a Count of Monte Christo, or any other hero of fiction can have no comfort for a miserable person. The divine intervention in behalf of Æneas, as portrayed in the Æneid, would not inspire with the expectation of a like divine assistance anyone who did not believe in the reality of the wanderings and deliverance of Anchises' son. Just so, a supposititious deliverance of an imaginary Daniel from the tyrannical edicts of a king of whose very existence the Jews were not aware, would be a poor consolation in the midst of the cruel torments of the atrocious Epiphanes. The critic draws too much on our credulity, when he asks us to believe that the contemporaries of the heroic Judas Maccabeus would have been encouraged for their deadly conflict by any old wives' fables, or the cunningly devised craftiness of any nameless writer of fiction, however brilliant. People do not die for fiction but for faith. The writer of the First Book of Maccabees, the best and only first-class Jewish authority upon the history of the wars of the Jews against the Seleucids, states that Mattathias stirred up his followers to revolt against the tyrant by an appeal to the deliverance of the three children from Nebuchadnezzar's wrath. To have had any effect upon the auditors, they must not merely have known of, but have believed as true, the story to which he appeals by way of example to prove God's interest in his people. To have believed it, they must have known it. So, also, when the writer of First Maccabees uses the story of the den of lions and Daniel's deliverance from it to encourage his readers, not he only, but they, must have believed in the actuality of that story. This belief would involve a belief in the existence of Darius the Mede. This belief must have been founded upon some knowledge of him, as well as of Daniel. Such a knowledge is best to be accounted for by supposing that the book of Daniel, certainly at least that portion of Daniel which mentions him, or some other book now lost but then known to his readers, and from which the author of our present book of Daniel derived his information, was in existence before the time of the Maccabees. In the absence of all other books which mention him, and in view of the generally admitted unity of the book, and of the claims of that book to be the record of actual events occurring in the life of Daniel, many of which are such as could have been known to him alone, we can rest our case as far as the story of Darius the Mede is concerned, by saying, first, that the Jews who first read the book must have believed that Darius the Mede existed and reigned; and secondly, that they must have believed that a Daniel once lived in the time of that Darius who suffered such indignities for God's sake and was by Him delivered from the tyrant's power. But if the writer and his readers believed in the existence of Darius the Mede, they can scarcely have failed to have had knowledge also of the Darius "the Persian" of Neh. xii, 22. These Jews were fighting not merely for the law but for all the sacred writings. The second book of Maccabees (chapter one) refers to Nehemiah, and Jesus ben Sira numbers him among his great men of Israel (ch. xlix, 13). The author of Daniel, if he wrote after the book of Nehemiah was written, must have meant another king than Darius the Persian by his Darius the Mede. He must have known of Cyrus, also; for he mentions him by name three times. He can hardly have been ignorant of Xerxes, son of Darius Hystaspis; for he is mentioned not merely in Esther, but in Ezra iv also. Nor can he have been unacquainted with the name of Artaxerxes,—a name occurring twelve times in Ezra and three times in Nehemiah. Since, then, all are agreed that a writer living in the second century B. C. must almost certainly have known the names of four kings of Persia, that is, Cyrus, Darius, Xerxes, and Artaxerxes, he who believes in the assumption that he knew only one each of the kings who bore these names must assume also:

(1) That the writer of Daniel can have thought that all of the kings of Persia mentioned in the books of Ezra-Nehemiah, Haggai, and Zechariah under the name of Darius were the same person.

(2) That he must have been ignorant of Cambyses, of the Pseudo-Smerdis, of two of the three kings named Artaxerxes, of two of the three kings named Darius, and of Xerxes II, Sogdianus, and Arses.

(3) That he must have thought either (a) that Darius the Mede was a king of Persia and the same as the Darius of Ezra-Nehemiah and as the Darius of Haggai-Zechariah, and that these last two Dariuses were the same person, or (b) that Darius the Mede was a Median king who succeeded the Chaldean kings and preceded the Persian kings as monarch of the Babylonian empire, or finally (c) that Darius the Mede was a sub-king under Cyrus, who succeeded Belshazzar as king of Babylon, or of the Chaldeans, or of both the Babylonians and Chaldeans.

That is, the assumption that the writer of Daniel knew of only four kings of Persia would involve the assumptions one, two, and three (a), (b), or (c). Not

merely one of the three assumptions but the first two
and one of the suppositions under three. That Darius
the Mede was a Median king who became monarch of
the Babylonian empire before, and independent of,
Cyrus [(3) (b) above], is supported by no good evidence;
and claimed nowadays by no one. So we may rule
it out.

Can we suppose that in an age when Jewish scholars
who knew Greek were flourishing in Egypt and Syria
and Babylonia, that these Græcized Jews would be so
ignorant of the classical Greek historians as to accept
as genuine and canonical the work of an author who
thought that there had been only four kings of Persia?
Can we suppose that the educated Jews of Egypt
were so ignorant of the Egyptian history and monuments as not to know that from Cambyses to Darius
Codomannus there had been many Persian kings who
ruled over Egypt, among them three Dariuses?[1]

Can we believe that among the Jews in Babylonia—
where cuneiform was written and read as late as the
first century B. C.—there were none who could read the
documents of their adopted country well enough to reject as fabulous the supposititious history and falsely
claimed predictions of the so-called Pseudo-Daniel?
Are we to believe, that 150 years after the time when
Berosus had written the history of Babylon, and
Menander that of Tyre, and Manetho that of Egypt,
that in the age of Polybius and Diodorus Siculus and a
host of other great historians writing in the *lingua
franca* of the educated world; are we to believe, I repeat,
that the nation of the Jews throughout the world,

[1] The Egypto-Aramaic papyri already known contain part of the
Behistun inscription of Darius Hystaspis, and mention by name, Cambyses, Darius I, Xerxes, Artaxerxes I, and Darius II.

many of whom certainly spoke and read Greek, should be so unacquainted with the history of the world in which they lived, as not to be able to detect and expose the falsities of such a pseudograph and to confute its claims to historicity and canonization? Why, 164 B. C., or thereabout, when some critics claim that the book of Daniel was written, was 16 years later than the time when Jesus ben Sira, according to the same critics, wrote the book of Ecclesiasticus, and just 32 years before the time when the same book was translated into Greek by his no less thoroughly enlightened grandson. It was just a short time before the time when the first books of the Maccabees were written. It was the time when, according to these same critics, much of the Old Testament was written. Can we believe that, at such a time, credence and canonization can have been given to a book, claiming to be historical, but which was at variance with what was known about such easily ascertained matters as the number and names of the kings of Persia? Let those believe who can, that the foisting of such a pseudograph upon the public of that time was possible; but let all remember that such a belief is based on pure assumption, and has no foundation in any known facts, nor in any reasonable probability, to be derived either from the text of Daniel, from a sensible interpretation of the books of Ezra-Nehemiah and Haggai-Zechariah, or from a likely supposition as to the knowledge of profane history current among the Jews of the second century B. C.

III. However, even if it could be proven that the other Old Testament scriptures mention only four kings of Persia, this would not indicate that the author of Daniel thought that Darius the Mede was one of them. Those who assert that the author of Daniel was of the opinion that Darius the Mede was a king of Persia[1] base their assertion upon the following further assumptions:

1. That "the realm of the Chaldeans" was the same in extent as the "empire of the Persians."

2. That "from the fact that in vi, 25, Darius the Mede is represented as the absolute ruler of the Babylonian empire and in vi, 1 as having divided this empire into 120 satrapies, the temptation is strong to suspect that the author has confused Darius the Mede with Darius Hystaspis who actually organized the Persian empire into 20 to 29 satrapies."

3. That "the author of Daniel supposed Xerxes to be the father and not the son of Darius."[2]

1. In answer to assumption number one, that the "author of Daniel thought the realm of the Chaldeans to be equivalent to the empire of the Persians," it is sufficient to say, that it is an assertion absolutely unsupported by evidence. If we assume that he meant them to be the same, we are met by a host of difficulties, inasmuch as such a king as Darius the Mede preceding Cyrus in the government of the Persian empire is unknown in both the Hebrew Scriptures and in the Persian, Greek, and Babylonian records. But if we allow that the author meant them to connote different dominions, the one local, the other the vast empire of Cyrus, extending from the Ægean Sea to the River Indus, embracing within its limits, as a part of it, the former kingdom of Nebuchadnezzar, no inconsistency is found between the statements of Daniel and the other biblical or extra-biblical sources. Let it be remembered by the reader, that in testing with other

[1] See p. 162.   [2] See IV, p. 199 and VII, p. 264.

testimony the veracity or consistency of a document, it is not fair to take the statements of the document in a sense different from that which the words most naturally imply; nor of two possible interpretations of a passage to take the one which is inconsistent with veracity, while casting aside the one which is consistent. The burden of proof rests upon the man who impugns another's veracity or the truth of his statements. Pennsylvania is not the United States of America. Prussia is not Germany. England is not the British Empire. Nor was the realm of the Chaldeans even at the height of its glory ever equal in extent, or equivalent in power or dominion to the empire of the Persians. Nor can we believe that any of the critics, nor that any writer of history, sacred or profane, early or late, ever thought that they were the same. The critic may call the author of Daniel an ignoramus doubly dyed; but such an assertion does not prove that the author ever said, or thought even, that the Chaldean kingdom had the same extent as the Persian empire.

2. But, says the critic, does not Daniel say that Darius is represented in vi, 25, as absolute ruler of the Persian empire, and in vi, 1, as having divided this empire into 120 satrapies?[1] To both of these questions I answer: No.

(1) For, first, no such representation as that Darius the Mede was ruler of the Persian empire is made in vi, 25. This verse in the Revised Version reads as follows: "Then king Darius wrote unto all the peoples, nations, and languages, that dwell in all the earth: Peace be multiplied unto you." Now, it is a fact that can scarcely need more than a statement from us, that the Aramaic word here translated "earth" may just as

[1] See p. 162.

well be translated "land." The corresponding word in Hebrew, Assyrian, and Arabic may, also, have either of these senses. "All the earth" may mean simply "all the land." Instead, therefore, of meaning "empire," as Dr. Driver implies, it is doubtful if a single example of its use in this sense can be found in any literature of any age.[1]

(2[2]) As to Daniel vi, 1, on the basis of which it is asserted that Darius the Mede divided the Persian empire into 120 satrapies, the verse says merely that he placed these satraps over (literally "in") all the kingdom. The natural interpretation of this kingdom would be, of course, the kingdom over which he ruled. As we have shown above that by this kingdom was not meant the Persian empire, the only further inquiry needed is as to whether or not the sub-kingdom above defined could have had 120 satraps. This inquiry demands a consideration of the meaning of the word satrap and of the extent of country over which a satrap may have been placed.

The word satrap is derived from the old Persian *Khshatrapavan*, which according to Spiegel is compounded of *khshatra*, "kingdom," and *pa*, "to protect." Its meaning, then, would be "protector of the kingdom." It is used twice only in the Persian inscriptions: in Behistun, iii, 14, where a Persian Dadarshish is called the servant of Darius and satrap of Bactria; and in iii, 55, of the same, where the Persian Vivana is called the servant of Darius and satrap of Arachosia. In the Avesta, the corresponding word is *shoithrapan*, which

---

[1] In support of this statement, see the Excursus at the end of this chapter, pages 186–192.

[2] See p. 161.

Justi, with whom Bartholomae agrees, renders "protector of the country" (*Beschützer des Landstrichs*) and derives from *shoithra-pa*. *Shoithra* he defines as "dwelling place, *Wohnort*, *rus*, *pagus* in opposition to city, about the extent of country occupied by a *zantu*." *Zantu* he defines as a "communion of thirty men and women."

Now, if we accept of these derivations and definitions, a satrap may have been originally merely a chief of a small body of wandering Medes, or Persians. According to Justi, a *daqyu* was a region (Gaubezirk) containing several *zantus;* so that each *daqyu* might have had several satraps. This *daqyu*, however, is said by Spiegel to be the same as the Old Persian *dahyu* of the monuments, which means both country and a subdivision of a country. We have seen above that on the monuments *dahyu* is always used in the singular to denote a country like Media, Bactria, Babylonia, Assyria, etc., and the subdivisions, or provinces of the same. So that a country like Media may have had many subdivisions each called *dahya* and each of these may have had several *satraps*. When Cyrus and Gobryas took Babylon, Gobryas who was already governor (*pihatu*) of the land of Gutium, a part of Media (?), was made governor of Babylon also. If Gobryas is the same as Darius the Mede, then, according to Dan. vi, 1, he may have become king of Chaldea, also, at the time including probably a part of Elam. According to the Cyrus chronicle this Gobryas, himself a pihatu of Cyrus, appointed pihats under him. According to the same chronicle somebody (most probably Cyrus) broke into the land of Accad from Elam at an earlier time and placed a *shaknu*, or governor, in Erech. This *shaknu* of Erech and others, who were probably placed over other cities, as well as the pihat placed in Babylon by Gobryas, might all very well be called *satraps* in Persian for all anyone *knows* to the contrary. Remember, that satrap occurs nowhere on the Persian monuments save in the two places of the Behistun Inscription mentioned above, to wit, Col. iii, lines 14 and 55. While Darius in the Behistun Inscription mentions the names of 23 countries over which he reigned and in the *Naksh-i-Rustam* inscription mentions 29 of them, it is not said in either that he had set satraps over them; but that he ruled them himself and that they brought tribute directly to him. Besides, even if Darius had called the men who ruled these countries under him by the name of satrap, this would not prove that the rulers of the provinces in these countries may not also have been called satraps by him; and certainly it would not prove that at an earlier time the word may not have been used to denote them. For all we know from the Old Persian inscriptions, it was the only proper Persian title to apply to them.[1]

---

[1] In proof of this statement, we have carefully gone through all the old Persian inscriptions, with the result that we find there the following words for government officials: *Khshayathiya*, "king," *khshatrapavan*, "satrap," *aura* Lord (used only once and then of Auramazda, the supreme God), *framatar* "commander" (used only of the king of kings and only in the phrase, "the unique, or only, commander of many"), and *mathasta*, literally "the greatest," the general-in-chief of an army. The word *fratama*, which in Daniel means "prince," is always used in the Persian inscriptions as an adjective and only in the phrase *fratama martiya an'ushiya* (literally, "the chief man followers"). There is no reference, however, to his official position or duties. We have seen above that the Old Persian word for country, *dahya*, was used, also, to denote a part of the country; that is, we have *dahya*, "country," and *dahyava dahyaush*, "the countries (or provinces) of a country"; and that Gobryas, the *pihatu* (or governor) of Babylon under Cyrus king of Persia, had under him other *pihatus* (or governors). The only Persian word of the inscriptions which corresponds to *pihatu* is the word *satrap*,

In view of this fact, our readers will doubtless consent to the statement that there is no reason why Darius the Mede may not have appointed 120 satraps to rule under him in the kingdom which according to vi, 1, he had received, and over which according to ix, 1, he "had been made king," as we suppose, by his over-lord Cyrus king of Persia. Notice, whether the kingdom was greater or smaller in extent than Babylonia merely, he may have had satraps under him, and the number of these satraps may have been as large as one hundred and twenty, for all we know to the contrary; and so the statement of Daniel vi, 1, stands unimpugned.

Before closing the discussion of the word *satrap*, it might be well to ask whether the use of the word would

---

as in §45 of the Behistun Inscription. So that writing in Persian we would say that Gobryas the *satrap* of the *dahyaush* of Babylon under Cyrus appointed under himself other satraps of the dahyava, or sub-divisions of his satrapy. In other words there were small countries within a larger country and small satraps under a great satrap, just as there was a *Shah-in-Shah*, or king of kings; just as there used to be a king of Oudh and other sovereigns under the headship of the queen of England. What has thus been shown to be true of the Old Persian inscriptions is true, also, of the Persian of the Avesta. It contains four words for king; to wit, *kavan*, *khsaeta*, *khshaetar*, and *khshathia*; according to Justi, the first of these, *kavan*, is a title which has been found used only for the one dynasty beginning with Kavata. The others are all connected with the *khshayathiya*, of the inscriptions. For satrap, the modernized *shoithrapan* is found. Other words for governor are *shoithrapaiti*, "lord of a district" (Herr eines Landstriches); *danhupaiti*, "lord of a country" (Herr eines Gaues); *Zantupaiti*, "chief" (Herr einer Genossenschaft); *fraçaçtar*, "ruler"(Herrscher); *ratu*, "leader"(Führer); *hara*, "protector" (Beschützer); *fratema*, "chief." There would seem to be an order of rank in *shoithrapaiti*, *danhupaiti*, and *zantupaiti*, corresponding closely to our governor, mayor, and alderman or magistrate. We see no reason why any one of these three might not have been called a *shoitrapan*, "satrap," just as our governors, mayors, and aldermen may all be called "protectors of the law." The king was above all satraps of every kind, just as the president is above all governors, mayors, and aldermen.

best agree with the dating of the book of Daniel in the latter part of the sixth century, say 535 B.C., or with the date 164 B.C., when many think that the book must have been written.

As to the earlier of these dates, 535 B.C., the only objections to its use at that time are, first, that the writer could scarcely employ the word in an Aramaic document so soon after the Persian conquest of Babylon, which had been accomplished in 538 B.C.; and secondly, that he would hardly have used a Persian word to denote officers of Nebuchadnezzar.

As to the former of these objections, it may be said, that the question is, not whether an author writing in *Babylonian* would have probably made use of the Persian word satrap in the year 535 B.C.; but whether a man writing for the Aramaic-speaking Jews living at the time might have used it. We must remember, that the Aramean inscriptions go back to about 1000 B. C.; that the Aramean tribes had been largely subject peoples from the time of Tiglath-Pileser in 1100 B.C.; that their vocabulary in all stages of its existence was more or less filled with the words of their conquerors, especially in the sphere of governmental terms.[1]

---

[1] It must be remembered, also, that these Aramean tribes extended from the Persian Gulf to the Mediterranean, and included the Syrians of the Old Testament, as well as the Arameans of the Assyrian monuments; that the Jews for whom Daniel wrote had been brought into contact with them from their earliest history down; and that many of the Jews as early as the middle of the sixth century certainly had learned the Aramaic tongue, the *lingua franca* of the period. We must remember, further, that many of the Jews had been settled about the middle of the eighth century B.C. in the cities of the Medes; that the language and government of the Medes are known to have been similar to, and in many respects the same as, those of the Persians; that some Aramean tribes, at least, had probably been subject to Median rulers since the destruction of Nineveh about 606 B.C.: that these Arameans

Finally, let it be noticed that an "*and*" is inserted in the text between the second and third words of Dan. iii, 2, as if the author intended to say "to the satraps, both deputies and governors." The last two words are the Assyrio-Babylonian *shaknu* and *pihu* (*pihatu*), the ordinary words for the rulers deputed by the king to rule over subject cities and provinces. The former of these words, *shaknu*, is found once in the Tel-el-Amarna letters of about the year 1500 B.C., and twice in its Phenician equivalent, on one of the two earliest specimens of Phenician writing which have come down to us, dating from the eighth century B.C., at the latest.[1] It is found, also, on the Egypto-Aramaic papyrus D14, dating from the sixth year of Artaxerxes I, *i. e.*, 459 B.C., and in the Sachau papyri seven or eight times. In Hebrew and in late Aramaic, it is not used to denote a deputy governor, but a deputy priest. The latter of the two, *pihu*, occurs in the Hebrew, referring to the reign of Solomon (1 Kings x, 15); in the Aramaic of the Sendshirli inscriptions of about 720 B.C.; and once in the Aramaic recension of the Behistun Inscription from the fifth century B.C. Both terms, therefore, suit the age of Cyrus, since

---

and Jews would naturally adopt the native terms of their Median rulers; and hence that the word *satrap* may have been familiar to the captive Jews since the middle of the eighth century B.C.; and to the conquered Aramean tribes of that portion of the Assyrian empire which fell to them from 606 B.C. Further, we must remember, that while Cyrus did not take the city of Babylon until 538 B.C., he had conquered Media and Assyria as early as 553 B.C., the third year of Nabunaid (see Abu-Habba insc., Col. i, 28–33), and that the Jews and Arameans in those countries would thus have been ruled by satraps, long enough before the writing of the book, about 535 B.C., to be familiar with the meaning of the term satrap.

[1] Cooke, *North Semitic Inscriptions*, p. 53.

they would then be understood by everyone, inasmuch as all that part of the world had been ruled for hundreds of years by kings using these terms to denote their subordinate officials. The newer Persian word, satrap, may very well have been explained by the two old Babylonian terms, *shaknu* and *pihu*. In fact, we find the latter of these employed by the Aramaic version of the Behistun Inscription as well as by the Babylonian in rendering the old Persian *Khshatrapavan*, or satrap.[1] The author of Daniel, then, merely collects for his Judeo-Aramaic readers of all sections the various terms for governor known to each or all of them, in order to convey to them the sense of the proclamation of Nebuchadnezzar.[2]

It is not sufficient to reply to this, that the word satrap has not been found in the inscriptions from his time; for these inscriptions, except the Aramaic dockets, are all in Babylonian. They are either building inscriptions or contract tablets, with the exception of the broken historical tablet recording the Egyptian campaign, and this fragment contains only one word for ruler, the ordinary word for king, *sharru*, and but one word for any other official, the word *abkallu*, "general of the army (?)." The building inscriptions of Nebuchadnezzar, moreover, are not concerned especially with political matters,[3] and so far as can be known, Nebu-

---

[1] Sachau, *Aramäische Papyrus*, p. 191.

[2] Nebuchadnezzar may have used in Babylonian such a phrase as *ana naphar kepani* (or *malki*), *shaknuti, u pihate*, etc., *i. e.*, to the totality of officers (or kings), deputies, and governors.

[3] The only titles for rulers besides king and the titles of the gods and kings of Babylon to be found in all the published building inscriptions of Nebuchadnezzar, are *pihati* in Langdon, number xvii, Col. ii, B 10; and *shagganakku mati Hattim* "chiefs of the land of the Hittites" (*id.*, Col. iii, 8).

chadnezzar may have used *satrap* in his proclamations, even in the Babylonian rendition of them.[1]

But as to the Aramaic translations of the proclamations of the Babylonian kings, whenever such translations may have been made, it was absolutely necessary to employ foreign words to express governmental ideas, inasmuch as the pure Aramaic did not possess a native vocabulary sufficient for expressing them.[2]

When the Arameans came under subjection to any foreign potentate, we find them uniformly adopting some of the governmental terminology of their latest conquerors, and gradually eliminating from their literature the linguistic traces of former subjugations.[3]

The *satrap* of Ezra iii, 2 (Peshitto), of Ephraem Syrus, and of Julian the Apostate, is evidently taken over from the Greek and not directly from the Persian; so that the use of the word in Syriac does not prove a continuous use of the term in Aramaic from the Achæmenid period down, but rather the contrary.   Further, along this line, may be noted the fact, that if we place the writing of the book of Daniel in the second century B.C., it is impossible to account for the manner in which

[1] However, it is worthy of remark, that, in the Babylonian after the Persian conquest the word satrap has not been found at all. Even in the Babylonian version of the inscriptions of the Persian kings the only words for governmental officials are *sharru* "king," *rabu* "general" (Behistun, 42, 82), and *bel* "lord" (Behistun: Small Insc., 9).

[2] The pure Aramaic has the word for king, *malka*, the word for ruler, *shalliṭ* or *shilṭon*, the word for judge, *dayyan*, the word *rab*, magnate, the words *resh* and *rashan*, "head, or chief," and the word *mar*, "lord" or "sir."

[3] Thus, the word translated governor in Dan. iii, 2, is the Assyrian *pihu* and is found in Aramaic first in the inscription of Panammu which was written about 725 B.C. and in the Aramaic recension of the Behistun Inscription; and is last used in Daniel and Ezra. Again, *sagan*, the

the word rendered *satrap* is spelled in the original, except on the assumption that the author copied the word from the Hebrew of Esther or Ezra; simply changing the ending to suit the Aramaic form. For notice, that the word, as *spelled* in Daniel, cannot have been transliterated from the Greek satrap, nor apparently from the Babylonian, nor from the later Persian form found in the Avesta. Whenever the word came into the Hebrew and Aramaic of the Old Testament, it must have come directly from the Old Persian, which is known to us only from the inscriptions of the Achæmenids, and in the case of this particular word from the Behistun Inscription of Darius Hystaspis alone.

For first, the word *satrap* in its Greek form has for its first letter a sigma, or *s* sound. Now, in the transliteration of Greek words taken over into Hebrew

---

"deputy" of Dan. iii, 2, is found, perhaps in a political sense, in the Tel-el-Amarna letters and again in the Egypto-Aramaic of the fifth century B.C. It occurs, also, in the earliest Phenician inscription, to be dated certainly no later than the eighth century B.C. Its most recent use in this sense in Aramaic is in Daniel, though it is found in the Hebrew of Nehemiah and Ezra. The Greek *strategos*, "general," is found on a Nabatean monument of 37 A.D., on Palmyrene monuments from the third century A.D., and in ancient Syriac frequently before the Mohammedan conquest. In the Targum (2 Chron. xxviii, 7) and in a Palmyrene inscription from 264 A.D., when Palmyra was at times under the influence or domination of the Persian Sassanids, *argabat*, or *arqabat*, a late Persian word not found in the Avesta nor in the old Persian inscriptions (de Vog., *La Syrie Centrale*, 26), is used in the sense of satrap, or deputy. In the same inscription we find the Latin *ducenarius* and the Greek *epitropos* and *hippikos*. In Roman times, also, *dux* "duke" and *comes* "count" are found in Syriac. After the Arab conquest, we find the Arabic words *kalifah*, "caliph," *wazir*, "vizier," and *ḳadi*, "cady." In later times, are found the Turkish, Kurdish, and Persian words *shah*, "king"; *agha*, "lord of a village"; *mudir*, "deputy-governor"; *wazir*, "minister, or governor"; *sultan*, "sultan"; *mutasarip*, "sub-governor"; *wali*, "governor-general"; *wali'ad*, "crown-prince." Many of these last were originally Arabic.

or Aramaic or Syriac, not a single one begins with an
Aleph, followed by a Heth, followed by a Shin, as
does this word 'aḥashdarpan in the Hebrew and Aramaic of the O. T. Nor does a single word begin with
Heth followed by a *Shin*. Nor does one begin even with
a Shin. This statement may be tested by anyone who
will take the trouble, as the writer of this chapter has
done, of looking over all the words beginning with the
above-mentioned letters, as they are to be found in
Dalman's *Aramäisch-neuhebräisches Wörterbuch* and
Brockelmann's *Lexicon Syriacum*.

On the other hand, we are fortunate enough to be
able to certify to the manner in which the Hebrew and
Aramaic of the Old Testament transliterated an Old
Persian word beginning with the same letters in Persian
as does the word for satrap. The Old Persian word
which the Greek renders by Xerxes, has on the Achæmenid inscriptions the letters *khshayarsha;* the word for
satrap is *khshatrapavan*. It will be noted that these
words both begin with a *kh* (Hebrew Heth) followed
by a *sh* (Hebrew Shin). Now, anyone can see in a
Hebrew Bible, or Dictionary, that Xerxes in its Hebrew
form begins with Aleph, followed by Heth, followed by
Shin, just as the word for satrap does. In like manner,
we might reason, that the Hebrew and Aramaic did
not take over the word through the medium of the
Babylonian; for, if we look at the way in which Xerxes
was transliterated in Babylonian, we find at least
twenty-four different ways of spelling the whole word
and four different ways of reproducing the first two
letters. Only one of these twenty-four ways corresponds to the Hebrew and Aramaic transliteration, and
written in this way the word occurs but twice, and

even there has a difference of one consonantal letter (Evetts, 3, 5).[1]

As to the Aramaic form of the word used in Daniel having been derived from the later Persian of the Avesta, this is ruled out by the fact that in this Middle Persian the word for satrap is spelled *shoithrapan*, a form which might be transliterated into Hebrew with a prosthetic Aleph, but never with a prosthetic Aleph and Heth both.   Finally, there is no evidence that the word satrap was used in any Aramaic dialect from Greek or Roman times, except in the Syrian.   Here, the forms *satrāpā* and *satrāpīs* show clearly that the Syriac took over the word from the Greek.

From the above induction of evidence bearing on the word satrap, we may conclude, that the word satrap can have been used by a writer in the latter part of the sixth century B.C., because:

First, the form of the word as spelled in the book of Daniel corresponds with the spelling of the Persian of the inscriptions; whereas the spelling of the word in Syriac, the only Aramaic dialect from Greek or Roman times that employs it, shows that the Syriac imported the word from the Greeks.

Secondly, because this spelling shows, that the word as used in Daniel cannot have been taken over from the Greeks, nor from the Persian of the Avesta or later times, nor, most probably, from the Babylonian; but directly from the Old Persian to which it exactly corresponds.

---

[1] For the different ways of writing Xerxes in Babylonian, see my article in the *Princeton Theolog. Rev.*, vol. iii, p. 161; to which add the readings of the tablets given in the *Vorderasiatische Schriftdenkmäler*, vols. iii, iv, v, and vi.

Thirdly, because the sense of the word as used by Daniel has nothing inconsistent with the derivation and use of the word among the Persians themselves.

IV. The assumption that the author of Daniel supposed Xerxes the Great to be the father of Darius the Mede, after having confused the latter with Darius Hystaspis, is so unwarranted, that it may be safely left to the judgment of the reader.[1] There is absolutely no evidence in support of such an assumption.[2]

Excursus on the words for land, people, and nation.

In support of my contention, that the words for land do not denote the idea of empire in the sense that this latter term is used by Dr. Driver, I append the following data. In all of the building inscriptions of Nabopolassar and Nebuchadnezzar, *irṣitu* is found numerous times in the phrase "king of the gods of heaven and earth" applied to the god Merodach.[3] Once[4] Nebuchadnezzar says that he laid the foundation of his palace upon the bosom of the broad earth (*irṣitim*), and sometimes he uses it in the phrase "land of Babylon."[5] The other and usual Assyrio-Babylonian word for land, *matu*, is used frequently in these and other inscriptions; but, in the singular, it always refers to *one* land only;[6] the plural *matati*, or *matan*, being used when the rule of the king of Babylon over other lands is mentioned.[7] This is true, also, of the contract

[1] See p. 162.
[2] For a discussion of this matter see p. 264.
[3] Langdon, 84, 122, 114.
[4] Langdon, p. 88.
[5] *Id.*, pp. 134, 176.
[6] Langdon, pp. 54, 60, 90 *et al.*
[7] *E.g.*, Langdon, pp. 88, 120, 148.

tablets from Nebuchadnezzar down, including those from the time of the Persian kings of Babylon. That is, when the king of the land, or city, of Babylon is meant, the singular is used; and when the king of the lands is meant, the plural is used. So, also, in the *Annals of Sargon* (Winckler's edition), the singular for land (*matu*) occurs 279 times, always of a country such as Elam, Assyria, or the Medes; or of a part of a country—a district. In this last sense, it is employed sometimes before *nagu* "district," though *nagu* may be employed alone in this sense.[1] There might also be a land within a land, as "the land of Yatbur in the land of Elam";[2] or districts within a land, as "six districts (*nage*) of the land of Gambuli."[3] Or there might be two names united under the head of one land, as "the land of Shumer and Accad."[4] Before this last combination of names we find also the two names for land combined as *irṣit mati Shumer u Accadi*, "the land (surface) of the country of Shumer and Accad."[5] Or there might be such a phrase as "the land of the district of the land of the Medes which is of the region of the land of Illibi";[6] that is, a land within a land within a land.[7]

In the Babylonian inscriptions of the Persian kings,

---

[1] See *Annals of Sargon*, lines 173, 227, 375.

[2] *Id.*, l. 291.   [3] *Id.*, l. 264.

[4] *Id.*, ll. 313, 314. Compare the kingdom of Great Britain and Ireland.

[5] *Id.*, ll. 235, 241.   [6] *Id.*, l. 158.

[7] The plural "lands" is used but eight times in Sargon's *Annals*, usually in the phrase "people of the lands," e. g., *niši matate* (ll. 16, 71, 177, 227). The other uses are "kings of the lands" (l. 437); "Bel, lord of the lands" (l. 436): "I passed through those lands" *i. e.*, those mentioned in the preceding context (ll. 58–60); the "lordship of the lands" (l. 181). In this last example, the text is much broken; but it seems to indicate that the lands meant are all parts of the land of Kammanu spoken of in l. 179.

also, "land" is never used for "lands"; but the former always means a single division of the empire which embraced the lands under the dominion of the great kings of kings. For the empire as a whole the following expressions are used: "lands";[1] "lands of the totality of tongues";[2] "lands of the totality of all tongues";[3] "the great wide earth's surface";[4] "all the totality of the lands;"[5] "the totality of all lands";[6] "earth's surface"[7]; "this great wide earth's-surface of many lands";[8] "the land of Persia and the land of Media and the other lands of other tongues of the mountains and the land this side the sea and beyond the sea, of this side the desert land and beyond the desert land";[9] "this great broad earth's surface";[10] "the totality of lands";[11] "the totality of all tongues";[12] "the great broad earth's surface";[13] "the lands which are upon all the earth's surface."[14]

In these inscriptions, earth as opposed to heaven is denoted by *irṣitu* in NR. 1, H. 2, Ca. 2, Cb. 2, K. 3; and by *kakkaru*.[15]

---

[1] *Mạtati*, Behistun Inscription, 7, 8, 14, 40, NR. 4, 8, 20, 25, D 18.

[2] *Id.*, D 7, E 5.

[3] *Matati sha naphar lishanu (lishanati) gabbi (id.*, NR. 4, B. 2, O. 15, Ca. 6, Cb. 9).

[4] *Kakkar ruktum rabitu (id.*, NR. 5).

[5] *Kullu napharisun (id.*, NR. 26).

[6] *Naphar matati gabbi (id.*, Ca. 4, Cb. 7, K. 8).

[7] *Kakkaru* (O. 2).

[8] *Kakkar agaa rapshatum sha matati madietum (id.*, H. 5).

[9] H. 6-12, 15-20. Bezold, p. 39.

[10] *Kakkari agata rabiti rapshatum (id.*, Ca. 6, Cb. 11, F. 16).

[11] *Naphar matati (id.*, F. 15).

[12] *Naphar-lishanu gabbi (id.*, K. 12).

[13] *Kakkari rabitum rapshatum (id.*, K. 12).

[14] *Matati sha ina muhhi kakkar gabbi (id.*, S. 2).

[15] Heb. *Karka*, ground. To denote land the Babylonian uses, also, *dadmu, kibratu, nagu,* and *pihatu.*

In the Persian of the Behistun Inscription *bumi* is employed to render both *irṣitu* and *ḳaḳḳaru; dahya* for *matu;* and *zana* for *lisanu.* The Susian inscriptions make similar and consistent distinctions, using *murun* for earth, *tayiyaus* for land, and *zana* for tongue.

In Arabic, *balad* came to be used in the sense of *matu;* but *'arḍ* had the double meaning of earth as opposed to heaven, and of the land in which we live.[1]

In Hebrew, the one word *'arṣ* had to do service in both senses. It meant earth as opposed to heaven as in Gen. i, 1; but it was used, also, for land, as in Gen. iv, 16, "land of Nod."[2]

The plural "lands" was used appropriately when a number of countries was meant. A good example is to be found in Gen. xxvi, 3, 4, where the Lord says to Isaac: "Sojourn in the land . . . ; for unto thee and unto thy seed I will give all these lands . . . ; and in thy seed shall all the nations of the earth be blessed." Another is the familiar phrase "kings of the lands" as used in Ezra ix, 7.[3]

[1] For the latter use, see the Koran vii, 107; xiv, 16; xx, 59, 66; xxvi, 34; xxviii, 57; xxxi, 34; xxxiii, 27.

[2] So, also, "Land of Shinar," Gen. x, 10, 11, xi, 2; "land of Canaan," xi, 31, xii, 5; "Land of Egypt," xiii, 10; and often of other lands, as Philistina, xxi, 32, Edom, xxxvi, 16, Goshen, xlv, 10, Midian, Ex. ii, 15, Gilead, Num., xxxii, 1, Moab, Deut. i, 5, Ephraim and Manasseh, xxxiv, 2, Judah, xxxiv, 2, Hittites, Jos., i, 4, Mizpeh, xi. 3, Zebulon, Jud. xii, 12, Ephraim, xii, 15, Benjamin, xxi, 21, Shalisha, 1 Sam. ix, 4, Shalim, *id.*, Zuph, ix, 5, Gad, xiii, 7, Shual, xiii, 17, Israel, xiii, 19, Beni Ammon, 2 Sam. x, 2, Hepher, 1 Kings iv, 10, Galilee, ix, 11, Naphtali xv, 20, Hamath, 2 Kings xxiii, 33 Bashan, 1 Chron. v, 11, Chittim, Isa. xxiii, 1 Chaldeans, xxiii, 13, Assyria, xxvii, 13, Uz, Jer. xxv, 20, Pathros, xliv, 1, Babylon, l, 28, Magog, Ezek. xxxviii, 2, Nimrod, Mic. v, 6, and others.

[3] Compare, also, the phrases "people of the lands," Ezra iii, 3, ix, 1, 2, 11, Neh. ix, 30, x, 29; "kingdoms of the lands," 1 Chron. xxix, 30, 2 Chron. xii, 8, xvii, 10, xx, 29; "families of the lands," Ezek. xx, 32; and

In Aramaic and Syriac, *'ar'*, the word corresponding to the Hebrew *'arṣ*, has the same variety of meanings.

It requires, therefore, more than an *ipse dixit* to show that the author of Daniel meant that Darius the Mede made his decree for more than a limited portion of that great empire which was ruled over by Cyrus and by Darius Hystaspis. For the word employed in Daniel vi, 25, *'ar'* might be used for the land of a city, of a tribe, of a people, or of peoples and nations, as well as to denote earth as distinguished from heaven. The Hebrews consistently employ the word *kingdom* or *realm* to denote empire or dominion; but the words used to express the idea are limited in the extent of meaning from a city to a province, or a country, or a number of countries. The nearest approach in Hebrew to a phrase equivalent to our "Persian empire" is to be found in Ezra i, 2, and 2 Chron. xxxvi, 23, where we read: "Thus saith Cyrus, king of Persia, The Lord God of heaven hath given me all the kingdoms of the earth." This phrase "all the kingdoms of the earth" is used in the widest sense in 2 Kings xix, 15, 19,[1] where Jehovah is said to be God alone of all the kingdoms of the earth; and again in Isa. xxiii, 17, where it is said of Tyre that "she shall commit fornication with all the kingdoms of the earth which are upon the face of the ground"; and in Jer. xxxiv, 1, where it is said that "Nebuchadnezzar king of Babylon, and all his army, and all the kingdoms of the earth that were under his dominion (*memsheleth yado*), and all the peoples

---

especially, 2 Chron. xxxiv, 33, where we read, "And Josiah took away all the abominations out of all the countries that pertained to the children of Israel."

[1] Isa. xxxvii, 16, 20 *id.*

(*ha'ammim*) fought against Jerusalem." In a similar sense, the phrase is employed where it is said in several places, that God would scatter the children of Israel among "all the kingdoms of the earth."¹ In 2 Chron. xvii, 10, it is said, that "the fear of Jehovah was upon all the kingdoms of the lands which were round about Judah." In 2 Chron. xx, 29 this fear is said to have been upon "all the kingdoms of the lands" which heard of the slaughter with which Jehovah had caused the sons of Ammon and the inhabitants of Mount Seir to destroy one another, in answer to the prayer of Jehoshaphat recorded in the sixth verse of the same chapter, where he asks Jehovah, God of his fathers, "Art thou not God in heaven? and rulest thou not over all the kingdoms of the nations?" In 1 Chron. xxix, 29, 30, it speaks of the books which recorded the acts of David "with all his reign and his might and the times that went over him, and over Israel, and over all the kingdoms of the lands." In 2 Chron. xii, 8, Israel was delivered into the hand of Shishak, king of Egypt, that they might know Jehovah's "service, and the service of the kingdoms of the lands." This phrase "all the kingdoms" is found, also, in 1 Kings iv, 21, where Solomon is said to have "ruled over all the kingdoms from the River [Euphrates] unto the land of the Philistines and unto the border of Egypt." "All the kingdoms of Canaan" are spoken of in Ps. cxxxv, 11; and "the kingdoms of Hazor" in Jer. xlix, 28.

From the above examples, it is evident that if the writer of Daniel had wished to indicate that the decree of Darius in chapter vi, 25, was meant for the Persian empire, he could have used such a phrase as "all the kingdoms of the earth," as Cyrus did in his decree of

¹ Deut. xxviii, 25, Jer. xxv, 4, xiv, 9, xxix, 18, xxxiv, 17.

Ezra i, 2, and Hezekiah in his prayer; or more definitely
still, the phrase of Isaiah xxiii, 17, "all the kingdoms
of the earth which are upon the face of the ground."
Or, he might have said "all the kingdoms of the lands,"
or "all the kingdoms of the nations" or, after the manner of Esther i, 1, "all the kingdoms of the earth from
India even unto Egypt." But, as he uses simply
"all the earth," the presumption is that he meant the
land (*'arṣ*), or country, over which he ruled, without
defining the extent of the country. It might have been
merely Babylonia, or Chaldea, or Media, or any two, or
all three, of these. According to any fair interpretation,
however, it must be made to harmonize with the rest of
the book of Daniel as explained in the light of its
own evidence; unless and until sufficient evidence shall
be gathered to convince unbiassed judges that the *'arṣ*
of chapter vi, 25, *must* have meant the empire of
Persia.

But, someone may say, is not this shown conclusively by the use of the words "peoples, nations, and
languages" of this very verse? To which the answer is,
Certainly not. For these words also must be limited
by their context. In Dan. iii, 4, 7 *bis*, 31, they are
employed to denote the inhabitants of the provinces of
the kingdom of Nebuchadnezzar; and in v, 19, Daniel
is represented as saying to Belshazzar, that "all peoples,
nations, and languages trembled and feared before"
Nebuchadnezzar. Here, of course, the Median and Lyd-
ian empires can scarcely have been meant. In Dan.
vii, 14, where it is said that "all peoples, nations and
languages, should serve" the son of man forever, it was
probably used in the most general sense. But we
contend that they do not necessarily, even in themselves, have this universal sense.

For the words here translated peoples are employed in Hebrew, Phenician, Arabic, and Aramaic in a narrower meaning which will suit the boundaries of the land of a sub-king of a province, as well as the empire of the king of kings.

For example, 'am, ' people" is found in Phenician for the people of the city of Tyre;[1] for the people of the city of Sidon;[2] for the people of the city of Maktar;[3] and for those of the city of Carthage.[4] In Arabic, the word 'am means "a company of men," or as some say "of a tribe."[5] In the Arabic version of Isaiah 'am is rendered by sa'b, "tribe," in chapter xxv, 3; xxxiii, 3; xlv, 1, and also in Saadya's version in Deut. xxxiii, 3. The Arabic has six or more divisions and subdivisions of the tribe and several more of the nation.[6]

In the Aramaic of the Targum of Jonathan to the prophets, and in the Peshitto, 'am translates the corresponding Hebrew word and also usually goy, "nation." E. g., Isa. xiv, 6, xxv, 3, xxxi, 28, xlii, 6.[7]

Goy, the ordinary Hebrew word for nation, is rendered malkuth in Isa. xi, 10; xxxiii, 3; xlix, 22, by the Targum of Jonathan. L'om is always rendered by maleku in Onkelos.[8] 'Am is rendered by shevet in Gen. xxviii, 3, xlviii, 4, and Deut. xxxiii, 3, where it refers to the divisions of Israel.[9] Mishpachah, the

[1] CIS i, 7.5.   [2] Cooke, North Semitic Insc., p. 95.   [3] Id., 151.
[4] Id., 134.   [5] Lane, vol. i, p. 2149.   [6] Lane, p. 1536.
[7] In the Nabatean royal inscriptions, 'am is used ordinarily in the phrase "lover of his people." See Cooke, pp. 217, 220, 225, 226, 227 et al.
[8] The Aramaic version of the Pentateuch in common use among Jews of the early Christian centuries and until about 200 A. D.
[9] Shevet is the transliteration of the Hebrew shevet and the translation of matteh meaning a tribe of Israel, both in the Aramaic Targums in the Syriac and Samaritan dialects, and with the change of the sibilant in Arabic also. In both Aramaic and Arabic the word shevet is commonly used only for a tribe of Israel.

13

Hebrew word for family, is rendered in Onkelos by the word for seed. The Samaritan usually transliterates,[1] but at other times renders by the peculiar word *karn*. The Arabic version employs *'asirat*, the word in Arabic for the next greatest division of a tribe.[2] For the Hebrew "house" in the sense of household, or family, Onkelos uses[3] "the men of his house." The Syriac has seven words for "gens"; four for family; two for nation; four for "populus."[4] In Hebrew, we have a much larger number of words for nation, people, etc., such as *goy* nation, *l'om* people, *'am* people, *'anashim* men, *banim* sons, *'ummah* tribe, *shevet* tribe, *matteh* tribe, *chayyah* tribe (Psa. lxviii, 11), *mishpachah* family, and *beth* house. Perhaps, also, *pachad* means tribe in Gen. xxxi, 42.

'Ummah occurs but twice in the Hebrew bible and in both cases it is used to denote a subdivision of the *'am;* in Gen. xxv, 16, it denotes the twelve divisions of the Ishmaelites, and in Num. xxv, 15, Zur the father of Cozbi is said to have been head of the *'Ummoth* of a father's house in Midian. As Midian is called an *'am* in Ex. ii, 15, it is plain that the *'ummah* was a subdivision of the *'am*, whatever the exact relationship to a "father's house" may have been.

In Babylonian, the ordinary word for people is *nishu*, which is probably of the same origin as the Hebrew *enosh* and the Syriac *nosho*, the usual word for man (*vir*) as distinguished from woman. The word is used of the people of a city;[5] or of a land.[6]

---

[1] As in Num. xxvii, 7 *et al.*

[2] Lane, p. 1556, compared with p. 2053. Steingass in his English-Arabic dictionary gives 5 words for nation, 10 for people, 4 for family; and Lane in his Arabic dictionary gives 9 subdivisions of "tribe."

[3] *E. g.*, Gen. xii, 17.

[4] See Brockelmann's Lexicon Syriacum *in loco*.

[5] E. g., *nishim Babilam-ki* (Muss-Arnolt, p. 737b).

[6] E. g., *nish Sumerim u Akkadim*, "people of Shumer and Accad" (*id.*,

Less frequently we find the word *ummanu*, which probably is from the same root as '*am*. Langdon translates *ummanati* by "people."[1]

A third word for people is *ummatu*;[2] a fourth, *tenišetu*, in such phrases as *Ea bel tenišetu* "Ea lord of mankind";[3] a fifth word is *dadmu* which is used in parallel inscriptions instead of *tenišetu* in such phrases as *kal dadmi*, "all men,"[4] or alone for people as in Sargon inscriptions.[5] A sixth way of expressing the people of a city, or country, is by the word *mare*, "sons," followed by the name of the city or land as in the phrase *mare ali*, "sons of the city," *mare Nina*, "sons of Nineveh," *mare Babili*, "sons of Babylon," *mare mati Ashshur*, "sons of the land of Assur."[6] A seventh way is *amelu*, employed before the name of a city or country to denote the inhabitants of it.[7]

737a); *nishim mati Babili*, "peoples of the land of Babylon" (Langdon, p. 59); and in the phrase land and people (*id.* 59: 12; 61: 12; 91: 9; 103: 23; 123: 26); for many nations *e. g.*, in the phrase *nishim rabeatim* (*id.*, 89: 28), or *nishim rapashtim* (71 : 12; 83 : 10; 89 : 11; 117 : 19; 149 : 12); for all nations *e. g.*, in the phrase *kullat nishim*, (*id.* 59 : 17; 89 : 24; 171 : 35 (?)); or *kishshat nishi*, "host of nations" (*id.* 119 : 42; 121 : 64; 141 : 50); or *nishi matati* (Muss-Arnolt, 737a); or simply *nishi* in the phrase *Ea patik nishi*, Ea creator of mankind. (KB iii, 11).

[1] So on p. 53, vol. iii, 4. See, also, Delitzsch, HWB., p. 87a. We find, also, the phrases *ummanat Bel*, people or servants of Bel, and *ummanim shadleatim* (*id.* 59 : 25), "the numerous or obedient peoples" (Langdon, p. 51, vol. ii, 2; Delitzsch, HWB., under shadlu, vol. ii, p. 644).

[2] Muss-Arnolt, 64a.

[3] Compare *tenišeti* "people" (Sargon *Annals*, 373), *tenišeti nakiri* "hostile peoples" (*id.* 414, xiv.27), *tenišeti matitan* "people of the lands" (*id.* 428); *kala tenišeti* "all men" (Del., HWB. 106) to denote tribe or family; *kullat tenišeti* (*id*). *Tenišet ameli Kaldi* and *tenišet mati Kaldi* "people of the men" or "of the land of the Chaldeans" (*id.* 106).

[4] Del., HWB., 211, e. g., *dadmi matitan* "the people of the lands" (Sargon, Pr., 165).   [5] E. g., *Annals*, 427, 454, xiv, 76, pp. ii, 40, iv, 121.

[6] Del., HWB., p. 391.

[7] E. g., of cities as in Sargon's *Annals* 40, 50, and of countries as in

To denote tribe, the Assyrio-Babylonian employs the words *nishatu, kimtu, salatu, emutu, limu,* (Hebrew *l'om*), *ummatu* (Hebrew *'ummah*), *salmat gagadim, salmat kakkadi,* and *lishanu.*[1]

In the Persian of the inscriptions, the following words are used for people etc.: *Kara* "people";[2] *karu Mada* "the Median people,"[3] a word used of the divisions of the Medes and Persians; *tauma* "family," especially of the family of the Achæmenidæ;[4] *citra* "seed, race" of the Aryan race only, as in NRa 14; *par'uzana* "of many tribes, or tongues," in the phrase "lands of many tribes, or tongues,"[5] equivalent to the Babylonian "lands of the totality of all tongues," and *martiya* a word corresponding to our word "man."

The New-Susian inscriptions of the Persian kings have the same variety of words to denote the people and the subdivisions of the people, as we have found in the Old Persian.[6]

---

the *Annals*, 242, Pr., 37.   The abstract word *amelutu* is used to denote "the human race" (Muss–Arnolt, 57B).

[1] Phrases used to denote the idea of mankind in a more or less limited sense are as follows: *amelutum nishi salmat kakkadu* "men of the people of the dark race"; *kibrati sha kala tenisheti* "the regions of all mankind" (Langdon, p. 141); *nishi kibrati arbatim* "men of the four regions" (*id.*, 153:21); *naphar nishi dadmi rapshatim* "the totality of the people of scattered habitations," or "of many peoples" (151:19) *gimir salmat kakkadu* (Sargon xiv, 69, 70), "the totality of the black headed (people)," and most detailed of all "*kullat matatan gimir kala dadmi ultu tiamtim eletim adi tiamtim shaplitim matati ragatim nisi dadmi rapsatim sharrani shadi neshutim u nagi bierutim,* etc., *ummanat Shamash u Marduk*" (Langdon 149 : 17–35) "all lands; the totality of the people from the upper sea to the lower sea, the far away lands, the people of many habitations, kings of distant mountains and remote regions, etc., the subjects (peoples) of Shamash and Marduk I summoned etc."

[2] *Beh.*, i, 50, 66, 75, 78.   Compare, also, *kara har'uva* "the whole people" (*id.*, i, 40, ii, 75, 90).   [3] *Id.*, i, 69, 71 *et al.*

[4] *Beh.*, i, 16 *ct al.*   [5] Elwend 75, Suez, b 5 *et al.*

[6] See F. H. Weisbach, *Die Achamenideninschriften Zweiter Art.*

So, also, with regard to the use of the terms to denote mankind and its divisions and subdivisions, the evidence shows, that coördinate, or equivalent, words denoting the same ideas did not exist among all nations, nor in all languages. The meanings of terms, then as now, were dependent upon social and political conditions. The Arabs, having one kind of society and circumstances, have a suitable vocabulary to express their political and social divisions. The Hebrews, with different conditions, have a different vocabulary. The Persians have another, and the Babylonians still another. Among the Aramaic .dialects, we find the Syrians with a different vocabulary from that of the Targums and from that of Ezra and Daniel. In considering, therefore, the meaning of the terms employed by Daniel to denote the political divisions of the population of the "land" or "earth," we must limit ourselves, not to the words employed in Greek, Latin, German, or English, nor even to those found in Arabic, Hebrew, Babylonian, or Persian; but to a consideration of the words found in the Aramaic itself. When we do this, we find, that 'am and' ummah are the only words in Ezra, Daniel, or the Targums, to express the people of a country, or of its subdivisions. If the book of Daniel had been written in some other language, more terms might possibly have been employed to express these ideas. As it is, who can deny that Babylonia itself, or a kingdom, or sub-kingdom, consisting of Babylonia, Shumer and Accad, Chaldea, Susiana, and possibly of Mesopotamia, Gutium, and parts at least of Media and Syria, over all of which it is more than possible that Darius the Mede may have reigned as sub-king under Cyrus,—who can deny, I say, that this kingdom may have had in it many peoples and clans and tribes? For example, there was the people, or *'am*, of the Arameans. One tribe, or *'ummah*, of these certainly dwelt in Damascus, others lived in the vicinity of Babylon, others probably had already possessed parts of Mesopotamia. So with the Medes, Darius Hystaspis and Herodotus speak of the people of the Medes and of their clans. Then there were the Arabs, who were not merely a separate *'am* but had always their distinct tribes. Other peoples would be the Babylonians, the Assyrians, the Elamites, and perhaps Scythians, Armenians, and Cimmerians.

So, also, with the languages, or tongues, spoken of in Daniel. It is perfectly consistent with the facts revealed by the monuments to suppose that decrees put forth at Babylon in the sixth century B.C. would be issued in several tongues, such as the Babylonian, the Susian, the Aramean, and the Median. Darius Hystaspis and his successors have made their inscriptions in three or more languages.[1] After the Macedonian conquests, many decrees and inscriptions were made in two or more languages, as witness the Rosetta stone, and many of the Palmyrene inscriptions. In a polyglot community, like that of Babylon in the sixth century B.C., any king who really wanted his subjects to obey his decrees must have issued them in languages which they could understand; and so we can well believe that Darius the Mede may have issued his decrees, not merely in Babylonian, or Median, or Persian; but, also, it may be, in Aramaic, and Hebrew, and Susian, as well as in other tongues.[2]

[1] Darius in his Behistun Inscription, § 70, says that he sent it into all lands. See Weissbach, *Keilinschriften der Achaemeniden*, p. 71.

[2] The inscription of Behistun is in three languages and an Aramaic version of it has been found at Elephantine in Egypt. The Suez inscriptions of Darius are in four languages.

Having thus shown that when the author of Daniel says in chapter vi, 25, that Darius made a decree for "all peoples, nations, and languages that dwell in all the *'ars*" he may have meant merely for that part of the Persian empire over which he ruled, we shall rest our case, and advise our readers to do the same, until those who assert that the whole empire of Persia is meant shall produce some evidence to support their claim. Let the readers of this article remember that every part of a document, especially one as to which, as in the case of the book of Daniel, the unity is generally admitted, must be interpreted in harmony with the rest of the document. The only exception to this rule of evidence is in the case of parts as to which it can be shown by convincing evidence that they have been forged and interpolated in the original text. No such claim has ever been made for this and similar verses. Till such a claim shall have been made and the evidence for it produced, we may be allowed to believe that Darius the Mede is not represented in the sixth chapter of Daniel as the absolute ruler of the Persian empire. A sub-king to Cyrus, king of Persia, may have issued the decree in the terms of the text, without exaggeration of language, or any departure from the truth, or any stretch of his authority, or of the legal bounds within which his writ could run.

CHAPTER X

DARIUS THE MEDE NOT A CONFUSION WITH DARIUS HYSTASPIS

V. As to the question, whether the author of Daniel confused Darius the Mede with Darius Hystaspis,[1] based upon the assumption that because Darius the Mede is said in vi, 1, to have organized the empire into 120 satrapies, he has confounded him with "Darius Hystaspis who actually organized the Persian empire into satrapies, though much fewer than 120," and "who established the system of satrapies" of which "the Behistun Inscription enumerates 23, etc.,"[2] the answer is:

First. The author of Daniel does not speak of organized satrapies, but simply of satraps. He does not mention the extent of their dominions, nor the limits of their authority, except by saying that "Darius set them over the kingdom." The word "kingdom" as here used, like "land" in vi, 25, must be defined by the context. All that the context teaches us is that Belshazzar the Chaldean was killed and Darius the Mede received the kingdom; that is, obviously, Belshazzar's kingdom. This kingdom was, probably, Chaldea, Babylon, Accad, and Susiana. In addition to this, as the title "the Mede" implies, and as would

[1] See p. 162.   [2] Driver, p. 500.

certainly be true if Darius the Mede be identical with
Gobryas, he was also governor or sub-king of Gutium as
the Cyrus *Chronicle* relates.   Gutium was a country of
undefined extent, but probably embracing all the
territory between Babylonia on the one side and
the mountains of Armenia to the north and Mt.
Zagros to the northeast on the other, and perhaps even
the country beyond Mt. Zagros whose capital city was
Ecbatana.[1] Secondly, it can scarcely be said, in conformity with the facts of history as revealed on the monuments, that Darius Hystaspis established the system
of satrapies, if by this is meant, as Dr. Driver seems
to imply, that a system of government by officials
mostly of the governing race, appointed by the central
or predominant authority, was originated and first
introduced by Darius Hystaspis as a method of governing subject races.   However it may have been with the
monarchs who preceded Sargon who reigned as king of
Assyria from 722 to 705 B. C., it is certain that his system of governing the subject cities and peoples was by
means of officials, mostly Assyrian, appointed by him,
upheld by his armies and authority, ruling as his
representatives and paying tribute to the dominant
central power.   Certain it is, also, that this system
continued to be used by his successors in the kingdom
of Assyria, and later, by the kings of Babylon and by
Cyrus.   To give all of the proofs for these statements
would too much enlarge the extent of this chapter.

---

[1] See the Cyrus *Cylinder*, 13.   Winckler makes Gutium a term to
denote the country north of Babylonia probably of undefined and shifting limits, but embracing in the time of Cyrus the whole country between the Euphrates and Tigris (*Untersuchungen*, p. 131).   It has
been shown above that there may well have been 120 satraps in this
kingdom, whether it were of the larger or smaller extent.

Sufficient, however, will now be given to satisfy the unprejudiced reader, that aside from the mere change of the names of the officials from Assyrio-Babylonian to Persian, no change, except along the line of development of Sargon's original conception and organization, can be traced to Darius Hystaspis. Notice, we admit that Darius Hystaspis was the first to thoroughly organize the Persian government as Canon Rawlinson has clearly shown,[1] and that he carried on the government by means of subordinates commonly called satraps: but we claim, that such a system of government, less perfectly organized, was in existence for at least two hundred years before this time, and that while the Persians did introduce a new name for the subordinate rulers of the subject states, they did not essentially change the system in vogue before this time. They simply perfected a system which was already in existence, and which has been called from them the satrapial system. This system involved three principles:—a government by officials representing the king and appointed by him, a fixed burden of tribute, and "the establishment of a variety of checks and counterpoises among the officials to whom it was necessary that the crown should delegate its powers."[2] As bearing upon the present discussion, it is only necessary that we should bring forth evidence to show that the first of these three principles,—to wit, government by officials representing the king and appointed by him, was in existence before the time of Darius Hystaspis, and especially that it was in existence under Cyrus, and that it would have been used by a sub-king of Cyrus, such as we believe Darius the Mede to have been. Before citing our evidence, it may be well to summarize

---

[1] *Ancient Monarchies*, vol. iii, 416 *seq.*   [2] Rawlinson, *id.*, iii, 417.

the main points of the satrapial system of government as they are given in that most excellent work of the late Canon Rawlinson, Professor of Ancient History in the University of Oxford, which he gives us in the third volume of his *Ancient Monarchies*, in the seventh chapter of his history of the Fifth Monarchy, in his account of the organization of the empire of Persia. For convenience of comparison with the system of the predecessors of Darius Hystaspis, what Prof. Rawlinson says may be treated under the following captions.

First, the satraps were appointed by the king, but the native kings sometimes were allowed to reign as subordinates.

Secondly, they had some of the powers and pre-rogatives of a king, *i. e.*, they had armies, levied taxes, and possessed palaces and seraglios.

Thirdly, the subject nations were allowed "to retain their languages, habits, manners, religion, laws, and modes of local government."

Beginning our evidence that the Assyrians had a government similar to that of the Persians with Sargon, the king of Assyria, who reigned from 722 to 705 B.C., we find:

1. That he also appointed governors of the subject provinces and cities and sometimes allowed the native kings to reign as subordinates.

(a) As to provinces, he is found using the frequently recurring phrase "my officers I set as governors over them," *e. g.* in the *Annals* (lines 7–10, Winckler's edition), Sargon says that he appointed his officers to be governors over the lands of Rapiku, all Chaldea, Hasmar, the distant Medes, Namri, Illibi, Bit-Hamban, Parsua, Man, Urartu, Kasku, Tabal, and Muski.[1]

---

[1] *Amelu shuparshakishu shaknuti ileshunu ishtakkanu.* So also in the

In line 19 of the same inscription, he speaks of the shaknu, or deputy-governor, of the city of Babylon and of the shaknu of the land of Gambuli, and in line 12 of placing an officer as bel piḥati over the whole of the broad land of Miluhhi (Ethiopia) including Egypt (unless Ashdod alone is meant in the passage). In the *Display* inscription 17–22, he speaks of setting his officers as governors (bel piḥati) over Jatnana, Muski, the broad land of Aḥarri (Amurri), the entire land of the Hittites, all Gutium, the distant Medes, Illibi, Rashi, the tribes of the Lu', the Rubu', the Harilum, the Kaldudu, the Hamranu, the Ubulum, the Ru'ua, the Li'ittaui, the Gambulu, the Hindaru, the Pukudu, all the desert-dwelling Suti of Jatburi, certain cities of Elam, the land of Ganduniash, upper and lower, the land of Bit-mukkani, the land of Bit-Dakkuri, the land of Bit-Shilani, the whole land of Bit-Sa'alla, all the land of Kaldi, the land of Bit-Jakin, and the region of Dilmun.[1]

---

inscription from *Hall* xiv, p. 29, he says he had appointed his officers to be deputies (*shaknuti*) over Media, Illipi, Andia, Zikirtu, Man, the Hittite lands of Gargamish and Kummuh and Kammanu, and his governors (*bel piḥati*) over Gamgumi, (perhaps) Egypt, and Miluhhi (certainly), Ashdod, Bit-Humri, Kasku, Tabal, Hilakku, Muski, Gaza, the sub-kingdoms of Jatnana, Kaldu,—the totality of which proud land he divided between the deputies (*shaknuti*) of Babylon and Gambulu, —Dilmun, Sharru, Hatti, Gutium, Rashi, Elam, the Arameans on the Tigris, the Suti, Jutluri, Sam'una, Ganduniash, and Bit-Jakin.

[1] For similar statements, see, also the *Pavement* inscription ii, 4–16, iii, 5–22, v, 14–27. On the *Pavement* inscription iv, 16–27, he says that he placed governors (*shaknuti*) over Shurda, Harhar, Media, Illipi, Andia, Zikirtu, Man, Amatti, Kummuhi, and Kammanu; and on *IV* he says further, that he put his governor (*bel piḥati*) over Bit-Humria, Jamnaai, Kasku, all Tabal, Hilakku, Muski, Rapihi, Ja' Jatnanu, Kaldi, Babylon, Gambuli, Dilmun, Amurru, Hatti, Gutium, Media, Illipi, Rashi, the people of Itu; Rubu', Harilum, Kaldudu, Hamranu, Ubulum, Ru'ua, Litaai, Hindaru, Puḳudu, the desert-dwelling Suti of the

Frequent mention also is made by Sargon of governors of particular countries. Thus, in the *Annals*, line 188, he gave over the land of Kammanu to his officer (*amelu shuparshakia*); in line 214, he sets an officer (*amelu shuparshakia*) as bel pihati over the new inhabitants of the land of Gamgumi; in line 372, he speaks of his officer the deputy governor of the land of Ḳui;[1] in line 401, he says he numbered Muttallu of Kummuh among the governors of his land;[2] in the stele inscription i, 63, he speaks of putting his officer as governor (*shaknu*) over the land of the Assyrians whom he had settled in the land of Hammath.

(b) As to cities, also, we find a similar phrase, "I set my officer as governor over it," e. g., *Annals*, lines 11–17, "my officer I set as deputy[3] over the city of Samaria." Line 68, he sets an officer as governor (*bel pihati*) over Kishshim and in line 72 he does the same for Harhar; in line 399 he does the same for Uliddu which he settled with people from Bit-Jakin and reckoned this governor among the governors of his land (line 401).

(c) Or, the governor or deputy, may have been set over several cities, e. g., in *Annals*, line 22, he sets his officer as governor (*bel pihati*) over Ashdod, Gaza, and Asdudimmu.

(d) Also, there might be one deputy appointed over a number of native rulers of one land, e. g., in *Annals*, 254–259, he puts over the sheikhs (*nasikati*) of Gambuli one of his officers as governor (*bel pihati*).

---

land of Jatburi, Sam'una, Ganduniash upper and lower, Bit-Amukkani, Bit-Dakuri, Bit-Shilani, Bit-Sa' alla, all the land of Kaldi, Bit-Jakin, and Dilmun.   [1] *Amelu shuparshakia amelu shaknuha mati Ḳui.*

[2] *Itti amelu bel pihati Matiya.*

[3] *Shaknu;* but *Display* inscription i, 22 *bel pihati.*

(e) Also, there might be several deputies in one land, *e. g.*, in the *Display* inscription i, 38, Sargon speaks of the great deputies (*shaknuti rabuti*) of the land of the Manneans.

(f) We find, also, that the native kings were in some cases permitted to continue their reign as subordinates to the central authority at Nineveh. *E. g.*, in the *Annals*, lines 97, 98, it is said that Sargon received tribute from Pharaoh, king of Egypt, Samsi, queen of Aribbi, and It'anna, king of the Sabeans. In line 215–219, Sargon tells how he deposed Azuri, king of Ashdod, and set up his brother Ahimiti in his place. In the *Display* inscription, lines 145–149, he tells of the submission and tribute of the sub-kings of Ja' in Jatnuna (Cyprus).

(g) The extent of the country ruled over by these satraps varied from time to time. *E. g.*, in the *Annals*, 42–45, Sargon says that he captured Shinuhtu, the capital of Kiakki, and gave it to Matti of the land of Atun. In 66 and 67 he conquered certain districts of the land of Naksama and added them to the province of Parsuash.[1] In 67–70, he conquered the land of Bit-Sagbat, and several others, and joined them to the government of Kisheshim, whose name he had changed to Ḳar-Aden. In 70–73, he conquers the Urikatu and five other districts (*nagi*) and adds them to the prefecture of Harhar, changing the name to Ḳarsharrukin. In 99, 100, he takes two fortresses from Mita, king of Muski, and adds them to the land of Kui. In 365–369, he conquers parts of Elam and gives them into the hands of his officials the deputies (*shaknuti*) of Babylon and Gambuli.

---

[1] *Eli pihat mati Parsuash.*

2. The governors of Sargon, like the satraps of Persia, had many of the powers and prerogatives of a king.

(a) They had armies under their command. For example, Sargon says in his *Annals*, 304–307, that he sent his governors (*bel pihati*) against the Hamaranai who had taken possession of Sippar. In 371–379, he says, that while he himself had been conquering the Chaldeans and Arameans, his official, the deputy of Kui, had been sent against Mita, king of Muski, had conquered him and brought some thousands of his warriors as prisoners before him in Elam. In 386, he sends a trusty officer with chosen troops on an expedition apparently to Cyprus, and he brings back the booty to Sargon in Babylon. In 388–399, he sent his officers with their troops against Muttallu of Kummuh, who conquered him and brought the booty to Sargon at Kalhu, and he made his officers governors over the newly conquered country. In 408 he sent some of his governors (*bel pihati*) to aid Ispabara in the war against the king of Elam.

(b) They levied taxes. This is implied in the fact that they all paid tribute to the king of Assyria. E. g., in *Annals*, 10, it is said, that Sargon placed his governors over the lands of Chaldea, Media, Tabal, and others, and placed upon them a tribute. This tribute they levied as they saw fit, the Assyrian kings caring more for the money than for the means by which it was gotten. A good example of the fact that the governors levied taxes is found in the *Annals* of Ashurbanipal, Col. ix, 117, where it says, that the people of Usu had shown themselves disobedient to their governors and had given them no tribute; whereupon Ashurbanipal himself punished the rebellious people.

(c) They had palaces. For example, when the king

of the city of Ashdod refused to give tribute, Sargon besieged and conquered it and spoiled the treasure of his palace.[1] Kiakki, also, of the city of Shinuhtu was thinking of not paying his tribute, when Sargon conquered him and captured his wife, sons, daughters, and his palace servants.[2] Pishiri of Carchemish rebelled and Sargon captured the treasures of his palace;[3] so, also, with Bel-shur-uṣur of Kisheshim.[4] Again, Ashurbanipal says in his *Annals*[5] that he captured the treasure of the palace of Dunanu of Gambuli.

(d) They had seraglios. For example, Dalta, king of Illipi, had at least two wives; for Nibi and Ispabara are called the sons of his wives.[6] Again, Ashurbanipal says in his *Annals*[7], that he captured Dunanu of Gambuli, a rebel, and his wife, his sons, his daughter and his concubines, his male and female musicians, etc.

3. The subject nations retained their own religion and local government. This is plain from the history of Israel and Judah as recorded in the Old Testament; and it was true of every other nation, so long as they did not by rebellion force the Assyrians to destroy them utterly. For example, the *nisakkus* of the Aramaic tribes retained their names and deities after they were compelled to pay tribute;[8] so with those of Gambuli,[9] and Jatbur.[10]

So also, the Egyptians, Babylonians, Arameans, Arabs, Medes, and all others were allowed to retain their own gods and worship, so long as they did not enrage the kings of Assyria beyond endurance by their rebellions. In case only of a war to the death, were the

---

[1] *Annals*, 215–226.   [2] *Id.*, 42–44.   [3] *Id.*, 46–50.
[4] *Id.* 68–70.   [5] *Cyl.* D, Col. vi, 22.
[6] *Annals* of Sargon, 404.   [7] *Cyl.* B, Col. vi, 10–23.
[8] *Annals*, 264–270.   [9] *Id.*, 255–264.   [10] *Id.*, 280–284.

gods of the enemy carried away, as was done with 20 gods of Elam, when Susa was conquered and destroyed by Ashurbanipal.[1] Once, Ashurbanipal imposed the earlier worship (?) and religious customs (?) of Ashur and Belit and the gods of Assyria upon the people of Akkad, Chaldea, Aram, and the sea-lands.[2]

Secondly, having thus shown, that the government of the Persian empire under Darius Hystaspis did not differ essentially from that of the Assyrian empire under Sargon; and that the sameness of the methods of government of the Assyrians and Persians will be evident to anyone who substitutes the word "satrap" for deputy (*shaknu*) and governor (*bel pihati*) in Sargon's inscriptions, or *vice versa*, the Assyrian words for deputy and governor for satrap in the records bearing upon the form of government among Persians,—in other words that the difference between the two systems is one of nomenclature, or language, rather than one of essence, or fact; we come next to a consideration of whether there could have been 120 satraps in the sub-kingdom of Darius the Mede. We have seen above that the sub-kingdom most probably embraced Gutium, over which Gobryas had been governor before the taking of Babylon by the Persians, Chaldea, Accad, and Susa, over which Belshazzar had most likely reigned as sub-king to Nabonaid, and Babylon, over which Belshazzar had been *de facto* king after the capture of his father Nabunaid and over which Cyrus made Gobryas governor after its conquest. Having been given so much of the Babylonian empire, it is altogether probable, also, that Cyrus, who was busied with the affairs of his wars and much greater empire, extending from the Indus to the Bosphorus, may have entrusted the whole of the

[1] Rassam *Cylinder*, Col. vi, 30–44.　　[2] *Id.*, Col. iv, 97–107.

14

realm of Nabunaid to Gobryas, this trusty servant and able general, to administer in his behalf and as his representative. At any rate, no one knows anything to the contrary. It is probable, again, that Cyrus, when he had seized Ecbatana, after the defeat and capture of Astyages,[1] would deliver the governorship of Media into the hands of one of the Medes who had been a partisan of his cause during the conflct with Astyages. As late, certainly, as Darius Hystaspis, subjects other than Persian, especially Medes, were at times made deputy rulers for the king of Persia. For example, Dadarshish, an Armenian, was the general of Cyrus in command against the rebellious Armenians.[2] This Dadarshish may be the same man who is later called a Persian, who was satrap of Bactria.[3] Again, Takhmaspada and Vindafra, both Medes, were generals of Darius Hystaspis in his wars against the rebellious Sagartians and Babylonians.[4] Further, Darius Hystaspis announces it as his policy and custom to favor all who are friendly to him and to his family.[5] The traditions of the Medes and Persians, as embodied in Herodotus and Xenophon, would lead us also to believe that Cyrus treated the Medes and their rulers as his especial favorites and with singular deference and kindness. So that, we can well believe that the realm over which this subordinate Median king, Darius the Mede, ruled may have been as great even as the realm of Sargon of Assyria. Now, then, for the point. Sargon of Assyria, on the inscriptions which have come down to us and which are published by Winckler, mentions by name one hundred and fifteen lands and seventeen

---

[1] See inscription of Abu Habba, i., 28–33, and the Cyrus *Chronicle*, 3, 1–3.   [2] *Behistun Insc.* ii, 29.   [3] *Id.*, iii, 13, 14.   [4] *Id.*, ii, 82 and iii, 83.   [5] *Id.*, i, 20–22, iv, 65–67.

peoples, which were tributary to him; and in most
cases states that these tributary countries and peoples
were ruled by deputies, or governors, appointed by
himself. Why, then, may not another king coming
between his time and that of Darius Hystaspis have
had one hundred and twenty deputies, or governors
(call them satraps, if you please), appointed by him
to rule the subject lands and peoples in his stead?
Even if Darius Hystaspis thoroughly organized the
satrapies and enlarged them and reduced their number
to twenty, as Herodotus implies,[1] this would not prove
anything as to the number which the kings of Assyria
after Sargon had, nor as to the number which the
kings of Babylon had, nor as to the number which
Cyrus and Cambyses had, nor as to the number which
a sub-king under Cyrus had. Granting that there was
a Darius the Mede, ruling a kingdom which was a
part of the Persian empire, who can say how many,
or how few, deputies and governors he may have
appointed to administer his kingdom for him? A rose
by another name would smell as sweet. So, whether
you call these legates of the king satraps or shaknus
or deputy-governors, it matters not. It is the thing
and not the name of the thing, that is important here.

But, again, when Dr. Driver says, that Darius Hystaspis on the Behistun Inscription enumerates in one
place (Col. i, par. 6) twenty-three satrapies and in the
later (sepulchral) inscription of *Naksh-i-Rustam* (lines
7–19) twenty-nine, he is begging the question at issue.
For, first, on neither of these inscriptions is it said that
Darius Hystaspis divided his kingdom into satrapies,
few or many. Countries only are mentioned. Thus
we read on the Behistun Inscription (Col. i, 13–27):

[1] Book III, 89.

These are the countries which submitted to me; through the might of Auramazda, I became their king; Persia, Susiana, Babylon, Assyria, Arabia, Egypt, which is on the sea, Sparda, Ionia, Media, Armenia, Cappadocia, Parthia, Drangiana, Asia, Chorasmia, Bactria, Sogdiana, Gandara, the Sacæ, the Sattagetæ, Arachosia and Maka, altogether twenty-three countries. Thus saith Darius the king. These are the lands which submitted to me; through the grace of Auramazda they became my servants, they brought me tribute, what was commanded them by me day or night, they fulfilled.

In the *Naksh-i-Rustam* inscription v., 19, we read:

Thus saith Darius the king; Through the grace of Auramazda, these are the lands, which I seized outside Persia; I ruled them; they brought me tribute; what I commanded them, they did; my law was observed; Media, Elam, Parthia, Aremu, Bactria, Sug'da, Chorasmia, Zaranka, Arachosia, Sattagytia, Gandaria, India, the Saka Humavarka, the Saka Tigrakhauda, Babylon, Assyria, Arabia, Egypt, Armenia, Cappadocia, Sparda, Ionia, the Saka who are beyond the sea, the Sk'udra, the Ionians Takabara, the Patiya, the K'ashiya, the Maciya, the Karkas.

Dr. Driver might have mentioned, also, the inscription of Persepolis,[1] where we find:

Thus saith king Darius; Through the grace of Auramazda, these are the lands which I rule with my Persian army, which feared before me and brought me tribute; Elam, Media, Babylon, Arabia, Assyria, Egypt, Armenia, Cappadocia, Sparda, Ionia of the continent, and those of the islands; and these lands in the East, Asagarta, Parthia, Zaranka, Aria, Bactria, Sug'da, Chorasmia, Sattagytia, Arachosia, India, Gandara, Saka, Maka.

[1] Spiegel, *Altpersische Keilinschriften.* p. 49.

As to the rulers of these countries, he speaks twice
only of satraps, once of Dadarshish, a Persian, who was
a satrap in Bactria, and once of a Vivana who was
satrap in Arachosia. Notice, that we have said *in*
Bactria and *in* Arachosia, not *of* Bactria and *of* Arachosia. For Spiegel and Weisbach and Bang translate
the words for Bactria and Arachosia as if the cases were
locatives, rather than genitives. We confess that we
are not convinced that they *must* be locatives rather
than genitives. But, on the other hand, they *may*
be locatives as well as genitives. And, if they be locatives, then Darius Hystaspis says simply, that these
men were satraps, one in Bactria and the other in
Arachosia, admitting the possibility of one or more
satraps in either country. The case ending being
ambiguous, the testimony from the case ending must,
also, be ambiguous; so that as evidence on either side
in this controversy, it can determine nothing. If the
case be the genitive, then we must admit, that these two
countries, Bactria and Arachosia, each had a satrap at
some time before the Behistun Inscription was made.
This would not prove that the other countries had
them at all, much less that they each had but one. If,
on the other hand, it be admitted that the case is a
locative, then Bactria and Arachosia may have had more
than one satrap and the whole argument derived from
there being a satrap over each country and only about
thirty countries for satraps to rule over would fall to the
ground. Here, also, let me reiterate the statement,
that even if Darius Hystaspis organized his kingdom
into about thirty satrapies, this would not prove anything as to the number or organization before his time,
—under Cyrus, for example.

Further, we cannot gather from the Behistun Inscription, that these two satraps there mentioned were anything more than generals of the armies of their respective countries where they hailed from. Neither of them is ever spoken of as having performed any duties except as general of an army, Dadarshish against the rebellious Margians and Vivana against the Persians.

Nor are all the countries of his empire mentioned on any one of the inscriptions, but only those he conquered again. Again, it will be noted that no two of the lists agree exactly, either in the number or order of the countries mentioned; nor do all three lists together mention all the countries under the dominion of Darius Hystaspis, his own inscriptions being witness.

For first, the *Naksh-i-Rustam* inscription makes three divisions of the Sacæ and adds the names of the Skudra, Putiya, Kushiya, Maciya, and Karkas to those mentioned in the Behistun inscription, while it omits the Maka and Margiana. The Persepolis inscription[1] divides the Ionians into those of the continent and those of the islands and adds India to the list of conquered lands; but otherwise agrees in number and names with the Behistun, but not in the order of the names.

Secondly, it will be noted, that in the Behistun Inscription Darius Hystaspis mentions as subject to him countries other than those given in any of these lists. Such are the Autiyara (Beh. ii, 58). Kampada (Beh. ii, 27), Gandutava (Beh. iii, 65), Nisaya (Beh. i, 58), Paishiyauvada (Beh. iii, 42, perhaps a city), Patishuvar (NRc, a people), Raga (Beh. ii, 71), and Hyrcania (Beh. ii, 92). While most of these are, doubtless, subdivisions of the greater countries mentioned in the lists,

[1] H by Spiegel.

this can hardly be the case with Gandutava and Hyr-cania. Thus we see that Darius Hystaspis mentions in all thirty-four distinct countries; and that, count-ing the lands that were subdivisions, there are forty countries all told mentioned in the Persian inscriptions as being under the rule of the great king, or king of kings.

Dr. Driver further cites Herodotus,[1] as stating that Darius Hystaspis divided his kingdom into twenty satrapies. Herein, Dr. Driver is correct in his cita-tion. However, before discussing the bearing of this on the matter before us, we shall quote the passage at length and entirely from Herodotus, Book III, 89–97, Cary's translation. Darius

constituted twenty governments, which they called satrapies; and having constituted the governments and set governors over them, he appointed tributes to be paid to him from each nation, both connecting the adjoining people with the several nations, and omitting some neighboring people, he annexed to some others that were more remote. He dis-tributed the governments and the annual payment of tribute in the following manner. Such of them as contrib-uted silver were required to pay it according to the stand-ard of the Babylonian talent; and such as contributed gold, according to the Euboic talent. The Babylonian talent is equal to seventy Euboic minæ. During the reign of Cyrus, and afterward of Cambyses, there were no fixed regulations with regard to tribute, but they brought in presents. In consequence of this imposition of tribute, and other things of a similar kind, the Persians say Darius was a trader, Cambyses a master, and Cyrus a father. The first, because he made profit of everything; the second, because he was severe and arrogant; the third, because he was mild, and always aimed at the good of his people. (90).

[1] See Bk. III, 80.

From the Ionians, the Magnesias in Asia, the Æolians, Cari-
ans, Lycians, Milyens, and Pamphylians (for one and the
same tribute was imposed on them all) there came in a revenue of four hundred talents in silver; this, then, composed
the first division. From the Mysians, Lydians, Lasonians,
Cabalians, and Hygennians, five hundred talents; this was
the second division. From the Hellespontians, who dwell
on the right as one sails in, the Phrygians, the Thracians in
Asia, Paphlagonians, Mariandynians, and Syrians, there
was a tribute of three hundred and sixty talents; this was the
third division. From the Cilicians, three hundred and
sixty white horses, one for every day, and five hundred
talents of silver; of these a hundred and forty were expended
on the cavalry, that guarded the Cilicians' territory, and the
remaining three hundred and sixty went to Darius; this
was the fourth division. (91). From the city of Poseideium,
which Amphilochus, son of Amphiaraus, founded on the
confines of the Cilicians and Syrians, beginning from this
down to Egypt, except a district belonging to Arabinas,
which was exempt from taxation, was paid a tribute of three
hundred and fifty talents; and in this division is included all
Phœnicia, Syria which is called Palestine, and Cyprus; this
was the fifth division. From Egypt and the Libyans
bordering on Egypt, and from Cyrene and Barce (for these
were annexed to the Egyptian division), accrued seven
hundred talents, besides the revenue arising from Lake
Moeris, which was derived from the fish; in addition, then,
to this money, and the fixed supply of corn, there accrued
seven hundred talents; for they furnish in addition 120,000
measures of corn for the Persians who occupy the white
fortress at Memphis, and their allies; this was the sixth
division. The Sattagydæ, Gandarians, Dadicæ, and
Aparytæ, joined together, contributed one hundred and
seventy talents; this was the seventh division. From Susa,
and the rest of the country of the Cissians, three hundred
talents; this was the eighth division. (92). From Babylon
and the rest of Assyria there accrued to him a thousand

talents of silver and five hundred young eunuchs; this was the ninth division. From Ecbatana and the rest of Media, and the Paricanians and Orthocorybantes, four hundred and fifty talents; this was the tenth division. The Caspians, Pausicæ, Pantimathians, Daritæ, contributing together, paid two hundred talents; this was the eleventh division. From the Bactrians as far as the Aeglæ was a tribute of three hundred and sixty talents; this was the twelfth division. (93). From Pactyica, and the Armenians, and the neighboring people as far as the Euxine Sea, four hundred talents; this was the thirteenth division. From the Sagartians, Thamanæans, Sarangeans, Utians, Mycians, and those who inhabit the islands of the Red Sea, in which the king settles transported convicts, from all these came a tribute of six hundred talents; this was the fourteenth division. The Sacæ and Caspians paid two hundred and fifty talents; this was the fifteenth division. The Parthians, Chorasmians, Sogdians, and Arians, three hundred talents; this was the sixteenth division. (94). The Paricanians and Asiatic Ethiopians paid four hundred talents; this was the seventeenth division. The Matienians, Saspires, and Alarodians were taxed at two hundred talents; this was the eighteenth division. From the Moschians, Tibarenians, Macronians, Mosynœcians, and Marsians, three hundred talents were demanded; this was the nineteenth division. Of the Indians the population is by far the greatest of all nations whom we know of, and they paid a tribute proportionally larger than all the rest—three hundred and sixty talents of gold dust; this was the twentieth division. (95). Now the Babylonian standard, compared with the Euboic talent, makes the total nine thousand five hundred and forty talents; and the gold, estimated at thirteen times the value of silver, the gold dust will be found to amount to four thousand six hundred and eighty Euboic talents. Therefore, if the total of all these are computed together, fourteen thousand five hundred and sixty Euboic talents were collected by Darius as an annual tribute; and passing over sums less than these, I do not mention them. (96). This tribute accrued to Darius from Asia and a small part of Libya; but, in the course of time, another tribute accrued from the islands and the inhabitants of Europe as far as Thessaly. This tribute the king treasures up in the following manner; having melted it, he pours it into earthen jars, and having filled it, he takes away the earthen mold, and when he wants money, he cuts off so much as he wants from time to time.

(97). These, then, were the governments and the imposts on each. The Persian territory alone has not been mentioned as subject to tribute, for the Persians occupy their land free from taxes. They, indeed, were not ordered to pay any tribute, but brought gifts. The Ethiopians bordering on Egypt, whom Cambyses subdued when he marched against the Macrobian-Ethiopians, and who dwell about the sacred city of Nysa, and celebrate festivals of Bacchus— these Ethiopians and their neighbors use the same grain as the Calantian Indians, and live in subterraneous dwellings —both these bring every third year, and they continued to do so to my time, two chœnices of unmolten gold, two hundred blocks of ebony, five Ethiopian boys, and twenty large elephants' tusks. The Colchians numbered themselves among those who gave presents, as well as the neighboring nations, as far as Mount Caucasus; for to this mountain the dominions of Persia extend; but the people to the north side of the Caucasus pay no regard to the Persians. These, then, for the gifts they imposed on themselves, furnished even to my time, every five years, one hundred boys and one hundred virgins. The Arabians also furnished every year a thousand talents of frankincense. These, then, brought to the king the above gifts, besides the tribute.

By comparing these satrapies of Herodotus with the countries mentioned in the Persian inscriptions, it will be seen, first, that Herodotus sometimes includes two or more of the countries named by Darius in one of his satrapies. For example, the sixteenth satrapy of Herodotus embraces four countries of the inscriptions, Parthia, Chorasmia, Sogdiana, and Aria; the seventh contained the Sattagytæ, and the Gandarians as well as two other peoples not mentioned on the monuments, to wit, the Dadicæ and the Aparytæ; and the fourteenth contained the Sarangians (Drangians) and Mycians (Maciya) of the *Naksh-i-Rustam* inscription, and, also, the Sagartians, Thamaneans, Utians, and the inhabitants of the islands of the Red Sea.

Secondly, the monuments mention some countries which Herodotus does not. For example, Arachosia, Maka, Sparda (?), the Patiya, the Kushiya (Cissians?), and the Karkas.

Thirdly, Herodotus names many countries and even whole satrapies which are not named on the monuments. For example, of the five countries named as in the second division, or satrapy, of Herodotus, not one is found on any of the inscriptions. Two of these countries are those of the familiar Mysians and Lydians and the others are those of the unfamiliar Lasonians, Cabalians, and Hygennians.

Again, Herodotus divides Asia Minor, on the near side of the river Halys, into four satrapies; whereas in this region, the inscriptions of Darius Hystaspis mention only the Ionians and the Cappadocians.

It will be seen that the testimony of Herodotus does not agree with that of the Persian inscriptions as to the number and limits of the satrapies, even if we should admit that the inscriptions do refer to satrapies at all, when they name the countries which submitted to the rule of the Persian king.

Further, and finally, let us say that it seems to us

impossible, with our present knowledge of the whole subject, to reconcile the statements of Herodotus as to the number and extent of the satrapies as recorded in Book III, 89–97, with those made by him in other places, or with those made by Thucydides, Xenophon, Arrian, and Strabo. The evidence seems to show that like the governments of Sargon the number and extent of the satrapies was a shifting quantity; that a satrap might have satraps under him; that the name satrap was indefinite, and corresponded not merely to the *shaknus* and *bel pihatis* of the Assyrio-Babylonians, but to the satraps, archons, and hyparchons of the Greeks and to the satraps, sagans, and pehoths of the Aramaic of Daniel: so that, in conclusion, we may say with some degree of confidence, that the case against the possibility of the appointment by Darius the Mede, a sub-king, satrap, or *bel pihati*, under Cyrus, of 120 satraps under him "to be in all his kingdom" is not supported by the evidence.

The book of Daniel says that such an appointment was made. We have endeavored to show, that there is nothing in language or history against the possibility of such an appointment. Until, therefore, *proofs*, not *ipse dixits* and assertions, can be produced to show that the book of Daniel is wrong, and that this statement with regard to satraps cannot be true, we hope, that our readers will agree with us, that according to the laws of evidence, we are justified in holding to the veracity and historicity of Dan. vi, 1, when it says: that "it pleased Darius [the Median, chap. v, 31] to set over the kingdom an hundred and twenty princes (satraps) which should be over the whole kingdom." The burden of proof rests upon those who assail the veracity of this statement.

CHAPTER XI

DARIUS THE MEDE NOT A REFLECTION OF DARIUS HYSTASPIS

VI. It is assumed, further, that "Darius the Mede is a reflection of Darius Hystaspis."[1]

Can the author of the charge of this confusion of the relationship between Darius and Xerxes not see, that if the author of the book of Daniel did not know more about Darius Hystaspis than to suppose that he was the son instead of the father of Xerxes, that Darius Hystaspis was a poor subject for reflection into the past? Such discrepancies between reflector and reflected are to us sufficient proof that no such reflection was made. Let us inquire then: What evidence have we, in the book of Daniel, that its author knew anything about Darius Hystaspis? or that he reflected back the words and deeds and circumstances of Darius Hystaspis to his supposititious homonymous Mede? All that is recorded in the book of Daniel with regard to Darius the Mede are the following facts:

First, he received the kingdom, apparently as the immediate successor of Belshazzar, the Chaldean king (chapter v, 31).

Secondly, he was made king over the realm of the Chaldeans (ix, 1).

[1] See p. 162 above.

Thirdly, he was about 62 years of age at the time he became king of this realm (v, 31).

Fourthly, it pleased this Darius to set over his realm 120 satraps who should be throughout the whole kingdom (vi, 1).

Fifthly, over these satraps there were three presidents (vi, 2).

Sixthly, these satraps were to give account to these presidents that the king should have no damage, (vi, 2).

Seventhly, Daniel was one of these presidents (vi, 2).

Eighthly, Daniel was a friend to the king (vi, 14, 16, 20, 23).

Ninthly, Daniel confirmed and strengthened the king (xi, 1).

Tenthly, Darius sought to set Daniel over the whole realm (vi, 3).

Eleventhly, Daniel prospered in the reign of Darius and in the reign of Cyrus the Persian.

Twelfthly, this Darius made four decrees: one, that no man should pray to any god but himself (vi, 5–9); a second, ordering Daniel to be cast into the den of lions (vi, 16); a third, commanding the accusers of Daniel to be cast into the same den from which Daniel had been delivered (vi, 24); and a fourth, magnifying the God of Daniel because of the manner in which he had delivered his servant Daniel (vi, 25–27).

Thirteenthly, this Darius was a mixture of weakness and cruelty, as is shown in his treatment of Daniel and his accusers.

Fourteenthly, Darius the Mede was a son of Ahasuerus (Xerxes) of the seed of the Medes (ix, 1).

Fifteenthly, Darius the Mede reigned either before, or along with, Cyrus the Persian.

Now, on the basis of these statements of the book of

Daniel with regard to Darius the Mede, the question to ask in this connection is: Do we know anything of the life of Darius Hystaspis which will cause us to conclude that these statements were reflections of his words and deeds and character?

In answering this question, it will be sufficient to consider the following matters.

First, the name Darius and the family relationships of the two Dariuses, the Mede and the Persian.

Secondly, the age at which they respectively became kings (Herod., I, 209).[1]

Thirdly, the manner in which they became king.[2]

Fourthly, the kingdoms over which they ruled.[3]

Fifthly, their relations to other kings.[4]

Sixthly, the methods of government pursued by each.[5]

Seventhly, the possibility of a man like Daniel standing in such a relation to the king as the book of Daniel says that he did.[6]

Eighthly, the characters of the Dariuses.[7]

First, then, what do we know about the family of Darius Hystaspis, which would cause us to believe that the author of Daniel reflected him back into the period preceding, or contemporaneous with, Cyrus the king of Persia who conquered Babylon? Fortunately, on the father's side, we can be as sure of the origin of Darius Hystaspis, as it is possible to be with regard to any man. At the very outset of the Behistun Inscription, he says of himself:

I am Darius, the great king, the king of kings, the king of Persia, the king of lands, the son of Hystaspis, the grandson of Arsames, the Achæmenid. Darius the king says: My father is Hystaspis, the father of Hystaspis was Arsames, the father of Arsames was Ariaramnes, the father of Ariaramnes was Teispes, the father of Teispes was Achæmenes.

He repeats this genealogy exactly in the first of the smaller inscriptions of Behistun and in the first of the Persepolis inscriptions. In nearly all of the other inscriptions of Darius, he is called the son of Hystaspis, the Achæmenid. In the *Naksh-i-Rustam* inscription, he adds that he was "a Persian, the son of a Persian, an Aryan of Aryan seed." In the Suez inscription C, he adds: "I am a Persian." In the Behistun Inscription, he says, "our family from old has been royal, eight of my family have before this been kings. I am the ninth. In two lines, we are nine kings."

It will be noted that in these inscriptions Darius makes the following points with regard to his genealogy: that, he was an Aryan by race, a Persian by nationality, an Achæmenid by family, a king by right of birth, and the son of a man called Hystaspis. On the other hand the book of Daniel says, that his Darius was a Mede by nationality and race (for he was of the seed of the Medes, ix, 1), and that his father was called Ahasuerus (Xerxes). Except the name and the race for the Medes and Aryans therefore, there is no similarity between the two Dariuses, as far as genealogy is concerned.

But, it will be said, it is absurd to suppose, that the author of the book of Daniel gained his information with regard to Darius from Persian sources. The Greeks, however, give the same genealogies as the Persians themselves. For, Herodotus says,[1] that Darius was the "son of Hystaspis, son of Arsames, one of the Achæmenides," and that Hystaspis "was governor

Book I, 209.

(*hyparchos*) of Persia,"[1] and that Darius was a Persian.[2] All the other classical authorities agree with Herodotus in these particulars with reference to Darius Hystaspis; so that the author of Daniel could not have derived his information from them and have been ignorant of these family relationships. The reflection of Darius Hystaspis' genealogy cannot, therefore, have been derived from Greek sources.

There remains, then, nothing but the Hebrew sources of information, and here the only sources of which we know, outside of Daniel itself, are Ezra, Nehemiah, Haggai, and Zechariah. Without discussing the subject of which Darius they mean, it is sufficient to say that they speak of Darius simply[3] or of Darius the king[4] or of king Darius,[5] or of Darius, king of Persia,[6] or of Darius, the Persian.[7]

Since, lastly, the Babylonian monuments give us no information with reference to the genealogy of Darius Hystaspis, apart from the duplicate of the Persian inscription mentioned above, never calling him by any title except "king of Babylon" or "king of the lands," or a combination of the two; it is obvious that the author of the book of Daniel, even granting, for the sake of argument, that he did live in the second century B.C., could not, so far as we know, have had any information with regard to Darius Hystaspis, which would have caused him to call him a Mede, or the son of Xerxes.

[1] *Id.* III, 70.
[2] III, 73. Sometimes, in a loose sense, the Greek historians speak of a king of Persia as "the Mede." But this appellation never occurs in genealogical statements.
[3] As in Ezra v, 5, vi, 12, 14 (?), Hag. ii, 10, Zech. i, 1, 7.
[4] As in Ezra v, 6, 7, vi, 1, 13, 15, Hag. i, 1, 15.
[5] As in Zech. vii, 1.
[6] As in Ezra iv, 5, 24, vi, 14 (?).　　　　　　[7] As in Neh. xii, 22.

The genealogy of the Darius of Daniel may have been a creation of the imagination, but it cannot have been a reflection of that of Darius, the son of Hystaspis, the son of Arsames, the son of Ariaramnes, the son of Teispes, the son of Achæmenes,—of the Darius who was a Persian, the son of a Persian, an Aryan, of Aryan seed.

Again, it is assumed, that the author of Daniel supposed Xerxes to be the father and not the son of Darius. This is a fine example of what is called begging the question. Of course, it will be admitted by everyone, that, if the author of Daniel meant Darius Hystaspis by his Darius, then he made a mistake in saying that the father of Darius Hystaspis was Xerxes (Ahasuerus). For, there is no doubt that Darius, the first Persian king of that name, was the son of Hystaspis. He calls himself the son of Hystaspis on nearly every one of his inscriptions. He claims also to be a Persian of the family of the Achæmenids.[1] This is the testimony, also, of Herodotus;[2] and, so far as we know, of every other witness. It has never been denied. Nor has it ever been denied that Xerxes the commander of the expedition which terminated at Salamis and Platæa was a son of Darius Hystaspis. This, Xerxes himself says in all but one of his own inscriptions; and in that one he is called simply "Xerxes the great king." Herodotus, also, calls him the son of Darius.[3]

But the question here is not about Darius the Persian; but, about Darius the Mede. If the latter were a reflection backward of Darius Hystaspis, we might well ask why the author of Daniel called him Mede and why he

---

[1] See especially *Behistun*, i, 1-6, A 1-8; *Elwend*, 62-70; *Persepolis*, i, 1-5, B 1-4; *Suez*, b, 4-8; *Naksh-i-Rustam*, A, 8-15.
[2] VII, 11, I, 209, III, 70, IV, 83, VII, 224 *et al.*   [3] VII, 2, 11 *et al.*

called him the son of Xerxes, and why he said he was
of the seed of the Medes.   For the first Darius, king of
Persia, is explicit in all three of these points.   He says
he was a Persian, the son of Hystaspis, the son of a
Persian, and of Aryan seed.[1]   In all of these points,
except the last, Daniel and the inscriptions of Darius
differ.   As to the last, since the Medes were a division
of the Aryans,[2] it is clear that both the Dariuses   are
represented as Aryans.   But here the sameness of
description of them ends.   One was a Mede; the other,
a Persian.   One was the son of Xerxes; the other the
son of Hystaspis.   One had a son named Xerxes, who
succeeded him on the throne of Persia; the other, may,
or may not, have had a son, and if he had, we know not
his name, nor whether he succeeded to the government
of any part of his father's dominions.

It is no proof that a Xerxes was not the father of
Darius the Mede, to say that we know nothing from
any other source about the existence of this Xerxes.

Having thus shown clearly that there is no doubt,
nor ever was any doubt, as to who Darius Hystaspis
was as to race, nation, family, and paternity; and that
the Darius the Mede of Daniel, whoever he may have
been, cannot have been in these respects a reflection of
Darius Hystaspis; we might ask whether after all it is
true that history affords us no hint as to who Darius the
Mede may have been.   Can such a Darius have existed?
May he have had a father called Xerxes?   May he have
been of the seed of the Medes?

Taking these three questions up in order, we ask,
first, whether a Mede called Darius may have reigned
for a time over Chaldea and Babylon as a contemporary
of Cyrus and a sub-king under him?   Having already

---

[1] See *Naksh-i-Rustam* inscription, a, 8–15.   [2] Herodotus, VII, 62.

shown above the possibility of someone's having thus reigned, we shall here confine ourselves to the question of whether this sub-ruler may have been called Darius.

In the first place, then, let it be said, that four of the kings of Persia who called themselves Darius or Artaxerxes assumed these names at the time of their accession. They were to them regnal names. Just as Octavianus assumed the name Augustus, or the first and third Bonapartes took the name Napoleon as their regnal name; so, we are told that the two Ochuses, and Arsaces the son of Darius Ochus, and Codomannus, all changed their names, or at least assumed another name when they became king. Thus Darius the Second was at first called Ochus by the Persians. By the Greeks, he is called Nothus. On the inscriptions, he is called simply and always, Darius "king of the lands."[1] Arsaces, his son, the brother of Cyrus the Younger, changed his name to Artaxerxes, when he became king; but was known to the Greeks as Artaxerxes Mnemon. On the inscriptions, he is known simply as Artaxerxes. Thus on the Susa inscription, we read, "Artaxerxes, the great king, the king of kings, the king of the lands, the king of the earth, the son of king Darius," etc. On a contract tablet from his reign, he is called simply Artaxerxes, the king of the lands.[2]

Artaxerxes the Third was called Ochus before he became king and continued to be so called by the Greeks even after his accession. Lastly, Darius Codomannus is said to have assumed the name of Darius when he became king.[3]

---

[1] See the subscriptions to the tablets from his reign published in BE., vol. viii, Prof. A. T. Clay, editor.

[2] See BE., vol. x, p. 2, and vol. ix, No. 1, 1. 33.

[3] Rawlinson: *Anc. Mon.*, iii, 515.

This custom of thus changing one's name upon ascending the throne, may account for the fact, that so many
of the rebels against Darius Hystaspis are represented
by him as changing their names as soon as they raised
the standard of rebellion. Thus, Nadintu-Bel and
Atrina changed their names to Nebuchadnezzar, and
claimed to be sons of Nabunaid; Martiya is said to have
taken the name Imanish; and Fravartish assumed the
name Khshatrita.[1] So, among the kings of Assyria, Pul assumed Tiglath-Pileser as his regnal
name; Sargon was probably the regal name of a
man who had some other name before he became
king; Ashurbanipal probably reigned in Babylon
under the name Kandalanu; the great Cyrus himself
is said by Herodotus to have had another name by
which he was known while a boy.[2] Astyages according to Ctesias had also the name Aspodas. Cambyses
the father of Cyrus the Great is called Atradates by
Nicolaus Damascenus.[3] Lastly, Artaxerxes II was called
Arshu and Artaxerxes III Umasu before they became
kings.[4]

From all the above facts, we may conclude that it is
certainly probable that Darius the Mede was known
by some other name before he became king. If we
assume that the pre-regnal name was Ugbaru (Gobryas),
then we have a man whose history as revealed by the
Cyrus *Cylinder*, by Xenophon in his *Cyropædia*, and

[1] *Behistun Inscr.*, iv, 10–31.   [2] Bk. I, 113.
[3] Rawlinson: *Ancient Monarchies*, iii, p. 368.
[4] See the astronomical tables published by Kugler in *Sternkunde und
Sterndienst in Babel*, page 82, where we read: *ultu shatti 18 KAN Arshu
sha Artakshatsu sharru shumushu nabu adi qat shatti 13 KAN Umasu
sha Artakshatsu sharru nabu*, i. e., from the 18th year of Arshu, whose
name was called Artaxerxes the king, till the 13th year of Umasu, whose
name is called Artaxerxes the king.

by the book of Daniel, is perfectly consistent with itself and with all the information revealed in all the sources.

But, did Ugbaru have a father named Xerxes? We have no information on this subject, except that the writer of Daniel says that the father of his Darius was Xerxes. Now, it is perfectly certain, that if there was a Darius the Mede at all, he must have had a father, and this father must have had a name. Why not, then, a father named Xerxes? There is nothing known about the naming, or the name, of Xerxes the son of Darius Hystaspis to show that he was the first of that name; and we know from the fact that there was a Xerxes the Second the son of Artaxerxes Mnemon, that Xerxes the Great was not the last, nor the only, one of that name. Why, then, may there not have been a third of the name, preceding the first, and a Median, as the second and third of the name were Persians?

It is not enough simply to assert that the writer of Daniel became confused and stated by mistake that Xerxes was the father instead of the son of Darius. This might be accepted as an explanation of an error of the kind, after the error had been proven. But to make the assertion of confusion in order to prove the error is contrary to all the laws of evidence and common sense. That John Smith's son is named Peter does not prove that another Peter Smith's father was not called John. That a Henry king of England followed a Richard does not prove that a Richard had not followed a Henry sometime before. Blessed is the man who knows his own father; twice blessed is he, who knows the father of a man living more than two thousand years ago.

It might be well just here to ask how two Medes

could have had names which we certainly know were
each the name of several kings of Persia. That is,
could two Medes of the time of Cyrus have had the
names Xerxes and Darius? Or, are not these names
in themselves evidence of a reflection backward of
Darius Hystaspis and his son Xerxes, and of a confusion between their relationship to each other? The
possibility of cogency in this argument will appear
if we suppose that the author had called them by the
Greek names Philip and Alexander, or Antiochus and
Seleucus. Is there, then, not the same cogency in the
use of Persian names for two men of supposedly
Median race?

No. There is not. Because the Medes and the
Persians were closely allied in race and language. Darius Hystaspis asserts that he, a Persian, was of Aryan
race; and Herodotus says, that the Medes were Arians.[1]
Besides, the same proper names are found in use among
both Medes and Persians. Thus, Harpagus, a Mede,
led the revolt of the army of the Medes which went
over to Cyrus;[2] and Harpagus, a Persian general of a
considerable army, is said to have taken Histiæus the
Milesian prisoner.[3] The Gobryas of Xenophon, whose
name is the Greek form of Ugbaru the governor of
Gutium of Cyrus, was most probably a Mede; whereas
the Gobryas who was one of the seven conspirators
against Smerdis, the Magian, was a Persian, as was
also a Gobryas, the son of Darius Hystaspis. Artembares, whose son was a playmate of Cyrus, was a Mede;[4]
whereas, the Artembares mentioned later was a Persian.[5]
Vindafra was a Mede who commanded the army which
Darius Hystaspis sent against Babylon when it revolted

[1] VII, 62. [2] Herodotus; Bk. I, 80, and after.
[3] Id., Bk. VI, 28. [4] Herodotus, I, 114. [5] Book IX, 122.

from him the second time;[1] Vindafrana was a Persian and one of the seven conspirators against Smerdis.[2] Citran-takhma, who claimed to be of the family of Uvakhshatara (*i. e.*, Cyaxares, the Median), revolted in Sagartia, and Darius Hystaspis sent against him Takhma-spada, a Median; whereas Tritan-taikmes (part of whose name is the same as Takhma-spada and part of each perhaps the same as the latter part of Citran-takhma) is called by Herodotus a son of Artabanus who was a brother of Darius Hystaspis. Further evidence that the Persian and Median languages were closely allied may be found in Rawlinson and others, though it is generally admitted that they had many dialectical differences. There is no reason, however, why the names Xerxes and Darius may not have been borne as proper names in the time of Cyrus; and by Medes.

Before leaving this subject, we might turn the question about and ask, whether there be any probable reason why the two Persian kings were called Darius and Xerxes. Could these names, possibly, have had any connection with the Xerxes and Darius of Daniel, arising from a possible relationship of blood between them? Now, we are perfectly aware, that in what follows we are treading on dangerous ground. But we feel that we are in good company; and hope that Prof. Sayce and Winckler, and the shades of a host of others, will pardon us, if we thrust ourselves forward for a little along the line which they have followed with so much brilliancy. Returning, however, to our subject, let it be said, that it has struck us with much force, that the claimants of the throne of Media and Sagartia, who rebelled against Darius Hystaspis, both assert that

---

[1] *Behistun Inscr.* ii, 83–87.   [2] *Id.*, iv, 83.

they were of the family of Cyaxares, not of that of
Astyages; whereas the claimants to the throne of Babylon assert that they were the sons of Nabunaid. Why
did the former claimants not assert their right to
succeed Astyages, who, according to Herodotus, had
been the last preceding king of Media, just as these
latter claimed to succeed Nabunaid the last *de jure*
king of Babylon? Most probably because, as Profs.
Sayce and Winckler have shown and the inscriptions
of Nabunaid and Cyrus certainly seem to imply, Astyages was not a Median king at all; but the king of the
Manda, or Scythians. If we take Astyages to have
been a Scythian, one of a race that had conquered and
held in subjection the kindred peoples of the Sagartians,
Medes, and Persians, we shall account reasonably for
many facts that are otherwise hard to understand.
Astyages, the Mandean, marries his daughter Mandane (the Mandean?) to Cambyses the king of Anshan,
but seeks to slay their son Cyrus, whom he looked upon
as a dangerous possible rival; doubtless, because Cyrus
the Achæmenid of royal line was the legitimate head of
the subject peoples, or at least, of the Persian branch
of them. Harpagus, the Mede, along with another
Mede named Mitradates, saves Cyrus. For this reason Harpagus is served with soup made from his own
son by order of Astyages. Harpagus enrolls the
Medes in a conspiracy against his master and calls
in Cyrus the Persian to lead the revolt. During
the classic battle, Harpagus, with the Medes under
him, goes over to Cyrus, and Astyages is captured
and dethroned. Cyrus, then, succeeds to the throne of
Media and is royally served all through his reign, and
his son Cambyses during his reign, by the Medes, who
had joined with the Persians in overthrowing the

power of the Mandeans. The Mandeans had conquered a large part of the old Assyrian empire and when Cyrus overthrew Astyages, Nabunaid of Babylon recaptured a large part of the region about the Euphrates and Tigris, including, perhaps, the country of Gobryas, the governor or king of Gutium, who, judging from his name, was probably a Mede. Gobryas calls in Cyrus to his aid, and the united armies conquer Babylon; whereupon, Cyrus appoints Gobryas governor of Babylon and successor to Belshazzar, the king of the Chaldeans. Gobryas assumes the name of Darius as his regnal name, and rules under Cyrus over as much of his empire as was once under the 'Babylonian or Assyrian kings. Cyrus, however, upheld his position as overlord, and Cambyses, his son, grasped the hand of Bel of Babylon, as the legitimate successor of his father, Darius-Gobryas being under Cyrus, and probably under Cambyses, the sub-king. Contracts, however, are dated only with the name of the overlord, as they were subsequently when Zopyrus was governor of Babylonia under Darius and Megapanus under Xerxes.

This Gobryas of Gutium had a daughter who was given in marriage to Hystaspis, one of Cyrus' Persian generals, the father of Darius Hystaspis, and the governor, under Cambyses and Smerdis the Magian, over the country of Persia. Darius the Persian would thus be named after his maternal grandfather's regnal name. Then Darius the Persian marries a daughter of Cyrus, whose oldest son, born after Darius became king, he calls Xerxes, the name which according to Dan. ix, 1, had been borne by his great-grandfather. There thus unite in Xerxes all the royal families which might have laid claim to the throne. Through Mandane, the mother of Cyrus, by way of Cyrus and his daughter

Atossa, Xerxes succeeds to the right of Astyages the Mandean. Through his grandmother, the wife of Hystaspis and mother of Darius Hystaspis, he succeeds to the right of Darius Gobryas, the Mede, the son of Xerxes the Mede. Through his father Darius, the son of Hystaspis, the son of Arsames, the Achæmenid, he succeeds to the right of Cyrus and Cambyses the Achæmenids, his cousins of the royal line of Persia and Anshan. Through Darius the Mede he probably succeeded not merely to the throne of Gutium, but to that of all the Median kingdom as well. For, let it be noticed, that the Xerxes of Dan. ix, 1, is possibly the same as Cyaxares. At any rate, the Medo-Persian root *khsha* is found in both; and it is possible, at least, that Xerxes and Cyaxares are the Median and Persian forms of the same name.[1]   If, then, Darius-Gobryas the Mede were the son of Xerxes-Cyaxares the last king of Media before Astyages the Mandean conquered it, he would be the legal successor to Cyaxares, and Xerxes the son of Darius Hystaspis would succeed to the Median right through him, as his father Darius Hystaspis had done before him.   The importance of securing the right to the succession is obvious, when we remember, that Citrantakhma who revolted against Darius Hystaspis in Sagartia, and Parumartish who revolted against him in Media, both based their claim to the throne on the ground that they were of the family of Cyaxares.

If we accept such a genealogy for Darius Hystaspis, it will account for the fact that he and Xerxes are called Medes as well as Persians by the Greeks, although Cyrus and Cambyses are not so called; and that Xerxes is called king of Persia and of the Medes in the sub-

[1] Compare Tobit xiv, 15, where Cyaxares is called Assuerus, that is, Xerxes.

scriptions of several Babylonian tablets.[1] It will account, also, for the loyalty of the Medes to the Persian kings, for the appointment of two of them, Vindafra and Takhmaspada, to put down the great revolts in Babylon and Media under Darius Hystaspis; for the appointment of a Mede, Datis, to command the expedition against Athens, which culminated at Marathon; and for the putting of the Medes in a peculiar position next to the Persians both by the classical writers, by Darius in the Behistun Inscription, and by the Babylonians in the subscriptions to the tablets from the age of Xerxes.

This rather lengthy excursus will, we hope, make it clear to all why we believe that the statements of the author of Daniel with reference to "Darius, the Mede, the son of Xerxes, of the seed of the Medes," are consistent with what is known of the history of the times which center about Cyrus the Persian, and the fall of Babylon. We believe, that it is entirely possible to harmonize every statement of the sixth chapter of Daniel with any *facts* that have been ascertained from the monuments of Persia and Babylon, or from any other reliable sources whatsoever. It is wrong and unfair to call any man a knave or a fool, a liar or an ignoramus, unless we have certain and sufficient proofs to substantiate our assertion. It is wrong to assert that the author of Daniel attempted to reflect backward the life and acts and character of Darius Hystaspis upon a fictitious and supposititious Darius, unless we can prove it. It is wrong to say that having attempted it, he confused the persons thus reflected, so as to confound the relationship existing between them.

---

[1] *I. e.*, in VASD, v, 118, 119; iv, 193, 194; Strassmaier, in *Acts of 8th Congress of Orientalists*, Nos. 19, 20.

And, finally, while one could well be pardoned for doubting whether all of these statements were written without
unintentional errors, or have been transmitted without
corruption of text; yet, in view of the evidence, we
think it is manifestly unfair, to accuse the author of
them either with lack of intelligence, knowledge, candor,
or consistency, or with confusions, reflections, inaccuracies, and exaggerations.

CHAPTER XII

DARIUS THE MEDE NOT A REFLECTION (*Continued*)

SECONDLY, the author of the book of Daniel cannot have reflected backward the *age* of Darius Hystaspis at the time when he became king of Persia.[1] In Dan. v, 31, it is said, that Darius the Mede received the kingdom when he was about 62 years of age. Herodotus states that Darius was only "about 20 years of age" when Cyrus just before his death had passed the Araxes on his fatal expedition against the Massagetæ; and that Darius "had been left in Persia, because he had not yet attained the age of military service."[2] He further says,[3] that Hystaspis, the father of Darius, was governor (*hyparchos*) of Persia, at the time when Darius arrived at Susa when Otanes and Gobryas, "the noblest of the Persians," were preparing their conspiracy against the false Smerdis. As the false Smerdis was killed in 521 B.C., this would make Darius to have been 79 years of age at the death of Smerdis and his father about 100 if the former had been 62 at the time of the death of Cyrus.

Further, Darius in his Behistun Inscription[4] speaks of his father Hystaspis as being still in active service as general of his forces in the war against the rebellious Parthians and Hyrcanians. His words are as follows:

[1] See p. 223.   [2] Bk. I, 209.   [3] Bk. III, 70.
[4] Col. ii, 92–Col. iii, 10.

238

Thus speaks king Darius: Parthia and Hyrcania rebelled and went over to Fravartish. Hystaspis, my father, was in Parthia; the people left him and rose in insurrection. Then Hystaspis took the people who stood by him and drew out. There is a city in Parthia called Vispauzatish; where a battle with the rebels took place. Auramazda helped me. Through the grace of Auramazda, Hystaspis smote the rebels hard. On the twenty-second day of the month Viyakhna the battle was fought. Then I sent a Persian army to Hystaspis from Raga. When this army came to Hystaspis, he drew out with this army and fought a battle with the rebels at a city of Parthia called Patigrabana. Auramazda helped. Through his grace, Hystaspis smote the rebel host. On the first day of the month Garmapada, the battle was fought; whereupon the province became mine. This is what I did in Parthia.

It is obvious that a man who must have been at least about 80 years of age, if his son were 62 and more, could not have carried on in person such an arduous campaign.

Finally, it is scarcely within the range of probability that Darius Hystaspis himself could have conducted so many expeditions as both his own inscriptions and the records of the classical writers impute to him, if he had been 62 years old at the time of the death of Belshazzar in 538 B.C. or at that of his succession to the throne of Cyrus in 521 B.C. If he had been 62 years old in 538 B.C., he would have been 114 at the time of his death in 486 B.C.; if he were 62 at the death of Smerdis in 521 B.C., he must have been 97 at the time of his death. It is not probable, that the Greek historians would not have noted this extreme old age in one so well known as he, and especially in one so active as he was even up to the time of his decease. So that we think that we are justified in concluding that whatever may have been the source or the object or the date of the writer of Daniel, he could not have meant to reflect to his Darius the age of Darius Hystaspis at the time of his accession.

Thirdly, the same may be said as to the *manner* in which the two Dariuses are said to have become king.[1] Herodotus, who shortly after the death of Darius Hystaspis was born at Halicarnassus in Asia Minor, a city subject at that time to the Persians, and who had traveled extensively in the Persian empire and studied the stories of its origin, has given us the longest, most thorough, and probably the most reliable account of the life of Darius Hystaspis. In his relation of the accession of Darius to the throne of Persia, he is explicit in stating how he succeeded the false Smerdis, the Magian; and by what a marvelous series of events, he and his fellow conspirators among the nobility of Persia, whose names also he gives, succeeded in wresting the domination of Western Asia from the usurping power of the Medes and the Magi.[2]

Not one word is said about Belshazzar, or about any other Babylonian or Chaldean king in all of this long account. Moreover, the Darius of Herodotus was the Persian leader of the Persians against the Magian leader of the Medes, and not a Median ruler succeeding to a Chaldean king.

These statements of Herodotus are confirmed as to these points by the inscriptions of Darius. The Behistun Inscription tells at length how the false Smerdis, having rebelled against Cambyses, assumed and maintained the kingship. On Col. i, lines 38–72, he says:

When Cambyses had gone to Egypt, the army became hostile and lying increased in the country, both in Persia

---

[1] See p. 223.   [2] See his *History*, Book III, 61–88.

and Media and the other countries. Then a man, a Magian, of Paishiyauvada called Gaumata rebelled at a fortress called Arakadrish. In the month Viyakhna, on the 14th day of the month, he rebelled. He lied to the people and said: "I am Bardiya, the son of Cyrus and brother of Cambyses." Therefore, the whole kingdom broke into rebellion, going over to him from Cambyses, both Persia and Media as well as the other lands. He seized the government. On the 9th day of the month Garmapada he seized the government. Then Cambyses died by suicide. This government which Gaumata seized,—this government has been from of old in our family. Then Gaumata the Magian took from Cambyses both Persia and Media and the other countries. He acted as he pleased. He was king. No one, neither Persian nor Mede, nor any one of our family would have snatched the kingdom from Gaumata the Magian. The people feared him on account of his cruelty. He would have killed many people who had known Bardiya; he would have killed them, "so that no one should know, that I am not Bardiya the son of Cyrus." No one dared to speak about Gaumata the Magian, until I came. Then I cried to Auramazda for help. Auramazda granted me aid. In the month Bagayadish, in the tenth day, I and a few men killed that Gaumata the Magian and those who were his noblest adherents. At a fortress called Sikayauvatish in the district of Media called Nisaya; there I killed him and took the kingdom away from him. Through the grace of Auramazda, I became king. Auramazda gave over to me the kingdom. The government which had been wrested from our family, I reëstablished as it had been before. The places of prayer which Gaumata the Magian had destroyed I preserved to the people. The pastures, the hearths, the dwellings of the clans which Gaumata the Magian had taken away, I restored. I restored all things as they had been before. Through the grace of Auramazda, have I done this. I have worked until I have placed our clan again in its place, as it was before. I have worked through the

16

grace of Auramazda, so that it was as it was before Gaumata the Magian had robbed our clan.   This is what I did when I became king.

Another point at which Herodotus' account of the conspiracy against the false Smerdis is confirmed by the inscriptions is in the list of the names of the conspirators.   According to Herodotus III, 70, there were six of these, to wit: Otanes, Aspathines, Gobryas, Intaphernes, Megabysus, and Hydarnes.   The names of five of these are given by Darius on Col. iv, 80–86,[1] of the Behistun Inscription, where we read:

Thus saith Darius the king: These are the men who were present when I slew Gaumata the Magian, who called himself Bardiya.   At that time these men helped me as my adherents: Vindafrana, the son of Vayaspara, a Persian; Utana, the son of Thukhra, a Persian; Gaubaruva, the son of Marduniya, a Persian; Vidarna, the son of Bagabigna, a Persian; Bagabukhsha, the son of Daduhya, a Persian; Ardumanish, the son of Vahauka, a Persian.

It will be seen that all but the second of the names as given by Herodotus are easily recognizable in the list given in the inscription, and that there is but a slight difference in the order of the names; and the spelling in one case is Greek and in the other Persian.   As to Aspathines, however, we find his name given by Darius on the *Naksh-i-Rustam* inscription as that of one of the companions of the king; so that it is possible, that he had two names, Aspathines and Ardumanish (Artabanus).

From the explicitness, then, of the accounts of the manner of the accession of Darius Hystaspis to the throne of Persia, it is impossible to suppose that a late

[1] Weissbach, *Die Achämeniden Inschriften*, §68.

writer who wished to reflect backwards the history of his succession to the kingdom could have said in the language of the book of Daniel: "That same night was Belshazzar the Chaldean slain; and Darius the Median received (or took) the kingdom" (v. 30, 31), or, as it is said in ix, 1, "Darius the son of Ahasuerus of the seed of the Medes which had been made king over the realm of the Chaldeans."

Fourthly, the author of Daniel does not reflect backward the *name of the kingdom* over which Darius Hystaspis had been made king.[1] In his own inscriptions, Darius Hystaspis calls himself "king of Persia";[2] "king of lands";[3] "king of the lands of many tongues";[4] "king of the lands of all tongues";[5] "king of the great wide earth";[6] and "king of numerous countries."[7] On the Babylonian tablets, he is uniformly called "king of lands," "king of Babylon," or "king of Babylon and of the lands."[8] So, likewise, Herodotus and the classical writers uniformly call him king of Persia.[9] Never once anywhere is he called "king of the Medes," "king of Babylon," or "king of the Chaldeans." In glaring contrast with this, the Darius of Daniel is called a Mede,[10] which may possibly mean that he was a Median by race, or a king of the Medes, or at least of a part of the Medes; also, "king over the realm of the Chaldeans";[11] and by implication, at least, king of

---

[1] See p. 223. [2] *Behistun* i, 2, A 2.
[3] *Id.* 1, 2, A 3; Persepolis inscr. i, 3. [4] Elwend, 14–16; Suez, b, 5.
[5] NR, a 10. [6] NR, a 11–12. [7] Persepolis, i, 3–4.
[8] So on all those published by Strassmaier and in all in the "Cuneiform Texts" and in the *Vorderasiatische Schriftdenkmäler.*

[9] See the author's articles on the Titles of the Kings in the *Princeton Theological Review* for 1904–5, and his article on the Titles of the Kings of Persia in the *Festschrift Eduard Sachau*, 1915.

[10] Dan. v, 31. [11] Dan. ix, 1.

Babylon, since he received apparently the kingdom of Belshazzar,[1] and Belshazzar is called "king of Babylon."[2] When we remember, that the author of Daniel is careful to distinguish Nebuchadnezzar as "king of Babylon";[3] Cyrus, as "the Persian,"[4] or as "king of Persia";[5] and Belshazzar as "the Chaldean,"[6] or as the "king of Babylon";[7] the fact, that Darius is called "the Mede,"[8] or king "over the realm of the Chaldeans,"[9] is especially worthy of notice. Particularly, is this careful discrimination of titles to be noted in view of the fact that a "Darius king of Persia" is mentioned by Ezra[10] and a "Darius the Persian" in Nehemiah xii, 22; one of which is most probably Darius Hystaspis. Accordingly, the author of Daniel cannot have gotten his knowledge of a Darius the Mede from the Scriptures. That is, since the Scriptures outside of Daniel speak only of a Darius the Persian, or a Darius, king of Persia, the author of Daniel did not reflect him back into his Darius the Mede, whom he never calls a Persian nor a king of Persia. So that here again we find that there is no evidence either on the monuments, or in the classical writers, or in the Scriptures, that Darius the Mede was a reflection of Darius Hystaspis.

Fifthly, nor does the Darius of Daniel reflect the *relations* of Darius Hystaspis *to other kings.*[11]

According to the Behistun inscription, Darius Hystaspis conquered two men who had rebelled against him and usurped the throne of Babylon. Each of these

---

[1] Dan. v, 31, vi, 1.

[2] Dan. vii, 1, where Theodotion, however, reads "king of the Chaldeans." [3] See i, 1. [4] VI, 29. [5] X, 1. [6] V, 30.

[7] vii, 1, where, as we have before mentioned, Theodotion reads "king of the Chaldeans." [8] VI, 1. [9] IX, 1.

[10] IV, 5, 24, vi, 14 (?). [11] See p. 223.

called himself Nebuchadnezzar and claimed to be a son of Nabunaid. The first of these is called by Darius "Nadintu-Bel the son of Aniri,"[1] and the second "Arakha, the son of Haldita an Armenian."[2] To show that the author of Daniel in his account of the overthrow of Belshazzar the Chaldean cannot have reflected backward the conquest of either of these rebel kings by Darius Hystaspis, I shall insert here at length the accounts of the rebellions of these men, as they appear in the Persian recension of the Behistun Inscription in the words of Darius Hystaspis himself.

After the death of Gaumata the Magian, Susiana revolted and a man named Atrina, the son of Upadarma, set himself up as king. At the same time, a Babylonian called Naditabaira[3] the son of Aniri, rebelled in Babylon and deceived the people, saying: "I am Nebuchadnezzar, the son of Nabunita." The whole Babylonian people went over to this Naditabaira. Babylon was rebellious and he seized the government in Babylon. Darius, therefore, sent an army against Susiana while he himself advanced against Naditabaira whose army held the (fords of the) Tigris, there awaiting his attack on ships. Through the grace of Auramazda, Darius passed the Tigris and defeated the army of Naditabaira on the 27th of the month Atriyadiya. Then he advanced to Babylon, fighting on the way a battle at Zazana on the Euphrates, driving a portion of the Babylonian army into the river which carried it away. This battle was on the 2nd day of the month Anamaka. Naditabaira escaped with a few horsemen to Babylon, whither Darius followed him, seized Babylon; and captured and killed Naditabaira in Babylon.

Sometime after, while Darius was in Persia and Media,[4] "the Babylonians rebelled a second time

---

[1] *Beh. Insc.* § 16.   [2] *Id.,* § 49.   [3] *i. e.,* Nadintu-Bel.
[4] *Beh. Insc.* § 49.

under the leadership of Arakha an Armenian, son of
Haldita, whose headquarters were in the district of
Dubala." He deceived the people, saying:

"I am Nebuchadnezzar, the son of Nabunita." The
Babylonian army (or people) rebelled and went over to him
and he took, and became king in, Babylon. Therefore,
Darius sent an army against Babylon, under the command
of Vindaparna, a Mede, his servant whom he had made general. Through the grace of Auramazda, he captured Babylon on the 2nd day of the month Markazana. "This"
says Darius, "is what I did in Babylon."

Herodotus, also, describes at length[1] a capture of
Babylon by Darius in addition to the first which had
been made by Cyrus.[2] It is most probable that the
first revolt under Nadintu-Bel is the one meant by
Herodotus inasmuch as he makes Darius to have commanded in person; and according to the Behistun
Inscription, this was done only in the first revolt; but
he seems to have confused in a measure the two revolts,
since he says, that Darius started on his expedition
against the Scythians "after the capture of Babylon,"[3]
and the inscription would indicate that this Scythian
expedition did not take place till after the second revolt.
Herodotus does not mention any name for the leader
of the rebellious Babylonians. He does state, however, that the city was captured through the ingenuity
of Zopyrus, a son of Megabysus, one of the seven noble
Persians who had conspired against the Magian; and
that as a reward Darius gave Zopyrus the government
of Babylon "free from taxes during his life," and that he
"every year presented him with those gifts which are

[1] Book III, 150–159.   [2] Id., Book I, 188–192.
[3] Id., Book IV, 1.

most prized by the Persians," "and many other things in addition."

In the Old Testament outside of Daniel, the only mention of a Darius along with and in relation to any other king is in Ezra vi, 14, where it is said that the temple was built at the command of the God of Israel and at the command of Cyrus, Darius, and Artaxerxes, kings of Persia.

In the book of Daniel, however, Darius the Mede is said to have succeeded Belshazzar as king of Babylon and as king over the realm of the Chaldeans;[1] and to have reigned before, or contemporaneously with, Cyrus king of Persia.[2] So that we can safely affirm with assurance that, as to his relations to other kings, the Darius of Daniel was not a reflection of Darius Hystaspis.

Sixthly, the same is true, also, with reference to their methods of government.[3] As we have shown above, the satrapial system had been in use as early as the time of Sargon, and it was employed by every king between Sargon and Darius Hystaspis, and by every king of Persia after Darius Hystaspis. Nor was it substantially modified, so far as we know, by Alexander or by the Greek Seleucid rulers; and in fact, it has continued in use in that part of the world through all changes of government, Persian, Seleucid, Parthian, Sassanid, Arab, and Turk, down to the present time. It is the method of absolute, autocratic monarchies, and always has been, and always will be. There may be differences of names and modifications in minor particulars of administration; but the system itself from its very nature will always remain unchanged in its essential features. As to the number, character, and

---

[1] V, 30, 31, ix, 1.   [2] VI, 29.   [3] See p. 223.

authority of the satraps said to have been appointed by Darius the Mede, there is, however, no evidence of a reflection from Darius Hystaspis. Nor is it otherwise with regard to the three presidents appointed by the Darius of Daniel and as to the governors and deputies and other officials, who are said to have taken part in the administration of his kingdom. The inscriptions of Darius Hystaspis, as we have seen above, mention satraps and generals alone; and Herodotus speaks of archons, hyparchons, monarchs, and epitropoi, beside generals and admirals with their subordinates. From any source of information that we possess with regard to the administration and names of officials of Darius Hystaspis, it is utterly impossible for anyone to construct the system of government or the names of officials, recorded in the sixth chapter of Daniel. The system of government of Darius the Mede, and the names of the officials, half Persian, half Babylonian, accord excellently with a period of transition from Babylonian to Persian rule. But in the points wherein the government of Darius the Mede corresponds with that of Darius Hystaspis, it corresponds, also, with any other satrapial system; and in the points where it disagrees, it cannot be a reflection of the latter. And if anyone should say, that these disagreements exist merely because of our lack of complete information as to the particulars of the system introduced, or organized, by Darius Hystaspis, we answer: When the evidence is forthcoming, we shall yield the point. But until evidence be produced, let it be observed, that here also there is no reflection of Darius Hystaspis to be found in the Darius of Daniel.

Nor is it different with regard to the laws and the decrees of the Darius of Daniel. To be sure, Darius

Hystaspis says in the Behistun Inscription, iv, 64, that
he ruled according to the law, and Darius the Mede is
apparently bound by the law of the Medes and Persians
which changeth not.   But Herodotus says that Cambyses, likewise, was bound by the law in the same way
(Book III, 31).   And, in fact, it is not for one moment
to be supposed, that there ever was a king that did not
rule his kingdom in accordance with some system of
laws and customs which he could not transgress if
he would, except in peril of losing his throne.   The
Babylonian kings from Hammurabi to Nabunaid boast
of their observance of the laws of the lands which they
ruled; and the cause of the overthrow of the latter is
said in the Cyrus Cylinder to have been that he had
not observed the laws.   What it is necessary to show,
however, in this connection is, not that Darius Hystaspis and the Darius of Daniel both observed laws; nor
that they were both bound by laws beyond their control;
but that Darius Hystaspis issued some particular edict,
or broke some particular law, which the author of Daniel asserts to have been done by Darius the Mede.   So,
also, with regard to the edicts of the Darius of Daniel, it
will not suffice to prove that he is a reflection of
Daniel Hystaspis to show that both issued edicts; but,
it must be shown at least that they issued the same,
or similar, edicts with reference to the same or similar
subjects in the same or similar circumstances, and
with the same or similar enacting clauses.   Now, it is
absolutely certain that this cannot be shown; and
until it be shown, we can confidently believe, that
Darius the Mede is in this respect, also, no reflection of
Darius Hystaspis.   For example, it would not be
enough to show that Darius Hystaspis had a den of
lions, and that he punished offenders by throwing them

to these lions, to render it certain that the den of lions of the book of Daniel was a reflection of that of Darius Hystaspis. It would need to be proven that other kings before and after Darius Hystaspis did not possess such a den. The probability is that if one king had a den of lions, another, also, would have one, and not the reverse. And, if a king had a den of lions, they must be fed; and so it is not far to the cry: "The Christians to the lions." It would be an exemplary, condign, and effective, punishment. It would save the double expense of the executing of the criminal and of the food for the lions!

But since the author of Daniel represents his Darius as casting a man into a den of lions a similar case with the same name and offense and punishment found recorded as having occurred in the reign of Darius Hystaspis would afford a strong presumption that one had been copied, or was a reflection of the other; but it would still have to be proven (even if it were admitted, that the two accounts referred to the same event) which of the authors it was who copied from the other. If, for example, Herodotus had said that Darius Hystaspis had cast a man called Daniel into a den of lions, it would be possible, that Herodotus had made a mistake as to his Darius. It would not prove, that the author of Daniel had made a mistake in saying that another Darius did so. Much less would it prove, that a late author had simply reflected back this story from the later to a supposed earlier Darius. Besides, each king may have cast a man, or many men for that matter, into a den of lions; and there may have been a mistake in names merely. Take, for illustration, the cases of the Decii and of the two Henrys mentioned by Prof. Edward A.

Freeman in his *Methods of Historical Study.*[1] He says:

The practice of rejecting a story merely because some thing very like it happened once before is one that must be used with great caution. As a matter of fact, events often do repeat one another; it is likely that they should repeat one another; not only are like causes likely to produce like results, but in events that depend on the human will it is often likely that one man will act in a certain way simply because another man acts in the same way before him. I have often thought how easily two important reigns in our own history might be dealt with in the way that I have spoken of, how easily the later reign might be judged to be a mere repetition of the former, if we knew no more of them than we know of some other parts of history. Let us suppose that the reigns of Henry the First and Henry the Second were known to us only in the same meager way that we know the reigns of some of the ancient potentates of the East. In short and dry annals they might easily be told so as to look like the same story. Each king bears the same name; each reigns the same number of years; each comes to the crown in a way other than succession from father to son; each restores order after a time of confusion; each improves his political position by his marriage; each is hailed as a restorer of the old native kingship; each loses his eldest son; each gives his daughter Matilda to a Henry in Germany; each has a controversy with his archbishop; each wages war with France; each dies in his continental dominions; each, if our supposed meager annals can be supposed to tell us of such points, shows himself a great lawgiver and administrator and each, to some extent, displays the same personal qualities, good and bad. Now when we come really to study the reigns, we see that the details of all these supposed points of likeness are utterly

[1] Pp. 138, 139.

different; but I am supposing very meager annals, such as are very often all that we can get, and in such annals, the two tales would very likely be so told that a master of the higher criticism might cast aside Henry the Second and his acts as a mere double of his grandfather and his acts. We know how very far wrong such a judgment would be; and this should make us cautious in applying a rule which, though often very useful, is always dangerous in cases where we may get utterly wrong without knowing it.

Again, he says, on page 135 of the same work: There is

in some quarters a tendency to take for granted that any story which seems to repeat another must necessarily be a repetition of it, a repetition of it in the sense which implies that the second story never happened. I have read a German writer who holds that the devotion of the second Publius Decius at Sentinum is simply the devotion of the first Publius Decius by Vesuvius over again. Now, setting aside whatever amount of evidence we may think that we have for the second story, if we bring it to a question of likelihood, there is certainly the likelihood that the exploit of the father should be told again as an exploit of the son; but there is also the likelihood that the son, finding himself in the like case with his father, should be stirred up to follow the example of his father. Most people, I fancy, accept the story of the second Decius.

While the Decii and the first two Henrys of England may thus be taken as examples of the fact that men of the same name may perform different deeds in a like way, we may take the various recorded captures of Babylon as illustrating how like events may be performed by different persons and in widely different times. Passing by the successive seizures of the city of Babylon by Tiglath-Pileser, Sargon, Sennacherib, Esarhaddon, and Ashurbanipal—all of which had points of similarity,—attention may be specially called to the different captures by the Persian kings, Cyrus, Darius (at two different times), and Xerxes. From the scanty information in our possession, it is utterly impossible for us to distinguish many of the features of these numerous seizures and capitulations, although we are certain as to the fact of their occurrence. To be noted is the fact, that the position of Babylon and its power rendered it the head center of rebellious forces and the objective of the attack of the contending powers.

So, then, even if it could be shown that it was recorded of Darius the Mede, and likewise of Darius Hystaspis, that each of them had cast a man into a den of lions, this would not prove that one of these accounts was copied from the other, or that one of them had not cast a man to the lions. It would rather raise a presumption that the kings of those times were in the habit of casting men to the lions. Fortunately for our present argument, there is no record of the casting of men to the lions on the part of Darius Hystaspis, nor in fact by any other Persian king; and hence the account in Daniel cannot, so far as we know, be a reflection, a casting back upon the canvas depicting the deeds of Darius the Mede, of an event which really transpired under another's reign. Nothing reflects nothing, whether in the realm of matter, or in that of history, or in that of fiction.

Seventhly, is it possible that a man like Daniel may have stood in such a *relation to Darius* the Mede as the book of Daniel represents?[1] Or, putting it in other words, if it be impossible that a man like Daniel could have occupied such a relation, wherein consists the

[1] See p. 223

impossibility? Is it because no man could have occupied such a relation to him? Or, because Darius the Mede was such a king that no man could have stood in such a relation to him? Or, is it because Daniel was such a man that he could not have stood in such a relation to a king? Let us answer the above questions in their order.

(1) It is not impossible that a man should stand in such a relation to a king as Daniel is said to have occupied to Darius the Mede. The very fact that the writer of Daniel says that he occupied this relation argues for its possibility. For, whatever and whoever the writer of Daniel was, he was certainly anything but a fool. Whether he has written history or fiction, he must have thought this relation possible.

Besides, the critics who deny the historicity of Daniel claim that he wrote to comfort the Jews of Maccabean times with a fictitious narrative bearing the similitude of truth. To those Jews for whom Daniel wrote the account, such a relation must, therefore, have seemed to be possible. Otherwise, the whole story of the book would have been absurd, and the purpose for which it was written would have been made of no effect. But no one has claimed that it was of no effect. On the contrary, all admit that few books have exerted a greater influence upon after times than has this book of Daniel. It has remained for the modern critic to discover that one of the main features of the story—Daniel's relation to Darius the Mede—was impossible. Apparently, this view of the case never struck the people who lived in the times when there were kings of Persia, and others of like character. To them it seemed to be in harmony with what they knew of kings, that they should have men like Daniel occupying such relations to them.

But to specify and illustrate. If it were impossible

for Daniel to have stood in such a relation to Darius, how was it possible for Joseph to have been in such relations with the king of Egypt as Genesis represents him to have been? If this last relationship, also, is said to have been impossible, for what purpose, then, did the author say that it actually existed? He, at least, must have thought that it was possible.

Again, if this story of Daniel in relation to Darius is impossible, how about Achikar, the sage of Nineveh, in his relation to Sennacherib and Esarhaddon, kings of Assyria? The author of this story certainly thought that it was possible for a man like Daniel to have occupied such a relation to a king. Again, the Arabian Nights, that best of all illustrators of Eastern manners and customs, gives us numerous examples of just such men as Daniel occupying the same relations to the king they served. Such men are the sage Douban in his relation to the Grecian king, and the vizier Giafar in his relation to the caliph Haroun al Rashid.[1]

What we know of the kings of Persia, also, shows us that they did have such counsellors. It is necessary only to mention Democedes under Darius Hystaspis, Demaratus under Xerxes, and Ctesias under Artaxerxes.

(2) Secondly, is the character of Darius the Mede such as would justify us in supposing that Daniel could not have stood in the relation to him that the sixth chapter of Daniel describes?

The answer to this question must be derived from the account of Darius given in the sixth chapter of Daniel; and, if we identify Darius with Gobryas, from the records of the Cyrus Cylinder also. From these sources we learn that he had the following characteristics:

[1] See Lane, vol. i, 37, 61.

First, he was a good and successful general.

Secondly, he was deemed worthy to receive from Cyrus the realm of Belshazzar the Chaldean.

Thirdly, he showed great ability as an organizer.

Fourthly, he listened to and followed the advice of his counsellors.

Fifthly, he showed wisdom in the choice of a prime minister; for he preferred Daniel, because an excellent spirit was in him.

Sixthly, he was faithful to his friends, as is shown by the way he sought to release Daniel.

Seventhly, sometimes, at least, he was weak and easily deceived, as is shown by the way he allowed himself to be imposed upon by the enemies of Daniel.

Eighthly, he was pious; for he believed that the God of Daniel was able to deliver him out of the mouth of the lions.

Ninthly, he was vain and filled with a heathenish sense of the divinity of kings; else, he would never have allowed a decree to have been made that no one should ask a petition of anyone for forty days, save of him.

Tenthly, and yet he was just. When things went wrong, he was sore displeased with himself. He obeyed the law, even when it was against his will and judgment. In accordance with the *lex talionis*, he punished those who had sought to encompass the death of Daniel with the same death that they had attempted to inflict on him; and he apparently restored Daniel to the position from which he had been unjustly deposed.

Eleventhly, he was sorry when he had done wrong. He was sore displeased with himself, and fasted and lay awake all night; and was exceedingly glad when Daniel was saved.

Twelfthly, he was laborious. He organized the kingdom, receiving reports from his counsellors, labored all day to deliver Daniel, rose early in the morning to hasten to the den of lions, and himself wrote a decree to honor the God of Daniel.

In short, Darius the Mede was no fickle, vengeful, lustful, oriental tyrant; but a wide-awake, beneficent, and very human ruler. Why should it be thought an impossible thing that such a king should have selected for his chief adviser and administrator such a man as Daniel?

(3) Thirdly and lastly, the alleged impossibility of Daniel's having stood in the relation to Darius in which the book of Daniel represents him to have been, cannot be shown from what is said of Daniel himself. For, first, it could not have arisen from the fact that he was a Jew. If it did, we would have to reject the stories of Ezra, Nehemiah, and Mordecai, as well as that of Daniel; for these all were Jews who are said to have occupied high official positions at the Persian court. Furthermore, the story of Joseph, also, implies the possibility of an Israelite's rise to the highest position at a heathen court. The stories of Tobit and Achikar and Aristeas, also, show that the Jews thought at least, that Israelites could be promoted to the first places in the gift of the kings of Egypt and Assyria. Finally, the Jewish writers would scarcely have introduced Jews as playing such rôles in their works, even if these works were purely fictitious, unless they knew that such positions were open to Jews.

Nor, secondly, would such a position be impossible to Daniel because he was a slave; for from time immemorial all the officers of an oriental king had been looked upon as his slaves. Thus, in the Tel-el-Amarna letters, all of the officers and sub-kings of the king of Egypt are called

his slaves.   Cyrus even is called by Nabunaid the little
slave of Astyages. [1] Darius Hystaspis, also, speaks of
Wohumis, one of the greatest of his generals whom he
had selected to put down the rebellion of the Armenians,
as his slave. [2]

Further, we may cite the instances of Tobit and Achikar, who are said to have been captives and slaves, and
notwithstanding this to have been elevated to the
highest positions at the Assyrian court, the former as
purveyor, the latter as counsellor or vizier.   The
Arabian Nights contain not infrequent examples of
such promotions of slaves; and the history of India gives
numerous instances of it.   Unfortunately, the Babylonian and Persian records contain so little information
about the officers of the kings that it is impossible to
find out much about their origin, race, social position,
or even their names.

Nor, thirdly, can it have been because Daniel was not
capable of performing the duties that he is represented
as performing.   According to the only account of his
education, that we possess, he had been specially prepared to stand before the king, and God had given him
the knowledge and wisdom necessary for the work in
life to which he was afterwards called.   Furthermore,
according to this same account, he discharged his
functions so well under Nebuchadnezzar, that he was
continued in high service until the reign of Cyrus.
Lastly, Ezekiel, the only other biblical record that
mentions him, puts him on a par with Noah and Job
as one of the three well known wise men to whom the
prophet could refer his hearers. [3]

[1] KB. ii, iii, ii, 98.
[2] Bab., *gallu*; Aram., *'elam*.   See *Behistun Insc.*, xxv.
[3] Ezek. xiv, 14, 20; xxviii, 3.

For all these reasons one may justly conclude, that it is entirely possible that a man like Daniel may have stood in such a relation to Darius the Median king as that in which the book of Daniel represents him to have stood.

Eighthly, nor is there any evidence of a reflection when we come to consider the *character of the two Dariuses.*[1] The principal trait in common is, that they were both organizers. But this common feature was rendered necessary by the fact that a common situation confronted them. They were both kings of a newly conquered kingdom, whose government had to be reduced to order. If the Ugbaru (*i. e.*, Gubaru, Gobryas) of the monuments be Darius the Mede, we have the evidence that he did organize the country of Babylon by appointing governors under himself, he himself being under Cyrus. So Darius Hystaspis organized his greater kingdom. There is no inconsistency in the statement that they each organized their respective governments; neither does it follow that the author who says that either of them did thus organize his kingdom was reflecting merely the organization made by the other. There must have been an organized government during the reign of Cyrus and Cambyses and their subordinates; there must have been a reorganization by Darius Hystaspis after he had reconquered the empire which had gone to pieces on the death of the Magus. Each organization was absolutely necessary and neither is a reflection of the other.

Nor, can it be said that the friendship and loyalty which the Darius of Daniel showed to Daniel was a reflection of the character of Darius Hystaspis. True, Darius Hystaspis was, in this respect, and in every

[1] See p. 223.

respect, one of the noblest and best of the rulers of all time. He justified his boast: "the man who was my friend, him have I well protected."[1] His treatment of Sylosen, whom he made tyrant of Samos because he had given him a cloak in Egypt before he became king;[2] his generosity to the Greek Physician Democedes who had healed him and his queen Atossa of their complaints;[3] his faithfulness to Histiæus the Milesian during all of his tergiversations;[4] his treatment of Zopyrus and Megabysus,[5] and of his fellow conspirators[6] all attest this characteristic and approve his claim. But he was not the only monarch who was friendly to his friends. Cyrus, also, was thus faithful and kindly. According to Xenophon in his *Cyropædia*, he was a model in his respect. Herodotus tells of the position of honor he gave to Harpagus, who aided him in the overthrow of Astyages; and of his kind treatment of Astyages and Crœsus. He himself speaks in his *Cylinder Inscription* of his kindness to Nabunaid and of his faithful conduct to Ugbaru. Besides, the other kings of Persia such as Artaxerxes I and II and Darius Nothus have left many examples of their generosity and faithfulness. These are not such uncommon traits in kings, that the fact that two kings are said to have had them is evidence that someone has reflected to his hero the lineaments of the other.

The same may be said of the piety, belief in God or the gods, manifested in the Darius of the sixth chapter of Daniel. "Thy God," says Darius to Daniel, "whom thou servest continually, he will deliver thee." This

---

[1] *Behistun Inscr.*, i, 21.   [2] Herodotus, Bk. III, 139–149.
[3] *Id.*, Bk. iii, 129–138.
[4] *Id.*, Bk. IV, 137–141, V, 11, 23, 24, 30, 38, 105, 107, VI, 1–5, 26–30.
[5] *Id.*, Bk. III, 160; iv, 143.   [6] *Behistun, Ins.* iv, 80–86.

sentiment cannot be paralleled in the inscriptions of
Darius Hystaspis. It is true that he has what might
be called a *general* piety, a trust in the favor which
Auramazda, his god, had for him, expressed in such
phrases as: "Through the grace of Auramazda I am
king"; "Auramazda gave me the kingdom";[1] "Then
cried I to Auramazda for help. Auramazda assisted
me";[2] "Through the grace of Auramazda, I did it,
I have wrought, until I have placed again this our
family in its place, as it was before; so have I done
through the grace of Auramazda"; and others of a
like nature. Or, as it is expressed in the inscription of
Elwend: "A great god is Auramazda, who creates this
world, who creates yon heaven, who creates mankind,
who creates pleasure for men, who made Darius king,
the only king among men, the only lord of many,"[3]
But, Xerxes and Darius Ochus and Artaxerxes I and
II have similar phrases in their inscriptions, and have left
us many proofs of a similar piety and trust in their god
or gods. Cyrus says that Marduk called him to the kingdom of the totality of all (the world) (*Cylinder* 10–12);
that he looked upon his (Cyrus') deeds and subdued
under him the host of Manda and all men (13–14); that
he commanded him to go to Babylon and like a friend
and helper went along at his side(15); that he who makes
the dead alive approached him graciously (19); that
Merodach, his lord whom he worshiped, had drawn
nigh to him graciously (27–35). The inscription of
Antiochus Soter, who reigned from 280 to 260 B. C., is
full, also, of similar pious expressions.[4] So that it is
obvious, that a general piety which all kings of the

---

[1] *Behistun,* i, 11, 12; 59, 60.   [2] *Id.,* i, 54, 55.
[3] So also in the similar inscription of Persepolis and *Naksh-i-
Rustam.*   [4] See Schrader, KB., iii–ii, 136–139.

Orient showed toward their gods, or god, cannot be produced when found in any particular one as an argument
to show that his piety was reflected from theirs or theirs
from his.   They were all more or less pious, or, if you
prefer, superstitious.   Darius Hystaspis, being a Persian, and the Darius of Daniel, being a Mede, and thus of
the same family of nations, and with, perhaps, the same
religion, may well have worshiped the same god, or
gods; but there is no evidence anywhere except perhaps
in Ezra, that Darius Hystaspis ever honored the God of
Daniel, the God of Israel, or declared his belief in that
God's ability to save a man from anything and certainly
not from a den of lions.

Again, there is a semblance of weakness, of dependence upon others, of susceptibility to flattery, about
the Darius of Daniel, for which no parallel can be found
in Darius Hystaspis.   Neither his inscriptions, nor
any of the other sources of information which we have
concerning him, give us the slightest intimation, that
he was anything other than a strong, independent, self-
reliant, conquering hero, a man preëminently sane
and free from that susceptibility to flattery which doth
surround a throne.   All the evidence goes to show that
the vacillating, troubled, penitent, sleepless Darius of
the realm of the Chaldeans, whatever else he may have
been, cannot have been a reflection of the self-satisfied,
dominant, and enterprising son of Hystaspis who
founded and ruled triumphantly the greatest empire
that the world till then had ever seen.

And lastly, we do not know anything in the
history of Darius Hystaspis which would cause us to
conclude that he ever had under him a ruler like Daniel
from whom a late writer might have made a reflection
backward to his supposititious Daniel.   The monu-

ments of Darius fail utterly to reveal a man like Daniel
of any race or position.   In fact, the Persian kings were
in general free from the influence of favorites of all
kinds, Arses having been an exception in this regard.
An autocracy which depends for its existence upon
the skill and power of the monarch is not calculated
to cultivate such men.   So, we find, that in Assyria,
Babylonia, and Persia, weaklings soon ceased to reign.
Some more aggressive, self-assertive, or intelligent
brother, or rival, speedily made an end of them by
assassination or rebellion.   Witness Evil-Marduk, La-
bashi-Marduk, Xerxes II, and Sogdianus and Arses and
even Astyages and Nabunaid.   When an autocrat
ceased to be a real autocrat, his doom was sealed.
Richard II, Edward II, and Henry VI are more recent
examples.   But a Darius Hystaspis!   A man, one of
the most strenuous, self-dependent, active, intelligent,
and successful of all the autocratic monarchs who ever
lived!   We would not expect to find, we do not find, in
any records of Greek, or other, source, any intimation,
that he ever submitted for a moment to give over the
government of his kingdom into the hands of another,
as Darius the Mede is said in Daniel to have done.
In so far as Darius the Mede did this, he cannot have
been a reflection of Darius Hystaspis.

CHAPTER XIII

OTHER ALLEGED CONFUSIONS OF KINGS

VII.[1] It is assumed that when the author of Daniel makes the fourth of the Persian kings mentioned in Chapter xi, 2, to "be exceedingly rich and to provoke a mighty war against Greece," it is clear that he has confused Xerxes and Darius Hystaspis by making them one and the same person.[2]

In support of this assumption, appeal is made to Dan. xi, 2, with which it is said, Dan. vii, 6, is confused. The latter verse reads in the Reviser's text: "After this I beheld, and, lo, another, like a leopard, which had upon the back of it four wings of a fowl; the beast had also four heads; and dominion was given it."

The natural interpretation of this figure is that the wings denote velocity and the heads voracity. There is absolutely no proof that the wings denote swiftness and the heads four kings, as Von Lengerke and others assert. Besides, it is an assumption, which itself needs to be proven, that the leopard is meant to denote Persia, and not Alexander the Great. Since the Scriptures outside of Daniel, as well as the monuments and the classical authors, uniformly represent Cyrus as the one who overthrew the Babylonian empire, it is

---

[1] See p. 162.   [2] Cornill, Introduction, p. 385.

impossible for us to conjecture where the author of Daniel could have received the false information which would have led him to believe that a Median empire intervened between the Babylonian and the Persian. Even if he had been writing a fiction, as the writer on Daniel in a recent Bible Dictionary affirms that he did, he would scarcely have made so unnecessary a blunder and one so easy to be detected. We can only conclude, then, that he was an ignoramus, who knew nothing about the sources of information which were easily accessible to him; or an impostor, who presumed on a crass and impossible ignorance of their own, as well as of Persian history, on the part of the Jews of Maccabean times; whom, according to his modern critics, he was wishing to comfort and encourage by his "edifying religious narrations." But, how can a man who is supposed to have known that "the names of only four Persian kings are mentioned in the O. T." have been so ignorant of the contents of the Old Testament as not to know that they uniformly represent Cyrus as the conqueror of Babylon and the Persians as the immediate successors of the Babylonians? However late the second part of Isaiah may have been written, no one can doubt, that it was written long before the middle of the second century B.C., and that it represents Jehovah's servant Cyrus as fulfilling his will upon Babylon.[1] In Ezra and 2 Chronicles, also, Cyrus is the one uniformly designated as the conqueror of Babylon.[2] No mention is made anywhere in the Bible outside or inside of Daniel of the name of any king of Media, nor of any special conquest of Babylon by the Medes

[1] Isa. xliv, and xlv.
[2] Ezra i, 1, 2, 7, 8; iii, 7; iv, 3, 5; v, 13, 14, 17; vi, 3, 14; 2 Chron. xxxvi, 22, 23.

alone, nor of any ruling of Median kings over Babylon. Appeal is made to Isaiah xiii, 17, and xxi, 2, and to Jeremiah, li, 11, 28, to show that these were the sources of his information. Isaiah xiii, 17 reads: "Behold, I will stir up the Medes[1] against them [*i. e.*, the Babylonians.]" Isaiah xxi, 2, reads: "Go up, O; Elam besiege, O Media," and verse 9 shows that Babylon is the object of the attack. In Jeremiah li, 11, we read, "The Lord hath stirred up the spirit of the kings of the Medes, because his device is against Babylon to destroy it." In Jeremiah li, 27–29, we read:

Set ye up a standard in the land, blow the trumpet among the nations, prepare the nations against her, call together against her the kingdoms of Ararat, Minni, and Ashkenaz: appoint a marshal[2] against her; cause the horses to come up as the rough canker-worm. Prepare against her the nations, the kings of the Medes, the governors[3] thereof, and all the deputies[4] thereof, and all the land of their dominion. And the land trembleth and is in pain; for the purposes of Jehovah against Babylon do stand, to make the land of Babylon a desolation, without inhabitant.

Further in 2 Kings xvii, 6, and xviii, 11, it is said that the king of Assyria, in the time of Hezekiah and Isaiah, settled the captive children of Israel in the cities of Media. From these passages it is evident that Media must have been well known in the time of Isaiah and we may well believe to every succeeding Jewish writer of any ordinary intelligence. The better one knows the history of the land of Media, the better also will he recognize the appropriateness with which Isaiah and Jeremiah

---

[1] Heb. *Maday.*
[3] Hebrew, *păhôth.*

[2] Hebrew, *tifsar.*
[4] Hebrew, *sagan.*

use the designation. According to Winckler,[1] the conquering Aryans, who were conquerors of the Persians, assumed, or were given by their neighbors, the name of the country and people that they had subdued. During the time of the Assyrian dominations, it was, and remained unto classical times, the name of the northern part of the plateau of Iran; the latter being the new name afterward given to it from its Aryan conquerors. Elam, on the other hand, was the well known designation of the country between the Median or Iranian plateau and the Persian Gulf; and included not merely Susiana (the Uvaya of the Persian recension of the Behistun Inscription), but Anshan, the land which Cyrus and his ancestors ruled, and Persia proper, which Darius and his ancestors ruled for a century or two before the capture of Babylon by Cyrus. The Behistun Inscription also puts Elam under the Persian dominion; though Herodotus calls it part of Susa and the rest of the country the land of the Cissians.[2] The other lands mentioned by Jeremiah—Ararat, Minni, and Ashkenaz—constituted what Winckler has identified as having been called Gutium by the Babylonians; though the name had probably been changed as to the extent of the country denoted by it at the time when Ugbaru was its satrap, or sub-king. It will be noted, also, that Jeremiah speaks of Media as having kings and not a king, when it is stirred up against Babylon. This harmonizes with our views as to the relation in which Ugbaru stood to Cyrus. He was one king of many who were under the king of kings. Another, according to the Behistun Inscription, must have been Hystaspis the father, or Arsames, the grandfather of Darius Hys-

---

[1] *Untersuchungen zur altorient. Geschichte*, p. 117.
[2] Bk. III, 91.

taspis; for Darius declares in both the great inscriptions at Behistun and the lesser one, called A, that eight of his ancestors had been king before him, and Herodotus states that Hystaspis was governor (*hyparch*) of Persia in the time of Smerdis the Magian.[1]

From the above discussion, it will appear, then, to be true, that while Isaiah, Jeremiah, and Daniel all use the name Media correctly, and say only what is absolutely exact with regard to it; that it would have been impossible for anyone in later times to have constructed out of the meager details afforded by the first two, such an account as we find recorded in the book of Daniel. They are all three perfectly in harmony with what we have from other sources; but no one of them could have drawn his information from the others,—least of all Daniel. There being, then, no statement anywhere in the Scriptures to the effect that there ever was an independent Median kingdom, which included in it the land of Babylon; nor of any king of a Median empire, who ever conquered it, or ruled over it; it seems far-fetched to maintain, that the author of Daniel ever imagined that a Median kingdom came in between the Babylonian and the Persian. In Daniel i, 21, it is said that Daniel continued unto the first year of king Cyrus; in vi, 28, it is said that he prospered in the reign of Darius and in the reign of Cyrus the Persian. Since Isaiah xliv and xlv had attributed the conquest of Babylon to Cyrus; Isaiah xiii,17, to the Medes; Isaiah xxi, 2, to Elam[2]; and Jeremiah li to Medes and others[3]; it is easy to reconcile all the statements by supposing that all of these people together, under Cyrus as king, were engaged in the attack on Babylon. There is every

[1] Bk. III, 70.   [2] *I.e.*, Anshan where Cyrus ruled.
[3] *I.c.*, Cutium, of which Gobryas was governor under Cyrus.

reason, however, for believing that native kings, who submitted to Cyrus and the other Persian kings after him, were not disturbed in their sovereignty over their *subjugated* states. Witness the Syenneses, kings of Cilicia, one of whom was and remained king under Cyrus,[1] another under Darius,[2] and a third under Xerxes.[3] Witness Damasithymus, king of the Calyndians who served in the Persian fleet and was killed at Salamis.[4] Witness the kings of Cyprus,[5] Gorgus, king of the Salaminians;[6] Aristocyprus, son of Philocyprus, king of Soli.[7] Witness Thannyras, the son of Inarus, the Libyan, and Pausiris, the son of Amyrtæus, who received from the Persian king the governments which their fathers had; "although none ever did more injury to the Persians than Inarus and Amyrtæus"; for "the Persians are accustomed," says Herodotus, "to honor the sons of kings, and even if they have revolted from them, nevertheless bestow the government upon their children."[8] So, Cyrus says in his *Cylinder*-inscription, line 29-31, that the kings brought to him their rich tribute. The kings who were dethroned were not ordinarily killed, unless they aimed, not at independence, but at the supreme sovereignty. Thus Astyages, king of the Medes (or Mandeans); Crœsus, king of Lydia; and Nabunaid, king of Babylon, were all spared by Cyrus[9]; and according to Abydenus, the last of these was given the government of Carmania.

From the above, it will be clear to our readers, that Cyrus may have had a king of Media, or a Median

---

[1] Herodotus, I, 74.   [2] *Id.*, V, 118.   [3] *Id.*, VII, 98.
[4] *Id.*, VII, 98, VIII, 87.   [5] *Id.*, XII, 100.
[6] *Id.*, V, 104.   [7] *Id.*, V, 113.   [8] *Id.*, III, 15.
[9] Herodotus, I, 130, 208; Abu Habba *Cylinder*, i, 32, 55; Nabunaid-Cyrus *Chronicle*, obverse Col. ii, 2, reverse Col. ii, 16.

king, ruling a part of his empire under him.   But further, before leaving this subject, let it be remembered, that it is not fair to accuse the Scriptures of making statements about the Medes having conquered Babylon; whereas, as a matter of fact, the Persians did it.   For, it is evident, that the subjects and neighbors of the Persian government both looked upon the Achæmenid kings as kings of the Medes, also, and addressed them as such. For example, Herodotus says that Tomyris, queen of the Massagetæ, addressed Cyrus as "king of the Medes,"[1] and the two Spartans who went to Susa to make satisfaction for the death of the Persian heralds who had perished at Sparta, addressed the king as "King of the Medes."[2]   Moreover, Xerxes, as we have shown above, is called "king of Persia and Media," "king of Medo-Persia,[3] etc., on a number of Babylonian contract tablets.   Herodotus and Thucydides, also, represent the Greeks as using the names almost indiscriminately for the allied peoples and for their kings as well; and both the monuments of the Persian kings and the classical writers place the Medes in a position little inferior to the Persians but much superior to any other nation in the kingdom of the Achæmenids.   Both by Cyrus and Darius Hystaspis, a large number of Medes as well as Persians were entrusted with the highest commands in the empire; while but a few exceptional cases can be cited where a man of any other nation received an appointment to a high command. So that the old designation of Medo-Persian may' well be employed to designate the kingdom founded by Cyrus; though, perhaps, Perso-Median would be better still.   If then, the Medo-Persian empire was *one*, and succeeded immediately to that of Babylon, the interpre-

[1] I., 205.   [2] *Id.*, XII, 134–136.   [3] *Shar Par-sa, Mada.*

tation of Daniel vii, 5, 6, which makes the bear to mean Media and the leopard Persia, falls to the ground; and so also does the interpretation which makes the four heads of the leopard refer to four kings of Persia. It follows that Daniel vii, 6, cannot be used to prove that in Daniel xi, 2, we find the author "attributing to the Persian empire only four kings," and that consequently he must have confused Darius Hystaspis and his son Xerxes when he makes the fourth king stir up all against the realm of Greece.

Dan. xi, 2, which is the only text except vii, 6, which is cited by Prof. Cornill to prove this confusion of the two kings reads as follows:

And now, I will show thee the truth. Behold, there shall stand up yet three kings in Persia; and the fourth shall be much richer than they all; and when he is waxed strong through his riches, he shall stir up all against the realm of Greece.

The first verse of this chapter says that this vision was in the first year of Darius the Mede. Since, as we have endeavored to show, Darius the Mede was never an independent king, but was merely a sub-king under Cyrus, it seems best to consider Cambyses, Smerdis the Magian, and Darius Hystaspis, to be the three kings meant by the author of this verse. The fourth would then be Xerxes; though it may possibly be Darius, if we count Cyrus as the first. The confusion, however, if there be any, is with us and not with the author. That is, we may not know which of the two he meant; but this does not prove that *he* did not know which of the two he meant. Remember, *no names are given*. The naming of the kings of the vision rests with the interpreters of it. It is not necessary to maintain that the prophets were themselves able clearly to distinguish the persons of their visions. We are told by Peter,[1] that the prophets searched diligently to find out what the visions which they saw might mean. There would be no possible objection, therefore, to this verse, even if it were indefinite and somewhat confused, provided that we could only recognize that it was prediction; and not try to force it to be an account written in the second century B.C.

VIII. But eighthly, it is said, that not merely did the author confuse Xerxes and Darius Hystaspis, but that this confused fourth king of Persia was further confused with Darius Codomannus, the fourteenth and last king of Persia, who was overthrown by Alexander the Great.[2] This confusion is said to be shown by Daniel xi, 2, which reads: "And a mighty king shall stand up, that shall rule with great dominion and do according to his will." Taken in connection with the verse preceding it, we admit and all admit, that this refers to Alexander of Macedon. But we fail to see the confusion. The prophecy might have been more explicit, but it is not confused. It does not say when this mighty king should arise. It does not say that he would have any direct or personal relation with the fourth king of Persia; though it may and, we think, does indicate and mean, that the great king would be instigated to his course of conduct by the activities of the fourth king against the dominion of Greece. As a matter of fact, Alexander the Great is said both by Arrian and Quintus Curtius to have declared that he undertook his expedition against Persia in order to avenge the earlier assaults on Greece and Macedon made by Darius Hystaspis and his son Xerxes. And who can or would do other-

[1] 1 Pet. i, 10, 11.   [2] See p. 162.

wise in thinking of the two great expeditions, than to put them in contrast and in a certain juxtaposition and relation of cause and effect with each other? Herodotus begins his great history by an attempt to show what was the original cause of the enmity between the Greeks and the Asiatics; and he says that the Persians ascribed to the capture of Troy, to the expedition of the Greeks into Asia about five hundred years before that of Darius Hystaspis against Greece, the commencement of their enmity to the Greeks.[1]

But even if there were a confusion of these kings of Persia in the statements of the book of Daniel, it must be evident to all, that, while this might be looked upon as a reason for distrusting these statements, it certainly cannot be used to prove that the author wrote after rather than before the history was enacted. We object, therefore, to the bringing forward of this claim of confusion as a proof of the late date of the book. And we object especially in this charge against the author of Daniel that he confused the composite Darius Hystaspis-Xerxes with Darius Codomannus, to laying stress upon an interval of time between the cause and the effect, between the attack on Greece and the counter attack on Persia; inasmuch as no one in his senses would think of charging Herodotus with confusion because he skips over the five hundred years between the attack on Priam's citadel and that on the Acropolis, or of charging Alexander the Great with confusion or ignorance, because he declares his attack on Darius Codomannus in 334 B. C., to have been an act of vengeance for the attacks of Darius Hystaspis and Xerxes upon Greece and Macedon in the wars which culminated at Marathon and Salamis.

[1] See Bk. I, 1–5.

18

IX.[1]   Ninthly, and lastly, it is assumed, that the
author states that the war of the fourth king of Persia
against Greece ended "in a triumphant repulse of this
attack by the Greek king Alexander the Great" and in
the defeat and dethronement of the fourth king.[2]

It is a sufficient answer to this assumption to repeat
the verse upon which it is founded: "A mighty king shall
stand up and shall rule with great dominion and do
according to his will."[3]   Here, is no mention of the
defeat and dethronement of any king, let alone the
fourth king of Persia alluded to in the preceding verse.
Here is no mention of the name of Alexander of Macedon, nor of his having repulsed any attack nor of his
being a great king.   The whole verse is absolutely
within the sphere of ordinary predictive prophecy, and
puts one in mind in its indefiniteness of the verse of
Balaam: "There shall come forth a star out of Jacob"[4];
and of the verse in Jacob's blessing: "The scepter shall
not depart from Judah," etc.[5]

CONCLUSION

In the discussions of the last five chapters, we have
attempted to show that the author of Daniel does not
attribute to the Persian empire a total of only four
kings; that it is scarcely possible that the author of
Daniel, if he wrote after the time of Alexander the
Great, can have thought that this empire had only four
kings; that it is not proven that only four kings of Persia
are mentioned in the Old Testament outside of Daniel;
that Darius the Mede cannot have been a reflection of
Darius Hystaspis; that the author of Daniel has not

[1] See p. 162.   [2] Cornill, p. 385.   [3] Dan. xi, 3.
[4] Num. xxiv, 17.   [5] Gen. xlix, 10.

confused Darius Hystaspis and Xerxes his son; that he does not mistake Darius Hystaspis for Darius Codomannus; and that he does not state that the war of the fourth king of Persia against Greece was repulsed by Alexander the Great. We leave the reader to judge whether we have succeeded in our attempt.

CHAPTER XIV

SUSA

WHEN a man is charged with having with his own hand committed a murder, the most conclusive defense is to prove an *alibi*, that is, that the accused was not at the place at the time when the murder was committed. Similarly, when it comes to historical statements, if it can be shown that the man about whom the statement is made did not live at the time or that he could not have been in the place where the event is said to have transpired, it is sufficiently clear that the statement connecting him directly with the event is false. Again, if an event is said to have been enacted in a certain building in a certain city at a certain time by a certain person, the statement is proved false if it can be shown that the person, or the building, or the city, did not exist at that time; or that if it did exist, its condition and circumstances were different from those described in the record. Further, if a document purports to have been written at a certain time by a certain person in a certain language, it would be sufficient to disprove its genuineness, if it could be shown that the person did not exist at that time, or that the language is such as that the document could not have been written at that time. Of course, this last statement would be subject to the proviso that the document in hand was not a later revision, or a translation, of the original.

In this and the following chapter I am going to consider some of the attacks made upon the genuineness of
the book of Daniel on the ground that it contains
anachronisms, that is, that it contains statements which
could not have been written in the time of Cyrus.

Objections Stated

"The author was guilty of an anachronism in making Shushan (Susa) subject to Babylon."[1]

Or, as Cornill says, "Of the fact of Susa also having
been a seat of the Babylonian court there may be a
reminiscence in viii, 2."[2]

Assumptions Involved

There are in these objections two assumptions: 1,
that in the time of Daniel, Susa was not subject to
Babylon; 2, that Daniel viii, 2, implies the anachronism that Susa was in Daniel's time a seat of the Babylonian court.

Answer to Assumptions

1. (a) As to the first assumption, discoveries made
since Bertholdt's time would indicate that Susa was
subject to Babylon in the time of Daniel. For as
Winckler says of the division of the Assyrian empire
between the Babylonians and the Medes: "All the
country to the north of the river region from Elam to
Asia Minor fell to the Medes." "Elam itself appears,
as in the earliest times, to have fallen to Babylonia."[3]

[1] Bertholdt: *Daniel*, p. 34.
[2] *Introduction to the O. T.*, p. 185.
[3] Winckler's *History of Babylon and Assyria*, Craig's Translation,
p. 384.

If we can accept the translation of Mr. Pinches, the Cyrus Cylinder supports this view of Dr. Winckler; for according to this translation, the city of Susa was one of those to which Cyrus returned its gods after he had captured Babylon and had received the homage of the nations, that had up to that time been subject to Babylon, in Shu-anna the citadel of the city of Babylon.[1] The province of Elam spoken of in viii, 2, of which Susa was the capital will thus appear to have been a part of Babylonia during the period of the Babylonian monarchy.

(b) But, even if Susa did not fall to Babylon in the division of the Assyrian empire, we must remember that it is possible (1) that Daniel was there in vision merely, or (2) that he may have gone thither on private or official business. In favor of (1) is the probable meaning of chapter viii, 2, which reads: "I saw in the vision; now it was so, that when I saw, I was in Shushan the palace, which is in the province of Elam." In favor of (2) is the fact that the cities of Babylon and Susa were separated by only a little over 200 miles and that for at least 1500 years the two cities had been bound together by the closest political and commercial relations. Susa lay on the direct land route from Babylon to India, and Babylon on the route from Susa to the Mediterranean. So that there may have been many reasons of a public or private nature why a man of Daniel's position may have visited Susa. In his official capacity also as ruler "over the whole province of Babylon,"[2] he may have been investigating the methods of government in the province of Elam. Or, if we take the reading of the Latin Vulgate, "province" or the LXX reading, "affairs"

---

[1] See Pinches: *The O. T. in the Light of the Hist. Records*, etc., p. 422, and KB. iii, ii, 126.   [2] Dan. ii, 48.

of Babylonia (a reading which depends merely upon a change in the pointing of the Hebrew original), Daniel may have had oversight at this time of the governors of all the provinces, or affairs, of the empire. Or, Daniel may have been transferred from the government of the province of Babylon to that of Elam. It is altogether probable, that as Nabunaid, the son of Nabunaid, had been made sub-king of Harran in the extreme north of the Babylonian empire,[1] so also, Belshazzar had been made king of Accad, Shumer, Chaldea, and Elam in the south. This would account for the *third* year of Belshazzar the king spoken of in Daniel viii, 1. It was the third year of Belshazzar as the king of the Chaldeans.

The presumptuousness of making hasty statements, unsupported by any proper evidence, with regard to the events which happened, and the state of affairs in that distant past in which Daniel lived, cannot be better illustrated than in the assertions which Bertholdt made in the introduction to his commentary on Daniel, which was published in 1806. We read:

The book of Daniel contains mistakes which it would have been impossible for Daniel to compose and which can be explained only on the supposition that the book was written long after the occurrence of the events described. In Chapter 8: 1, 2, Daniel says of himself: "In the third year of the reign of Belshazzar the king, I found myself in Shushan the palace, in the province of Elam." In the 27th verse he says that he had royal business to transact in that place. In these words lies an insoluble difficulty, if Daniel has written them. Elymais never belonged to the Chaldean court of Babylon. Later, under Cyrus, Daniel may indeed have come into this land; but how

[1] See Pognon: *Inscriptions Sémitiques*, Part 1.

could he already much earlier have had to transact there the business of king Nabonned? One might perhaps say that he went thither as an ambassador to the Persian court. But only if it were not certain that the kings first after Cyrus made it their winter residence—that Darius Hystaspis first caused the buildings requisite for this to be erected, that thus in Nabonned's time there did not exist a court or a royal palace (*Burg*) in the chief city of Elymais! Clearly a later composer betrays himself here who has confused either the later Persian residence city Susa with Babylon, the capital of the Chaldean kings, or indeed Nabonned with a ruler of the Persian dynasty, or a later event from the life of Daniel with an earlier.[1]

The only answer needed to this self-raised difficulty is found in Herodotus III, 70, where we read: "Darius, the son of Hystaspis, arrived at Susa from Persia, where his father was governor (*hyparch*)." From which we gather, first, that, at the time before Darius Hystaspis became king, Susa existed; and secondly, that it was not *in* Persia even then, but in Elam. So that Bertholdt's great insoluble difficulty was all in his own mind!

2. The assumption that Susa was in Daniel's time a seat of the Babylonian court is based upon two further assumptions: (1) that Belshazzar was at this time a Babylonian king, or king of the Babylonians, and (2) that the Hebrew *bira* here means "palace."

(1) As to the first of these assumptions, it is sufficient to remember that Belshazzar is never called a Babylonian king. In Daniel v, 30, he is called "the Chaldean king," and the narrative in the fifth chapter implies merely that he was for a short time in some sense the king of Babylon. Chapter seven, verse one, speaks of his first year as king of Babylon. All the statements

---

[1] See Bertholdt, *Daniel*, pp. 34, 35.

with regard to the reign of Belshazzar can be reconciled only by supposing that his third year, spoken of in Daniel viii, 1, was his third year as second ruler in the kingdom, or as a sub-ruler under Nabunaid. As the Nabunaid-Cyrus Chronicle says, that a son of the king, *i. e.*, of Nabunaid, was commander of the army in Accad, and as it is generally believed that this son was Belshazzar, the residence of Belshazzar may very well have been at Susa, the largest city next to Babylon in the southern part of Nabunaid's dominions. Daniel may have been on business in Susa, either by commission from the sovereign, king Nabunaid, or as an official under Belshazzar. The court of Susa, then, if court there was, would have been not the Babylonian court of Nabunaid, but the court of Belshazzar the Chaldean. That the years of a sub-king of a sub-kingdom might be dated otherwise than from the time of the accession of the chief ruler, is evident from the fact that the years of the reigns of the kings of Israel and Judah are reckoned from the year of the accession of the subject and not of the sovereign king. Sometimes, the year of the reign of each is given, as in Jeremiah xxv, 1. And again, the documents of Babylon under the reigns of Shamashshumukin *et al.*, although they reigned as subordinates to the kings of Assyria, were dated according to the years of the sub-kings and not after the years of the overlord.

(2) It is an assumption, however, that a court is spoken of at all in Daniel viii, 2. The Hebrew word *Bira* is certainly a loan word from the Assyrio-Babylonian, where it does not mean "palace" but "fortress," and is a synonym for *halṣu*, "fort," and for *karashu*, "camp." It is more probable, therefore, that in Daniel viii, 2, the phrase is to be rendered "the fortress of

Susa," rather than "the palace of Susa." With this translation, the assumption that there is any reference to a court falls to the ground.

Conclusion

The above discussion has shown that the statements of the book of Daniel with regard to Susa are, so far as is known to-day, in exact harmony with the facts revealed on the monuments.

CHAPTER XV

NEBUCHADNEZZAR'S MADNESS

WAS Nebuchadnezzar mad? Can he have had such a madness as is described in the book of Daniel? Can he have been mad for as long a time as Daniel says he was? And may his kingdom have been preserved for him during the time that he was ill? Such are the main questions to be considered in the present chapter. Being no specialist in diseases of the mind, it will be necessary to cite medical authorities in answer to the question as to the possibility of a madness such as the author of Daniel describes. As to the other objections made by the critics, it will be observed that in lieu of proof they have recourse to the old phrases "cannot" and "no proof needed to show incredibility." Those of my readers who think that the bare opinion of any man is sufficient to show that an event recorded by an historian is impossible or incredible, need not take the trouble of reading farther than the objections cited below. Those who believe that proof is needed will find, if they read, that nothing either impossible or incredible has been recorded by the author of Daniel as having taken place. It will be further observed that the critics found one of their main objections upon an interpretation of one of the terms used by Daniel,—that which is translated "times" in the English versions of Daniel iv, 25. It will be shown that there is no foundation in

283

the usage of language for the critics' interpretation of this word as meaning "years"; but that even if this were the meaning of the word in this place, the history of Nebuchadnezzar, as far as it is known at present, does not render it impossible to believe that he may have been ill ror seven years.

The objections as made by the critics and the assumptions involved in them are as follows:

OBJECTIONS STATED

"Nebuchadnezzar's madness during seven years cannot be taken literally."[1] To which I add from Professor Cornill as follows: "No proof is needed to show the incredibility attaching to the supposed incapacity of this king for governing, owing to madness, for the space of seven years."[2]

The question then is, can Nebuchadnezzar have been mad for seven years? We might content ourselves here with quoting Dr. Driver's excellent remark with reference to Nebuchadnezzar's madness and "some other similar considerations."

Our knowledge [says he] is hardly such as to give us an objective criterion for estimating their cogency. The circumstances alleged will appear improbable or not improbable according as the critic, upon independent grounds, has satisfied himself that the book is the work of a later author, or written by Daniel himself. It would be hazardous to use the statements in question *as proof* of the late date of the book; though, if its date were established on other grounds, it would be not unnatural to regard some of them as involving an exaggeration of the actual fact.[3]

[1] See *Jewish Encyclopedia*, Art. Daniel.
[2] See *Introduction to the Old Testament*, p. 385.
[3] See *Literature of the Old Testament*, p. 500.

But, for the sake of those who will not accept Dr. Driver's very sensible remarks upon this subject, it may be well to consider the following assumptions that are involved in the objections.

Assumptions Involved

1. It is assumed that no man can have suffered from such a madness as that attributed to Nebuchadnezzar in the fourth chapter of Daniel.
2. It is assumed that Nebuchadnezzar cannot have had such a malady for seven years.

Answer to Assumptions

In this chapter we shall be confronted with the same kind of objections and assumptions that have been considered in the last. Professor Cornill is master of all the arts of debate. His pages on Daniel are as full of the words "no proof is needed," "impossible," "incredible," as an illuminated manuscript of gold letter heads. Several times on a single page is the word "impossible" employed by him to characterize the statements of Daniel; several times, the phrase "no proof is needed" to show their incredibility, obscurity, etc. It seems amazing how such a conglomeration of absurdities, such a congeries of impossibilities, should have befooled both Jew and Christian alike for 2000 years or more! Why could not their learned men at least have seen that such things were impossible? And if they are impossible, and if no proof is needed to show this impossibility, why is it that millions to-day, including some who have every right to claim an equality with Professor Cornill and his coadjutors in knowledge,

wisdom, and grace, should still believe them possible?
Is no proof needed to convince Professor Cornill's
opponents? Perhaps, he thinks, they are not worth
trying to convince. Then why did he write his book?
Perhaps he thinks that the majority of people to-day
will accept the opinion of a professor as they used to
accept that of an emperor, or a council. And most
likely the majority of his readers will. On behalf,
therefore, of this majority that does accept opinion as
authority, as well as on behalf of the minority who
demand proofs and are willing to abide by the evidence,
I appeal from the critics' opinion to the documentary
evidence. The writer of Daniel, purporting to give
contemporaneous testimony, says that Nebuchadnezzar
king of Babylon was mad during a space of seven times.
The critics, interpreting the word for "times" as meaning years, say this is impossible.

In the discussion of this question, I shall consider—

First, whether any man can have suffered from such a
madness as that attributed to Nebuchadnezzar?

It would be madness in one who is not a specialist in
diseases of the mind to attempt to answer this question.
After consulting with some of the most eminent specialists in the line of so-called insanity, and the reading of
the best works on the subject that could be found in the
libraries of Philadelphia, I have come to the conclusion
that there is a general agreement among them as to the
possibility of such a disease, or form of insanity, as that
with which Nebuchadnezzar is said to have suffered.
D. H. Tuke, in his *Dictionary of Psychological Medicine*,
page 5, says that

the complete loss of personal identity, and the conviction
of being changed into one of the lower animals, accom-

panied frequently by a corresponding belief on the part of the beholders, is one of the most remarkable facts which the psychological history of the race reveals.

In the article on Lycanthropy, page 752 of the same dictionary, he cites a well-accredited case of a man who imagined himself to be a wolf, and attempted to act like one, as late as 1852 A. D. The case is described at length by the sufferer's physician, a French specialist of note named Morelle. Dr. Chapin, who was till lately at the head of the Pennsylvania Hospital for the Insane, defines insanity as a "prolonged change of a man's ordinary way of thinking and acting, resulting from disease." Dr. Chapin says that the best article upon the insanity of Nebuchadnezzar of which he knows is one by D. R. Burrell, M. D., of Binghampton, N. Y., in the *American Journal of Insanity* for April, 1894, pages 493–504. In this article, Dr. Burrell says among other things of interest bearing on our subject, as to which we refer the reader to the volume cited, that the fourth chapter of Daniel contains "one of the most beautiful and accurate descriptions of the premonition, the onset, the course, and the termination, of a case of insanity that is recorded in any language"(p. 504).

Nothing can be truer to nature and the daily manifestations of the insane than the account of the recovery of the king; the coming out of chaos, or self-absorption; the return of understanding; and then a heart overflowing with thankfulness (*id.*, p. 504).

As to the king's eating grass, he says: "He ate grass—in imitation of the animal he claimed to be—in imitation only—as those now who think they are animals eat in imitation of these animals, but subsist upon the food of man." Dr. Burrell thinks, also, that the treatment afforded to the king was the best possible; and that he never forgot, during the long period of his mental confusion, that he was still Nebuchadnezzar, king of Babylon (*id.*, pp. 502–3).

Resting this part of our case, then, with the testimony of these noted specialists, we proceed to the second question, as to whether Nebuchadnezzar can have had this disease for seven years. The medical experts, as we have seen above, raise no question as to the possibility of a man's suffering from this form of insanity for seven years; but the historical critics have raised the question as to whether the monumental evidence permits us to believe that Nebuchadnezzar can for seven years have been incapacitated from directing the affairs of state. Before entering upon the discussion of this subject from the historical point of view, we want to express our dissent from the statement made by Dr. Burrell in his article on "The Insane Kings of the Bible," cited above, to the effect that "the king may have thought he was an ox, but may have been perfectly sane on other matters." While we would not dogmatically deny that an interpretation of the Aramaic imperfect forms of the verbs found in verses 31 and 33 as frequentatives rather than inceptives, might allow of this view; nevertheless we are decidedly of the opinion that the translation of the English versions is correct, and that the writer meant us to understand that Nebuchadnezzar had not merely a monomania, or craze on one point, but that he was rendered completely incapable of conducting the government. What other sense can be put upon the words, "The kingdom is departed from thee"?

With regard to this question, then, it may be said:

(1) That the translation "seven years" is possible, but not necessarily correct. The word rendered "years" is not the ordinary word for year (*shana*), but a word which means merely a fixed or appointed time (*'iddan* or *'adan*). It seems to be a word of Babylonian origin, meaning "fixed time," and is equivalent often to the Greek *kairos*. In R. C. Thompson's *Reports of the Magicians and Astrologers of Nineveh and Babylon*, number 251, Rev. 3–6, we read, "let not the king go into the street on an evil day, until the time (*'adan*) of the omen has passed. The omen of a star lasts for a full month."[1]

To be sure, the old version of the Seventy renders this passage by "seven years"; but the version of Theodotion has "seven seasons" (*kairoi*), the Latin Vulgate has *tempora*, and the Arabic has "times" (*'azminatin*).

But even if it be insisted upon that it should here be interpreted as meaning "seven years," why can it not be taken literally? The only sources of information as to the reign of Nebuchadnezzar which we possess outside the Scriptures, are some contract tablets, some building inscriptions, one historical inscription, and six or more sources belonging to profane history, all of these last sources coming to us at second hand. Thus, Josephus cites (1) "the archives of the Phenicians" as saying concerning Nebuchadnezzar that he conquered all Syria and Phenicia and began the siege of Tyre in his seventh year and continued the siege for thirteen years; (2) Philostratus, as mentioning in his history the siege of Tyre for thirteen years; (3) Megasthenes, as pretending to prove in the fourth book of his *Indian History* that Nebuchadnezzar was superior to Hercules in

[1] "Sharru a-na su-u-ku la uṣ-ṣa-a (4) adi a-dan-shu sha it-ti (5) it-ti-ku (6) it-it sha kakkab a-di arah ume."

19

strength and the greatness of his exploits, and as saying that Nebuchadnezzar conquered a great part of Libya, and Iberia also; and (4) Diocles, as merely mentioning Nebuchadnezzar in the second book of his *Accounts of Persia*. To these may be added (5) the accounts which Josephus has taken from Berosus, and (6) those which Eusebius has taken from Abydenus. These last two both refer to the illness of Nebuchadnezzar, but give us no note of time (none at least as to the length of the illness) though they do imply that it occurred near the end of his reign.

The contract tablets give us no facts as to the private or public life of Nebuchadnezzar, except to imply that the regular machinery of government at Babylon ran on uninterruptedly throughout his reign. This implication is gathered, however, from the fact that the tablets are dated continuously throughout every one of the 43 years of his reign, from 604 to 561 B.C., and not from any direct allusions to the political events of the time.

According to Langdon, there is but one of the building inscriptions that should be put between 593 and 580 B.C., and only three between 580 and 561. The one historical inscription which we possess records the invasion of Egypt in the 37th year of Nebuchadnezzar, that is, in 567 B.C. Before the expedition to Egypt took place, Nebuchadnezzar may, *for all we know* from the monuments and other sources, have been incapacitated for seven years through insanity. It might be well to note, also, that in an addition at the beginning of the Septuagint version of the fourth chapter of Daniel, it is said that the dream occurred in the 18th year of Nebuchadnezzar, that is, in 586 or 587 B.C. As the insanity is said to have commenced a year later (Dan. iv, 29), this would make the disease to have extended from 586 (5) to 580 or 579 B.C. No known objection can be made to these dates.

It is marvelous how much Bertholdt and others have made out of the fact that Berosus does not expressly and precisely mention the madness of Nebuchadnezzar. In the excerpts from Berosus which have been preserved for us in Josephus and Eusebius, it is said that Nebuchadnezzar "having fallen into weakness died." While we would not argue from this phrase, as Hengstenberg did, that Berosus thus, euphemistically as it were, refers to the madness of Nebuchadnezzar; yet, on the other hand, it is absurd to assert that, inasmuch as Berosus, in the few words concerning Nebuchadnezzar which have come down to us, does not state expressly that Nebuchadnezzar had been mad, that therefore he never was mad. Even if it were true, as Bertholdt asserts, that Berosus knew nothing of his madness, this would not prove that he had not been mad. For it is almost certain that the Babylonian sources from which Berosus derived his information would contain nothing about this great calamity. People never have on their monuments, and very few in their records or autobiographies, the records of their vices, crimes, or weaknesses. De Quincey and Rousseau, each for a reason best known to himself, portrays in fine literary style what most men would conceal, even if true. Cowper, in order to exalt the greatness and goodness of God, refers in one of his poems to his madness, just as Nebuchadnezzar is said to have done to his. But the weaknesses of our friends and of great men are mostly interred with their bones, and we speak no ill of the dead. One would search in vain for a tombstone recording that the inmate of the sepulcher had been for seven times (years or months) in an insane asylum.   Berosus, writing a history of his own country—for according to Josephus "he was by birth a Chaldean"—would naturally want to soften down the character of the calamity which had befallen the greatest of the Chaldean kings.   His negative testimony, therefore, must be discounted, and, in an euphemistic manner of speech, his phrase "having fallen into a weakness" may well have referred to his madness.

But says Bertholdt again,

is it credible that without any scruple, or any fear of a relapse, such as according to common experience in diseases of this kind most frequently occurs, they would have entrusted to the hands of a man that had for many years been bereft of his reason the reins of government, and therewith the lives of many millions of persons? . . .
If Nebuchadnezzar became crazy through discontent (*Unmuth*) and distraction, what wonder that he did not commit suicide![1]

The first assumption here is that the word for time must mean year; but we have seen above that it means simply a fixed time, and that in Assyrian it is defined in one case at least as meaning a month.   It is to be said also, that, as Calvin says, their opinion is probable who think that the number *seven* is indefinite, *i. e.*, until a long time had passed.

The second assumption is that insane persons are wont to commit suicide; whereas, as everyone knows from his own knowledge of the insane, but a very small proportion of them desire to commit suicide.

The third assumption is that the government may

---

[1] *Comm. on Dan.*, pp. 301–302.

not have been carried on for him during his period of insanity. According to verse 36 (33 in the Aramaic) his counselors and lords began to consult him again, as soon as his reason began to return. This implies that they had conducted the government without consulting him, so long as he was incapacitated by his disease.

The fourth assumption is that an insane person would necessarily be deposed. Such a deposition has happened at times in the history of the world, that is true; and even a violent deposition resulting in the death of the ruler, as in the case of Paul of Russia. But how about the Cæsars, and George III of England, and King Louis of Bavaria, not to mention a dozen or more others who may most charitably and reasonably be adjudged to have been insane, and that not in an innocuous sense, but violently and outrageously and homicidally insane? May not a regency have been deemed preferable to an Evil-Merodach, or to possible anarchy?

The fifth assumption is that an insane person would be looked upon and treated in ancient Babylon as such an one might possibly be treated in modern Europe. But we must remember that in antiquity a king was often looked upon as a god and insanity as possession by a god.

We must not be surprised [says Eusebius] if the Greek historians, or the Chaldeans, conceal the disease, and relate that he was inspired, and call his madness, or the demon by which he was possessed, a god. For it is the custom to attribute such things to a god, and to call demons gods.[1]

[1] *Chron. Arm.*, p. 61.

In accordance with this belief we can understand why Abydenus relates that the Chaldeans said that Nebuchadnezzar having ascended to the roof of his palace became inspired by some god. But not only insane kings, but all kings, were considered in many countries to be divine. So it was with the kings of Egypt. So, also, with the Seleucid kings of Babylon. Because of these beliefs, probably, the subjects of Cambyses so long endured his raging manias.

The sixth assumption is that he would not be permitted to resume his royal functions and glory, if at any time his normal sanity were restored. We would like to know who would have, or could have, attempted to prevent him from resuming his power. To maintain that he would have been thus prevented, we must assume that he was hated or feared by his subjects to such an extent as to have caused them to rebel against his authority. Why then would they not have rebelled and killed him like a mad dog while he was still insane? Having spared him while helpless, we judge that they would not resist him after his reason had returned. Nor do we judge that then any more than now, the physicians can have been positively certain that one attack of insanity would inevitably be followed by another. Of one thing at least we may be certain, that no physician of that day would have thought of advising that Nebuchadnezzar should be excluded from taking up again the reins of government. If one had so advised, it is probable that he would have been hanged higher than Haman!

CONCLUSION

From the above discussion it is evident that the madness of Nebuchadnezzar may be taken literally;

that he may have been mad for seven years, or times;
and that proof is needed to show the incredibility
alleged as attaching to his supposed incapacity for
governing.

CHAPTER XVI

WERE THE EDICTS OF THE KINGS IMPOSSIBLE?

ONE of the commonest tricks in all kinds of discussion is to assert that the view of your opponent is impossible (*unmöglich*), and that your own is self-evident (*selbst verständlich*). How frequently has the word *impossible* been used to silence the questionings and incredulity of the hearer? And yet, what is impossible? Why even should it be thought a thing impossible with God that *he* should raise the dead? Are not all things possible with him, except to deny himself, to do something contrary to his nature? At least, is it not fair to demand, whenever anyone says that a thing is self-evident or impossible, why he thinks it is thus or so? A few years ago even scientists of note deemed airships impossible. To-day they exist. Let us then be no longer silenced by these imposing words, by whomsoever used. They mean no more, at most, than that to him who uses them a thing *seems* to be self-evident or impossible. In all such cases let us consider it proper to ask: Why is it deemed impossible? Why does it seem to be self-evident? For few truths are self-evident. No historical facts are ever self-evident. But every event that has been recorded as having transpired is evidenced by the document that records it. There may be but one documentary witness to testify that the given event occurred, but this in itself does not necessarily make it improbable, and certainly not impossible of occurrence. Two witnesses would make the event more probable; three or four, more probable still. No number of witnesses would render an event so certain as to remove all doubt as to its having taken place; but in ordinary cases, "out of the mouth of two or three witnesses shall every word be established."

Certain, also, is it that no event that has been recorded can be rejected as impossible, simply because there is but one witness to the fact of its occurrence. A thing may have happened even if there were no record of it. Countless things, indeed, have happened of which no record at all exists. Even the events of a novel like "She" *may* have transpired. The ingenuity with which the author keeps within the sphere of the possible, while transgressing the radius of the probable, is what carries the reader spellbound to the catastrophe at the bitter end.

After these preliminary remarks on the unreasonableness of rejecting a recorded fact simply because it seems to someone to be impossible, it might be considered needless for us to discuss the assertion that it is impossible that the edicts of the kings recorded in Daniel were ever issued. But inasmuch as this accusation has been made by one of great influence and of great scholarship and high position, let us waive all preconceived opinion and proceed in the usual manner to the discussion.

OBJECTIONS STATED

No proof [says Professor Cornill] is needed to show the impossible character of the edicts ascribed in chapters iii and iv to Nebuchadnezzar and in chapter vi to

Darius, and the absurdity of the wish attributed to Nebuchadnezzar in chapter ii.[1]

The reader will recall that the first of these edicts,
that of the second chapter, was that the wise men of
Babylon should be killed, inasmuch as they could not
discern and interpret the dream which the king had
concealed or forgotten. The decrees in the third chapter were that all who refused to bow down to the image
which had been set up should be cast into the midst of a
burning fiery furnace, and that every people, nation,
and language, "which speak anything amiss against
the God of Shadrach, Meshach, and Abed-nego, shall be
cut in pieces," etc. (v. 29). The decree of the fourth
chapter is a general decree covering the whole chapter
and directing the nation to praise God because of the
signs and wonders he had wrought. The decrees of
Darius in the sixth chapter were the one in which anyone praying to any god but himself for thirty days
should be cast into a den of lions, and the one wherein he
exalts the God who had delivered Daniel from the den
of lions (v. 25-27). We have here six decrees, the three
exalting God (iii, 29, iv, and vi, 25-27), and the three
concerning the killing of the wise men, concerning the
fiery furnace, and concerning the den of lions.

ASSUMPTION INVOLVED

The great assumption here is that no proof is needed
to show that these edicts or decrees are impossible.

ANSWER TO ASSUMPTION

There are four kinds of impossibility which ought
here to be considered: For these decrees might involve

[1] See *Introduction to the O. T.*, p. 385.

(1) a moral impossibility based on what we know of the character or knowledge of kings and potentates in general or of these kings in particular; or (2), a legal impossibility derived from what is known of the laws of Babylon and Persia; or (3), a physical impossibility based on the difficulty of carrying out such decrees; or (4), an historical impossibility, arising from the fact that there is conclusive evidence that such decrees cannot have been made.

I. As to any one of the decrees presenting a moral impossibility, it certainly cannot be asserted that such decrees are not paralleled by many similar cases in the history of mankind. It does not prove that a decree is impossible to assert, or even to prove, that it is absurd or senseless (*unsinnig*) as Von Lengerke declares the edict of Nebuchadnezzar with regard to the wise men to be. Tyrants have always suffered from the disease which has been fitly named megalomania. Froude and others have put forth the view that almost all of the so-called Cæsars after Augustus were afflicted with this form of insanity. Monarchs and autocrats are most likely to suffer from attacks of this complaint, whether from fear of losing their power or their lives, or from the supposed necessity of upholding their authority or dignity. It must be admitted, also, that persecutions have arisen from the conscientious belief that the opinions of a world-ruler, whose right is claimed to be divine, must and ought to be imposed upon the governed. The Roman emperors from Nero to Galerius persecuted their Christian subjects with edicts and punishments akin in purpose, cruelty, and severity, to those of Nebuchadnezzar and Darius recorded in Daniel iii, iv, and vi. Indeed, the edicts are so similar that one might well believe that the emperors had copied and emulated the prototypes of Daniel. The decrees of the emperors demanded that all their subjects should burn incense before the statues of the Cæsars. Refusal to do so was followed by confiscation of property and death of the obstreperous.[1] Under Marcus Aurelius, the best of the heathen emperors, the aged bishop Polycarp "was burned at the stake because he would not consent to curse that Lord whom for 86 years he had served"; "Blandina, a delicate female slave, was scourged in the most dreadful manner, roasted on a red-hot iron chair, thrown to the wild beasts, and then executed"; "the dead bodies of the Christians lay in heaps on the streets." Under Septimius Severus, Perpetua was condemned to be gored by a wild cow. Under Decius, one of the ablest of the Roman Cæsars, "every conceivable means—confiscation, banishment, exquisite torture, and death—was employed to induce Christians to apostatize." Now, we can only explain the fact that such noble and great men, as many of these emperors certainly were, resorted to such terrible and terrifying measures to secure the extinction of Christianity and the unity of worship which was involved in the burning of incense to the statues of the Cæsars, on the supposition that they really believed that the safety of the state for whose welfare they were responsible was endangered by what to them appeared to be a godless and abominable sect. It is not fair to call these persecutions of the early Christians senseless (*unsinnig*) from the point of view of the emperors, with their idea of what the state was,

[1] Galerius proposed that everyone refusing to offer sacrifice should be burnt alive. Diocletian denounced punishment of death against all holding secret assemblies for religious worship. See Gibbon's *Decline and Fall of the Roman Empire*, ii, 63, 64.

and of how it was imperiled by the followers of the despised Jew of Nazareth.

Another parallel to the persecution of the Christians by the Roman emperors may be found in the intolerance of heresy by the Roman hierarchy. It is well for those who protest against the claims of the pope of Rome to be the vicar of Christ to remember that he has made himself responsible for all of the cruel acts of the Inquisition; and that the policy and deeds of the Inquisition, the persecution of the Waldenses, the suppression of the Albigenses, the massacre of St. Bartholomew, the destruction of Jews, Moriscoes, and heretics in Spain, and all similar methods of punishing unbelievers, are still upheld by the Roman hierarchy as justifiable on the ground of their divine right and obligation to suppress heresy in every form. Prof. Marianus de Luca, of the Society of Jesus, has recently published a work entitled *Institutions of Public Ecclesiastical Law.*[1] The work was highly commended by Leo XIII in a letter addressed to Professor de Luca and published on the covers of the volumes. In this work, the author maintains that it is still a Catholic tenet "that the church may justly inflict on heretics the penalty of death," and he endeavors to justify this tenet by an appeal to the Scriptures, to the Fathers, to the councils, to the idea and practice of the church, and to reason itself.[2]

In view, then, of these two great outstanding examples of religious intolerance based upon fundamental principles of political, or ecclesiastical, government, we are convinced that the decrees of Nebuchadnezzar and

[1] *Institutiones Juris Ecclesiastici Publici,* Neo-Eborici, 1901.
[2] See for a discussion of this work, Prof. C. H. H. Wright's *Daniel and the Critics*, Appendix III.

Darius (Daniel iii, iv, and vi) were neither senseless nor irrational from their point of view, nor from that of most of their subjects. Cannot anyone see in Nebuchadnezzar, when he forbids on penalty of death that anyone shall worship any other god than the image which he has set up, a prototype of Henry VIII of England, or Philip II of Spain,[1] or Louis XIV of France?[2] No one can read the history of Babylonia and Assyria without seeing how intimately the rise and fall of nations were bound up with the rise and fall of the gods which the people worshiped. "Where," says Sennacherib, "are the gods of Hena and Ivah?" "and shall the god in whom thou trustest deliver thee?" The prayers and records of all the Assyrian and Babylonian and Persian kings show clearly their belief that their power and prosperity were due to the favor of the gods they worshiped. Let one read, for example, the inscriptions of Ashurbanipal, Nebuchadnezzar, and Darius Hystaspis, and he will be convinced that they one and all attributed their elevation, their success, the continuance of their life and reign, and the failure or endurance of their prosperity and kingdom, to the favor or disfavor of their gods. When, then, a man flouted at the image of their god, or refused to worship as the king decreed, it was rebellion against the constituted authority in church and state; and the rebellion must be suppressed instantly, and in such a manner as to inspire terror in all other possible offenders. Granted the views of autocracy and of the relation of the gods

---

[1] According to the decree of Philip II, any Morisco found within ten miles of Granada, if above seventeen years of age, was to incur the penalty of death (Prescott: *Philip the Second*, iii, 265).

[2] At the revocation of the Edict of Nantes, the pastors were hanged or burned (Guizot: *History of France*, iv, 338).

to that autocracy which prevailed all through the
ancient world, there was nothing else for Nebuchadnezzar nor for Darius the Mede to do, but to proceed to
execute summarily the penalty affixed to the transgression of their decrees. As to their decrees, they were
perfectly in harmony with the views of the gods and of
government which existed among men at the times in
which they lived.

As to the character of Nebuchadnezzar, we know
from 2 Kings xxv, 7, that he slew the sons of the captive
Zedekiah, king of Judah, before his eyes and then put
out the eyes of Zedekiah himself and bound him with
fetters of brass and carried him to Babylon; and that
afterwards he slew Seraiah the chief priest and Zephaniah the second priest, and about seventy other important
persons at Riblah in the land of Hamath. Jeremiah
adds (chapter lii) that he kept Zedekiah in prison to
the day of his death and that he slew all the princes
of Judah. Besides, he kept Jehoiachin in prison for
thirty-seven years, he being freed only after Nebuchadnezzar's death by his successor Evil-Merodach.

The building inscriptions of Nebuchadnezzar throw
much light on his character. Those who wish to read
the whole of these we refer to Mr. Stephen Langdon's
work entitled *The Building Inscriptions of the Neo-
Babylonian Empire*. They will there find that he was a
most devoted worshiper of the heathen gods, especially of Marduk and Nebo. He expended a large part
of the wealth of the subject nations upon the restoration of the great temples of Babylonia and especially
of Babylon.[1]

---

[1] On pages 172 and 174 of Langdon's work Nebuchadnezzar speaks of
"an image of his royal person," which, possibly, he had set up "before
Marduk the king." On page 149 he says that he undertook to raise the

He undertook nothing, however, but at the command of the gods. His authority was derived from them. His works were executed through their help. His conquests were made by their help. His rule was established and his reign secured by them. The fear of his

top of the temple called E-temen-an-ki toward Heaven and to strengthen it, and for this purpose, says he, "the far dwelling peoples over whom Marduk my lord had appointed me and whose care was given unto me by Shamash the hero, all lands and the totality of all men from the upper to the lower seas, distant lands, the men of wide-spread habitations, the kings of distant mountains and remote regions who are between the upper and the lower sea with whose strength Marduk my lord had filled my hands that they might bear his yoke, I summoned together with the worshippers (*ummanat*) of Shamash and Marduk to make E-temen-an-ki." On pages 68, 69, he prays to "Ninkarraka, majestic mistress, to command before Marduk, lord of heaven and earth, the destruction of his foes and the ruin of the land of his enemies" (i, 38–49); and in 2 Col. iii, 30–47, that "Lugal-Marada, his god, may smite the evil-minded, break their weapons, devastate all the land of my enemies and slay all of them. Before Marduk, lord of heaven and earth, make my deeds appear acceptable, speak for my favor." On page 97 we read, "Nebuchadnezzar, who has learned to fear the gods, who causes to exist in the mouths of men the fear of the great gods, who keeps in order the temples of the gods." On page 98 he says, "I consulted all the hidden advice of Shamash, Ramman, and Marduk"; on page 151, "All men of wide-spread habitations I compelled to do service for the building of E-temen-an-ki." And further, on the same page: "Oh Marduk, at thy command the city of the gods has been builded, by thy mighty order that changes not may it prosper; may the work of my hands endure." On page 89, he speaks of "the numerous peoples which Marduk gave into his hands, of gathering all men under his shadow in peace, and of receiving in Babylon the tribute of the kings of all regions and nations." On page 93, he says that Marduk sent him to care for his work, that Nebo caused him to seize a scepter of justice; on page 101, he says that "his ears are attentive to the wisdom of Ninib, the hero, and that he is regardful of the sacred places of Ninib and Ishtar"; and on page 103, he says that "he adorned with gold the shrine of Sarpanit, Nebo, and Marduk, and rebuilt the temples of Nin-mah, Nebo, Ramman, Shamash, Sin, and Ninlilanna," and on page 107, "the temple of Shar-zarbi, Anu, Lugal-marada, and Ishtar." See also the prayers on pages 121, 69, 97, and 89, and for his superstition, pages 93, 99, 109, 121, 123.

gods was in his heart and in the heart of all the peoples
subject to him, so that they obeyed his will and did his
works. He prayed to them and they revealed to him
their will. His offerings to them were more numerous
than those of any who had preceded him and their
favors to him excelled those that they had granted to
any others. Through their favor, he slew all his
enemies and subdued all his foes.[1]

With reference to the belief of Nebuchadnezzar in
dreams and visions, which really lies at the foundation
of his strenuous insistence upon their correct interpretation, it may be said and emphasized that no one
can get a right view of ancient history without fully
realizing that the heroes of those times were the born
and bred children of superstition, that the greatest kings

[1] As to the demand of the wise men, that they should discover the
dream before they attempted to interpret it, Dr. Behrmann, in his
commentary on Daniel, has called attention to a parallel case mentioned
in Ibn Hisham's *Life of Muhammed*. For the benefit of those of our
readers who have not access to this work, either in its Arabic original
or in Wüstenfeld's German translation, we subjoin a translation of this
passage: "Rabia son of Nassr, was one of the weakest of the Toba kings
of Yemen. He saw a frightful vision and was exceedingly troubled by
it. So he called the prophets, enchanters, soothsayers, and astrologers
of all his kingdom and said to them: I have seen a frightful vision and am
exceedingly troubled by it. Tell me it, therefore, and its meaning.
And they said: Relate it unto us and we will tell its meaning. And he
said to them: If I tell you about it, I cannot be certain about your
telling its meaning. Behold, he cannot know its meaning who knows
not it before I tell it to him."

To this parallel, we would add another from the Arabian Nights
taken from the story of Seifelmolouk, which illustrates the rage of
an eastern potentate when his wise men have failed him. When King
Asim heard that his son was ill, he summoned the sages and astrologers
and they looked at him and prescribed for him; but he remained in the
same state for a period of three months. So King Asim was enraged
and said to the sages: "Woe to you, O dogs! Are ye all unable to cure
my son? Now, if ye cure him not immediately, I will slay you all!"
(Lane's *Arabian Nights*, ii, 290.)

20

and generals believed in dreams and visions and followed the advice of dream interpreters and soothsayers of all sorts.

For example, Ashurbanipal, the last great king of Assyria, says in his *Annal* inscription,[1] that Ashur revealed Ashurbanipal's name to Gyges, king of Lydia, in a dream, saying: "Embrace the feet of Ashurbanipal, king of Assyria, and thou shalt conquer in his name thine enemies." "On the same day on which he saw the dream, he sent his horsemen to greet me and sent this dream which he had seen through his ambassador and told it to me. From that day on, from the time that he embraced my feet, he conquered the Cimmerians." On Col. iii, 118, he says that

On the same night in which his brother Šamaššumukin rebelled against him, a seer of dreams lay down at night upon the earth and saw a dream, as follows: Upon the face of the moon stood written: "Whoever plans evil against Ashurbanipal, king of Assyria, and undertakes a battle against him, to him will I cause an evil death to come; through the lightning-like sword, firebrand, hunger, and the rage of Gira, will I put an end to his life." This I heard, and I trusted on the word of Sin, my Lord.

On Col. v, 97–103, he says that in his campaign against Ummanaldis, king of Elam, his troops feared to pass the rushing flood of the river Ididi; but Ishtar that very night caused the troops to see a dream and in it said to them, "I am going before Ashurbanipal, the king, whom my hands have formed." Trusting in this dream the troops crossed the Ididi in good spirits (*shalmish*). Finally, Col. x, 51–120, he speaks of rebuilding the *Bit-riduti*, or palace, "in which upon his bed the gods

[1] Col. ii, 95–104.

had given him favorable dreams by night and good thoughts by day."

According to Herodotus, the war of Xerxes against Greece was instigated by some most singular dreams which came to him and his uncle, Artabanus; and without the influence of these dreams, Herodotus says that the war would not have been undertaken (Bk. VII, 12–18). Alexander, also, is represented by his biographers, as having been guided in his undertakings by dreams, visions, and omens; and as having a prophet (*mantis*) always with him.[1] So, Nebuchadnezzar speaks of Ninkarrak, his beloved mistress, who gives him good visions;[2] prays to Shamash to answer him honestly by dreams and visions;[3] says that his father had cleaned the foundations of the *zikkurat* of Babylon by oracular commission[4] and that he restores the temple of Shamash who in visions announces the truthful reply;[5] and uses many other similar phrases, showing his belief in and obedience to the will of the gods as revealed in visions and responses.

Nabunaid says in the great inscription from Ur, Col. ii, 45–51, that Ishtar of Agani, his mistress, sent him a dream through which to discover the foundations of Iulbar. In the inscription from Abu-Habba, Col. i, 16–33, he says that

in the beginning of his kingdom, the gods caused him to see a dream (*ushabru' inni shutti*). Marduk, the great god, and Sin, the light of heaven and earth, stood on either side, and Marduk spoke to me: "Nabunaid, king of Babylon, with the horse of thy wagon bring bricks and build Ihulhul

---

[1] See Arrian's *Expedition of Alexander, passim.*
[2] Langdon, Nk., i;   Col. iii, 5–8.   [3] *Id.*, xii;   Col. iii, 20–22.
[4] *Id.*, xvii;   Col. i, 44–50.   [5] *Id.*, xix;   Col. vii, 62–66.

and cause Sin the good lord to occupy his dwelling place therein." Reverently spake I to the lord of the gods: "That temple which thou hast commanded to build, the Scythian surrounds it, and extensive are his troops." But Marduk said to me: "The Scythian whom thou hast mentioned—he, his land, and the kings, his helpers, are no more." In the third year, they caused him to go to war, and Cyrus, the king of Anzan his little vassal, scattered with his few troops the far-extended Scythians. Astyages the king of the Scythians he captured and brought as a prisoner to his own land.

On Col. ii, 59–61, he says that "Shamash, the great god of Ibara, showed to him the dwelling place of his heart's joy, in Tashrit, on the favorable month, on the lucky day, which Shamash and Ramman had made known to him in a dream."

Astyages, the contemporary of Nabunaid, and the grandfather of Cyrus, saw two dreams which the dream-interpreters explained as prefiguring the conquest of all Asia by his grandson, Cyrus.[1]

We may truly say that the men of that time, even the greatest of them, lived and moved in a world of dreams. The greater the man, the more important his dreams, both in consequences to himself and to those about him. Hence, we can in a measure imagine the wrath and uncontrollable indignation of Nebuchadnezzar when he finds that he cannot trust the ability of his wise men to explain the dream that troubles him. One great part of his system of kingcraft seemed to have collapsed. How could he, henceforth, find out the will of those gods on whom he depended and whose commands and wishes he followed, if this great means of revealing their will through visions and dreams was

[1] Herodotus, I, 107.

rendered nugatory through the ignorance or incapacity of the interpreters of dreams? No wonder he was beside himself with rage with what was to him, perhaps, the first consciousness of utter helplessness he had ever felt! This will account, also, for his extravagant outbursts of praise in honor of Daniel and his God. From the above statements as to the beliefs and declarations and acts of Nebuchadnezzar gathered from his own and contemporary documents, it is evident that there is no moral impossibility of his having issued the edicts recorded in the book of Daniel as having been issued by him.

As to Darius the Mede, inasmuch as no one knows anything about his character except what is to be derived from the book of Daniel, we are content to leave to the judgment of our readers the answer to the question as to whether the man whose life is portrayed for us in the sixth chapter could have been induced to issue the decree about the prayers to himself and about the punishment of being thrown into the den of lions for disobedience to the same, or the decree ordering all nations to fear the God of Daniel. We believe that the question can be answered as well by the ordinary reader as by the most learned professor. For it is not a question demanding scholarship for its answer, but simply common sense.

The only other question with reference to the moral possibility of such decrees that might be reasonably raised would arise from the doubt as to whether a king of Media or Persia would probably make a decree forbidding anyone to pray to, or make request of, any god or man save of himself, or a decree commanding the nations to fear the God of Daniel. Those who deny the possibility of such decrees, assume that enough is known

of the religious ideas of the kings of Media and Persia
to enable us to assert that such decrees would have
been utterly repugnant to their beliefs. It is assumed
that their belief was an unadulterated Zoroastrianism,
and that the Zoroastrianism of that time as well as of
later times forbade the worship of any god save Auramazda, the only and supreme god. But whatever
the general belief may have been, it can scarcely be
claimed that Cyrus, Cambyses, Smerdis the Magian,
Astyages, and the Achæmenian kings of the family of
Darius Hystaspis, or any of the kings of Persia, recognized no other god but one. For example, Cyrus in
the Cylinder Inscription says that it was Marduk, the
god of Babylon, who in his anger at Nabunaid troubled
himself to call Cyrus, king of the city of Anshan, to the
dominion of all the world (10–12). Marduk, also, en-
abled him to subdue the land of Kuti and the Scythians,
commanded him to make his expedition to Babylon and
as a friend and helper at his side, caused him to enter
Babylon without a battle, delivered Nabunaid into his
hands, and showed himself gracious unto him (13–21).
Bel and Nebo, also, are said to love his rule and to have
desired with joyful heart his dominion (22). Cyrus
concludes the inscription with the prayer that all the
gods may daily make known before Bel and Nebo the
length of his days, may speak the word of his grace, and
say to Merodach, his lord, a prayer for Cyrus the king,
who honors them, and for Cambyses his son. In the
Cyrus Chronicle, no mention of the religious views
of Cyrus occurs; but his breadth of view as to polythe-
ism is implied in the statement on the *Reverse*, line 21,
that as soon as he became king of Babylon, the gods
of Accad, which Nabunaid had caused to be carried to
Babylon, were brought back to their own cities.

Nothing further is known from the Persian and Babylonian monuments as to the religious views of Cyrus and Cambyses.

The Egyptian records, however, tell us that Cambyses came to Egypt, "willing to conform to the local worships that he found."[1]

He worshiped before the holiness of Neit with much devotion, as all the kings had done; he made great offerings of all good things to Neit, the great, the divine mother, and to all the gods who dwell in Sais, as all the pious kings had done.[2]

Darius Hystaspis is said on the same inscription to have continued the policy of Cambyses.

His Majesty, the king of Upper and Lower Egypt, Darius, ordered me [i. e., *Uza. hor. res. neit*] to go to Egypt while his Majesty was in Aram [Syria] in order to reëstablish the school of sacred scribes. His Majesty did this because he knew the virtue of this work of restoring all that he found wrecked, and to restore the names of all the gods, their temples, their endowments, and the management of their feasts forever.[3]

Nothing whatever is known from the monuments as to the views of Smerdis the Magian, and Darius Hystaspis, except what Darius tells us in his Behistun and other inscriptions. That Darius was a polytheist appears in the Persepolis Inscription H, where he prays: "Let Auramazda and the clan-gods help me," "that an enemy may not come to this country, nor an army, nor a dearth nor a rebellion; for his favor I beseech Aura-

---

[1] Petrie: *History of Egypt*, iii, 361.

[2] *Id.*, 361, 362. Translated by Petrie from the inscription on the statue of *Uza. hor. res. neit.*   [3] *Id.*, 362.

mazda and the clan-gods; may Auramazda and the clan-gods grant me this." So Xerxes, in inscriptions E, A, C, and K of Spiegel, prays that "Auramazda and the gods may protect him and his kingdom." Artaxerxes Longimanus, who ruled immediately after Xerxes, from 465 to 425 B.C., prays in the only inscription of his that we have that Auramazda, Anahita, and Mithra may protect him. Artaxerxes Ochus prays that Auramazda and Mithra may protect him and his land.

Let us remember, too, that it was not an unheard-of thing for kings to be looked upon as gods. The kings of Egypt were worshiped as such from immemorial times. The idea of Divus Cæsar is closely connected with the divine right of kings. Both gods and kings were lords. Both were absolute monarchs and autocrats. The difference between the power of a god and that of a king might easily be looked upon as one of degree and not of kind. That kings could be called gods is witnessed by Pharaohs, Ptolemies, Seleucids, Herods, and Cæsars. It is, therefore, neither unnatural, grotesque, nor improbable, that the courtiers of this Median king should have flattered him with the same ascriptions of godlike power.

Finally, whatever may have been the belief of the Persians, or of the Medes, as to one or more gods, the decrees of Darius the Mede were meant to apply not merely to the Persians and Medes among his subjects, but to the Babylonians, Assyrians, Jews, and all other nations as well. Many of these nations had many gods. The first edict of Darius forbids anyone of any nation from making request of any god or man, save of himself. This may, or may not, imply that the king himself, or any of his subjects, considered Darius to be a god.

It certainly prohibits one and all from praying to anyone for, or asking from anyone, anything, except from
the king, leaving aside the question as to the belief of
the person praying.[1]

From whatever side considered, therefore, there is
nothing in what we know of the character of either
Nebuchadnezzar or Darius the Mede, to make it impossible to believe that such decrees as those recorded
in Daniel were actually made. A *moral* impossibility
against such decrees is a figment of the objector's
imagination.

II. As to the *legal* impossibility against the issue
of such decrees, one need only say that the evidence
shows that the doctrine of the divine origin and authority of their kingship was always claimed as the ground
of the right of the kings of both Babylon and Persia
to rule.

All that we know of the kings of ancient Babylon
shows us that the laws of the land were formulated by
the kings, without any control except what was exercised by the gods, doubtless through the medium of
the priests. For example, Hammurabi speaks of the
judgments of the land which he had pronounced and the
decisions of the land which he had rendered;[2] and he
expresses the hope that future kings may pronounce
judgments for the black-headed people and render their
decisions.[3] So, also, Nebuchadnezzar refers again
and again to the fact that he had been appointed by

---

[1] The decree of Darius the Mede, commanding his subjects to tremble
before the God of Daniel, is paralleled in the Scriptures by the decree of
Cyrus recorded in 2 Ch. xxxvi, 23, and Ezra i, 2–4, by the decree of Darius recorded in Ezra vi, 8, acknowledging the God of heaven, and by
the decrees of Artaxerxes found in Ezra vii, 12–26, and Neh. xi, 23, and
ii,7, 8.

[2] Harper: *Code, Epilogue*, 68–71.   [3] *Id.*, 85–90.

Marduk to rule over all peoples; and he prays to Shamash, "who makes successful faithful decisions," to
grant him "a scepter of righteousness, a good rule,
and a just sway."[1]   So, also, the Persian kings in the
formulation and promulgation of their laws admitted
no other control than that of Auramazda.   Thus
Darius says: "These are the lands which submitted to
me; what was commanded them by me was carried out.
Through the grace of Auramazda have their lands been
constituted according to my law: as it was commanded
them by me, so was it done."[2]

The fact, also, that the kings never acknowledge
any laws of men as binding upon them, but appeal
always for their right to make decrees and for their
authority to execute them to the revealed will of the
gods whom they served, shows that they recognized
no such human laws as binding upon them.   Appeal is
made, it is true, in Daniel vi, to the laws of the Medes
and Persians; but in the same chapter it is shown how a
king could decree a law which annulled in its practice
all the laws and customs as to the worship of Auramazda, Marduk, and all the other gods, which had
prevailed up to that time.   In Esther, too, we are
shown how laws once made could be circumscribed and
circumvented by new laws which rendered their execution practically impossible.   The case of Cambyses,
recorded by Herodotus (Bk. III, 31), when "he summoned the royal judges and asked them if there was any
law permitting one who wished to marry his sister," is
not against the theory that the king was autocratic; for
the judges, while saying, "they could find no law permitting a brother to marry his sister," said also, that
"they had discovered another law which permitted the

[1] Langdon, *op cit.*, p. 99.   [2] *Beh. Ins.* i, 7, 8.

king of Persia to do whatever he pleased." In the inscriptions of both Nebuchadnezzar and Darius Hystaspis the view of *"L'état c'est moi"* (I am the state) is observable everywhere. As was said to be true of a recent writer, the fonts of type would scarcely have enough capital *I's* to enable the printer to set up the translation of the inscriptions of Nebuchadnezzar; and as for Darius, he begins every sentence with a "thus saith Darius the king." The history of Herodotus, also, shows that the kings of Persia were absolutely autocratic, monarchs beyond control, except through their superstitions and their fears.

III. As to the carrying out of these decrees having been *physically* impossible, a few words only need be said; and we shall say these words under three heads corresponding to the three principal decrees.

1. As to the decree of Nebuchadnezzar in chapter two that all the wise men of Babylon should be killed, it is perfectly certain that it was practically possible of accomplishment. The wise men were probably distinguished by a peculiar dress. At any rate, they would belong to guilds, or classes, whose members would be known by name as well as by vocation. We may compare with this edict for their destruction the similar edict of Saul to destroy the witches, and the massacre of the Magians by Darius, and the annihilation by the new régime of Egyptian kings of the followers of the new cult of the sun disk established by Amenophis IV.

2. The decree of Nebuchadnezzar in chapter iii, according to which those who refused to obey his commands were to be burned in a fiery furnace, was easy to carry out and was apparently in agreement with Assyrio-Babylonian custom. For we are told that Shamashshumukin the brother of Ashurbanipal threw

himself into a furnace of fire.[1] Ashurnaṣirpal, also, speaks frequently of the burning of people in a fire.[2]

3. The decree of Darius the Mede with regard to the den of lions was easy of execution, inasmuch as at that time lions were common in all that part of the world. The Assyrian kings were wont to hunt lions as a pastime. Thus Tiglath-Pileser I says that he killed 920 lions in one hunting expedition;[3] and Ashurnaṣirpal says that he killed at one time 120 lions and that at another time he captured 50 young lions and shut them up in Calah and in the palaces of his land in cages and let them produce their young.[4] At another time he killed 370 strong lions.[5] In his menagerie, he says, also, that he had herds of wild oxen, elephants, lions, birds, wild asses, gazelles, dogs, panthers,[6] and all animals of the mountains and of the plains, to show to his people.[7] Moreover, the Hebrew poets and prophets were familiar with lions; the people, also, made proverbs concerning them; and their heroes, such as Samson and David, are said to have slain them. So, also, the oldest story in the Aramaic language (that of Achikar from the fifth century B.C.) treats the lion as a well known animal.[8] Herodotus says that lions interfered with the march of Xerxes' army to Greece.[9] Surely, if we can believe that the Romans imported lions from Africa and threw the Christians to them in the Coliseum, we can readily believe that a Median king of Babylon may have had a den of lions into which to throw those who had

[1] KB. ii, 190.   [2] *E. g.*, KB. i, 71, 75, 77, 81, 91.
[3] KB. i, 39.   [4] *Id.*   [5] *Id.*
[6] This word *nimru* may denote also leopard or tiger.   [7] *Id.*
[8] See Sachau: *Aram. Pap.*, p. 181.   [9] Bk. VII.

disobeyed his laws.   Certainly, at least, there was no
physical impossibility in the matter.

IV.   As to its being *historically* impossible that the
edicts recorded in Daniel should have been issued, it need
only be asked what evidence there is against them.
Not one edict of Nebuchadnezzar or of any other New
Babylonian king, is recorded in any contemporaneous
document that has come down to us.   Several commands, or orders of the day, of Nebuchadnezzar are
found in the Scriptures.   Thus, at his command, Zedekiah and Ahab were roasted in the fire;[1] the children
of Zedekiah king of Judah were slain before the eyes
of their father, whose eyes were then put out;[2] and
Jehoiachin was carried to Babylon in chains and kept
in prison for thirty-seven years.[3]

In Nebuchadnezzar's own inscriptions, there are the
following orders, but no formal decrees.   He summoned (*ikbi*) the peoples that he ruled to build one
of his temples and compelled them to do service,[4] and
he regulated (*manu*) the offerings to the god Marduk.[5]
So, also, Nabunaid orders the workmen (*ummanati*) of Shamash and Marduk to build Ebarra;[6] and
commands the wise men of Babylon to seek the old
foundation of Ebarra in Sippar.   Cyrus, moreover,
proclaimed peace in Babylon just after he entered it
as conqueror.[7]   Darius I issued a grant for the rebuilding of the college of physicians at Sais.[8]   Xerxes
commanded that the inscription of Van should be made.[9]

It will thus be seen that not merely have no decrees

---

[1] Jer. xxix, 22.   [2] *Id.*, lii, 11.   [3] 2 Kings xxv, 27.
[4] Langdon, 148–151.   [5] *Id.*, 159.   [6] *Id.*, p. 241.
[7] KB. iii, 2, 135.
[8] *Zeitschrift für Ägyptische Sprache*, xxxvii, 72–74.
[9] Spiegel: *Altpers. Keilinschrift.*, p. 66.

strictly so-called of the kings of Babylon and Persia come down to us; but that few even of their commands have been preserved to us, except such as are given in the Greek historians. There must have been thousands of decrees made by these kings. What these decrees were we cannot know. To deny that the decrees recorded in Daniel were made would involve a knowledge of all the decrees that these kings made. Such a knowledge will never be ours. It is futile, therefore, to say that it was impossible that Darius made a decree about the lions, or Nebuchadnezzar about the image, or Belshazzar about the promotion of Daniel. One can at best merely deny that there is outside of Daniel any evidence that these decrees were made. This, indeed, is admitted. It is maintained, however, that lack of evidence for is not evidence against. Unless Daniel's positive and explicit statements can be disproved, their veracity stands unimpeached.

CONCLUSION

It is evident, then, that the edicts of the kings as recorded in Daniel are not merely not impossible, but that they are very probable. They certainly may have been enacted. Daniel says they were. It has not been shown, it cannot be shown, that what he says is not true. But it has been shown that it is not impossible for them to be genuine. It has been shown, further, that they very probably are genuine, inasmuch as they harmonize with what we would expect from such kings as Nebuchadnezzar, Belshazzar, and Darius the Mede and from the conditions under which they lived and reigned.

CHAPTER XVII

THE CHALDEANS

It is futile to suppose that we can define the vocabulary which the writer of an ancient document must have used. To say that a given ancient record cannot have been written before a certain date because a certain word or phrase occurs in it, is to assume a knowledge which we to-day seldom possess. Almost every new find of documents in whatever language written presents to us a number of words which before its discovery were unknown to us. Thus, the papyrus containing the Mimes of Herodas, first published in 1891, revealed a large number of Greek vocables which were not made known in other Greek works of antiquity and were not to be found in our standard classical dictionaries. So, also, the Greek papyri, ostraka, and inscriptions have enlarged our knowledge of the so-called Hellenistic Greek, until it has required the rewriting of our grammars and a readjustment of all our conceptions of the origin and use of the common Greek language of New Testament times.

The recent finds of Aramaic documents in Egypt have in like manner caused a revolution in our ideas of the Aramaic of the times of Ezra. Not merely do they necessitate a revision of all of our previous theories with regard to the orthography, phonology, morphology, and syntax of the Aramaic language; they also supplement the vocabulary with a large number of hitherto undiscovered terms. Above all, they make known to us a large number of foreign words which the Arameans of that time and country had adopted from their rulers and neighbors. So that, when we survey the whole field of foreign words in the various Aramaic dialects, and especially in Egypto-Aramaic, there are found among other peculiarities the following:

I. 1. Many foreign words are to be found in use in but one Aramaic document.

2. Some words known to be foreign can be identified with no terms found as yet in the original language from which they are known to be derived.

3. Some words, whose foreign origin is certain, are found in use in Aramaic documents long before they are found in use in the original language from which they were derived.

4. Some foreign words are found in use in an early document although they are not found again for hundreds of years.

5. Aramaic words which have been supposed to be borrowed are sometimes found to have been native, or at least to be Semitic.

6. Some are found in different documents and in different dialects, but are confined to one age and derived from one source dating from the same period.[1]

---

[1] In illustration of the above statements the following examples may be given:

I. 1. (1) *Astabid* is found in the Syriac Aramaic of Joshua the Stylite (sec. lix) and there only. It is a Persian word said by Joshua to mean *Magister*, or "master of the soldiery."

(2) *Chartummin* (Dan. ii, 10, 27; iv, 6; v, 11), denoting one kind of soothsayer, is found nowhere else in Aramaic. It seems to have been taken over by the author of Daniel from the Hebrew of Genesis, the only place where it occurs in the Hebrew of the Old Testament. It

II. 1. Further, of pure Aramaic words, some are found in the early documents which are not found again in the Aramaic dialects for hundreds of years.

2. Secondly, some are used in one dialect alone.

---

is derived apparently from the Egyptian, though not identified with any known Egyptian word.

2. (1) *Nopata*, "ship-master," of Sachau Papyrus No. 8, from Persian *Nav* "ship," and *pati*, "lord." This compound word is found in no other Aramaic document, or dialect; nor does it occur in Hebrew, nor in Phenician, early or late; nor, in fact, has it been found in Old, Middle, or New Persian. The sense of the context in Papyrus 8, and of a word of like meaning in New Persian, and the meaning of the parts of the compound, seem, however, to justify the form and meaning of the word in this place as given by Dr. Sachau.

(2) *Sewnekanin* "Syenese" of the Sac. Pap. No. 4, formed by affixing the Persian ending *kan* to the word Syene, and then putting on the Aramaic plural ending *in*.

(3) *Patbag* "delicacies" has not been found in Persian either ancient or modern.

(4) Further examples of this kind are the Greek words *kerkiesis* and *kerkesiris*, from the Ptolemaic period, composed of the Aramaic word *kerk* "village" and the nouns *Isis* and *Osiris*. These Aramaic words which are thus made known by the Greek papyri have never been found in any other Aramaic documents.

3. (1) *Dathbar* (Dan. ii, 2, 3) "judge," is certainly derived from the Persian *dath*, "law," and *bar* "to bear." It is found in Babylonian, also, but not in the Old Persian of the inscriptions, nor in the Avesta. (See Davis in *Harper Mem. Volume.*)

(2) *Artabe* a kind of measure, is said by Herodotus (Bk. I, 192) to be a Persian word taken over into Greek. Herodotus uses it before 424 B. C.; but it does not occur in any document in Old or Middle Persian. It is found under the form *ardab* in the Aramaic of the Sachau Papyrus, No. 25, 4, *et al.*

(3) *Pitgam* "command, " "word," (Dan. iii, 16, iv, 14), is found in Armenian under the form *padgam*. It is not found in the Persian of the inscriptions nor in that of the Avesta.

4. As examples of foreign words found in use in an early document of a language and not found again for hundreds of years we may note:

(1) *Zarnika* "arsenic" occurs in Sac. Pap. No. 8, and not again in Aramaic till after 200 A. D. According to Lagarde (G. A., 47, 117) this is a Persian word. (See Brockelmann, *Lex. Syr. in loc.*)

21

3. Thirdly, some are used in documents from one age alone.[1]

Since no one of these nine statements can be denied, it will be a reckless man who will assert that a word cannot have been used by a writer of the sixth century

---

(2) *Kebritha*, "brimstone" is a second example of the same kind. Sac. Pap. 9,17, 21.

(3) *Stater* is a Greek word used in the Egyptian papyri of the fifth century B.C. a number of times, but not found again in Aramaic till 200 A.D. Sac. Pap. 15, 29, 3; 34, 4, 7, 9, 60, 9; 11, 12.

5. As examples of words supposed to have been derived from one language but which have been discovered later to have been derived from another, are:

(1) *Mdy*, "a measure," which was formerly supposed to have been borrowed from the Latin *modius*. Inasmuch as it occurs in Sac. Pap. No. 8, of the year 412 B.C., it seems impossible to hold longer this view. It is better to take it from the Assyrian *madadu* or from the Hebrew *mada*, "to measure."

(2) So, *iggereth*, "letter," which Marti in his *Kurz. Gram. der Aram. Sprache*, Berlin, 1911, p. 57, compares only with Iranian, New Persian, and Greek, is surely Assyrio-Babylonian. It is found, for example, in Harper's letter 931, obv. 13, written about 650 B.C. See, also, letter 414, obv. 18.

6. As examples of words used in a certain age alone may be mentioned ארגבטא (de Voguë 26, A.D. 264)=ארקבטא in Targum to 2 Chron. xxviii, 7.

---

[1] In illustration of the statements under II, the following examples may be given:

1. As examples of Aramaic words found in the Egypto-Aramaic which are not found again for centuries, may be mentioned:

(1) *Sefina*, "ship" (Sac. Pap. 8); and

(2) *Peshka*, "handbreadth" (*id.*).

2. As examples of words used in one dialect alone may be mentioned:

(1) *Ducenarius*, found in Palmyrene alone, see de Voguë 24, 2 (A.D. 263); *id.*, 25, 2 (A.D. 263); *id.*, 26, 2 (A.D. 264).

(2) *Degel*, "regiment," found in this sense in the Egypto-Aramaic alone (Sac. Pap., 15, 29, 2 *bis*; 26, 27, 3 *bis*; 32, 2; 59, 4, 2; 60, 3, 2; 71, 12; 33, 33, 2; 58, 3, 2; 52, 1), though it occurs also in New Hebrew.

3. As examples of words used in documents of one age alone, see *gazerin* (Dan. ii. 27, iv,4, v,7, 11) for the augurs of Babylon, and *'hinâ*, " opportunity" in *Joshua the Stylite*, xiii and lix.

B.C., because that word has been found in no other known author of that time, or in fact, of any other time. We simply do not know enough to make these assertions, and we might as well admit it. To say that a writer of Aramaic of the sixth century B.C. cannot have used the word "Chaldean" or the Greek names of three musical instruments is merely to make an assertion that lies beyond the bounds of proof. The desire to find fault and to depreciate the genuineness of Daniel overrides the historico-philological judgment of those who say it. Neither history nor philology supports such an assertion, as I shall attempt in the following discussion to show. Before entering upon this discussion, however, the following *caveat* must be entered, to wit: that even though it may be impossible to demonstrate when or how certain foreign words came into a language, the time of their coming there cannot commonly be determined by the date at which they first appear in another document, whether this other document be in the language from which the word has been derived, or in the language that has derived the word. All analogy, based on records already found, would lead us to believe that hundreds of both native and foreign words were used by the ancient Arameans that have hitherto been discovered in no Aramaic document.[1] The accumulating finds in Greek teach us that there were doubtless thousands of Greek words in common use that have never been used by the classical writers

---

[1] For proof of this statement, it is only necessary to attempt to translate Sachau Papyrus 8 which is full of Persian and Egyptian words, many of them of unknown meaning; and also of good Aramaic words, as to which Prof. Sachau well remarks: "was man sonst aus dem Aramäischen oder Hebräischen weiss und zum Vergleich heranziehen kann, ist nicht genügend, um das Verständnis dieser Urkunde zu erschliessen." (See Sachau: *Aram. Pap.*, p. 47.)

that have come down to us. Any one of these words might have been borrowed by the Arameans and others who came in contact with the Greeks who used them. Again, new discoveries in the Egyptian, Babylonian, Persian, and all other ancient languages are always revealing to us afresh our ignorance of the fullness of their vocabularies, and of the origin and use of their words. Cognizant of this universal lack of knowledge of the limitations of the vocabularies of ancient languages, and refusing to be bound by mere assertions that a given word cannot have been used by a given writer at a given time, inasmuch as we do not happen to know that some other writer of that same time or of some time previous used it, I pass on to a consideration of the objections made to the book of Daniel on the assumption that its author has employed certain words which could not have been used in the sixth century B. C. I shall, at present, confine myself to a discussion of the word "Chaldean," as to which the critics of Daniel assert that it cannot have been used as early as the sixth century B. C. to denote the Babylonian astrologers, inasmuch, they say, as it is not found in use in this sense until a much later time.

OBJECTIONS STATED

Professor Cornill says: "The manner in which the term *kasdim* (Chaldean), exactly like the Latin Chaldæus, is used in the sense of soothsayer and astrologer (ii, 2, 4, 5, 10; iv, 4; v, 7, 11) is *inconceivable* at a time when the Chaldeans were the ruling people of the world."[1]

Professor Driver states the objection as follows:

[1] *Introduction to the Old Testament*, p. 387.

The "Chaldeans" are synonymous in Daniel (i, 4; ii, 2; etc.) with the caste of wise men. This sense "is unknown to the Ass. Bab. language, has, wherever it occurs, formed itself after the end of the Babylonian empire, and is thus an indication of the post-exilic composition of the Book" (Schrader, *The Cuneiform Inscriptions and the Old Testament*, 2nd edition, p. 429). It dates, namely, from a time when practically the only "Chaldeans" known belonged to the caste in question (comp. Meinhold, *Beiträge*, p. 28).[1]

Professor Meinhold, to whom Dr. Driver refers, says in the passage cited as follows:

Wonderful above all things appears to us the use of the name *Kasdim*. For while *Kasdim* everywhere else in the Old Testament is a designation of the Babylonian people, we find here alongside of this common meaning (iii, 8: v, 30) that of Magians which is also known from the profane historians. As to what particular kind of Magians these are is not clear, since *Kasdim* is at times the general designation of the totality of all classes of wise men (ii, 10) and at times is a special designation of a division of the same (iv, 4; v, 10). This striking appearance is only to be explained by the fact that the Jews of the exile had first learned something of the Chaldeans as a special division of the wise men within the totality of the Babylonian nation. Everywhere in the Old Testament *kasdim* appears rather as the most general name of the whole people.

The more specific meaning, however, shows that the knowledge of the kingdom of the Chaldeans had only been retained in the memory of the priests and wise men of succeeding times. While everything else had soon passed away and disappeared in the course of time, the castes, because of a religious kind, could still long be retained in remembrance. They were the only remains of the Chaldeans. They were the Chaldeans. Thus is explained the

[1] *Literature of the Old Testament*, p. 498.

later use of the name. An exilic author could, however, not write thus.[1]

ASSUMPTIONS INVOLVED

There are here the following assumptions:

I. That the term *kasdim* to denote the ruling nation in Babylon passed away from the remembrance of succeeding times, while the use of it to denote the wise men remained.

II. 1. That the original of the word *kasdim*, in the sense of a priestly class, is not found on the monuments.

2. That the word Chaldean as used for priest, or wise man, is of the same origin, or meaning, as the word Chaldean as used to denote a people.

3. That the absence of the term in its priestly sense from the Assyrio-Babylonian monuments proves that it was not employed by the Babylonians in common speech to denote a certain class of wise men.

III. That the apparent absence of the word from the Assyrio-Babylonian language is a proof that it was not used in the Aramaic language.

ANSWER TO ASSUMPTIONS

I. Taking up the assumptions in the order named, we shall discuss the first under two heads: first, the use of the word to denote a people, and secondly, its use to denote a priestly class.

---

[1] It is admitted that in the Scriptures outside of Daniel, the word always denoted a people.

The places where it is employed in this sense are, Gen. xi, 28, 31; xv, 7; 2 Kings, xxiv, 2; xxv, 4, 5, 10, 13, 24, 25, 26; 2 Chron. xxxvi, 17; Neh. ix, 7; Job i, 17; Is. xiii, 19; xxiii, 13; xliii, 14; xlvii, 1, 5; xlviii, 14, 20; Jer. xxi, 4, 9; xxii, 25; xxiv, 5; xxv, 12; xxxii, 4, 5, 24, 25, 28, 29, 43; xxxiii, 5; xxxv, 11; xxxvii, 5, 8, 9, 10, 11, 13, 14; xxxviii, 2, 18, 19, 23; xxxix, 5, 8; xl, 9, 10; xli, 3, 18; xliii, 3; l, 1, 8, 10, 25, 35, 45; li, 4, 24, 35, 54; lii, 7, 8, 14, 17; Ezek., i, 3; xi, 24; xii, 13; xxiii, 14, 15. 16. 23; Hab. i, 6.

1. It is admitted that in the Scriptures outside of Daniel the word always denoted a people. In Daniel, also, it is employed to denote a people; once in the Hebrew portion, chapter ix, 1, where it is said that Darius had been "made king over the realm of the Chaldeans"; and once in the Aramaic, in chapter v, 30, where it is said that "Belshazzar the Chaldean king (or king of the Chaldeans) was slain." In Daniel i, 4, the Chaldeans *may* be the people, but it is more probable that the priestly class is meant.

On the monuments we find this sense, with one or two possible exceptions, only in those inscriptions which come from Assyria. The documents from the Persian, Greek, and Parthian periods never use it to denote a people; and those from the Babylonian of the time preceding Cyrus never employ it in this sense, save perhaps once. This exception is in an inscription of Nabunaid addressed to the gods Shamash and Ai of Sippar, in which he mentions the cedars (*erinu*) of Amanus and of the land of Kal-da.[1] Since we have no evidence from any other source that cedars were a product of the Chaldea south of Babylon, it is most probable that some other land with a similar name was meant by Nabunaid. It is a most remarkable circumstance that none of the documents from Babylonia, not even those of the Chaldean kings themselves, with the possible exception of this one instance just noted, ever speak of either the Chaldean land or people.

The Assyrians, however, frequently mention both the land and the people of the Kaldu, from the time of Ashurnasirabal (885–860 B.C), down to the time of Ashurbanipal (668–626 B.C.).

After the time of Ashurbanipal neither the land nor

[1] Zehnpfund-Langdon, NK, p. 231; Col. i, 23.

the people of the Chaldeans is mentioned till the time of Sophocles[1] and Herodotus (464–424 B. C.), the latter of whom says that the Chaldeans served among the Assyrians who went against Greece in Xerxes' army, under Otaspes, son of Artachæus.[2] The Chaldeans of whom Xenophon speaks[3] were near the Black Sea and may possibly have been the descendants of the Chaldeans of Bit-Yakin whom Sargon carried away and settled in Kummuh. The next writer to speak of the southern Chaldeans is Berosus, himself a Chaldean priest who lived in the time of Alexander the Great. In his *Chaldean History*, he speaks of a great number of people as inhabiting Chaldea, and of ten early kings of the Chaldeans who ruled before the time of Abraham, and of the Chaldean language, and of Chaldean kings beginning with Nabonasar.[4] He says further that Nebuchadnezzar exceeded in his exploits all that had reigned before him in Babylon and Chaldea and that his father, Nabopolassar, was king of Babylon and of the Chaldeans.[5] Strabo, who was born about 54 B. C., says in his *Geography*[6] that there was a tribe of Chaldeans and a district of Babylonia inhabited by them near the Persian Gulf; and further, that Babylonia was bounded on the south by the Persian Gulf and the Chaldeans.[7] Again, he says that the Babylonians and the nation of the Chaldeans possessed the country at the mouth of the Euphrates.[8] Again, he speaks of a city called Gerra in a deep gulf inhabited by Chaldean fugitives from Babylon,[9] and of the marsh lands of the Chaldeans made by the overflowing of the Euphrates.[10]

---

[1] 468 B. C., *Fragments*, 564. [2] Bk. VII, 63.
[3] Bk. IV, 3. [4] See Cory, *Fragments*, pp. 21–36.
[5] Josephus; *Contra Apion.*, i, 19. [6] Bk. XVI, 1. [7] *Id.*
[8] *Id.*, xvi, 3. [9] *Id.* [10] *Id.*, xvi, 4.

Josephus, in his *Antiquities of the Jews*,[1] calls Nebuchadnezzar "king of Babylon and Chaldea," and speaks of the "kings of Chaldea."[2] Alexander Polyhistor, who lived in the second century B.C., speaks of Saracus king of the Chaldeans, and of Nabopolassar who obtained the empire of the Chaldeans.[3] Polyhistor states, also, that after the deluge, Evixius held possession of the country of the Chaldeans during the period of four *neri;* that 49 kings of the Chaldeans ruled Babylon for 458 years; that there was a king of the Chaldeans whose name was Phulus (Pul); that Sardanapalus the Chaldean reigned 21 years; and that Neglisarus reigned over the Chaldeans four years.[4]

It will be seen from the above references that the people and country of the Chaldeans are mentioned on the monuments as existing from about 850 B. C., and in the Greek historians as existing from immediately after the flood, to the time of Christ.

2. Secondly, we shall consider the use of the word "Chaldean" to denote a priestly class. In this sense the word is found in Daniel in the following places.

(a) In Hebrew, (1) in i, 4, where it is said that the king of Babylon commanded the master of his eunuchs to teach certain Jewish youths "the *language* and the tongue of the Chaldeans."

(2) In ii, 2, "the king commanded to call the magicians, and the enchanters, and the sorcerers, and the Chaldeans, for to tell the king his dreams."

(3) In ii, 4, the Chaldeans speak to the king "in the Aramaic language."

(b) In Aramaic, (1) in ii, 5, "The king answered and said to the Chaldeans."

---

[1] Bk. X, chapter ix, 7. [2] *Id.* X, chapter x, 2.
[3] Cory: *Fragments*, p. 59. [4] *Id.*, 63.

(2) In ii, 10, "The Chaldeans answered before the king and said, There is not a man upon the earth that can show the king's matter, forasmuch as no king, lord, or ruler, hath asked such a thing of any magician, or enchanter, or Chaldean."

(3) In iii, 8, "Certain Chaldeans came near and brought accusation against the Jews."

(4) In iv, 7, Nebuchadnezzer says, "Then came in the magicians, the enchanters, the Chaldeans, and the soothsayers; and I told the dream before them."

(5) In v, 7, "The king [Belshazzar] cried aloud to bring in the enchanters, the Chaldeans, and the soothsayers. The king spake and said to the wise men of Babylon," etc.

(6) In v, 11, 12, the queen says that Nebuchadnezzar had made Daniel "master of the magicians, enchanters, Chaldeans, and soothsayers; forasmuch as an excellent spirit, and knowledge, and understanding, interpreting of dreams, and showing of dark sentences, and dissolving of doubts, were found in the same Daniel."

In the classical writers, it is used in this sense first by Herodotus, who flourished from 464 to 424 B. C.; that is, contemporaneously with the whole reign of Artaxerxes I, called Longimanus, the successor of Xerxes the son of Darius Hystaspis. It will be noted that Herodotus died about one hundred years after the death of Cambyses the son of Cyrus, and little more than a century after the death of the Daniel who is the hero and supposed author of our book. Herodotus never mentions a Chaldean people save once, and that incidentally; but he does speak at length of the Chaldean priests. His statements are as follows:

In the middle of each division of the city of Babylon, fortified buildings were erected, in one of which was the precinct of Jupiter Bel, which in my time was still in existence. In the midst of this precinct was a tower of eight emplacements and in the uppermost of these a spacious temple in which was a large couch handsomely furnished, but no statue; nor did any mortal pass the night there except only a native woman, chosen by the god out of the whole nation, as the *Chaldeans, who are priests of this deity,* say. These same priests assert, though I cannot credit what they say, that the god himself comes to this temple. There is, also, another temple below, within the precinct at Babylon; in it is a large golden statue of Jupiter erected, and near it is placed a large table of gold, the throne also and the step are of gold, which together weigh 800 talents *as the Chaldeans affirm.* Outside the temple is a golden altar and another large altar where full-grown sheep are sacrificed; for on the golden altar only sucklings may be offered. On the great altar the Chaldeans consume yearly a thousand talents of frankincense when they celebrate the festival of this god. There was also at that time within the precincts of this temple a statue of solid gold, twelve cubits high. I, indeed, did not see it. I only relate what is said by the Chaldeans.

Ctesias, the Greek physician of Artaxerxes II, who wrote about 400 B. C., speaks of the Chaldeans as having hindered Darius Hystaspis from viewing the dead body of Sphendidates the Magian.[1] Aristotle, who was the tutor of Alexander the Great, mentions the Chaldean astrologers.[2]

Arrian, in his great work on *The Expedition of Alexander,* has much to say about these Chaldean priests. This Arrian was a Greek historian, a Roman general, prefect of Cappadocia under Hadrian, who reigned from 117 to 138 A.D. He was conversant with philosophy,

---

[1] See *Fragments* by Bähr, pp. 68 and 140.   [2] See *Frag.,* 30.

being a pupil of Epictetus and publisher of his lectures. He wrote a treatise on military tactics, another on the geography of the Black Sea, and another on that of the Red Sea, and was a friend and correspondent of Pliny the Younger. He was, therefore, well fitted to write a history of the expedition of Alexander against Persia. This he has done in seven volumes which he claims in his proem to be based upon a work by Aristobulus, who marched along with Alexander; and on another work by Ptolemy Lagus, who not only marched with him, but, as Arrian says, "since he was a king, it would have been shameful for him to lie." Both, he says, wrote without expectation of any reward, since Alexander was already dead when they composed their memoirs. So Arrian pronounces them both most worthy of credence. Trained geographer, philosopher, historian, politician, general, and writer, as he was, he might well be trusted to have transcribed the essence at least of his authorities; and having proclaimed and praised the truthfulness and trustworthiness of his sources, it may be supposed that he tried himself also to be truthful. Senator, consul, and prefect of Rome, it is altogether probable that he was a capable, as well as an experienced, judge of documentary, as well as oral, testimony.

Arrian, then, says with reference to the Chaldeans, as follows:

Alexander, having hastened from Arbela, went forward straight to Babylon; and when he was not far from Babylon he led his army drawn up in battle array; and the Babylonians in a body met him with their priests and rulers bearing gifts as each one was able, and surrendering the city, and the acropolis, and the treasure. And Alexander, having come to Babylon, gave orders to build again the temples which Xerxes had destroyed, both the altar and also the temple of Bel, who is the god whom the Babylonians deem especially worthy of honor. There indeed, also, he met the Chaldeans, and whatever seemed good to the Chaldeans with reference to religious matters in Babylon he did; both other things, and to Bel, also, he sacrificed as these directed.[1]

Later, he says that when Alexander was returning from India and was marching to Babylon,

the wise men of the Chaldeans met him and, drawing him aside from his companions, besought him to hold up his advance on Babylon; for an oracle had come to them from the god Bel that his going to Babylon at that time would not be for his good. Alexander answered them: "Who guesses well, is the best prophet." Whereupon the Chaldeans said, "Do thou, oh king! not go to the west nor come hither leading an army of occupation; but go rather to the east." (Bk. VII, 16.)

He says further that

Alexander was suspicious of the Chaldeans, because at that time they managed the affairs of Bel, and he thought that the so-called prophecy was meant for their profit rather than for his good.[2] Refusing to follow their advice but attempting to evade the consequences predicted, he nevertheless did as their prediction had implied that he would.[3]

Berosus, our next witness, informs us concerning himself, that he lived in the age of Alexander the son of Philip. He speaks of the writings of the Chaldeans[4] and of their wisdom,[5] and "of a certain man among them in the tenth generation after the deluge who was

[1] Bk. III, 16. [2] Id., 17. [3] Id., 21–27.
[4] Cory, Fragments, p. 26. [5] Id., 32.

renowned for his justice and great exploits and for his skill in the celestial sciences";[1] and of their having been accurately acquainted only since the time of Nabonassar with the heavenly motions.[2] He says that the affairs of Nebuchadnezzar had been faithfully conducted by Chaldeans and that the principal person among them had preserved the kingdom for him after the death of his father and before his return from Palestine.[3]

Megasthenes, who lived and occupied important official positions under Seleucus Nicator, wrote about 300 B.C., that the Chaldeans related certain facts about Nebuchadnezzar's having been preserved by some god, so as to foretell to them the downfall of Babylon through the Medes and Persians.[4]

Abydenus, a pupil of Berosus, speaks of Pythagoras, who lived about the time of Daniel, as a "follower of the wisdom of the Chaldeans."[5]

Strabo, who flourished from 54 B.C., one of the most reliable of ancient writers, says that

in Babylonia there was a dwelling place for the native philosophers, called Chaldeans, who are for the most part concerned with astronomy; but some also are given to casting nativities, which the others do not permit. There is also a tribe of the Chaldeans and a district of Babylonia near to the Arabs and to the Persian Sea. And there are of the Chaldean astronomers several kinds. For some are called Orchenoi, and others Borsippenoi, and there are others more, as it were, in sects, holding different dogmas concerning the same things.[6]

Diodorus Siculus, who lived in the time of Cæsar and Augustus, in his History, Book II, 9, says that

[1] *Id.*, 16.   [2] *Id.*   [3] *Id.*, 89.
[4] Cory: *Fragments*, 44–45.   [5] Cory, 65.   [6] XVI, I.

"the Chaldeans made observations of the stars from the
tower of the temple of Jupiter, whom the Babylonians
call Bel." Again, he says in chapter 24, that

Belesus, who understood how to destroy the hegemony
of the Assyrians, was the most notable of the priests whom
the Babylonians call Chaldeans. Having, then, the greatest experience in astrology and soothsaying, he foretold
the future to the multitude just as it fell out.

In chapter 29, he says

that it does not seem out of place for him to narrate a few
words concerning those who were called in Babylon Chaldeans and their antiquity, that he may omit nothing worthy
of mention. The Chaldeans, then, being the most ancient
Babylonians have a position in the determination of the
policy of government something like that of the priests of
Egypt. For being assigned to the service of the gods they
pass their whole life in philosophizing, having the greatest
glory in astrology. They pay much attention, also, to soothsaying, making predictions concerning future events, and
purifications, and sacrifices, and with various kinds of incantations they attempt to bring about the avoidance of evil
and the accomplishment of good. And they have experience also in divination by birds and show the interpretation
of dreams and omens. Not unwisely, also, do they act in
matters concerning hieroscopy and are supposed accurately
to hit the mark. This philosophy is handed down from
father to son in a race which is freed from all other services.

Finally, Quintus Curtius Rufus, probably of the
second century A.D., says that early in the expedition of
Alexander "The Chaldeans had explained a singular
dream of Pharnabazus to mean that the empire of the
Persians would pass over to the Greeks."[1] Further

[1] See the *Life and Expedition of Alexander the Great*, III, iii, 6.

on, he says that "as Alexander was approaching Babylon, he was met by Bagophanes, the custodian of the
citadel, who was followed by gifts of herds of sheep and
horses; and next to these came the Magi, singing their
native song according to their custom. After these,
the Chaldeans and not only the seers (priests) of the
Babylonians, but even the skilled workmen, advanced
with the harps of their own class; the last mentioned
were wont to sing the praises of the kings; the Chaldeans
to manifest the movements of the stars, and the fixed
changes of the seasons. Then, last of all, marched
the Babylonian horsemen, with their own peculiar dress
and with special horse-trappings, required more for
luxury than for magnificence."[1] Further he says that

"when Alexander, on his return from India, was 300 stadia
from the city [Babylon], the seers warned him not to enter
since there was a portent of danger. But he scorned
their predictions as being vain and mere fabrications.
Therefore when the envoys had been given audience he set
sail for the land of the Arabs, laughing at the Chaldeans,
who predicted danger in the city."[2]

Afterwards, when Alexander was brought dead to Babylon, it was the Babylonians who "looked down, some
from the walls, others each from the roof on his own
house, to see the funeral cortège pass through the
streets";[3] but the Egyptians and Chaldeans were
"ordered to attend the dead body in their own
fashion."[4]

From the above extracts, it is evident that Quintus
Curtius, whatever may have been the sources of his
information as to the life of Alexander, sought to make
a clear distinction between the Babylonians and the

[1] Id., V, i, 4.   [2] Id., X, iv, 11.   [3] Id., X, v, 14.   [4] Id., X, x, 26.

Chaldeans who were in Babylon at the time of Alexander's conquest of Persia. According to him, therefore, the former were the people and the latter were the priestly class as early as 330 B.C.

Summing up, then, the testimony of the ancient classical writers who have written about Babylon, we find that they make a distinction between the Babylonian, or Chaldean, people or peoples on the one hand, and the Chaldean priests or astrologers on the other; and that this distinction is held by them to have existed from the earliest times to the time in which they respectively wrote.

II. We shall consider together the assumptions as to the origin, meaning, and use of the word Chaldean upon the Babylonian monuments.

It may justly be asked in view of all the references in the classical writers of Greece and Rome to the Chaldeans as the wise men of Babylon, if there is no evidence on the monuments to corroborate the other authorities. If there were no evidence on the monuments from Babylon, we must remember, that the case would be the same as to the Chaldeans as astrologers that it is as to the Chaldeans as a nation. But we are in better case with regard to the use of the term to denote astrologers, than we are with regard to its use to denote a nation. For we are still inclined to believe that a good argument can be made in favor of the *galdu* of the inscriptions being the same as the Chaldean priest of classical sources and of the Chaldeans of Daniel. It may be argued:

First, the *galdu* in Babylonian would according to the laws of phonetic change become *kaldu* in Assyrian, *Chaldaios* in Greek, and *kasday* in Hebrew and Aramaic. The change of *g* to *k* is found in the word *e-gal*, "great

22

house," "palace," or "temple," which becomes *e-kal* in Assyrian, and *hekal* in Hebrew. Compare also the Greek *kamelos*, "camel," in Assyrian, *gammalu*.[1]

The change from *l* to *s* before *d* is found in the Hebrew *Kasdim* for the Assyrian *Kaldi*, from an original Babylonian *Kaldu* or *Kasdu*. After the analogy of the change from *Kaldu* to *Kasd* the Hebrew would change *galdu* to *kasd*. *K* in Assyrian and Hebrew frequently is represented by *ch* in Greek and Latin. So that there is no reasonable ground for denying that *galdu* might be Chaldean, as far as the phonetics are concerned.

Moreover, it shows an ingenuity almost surpassing belief in a writer of the middle of the second century B. C., who derived from the Greeks the notion of what the *Chaldaioi* were, to suppose that he would deliberately change *Kaldim* to *Kasdim*. This was a law of change in Babylonian, Assyrian, and Hebrew, but not as between Greek and Hebrew, or Greek and Aramaic.[2]

The Aramaic versions and dialects outside of Daniel consistently use *Kaldi* to denote the astrologers and *Kasdi* to denote the people of Chaldea.[3] The author of Daniel, forsooth, was the only writer who confounded the distinction between them! It seems more likely that an author living in Babylon in a time when words which had a sibilant, or an *l*, before a dental were often

---

[1] This change of Assyrio-Babylonian *g* to Hebrew and Aramaic *k* is not so frequent as the change of *k* to *g*. The latter is found in Mukina—Mugin; Sharukin—Sargon; Tikulti—Tiglath; Mannuki—Manug; Shakan-Sagan.

[2] In words derived from the Greek which have an *l* before a dental, the New Hebrew, the Syriac, and the Aramaic of the Talmuds, never change the *l* to *s* or *sh*. See Dalman *Aram-neuhebr. Wörterbuch*, pp. 53, 188, 226, 228, 320, 321, and 364; and Brockelmann's *Lex. Syr.*, *in loc.*

[3] See dictionaries of Levy and Jastrow, *sub verbis*.

written in both ways (as *iltu, ishtu; iltanish, ishtanish*) would have written *Kasdim* for *Kaldim*, than that an author living in the second century in Palestine and deriving a word and its meaning from the Greek should have changed *ld* to *sd*, contrary to the usage of the Greek in words derived from the Aramaic languages, and of the Arameans and Hebrews in words derived from the Greek.[1]

Secondly, that old Accadian double words like *gal* and *du* were often taken over into Semitic, still preserving the double sense of the original compound words, may be abundantly shown. E. g., *e* = "house," *gal* = "great," *e-gal* = "palace" (Hebrew, "temple," also); *e* = "house," *kur* = "land" or "mountain," *e-kur* = "temple of the land, or mountain"; *dup* = "tablet," *sar* = "writer," *dupsar* = "writer of tablets"; and many others.

Thirdly, that the meaning of *galdu* can be reconciled with the duties of the Chaldeans is certainly probable; at least, we can see no sufficient reason for denying on this ground that Gal-du and Chaldean are the same.

III. The last assumption, that is, that "the absence of the term from the Babylonian monuments[2] would prove that it could not have been used by the Aramean and Hebrew writers," is a most unjustifiable assertion. We could multiply analogies to show that writers in foreign languages often use terms when speaking of a given nation and its affairs, which a writer in the language of the nation spoken of would never use. For example and in point, Dr. Meinhold, in his statement of this very objection to the book of Daniel of which we

---

[1] Cf. Brockelmann's *Lex. Syr.*, pp. 17–21, 29, and Dalman's *Aram.-neuhebr. Wörterbuch.*, 29–37.

[2] That is, in monuments written in the Babylonian language.

are now speaking, uses the term "Magian" as a designation of the wise men of Babylon. Yet this word never occurs on any Babylonian monument and is never found in Babylonian at all except in the Babylonian recension of the Behistun Inscription of Darius Hystaspis. There Darius used it correctly to describe the Magian usurper Gumatu, or Smerdis. But why should Dr. Meinhold call the Babylonian wise men by this Medo-Persian word? Simply because the term has been adopted into the German language as a designation of a class of heathen priests practicing certain arts. So, also, the Arameans and Hebrews probably used the word Chaldean to denote a certain class of wise men in Babylon, who practiced certain arts. They may have derived the term from *galdu*, "the master-builder," or from the *Kaldu*, the conquering tribe of Nabopolassar, because of certain arts practised by them. The term Chaldean to denote this class may not have been used in Babylonian at all any more than Magian was. But will anyone tell us by what term this class should have been designated by an Aràmean writer of the sixth century B.C.? If we go to the Syriac for information, no term will be found that would cover such a class of star-gazers and dream interpreters and fortune tellers as the Chaldeans of Daniel probably were. No other Aramaic dialect will help us to a term. The ancient versions suggest no other equivalent designation to take its place. Pray, what term would the critics of Daniel suggest as a substitute? The ancient Hebrews, the Arameans, the Greeks and Romans, early and late, all use the word Chaldean in some form or other to denote this special class of Babylonian wise men. It is appropriate, distinctive, and general, in its meaning and use. As to its origin and antiquity no one knows for certain anything *except negatively.* And let it be remembered that no amount of negative evidence from the *Babylonian* can ever countervail the positive evidence to be derived from the fact of the use of this term in the Aramaic of the book of Daniel.

CONCLUSION

The conclusion of the discussion about the use of the word "Chaldean" by the author of Daniel is that there is no evidence to show that he does not employ the term consistently and that it may not have been used in Aramaic as a designation of a class of Babylonian wise men, or priests, as early as the sixth century B.C.

Excursus on the Chaldeans

All are agreed that the sign *gal* may mean in Semitic Babylonian *rabu*, "great, chief." The sign *du* denotes the idea of "making," of " building," or "constructing," being used in Assyrian for such words as *banu, epešu, šakanu, zakapu, elu, emu, nadu, pataku,* and *ritu.* The compound *gal-du* might, therefore, be rendered "*rab banie* in Babylonian, *i. e.,*" chief of the builders," or "constructors," and the plural would be "the chiefs of the constructors." So far all interpreters would probably agree. It differs from *dim-gal = banu-rabu* which means "chief builder"; just as *bitu rabu,* "great house," differs from *rab biti,* "major domo," or "master of the house."

The standard passages to determine the use of *dim-gal* are the *Nies* inscription of Sargon,[1] the *Prism* inscription of Sennacherib, Col. vi, 40–46, the building inscriptions of Esarhaddon, and the *Zikkurat* inscription of Nabopolassar, Col. ii, 14–37. The first reads:

[1] See the *Yale Oriental Series,* Babylonian Texts, i, 62.

The king says that " according to the command of the god Mur the *dim-gal-la* and *ummanu* knowing the command (or work), with bright bricks he (*i. e.*, Sargon) elevated its turrets (*i. e.*, of the temple of Eanna) and completed its work." [1]

The *Prism* inscription of Sennacherib reads:

In a favorite month, on an auspicious day, I caused to be made on this foundation in the wisdom of my heart a palace of *pilu*-stone and cedar-wood in the style of the land of the Hittites and as the seat of my lordship, by the art of skillful master-builders (*tim-kal-li-e*), a lofty palace in the style of Assyria which far surpassed the former one in size and ornamentation.

Esarhaddon mentions them twice. In the first passage, he says "The wise master-builders (*dim-gal-li*) who form the plan, I assembled and laid the foundation of Esaggil and fixed its cornerstone . . . I made its measurements according to its earlier plans." [2] In the second passage he speaks of "(the wise architects) who formed the plan." [3]

In Nabopolassar's *Zikkurat* inscription we read:

By the commission of Ea, by the advice of Marduk, by the command of Nebo and Nerba, in the great-heartedness which God my creator created within me, in my great chamber I called a council. My skilled workmen (lit. the wise sons of *ummani*) I sent out. I took a reed and with a measuring reed I measured the dimensions. The master-

[1] *Ina shipir ili Mur amel Dim-gal-la u um-me-e (i.e., ummanu)* [1] *mudie shipri ina libitti ellitim reshushu ullimi ushaklil shipirshu.*

[2] Col. iv, K. 192, Rev. lines 14–17. See Meissner-Rost, *Bauinschriften Asarhaddons*, B.A. iii, 246–247.   [3] *Id.*, K. 2711, 32.

[1] See *Brünnow's Classified List*, No. 3912.

builders (*ameluti dim-gal-e*) fixed the limits and established the boundaries. According to the advice of Shamash, Ramman, and Marduk I made decisions and in my heart I kept them. I treasured in memory the measurements. The great gods by a decision caused me to know the future days.

Before discussing these passages, we shall give two more, which do not mention the *dimgals*, but do speak of the wise *ummani* and the fortunate day and month. These are both from the time of Nabunaid. The first reads as follows:

The pinnacles of the temple [of the sun-god of Sippara] had bowed down and its walls were leaning [?]. I saw it and was much afraid and terrified. In order to lay aright the foundation, to establish the boundaries of his temple, to build a holy place and chambers suitable for his godhead, I prayed daily to him and yearly brought offerings, and sought from him my mandate (*purussia aprussu*). Shamash, the exalted lord, from of old had called me; Shamash and Ramman had laid upon me the grace of the fulfillment of my righteous mandate, of the accomplishment of my mission, and the establishment of the temple. I trusted entirely to the righteous mandate, which cannot be gainsaid, and grasped the hand of Shamash, my lord, and caused him to dwell in another house. Right and left, before and behind, I searched the holy place and the heart of the chambers. I assembled the elders of the city, the sons of Babylon, the wise mathematicians, the inmates of the house of Mummu [= the dwelling place of Ea, the god of wisdom] the guardian of the decree (*piristi*) of the great gods, establisher of the royal person [?]. I ordered them to the council and thus I spoke to them: Search for the old foundation; seek for the sanctuary of Shamash, the judge, that I may make an enduring house for Shamash and for Malkatu, my lords. With hearty prayer to Shamash, my lord, with supplications to the great gods, all the sons of the wise men (*ummanu*) laid bare the old foundation. . . . With joy and rejoicing I laid on the old platform, I strengthened its underground supports and raised its pinnacles like a lofty peak.[1]

The second reads thus:

In the tenth year, in the days of my happy reign, in my enduring kingdom, which Shamash loves, Shamash the great lord thought on the seat [of his heart's desire], he wanted to see the top of the tower of his habitation (?) raised higher than it had been before. . . . He commanded me, Nabunaid, the king, his care-taker, to restore Ebarra to its former place, to make it as in the days of old the seat of his heart's desire. At the word of Marduk, the great lord, the winds were let loose, the floods came, swept away the débris, uncovered the foundations, and revealed their contour.

Nabunaid, having been commanded to restore the temple, says:

I raised my hands and prayed to Marduk; O Bel! chief of the gods, prince Marduk, without thee no dwelling is founded, no boundaries are prepared. Without thee, what can anyone do? Lord, at thy exalted command may I do what seemeth good to thee. To build the holy place of Shamash, Ramman, and Nergal,—even that temple I sought, and a gracious oracle for the length of my days and the building of the temple they wrote. . . . Sufficient grace for the peace of my days . . . he fixed in my commission (*tertiia*) . . . the workmen (*ummanati*) of Shamash and Marduk . . . to build Ebarra, the glorious sanctuary, the lofty chamber, I sent. A wise workman (*ummanu mudu*) sought in the place where the foundation had appeared, and recognized the insignia (*simatim*). In a favorable month,

[1] KB. iii, ii, 110–112.   [2] KB. iii, ii, 90, 91.

on a lucky day, I began to lay the bricks of Ebarra . . .
according to the insignia upon (the foundation) of Hammurabi the old king. I rebuilt that temple as it had been
before.[1]

From these passages it is evident that the *dimgals*
made the measurements and designed the ornamenta-
tions of the palaces and temples. Arrian tells us that:

the expenses of the restoration of the temple of Bel which
Alexander had ordered were to be met by the revenues of the
lands and treasures which had been dedicated to that
god. These treasures had been placed under the steward-
ship of the Chaldeans, and had formerly been used for the
refitting of the temple and the sacrifices which were offered
to the god.[2]

The Chaldeans, then, of the time of Alexander (whom
Arrian in the same chapter carefully distinguished
from the Babylonians who had been ordered to clear
away the dust from the old foundations), not merely
prepared the sacrifices and farmed the revenues,
but directed the repairs and restorations of the temple
of Bel.

These skilled workmen, the wise sons of the *ummani*,
these wise *dimgals*, who fixed the limits and established
the boundaries, and by whose art (*shipru*, "commission") the size and ornamentation of the temples and
palaces were determined;—all acted under the commission (*shipru*) of Ea, according to the advice of Marduk
and the command of Nebo. As Bezaleel and Aholiab
did all things according to the pattern (*tabnith*) of the
tabernacle and the pattern of the instruments "which
the Lord had showed them in the mount," so, these

[1] KB. iii, ii, 90–92. See also, BA. iii, 234–237.
[2] *Exped. of Alex.*, vii, 17.

architects and artists of Nineveh and Babylon are said to have erected their buildings after the commissions, the advice, and the orders, of the gods. Just as God filled Bezaleel with wisdom and understanding and knowledge in all kinds of workmanship and gave to everyone who was wise of heart a heart of wisdom[1] to execute the work of the tabernacle; so, the *dimgals* and *ummanus* of Sennacherib and Esarhaddon and Nabopolassar and Nabunaid are said to have had wisdom and skill for their work from Ea, the god of wisdom, and Nebo the builder of cities, and Marduk the lord of all. These wise master-builders of the Babylonians, like the Bezaleels and Aholiabs of the Jews, were not building after their own patterns, but according to those that had been revealed to them by the chiefs of the builders, the Moseses, the Galdus, the Chaldeans, who had received them from their gods. The earthly temples were the copies of the houses in the skies.[2] The men who delimited the houses of the gods in the heavens; who fixed the boundaries of the temples, the earthly houses of the gods; who determined (as we shall see below) the horoscopes, the houses of the nativities, of men;—these were the astrologers, call them in your language by what special name you please. The classical writers and Daniel call them Chaldeans. The Assyrio-Babylonian *dimgal* and the Babylonian *galdu* would both be excellent names to denote this class of men, who on the heavenward side studied the will of the gods, the plans of their houses and their destinies for men, in the skies; and on their earthward side, revealed the plans of the temples and the destinies of men. The *galdus* and *dimgals* were the masters of the builders, the chiefs of the wise workmen, the master-builders, under whose di-

---

[1] Ex. xxxi, 1-11.   [2] Delitzsch: HWB, p. 654b.

rection the *ummanus* and *mashmashus* and *kali* worked
as subordinates,—unless, indeed, these last were
merely names of sub-classes of the former. The Greeks
and Daniel, and the Babylonian contract tablets,
would then agree in making frequent mention of the
genus *galdu;* whereas, as yet, we have found on the
astrological tablets the mention of the species alone.
An Aramean writer, when bringing a foreign term into
his native language, may well be excused for introducing
the general term; for it must be remembered that no
one of the specific Babylonian terms for astrologer has
as yet been found in any Aramaic dialect, unless the
asheph, or *ashshaph*, of Daniel be classed as one. Neither *mashmashu*, *kalu*, *baru*, nor *zimmeru*, has ever yet
been found in Aramaic. The chiefs of the builders,—
the heads of the department of astrology, would be
the natural ones for Nebuchadnezzar to call to his
council, just as Nabopolassar is said above to have sent
out his wise workmen from the council of his great
chamber. The Babylonian name for the chief of the
builders is *galdu*. The writer of Daniel may rightly
have called them in Aramaic *Chaldeans;* inasmuch
as the name *galdu* in the sense of master-builder is
found on the Babylonian tablets as early at least as
the 14th year of Shamashshumukin, king of Babylon,
who reigned from 668 to 648 B.C.[1]

Finally, that *banu*, the Babylonian equivalent of the
Sumerian *du*, "to build," was used in a tropical sense
for the construction of other than material objects
is evident. For, first, it often means "beget." In this
sense it is used of both gods and men, and this in
innumerable cases and in all times and places.

Again, it is used of oracles and decisions of the gods.

[1] See KB. iv, 168.

Thus Nebo is called the *banu pirishti,* "the creator of decisions"[1] and Damkina the *banat shimti,* "creator of fate"[2] and "the wise king the creator of fate."[3]

These decisions which had been created (*banu*) by the gods were, doubtless, made known in the houses of decision[4] where the gods decreed the days of eternity and the fate of one's life.[5] These decisions, also, are said to have been revealed to the *baru,* or seer, who was the special guardian of the decrees of heaven and earth, to whom the gods opened up (*petu*) or spoke (*tamu*) the word of fate (*tamit pirishti*).[6] So, Ninib is the god without whom the decisions (*purussu*) of heaven and earth cannot be decided;[7] as whose mighty priest (*ishipu*) Ashurnasirpal was called by Ninib himself,[8] whose father had been a priest (*shangu*) of Ashur. The decrees of fate (*shimati*) by which his fate (*shimtu*) was righteously decided, had come out of the mouth of the great gods.[9]

In view of the above statements about the decisions of the gods which directed the life of men, the question is natural to ask, how did the gods reveal their will? And the answer is, through the inspection of livers and cups, by dreams and visions, and by many other ways; but especially by the phenomena connected with the starry heavens. In the religious belief of the Babylonians, as Delitzsch and Winckler and Jeremias have clearly shown, the events of earth were directed by the gods whose seats were in the stars; and the things of

---

[1] Del., HWB, p. 543b.   [2] Muss-Arnolt 175a.
[3] *Sharru nemeki banu tashimti,* King: *Bab. Magic,* No. 413.
[4] *Bit pirishti* or *parak shimati* or *ashar shimati,* which Delitzsch calls the earthly copy of the heavenly *Upshukinnaku.*
[5] Nbk. Inscription, xv, Col. ii, 54–64. Langdon, p. 123.
[6] See Zimmern, *Ritualtafeln,* p. 89.   [7] *Ashurnasirpal,* i, 3.
[8] *Id.,* 21   [9] *Id.,* 36, 37.

earth were but the copies of the things in heaven. It was there, above, that was built by them the house of our fate. The movements of the stars, the eclipses of sun and moon, the appearances of clouds, the bursting of storms and thunder—such were some of the ways by which the gods declared their decisions which had been made, or built (*banu*), in the heavenly counsel-chambers. As the gods had built in heaven, the astrologers built on earth. Nebo, the spokesman and interpreter of the gods of heaven and earth, was the heavenly builder (*banu purishti*) and his earthly representative (the *banu*, or *gal-du*) constructed what he had revealed to them through star and cloud and storm and earthquake, and made it known to men.[1] The temple of the god on earth was built after the fashion of his house in heaven, and was oriented and constructed with the intention that the former house as well as the latter might be the means of revealing the will of the god. The chief of all the builders was he who showed men where and how to construct their buildings and their lives, the plans for which were mysteries (*pirishtu*) opened up (*petu*) for them to read in the prototypes and figures of heaven.

But, it will be said, why then do we not find this name, or these signs, employed in the astrological reports expressly and clearly to denote the astrologers?

No completely satisfactory answer can be given to this question. It can, however, be paralleled by some questions which are equally hard to answer. For

[1] "Weltenbild und Himmelsbild sind eins. Der Priester der zu den Astralgottheiten flehte, eignete sich eine genaue Kenntniss des gestirnten Himmels an; die Bewegungen der Himmelskörper und ihre Stellungen zu einander musste er erforschen, um den Willen der Gottheiten zu erkennen." (See Weidner: *Handbuch der babylonischen Astronomie*, Einleitung: Leipzig, 1915.)

example, why is it that the *gal-du* is not mentioned on any of the building inscriptions? Why is it that he is never mentioned anywhere as concerned even in any building operations or transactions? Why is it that the signs occur so often on the business tablets from Babylon, but in those from Assyria scarcely ever, if at all? Why is the name *Kal-du* used by the Assyrians to denote the Chaldean people and country and by the Babylonians not at all? Why is the land, or people, or even a single man, never expressly called Chaldean on the monuments of Babylon? On the contract tablets we have a large number of patronymics, such as Accadian, Aramean, Arabian, Assyrian, Babylonian, Hittite, Persian, and Egyptian.[1] Why not Chaldean? In Assyrian, we find *Kal-du* used for individuals, the country, and the people.[2]

Why do the Babylonians use the signs *dup-sar* to denote the scribe, and the Assyrians almost always *a-ba*? Why is *banu* the common word for builder on the contract tablets and in the Code of Hammurabi, but *ummanu* in the building inscriptions? Why does *dim-gal* denote builder on the building inscriptions (three or four times in all) and yet never occur on the contract tablets? Why were the astrological reports signed and prepared by the *azu*, and the *us-ku* and the *mashmashu* and the *aba* and the *dupsar* and the *rab aba* and the *rab dupsar* and the *rab ashipi* and the *mar Borsippi* and the *mar Urukai* and others? And may not all of these have been sub-classes of the *gal-du*, or Chaldean?

---

[1] Tallquist, NB. xxviii.

[2] For example, *Shuzubu amilu Kal-da-ai*—Shuzub the Chaldean. See Sennacherib *Prism Inscription*, Col. iii, 42, v, 8.

Mat Kaldi "land of Chaldea" (*id.*, i, 34).

Amelu Kal-du sha kirib Uruk "the Chaldeans who were in the midst of Uruk" (*id.*, i, 37).

Here is a fine list of questions all calling for an answer and as yet unanswerable. When we can answer them we may be able to answer the one about *gal-du* (=*rab banie*) and *dim* (=*banu*). Until then, let us all be willing to acknowledge that our ignorance as to the sign and meaning of a term, or as to the time when it was first used, proves nothing.

Finally, in view of the fact that the kindred peoples of Assyria and Babylonia use different signs and names to denote the same thing, why may not the Greeks and Arameans and Hebrews, also, have done the same? If we could prove that neither Assyrian, nor Babylonian, denoted the astrologer by the term Chaldean, how would this prove that others did not? Different nations, different customs. Different languages, different names.

Besides, it is to be noted in its bearing upon the Babylonian origin of the Aramaic of Daniel that the other names employed to denote the wise men whom Nebuchadnezzar called up before him are not as a whole found in any Aramaic dialect except that of Daniel, and some of them nowhere else but in Daniel. The word *Chartom* used in Hebrew first in the accounts of Joseph and Moses to denote the Egyptian soothsayer, is generally supposed to be an Egyptian word. It means possibly "sacred scribe," or "chief of the enchanters," or "spellbinder." If this be the true meaning, it corresponds very closely to the Babylonian *dupsar*, "tablet-writer," or "scribe," or to the Babylonian *baru*, "seer." *Chartom* is not found in Syriac; nor is it in common use in any Aramaic dialect, being used merely in versions and commentaries, or in references to the original Hebrew and Aramaic passages which contain it.

The second class mentioned in Daniel ii, 10, the *ash-*

shaph, is never found in any Aramaic dialect, except Syriac, and there but seldom.

The fourth class of Daniel ii, 27, the *gazerin*, is not called by this name in any other Aramaic dialect. In meaning, it would correspond to the Babylonian *mushim shimti*, "decider of fate."

The other class mentioned frequently in Daniel, that of the wise men (*hakkimin*), may be taken as a general term, or it may correspond to the *mudu*, or *imgu*, of the Babylonians, both words of frequent occurrence on the Assyrio-Babylonian monuments.

In the Hebrew portion of Daniel, *kasdim*, *chartom*, and *'ashshaf* are used to denote classes of wise men; and in addition, the term *mekashshefim* is found in Daniel ii, 2, where Nebuchadnezzar is said to have called the last named, among others, to make known and to interpret his dream. The root of this last word and several of its derivatives are found frequently in Assyrio-Babylonian as technical terms for witchcraft, one of its derivatives meaning "poison" or "philter." In Syriac, the only Aramaic dialect where the root is employed, it is used in a good sense, of prayer and supplication. It will be noted that Daniel is not said to have had anything to do with the *mekashshefim*, a wizard being expressly forbidden by the law of Deut. xviii, 10, and especially by the law of Ex. xxii, 17.

That a word having a purely physical signification should pass on to a second sense having a moral or religious meaning, is supported by the analogy of all languages. Such English words as deacon, minister, and baptize, illustrate this change of signification. The Semitic languages, also, are rich in this kind of words with transferred or developed meanings. We need not go outside the words relating to astrology and magic to find them. For example, *beth*, "house," becomes the division of the zodiac where a certain god is supposed to dwell; as, the house of Jupiter, etc. This use is found in Arabic,[1] and in Syriac.[2]

So the Babylonian *epeshu*, "to bewitch," is probably connected with *epeshu*, "to do"; then, "to be wise." So the Arabic *sana'a* and *bana*, "to make"; then, "to educate." So, also, the Babylonian *ummanu*, "workman"; then, a kind of priest. According to Behrens,[3] *ummanu* is a synonym of *mashmashu*, a kind of priest.[4]

This connection between "work" and sorcery may be seen perhaps also in *harrash*, which in Hebrew means "workman" and in Aramaic "sorcerer."

From the word for "builder" the Aramaic and New Hebrew derive the sense "builder of doctrine" (*Gelehrter*).

Another point in favor of the gal-du's being closely allied to the scribes and priests, is to be found in the fact that so often in its occurrence on the contract tablets after the name of a witness it is met with in the immediate vicinity of the name and title of *shangu*, "priest," and *dupsar*, "scribe."[5]

The *banu*, or builder, is seldom found in this position, but the *gal-du*, or chief of the builders, frequently.

Further, there is evidence on the contract tablets

---

[1] See Otto Loth in Fleischer's *Festschrift*, for 1875.
[2] See Bardisan on *The Laws of the Nations*, in the *Spicilegium Syriacum*.   [3] *Ass.-Bab. Briefe Kult. Inhalts*, p. 10.
[4] He cites in favor of this view as follows: *Apliya am. ummanu sha Ishtar sha Arbail* (Harper: *Assyrian Letters*, v, 533, 2 ff.), "*Apliya* the *umman* of Ishtar of Arbail"; and (*id.*, v, 447, R 11) *annuti IX sha itti ummani izzazum dullu sha bit am. marṣi ippashuni*, "These nine are those who assist the *umman* to perform the rites for the house of the sick"; and (*id.*, ii, 167, R 16) "1 Qa meal 1 Qa Wine for the *ummanu*."
[5] *E. g.* Cambyses, viii, 11, 12, xvi, 16; Darius, lxxxii, 14, ccccl, 15.

23

that the *galdus* stood to the *shangus* (*i. e.*, priests) in a blood relationship differing from that in which the *shangus* stood to the *banus* or ordinary builders.[1]

Now, Zimmern holds that the Babylonian priests formed a close corporation which transplanted itself from father to son. He bases this view (1) on a statement of Diodorus Siculus (ii, 29) that the knowledge of the Chaldeans was transmitted from father to son; (2) on the fact that the seers and other priests are frequently called "sons of seers," etc.; and (3) upon the strong emphasis placed in the ritual tablets upon the continuity of the priesthood and of its most holy traditions. The passage from Diodorus reads as follows: "Among the Chaldeans, philosophy is handed down in families (*ek genous*), a son receiving from his father, and being freed from all other public services."

Examples under (2) are found on the Ritual Tablets i, 1, 7, 38 *et al.* Under (3), Professor Zimmern shows[2] that the *baru* had to be of priestly blood and education and that it may be assumed that this was true of all the priests. Thus in the Ritual Tablets No. 24, we read:

The cunning wise man who guards the secret of the great gods causes his son whom he loves to swear on the tablet and before Shamash and Hadad, causes him to learn "When the sons of the seers" [that is, the tablets beginning with this phrase]. The *abkal* of the oil, of long genealogy, a scion of Enme-dur-an-ki, king of Sippar, establisher of the holy cup [and] elevator of the cedar [staff] a creature of Nin-har-sag-ga of priestly blood, of noble descent, perfect in

---

[1] For example, Gimillu-Gula the priest (*shangu*) is called the son of Shumukin the *galdu* (Nebuch., 335, 13); so, also, the priest Tabik-ziru is the son of a *galdu* (*id.*, 22, 12; *cf* 179, 327, 72, and 196); so, also, in Cambyses, 72, 14, 15, and 284, a priest (*shangu*) is called a grandson of a *galdu*. [2] *Ritualtafeln*, pp. 87–91.

stature and in growth, shall approach before Shamash and Hadad in the place of vision and decision.[1]

If then, Zimmern and Diodorus Siculus are right in stating that the Babylonian priests held their office by family inheritance (and we know certainly that the Hebrew and Egyptian priests did thus inherit their official rights), it is obvious that since *shangus* could be and were sons, or grandsons, of *galdus*, both must have been of the priestly race. It is well to call special attention to the fact that Diodorus calls these priests the Chaldeans. If, as we have argued above, *galdu* is the same as " Chaldean," the *galdu* might well be the general term; that is, all the *shangus* would be *galdus*, but *galdus* would not all be *shangus*,—just as all the Jewish priests were Levites, but the Levites were not all priests.

Further, we find no example of anyone who was called both a *banu*, and a *gal-du*. Nor among the hundreds of names mentioned in Tallquist's *Book of Names* (*Namenbuch*) is anyone at one time called a *galdu* and at another time a *banu*.[2]

Whether the *baru*, the *ashipu*, the *zimmeru*, and others performing priestly functions were also *galdus*, or in what relation any of these stood to either the *shangus*, or the *galdus*, the records give us no information.[3] No man whose name is given in the Tallquist tablets, is called either *baru*, *ashipu*, *zimmeru*, or *mashmashu;* while *shangu* and *galdu* each occur hundreds of times. If the sign *rid* in the inscriptions from the reign of

---

[1] See also Dhorme, *Textes Réligieux Assyro-babyloniens*, p. 142.

[2] Of course this is merely negative evidence. A *shangu* however, might be the son of a *banu*, as in the inscription of Evil-Merodach published by Evetts (*Bab. Texte*, vii, B. No. 19).

[3] But see Addendum to Excursus, p. 365.

Sin-shar-ishkun, king of Assyria, published by Evetts in his *Babylon. Texte*, p. 90, be read *nappahu*, then a priest in Assyria might be a son of a smith. But if we read the sign *ummanu*, it may mean an *ummanu* priest.[1] As to the relation in which the *dupsar*, or scribe, stood to the *galdu*, we are not prepared to make any positive statements. It is clear that a *galdu* might have a son who was a scribe.[2]

Lastly, if the *galdus* were priests we can account reasonably for such texts as that found in Peek's collection, number 4, which Pinches translates: "The fruit due, again applied for, in the district of Sippar, from the Chaldeans."[3] These *galdus* can scarcely have been a community of architects, but may well have been a fellowship of priests; since, as Dr. Peiser says in his *Sketch of Babylonian Society*,[4] certain portions of the land were given over into the possession of the temples, so that the support of the temples and priests to be derived from the income of the land might not be interfered with. The view of Dr. Peiser derived from the monuments is supported by the testimony of Arrian in his *Expedition of Alexander*,[5] where he says that

The Chaldeans did not wish Alexander to come to Babylon lest he should take away from them the income derived

---

[1] For this use of *ummanu* see Behren's *Ass. Bab. Brief*, p. 10, and Frank's *Studien zur Babylonischen Religion*, p. 17.

[2] For example, Peiser's *Babylonian Contracts* (*Bab. Verträge*) Nos. 5, 7, 16, 28, 45, 50, 51, 55, 61, 64, 70, 80, 83, 100, 101, 110, 114, 115, and 140. But a scribe might be descended also from a herdsman (Peiser, *Verträge* iii, 22); from a smith (*id.* 8); from a *ba'iru* (a fisher, constable, or press-gang officer, *id.*, 17, 22, 23, 65); or from a physician (*a-zu, id.*, 76); or even from an Egyptian (*id.*, 94).

[3] *Gal-du-mes* pl. Cf. VASD. vi, 20, 22.

[4] *Skizze der Bab. Gesellschaft*, p. 16. [5] Bk. 7, ch. 17.

from the possessions of the temple of Bel (to which much
land and much gold had been dedicated by the Assyrian
kings), that he might with it reconstruct the Temple of
Bel which had been destroyed by Xerxes.

As we indicated above, we shall now proceed to discuss more fully the question as to what these constructors built. The obvious answer would be, houses,
of course. But what kind of houses? Or, what were
the duties of the "chief of the builders" in their relation
to houses? It will, perhaps, not be known to all my
readers that among astrologers the word "house" was
used to denote the parts of the heavens. There was
the house of Mars, and the house of Jupiter, and the
house of the Sun, etc. An astrologer who constructed
horoscopes may very well have been called a builder,
or the chief of the builders. Unfortunately, the
astrological and magical texts so far published in
Assyrio-Babylonian give us no horoscopes in the
narrower sense of nativities; but the Arabic, Syriac, and
the Aramaic of Onkelos, all use the phrase "house of
nativity, or birth" to denote a child's horoscope.[1]
A better word than "builder" for the one who constructed this house cannot be suggested. Unfortunately,
again, the Assyrio-Babylonian texts so far published
give us no certain word for astrologer. *Baru*, "seer,"
may have included the duties of astrologer or star-gazer
but his functions were certainly much wider, as Zimmern
has clearly shown.[2] The *dupsar*, or scribe, was specifically the writer of a tablet, though he may, of course,
have been an astrologer also. The signs *A-BA*, which
in Assyrian denote the scribe, might denote the astrol-

[1] See Gen. xl, 20, in Syriac and Aramaic.
[2] *Ritualtafeln*, pp. 82–91.

oger, also; but no one is sure as yet how to read these signs in Assyrian, nor what they mean exactly. *Galdu*, because of its meaning as well as because of its being the phonetic equivalent of *Chaldaios*, may well have been the name for astrologer among the Babylonians. That the word should be spelled in its Aramaic, Hebrew, and Greek forms, in the same way as *kaldu*, the name of the nation, does not prove an identity of origin. The English word "host" has three distinct meanings, one derived from the Latin *hostia*, "sacrifice," one from the Latin *hostis*, "enemy," and one from the Latin *hospes*, "entertainer." Many words in all languages are homonymous and homophonous, without being homogenous, or homologous.

Moreover, the duties of astrologers were not confined to making horoscopes of nativities. It is clear from the monuments that someone was called upon to orient and lay out the temples and palaces, perhaps all houses, before they were constructed. The plans of the temples, at least, may well have been drawn up by someone connected with the worship of the god in whose honor the temple was to be built. As each god had his particular ceremonies and a distinctive temple for his proper worship, we can readily perceive how the records speak of a *galdu* of the god Shamash[1] and of a *galdu* of the god Marduk.[2]

As the streets, walls, embankments, and public buildings needed to be oriented and constructed, we can understand how, also, there could be a *galdu* of the city of Babylon.[3]

Moreover, since buildings could be commenced only on a lucky day and in a lucky month, it may well have

[1] Strassmaier: *Insc. of Nabunaid*, 351,1, VASD. vi, 22, 2.
[2] Strass.: *Insc. of Darius*, 457,12.　　　　[3] *Id.* 348, 19.

been the duty of the chief of the builders to determine
when the day had arrived on which it would be fortunate
to begin operations. Again and again the kings reiterate that a building was begun on a lucky day. Who
better than the astrologer could determine this? And
since building could not be commenced without his
permission, he might for this reason, also, be called
galdu—chief of the builders.

Again, Schrank says that the *mashmashu* and *kalu*
seem to have taken part in the festive initiation of new
buildings, canals, etc. Thus Sennacherib sends a
mashmashu and a *kalu* to open a canal and[1] a *kalu* takes
part in the rebuilding of temples.[2]

Further, it is frequently said that ceremonies took
place at the initiation of repairs, or the laying of the
foundation, or at the commencement of the removal
of the débris from the ruins of an old temple, or at the
dedication of a new, or renewed, building. For example,
at the laying of the foundation of the temple of Sin
in Harran, Nabunaid says that he did it with incantations and with the commission of the god Libittu,
the lord of foundations and bricks, on the fortunate day
and in the favorable month which Shamash and
Ramman had made known to him in a vision; and that
he poured out on its walls palm-wine, wine, oil, and
honey.[3]

Again, further on in the same inscription Nabunaid
says that he laid the bricks of the temple of the Sun at
Sippar upon the foundation of Naram-Sin which Shamash had made known to him in a vision (*biri*), with joy
and rejoicing, in a favorable month on a fortunate day,

---

[1] Meissner and Rost, *Die Bauinschiften Sanheribs* 27.
[2] See *Bab. Sühnriten*, pp. 12, 13.　　　　[3] KB. iii, ii, 100.

anointing with oil the written name of Naram-Sin
and offering sacrifices.[1] Further on, he speaks of having sanctified it and made it fit to be a temple of his
godhead.[2]

It will be noticed, also, that no step is taken by any
king, at least in regard to building, without some intimation of the will of the gods.[3]

Some of the names by which the mediums or interpreters of these communications from the gods were
called are *baru*, "seer";[4] *mahhu*, "priest";[5] *shabru*,
"interpreter" (?);[6] *ashipu*, "enchanter";[7] *kalu* or
mashmashu.[8]

No building operations seem to have been commenced without a sign from the gods through one of
these methods of communication. These priests and
seers, and others of like import, could cause or prevent
any building enterprises. They were the real masters
of the building trades unions, the "bosses of the jobs."
They could declare a strike or assumption of operations. Taking them all together, no better term could

---

[1] *Id.*, 104. [2] *Id.*, 108.

[3] This intimation comes by a word or command (*amatu*, KB. iii, ii. 78,
98, 126; *kibit*, KB. iii, i, 252, 254, 256, and very often everywhere; *zikru*,
KB. iii, ii, 264; *temu*, iii, ii, 124), by a dream or vision (*shuttu*, iii, ii, 98;
igiltu, iii, i, 252; *biru*, iii, ii, 101, 104; *shiru*, iii, ii, 84), or by a decision or
judgment (*parussu*, KB. iii, ii, 110; *shimatu*, iii, ii, 70, 72; *dinu*, KB. ii, 236;
or *teru*, iii, ii, 110, 118. *Reports of Mag. and Astrol.*, 186 R. 9, 187 R. 3),
or by a commission or sign however given (*shibir ashiputim*, Langdon,
p. i, 146, 148. Compare *shipir ish-ship-pu-ti*, "the commission of the
ish-ship priest," Ashurbanipal, *Rassam Cyl.*, iv, 86; *shipir Ish-tar* or
Ishtarate, "the commission of Ishtar" or "of the Ishtar priestesses,"
KB. ii, 252; *shipir mahhie*, "the commission of the *mahhu* priests," *id.*;
idatu, "signs," KB. ii, 252, and Del., HWB., 304).

[4] See Zimmern, *Ritualtafeln*, 86–91. [5] KB. ii, 252.
[6] KB. ii, 250.
[7] KB. 192; Frank, *Studien zur bab. Religion*, p. 23.
[8] Schrank, *Bab. Sühnriten*, 12.

be suggested by which to name them than *galdu, rab banie*, "the chiefs of the builders."[1]

Again, *banu* is used in series of synonymous expressions to denote the men who were connected with the oracles of the gods, with astrology, with building, and with the wise men in general. In so far as any of these wise men had to do with the construction of the houses of the gods;[2] or with the horoscope, or house of one's nativity; or with the building of temples; or with the building of "fates," or even of thoughts,—they might each be called a *banu*, or builder. Their chiefs might well have been called *gal-du = rab banie*, "chiefs of the builders." Inasmuch as this kind of building was their highest function, we can easily understand how

[1] A syllabary published on the *Cuneiform Texts from Bab. Tablets*, etc., in the British Museum, part xviii, plate 13, supports this view just stated. In the syllabary we find *banu* given as a synonym of *baru*, "seer"; *baru* as a synonym of *a-su*, "physician," and *mu-de-e ter-te*, "knower of oracles," "*Orakelkündiger*" (Zimmern, *R. T.*, 87); and these immediately followed by *dup-sar-ru*, "scribe," *en-ku*, "wise man," and *mu-du-u*, "learned, kenner." The Sumerian *a-zu*, as is well known, denotes in Assyrian, *asu*, "physician," *dupsar*, "scribe," and *baru*, "seer" (Zimmern, *R. T.*, 86); but *gi-hal = banu piristi* (the *gi* denoting *piristu = shimtu*, Br. 2402, 2410), a phrase used to describe Nebo, "the builder of fate." Compare what Ashurbanipal says in the *Rassam Cylinder* (x, 70, 71): "On my bed at night my dreams are favorable and on that of the morning my thoughts are created"; where *banu* is permansive, as *damka* is in the preceding clause (Vd. Del., Gr., sec. 89B). So *A-ZU = asu*, or *baru*. With the sign for god before them, the signs *ni-zu =* Nebo. Again, *me-zu = baru* or *mude terti* (Br. 10384, 10385). Lastly, the signs *nun-me-tag = enku, eppishu, hassu, mudu, bel terte, abkallum*, and *mar ummani*, and these all are probably synonyms of *baru* (Zimmern, *Ritualtafeln*, 86).

[2] This house of the gods is the same as the *bait* of *Al Kindi* (edited by Otto Loth for the *Festschrift* of Prof. Dr. H. L. Fleischer), and the *bet* of Bardesan's *Book of the Laws of the Countries* (published by Cureton in the *Spicilegium Syriacum*), the *oikos* or *doma* of Manetho's *Apotelesmatica*, and Maximus' *Anecdota Astrologica*, and the "house" of our own astrologers.

the foreign Greeks and Hebrews and Arameans may
have adopted the phrase used to denote the highest
officials of the cult, or profession, as a general term
including all the sub-classes subsumed under it. We
can understand, also, why the Babylonian contract
tablets name so many *galdus* and almost entirely fail
to mention the other classes named above, except the
scribes, or *dupsarri*. The *shangu* ("priest"), the *dupsar*, and the *galdu*, the three titles met with so often
on the tablets, will thus represent the learned classes,
who transacted the business of the community both
sacred and profane. And where visions and dreams
are concerned, as is the case in Daniel, the *galdu* would
be the man for the work.

Before closing the discussion of the meaning of the
word Chaldean, it may be well to call attention to two
remarkable facts to be gleaned from the astrological
and contract tablets. The first is that the signs *gal* and
du, which are found so often on the contract tablets of
Babylonia, are scarcely, if ever, found on any documents from Assyria.[1] Babylonia was the country of
the *galdu* according to the cuneiform documents; and

---

[1] The signs *A.BA.* of the Assyrian tablets are commonly employed
where the Babylonian use *dupsar*, "scribe." See tablets in KB. iv, pp.
100, 108, 110 *bis*, 112, 114 *bis*, 116 *bis*, *et al.* The *rab a-ba* of Nos. 74, 109,
266, of Thompson's *Reports of the Magicians and Astrologers of Nineveh and Babylon* would be the chief of the scribes, the same as the *rab
dup-sar* of Nos. 81, 259.

The *A.ZU* of No. 58 may also be read as *dup-sar*, "scribe" (see Brünnow, 11377 and 11379). The *rab asu* of No. 59 might then be "the
chief of the scribes." The only names left in Thompson's tablets that
might come under the class of the Chaldean priests are the *mashmashu* on Nos. 24, 83, 183, 243, and *kalu* on 134 (*kal-li-e* on No. 256.
Cf. rab kal-li-e, K. 316, KB. iv, 114) and possibly the *hal* of 18, 186, and
187, all of which, as we have seen above, may have been subdivisions
of the *gal-dus*.

it was the region of the Chaldean priests according to Daniel, Herodotus, Ctesius, Berosus, Strabo, Diodorus Siculus, and Arrian.

The other fact is the noteworthy agreement of Strabo and the Assyrian astrological reports with regard to the localities where the different classes of astrologers resided. Strabo says (Bk. XVI, 1) that there were many kinds of Chaldean astrologers, such as Orchenoi, Borsippenoi, and many others. Now, many of Thompson's *Astrological Reports* are by men who are called sons of Borsippa or sons of Uruk (*i. e.*, Orchenoi); and an *ummanu* of Borsippa is mentioned in Thompson's *Late Babylonian Letters*, i, obv. 6. The reports and letters were written in the 7th century B. C. During all this time the astrologers of Borsippa and Uruk held their place of preëminence as astrologers; and Strabo calls them both Chaldeans.

If, therefore, anyone object to deriving "Chaldean" from *gal-du*, chief of the builders," he may still hold that the name as used for priests was derived from the name as used for a people. For the name *Kaldu*, or Chaldean, for the people and country and individuals of Chaldea, is found from the time of Shalmanezer III, 850 B. C. to the time of Arrian and Quintus Curtius. During any part of this time, therefore, if we derive the name Chaldean as applied to the Chaldean priests from the name of the Chaldean people, these priests may have been found in Babylon exercising the functions of astrologers and have been called Chaldeans after the ruling people, just as other astrologers were found in Borsippa and Uruk, and named after the cities where they dwelt and performed their duties. That is, if the astrologers of Borsippa could be called Borsippenes, the astrologers of Chaldea may have been rightly called Chaldeans; the one from the city, the other from the country, or nation, to which they respectively belonged. The sub-classes are mentioned by Strabo as well as the general term; Daniel mentions the general term alone.[1]

In conclusion, let it be remembered that the astrological reports thus far published, which give the names of the writers, are almost all Assyrian; and that the astrological reports of Strassmaier, Epping, and Kugler do not give the native names for the astronomers who drew them up, nor even the signs used to denote those names. But even if they did give many signs, or names, to denote astrologers, it would not prove that Daniel was wrong in using Chaldean to denote them. For first, Daniel was writing in Aramaic and not in Babylonian; and secondly, the subscriptions of the writers of the *Astrological Reports* with half a dozen or more groups of signs and at least a dozen different ways of describing them, to denote the writers of the reports should warn us not to be too certain that *gal-du* may not also have been properly used to denote them.

In concluding this long discussion of the origin, meaning, and use of the word Chaldean to denote a priestly class, let us sum up by saying that we think we have shown that it is not certain that the word does not occur upon the Babylonian monuments inasmuch as it probably is the same as the word *gal-du* which is frequently found on them; that, secondly, if Chaldean be not the Aramaic and Hebrew form of *gal-du*, it may have been the same in origin, though different in meaning, as

---

[1] The use by the Arameans of the patronymic Kaldu or Kasdu to denote a priestly class or function may be compared with *medizein* in Greek to denote Greeks who favored the Medes and with "to jew down" in English.

the Assyrian *Kal-du*, which was employed to denote the tribe living south of Babylon whose kings ruled over Babylon in the time of Daniel, inasmuch as priestly functions were often delegated to a tribe, or class, as has been the case among the Jews, the Egyptians, the Medes, and the people of Lystra; and thirdly, that even if the word were absent from the Babylonian monuments as a designation of the astrologers, or priests, it would not prove that such a class with such a name did not exist, any more than the absence of the name as a designation of the tribe, or people, of the Chaldeans proves that such a people did not exist.

ADDENDUM TO EXCURSUS

Since writing the above the most important evidence to show that the *banu* and *gal-du* were included in the sodality of the priests and seers has appeared in the Yale cylinder of Nabunaid.[1] At the dedication of his daughter, Bel-shalti-Nannar, to Sin and Nikkal for the service of divination (*ina shibir ashipitim*) in the temple of Egipar, he says that he endowed the temple richly with fields, gardens, servants, herds, and flocks; and that "in order that the priesthood of Egishshirgal and the houses of the gods might not incur sin, he remitted the taxes, established the income, and purified and sanctified to Sin and Nikkal the chief priest,[2] the inspector of property,[3] the seer, the

[1] Published in the *Yale Oriental Series*, Babylonian Texts, vol. i, pp. 66–75. New Haven, 1915.

[2] See Frank, *Studien zur babylonischen Religion*, p. 5. For *ramkut* in the sense of priesthood and *kinishtum* in the sense of sodality, see the same, p. 60. For the latter, compare also *kenishta d'beth Y'huda* in the haggada to Psalm xxxviii, 12. (See Lewy's *Chaldäisches Wörterbuch*, i, 373.)

[3] See *Brünnow's Classified List*, 7820 and 10695.

engiṣu, the imprecator, the *gal -du*, the *banu*, the
dullaḫḫa, the overseer of the *gallum*, the custodian,
the *lagaru*, the maker of supplications, the singers
who rejoice the hearts of the gods,—the solidarity
of those whose names are named."[1]

From this passage it is manifest that the *gal-du*
and *banu* are said to be in the sodality, or assembly,
of the *ramku*-priests. Their names are placed after
those of the *enu-ishibi*, the *baru*, and the *ariru*, and
before those of the *lagaru*, and the *zammeru*. They
are said, also, to have been named with names,
that is, to have been dedicated to the service of the
gods with the giving of a new name, just as in the
same inscription the daughter of Nabunaid received a new name at her dedication.[2]

---

[1] 24 Ash-shum: 25 ra-am-ku-ut E-gish-shir-gal u batati ilani
26 e-nu i-shib-bi shabru ṣibṭi am . baru am . EN-GI-ṢU
27 am . a-ri-ru am . gal-du am . banu am . DUL-LAḤ-ḤA itu gal-lum
28 am . ti-ir-bit am . la-ga-ru sha-ki-in tak-ri-ib-ti
29 am . zammare mu-ḥad-du-u lib-bi ilani
30 am . ki-ni-ish-tum sha na-bu-u shu-ma-an-shu-un
31 i-li-ik-shu-nu ap-tu-ur-ma shu-bar-ra-shu-nu ash-ku-un
32 ub-bi-ib-shu-nu-ti-ma
33 a-na ili Sin u ili Nin-gal bele-e-a u-zak-ki-shu-nu-ti

[2] On column i, lines 24–25, Nabunaid says: I dedicated my daughter
to the *entu*-office. I called her name Bel-shalti-Nannar.

CHAPTER XVIII

DANIEL AND THE WISE MEN

WHEN Paul was at Philippi, he was accused of teaching customs which it was not lawful for the Philippians to observe, being Romans. Without a trial and uncondemned, he was beaten and imprisoned and put in the stocks. This illustrates the manner in which the critics accuse Daniel of becoming a Babylonian wise man, of observing customs which it was not lawful for him to observe, "being a strict Jew." They do not prove that the customs of the wise men were not lawful for a strict Jew to observe. To do this they should first show what a strict Jew might legally have been; and secondly, what there was in the customs and beliefs of a wise man of Babylon that made it impossible for Daniel to have been at the same time a strict Jew and a Babylonian wise man. This they have failed to show. They simply assert it, just as the Philippians asserted that Paul troubled their city by teaching unlawful customs.

Again, as we shall see, they have failed to show how it would have been impossible for a Jewish writer of the second century B.C.,—the time of the Maccabees and of the Assideans,—to have written a work whose hero would have been represented as being both a strict Jew and a Babylonian wise man, if there had been an inconsistency in a man's being at the same time both of them. They have failed even to consider how a strict Jew, writing a book of fiction for the consolation of strict Jews, to be accepted by strict Jews as a genuine history, could have said that a strict Jew was a Babylonian wise man, if there was anything unlawful or improper in a strict Jew's being a Babylonian wise man. Certainly a strict Jew of the middle of the second century B.C. was as strict as one of the middle of the sixth. Certainly, also, a Chaldean wise man of the second century B.C., was as bad as one of the sixth. Certainly, also, as we shall see, a wise man was at both times and at all times the subject of unstinted, unqualified, and invariable praise on the part of Jew and Babylonian and Greek. Certainly, last of all, if the critics were right in placing the completion of the law in post-exilic times, a strict Jew of the second century B.C. would be much stricter than he would have been in the sixth century B.C., before the law had been completed. For surely a strict Jew of the sixth century B.C. cannot be blamed by the critics for not observing a law that according to these same critics was not promulgated till the fifth or fourth century B.C. A writer living in Palestine in the second century B.C., composing a book with the intent of encouraging the Assidean party and the observance of the law, would scarcely make his hero live a life inconsistent with this very law which it was his purpose to magnify; whereas a Jew living at Babylon in the sixth century B.C., where the law could not be strictly observed, might have been excused even if he had transgressed the injunctions which it was impossible for him to observe. This is an *ad hominem* argument which is gladly left to the consideration of those who affirm that a strict Jew of the sixth century B.C., could not have been a Babylonian wise man, while one of the second might have been!

When Jesus was brought up before the High Priest two witnesses testified that he had said, "Destroy this temple and in three days I will raise it up." The evangelist admits that he had used these words but says that he had meant by them his own body and not the temple at Jerusalem. The witnesses, therefore, were false, not because they did not report correctly the words that had been said, but because they gave to them a sense different from that which had been intended and understood. So, as I shall proceed to show, the author of Daniel represents the prophet as having been a wise man indeed; but his wise man was one whose manner of life was in entire harmony with the teachings of the law and of the prophets, whereas the wise man of the critics is the baseless fabric of their own imagination. But let us to the proof.

OBJECTIONS STATED

A writer who makes a pious Jew and one true to the law to have been admitted into the society of the Chaldean Magicians can only have possessed very confused notions of the latter.[1]

Other indications adduced to show that the Book is not the work of a contemporary, are such as the following:— The improbability that Daniel, a strict Jew, should have suffered himself to be initiated into the class of Chaldean "wise men," or should have been admitted by the wise men themselves.[2]

How explain the assertion that Daniel, a strict Jew, was

[1] Cornill, p. 338. [2] Driver, p. 500, h.

24

made chief of the heathen sages of Babylon? (ii, 48, iv, 6).[1]

ASSUMPTIONS INVOLVED

There are several assumptions in these objections.

1. That a strict, or pious, Jew, and one true to the law, could not have been the chief of the "wise men" of Babylon without besmirching his reputation and injuring his character.

2. That a Jewish writer at the time of the Maccabees could have been capable of making the pious hero of a fiction to have been a member of the heathen society of magicians, or Chaldeans; but that it is improbable that a real Daniel of the sixth century B.C. can have been a member of such a class.

3. That an author thus writing can only have had very confused notions of what such magicians were.

4. That Daniel must have been initiated into the mysteries of such a society.

5. That the chief of such a society must himself have been guilty of practicing the black art.

6. That the wise men themselves admitted him into the class of the Chaldeans.

ANSWER TO THE OBJECTIONS

Before proceeding to the discussion of these assumptions, let us quote in full the statements of the book of Daniel with reference to Daniel's relation to the wise men.

1. Nebuchadnezzar had him trained in the learning and tongue of the Chaldeans (Dan. i, 3–5) so that he might be able to stand before the king, and the king approved of his education (i, 18–20).

[1] Bevan, *The Book of Daniel*, p. 21.

2. God gave him grace and mercy before the prince of the eunuchs (i, 9) and knowledge and discernment in all literature (book-learning) and wisdom (i, 17).

3. The king of Babylon found him ten times better than all the magicians and enchanters which were in all his kingdom in all matters of wisdom and understanding (i, 20).

4. When the king called the magicians, enchanters, sorcerers and Chaldeans to tell the king his dream, Daniel was not among them (ii, 4-9). It was only when the king commanded to kill all the wise men of Babylon that they sought Daniel and his companions to slay them (ii, 13).

5. The king made Daniel great and chief of the *sagans* over the wise men of Babylon (ii, 46-49).

6. In iv, 9, he is called *rab hartumaya* or chief of the magicians, or sacred scribes.

7. In v, 11, the queen says that he had been made master of scribes, exorcists, astrologers (mathematicians), and fortune tellers.

8. He interpreted dreams and omens by the power of God given in answer to prayer (ii, 17-23).

We find in these passages the following points regarding Daniel:

1. He was taught all the book-learning and the languages of the Chaldeans, so that Nebuchadnezzar found him to be ten times better than the sacred scribes and enchanters (the *hartummim* and *ashshafim*) that were in all his kingdom.

2. God gave him knowledge and discernment in all book-learning and wisdom and ability through prayer to interpret dreams and omens.

3. He was among the wise men (*hakkimin*) of Babylon, but is not said to have been among the sacred

scribes, the priestly enchanters or exorcists, the sorcerers, or wizards, nor among the Chaldeans, astrologers, or mathematicians.

4. He was chief of the sagans over the wise men (*hakkamin*) of Babylon; and, also, chief of the sacred scribes, priestly enchanters, Chaldeans, or astrologers.

The six assumptions with regard to Daniel's relation to the "wise men" are so inextricably interwoven that we shall make a general discussion of the whole subject, aiming to show that they all are false. And first, it may be asked, if the objectors really think that it was wrong for a pious Jew to be taught the learning and the tongue of the Chaldeans. If so, then Moses was wrong to be instructed in all the wisdom of the Egyptians and Paul to have studied in the heathen university at Tarsus. Besides, the book says (i, 17) that "God gave him [*i. e.*, Daniel] knowledge and skill in all learning and wisdom."

Or, can it have been wrong for him "to have understanding in all visions and dreams" (i, 17)? Then it must have been wrong for Joseph, also, to have interpreted the dreams of Pharaoh and his officers; and yet both Joseph himself and Pharaoh and Stephen attribute his ability to God. Besides, in the book of Daniel, both Daniel himself and the wise men and Nebuchadnezzar ascribe Daniel's power of interpreting dreams and visions to the direct intervention of God.

Or, did "the law" to which he is said to have been true, prohibit interpretations of dreams and visions?

As to dreams, one of the characteristics of the Elohist (E), as opposed to the Jehovist, is said to be his mentioning dreams so often. But this is always done without any blame being attached to the belief in them, or to an attempted interpretation of them. According to Dillmann, Numbers xxii, 6, belongs to the Jehovist. It reads as follows: "If there be a prophet among you, I Jehovah will speak unto him in a dream." Certainly there is no disapprobation here. In Deuteronomy, the only reference to dreams is in the thirteenth chapter, where a prophet or a dreamer of dreams who should tempt the people to serve other gods is condemned to death; the dreamer being put in the same class as the prophet.

As to visions, the Jehovist in Genesis xv, 1, represents God as speaking to Abraham in a vision, and nearly all the great early prophets assert that God spake to them in visions; so that it is obvious that a belief neither in dreams nor in visions, nor in the interpretation of them, can have been wrong, in the opinion of the prophets. That Daniel, also, is said to have seen visions, is in harmony with the strictest orthodoxy and the most devoted piety of those that were true to the law from the earliest times down to the time when in the New Testament the young men saw visions and the old men dreamed dreams.

If Daniel, then, did anything unbecoming a strict Jew, it must have consisted in the fact that he allowed himself to be found in bad company, that there was something in the dogmas, or practices, of the "wise men," that was inconsistent with a man of piety becoming a master of their wisdom, even though he may not have accepted their dogmas, nor taken part in their practices.

Now, let us waive for the present the question as to whether Daniel did actually become a member of the society of the Chaldean wise men, and consider simply what were the tenets and practices of these so-called "wise men." At the outset, let it be said, that there is much danger here of darkening words without knowledge, just because it is impossible for us with our present means of information to form a clear and correct conception of what the Babylonian wise men were. This difficulty is partly one of language, partly one of literature. As to literature, there is nothing from the Babylonians themselves bearing directly on the subject. As to language, it must be remembered that the terms in Daniel are either in a peculiar Aramaic dialect, or in Hebrew, and that it is impossible with our present knowledge to determine what Babylonian words are equivalent in meaning to the Aramaic and Hebrew expressions.

Taking up, first, the most general term used in Daniel, that which is translated by "wise men," we find that the Aramaic of Daniel expresses this idea by the word *hakkim*. This word and its congeners are employed in a good sense in every Aramaic dialect. So on the *Panammu Inscription* of about 725 B.C., from northern Syria, the king speaks of his *wisdom* and righteousness. So, also, in the Targum of Onkelos in Deut, i, 13, and after; where it regularly renders the Hebrew *hakam* "wise." So, also, the Samaritan Targum commonly translates the Hebrew word *hakam* by *hakkim;* an exception being Gen. xli, 8, where the Samaritan has the word קסם *sorcerer*. So, also, in the Syriac Aramaic, both in the Peshitto version of the Scriptures and elsewhere, the word is used in a good sense. This is true, likewise, in Arabic, both in the translation of the Scriptures and elsewhere. Lane, in his great Arabic dictionary, gives none but good senses for the root and its derivatives in general. *Hakim* is "a sage, a philosopher, a physician"; while *hikma* is "a knowledge of the true nature of things and acting according to the requirements thereof." In Hebrew, moreover, the word "wise" is never used in a bad sense.[1] The only "wise men" who are condemned are those who are wise in their own eyes and not in reality (Is. v, 21). In later Hebrew, too, the wise are commended, as in Ecclesiasticus vi, 32, and in the Zadokite Fragments 2:3 and 6:3.

In Babylonian, the noun from this root has not been found, but the verb, which has been found several times, is used always in a good sense. The Assyrio-Babylonian language, however, has a number of words, which may be rendered by "wise man"; but not one of these is employed specifically or by itself to denote any class of sorcerers or astrologers; much less were these sorcerers the only wise men.[2]

In Ethiopic, also, according to Dillman's dictionary *hakim* and *tabib*, the latter the ordinary word for wise man, are used only in a good sense.[3]

---

[1] Pharaoh, Gen. xli, 8, and Ex. vii, 11; the king of Babylon, Jer. l, 35, and li, 57; the king of Gebal, Ezek. xxvii, 9; the king of Tyre, Ezek. xxvii, 8; king Solomon and his son Rehoboam, 2 Ch. ii, 13; Ahasuerus, Es. vi, 13; and Moses and the children of Israel, Deut. i, 13, Ex. xxviii, 3; —all have their wise men. "Wise men" are commended in Prov. xii, 18, xiii, 20, xiv, 3.

[2] The most common of these words is probably *mudu* from the root *idu*, "to know," a root common to Ass. Bab. with Aramaic and Hebrew. This word is used of the gods, Nebo and Shamash, of the kings like Sargon, Sennacherib, and Nebuchadnezzar; and of other men, but always in a good sense.

Another word is *imku* (or *emku*) from a root also found in Hebrew meaning "to be deep." The inscriptions speak of the wise heart of Ea; of the wise princes Nabunaid and Nabu-balatsu-ikbi; of Nebuchadnezzar the wise one (often); of the wise master-builders, etc.

Ershu (or *irshu*) from a root meaning "to decide" is used as an appellation for the gods Sin and Ea and for kings like Sennacherib and Nebuchadnezzar. *Itpishu*, also, is used of the gods Damkina, Nebo, and Ninib, and of the kings Sargon, Sennacherib, and Nebuchadnezzar.

[3] *Ma'mer* from the verb *'amara* "to show, to know," is used often in the Ethiopic version of the Old Testament in the sense of "wizard"

From the uses of the words for wise men in the
various Semitic languages, it is clear, therefore, that
there can have been nothing wrong in belonging to the
class of wise men as such. Nor does the Bible, nor
Nebuchadnezzar, even intimate that there was. The
wise men of the book of Daniel were to be slain because
a tyrant in his wrath at a portion of them who claimed
to do more than they were able to perform, or of whom
at least the king demanded more than it was possible
for them to know, had failed to meet his expectations.
The decree to kill all was not justified by the offense of a
portion merely of the so-called wise men. But even if
it had been impossible for any of the wise men to meet
the demand of the king, it would not prove that it was
wrong for a pious Jew to be a wise man. What wise
man of to-day would be able to tell a man a dream that
he had forgotten? Such ignorance has nothing to do
with piety. It is simply a limitation common to humanity. For as Daniel truly says, "The secret which the
king was asking *no wise men* were able to make known,
but there is a God in heaven who revealeth secrets."
The wise men are not blamed for not knowing what
God alone could know.

As to the word '*ashshaph* (magician) in the Hebrew of
Daniel i, 20, ii, 2, and in the Aramaic of ii, 10, and
the word '*asheph* of ii, 27, iv, 4, v, 7, 11, 15, it may be
said, first, that neither derivative, nor root, occurs anywhere else in the Old Testament. Both the verb and
several nouns occur in Syriac in the sense of "enchant,
enchanter"; but not apparently in any other Aramaic

---

to translate the Greek γνωστής, Heb. *yidde'oni* and the Greek στοχαστης,
Heb. *ḳosem*. It renders, also, the Greek χαλδαιοι in Dan. ii, 2, and
γαζαρηνοι in Dan. iv, 3, v, 15. In most of these cases the Arabic versions use '*arraf*, "wizard," from the verb '*arafa*, "to know."

dialect, nor in Arabic, nor Ethiopic. In Babylonian, however, the root is met with in various forms; and the two forms corresponding exactly to *'ashshaph* and *'asheph* are found also.[1]

What, then, is the meaning of the root and of the forms as we find them in Babylonian?[2]

From the authorities that we possess and the texts cited by them, it is evident, that in the estimation of the Babylonians the office and functions of the *'ashipu* and of the *'ashshapu* were beneficent to the community. They removed bans and exorcised evil spirits and disease and caused good visions and dreams. A common verb to denote their method of activity is *pasharu*, "to loose"; the same verb that is employed in Daniel to denote what they were expected by Nebuchadnezzar and Belshazzar to do. It was part of their business to see that "bad depressing dreams" (*shunati nashdati*) did not appear, caused by demons who "seized the side of one's bed and worried and attacked one."[3]

Another term found in Daniel[4] is *hartom* or *har-*

---

[1] A most remarkable fact in its bearing upon the correctness of the sources and transmission of the text of Daniel, when we consider that these words are not found outside of Assyrio-Babylonian except in the book of Daniel. In the Peshitto version of Daniel, *'ashuph* is used to translate both *'asheph* and *'ashshaph*. *'Ashshaph* is found in New Hebrew nowhere but in commentaries on Daniel. See Jastrow's Dict. *in loc.*

[2] The best sources of our information are Tallquist: *The Assyrian Incantation-series Maklu;* Zimmern in his chapter on the ritual table for the *'ashipu* found on pages 122–175 of his work entitled: *Contributions to the Knowledge of the Babylonian Religion (Beiträge zur Kenntniss,* etc.); the work of Dr. Walther Schrank: *Babylonian Rites of Purifications, especially in their relation to Priests and Exorcists (Babylonische Sühnriten besonders mit Rücksicht auf Priester und Büsser);* and King: *Babylonian Magic.* [3] Frank, *Bab. Beschwörungsreliefs,* pp. 88, 90.

[4] In i, 20, and ii, 2, in Hebrew, and in ii, 10, 27, iv, 4, 6, and v, 11 in Aramaic.

tum. This word is found, also, in the Hebrew of Gen.
xli, 8, 24, and in Ex. vii, 11, 22, viii, 3, 14, 15, ix, 11
(*bis*).   Since this word occurs in no other Aramaic dialect except that of Daniel, no light upon its meaning in
Daniel can be derived from these sources.¹   When we
remember the part which the name bears in Egyptian sorcery, we can well believe, however, that their
chief sorcerers received their designation from the fact
that they had power in calling names,² and that the
Arameans and Hebrews adopted the name to denote
those who bound or freed by the power of names.

¹ In the Aramaic of the Targum of Onkelos, of the Samaritan Targum, and of the Syriac Peshitto, *hartom* is always rendered by *harrash*,
except in the Peshitto of Daniel v, 11, where it is rendered "wise men."
The Arabic of Saadya's translation of the Pentateuch renders it by
ulema, "wise men," except in Ex. vii, 11, 22, where it has *sahana*,
"enchanter."   The Arabic of Daniel always gives *rakka*, "charmer."
The usual translation in the LXX and Theodotion is *'epaoidos*, "enchanter"; though it is rendered by "wise men" in the LXX of Daniel i, 20, and
ii, 10.   The derivation and primary meaning of the word are so uncertain
that it is impossible to dogmatize about them.   Probably the majority
of scholars who have discussed the subject derive the word from *heret*,
"stylus," by affixing an *m*.   The meaning then would be scribe, or
engraver; and the word would correspond in sense to the Egyptian
sacred scribe spoken of by the Greek writers.

Hoffman compares it to an Arabic word with the same four radicals
meaning "nose," and would make the original sense to have been one
who sang through the nose, hence "chanter," "having the nose in the
air."   Lane defines the word as having the meaning "chief," "fore-
most in affairs and in the military forces."   Nearly everyone quotes
the opinions of Jablonsky and Rossi that it may be an Egyptian word
denoting "thaumaturgus" or "guardian of secret things"; but these are
both so far-fetched as to be most unlikely.   It would, according to the
rules of transliteration from Egyptian into Hebrew, be capable of derivation from *hr*, "chief," and *dm*, "to name," and would then mean
"chief of the spellbinders."¹

² Compare the significance attributed to the name of Solomon in the
Arabian Nights.

¹ See Wilkinson, *Ancient Egyptians.* i. 168; and Griffith's *Stories of
the High Priests of Memphis.*

This power of the name played a prominent part in Babylonian religion also. In the treatment of disease, the name of the demon or disease to be exorcised had to be mentioned, and, also, the name of the god by whose power the exorcism was accomplished. In order to gain the help of the god without which the devil or demon could not be expelled, the priests would recite his praises and chant their prayers and supplications; and from this essential factor of the art of exorcism arose perhaps the hymns of praise which are so often found among the incantations of the Babylonians.[1]

As to the meaning of *gazer*, the last term employed in Daniel to denote classes of wise men, very little can be said positively. The root does not occur in Assyrio-Babylonian; nor is a word from the root having a satisfactory meaning to be found in any other Aramaic dialects, nor in Arabic, Hebrew, or Ethiopic.[2]

[1] See Shrank: *Babylonische Sühnriten*, pp. 20–27; Thompson: *The Devils and Evil Spirits in Babylonia and Assyria, passim;* Jastrow: *Die Religion Babyloniens und Assyriens;* and Rogers: *The Religion of Babylonia and Assyria*, p. 146. Compare also the numerous cases of this kind of magic in the Arabian Nights.

[2] In Hebrew, the verb *gazar* is found in the meaning "decide, decree," in Job. xxii, 28, where Eliphaz says to Job: "Thou shalt also *decree* a thing and it shall be established unto thee"; and in Esther ii, 1, where it is said that Ahasuerus remembered Vashti and what had been *done* against her. The Targum of Onkelos uses it in Ex. xv, 25, to translate the verb "to establish" in the phrase "to establish a statute," as the equivalent of the Hebrew *sim*, to establish. This passage may afford us the missing link with which to connect the Aramaic *gazer* with the Babylonian, *shamu* = Heb. *sim*. The *mushim shimtu* is "the decreer of decrees, or oracles." We may compare the synonym of *shimtu*, i. e., *paristu*, "oracle," which is from a root meaning "to cut, decide," just as *gezira*, "decree," in Aramaic is from the root *gezar*, "to cut, decide." *Gazer*, then, would be the translation of the Babylonian *mushim*, or *paris*, and could mean a man who made out, or conveyed to men the decrees of the gods. He would be the earthly representative of the

The Hebrew word *mekashshefim* is never used of the wise men. In Daniel ii, 2, the only place in which it occurs in the book, the English version renders it by *sorcerers*. Neither the root of this word nor any derivation of the root was used in this sense in any Aramaic dialect.[1]

The Hebrew employs the noun *kashp* always in the bad sense of an "evil enchantment," and the *nomen agentis* of this is equivalent in meaning to the English "wizard, witch, or sorcerer." The word for "witchery or witchcraft" is found six times in the Hebrew Bible, to wit: in Is. xlvii, 9, 12; Mi. v, 11; Na. iii, 4 *bis*, and in 2 Ki. ix, 22. The word *mekashsheph*, "wizard or sorcerer," is found in Deut. xviii, 10, Ex. vii, 11; Mal. iii, 5, and Dan. ii, 2, while its feminine occurs in Ex. xxii, 17. The verb *kishsheph* is found only in 2 Ch. xxxiii, 6. All of these except the participial form are found in Babylonian and were probably borrowed from it; or possibly go back to a time when Babylonian and Hebrew were one. The Sumerian sign *uh* denotes the Babylonian words for "poison, spittle, blood, and *kishpu*." Perhaps the best illustration of the relation of witchcraft to the dream of Nebuchadnezzar is to be found in the prayer addressed to Marduk by a sick man through his priest (*mashmashu*). As King translates this portion of the prayer in his *Babylonian Magic*, p. 62, it reads:

---

heavenly "*mushim*" of Ea, or of Bel, and the other great gods who establish the fates. *Obelisk of Shalmaneser III*, obv. 5, 14.

His place of abode, and activity, may well have been the "Dul-Azag," "place of fates," "chamber of fates," of which Nebuchadnezzar speaks (Langdon, xv, Col. ii, 54, and Col. v, 12–14) and which Delitzsch thinks to have been "the earthly image of the heavenly Upshukkinnaku."

[1] In the Syriac the verb is used in a good sense for "to pray."

O my God, by the command of thy mouth may there never approach any evil, the magic of the sorcerer and of the sorceress (*upish kashshapi u kashshapti*); may there never approach me the poisons of the evil men; may there never approach the evil of charms of powers and portents of heaven and of earth.

In number 50, 22, of the same book Ashurbanipal prays that his god may free him from evil bewitchment (*pushir kishpiya*), using the same verb which we find so often in Daniel for "interpret." To practice sorcery was punishable with death by drowning, according to the law of Hammurabi.[1] This was the law also, among the Hebrews: "Thou shalt not suffer a witch to live" (Ex. xxii, 17). The question might be asked, then, why Nebuchadnezzar summoned the sorcerers to interpret his dream. The text given in Behrens[2] would explain this, if we accept the reading which permits the translation: "from before the wind may the king be bewitched."[3] According to this, a man might be bewitched for his good against some evil. This, then, may have been the reason why Nebuchadnezzar summoned the wizards. They sent bad dreams; therefore, they should explain them, and tell what they had sent.[4]

[1] Harper, *The Code of Hammurabi*, sec. 2.
[2] *Ass. Bab. Briefe Cultischen Inhalts*, p. 17.
[3] *Ishtu pan zigi sharru likashshaph.*
See also Harper, vii, 660, and i, 18, 11, and 25; and Behrens, p. 16.
[4] It must be remembered, too, that the *Piel* stem in Hebrew may express "the taking away of the object denoted by the noun," *e. g., chitte'*, "to take away sin"; *dishshen*, "to take away the ashes"; *sheresh*, "to root out." (See Cowley's Gesenius, §52h.) This usage is found, also, in Arabic, Aramaic, and New Hebrew (see Wright's *Arab. Gram.*, vol. i, §41 and Siegfried & Strack's *N. H. Gram*). If we take the intensive in this sense in *likashshaph*, it would mean "may [the king] be freed from witchcraft." This privative sense may possibly occur in the phrase

The results of this investigation of the names of the classes of wise men mentioned in the Book of Daniel might be summed up by saying that the *'ashephs* and *'ashshaphs* were certainly exorcists who used chants and purifications (?) to drive out disease and to avert calamity; that the *mekashshephs* were wizards, who bound their victims by means of philters, spittle, etc., and had power to send bad dreams and evil spirits among them, as well as to release them from the witcheries which they had caused; that the *gazers* and *kaldus* were astrologers and augurs, who told fortunes, foretold plagues, interpreted omens and dreams, forecasted horoscopes or nativities, etc.; that the *hartums* were sacred scribes who wrote prescriptions and formulas for the use of the sick and those who attempted to cure them, and "spellbinders" who bound and loosed by the power of names of potency; and that the *hakims*, or wise men, embraced all these and others who were not included in these classes. Daniel was found by Nebuchadnezzar to be ten times better than all the *'ashshaphs* and *hartums* of Babylon. He was made chief, or master, of the king's wise men (ii, 48), and of his *hartums* (v, 11), and of all the classes mentioned, except apparently the wizards,—as to whom it is not said, at least, that he ever had anything to do with them. It will be noted that nowhere in the Bible is connection with *'ashephs*, *'ashshaphs*, *hartums*, *gazers*, *kaldus*, or *hakkims*, expressly forbidden. Only the *hakkims*, *hartums*, and *mekashshephs* are ever mentioned outside of Daniel. The first of these three are always spoken of with praise; the second without praise or blame; and the last only

---

ramankunu ina pan ili la tuhattaa of K. 84, 24, *i. e.*, "Before God ye shall not free yourselves from sin"; and also in *dannati*, "distress," *i. e.*, "deprived of strength." (See King, *Magic*, p. 94.)

with condemnation. "A pious Jew," therefore, "and one true to the law," may certainly have studied, at least, the sciences and arts practiced by these uncondemned classes, without laying himself open to the charge of breaking the letter of the law. We see no reason, either, why he may not have studied all about the practices of the wizards without himself being a sorcerer.

Besides, we think it may be rightly doubted that a pious Jew, that is, one deemed pious according to the estimation of the Jews of the time of the author of Daniel,—whenever he lived and wrote,—cannot have been an astrologer and an exorcist and a dream interpreter. Josephus cites, apparently with approval, a statement of Berosus, to the effect that "Abram was a man righteous and great among the Chaldeans and skillful in the celestial science.[1] He says, also, that one of the Egyptian

sacred scribes (*hierogrammaticoi*), who were very sagacious in foretelling future events truly, told the king that about this time there would be a child born of the Israelites, who, if he were reared, would bring the Egyptian dominion low and would raise the Israelites; that he would excel all men in virtue, and obtain a glory that would be remembered through all ages.[2]

This same scribe attempted to kill Moses at a later time, when as a child and having been adopted by Pharaoh's daughter, he cast to the ground and trod upon the crown of Pharaoh which the latter had placed upon his head; thus attesting, said the priest, his prediction that this child would bring the dominion of

---

[1] *Antiq.*, I, vii, 2.　　　　　　[2] *Antiq.*, I, vii, 2.

Egypt low.[1] "Because of this prophecy the Egyptians abstained from killing him and later made Moses general of their army against the Ethiopians in response to their own oracles and presages."[2]

As to Solomon, moreover, God granted him to learn the science of demonology for the profit and service of men, and he composed epodes[3] by which diseases are assuaged; and he left behind him methods of treatment for exorcists by which those who are bound drive out the demons so that they never return, and this method of practice prevails with us even now; for I have seen a certain one of my own country whose name was Eleazar, in the presence of Vespasian and his sons and his chiliarchs and the multitude of his soldiers, releasing people who had been seized by these demons, the skill and wisdom of Solomon being thus clearly established.[4]

Josephus, moreover, professes that not merely he himself had prophetic dreams, but that he had a certain power in interpreting them.[5]

According to the Targum of Jonathan ben Uzziel, the king of Egypt in Moses' time had a dream in which he saw all the land of Egypt put in one scale of a balance and in the other a lamb which was heavier than all the land of Egypt; upon which he sent and called all the enchanters (*harrash*) of Egypt and told them his dream; whereupon Jannes and Jambres, the chiefs of the enchanters, opened their mouths and said to Pharaoh: "A boy is about to be born in the congregation of Israel,

---

[1] *Antiq.*, II, ix, 7. [2] *Id.*

[3] That is, chants, such as were used by the enchanters of Babylon and Egypt and by the Magi. Herodotus, I, 132.

[4] *Antiq.*, VIII, ii, 5.

[5] See *Wars of the Jews*, III, viii, 3, 9.

through whose hand all the land of Egypt is to be destroyed."[1]

In the book of Tobit, an evil spirit is said to have been exorcised by means of the liver of a fish.[2]

In the Acts of the Apostles,[3] Simon Magus practiced his arts of magic by using the power of *names* to drive out evil spirits.

The Lord, also, refers to such practices among the Jews of his time, when he says: "If I by Beelzebub cast out demons, by whom do your sons cast them out?"[4]

We have thus shown that according to the views of the Scriptures and of the ancient Jews at all times, there was nothing wrong either in dreams or in the interpretation of them; and that Jewish opinion as preserved in Josephus, the book of Tobit, the Targum of Jonathan ben Uzziel, and elsewhere, did not condemn the use of incantations and the practice of exorcism and other similar arts.

Finally, we come to consider the question as to whether Daniel is said to have been a member of any of these classes of dream-interpreters which are mentioned in his book. It will be noted that he is never called a *hartum* nor an *'ashshaph*, but is said to have been ten times better than all of them in knowledge and wisdom. It is not said either that he was an *'asheph* nor a *mekashsheph* nor a *gazer*, nor a *kaldu*. That he was a *hakim* is rightly inferred from the fact that he was sought for to be killed, when the decree went forth that all the wise men should be killed; but elsewhere he is always called chief (*rab*) of the wise men, or of the *hartums*, or of three or four classes together. He is, in fact, called chief of all classes, except of the *mekash-*

---

[1] See T. J. ben Uzziel to Ex. i, 15.   [2] See chapters vi and viii.
[3] See chapter viii.   [4] Matt. xii, 27.

25

shephs, the only class which is directly condemned by law. Once he is called chief of the *sagans* over all the wise men of Babylon. This phrase we shall discuss below. At present, let us look at the meaning of the word *rab*, "chief," in its relation to the objects, or persons, over which the *rab* was set. The only point we need to discuss in this connection, is whether the *rab* was necessarily of the same class and practicer of the same arts and crafts as those who were set under him. It might seem to most to be sufficient merely to state as an obvious fact not needing proof that he might have been chief of the *hartums* and others without himself being one. But as some have controverted it, and seem to think that Daniel must have been an individual of the same kind as those over whom he was set as chief, it may be well to pause and discuss the term *rab*, as it is used.

In Arabic *rab* is the most ordinary title of God, occurring in the Koran as a designation of the deity only less frequently than the word *Allah* itself. He is the lord of all creatures, not because he is like them or of them, but as their maker and preserver and ruler and owner. So a master of slaves is not a slave, but the owner of the slaves, the *dominus*. In Hebrew, *rab* meant captain, or master, or chief. Thus, Nebuzaradan was *captain* of the guard (Jer. xli, 10); Ashpenaz was *master* of the eunuchs (Dan. i. 3); Ahasuerus had *officers* of his house (Est. i. 8); Jonah's ship had its *master* of the ropes (Jon. i, 6). In Assyrio-Babylonian the word was of much more general use than in Arabic or Hebrew. There were *rabs* set over the gardens of the king, over the watering machines, over the treasury, over the stables, the courts, the flocks, the house, the temple, the cities, the prisoners; over the governors, the captains, the bowmen, and the divisions of the army; over the merchants, the builders (?), the seers, enchanters, and exorcists; there was a captain of the king, a chief of the captains, or princes, of the king, and a *rab* of the sons of the king, and a chief of the house of Belshazzar the son of the king.

It will be noted that the *'ashiph*, the *mashmash*, the *bari* (or seers), and the *zimmeri*, or enchanters, all have a chief. One should remark, further, that a *rab* does not necessarily perform the duties of the ones over whom he is set. The soldiers were directed by their *rab* and led by him; but doubtless did many menial duties from which he would be exempt. The *rab* of the sons of the king may have been beneath them in birth, but would be their teacher. No one would hold the *rab* responsible for all of the acts or beliefs of the scholar, any more than he would hold Seneca responsible for Nero, or Bossuet for Louis XV. The chief of the chiefs of the king would probably be the highest chief, or lord, next to the king, according to the common Semitic idiom for expressing the superlative by putting a noun in the singular before the same noun in the plural, as in the phrase "king of kings and lord of lords." From these examples, it is evident that a *rab* may or may not have been of the same knowledge, class, dignity, or practice, as those over whom he was placed. We have had secretaries of the navy who were not trained at Annapolis. England has had ministers of war who were not distinguished generals. France has had in her cabinet ministers of religion who were not ecclesiastics. So the fact that Daniel was made *rab* of the wise men, or of the *hartums*, and others, does not prove that he was one of them, or that he did what they did. The book of Daniel says he knew ten times more of real knowledge and wisdom than all the '*ashephs* and *hartums* of Babylon; and that he got his knowledge as dream-interpreter from God through prayer, and not by divination or sorcery. It never calls him a *hartum*, an '*ashshaph*, an '*asheph*, a *mekashsheph*, a *kaldu*, or a *gazer;* but a man who was made wise through study, abstinence, and the favor of God. He may have known all the mysteries of the Babylonian seers, priests, and enchanters; but there is no evidence in the book of Daniel, nor anywhere else, to show that Daniel practiced the black art, nor the heathen methods of divination in any form, nor to show that he became a member of any of these orders. It is said simply that he was the superior of these in knowledge and wisdom and in power of interpretation of dreams and omens. The means he used were proper according to the precepts and examples of the Scriptures.

As to his being *rab* of the Babylonian sorcerers of whatever class, this was an appointment of the king. What duties or functions were involved in the office we know not. It may have been simply an honorary title, or the grant of a position of precedency in court functions and ceremonies. That it did not imply a permanent position with onerous duties and continuous service, would seem to follow from the fact that the queen mother had to recall to Belshazzar that Nebuchadnezzar had ever made the appointment. So that, in conclusion, we can fairly claim that the case against the author of Daniel, on the ground that he makes his hero, though a pious Jew, to have been a member of a class of Chaldean wise men contrary to the Jewish law, has not been made out. The charge has not been proven. On the contrary, the account of Daniel has been shown to be entirely consistent with itself and with the prerequi-

site historical surroundings, supposing it to be a record
of events which took place at Babylon in the sixth
century B.C.

CONCLUSION

In the above discussion we have shown that the six
assumptions mentioned on page 370 are all false
and that the objection to the historicity of the book of
Daniel on the ground that a strict Jew cannot have been
made chief of the heathen sages of Babylon, nor initiated
into their class, is unsupported by the evidence drawn
from the Jews themselves, as well as from the monuments, as to what the character of the wise men really
was. We have shown, further, that the objection, if
valid, would militate as much against the ideas of the
pious Jews in the second century B.C., as against those
held by them in the sixth century B.C.; inasmuch as the
literary conception of such a character and the reception
of a work based on such a conception would be as much
against their ideas as the historical existence of such a
man would be. Moreover, we have shown that "the
confused notions" about Daniel in his relations to the
wise men of Babylon, as well as about these wise men,
are true not so much of the author of Daniel as of those
who criticize the statements of the book in reference
to them. And finally, we have shown that there is
no reason for believing that Daniel may not have been
and done all that the book of Daniel says that he was
and did, without any infringement of the law or the prophets, or contravention of the religious ideas of the
Jews at any time of their history.

BIBLIOGRAPHY OF PRINCIPAL WORKS CITED

AJSLL—*The American Journal of Semitic Literature and Language.*
American Journal of Insanity.
ANDERSON, SIR ROBERT. *Daniel in the Critics' Den.* New York.
ASSEMANI, J. S. *Bibliotheca Orientalis*, etc. Rome, 1719–1728.
——*Ephræmi Syri Opera omnia*, etc. Rome, 1737–1746.
BA—*Beiträge zur Assyriologie.* Leipzig, 1890.
BÄHR, J. C. F. *Ctesias Cnidius, Operum reliquæ.* Frankfurt, 1824.
BARTHOLOMAE, CH. *Altiranisches Wörterbuch.* Strassburg, 1904.
BE—*Babylonian Expedition of the University of Pennsylvania.*
Behistun Inscription. See BEZOLD, SPIEGEL, and TOLMAN.
BEHRENS, EMIL. *Assyrisch-babylonische Briefe kültischen, Inhalts aus der Sangonidenzeit.* Hinrichs, 1906.
BEHRMANN, GEORGE. *Das Buch Daniel.* Göttingen, 1894.
BEROSUS. See CORY, *Ancient Fragments.*
BERTHOLDT, L. *Daniel.* Erlangen, 1806.
BEVAN, A. R. *A Short Commentary on the Book of Daniel.* Cambridge, 1892.
BEZOLD, CARL. *Catalogue of the Cuneiform Tablets in the Koujundjik Collection of the British Museum, 1889–1899.*
——*Die Achämenideninschriften.* Hinrichs, 1882.
Br.—Brünnow, q. v.
BREASTED, J. H. *A History of the Ancient Egyptians.* New York, 1908.
—— *Ancient Records of Egypt.* Chicago, 1906.
BREDERIK, EMIL. *Konkordanz zum Targum Onkelos.* Giessen, 1906.
BROCKELMANN, C. *Lexicon Syriacum.* Edinburgh, 1895.
BRÜNNOW, R. E. *A Classified List of all Simple and Compound Cuneiform Ideographs*, etc. Brill, 1889.
BRUGSCH and BOURIANT. *Le Livre des Rois.* Cairo, 1887.
BURNOUF, E. *Dictionaire Classique, Sanscrit-Français*, Paris, 1866.
BURRELL, R. D., M.D. *The Insane Kings of the Bible.* See *American Journal of Insanity*, 1894.
Cam.—STRASSMAIER'S *Inschriften von Cambyses.*
CIS—*Corpus Inscriptionum Semiticarum.* Paris, 1881.
CLAY, ALBERT T. *Business Documents of the Murashu Sons of Nippur.* (See *Publications of the Babylonian Section of the U. of P. Museum*, vol. ii, 1912, and BE series A, vol. ix, 1898, vol. x, 1904.)

CLAY, ALBERT T. *Aramaic Endorsements on the Documents of the Marashu Sons* (in O. T. Studies in Memory of W. R. Harper). Chicago, 1908.

——— *Miscellaneous Inscriptions from the Yale Babylonian Collection.* New Haven, 1916.

——— *Yale Oriental Series, Babylonian Texts.* New Haven, 1915.

——— *Babylonian Records in the Library of J. Pierpont Morgan.* New York, 1912–1913.

COOK, S. A. *The Law of Moses and the Code of Hammurabi.* London, 1903.

COOKE, G. A. *A Textbook of North Semitic Inscriptions.* Oxford, 1903.

CORNILL, CARL. *Introduction to the Canonical Books of the Old Testament.* London and New York, 1907.

CORY, I. P. *Ancient Fragments.* London, 1832.

CT—*Cuneiform Texts from Babylonian Tablets, etc., in the British Museum.* London, 1896 f.

CURETON, W. *Spicilegium Syriacum.* London, 1855.

Cyr—STRASSMAIER'S *Inschriften von Cyrus.*

DALMAN, G. *Grammatik der jüdisch-Palästinischen Aramäisch.* 2d edition, Leipzig, 1905.

DALMAN, S. H. *Aramäisch neubehäisches Wörterbuch.* Frankfurt, 1901.

Dar—STRASSMAIER'S *Inschriften von Darius.*

DAVIS, JOHN D. See *O. T. and Semitic Studies.* Chicago, 1908.

DELITZSCH, FRIEDRICH. *Assyrisches Handwörterbuch.* Leipzig, 1896.

——— *Assyrische Grammatik.* Berlin, 1889.

DE LUCA, MARIANUS. *Institutiones Juris Ecclesiastici Publici.* Neo-Eborici, 1901.

DE WETTE—SCHRADER. *Einleitung in das Alte Testament.* Berlin, 1869.

DHORME, P. PAUL. *Choix de textes assyro-babylonien, etc.* Paris, 1907.

DILLMANN, C. F. A. *Lexicon Linguæ Æthiopicæ.* Leipzig, 1865.

DRIVER, S. R. *An Introduction to the Literature of the Old Testament.* Edinburgh and New York. 1st edit. 1891, 13th edit. 1908–1910.

Ecclesiasticus. See STRACK and SMEND.

EPHRAEM SYRUS. *Opera omnia quæ exstant, etc.* Romæ, 1737–1746.

EUSEBIUS. *Chronikon.* Ed. Schoene, Berlin, 1875.

EVETTS, B. S. A. *Inscriptions of the Reigns of Evil-Merodach, Neriglissar, and Laboroarchad.* Leipzig, 1892.

FARRAR, F. W. *The Expositor's Bible, the Book of Daniel.* New York, 1895.

FLEISCHER, H. L. *Morgenländische Forschungen, Festschrift, etc.* Leipzig, 1875.

FLÜGEL, G. *Concordaniæ Corani Arabicæ.* Leipzig, 1875.

FRANK, KARL. *Babylonische Beschwörungsreliefe.* Hinrichs, 1908.

——— *Studien zur Babylonischen Religion.* Strassburg, 1911.

GA—*Gesammelte Abhandlungen von Paul de Lagarde.* Leipzig, 1866.
GESENIUS, W. *Hebrew Grammar.* (Kautzsch-Cowley) Oxford, 1898.
GIBBON, EDWARD. *The Decline and Fall of the Roman Empire.* London and New York, 1898–1901.
GRIFFITH, F. L. *Stories of the High Priests of Memphis.* Oxford, 1900.
GUIZOT, F. P. G. *A History of France.* New York, 1885.
HARPER, R. F. *Code of Hammurabi.* Chicago, 1904.
—— *Assyrian and Babylonian Letters,* Chicago, 1892–1914.
IBN HISHAM. *Das Leben Muhammeds.* See Wüstenfeld.
JASTROW, A. *A Dictionary of the Targumin.* London and New York, 1886–1903.
JASTROW, MORRIS, JR. *Die Religion Babyloniens und Assyriens.* Giessen, 1905–1912.
JEREMIAS, A. *The Old Testament in the Light of the Ancient East.* London and New York, 1911.
Jewish Encyclopedia. New York, 1901–1906.
JOHNS, C. H. W. *Assyrian Deeds and Documents,* etc. Cambridge, 1898–1901.
—— *Babylonian and Assyrian Laws, Contracts, and Letters.* New York, 1904.
Josephus Flavius, Genuine Works, by Wm. Whiston. New York, 1824.
Opera. Niese Berlin, 1887–1897.
Julian the Apostate (or *Julianos der Abtrünnige*), by J. G. E. HOFFMANN. Leiden, 1880.
JUSTI, F. *Handbuch der Zendsprache.* Leipzig, 1864.
KAT—*Die Keilinschriften und das Alte Testament.* 2nd edition, Giessen, 1883.
KB—*Keilinschriftliche Bibliothek.* Berlin, 1889.
KING, L. W. *Babylonian Magic and Sorcery.* London, 1896.
KNUDTZON, K. L. *Assyrische Gebete an den Sonnengott.* Leipzig, 1892.
KOHLER and UNGNAD. *Assyrische Rechtsurkunden.* Leipzig, 1915;
——*Hundert Ansgewählte Rechtsurkunden.* Leipzig, 1911.
KOHLER, J., PEISER, F. E., and UNGNAD, A. *Hammurabi's Gesetz.* Leipzig, 1904–1911.
KU—Kohler and Ungnad.
KUGLER, F. X. *Sternkunde und Sterndienst in Babel.* Münster, 1907.
LANE, EDWARD WILLIAM. *The Thousand and One Nights or the Arabian Nights Entertainments.* New York, 1848.
——*An Arabic-English Lexicon.* London and Edinburgh, 1883–1893.
LANGDON, STEPHEN. *Building Inscriptions of the Neo-Babylonian Empire.* Günther, 1905.
LEVY, J. *Chaldäisches Wörterbuch.* Leipzig, 1881.
LIDZBARSKI, U. *Handbuch der nordsemitschen Epigraphik.* Weimar, 1898.

LOT—*An Introduction to the Literature of the O. T.* By Driver, q. v.

LOTH, OTTO. See Fleischer's *Festschrift.*

LOTZ, WM. *Die Inschriften Tiglath Pileser's I.* Leipzig, 1880.

MANETHO. See Cory's *Ancient Fragments.*

MANETHO, S. *Apotelesmatica.* Paris, 1862.

MARTI, KARL. *Kurzgefasste Grammatik der Aramäischen Sprache.* Berlin, 1911.

MAXIMUS. *Anecdota Astrologica.* Leipzig, 1877.

MEINHOLD, J. *Beiträge zur Erklärung des Buches Daniel.* Leipzig, 1888.

MEISSNER-POST. *Bauinschriften Asarhaddon's.* (See BA, iii, p. 189–362.)

MUSS-ARNOLT, W. *A Concise Dictionary of the Assyrian Language.* New York, 1905.

MVAG—*Mitteilungen der Vorderasiatischen Gesellschaft.* Berlin, 1896.

Nbp—STRASSMAIER'S *Inschriften von Nabopolassar.*

Nd—STRASSMAIER'S *Inschriften von Nabunaid.*

Ng—STRASSMAIER'S *Inschriften von Nergalsharuṣur.*

Ngl—*Id.*

Nk—STRASSMAIER'S *Inschriften von Nabuchodonosor.*

NÖLDEKE, TH. *Mandäische Grammatik.* Halle, 1875.

——*Grammatik der Neusyrischen Sprache.* Leipzig, 1868.

NORBERG, M. *Lexidion Cod. Naz.* Hofniae, 1817.

OLMSTEAD, DR. A. T. *Western Asia in the Days of Sargon of Assyria.* New York, 1908.

Onkelos, Targum of. See Walton's *Polyglot.*

Peek, Collection of Sir Henry. Inscribed Babylonian Tablets. Part II, edited by T. G. Pinches, London (no date).

PEISER, F. E. *Babylonische Verträge der Berliner Museums,* etc. Berlin, 1890.

——*Skizze der Babylonischen Gesellschaft.* MVAG, 1896.

PESHITTO. See Walton's *Polyglot.*

PETERMANN, H. *Pentateuchus Samaritanus.* Berlin, 1872.

PETRIE, W. M. F. *A History of Egypt.* London, 1896.

PHILLIPS, GEO. *The Doctrine of Addai the Apostle.* London, 1876.

PINCHES, T. G. *The Old Testament in the Light of the Historical Records of Assyria and Babylonia.* London and New York, 1902.

POGNON, H. *Inscriptions Sémitiques de la Syrie.* Paris, 1907.

POLYHISTOR, ALEXANDER. See Cory's *Ancient Fragments.*

PRESCOTT, W. H. *History of Philip the Second.* 1855.

PRINCE, J. D. *A Critical Commentary on the Book of Daniel.* Leipzig, 1899.

PSBA—*Proceedings of the Society of Biblical Archœology.*

PTR—*Princeton Theological Review.*

R—*The Cuneiform Inscriptions of Western Asia.* London, 1861 f.

RANKE, H. *Early Babylonian Personal Names.* Philadelphia, 1905.

RAWLINSON, GEORGE. *The Five Great Monarchies of the Ancient Eastern World,* 1862–67.

——*Bampton Lectures for 1859* (The Historical Evidences of the Truth of the Scripture Records Stated).

Records of the Past. London, 1875 and 1873–1881.

Révue d'Assyriologie.

ROGERS, R. W. *The Religion of Babylonia and Assyria.* New York, 1908.

Saadya's Version of the Pentateuch. See Walton's *Polyglot.*

SACHAU, EDWARD. *Festschrift.* Berlin, 1815.

—— *Aramäische Papyrus.* Berlin, 1911.

Samaritan Targum. See PETERMANN.

SAYCE, A. H. *Higher Criticism and the Verdict of the Monuments.* London, 1894.

SCHECHTER, S. *Documents of Jewish Sectaries. Fragments of a Zadokite Work.* Cambridge, 1910.

SCHORR, MOSES. *Altbabylonische Rechtsurkunden.* Wien, 1907.

SCHRANK, W. *Babylonische Sühnriten,* etc. Leipzig, 1908.

SCHRÖDER, P. *Die Phönizische Sprache.* Halle, 1869.

SIEGFRIED and STRACK. *Lehrbuch der neuhebräischen Sprache.* Leipzig, 1884.

SMEND, R. *Die Weisheit des Jesus Sirach.* Berlin, 1906.

Smith's Dictionary of the Bible. New York, 1870.

SMITH, W. ROBERTSON. *Kinship and Marriage in Early Arabia.* Cambridge, 1885.

SPRIEGEL, FR. *Die altpersischen Keilinschriften,* etc. Leipzig, 1881.

STEINGASS, F. *English-Arabic Dictionary.* London, 1882.

STRABO. *Rerum Geographicarum,* etc. Leipzig, 1829.

STRACK, HERMANN L. *Die Sprüche Jesus', des Sohnes Sirachs.* Leipzig, 1903.

——*Lehrbuch der neuhebräischen Sprache.* See SIEGFRIED.

STRASSMAIER, J. N. *Die Inschriften von Nabuchodonosor, Nobonidus, Cyrus, Cambyses, and Darius.* Leipzig, 1889–1897.

SWETE, H. B. *The Old Testament in Greek.* Cambridge, 1899.

TALLQUIST, K. L. *Neu-babylonisches Namenbuch zu den Geschäftsurkunden aus der zeit des Šamaššumukin bis Xerxes.* (Acta. soc. F., Tom. xxxii, No. 2, 1905.)

—— *Die Assyrische Beschwörungsserie Maklu.* (Acta Soc. F., Tom. xx, No. 6, 1894.)

Targum of Jonathan ben Uzziel. See Walton's *Polyglot.*

Theodotion's Translation of Daniel in Swete's edition of the LXX.

THOMPSON, R. C. *The Devils and Evil Spirits in Babylonia,* etc. London, 1903–1904.

THOMPSON, R. C. *The Reports of the Magicians and Astrologers of Nineveh and Babylon.* London, 1900.

TIELE, C. P. *Babylonische-Assyrische Geschichte.* Gotha, 1886.

TOLMAN, H. C. *Ancient Persian Lexicon,* etc. New York, 1908.

TUKE, D. H. *Dictionary of Psychological Medicine.* 1892.

VAB—*Vorderasiatische Bibliothek.*

VASD—*Vorderasiatische Schriftdenkmäler.* Leipzig, 1907.

Victoria Institute, Transactions of.

VOGUË, LE CONTE DE. *Inscriptions Sémitiques, Syrie Centrale.* Paris, 1868–1877.

VON LONGERKE, C. *Das Buch Daniel.* Königsberg, 1855.

Vorderasiatische Schriftdenkmäler. Leipzig, 1907.

VSD—*Vorderasiatische Schriftdenkmäler.* Leipzig, 1907.

Vulgate, Latin. See Walton's *Polyglot.*

WALTON, B. *Biblia Sacra Polyglotta.* London, 1657–1661.

WEIDNER, E. F. *Handbuch der Babylonischen Astronomie.* Leipzig, 1915.

WEISSBACH, F. H. *Die Keilinschriften der Achämeniden.* See VAB. Leipzig, 1911.

WEISSBACH, F. H. *Die Achämenideninschriften zweiter Art.* Leipzig, 1890.

——*Die Altpersischen Keilinschriften.* Leipzig, 1893–1908.

WELLHAUSEN, JULIUS. *Prolegomena to the History of Israel.* Edinburgh, 1885.

WILCKEN, ULRICH. *Griechische Ostraka aus Aegypten und Nubien.* Leipzig, 1899.

WILKINSON, J. G. *The Manners and Customs of the Ancient Egyptians.* Boston, 1885.

WINCKLER, H. *Der Thontafelfund von El-Amarna.* Berlin, 1889.

—— *Tel-el-Amarna Letters.* New York, 1896.

—— *Die Keilinschriften Sargons.* Leipzig, 1889.

WRIGHT, C. H. H. *Daniel and Its Critics.* London, 1906.

WRIGHT, W. *The Chronicle of Joshua the Stylite.* Cambridge, 1882.

—— *Arabic Grammar.* Third Edition, Cambridge, 1896.

WÜSTENFELT, FERDINAND. *Das Leben Muhammed's nach Muhammed Ibn Ishak,* etc. Göttingen, 1858.

Yale Oriental Series, Babylonian Texts. New Haven, 1915.

ZA—*Zeitschrift für Assyriologie.*

ZDMG—*Zeitschrift der deutschen morgenländischen Gesellschaft.*

ZEHNPFUND-LANGDON. *Die neubabylonischen Königsinschriften.* Leipzig, 1912.

Zeitschrift für Aegyptische Sprache.

ZIMMERN, H. *Beiträge zur Kenntniss der bab. Religion.* Leipzig, 1901.

INDEX OF SUBJECT MATTER, SOURCES, ETC.

A

Abgar, 32, 141
Abu-Habba cylinder, 17, 122
Abydenus, 33, 48, 57, 58, 289, 334
Accadian words in Babylonian, 339
Adad-Nirari, 11
Alexander, 163, 165, 272, 274, 335-337
Amasis, 39
Amelu, 121
Anachronism, 276
Antiochus Epiphanes, 167
Aramaic, 30, 31; words for king in, 94, 113, 182, 183, 192; *rada* and *kavash* not Aramaic, 96; foreign words in, 319-322; words for wise in, 374-377
Aramean, 179
Ararat, 116
Arrian, 6, 165
Artaxerxes I., 170
—— II., 136, 140, 228
—— III, 136, 228, 229
Asharidu, 36
Ashkenaz, 155
Ashurbanipal, 12, 40, 67, 112, 116, 139, 306
Ashuretililani, 40, 136
Ashurnaṣirpal, 36, 67
Asnapper, 6
Assyrian records, 4, 14, 16, 20, 22, 25, 26, *et al.*
Astyages, 38, 67, 269
Azariah, 10.

B

Babylon, records of, 12, 20, *et al.*; two kings of, at the same time, 106, 107-108; different meanings of the phrase "king of Babylon," 112, 113; difference between "king of Babylon" and "king of Chaldea," 114; conquest of, by Cyrus, 149; taken by Medes, 151; conquest of, by Darius Hystaspis, 244-247
Banu, 341 f., 347
Bartholomæ, 139
Behistun inscription, 15, 39, 121, 142, 154, 156, 177, 214, 238, 242, 245, 249, 261
Behrmann, 161
Belshazzar, spelling of name no indication of late date, 10-15; testimony of the monuments as to a man of that name, 101-103; not king over the empire of Nabunaid, 106; king of Babylon part of one year, 106; king of only part of Nabunaid's dominion, 107-110; son of both Nebuchadnezzar and Nabunaid, 117-122; in what sense treated as king by his contemporaries, 122-126; not mentioned in the Greek historians, 167
Belteshazzar, 30-36
Berosus, 3, 48, 55-58, 119, 289, 291, 334
Bertholdt, 86, 277, 279
Bevan, 44, 63, 370
Bezold, 121, 130
Bira, fortress, not court, 280-282
Breasted, 79

C

Cambyses, 39, 164, 170
Carchemish IX, 50, 52, 54-56, 60, 64, 74-80
Chaldeans, excursus on the, 341-366; king of, 114; Darius the Mede made king of, 151; kingdom of, different from that of the Persians, 173, 174, 200; and

Chaldeans—*Continued*
  from that of Babylon, 114;
  people of, 326-329; priests of,
  330-337; in the Scriptures,
  329-330; in the classics, 330-
  339; in Babylonian, 337-339;
  in Aramaic, 339-341; wise men
  of, 367-389
Chronicles, the Book of, and
  the reign of Jehoiakim, 52, 53,
  64-66; and the expedition
  against Jerusalem, 73
Chronology. Different ways of
  reckoning the years of a king,
  viii, 68; years of the beginning
  of the reign, 49; different
  datings of the reign of same
  king over different countries,
  115-117; double dating of the
  same document, 129-133; meaning of *iddan* "time," 289-291
Clay, Albert T., 121, 125, 130
Codomannus, 228, 272
Confusion, fallacy of asserting, 128
Conspirators against Smerdis, 39,
  164, 170
Cook, S. A., 118, 120
Cornill, 63, 99, 150, 157, 158, 161,
  165, 264, 271, 272, 277, 284, 297,
  324, 369
Curtius, Quintus, 165, 335 f.
Cylinder of Antiochus, 122; of
  Cyrus, 15, 17, 39, 122, 126, 141,
  153, 260
Cyrus, 17, 34, 38, 39, 67, 103, 109,
  112, 116, 124, 129, 134, 164,
  169, 233 f., 307; religious views
  of, 310; conquest of Babylon,
  149, 265-272; suzerain to
  Darius the Mede, 133-135

D

Daniel, name not mentioned on
  the monuments, vi; nor is his
  name likely to be found on
  them, 25; called Belteshazzar,
  vi; Belshazzar, the abbrevi-
  ated form of Belteshazzar,
  found on monuments, vii, 34;
  ancestors not known, vii, 30
Daniel, book of, on the expedition
  of Nebuchadnezzar, 64; on the
  life of Darius the Mede, 221 f.;
  use of term Chaldean in, 329 f.;
  statements as to the wise men,
  370 f.

Darius Codomannus, 272
Darius Hystaspis, 29, 38, 39, 40,
  119, 164; and the war against
  Greece, 164-165; treats Medi-
  ans as equals of Persians, 154;
  not confused with Darius the
  Mede, 160-162; his system of
  government, 201-203, 211-220;
  not reflected in Darius the
  Mede, 220 f; family of, 223-
  237; age when he became king,
  238-240; manner in which he
  became king, 240-243; names
  of kingdoms over which he ruled,
  243-244; relations to other
  kings, 244-247; conquest of
  Babylon by, 244-246; method
  of government, 247; decrees of,
  248; character of, 259 f.; not
  confused with Xerxes, 264,
  272; religious views of, 31;
  proper names in his inscriptions, 39
Darius the Mede. Meaning of
  the word Darius, 139; sub-king
  under Cyrus, 129-134; probably same as Gobryas, 133-
  143; no tablets dated from his
  reign, 134-137; new tablet of
  Gobryas, 136-137; age when
  he became king, 137; a Mede,
  141; king of the Chaldeans,
  but not of Media, or Persia,
  157-158, 173-174, 186-192; not
  one of the four kings of Persia
  of Dan. 2, 173; not confused with Darius Hystaspis,
  200-220; not a reflection of
  Darius Hystaspis, since they
  were of different nationality,
  224; family, 224, and age, 238;
  became king in different ways,
  240, ruled over different kingdoms, 243; had different relations with other kings, 244,
  pursued different methods of
  government, 247, had different
  relations with those about them,
  253, and were different in
  character, 259; not mentioned
  in the Greek historians, 167-
  169; statements of Daniel with
  regard to, 221-223; and the den
  of lions, 249-253, 316; relation
  to Daniel, 253-259; character of,
  259; decrees of, 298, 309-318

Darius II, 228
Dates, 52, 130–132
Delitzsch, 35
De Wette, 43
Dimgal, 341 f.
Diocles, 290
Diodorus Siculus, 334
Divinity of kings, 312
Driver, 45, 62, 69, 100, 161, 162, 200, 220, 284, 325, 369
Duplicates, 250–253

E

Ecbatana, 137, 141, 143, 153, 210
Edicts of the kings of Babylon not impossible, 296–298
Edicts of the Cæsars, 299–301; of the Inquisition, 301
Egypt, 7, 9, 10, 13–15, et al.
Elam, 156
Era, 130
Esarhaddon, 6, 12, 67, 107, 112
Eusebius, 3, 57, 291, 293
Evident, self, 296
Evil-Merodach, 65, 100, 123, 266

F

Fallacy of positing the sources of an author's information, 145
Farrar, Dean, vi, 18, 24–26
Freeman, Edward, 28, 251
Furnace, fiery, 311

G

G exchanged for k, 338
Gutium, 111, 141, 152–153, 201

H

Herodotus, 4, 8, 19, 21, 80, 107, 109, 138, 139, 153, 215, 238, 240, 242, 246, 249, 269, 331
Hostages, 32, 66
Hystaspis, 139, 140

I

Ibn Hisham, 305
Impossible, use of the term, 296
Inscriptions, building, 37, 38, 126; historical, 39, 126

J

Jehoiachin, 65, 66

Jehoiakim, 43–53, 60, 63, 107
Jeremiah, 61, 69–73; and the reign of Jehoiakim, 49–56, 66; and the Chaldeans, 69–73; and the expedition against Carchemish, 75–80
Jeroboam II, 11
Johns, C. H. W., 29, 118, 120
Josephus, 35, 54, 55, 289, 290, 291, and often
Justi, 176

K

K exchanged with g, 338
Killing of the wise men, 313
King, use of words for, 85–94, 112, 113
Kings, the book of, and the reign of Jehoiakim, 45–48; and the captivity of Judah, 66; and the expedition against Jerusalem, 73
Kings, married wives of predecessors, 119; frequently taken into captivity, 64, 65; two over same country at once, 106–108; the four kings of Persia mentioned in Daniel, 162; Persian kings mentioned in the O. T., 165–172

L

Land, 174–176; words for, in Babylonian, 189; Arabic, 189; Hebrew, 189–192; Persian, 189; Susian, 189
Lane, Edward, 35, 117
Langdon, 37, 111, 289, 303
Laws of kings of Persia, 313
Lengerke, von, 299
Letters of the Babylonians, 19, 125
Lidzbarski, 29
Limmu of Nineveh, 130
Lions, 249–253, 316

M

Maccabees, First book of, 168
—— Second book of, 168
Manasseh, 12, 65, 310
Manetho, 3
Mattathias, 168
Media, 151–158; kings of, 108; helped to conquer Babylon 149, 151–158; relation to Persi..

Media—*Continued*
    154, 231; Daniel never calls
    anyone king of Media, 156;
    Xerxes called king of Media on
    contract tablets, 154, 155
Megasthenes, 48, 57, 58, 289, 334
Meissner, 120
Menahem, 11
Menander, 3
Merenptah, 10
Merodach-Baladan, 10, 13, 124
Method pursued in this book, v
Minni, 156
Muss-Arnolt, 35

N

Nabopolassar, 37
Nabunaid, 13, 15, 17, 20, 38, 40,
    67, 101, 110, 111, 114, 121, 133,
    136, 307; last king of the
    Babylonian empire, 101; dreams
    of, 307; chronicle, 15, 17, 153;
    cylinder, 37
Names, ways of writing proper, in
    Babylonian, 28–36; in building
    and other inscriptions, 37–41;
    dual, 138–139; new, vi, xi, 30,
    366
Naqs-i-Rustam inscription, 143,
    177, 211, 214, 224, 242
Nebuchadnezzar, Aramaic form
    of the Babylonian Nebuchad-
    rezzar, 167; expedition in the
    third year of Jehoiakim, vii,
    ix; in Palestine when father
    died, viii; inscriptions of, 37;
    and the battle of Carchemish,
    64, 74–79; sons of, 100; early
    Greek historians do not mention
    him, 167; madness of, 283–295;
    mad "seven times," 289–291;
    dreams of, 297 f., 318; character
    of, 303–307
Necho, 37, 50, 52, 53, 65, 67, 75,
    80, 107; documents bearing on
    his reign, 53, 79; conquest of
    Carchemish, 75–79; supremacy
    over Palestine, 79–80
Nicolaus of Damascus, 3, 229

O

Oaths by gods and kings, 111, 125
Officials, 20, 181–183, 203–206

Omri, 11, 12
Opinion *versus* evidence, 128

P

People and nation, words for,
    192–199
Persepolis inscription, 212
Persia, Daniel not ignorant of its
    history, 147–149; Xerxes called
    king of, 154–155; Daniel's men-
    tion of, 157–158; reference to it
    in Dan. vii, 6, 163; the four
    kings of, referred to in Dan. xi,
    2, 164; system of government of,
    derived from the Assyrians,
    200–220; religion of, 309–312:
    laws of, 314
Persian documents, 19, 21, 39, 40
Person defined, 83
Petrie, 14, 80, 116
Phenicians, archives of, 289
Philostratus, 289
Pihatu, 160
Pinches, 102, 134, 136
Pittacus, 39
Pognon, 40, 110, 116, 117
Prince, 44, 129
Province, 142
Psammetichus, 12
PSBA, 125
Pythagoras, 334

R

Rab defined, 386 f.
Rameses II, 138
Ramessids, 13, 14
Reflection, argument from, re-
    futed, 220–263
Religion of Persian kings, 310–312
Resh, the letter, 104

S

S before d changed to l, 338
Samaria, 11, 12
Sargon, 5, 11, 18, 187, 201; estab-
    lished the satrapial system, 201,
    220
Satrap, 141–143, 175–186, 200;
    satrapial system of government
    derived from the Assyrians,
    200–220; one hundred and
    twenty satraps in kingdom of
    Darius the Mede, 209–211;

Satrap—*Continued*
satraps of Sargon, 203–209;
of Herodotus, 215–220; of Darius Hystaspis, 211–215
Sayce, 30, 100, 161
Schorr, 120
Schrader, 122
Scriptures, the principal passages
discussed:
Daniel i, 1: 43–59, 62–82, 86;
i, 17: 372; ii, 2: 324, 376–385;
ii, 13: 298; ii, 48: 370, 385–
389; iii, 6, 29: 298; iv, 1: 298;
iv, 25–36: 283–294; v, 1: 11,
29, 99–114, 117–122; v, 31:
151–153, 238–240; vi, 1: 134 f.,
175; vi, 7–9: 298; vi, 25–27:
298; vi, 29: 129; vi, 25: 173–
199; vii, 1: 114, 244; vii, 6:
160, 163, 264; viii, 2: 277–
282; ix, 1: 134; xi, 2: 160, 162,
163–172, 271; xi, 3: 274
Ezra iv, 10: 6
Chronicles, Second, xxvi, 6, 7.
73
Kings, First, xx, 14: 142
Kings, Second, xxiii, 36, 37;
45–48; xxiv, 1–7: 73
Jeremiah xxv, 1–9: 49–52, 68–
79; li, 27–29: 266
Sennacherib, 12, 33, 130
Septuagint, 35, 293
Sesostris, 138
Shabaka, 116
Shaknu, 180
Shalmaneser, 6, 7, 11, 47, 67,
139
Shangu, 30
Shin, 104
Shishak, 10
Silence, argument from, in general,
1–23; in the case of Daniel, 24–
42; in the case of the expedition
against Jerusalem, 43 f.
Sira, 168
Slave, 28
Smerdis, 39
Smith, W. R., 117
Sources of information bearing on
the book of Daniel xv, 3–5;
silence of, 5–22; with regard to
the name of Daniel, 27 f.; for
the reign of Jehoiakim, 45–58,
81; for the name and reign of
Belshazzar, 101–105, 123–126;
sources known to Daniel and

unknown to us, 145–150; es-
pecially of the history of Persia,
3–25, 166–172; and Assyria,
4–26
Spiegel, 38, 176
Strabo, 334
Strassmaier, 29, *et passim.*
Susa, subject to Babylon in time of
Belshazzar, 277; not a court
but a fortress, 280

T

Tablets, 27–36, 125, 134 *et al.*
Taharka, 12, 116
Tallquist, 27
Theodotion, 289
Thompson, R. C., 289
Tiglath-Pileser, 11, 20, 67, 116,
139
Times, 289–291
Tolman, 139
Tyre, 12

U

Ugbaru, 39, 40, 102, 109, 133, 230
Ummanu, 341 f.
Ushtanni, 137, 143

V

Vessels carried away by Nebuchadnezzar, 66
Vogüé, de, 27

W

Winckler, 139
Wise men, 367–389; Daniel's
relation to, 370–372; not wrong
for a Jew to be a wise man, 372–
374, 376; meaning of the word
in Aramaic, Arabic, Hebrew,
Babylonian, and Ethiopic, 374–
375; discussion of *ashshaph*,
gazer, and other words employed in Daniel ii, 376–383;
wise man might have been an
astrologer, 383–385

X

Xenophon, 138, 142, 209, 260
Xerxes, 155, 164, 226–236, 307;
spelling of name, 105; son of

Xerxes—*Continued*
  Darius Hystaspis, 227; not
  confused with latter by Daniel,
  160–162, 264 f.; dreams of, 307;
  and the expedition against
  Greece, 164–165, 272

Y

Yale cylinder of Nabunaid, 365–
  366

Year of the beginning of the reign,
  68; different ways of reckoning,
  68–69; of Daniel iii, more
  properly "time," 289

Z

Zedekiah, 31, 65, 66, 107
Zopyrus, 246
Zoroastrianism of the Achæ-
  menids, 310

STUDIES
IN THE
BOOK OF DANIEL

VOLUME II

BY

ROBERT DICK WILSON
Ph.D., D.D., LL.D.

BAKER BOOK HOUSE
Grand Rapids, Michigan

PHOTOLITHOPRINTED BY CUSHING - MALLOY, INC.
ANN ARBOR, MICHIGAN, UNITED STATES OF AMERICA
1972

INTRODUCTION

Those who are acquainted with the first volume of Dr. Wilson's *Studies in the Book of Daniel* will need no extended introduction to the present volume. "The method pursued," he tells us, "is to give first of all a discussion of some of the principles involved in the objections considered in the pages following; then to state the objections with the assumptions on which they are based; next, to give the reasons why these assumptions are adjudged to be false; and lastly, to sum up in a few words the conclusions to be derived from the discussion." Dr. Wilson was accustomed to say that he would not attempt to answer general or sweeping charges against the Bible. But where specific charges were made, reflecting upon the truthfulness of the Bible, and where evidence was presented in support of such charges, he was prepared to undertake the most painstaking investigations to test the correctness of the charges. He believed thoroughly in "scientific Biblical criticism." His method and aim were truly scientific. He was not only willing, but eager to ascertain the facts and all the facts. For he believed and showed again and again that the facts support the high claims of the Bible to entire trustworthiness as the Word of God. Consequently in his great debate with the critics he tried to single out the strongest and most serious charges as expressed by their most influential spokesmen, to state these objections in their own words, and then to deal with them as thoroughly as possible in the light of the evidence.

Dr. Wilson's original plan was to write three books on Daniel. The first which dealt with historical questions appeared in 1917. The second was to deal with the linguistic problem, the objections raised by the critics on the ground of "philological assumptions based on the nature of the Hebrew and Aramaic in which it was written." The nucleus of this volume might well have been the article on "The Aramaic of Daniel," which he had contributed to *Biblical and Theological Studies,* the Centennial Volume published by the Faculty of Princeton Theological Seminary in 1912. In this

3

article he had maintained against the higher critics and especially Dr. Driver that the Aramaic of the Book of Daniel is of the character which we would expect to have been spoken in Babylon in the Neo-Babylonian and early Persian period. About a year before Dr. Wilson's death in 1930, Mr. Harold H. Rowley published a book on *The Aramaic of the Old Testament* (Oxford, 1929) in which he took issue with Dr. Wilson's conclusions regarding Daniel and defended the critical views of Dr. Driver. Dr. Wilson spent much time during the last summer of his life in studying this book. From casual statements made to members of his family and to his colleagues at Westminster Seminary it was inferred that Dr. Wilson had practically completed his investigation, that he felt that he could satisfactorily answer Mr. Rowley, and that his reply was practically ready for publication. Consequently in the memorial articles which appeared in the *Sunday School Times* and in *Christianity Today,* shortly after his death, it was stated that Dr. Wilson's reply to Mr. Rowley would soon be published. Unfortunately, search for the manuscript of the reply was unsuccessful, nor were any data sufficient to form the basis for such an article discovered. Either Dr. Wilson's statements as to the shape in which his material stood were misunderstood, or the manuscript material was lost or accidentally destroyed. Whichever be the explanation, it is most regrettable that Dr. Wilson's own defense of his position could not be published. Especially is this to be regretted since Dr. Wilson's other studies in the philology of the Book of Daniel, which appeared in the *Princeton Theological Review,* in addition to being highly technical are hardly extensive enough to form anything but the nucleus of a volume on philology. And as they are there available to specialists, it has not seemed advisable to include them in a volume which deals with other subjects.

The contents of the present volume, consequently, represent the studies which Dr. Wilson intended for the third volume of the series: "In a third volume I shall discuss Daniel's relation to the canon of the Old Testament as determining the date of the book and in connection with this the silence of Ecclesiasticus with reference to Daniel, the alleged absence of an observable influence of Daniel upon post-captivity literature, and the whole matter of apocalyptic

literature, especially in its relation to predictive prophecy." Two of
the studies referred to had recently appeared in the *Princeton Theological Review,* and Dr. Wilson allowed the others also to appear
first in its pages without, however, relinquishing the plan with
regard to them, which he had stated in the first volume on Daniel.
In view of the fact that this plan was never carried out and since
with the lapse of years magazine articles tend to become inaccessible,
it has been deemed advisable to gather them all together, and present
them in the form which was originally intended by their author.
This has been made possible through the generosity of a personal
friend of Dr. Wilson's who is unwilling to have his identity
disclosed.

In view of my close and intimate association with Dr. Wilson, a
friendship begun in my student days and extending over a period of
more than a quarter of a century, it was thought appropriate that I
should prepare these articles for the press. I have counted it a privi-
lege to help in this way to make the writings of a great defender of
the faith more widely known. I have had the advantage of access to
copies of these articles which contained Dr. Wilson's notes, comments and corrections. It has not been possible to use all of this
material, and certain further changes have also seemed advisable.
It has been my aim however to make only such changes as I felt sure
that he himself would have approved. Thanks are due to Rev. Les-
lie W. Sloat, one of the last students privileged to study under Dr.
Wilson, for help in preparing the copy for the press, and for assistance in proof reading. Mr. Sloat has also prepared the index.

OSWALD T. ALLIS.

CONTENTS

CHAPTER   PAGE

I. THE BOOK OF DANIEL AND THE CANON   9

II. DANIEL NOT QUOTED   65

III. THE SILENCE OF ECCLESIASTICUS CONCERNING
     DANIEL   76

IV. APOCALYPSES AND THE DATE OF DANIEL   101

V. THE ORIGIN OF THE IDEAS OF DANIEL   117

VI. THE INFLUENCE OF DANIEL   157

VII. THE BACKGROUND OF DANIEL   233

VIII. THE PROPHECIES OF DANIEL   258

INDICES   281

STUDIES IN
THE BOOK OF DANIEL

CHAPTER I

THE BOOK OF DANIEL AND THE CANON

IN ALL recent works on the Book of Daniel the charge is made, that the position of the book in the Hebrew Canon points to the conclusion that the book was written at a time much later than that at which the Jewish and Christian churches have always and unanimously, until recently, supposed that it was written. Since the last six chapters are in the first person, and since they are dated from the reigns of Belshazzar, Darius the Mede, and Cyrus, no one can doubt that they claim to be the record of visions which can have been known only to Daniel himself. The first six chapters, though written in the third person, purport to record actual events in the lives of Daniel and his three companions during the reigns of Nebuchadnezzar, Belshazzar, and Darius the Mede. In ancient times, the claim of Daniel to be historical was contested only by Porphyry, a man who rejected all of the sacred books of the Old and New Testaments. Within the last two centuries, however, it has been frequently asserted, that the first six chapers of Daniel are at best but a series of traditions "cast by the author into a literary form, with a special view to the circumstances of his own time" [1]; and that the visions of the last six chapters are a narration of events already past, put in an apocalyptic form.

Among the specifications in this general charge against the historical character of Daniel, is the one which will now be considered: that the position of the Book of Daniel in the Hebrew

---

[1] S. R. Driver, *Literature of the Old Testament*, p. 511 (abbrev. *L.O.T.*).

Canon points "more or less decisively to an author later than Daniel himself." [2]

In the discussion of this specific charge, I shall pursue the following method: First, I shall state the charge in the words of those that make it. Secondly, I shall present the admissions and assumptions involved in the charge. Thirdly, I shall cite and discuss the evidence upon which these assumptions rest. And, lastly, I shall give the conclusions which the evidence seems to justify.

THE CHARGE

The first alleged proof of the late date of Daniel is "the position of the Book in the Jewish Canon, not among the prophets, but in the miscellaneous collection of writings called the *Hagiographa*,[3] and among the latest of these, in proximity to Esther. Though little definite is known respecting the formation of the Canon, the division known as the 'Prophets' was doubtless formed prior to the Hagiographa; and had the Book of Daniel existed at the time, it is reasonable to suppose that it would have ranked as the work of a prophet, and have been included among the former." [4]

In the Hebrew Scriptures "Daniel has never occupied a place among the prophetical Books, but is included in the third collection of sacred writings, called the Kethubim or Hagiographa. Of the history of the Jewish Canon very little is known with certainty, but there is every reason to believe that the collection of Prophetical Books, from which lessons were read in the Synagogue, was definitely closed sometime before the Hagiographa, of which the greater part had no place in the public services. That the collection of Prophetical Books cannot have been completed till sometime after the Exile, is obvious, and on the supposition that Daniel was then known to the Jews, the exclusion of this book is wholly inexplicable." [5]

[2] *Id.*, p. 497.

[3] The Hagiographa, or holy writings, consist, according to our present Hebrew Bibles, of the books—Pss., Prov., Job, Cant., Ruth, Lam., Eccl., Esth., Dnl., Ezra, Neh., 1 and 2 Chron.

[4] *Id.*, p. 497.

[5] A. A. Bevan, *A Short Commentary on the Book of Daniel*, p. 11.

"The place of the Book of Daniel among the Hagiographa favors also its late composition. If it had been written during the Exile, notwithstanding its apocalyptic character, it naturally would have been placed among the Prophets." [6]

"Not until the time of the LXX (which, moreover, has treated the text of Daniel in a very arbitrary fashion) does it find a place, after Ezekiel, as the fourth of the 'great' prophets, and thus it comes to pass that once in the New Testament Daniel is designated as a prophet." [7]

"The position of the book among the Hagiographa instead of among the Prophetical works would seem to indicate that it must have been introduced after the closing of the Prophetical Canon. . . . The natural explanation regarding the position of the Book of Daniel is that the work could not have been in existence at the time of the completion of the second part of the Canon, as otherwise, the collectors of the prophetical writings, who in their care did not neglect even the parable of Jonah, would hardly have ignored the record of such a great prophet as Daniel is represented to be." [8]

Among "objective reasons of the utmost weight, which render the view of its non-genuineness necessary," Cornill mentions "*the position of the book in the Hebrew Canon, where it is inserted, not among the prophets, but in the third division of the canon, the so-called Hagiographa.* If it were the work of a prophet of the time of Cyrus, no reason would be evident why there should be withheld from it a designation which was not denied to a Haggai, Zechariah, and Malachi—nay, even to a Jonah." [9]

"In the Hebrew Canon, Daniel is not placed among the Prophets, but in the Hagiographa, the latest section of the Canon; although Haggai, Zechariah, and Malachi, who were later than the time at which Daniel is described as living, are placed among

[6] E. L. Curtis, art. "Daniel," in Hastings' *Dictionary of the Bible*, Vol. I, p. 554f.
[7] Kamphausen in *Encyclopedia Biblica*, Vol. I, p. 1011 (Macmillan).
[8] Prince, *Commentary on Daniel*, pp. 15-16.
[9] *Introduction to the Canonical Books of the Old Testament*, pp. 384-386.

the prophets. Either the Jews did not regard the book as prophetical, or it was considerably later than Malachi, c. 444." [10]

ASSUMPTIONS

The assumptions involved in the above statements are as follows: 1. It is assumed that the position of a book in the Hebrew Canon determines the time of its writing, or at least 2. that the position of a book in the Hebrew Bible determines the time of its admission into the Canon and that the proximity of Daniel to Esther proves the late date of Daniel. 3. It is assumed that because a division of the Hebrew Bible called "Prophets" in our Hebrew Bibles was doubtless formed (i.e. collected and named) prior to the Hagiographa, therefore a book of prophecy originally not included in this division must have been written after this collection was completed. 4. It is assumed that, had the Book of Daniel existed at the time when the division called Prophets was formed, it is reasonable to suppose, that if it had been ranked among the prophetical books, it would have been placed in this division. 5. It is assumed that no reason is evident why there should have been withheld from a Daniel a designation which was not denied to a Haggai, a Zechariah, and a Malachi—nay, even to a Jonah. 6. It is assumed that Daniel never occupied a place among the prophetical books. 7. It is assumed that the collection of prophetical books from which lessons were read in the synagogues, was definitely closed before the Hagiographa were canonized. 8. It is assumed that the greater part of the Hagiographa had no place in the public services.

ADMISSIONS OF THE CRITICS

Before proceeding to a discussion of these assumptions, special attention should be called to the admissions of the critics on the matter of the evidence bearing on the assumptions; and on the character of the premises that justify these critics in their conclusions. First, as to the evidence, Driver admits that "little definite

[10] Bennett and Adeney, *A Biblical Introduction*, p. 225.

is known respecting the formation of the Canon." Bevan, also, admits that "of the history of the Jewish Canon very little is known." Secondly, as to the character of the premises from which they deduce their conclusions, it will be noted in the above citations, that Driver says, after having admitted that very little is known respecting the formation of the Canon, that the division known as the Prophets was "doubtless formed prior to the Hagiographa," and that "it is reasonable to suppose that the Book of Daniel would have been included among the former." Cornill says that "no reason is evident why Daniel should not be among the Prophets." Prince says that the position of the book would seem to indicate, that it was introduced into the Canon after the closing of the Prophetical Canon, and the natural explanation of its position is that it did not exist at the time of the closing of the Prophetical Canon. Bevan says that there is every reason to believe that the collection of Haphtaroth was made before the closing of the Hagiographa; and that on the supposition that Daniel was known, its exclusion from the Prophetical Canon is inexplicable, or not very easy to reconcile with the theory of the antiquity of the book.

It will be observed that, while admitting that little is known, the critics indulge in such phrases and words as "doubtless," "reasonable to suppose," "seem to indicate," "every reason to believe," "supposition," "not easy to reconcile," "inexplicable," "natural explanation," and so forth. All of these words and phrases are admissions on the part of the critics that their theory with regard to the Book of Daniel is not convincingly supported by the evidence, even themselves being witnesses.

EVIDENCE

The evidence bearing upon the divisions, number, order, and use of the books regarded by the Jews and Christians as canonical may, for convenience of treatment, be marshalled under two heads: 1, the evidence relating to the divisions, number, and order; and 2, that relating to the use.

1. Divisions, Number, and Order

1. *Ben Sira,* the elder, speaks a number of times of the Law, [11] and cites in order Josh., Jgs., Sam., Kgs., Isa., Jer., Ezk., Job, the Twelve, and Neh. He cites, also, from Chr., and mentions the Pss. of David and the Provs. of Sol.[12]

2. The Prologue to the Greek translation of *Ben Sira,* written about 132 B.C., refers three times to a threefold division of the Old Testament, as follows: (1) "The Law and the Prophets, and the other books which follow after them"; (2) "The Law and the Prophets and the other ancestral books"; (3) "The Law itself and the Prophecies and the rest of the books." Notice that he gives neither the number nor the names of the books in these divisions.

3. *First Maccabees* contains the following speech delivered by Mattathias, the father of the Maccabees, to his sons in the year 169 B.C, just before his decease:

"Now hath pride and rebuke gotten strength, and the time of destruction, and the wrath of indignation: now therefore, my sons, be ye zealous for the Law and give your lives for the covenant of your fathers. Call to remembrance what acts our fathers did in their time; so shall ye receive great honour and an everlasting name. Was not Abraham found faithful in temptation, and it was imputed unto him for righteousness? Joseph in the time of his distress kept the commandment and was made lord of Egypt. Phinehas our father in being zealous and fervent obtained the covenant of an everlasting priesthood. Jesus for fulfilling the word was made a judge in Israel. Caleb for bearing witness before the congregation received the heritage of the land. David for being merciful possessed the throne of an everlasting kingdom. Elias for being zealous and fervent for the Law was taken up into heaven. Ananias, Azarias, and Misael, by believing were saved out of the flame. Daniel for his innocency was delivered from the mouth of lions. And thus consider ye throughout all ages, that none that put their trust in him shall be overcome. . . ."[13]

[11] References to the Torah are found in xv, 1; xxxii, 15, 17, 18, 24; xxxiii, 2, 13; xli, 4, 8; xlii, 2; xlv, 5; xlviii, 3, 6; xlix, 4; l, 20.

[12] Chapters xliv-xlix. His citation from Chr. is mingled with those from Kgs. and Isa., and his references to the Pss. and Prov. are inserted in his account derived from Kgs. Notice that he puts Job among the Prophets, and gives the longest eulogy of all to the high priest Simon. He probably does not mention Daniel, Ezra, Esther, or Mordecai (See below Chap. III).

[13] ii, 49b-61.

Notice that Mattathias refers to events recorded in the Law, the Former Prophets, and in Daniel, esteeming all the records as of equal veracity. Did he not know of the Latter Prophets, since he does not quote from them, nor the Psalms, nor Job?

4. *Second Maccabees* contains a letter written in 124 B.C., in which the writer speaks of "the records and commentaries of Nehemiah, and how founding a library he gathered together the books concerning the kings and prophets and those of David and epistles of kings concerning votive offerings." [14] The Syriac version is slightly different and reads thus: "It is related in books and in memoirs that Nehemiah did thus: that he assembled and arranged in order the books of the kingdoms and of the prophets and of David and the letters of the kings which concern offerings and sacrifices." [15] Daniel could only have been in the division called "the prophets."

5. *Philo*, who died about 40 A.D., says that the sect of the Therapeutæ received "the Law, and the Oracles uttered by the Prophets, and the hymns and the other (writings) by which knowledge and piety are augmented and perfected." [16] Daniel was almost certainly in the division called "the prophets."

6. In the *New Testament* the following passages bear upon our subject: (1) In Luke xxiv, 44, the Lord speaks of those things which were written concerning Him "in the Law of Moses, and in the Prophets, and in the Psalms." (2) In John xv, 25, Psalm lxix, 5 is referred to as in "their Law." (3) In Luke xxiv, 27, the author speaks of "Moses and all the Prophets." With this compare the phrase, "the Law and the Prophets" (Matt. vii, 12; xxii, 40, cf. Jn. i, 45). (4) In Matt. xxiv, 15, mention is made of

[14] ii, 13.

[15] See Lagarde, *Libri Apocryphi Veteris Testamenti Syriace*, p. 216.

[16] *De Vita contemplativa*, ii, 475. (Cf. Westcott, *The Bible in the Church*, p. 33). The genuineness of this work has been defended in recent times by F. C. Conybeare, P. Wendland, and L. Massebieau; the last of whom has "shown with great thoroughness that in language and thought alike it is essentially Philonic." (See Art. by Bigg in *Encyc. Brit.*, xxi, 412). Philo cites from every book of the Old Testament, except Ruth, Est., Eccl., Cant., Lam. (*i.e.*, the Megilloth), Ezk., and Dnl. He expressly calls the author of Pss. xxiii and lxxxiii a prophet. In the headings David is called the author of the former and Asaph of the latter.

"Daniel the prophet." With this compare the mention of Asaph as "the prophet" (Matt. xiii, 35, cf. Ps. lxxviii, 2), of David "the prophet" (Acts ii, 30), "Isaiah the prophet" (Matt. iii, 3), "Jonah the prophet" (Matt. xii, 39), and "the prophet Joel" (Acts ii, 16). Compare also Mark i, 2; Luke xviii, 31; xxiv, 25; John vi, 45; Luke xvi, 16; Acts xiii, 35, Rom. iii, 21; and "in the book of the Prophets" (Acts vii, 42); "in the book of Psalms" (Acts i, 20).

7. *Josephus* has the following to say of the Canon:

"We have not an innumerable multitude of books among us, disagreeing from and contradicting one another, but only twenty-two books, which contain the records of all the past times; which are justly believed to be Divine; and of them five belong to Moses, which contain his laws, and the traditions of the origin of mankind till his death. This interval of time was little short of three thousand years; but as to the time from the death of Moses till the reign of Artaxerxes king of Persia, who reigned after Xerxes, the prophets, who were after Moses, wrote down what was done in their times in thirteen books. The remaining four books contain hymns to God, and precepts for the conduct of human life. It is true, our history hath been written since Artaxerxes, very particularly, but hath not been esteemed of the like authority with the former by our forefathers, because there hath not been an exact succession of prophets since that time; and how firmly we have given credit to those books of our own nation is evident by what we do; for during so many ages as have already passed, no one has been so bold as either to add anything to them or take anything from them. . . ." [17]

Josephus quotes all the Old Testament books except Job, Cant., Eccl., and Prov., and uses 1 Macc., though excluding it from the Canon. It seems clear that his third division of the Canon consists of Psalms, Proverbs, Ecclesiastes and Canticles.

Of Daniel himself, Josephus says:

"He was so happy as to have strange revelations made to him, and those as to one of the greatest of the prophets. . . . He retains a remembrance that will never fail, for the several books that he wrote and left behind him are still read by us till this time; and from them we believe that Daniel conversed with God; for he did not only prophesy of future events, as did the other prophets, but he also determined the time of their accomplishment; and while the prophets used to tell misfortunes, and on that account were disagreeable both to the

[17] *Contra Apion*, i, 8.

kings and to the multitude, Daniel was to them a prophet of good things, and this to such a degree, that, by the agreeable nature of his predictions, he procured the good-will of all men; and by the accomplishment of them, he procured the belief of their truth, and the opinion of (a sort of) Divinity for himself, among the multitude. He also wrote and left behind him what made manifest the accuracy and undeniable veracity of his predictions. . . . And indeed it so came to pass, that our nation suffered these things under Antiochus Epiphanes, according to Daniel's vision, and what he wrote many years before they came to pass. In the very same manner Daniel also wrote concerning the Roman government, and that our country should be made desolate by them. All these things did this man leave in writing, as God had showed them to him, insomuch that such as read his prophecies, and see how they have been fulfilled, would wonder at the honour with which God honoured Daniel." [18]

8. In The *Ascension of Isaiah,* is found the following partial list of Old Testament books:

"All these things, behold they are written in the Psalms, in the Parables of David the son of Jesse, and in the Proverbs of Solomon his son, and in the words of Korah and Ethan the Israelite, and in the words of Asaph, and in the rest of the Psalms which also the angel of the Spirit inspired. (Namely), in those which have not the name written, and in the words of my father Amos, and of Hosea the prophet, and of Micah and Joel and Nahum, and Jonah and Obadiah and Habakkuk and Haggai and Zephaniah and Zechariah and Malachi and in the words of Joseph the Just, and in the words of Daniel." [19]

The threefold division is not recognized and the order of The Twelve is different; Daniel is apparently among the prophets.

9. In the Latin translation of *Fourth Esdras,* (chap. i,) the Minor Prophets are enumerated in the following order: "Hos., Am. and Mic., Joel, Ob. and Jon., Nah. and Hab., Zeph., Hag., Zech. and Mal., which is called also an angel of the Lord." [20]

10. In his *Eclogues,* a collection of testimonies to Christ and Christianity made from the Old Testament, *Melito,* Bishop of Sardis about 175 A.D., gives a "catalogue of the books of the Old

[18] *Antiquities,* X, xi, 7.
[19] iv, 21-22. See *The Ascension of Isaiah* by R. H. Charles (pp. xliv-xlv). If we put these verses in the Testament of Hezekiah, they will have been written according to Charles between 88 and 100 A.D. If they belong to the Redactor, they were written about 200 A.D.
[20] This is the order of the Greek MS "B," but is not the Hebrew order.

Testament which it is necessary to quote." We have two recensions of this catalogue, one in the Church History of Eusebius,[21] and the other in the Syriac fragments published by Cureton. The Greek of Eusebius reads:

"Melito to his brother Onesimus, greeting: Since thou hast often, in thy zeal for the word, expressed a wish to have extracts made from the Law and the Prophets, concerning the Saviour, and concerning our entire faith, and hast also desired to have an accurate statement of the ancient books, as regards their number and order, I have endeavoured to perform the task, knowing thy zeal for the faith, and thy desire to gain information in regard to the word, and knowing that thou, in thy yearning after God, esteemest these things above all else, struggling to attain eternal salvation. Accordingly, when I went East and came to the place where these things were preached and done, I learned accurately the books of the Old Testament, and send them to thee as written below. Their names are as follows: Of Moses, five books: Gen., Ex., Nu., Lev., Dt.; Jesus Nave, Jgs., Ruth; of Kgs., four books; of Chr., two; the Ps. of David, the Prov. of Solomon, which also is Wisdom, Eccl., Song of Songs, Job; of Prophets, Isa., Jer.; of the Twelve Prophets, one book; Dnl., Ezk., Esdr." [22]

From the Syriac recension I shall give only the names in order:

"Of Moses, five (books), Gen., and Ex., and Nu. and that of the Priests, and Dt.; and again that of Josh. son of Nun, and the bk. of Jgs. and Ruth; and the bk. of four Kgs.; the bk. of two Chr.; and the Ps. of David; and of Sol., the Prov., which is Wisdom, and Koheleth, and the Song of Songs; and Job; and of the Prophets, Isa. and Jer., and the Twelve Prophets together, and Dnl., and Ezk. and Ezra."

Esther is omitted from Melito's canon, and Ezra as well as Daniel is among the prophets. The threefold division is broken by Ruth, Lam., Dnl., and Ezra.

11. In the *Talmud,* the following are the most important allusions to the Old Testament Canon:

(1) "The Rabbis have taught the order of succession in the Books of the Prophets runs thus: Josh., Jgs., Sam., Kgs., Jer., Ezk., Isa., and the Twelve. The order of succession in the Hagiographa is: Ruth, and the Bk. of Ps., Job and Prov., Eccl., the

[21] iv, 26.
[22] *Nicene and Post-Nicene Fathers,* Second series, I, 206.

Song of Songs, and Lam., Dnl. and the roll of Est., Ezra and Chr." [23]

(2) "All Sacred Scriptures [24] render the hands unclean. The Song of Songs and Ecclesiastes render the hands unclean." "All the Scriptures are holy." [25] "The Aramaic portions of Ezra and Daniel render the hands unclean." "The Sadducees said: 'we blame you Pharisees because you say Sacred Scriptures render the hands unclean, but the books of Hameram [26] do not render the hands unclean'. . . . They say that the bones of an ass are clean, but the bones of Jochanan the High Priest are unclean." "According to their value is their uncleanness, so that no one may make the bones of his father and mother into spoons." "So are the Sacred Scriptures; according to their value is their uncleanness. The books of Hameram, which are not valued, do not render the hands unclean." [27]

(3) "Rab Yehuda alleges that Shemuel said the book of Esther does not defile the hands. This is tantamount to saying that it was Shemuel's opinion that the book of Esther was not dictated by the Holy Spirit. But Shemuel asserted that the book of Esther was dictated by the Holy Spirit." [28]

(4) "Remember that man with respect; his name is Hananiah the son of Hezekiah. Had it not been for him, the Book of Ezekiel would have been suppressed, because its contents were contradictory to the words of the Law." [29]

(5) On the festival of the Year, three texts at least were read

[23] *Baba Bathra* 14b. Cf. Green, *The Canon*, p. 139. Note that the order of the Megilloth is broken, but follows a chronological arrangement.
[24] כתבי הקודש This phrase also in Tosefta *Sab.* xiii (xiv) and xvi, 15.
[25] *Yadayim*, iii, 5. Id. iv, 4.
[26] Perhaps Hameram is Homer.
[27] *Yadayim*, iv, 5.
[28] *Megilla*, fol. 7d. See Hershon, *Treasures of Talmud*, p. 44. On Esther, cf. Green, *Canon*, pp. 139f.
[29] Hershon, p. 45. *Moed Katan*, 5a. In a note, Hershon adds: "Rashi *in loco* points to Ezek. xliv, 31 and xlv, 20 as contradictions to the Law. From the former text it might be inferred that Israelites are allowed to eat that which was prohibited to the priests, and this would be a contradiction to the Law. The second passage contains an innovation of the prophet, for the Law says nothing about such a sacrifice as that on the second day of the month."

from the Law, three from the Psalms, and three from the Prophets.[30]

(6) On the day of Atonement, selections were read to the High Priest "in Job and in Ezra and in Chronicles. Zechariah, the son of Kebutal said, 'I often read before him in Daniel'." [31]

(7) "The Chaldee (Aramaic) passages in Ezra and Daniel defile the hands." [32]

(8) "All the Holy Scriptures may be saved from fire on the Sabbath." "This is interpreted as referring to the Hagiographa as well as to the Law and the Prophets." [33]

(9) All the books of the Old Testament are cited as Scripture in one or another of the tractates of the Mishna. The two usual formulas of citation are "It is written," and, "It is said," both being used alike for quotations from the Law, the Prophets, and the Hagiographa. For example, (a) "It is written": Deut. xvi, 14 in *Moed katon;* 1 Kings vi. 20 in *Megillah;* Dan. ii, 46 in *Sanhedrin;* Dan. iii, 12 in *Megillah.* (b) "It is said": Gen. xxiv, 42 in *Sanhedrin;* 1 Sam. xv, 32, *id.; Dan.* ii, 32, *id.*

(10) Especially to be noted is the citation of all of the so-called disputed books—Proverbs, Chronicles, Jonah, Ezekiel, Ecclesiastes, the Song of Songs, and Esther,[34] with the same formulas as those employed for the Law. E.g., 2 Chron. xxxiii, 13 in *Sanhedrin;* Proverbs iii, 2, 8, 16, 18, iv, 9, 22 in *Aboth;* Ezekiel xli, 22 in *Aboth;* Jonah iii, 10 in *Taanith;* Eccl. i, 15 in *Sukkoth* and in *Chagiga;* Song of Songs iii, 11 in *Taanith;* Esther ii, 22 in *Aboth.* A citation from the Song of Songs, iii, 9, 10 is introduced by the phrase "the explanation of the Prophets is" (*Sukkoth,* vi.).

(11) "Some desired also to withdraw (*ganaz*) the book of Proverbs because it contained internal contradictions [35], but the

---

[30] See Barclay, *The Talmud,* p. 157.

[31] *Yoma,* i, 6.

[32] *Yadayim,* iv, 5.

[33] *Shabbath,* xvi.

[34] Esther was translated into Greek by Lysimachus and brought to Egypt in the fourth year of Ptolemy and Cleopatra, *i.e.,* c. 178 B.C. (?). Cf. Swete, *Introduction to the O. T. in Greek,* p. 258. The schools of Hillel and Shamai united in the recognition of Esther (*Megilla,* 7a).

[35] E.g. xxvi, 4 and 5, "Answer a fool according to his folly," and "Answer not a fool according to his folly."

attempt was abandoned because the wise men declared: 'We have examined more deeply into the Book of Ecclesiastes, and have discovered the solution of the difficulty'." [36]

(12) "At first, they withdrew Proverbs, and the Song of Songs, and Ecclesiastes from public use, because they spoke in parables. And so they continued, until the men of the Great Synagogue came and expounded them." [37]

(13) "The wise men desired to withdraw (*ganaz*) the book of Koheleth, because its language was often self-contradictory." [38]

(14) Again, it was asserted that Ecclesiastes contradicted other Scriptures. Thus, in *Sabbath* 30a, where it is asserted that the Preacher contradicts the words of the Psalter: "O Solomon, where is thy wisdom? where is thy discernment? Doth it not suffice thee that many of thy words contradict the utterances of David, that thou contradictest even thyself?" [39]

(15) "Moses wrote his own book and the chapter of Balaam and Job. Joshua wrote his own book and the last eight verses of the Pentateuch. Samuel wrote his own book, and also Judges and Ruth. David wrote the Book of Psalms through the ten elders Adam, Melchisedek, Abraham, Moses, Heman, Jeduthun, Asaph, and the three sons of Korah. Jeremiah wrote his own book, as also the Kings and the Lamentations. Hezekiah and his company wrote the book of Isaiah, Proverbs, Canticles, and Ecclesiastes. The men of the Great Synagogue wrote Ezekiel, the twelve Minor Prophets, Daniel, and the book of Esther. Ezra wrote his own book and a genealogy which belongs to the Chronicles." [40]

(16) Next to the Law, most of the so-called disputed Books were most highly honoured in the services of the Temple. Thus, (a) Jonah was the only one of the Prophets of which the whole was read in the public services. On the Sabbaths and Feast days, selections, called Haphtaroth, were read from the other Prophets;

[36] *Sabbath,* 30 b.
[37] *Aboth di Rabbi Nathan.*
[38] *Sabbath,* 30. E.g., "sorrow is better than laughter" (vii, 3), and "I said of laughter, it is to be praised" (ii, 2).
[39] See Ryle, *The Canon of the O.T.,* p. 196.
[40] *Baba Bathra,* 14 b.

but the whole of Jonah was read on the day of Atonement,⁴¹ and Daniel was often read on this day.⁴² (b) Of the Haphtaroth in use among the Jews of to-day, twelve are selected from Ezekiel, sixteen from Isaiah, nine from Jeremiah, fifteen from the Minor Prophets (one at least from all except Hag.), three from Joshua, three from Judges, six from Samuel, ten from First Kings, and five from Second Kings. No Prophet, except Isaiah is more highly honoured in this respect than Ezekiel. (c) Aside from the Law and Jonah, only five other books were read in full in the public services of the Temple, and they were called by the special name "Megilloth" (rolls). These were all from the Hagiographa, and were: Ruth, read at the feast of Weeks; Lamentations, read on the day of the fast for the destruction of the Temple; Ecclesiastes, read at the Feast of Tabernacles; the Song of Songs, read at the Feast of the Passover; and Esther, read at the Feast of Purim. There is evidence that Esther was thus read as early as the middle of the second century B.C. (d) Parts, at least, of Chronicles were read to the High Priest during his preparation for the functions of the day of Atonement.⁴³ (e) Although the Book of Proverbs was not read in the public services, it is cited in the Mishna for proof texts more frequently than any other book of the Hagiographa, except the Psalter. E.g., in *Aboth* from sections iii, 14 to vi, 10 inclusive, there are citations of Proverbs iv, 2, xvi, 32, viii, 21, 14, xi, 22, iii, 35, iv, 22, 9, iii, 2, 8, 16, 18, i, 9, xvi, 31, xvii, 6, vi, 22, viii, 22, xvi, 3.

(17) The order of the books in the Hebrew Manuscripts varied, outside the Law, apparently at will. In proof of this statement see, e.g., the tables in Ryle and Ginsburg; also Swete, *Introduction*, p. 200.

12. *The Old Testament* Books as given in the principal *Greek Manuscripts.*

(a) They all agree in the number and order of the Pentateuch, to wit: Gen., Ex., Lev., Nu., Dt.

---

⁴¹ See the conspectus of the Haphtaroth at the end of any good edition of the Hebrew Bible.

⁴² *Yoma*, i, 6.

⁴³ See *Kippurim*, i, 6.

(b) For the rest of the books, the order is as follows:

(1) For Codex Vaticanus (B): Josh., Jgs., Ruth, Kingdoms a-d, Paraleipomena a-b, Esdras a-b, Ps., Prov., Eccl., Asma (the Song), Job, Wisd. of Sol., Wisd. of Sirach, Est., Jth., Tob., Hos., Am., Mic., Joel, Ob., Jon., Nah., Zeph., Hag., Zech., Mal., Isa., Jer., Baruch, Lam., Ep. of Jer., Ezek., Dnl.

(2) For Codex Alexandrinus (A): Joshua son of Nun, Jgs., Ruth (together books 7), Kingdoms a-d, Paraleipomena a-b (together six books); Prophets 16, Hos., Am., Mic., Joel, Ob., Jon., Nah., Hab., Zeph., Hag., Zech., Mal., Isa. (the) Prophet, Jer. (the) Prophet, Bar., Lam. (of Jeremiah), Ep. Jer., Ezk. (the) Prophet, Dnl. (+Prophet, 16 in *catalogue*), Est., Tob., Jth., Esdras a the Priest, Esdras b the Priest, Macc. a-d, Ps., Job, Prov. of Sol., Eccl., Song of Songs, Wisd. of Sol. (the Panaretos), Wisd. of Jesus son of Sirach, Ps. of Sol.

(3) For Codex Sinaiticus, so far as known: "Paraleipomenon a-(b), Esdras (a)-b, Est., Tob., Jth., Macc. a-d, Isa., Jer., Lam. of Jer., . . . Joel, Ob., Jon., Nah., Hab., Zeph., Hag., Zech., Mal., Ps. of David, Prov. (+of Solomon in *subscrip.*), Ecc., Song of Songs, Wisd. of Sol., Wisdom of Jesus son of Sirach, Job.

(4) For Codex Basiliano-Venetus (N & V): Josh., Ruth, Jgs., Kingdoms a-d, Paraleipomenon a-b, Esdras (a)-b, Est., . . . Job, Prov., Eccl., Song of Songs, Wisd. of Sol., Wisdom of Jesus son of Sirach, Hos., Am., Joel, Ob., Jon., Mic., Nah., Hab., Zeph., Hag., Zech., Mal., Isa., Jer., Bar., Lam., Ezk., Dnl., Tob., Jth., Macc. a-d.[44]

(5) The order of books in the Hexaplaric Syriac was: Law, Josh., Jgs., Kgs., Chr., Ezra, Est., Jth., Tob., Ps., Job, Prov., Eccl., S. of S., two Wisd., Twelve Prophets, Jer. (with Bar. Lam., and Ep.), Dnl., with Sus. and Bel, Ezk. and Isa.[44a]

13. The Armenian, Harkensian Syriac and Itala.

(1) The Armenian version has the following order: "Law, Joshua, Jgs., Ruth, Kgs. 4, Chr. 2, Esdras 1 and 2, Neh., Est., Jth.,

[44] For these lists, see Swete, *Introduction to the O. T. in Greek*, pp. 201f; and Ryle, *Canon of the O. T.*, p. 215f, where the order of the fragmentary uncials and cursives is given. On Constantinople Bible cf. Westcott, *The Bible in the Church*, p. 165.
[44a] Swete, *Introduction*, p. 113, and Conybeare's list.

Tob., Macc. 1-3, Ps., Prov., Koheleth, Song of Songs, Wisd., Job, Isa., Hos., Am., Mic., Joel, Ob., Jon., Nah., Hab., Zeph., Hag., Zech., Mal., Jer., Bar., Lam., Dnl., Ezk." In an Appendix, after the New Testament, it adds Sirach, 3 Ezra, Prayer of Manasseh, 3 Cor., John?, and the Prayer of Eithami.[45]

(2) The Ambrosian codex of the Harclensian Syriac contains the following: Ps., Job, Prov., Eccl., Song of Sol., the Two Wisdoms, the Twelve Prophets, Jer. (with Bar., Lam. and the Ep.), Dnl. (with Sus. and Bel), Ezk., Isa.

(3) The order in several fragments of the Itala is as follows: (a) In the Fragmenta Wirceburgensia: Hos., Jon., Isa., Jer., Lam., Ezek., Dnl., Bel. (b) In the Fragmenta Weingartensia: Hos., Am., Mic., Joel, Jon., Ezk., Dnl. (c) In the Fragmenta palimpsesta Vaticana: Hos., Joel, Am., Jon., Hab., Zeph., Zech. (d) In the Fragmenta Stutgardiana: Am., Ezk., Dnl.[46]

14. The lists in the Greek, Latin, and Syrian fathers are as follows:[47]

(1) Origen (d. A.D. 254): Gen., Ex., Lev., Nu., Dt., Josh. the son of Nun, Jgs., Ruth, Kgs. a-d, Paraleipomenon a-b, Esdras a-b, Bk. of Ps., Prov. of Sol., Eccl., Song of Songs, Isa., Jer. with Lam. and the Ep. in one, Dnl., Ezk., Job, Est.[48] And beside *(hexo)* these, is the Maccabees.

(2) The list of Athanasius (c. 367 A.D.; d. 373) is the same as that of Origen as far as the Song of Songs. After that we have: "Job; Prophets,—the Twelve, Isa., Jer. and with him Bar., Lam., Ep., Ezk., Dnl. There are also other books beside these, not canonized by the fathers, but approved to be read with those now listed: Wisd. of Sol., Wisd. of Sirach, Est., Jth., Tob." [49]

(3) The list of the Pseudo-Athanasius. Gen., Ex., Lev., Nu., Dt., Josh. the son of Nun, Jgs., Ruth, of Kgdms., a, b, of Kgdms. c, d, of Chr. a, b, Esdr. a, b, the Davidic Psalter, the Prov. of Sol.,

[45] See the edition of the Old Armenian Bible published in 1804.
[46] See Swete, *Introduction*, pp. 96, 97.
[47] For Melito, see above under 10.
[48] The Twelve is omitted, probably the mistake of a copyist. (Cf. Westcott, *Bible in the Church*, p. 135).
[49] The Syrian list by Cureton agrees with the Greek given by Zahn, II, p. 211.

Eccl. of the same, Song of Songs, Job, Twelve Prophets num-
bered as one: Hos., Am., Mic., Joel, Ob., Jon., Nah., Hab., Zeph.,
Hag., Zech., Mal.; and besides these, four others, Isa., Jer., Ezk.,
Dnl. And besides these, there are the antilegomena as follows:
Wisd. of Sol., Wisd. of Sirach, Est., Jth., Tob., four bks. of
Macc., the Ps. and Odes of Sol., Sus. And again there are the
apocrypha: Enoch, Patriarchs, Prayer of Joseph, Testament of
Moses, Ascension of Moses, Abraham, Eldad and Medad; and
the Pseudepigrapha of the prophet Elijah, of the prophet Zeph.,
of Zech. the father of John, of Bar., Hab., Ezk., and Dnl.

(4) The list of Cyril of Jerusalem (c. 348 A.D.; d. 386): The
first books, the five of Moses: Gen., Ex., Lev., Nu., Dt.; and
besides, Josh. the son of Nun (and) the book of Jgs. with Ruth;
and of the remaining historical books, Kgdms. 4, Chr. 2, Esdr. 2,
Est. (twelfth); and there are found five poetical books, Job, the
book of Ps., Prov., Eccl., the Song of Songs (seventeenth book);
and in addition five prophetical (books), the XII prophets, one
book, one of Isa., one of Jer. with Bar. and Lam. and the Ep.,
Ezk., Dnl. (twenty-second book).

(5) There are three lists of Epiphanius (c. 392 A.D.; d. 403),
no two of them alike. (a) Gen., Ex., Lev., Nu., Dt., Josh., Jgs.,
Ruth, Job, Ps., Prov. of Sol., Ecc., Song of Songs, Kdgms. 4,
Chr. 2, The Dodekapropheton, Isa., Jer., with Lam. and his Ep.
and Bar., Ezk., Dnl., Esdr. 2, Est. (b) Five Law books (the
Pentateuch and the Nomothesia Gen.-Deut.). Five Poetical books
(Job, Ps., Pro. of Sol., Ecc., Song of Songs). Another Pentateuch,
called Grapheia, and by some Hagiographa (Josh. the son of Nun,
the Book of Jgs. with Ruth, Chr. 2, Kgds. a, b, Kgdms. c, d).
The Prophetical Pentateuch (the Dodekapropheton, Isa., Jer.,
Ezk., Dnl.). Two others (two of Esdr., called one, Est.), that of
Solomon called the Panarete; the book of Jesus the son of Sirach.
(c) The Law as in (a). The (book) of Josh. the son of Nun,
Job, Jgs., Ruth, the Ps., Chr. 2, Kgdms. a-d, the book of Prov.,
the Preacher, the Song of Songs, the Dodekapropheton, of the
Prophet Isa., of Jer., of Ezk., of Dnl., of Esdr. a, b, of Est.

(6) The list of Gregory of Nazianzus (d. 390 A.D.). The twelve
historical books, Gen., Ex., Lev., Nu., Dt., Josh., Jgs., Ruth, Acts

of Kgs., Chr., Esdr. Five poetical books, Job, David, three of
Sol., (Eccl., Song, Prov.). Five prophetical books, the Twelve
(Hos., Am., Mic., Joel, Jon., Ob., Nah., Hab., Zeph., Hag., Zech.,
Mal.), Isa., Jer., Ezk., Dnl. Two and twenty books. Esther is
omitted.

(7) The list of Amphilochius (d. 395 A.D.). The Pent., Crea-
tion *(ktisis)*, Ex., Lev., Nu., Dt., Josh., Jgs., Ruth, Kgdms. a-d,
Chr. a, b, Esdr. a, b, Five Poetical books, Job, Ps., Three of
Solomon, (Prov., Eccl., Song of Songs). The Twelve Prophets,
(Hos., Am., Mic., Joel, Ob., Jon., Nah., Hab., Zeph., Hag., Zech.,
Mal.). The four Prophets,—Isa., Jer., Ezk., Dnl., the wisest in
deeds and words. To these some adjudge Esther.

(8) The list of Pseudo-Chrysostom. The historical (part).
The Octateuch, - Gen., Ex., Lev., Nu., Dt., Josh. the son of Nun,
Jgs., Ruth. The Kgdms. a-d, Esdr. The advisory (symboleutic)
part, as Prov., Wisd. of Sirach, the Preacher, the Song of Songs.
The prophetic (part), as the sixteen Prophets. Ruth (?) = Job
(?), David. Est. omitted.

(9) The Synopsis, revised by Lagarde.[50] The Mosaic. Gen.,
Ex., Lev., Nu., Dt. The others, Josh. the son of Nun, Jgs.,
Ruth = the Octateuch. The Tetrabasileion, a, b, c, d, Chr. a, b,
Esdr. a, b, Est., Tob., Jth., Job. Of Solomon, Wisd., Prov.,
Eccl., Song of Songs. The Twelve Prophets, Hos., Am., Mic.,
Joel, Ob., Jon., Nah., Hab., Zeph., Hag., Zech., Mal. The
four great Prophets, Isa., Jer., Ezk., Dnl. The end of the six-
teen Prophets. Wisd. of Jesus the son of Sirach. Psalms
apparently omitted.

(10) The list of the anonymous Dialogue of Timothy and
Aquila. The Mosaic Pentateuch, Gen., Ex., Lev., Nu., Dt. The
son of Nun, Jgs. with Ruth, the Chronicles, a, b, of the Kgdms.
a, b, of the Kgdms. c, d, Job, Ps. of David, Prov. of Sol., the
Preacher w. the Songs, the Dodekapropheton, Isa., Jer., Ezk., Dnl.,
Esdr., Jth., Est. Apocrypha: Tob., the Wisd. of Sol., the Wisd.
of Jesus the son of Sirach.

(11) The list of Junilius. Histories (17): Gen., Ex., Lev.,
Nu., Dt., Josh., Jgs., Ruth, Kgdms. a-d (many add: Chr. 2, Job

⁵⁰ *Septuaginta Studien*, II, p. 50f. Discussed by Zahn, II, 302-18.

1, Tobias 1, Esdr. 2, Jth. 1, Est. 1, Macc. 2). Prophecies (17) : Psalms (150), Hos., Isa., Joel, Am., Ob., Jon., Mic., Nah., Hab., Zeph., Jer., Ezk., Dnl., Hag., Zech., Mal., Prov. (2) : Prov. of Sol., of Jesus son of Sirach. (Some add the book of Wisdom, and the Song of Songs.) Dogmatics (1) : Eccl.

(12) The list of Leontius (d. 543, A.D.). The Historical Books (12) : Gen., Ex., Nu., Lev., Dt., Josh. the son of Nun, Jgs., Ruth, the Words (logoi) of the Kgdms. a-d, Chr., Esdr. The Prophetical (Books) (5) : Isa., Jer., Ezk., Dnl., the Dodeka- propheton. The Paranetic (Books) (4) : Job, Prov. of Sol. Eccl., the Song of Songs, the Psalterion. Esther is omitted. (MS #124 has Lev. and Nu. after Dt.)

(13) The list of John of Damascus. The First Pent., which also is Nomothesia (Gen., Ex., Lev., Nu., Dt.). The Second Pent., which is called Grapheia, but by some Hagiographa (Josh. the son of Nun, Jgs. with Ruth, of Kgdms. a, b, of Kgdms. c, d, of Chr. a, b). The Third Pent., the Poetical (sticherai) Books, (Job, the Ps., Prov. of Sol., Eccl. of the same, Song of Songs of the same). The Fourth Pentateuch, the Prophetical (the Dodekapropheton, Isa., Jer., Ezk., Dnl.). Two others: Esdr. a, b, Est. The Paranetic, that is, the Wisd. of Sol., the Wisd. of Jesus.

(14) The list of Nicephorus (d. 611 A.D.). (A) Writings approved by the Church and canonized: Gen., Ex., Lev., Nu., Dt., Josh., Jgs. and Ruth, of Kgdms. a, b, of Kgdms. c, d, Chr. a, b, Esdr. a, b, Ps., Prov. of Sol., Eccl., Song of Songs, Job, Isa., Jer., Bar., Ezk., Dnl. the Twelve Prophets. Together the 22 books of the Old Testament. (B) Books that are disputed and not approved by the Church: Macc. 3, Wisd. of Sol., Wisd. of the son of Sirach, Ps. and Odes of Sol., Est., Jth., Sus., Tobit which also is Tobias. Apocrypha of the Old Testament: Enoch, Patriarchs, Prayer of Joseph, Testament of Moses, Ascension of Moses, Abraham, Eldad and Medad, Elijah the prophet, Zepha- niah the prophet, Zechariah the father of John, The pseudepi- grapha of Baruch, Habakkuk, Ezekiel, and Daniel. (See Zahn II, 300.)

(15) List of the Canons of Laodicea. Genesis of the World,

Exodus from Egypt, Lev., Nu., Dt., Josh. the son of Nun, Jgs., Ruth, Est., of Kgdms. a, b, of Kgdms. c, d, of Chr. a, b, Esdr. a, b, the Bk. of Ps., Prov. of Sol., Eccl., Song of Songs, Job, Twelve Prophets, Isa., Jer. and Bar., Lam., and Ep., Ezk., Dnl.

(16) List of the Apostolic Canons. Five of Moses (Gen., Ex., Lev., Nu., Dt.), Joshua the son of Nun, Jgs., Ruth, four of Kgdms, two of Chr., two of Esdr., Est., Jth., three of Macc., Job, Ps., three bks. of Sol. (Prov., Eccl., Song of Songs), one of the Twelve Prophets, Isa. one, Jer. one, Ezk. one, Dnl. one. Besides, take care that your youths learn the Wisd. of the very learned Sirach.

(17) The list of the Cod. Barocc. Concerning the books of the LXX and those not included in them. Gen., Ex., Lev., Nu., Dt., Josh., Jgs. and Ruth, of Kgdms. a-d, Chr. a, b, Job, Ps., Prov., Eccl., Song of Songs, Esdr., Hos., Am., Mic., Joel, Jon., Ob., Nah., Hab., Zeph., Hag., Zech., Mal., Isa., Jer., Ezk., Dnl. . . . And in addition to the LXX, the Wisd. of Sol., the Wisd. of Sirach, of Macc. a-d, Est., Jth., Tob. And a large number of Apocrypha: Adam, Enoch, Lamech, Patriarchs, Prayer of Joseph, Eldad and Medad, Testament of Moses, Ascension of Moses, Psalms of Solomon, Apocalypse of Elias, Visions of Isaiah, Apocalypse of Zephaniah, Apocalypse of Zechariah, Apocalypse of Esther. (See Zahn II, 291.)

(18) The list of Ebedyesu. Gen., Ex., Bk. of Priests, Nu., Dt., Josh. son of Nun, Jgs., Sam., of Kgs., Book of Dabariamin, Ruth, Ps. of David the King, Prov. of Sol., Koheleth, Song of Songs, Son of Sira, Great Wisdom, Job, Isa., Hos., Joel, Am., Ob., Jon., Mich., Nah., Hab., Zeph., Hag., Zech., Mal., Jer., Ezk., Dnl., Jth., Est., Sus., Esdr., Dnl. Minor, Ep. of Bar., Bk. of the Tradition of the Elders, Prov. of Josephus, History of the sons of Samona, the Book of Maccabees (a-c).

(19) The list of Hilary, (d. 366 A.D.). i-v. The five books of Moses. vi, Joshua the son of Nun. vii, Jgs. and Ruth, viii, of Kgs. a-b, ix, of Kgs. c-d, x, Chr. a-b, xi, Accounts (sermons) of the days of Esdras, xii, Bk of Ps., xiii-xv, Prov. of Sol., Eccl., Song of Songs. xvi, The Twelve Prophets, xvii-xxii, Isa., Jer. w. Lam., and Ep., Dnl., Ezk., Job, Est., (xxiii-xxiv, Tob., Jth.).

(20) The list of Rufinus (d. 410 A.D.). The five books of Moses (Gen., Ex., Lev., Nu., Dt.), Joshua the son of Nun, Jgs. along with Ruth, Kings 4, Chr. (= Book of Days), of Esdr. 2, and Est., of the Prophets (Isa., Jer., Ezk., Dnl., the Twelve Prophets, one book), Job, Ps. of David, of Sol. 3 (Prov., Eccl., Song of Songs). These conclude the number of books of the Old Testament. Some other books called not canonical, but ecclesiastical, are Wisd. of Sol., Wisd. of Sirach (= Ecclesiasticus), Tob., Jth., the books of Macc.

(21) The list of Augustine (d. 430 A.D.). Histories. Five of Moses (Gen., Ex., Lev., Nu., Dt.), Joshua son of Nun, Jgs., Ruth, Four books of Kgs., Two books of Chr., Job, Tob., Est., Jth., Two books of Macc., Two books of Esdr., Prophecies. The Ps. of David, three bks. of Solomon (Prov., Song of Songs, Eccl.), Wisd., Ecclus., The Twelve Prophets (Hos., Joel, Am., Ob., Jon., Mic., Nah., Hab., Zeph., Hag., Zech., Mal.), the volume of the four Major Prophets (Isa., Jer., Dnl., Ezk.).[51]

(22) The lists of Jerome (d. 420 A.D.).

(a) In the *Prologus Galeatus* to his version of Sam. and Kgs. Jerome gives the following order for the twenty-two books: the Law, (Gen., Ex., Lev., Nu., Dt.); The Prophets (Josh., Jgs. w. Ruth, Sam., Kgs., Isa., Jer. w. Lam., Ezk., the Twelve); Hagiographa (Job, David, Sol. [Prov., Eccl., Song], Dnl., Chr., Ezras, Esth.)[52]

(b) In his *Institutio* Cassiodorus gives a list of Jerome's which differs from the above: Law (Gen., Ex., Lev., Nu., Dt.), Prophets (Josh., Jgs., Ruth, Sam., Isa., Jer., Ezek., Dnl., the Twelve), Hagiographa (Job, David, Sol. [Prov. Ecclus. (?), Song], Verba dierum id est Paralep. Ezras, Esth.).[53]

---

[51] The twelve Minor Prophets and the four Major are embraced by Augustine under the phrase "proprie Prophetae." Augustine follows his list with the remark: *His quadraginta quattuor libris Veteris Testamenti terminatur auctoritas.*

[52] Cf. Westcott, *Canon*, p. 529f, Wildeboer, *Canon*, p. 8off.

[53] This list omits Kgs. and according to the Bamberg Ms. it also omits Daniel. Zahn (*Geschichte*, II, p. 270) points out that the omission of Daniel must be a copyist's error since Daniel is needed to make up the twenty-two. Zahn raises the question whether the fact that the Bamberg text reads *de verba dierum* means that "de" is a corruption of "Daniel" and that Daniel

(23) The list of Innocent I (d. 417 A.D.). The five books of Moses (Gen., Ex., Lev., Nu., Dt.), Josh. son of Nun, Jgs., Four books of Kgs., Ruth, Sixteen books of the Prophets, Five books of Solomon, The Psalter, Histories: Job, Tob., Est., Jth., Two books of Macc., Two bks. of Esdr., Two books of Chr.

(24) The list of the Pseudo-Gelasius.[54] Five books of Moses (Gen., Ex., Lev., Nu., Dt.) Josh. son of Nun, Jgs., Ruth, Four of Kgs. Likewise the books of the prophets, sixteen in number (Isa., Jer., Ezk., Dnl., Hos., Am., Mic., Joel, Ob., Jon., Nah., Zeph., Hag., Zech., Mal.),[55] two of Chr., 150 Psalms, three books of Solomon (Prov., Eccl., Song of Songs), Bk. of the Wisd. of the son of Sirach, another following book of Wisd., likewise of Histories: Job, Tob., [Zahn (II, 262) adds—Esdras two], Esther, Jth., two bks. of Macc.

(25) The list of Cassiodorus, (d. 544 A.D.) Gen., Ex., Lev., Nu., Dt., Joshua son of Nun, Jgs., Ruth, Kings a-d, Chr. a-b., Ps., Five books of Solomon (Prov., Wisd., Ecclus., Eccl., Song of Songs), Prophets (Isa., Jer., Ezk., Dnl., Hos., Am., Mic., Joel, Ob., Jon., Nah., Hab., Zeph., Hag., Zech., Mal. which also is Angelus), Job, Tob., Est., Jth., Esdr. two books, two books of Macc. In all 44 books.

(26) The list of Isidorus. 1. Five books of Moses. 2. Josh. son of Nun, Jgs., Ruth. 3. Four of Kgs., Two of Chr., Tob., Est., Jth., Esdr., Two bks. of Macc. 4. Prophets: One bk. of Psalms, Three bks. of Sol. (Prov., Eccl., Song of Songs), Wisd., Ecclus., sixteen books of Prophets.

(27) The list of Mommsen, from the year 359 A.D. The canonical books: Gen., Ex., Nu., (sic!) Lev., Dt., Josh. son of Nun, Jgs., seven books. Ruth, Four of Kings, Two of Chronicles, Two of Macc., Job, Tob., Jth., Est., 151 Psalms of

---

should therefore precede Chron. as in the *Prologus Galeatus*. But he apparently favours the view that Daniel should follow Ezekiel in Jerome's list as given by Cassiodorus.

[54] There are four or five different lists of the decree of Gelasius discussed by Zahn (II, 259-67).

[55] Thiel gives the order from this on: Chron. two books, Ps., Solomon three (Prov., Eccl., S. S.), Wisd., Ecclus.

David, of Solomon, of Major Prophets: Isa., Jer., Dnl., Ezk., The Twelve.[56]

(28) List in the Codex Claromontanus (c. 300 A.D.) Gen., Ex., Lev., Nu., Dt., Josh. son of Nun, Jgs., Ruth, Four of Kgs., Chr. two, the Davidic Psalms, Prov., Eccl., Song of Songs, Wisd., Wisd. IHU (i.e. of Jesus ben Sirach), Twelve Prophets: Hos., Am., Mic., Joel, Ob., Jon., Nah., Hab., Zeph., Hag., Zech., Mal., Isa., Jer., Ezk., Dnl., Macc., First, Second and Fourth, Jth, Ezra, Est., Job, Tob.

(29) List of the Liber Sacramentorum (6th or 7th cent. A.D.) Gen., Ex., Lev., Nu., Dt., Josh., Jgs., Bks. of Women: Ruth, Est., Jth., two books of Macc., Job, Tob., Four of Kgs., Sixteen books of Prophets, Five of David, Three of Solomon, One of Esdras. The books of the Veteris make in number forty-three.

(30) The list of the Council of Carthage (397 A.D.) Gen., Ex., Lev., Nu., Dt., Josh. son of Nun, Jgs., Ruth, Four books of Kgs., Two books of Chr., Job, the Davidic Psalter, Five books of Sol., Twelve books of Prophets, Isa., Jer., Ezk., Dnl., Tob., Jth., Est., Two books of Esdr., two books of Macc.[57] Ballerini's text gives the order: Daniel, Ezekiel. See Zahn II. 252. And it omits the books of Maccabees.

15. The Old Syriac version, called the Peshito, has an order differing from all others. It puts Job before the Psalter and gives a unique arrangement of both the major and minor Prophets. The original Peshito seems to have omitted Chr., Ezra-Neh. and Est. but accepted Ecclus.[58]

16. Theodore of Mopsuestia omits Chr., Ezra-Neh., Est. and Job.

17. The Nestorians omit Chr., Ezra-Neh., and Est., but receive Job, Ben Sirach, and the additions to Dnl.

18. Some Monophysites take the same view as the Nestorians, but add Esther.

19. Barhebraeus takes no account of Chronicles.[59]

[56] From this list I have omitted some irrelevant matter.

[57] For the most part, these lists have been translated from the originals as given in Swete, *Introduction to the O.T. in Greek*, pp. 198-214.

[58] See Wildeboer, p. 85.

[59] For 16-19 above, cf Buhl, *Canon and Text*, pp. 53, 190.

20. The Ethiopic Bible, in a MS in the British Museum gives in order: the Law of Moses 5, Jgs. 3, Jub. 1, Kgs. 4, Chr. 1, Job 1, Bks. of Sol. 5, (Prov. is divided in two), Isa. 1, Jer. 1, Ezk. 1, Dnl. 1, The Minor Prophets 12, Ezra 2; Macc. 1, Tob. 1, Jth. 1, Assenath 1, Est. 1, Ecclus. 1, Ps. 1, Ozias 1. The sum of the Old Testament is 46.[60]

2. The Use

Since Bevan has appealed to the Haphtaroth, or selections from the prophetical books, to be read on the Sabbaths and feast days, as evidence that the Book of Daniel was not in existence when these selections were made, it seems best to give a list of these Haphtaroth so that the evidence may be forthcoming for the discussion of this view, which will be given later.

(1) The blessing before the reading of the Haphtara reads: "Blessed art Thou, Jehovah our God, the king of the world, who hast chosen good prophets and accepted their words, which were spoken in truth. Blessed art Thou who didst choose the Law and Moses thy servant and Israel Thy people and the prophets of truth and righteousness."

The blessings after the reading are:

(a) "Blessed art Thou Jehovah our God, king of the world, rock of all the ages, righteous in all generations, the faithful God, who sayeth and it is done, speaketh and it stands fast; for all His words are truth and righteousness."

(b) "Faithful art Thou, Jehovah our God, and faithful are Thy words, one word of thine shall not return back in vain; for a faithful king art Thou, O God. Blessed be Thou, Jehovah, the God who is faithful in all His words."

(c) "Comfort Thou Zion, for it is the house of our life. And for humility of soul do Thou save quickly in our days. Blessed be Thou, Jehovah, who rejoicest Zion with her sons. Make us to rejoice, O Jehovah our God, through Elijah the prophet thy servant, and through the house of David thine anointed, quickly let him come and let our heart rejoice. Upon his throne let not

---

[60] Cf. Westcott, *Bible in Church*, p. 238, where he follows Dillmann, *Cat. MSS. Aeth.* p. 4.

a stranger sit, and let not others inherit again his glory; for by thy holy name hast Thou sworn to him, that his light shall not be quenched for ever and ever. Blessed be Thou, Jehovah the shield of David."

(d) "For the *Law* and for the service *and* for the *prophets* and for this Sabbath day, which Thou hast given to us, O Jehovah our God, for sanctification and for rest, for glory and for beauty; for all, O Jehovah our God, we are thanking Thee, and blessing Thee. May Thy name be blessed by every living one for ever and ever continually. Blessed be Thou Jehovah, who sanctifiest the Sabbath." [61]

(2) The Haphtaroth selections in use among the modern Hebrews are as follows: 1). From Joshua. (a) i, 1-18. (b) ii, 1-24, (c) v, 2-vi, 27. 2). From Judges. (a) iv, 4-v, 31. (b) xi, 2-33. (c) xiii, 2-25. 3). From First Samuel. (a) i, 1-ii, 10. (b) xi, 14-22. (c) xv, 1-22. (d) xx, 18-42. 4). Second Samuel. (a) vi, 1-29. (b) xxii, 1-51. 5). First Kings. (a) i, 1-31. (b) ii, 1-12. (c) iii, 15-28. (d) v, 26-vi, 13. (e) vii, 13-26. (f) vii, 40-50. (g) viii, 2-21. (h) viii, 54-66. (i) xviii, 1-39. (k) xviii, 46-xix, 21. 6). From Second Kings. (a) iv, 1-23. (b) iv, 42-v, 19. (c) vii, 3-20. (d) xi, 17-xii, 17. (e) xxiii, 1-27. 7). From the First part of Isaiah. (a) i, 1-28. (b) vi, 1-13. (c) x, 32-xii, 6. 8). From Second Part of Isaiah. (a) xl, 1-26. (b) xl, 27-xli, 16. (c) xlii, 5-21. (d) xliii, 21-xliv, 23. (e) xlix, 14-li, 3. (f) li, 12-lii, 9. (g) liv, 1-10. (h) liv, 11-lv, 5. (i) lv, 6-lvi, 8. (k) lvii, 14-lviii, 14. (l) lx, 1-22. (m) lxi, 10-lxiii, 9. (n) lxvi, 1-24. 9). From Jeremiah. (a) i, 1-ii, 3. (b) ii, 4-28, iv, 1, 2. (c) vii, 21-viii, 12. (d) viii, 13-ix, 23. (e) xvi, 19-xvii, 14. (f) xxxi, 2-20. (g) xxxii, 6-27. (h) xxxiv, 8-22. (i) xlvi, 13-28. 10). From Ezekiel. (a) i, 1-28. (b) xvii, 22-xviii, 32. (c) xx, 2-20. (d) xxii, 1-16. (e) xxviii, 25-xxix, 21. (f) xxxvi, 16-36. (g) xxxvi, 37-xxxvii, 14. (h) xxxvii, 15-28. (i) xxxviii, 18-xxxix, 16. (k) xliii, 10-27. (l) xliv, 15-31. (m) xlv, 16-xlvi, 18. 11). From Hosea. (a) ii, 1-22. (b) xi, 7-xii, 12. (c) xii, 13-xiv,

---

[61] These prayers have been translated from the *Seder Birekhoth Hahaptarah* of the Jewish Year Book of Adelbert della Torre, published at Vienna in 1861, p. 50.

34   Studies In the Book of Daniel

7. (d) xiv, 2-10. 12). From Joel. ii, 1-27. 13). From Amos. (a) ii, 6-iii, 8. (b) ix, 7-15. 14). From Obadiah. vs. 1-21. 15). From Jonah. i, 1-iv, 11. 16). From Micah. v, 6-vi, 8. 17). From Habakkuk, ii, 20-iii, 19. 18). From Zechariah. (a) ii, 14-iv, 7. (b) xiv, 1-21. 19). From Malachi. (a) i, 1-ii, 7. (b) iii, 4-24.[62]

(3) In addition to the Haphtaroth in use among the modern Jews, which are to be found listed with their corresponding sections from the Law in the conspectus of the appendix of our Hebrew Bibles, the following Haphtaroth in use among the Karaites and the earlier Jews are mentioned in an article by Büchler in *The Jewish Quarterly Review*.[63] 1) Joshua (a) iii, (b) iv, 1-15. (c) 3-18. (d) xiv, 6. (e) xvii, 4. (f) xxi, 41. 2) Judges (a) ii, 7. (b) xi, 16-26. (c) xviii, 7. (d) xix. (e) xix, 20. 3) 1 Sam. (a) ii, 21-28. (b) vi, 6. (c) xii, 3-xiv, 2. (d) x, 24. (e) xv, 2. 4) 2 Sam. (a) v, 13-vi, 1. (b) xi, 5. (c) xiii. (d) xvi, 21. 5) 1 Kings (a) iv, 20. (b) x, 9. (c) xvii, 24. 6) 2 Kings (a) xii, 14-23. (b) xx, 8. 7) Isaiah, First Part. (a) iv, 6. (b) xxvii, 6. (c) xxix, 8-14. (d) xxx, 15. (e) xxxii, 18. xxxiii, 17. (f) xxxiv, 11. (g) xxxvii, 31-37. (h) xvii, 14-xviii, 7. 8) Second Part. (a) xlii, 12-17. (b) xliii, 1-7. (c) xlvi, 3. (d) xlviii, 12. (e) xlix, 9-13. lxiv, 1. (f) lxv, 10. (g) lxv, 23-lxvi, 8. 9) Jeremiah. (a) xii, 15. (b) xiv, 19-22. (c) xxix, 8. (d) xxx, 10-16. (e) xxxviii, 8. 10) Ezekiel. (a) xii, 20. (b) xvi. (c) xx, 41. (d) xiv, 11. (e) xlv, 1. (f) xlv, 12. 11). Hosea xii, 4-13. 12) Joel iii, 3. 13) Amos i, 3-15. 14) Micah (a) ii, 12. (b) vi, 3-vii, 20. (c) vii, 9. 15) Nahum i, 12-ii, 5. 16) Zephaniah (a) i, 12. (b) iii, 9-19. 17) Zech. x, 6-11.

(4) *The New Testament.* 1. In Luke iv, 17, we are told that Jesus "went to the synagogue, as was His wont every sabbath day, and stood up for the purpose of reading. And there was given to Him the book of the prophet Isaiah, and He opened the book, and found the place where it is written: "The Spirit

[62] For the list here given, see the Conspectus Haphtararum in the Appendix to any good edition of the Hebrew Bible. (The minor variations between the Sephardim and the Ashkenazim are not noted.)
[63] Vol. VI, pp. 1-73.

of the Lord is upon me," etc. (Isa. lxi, 1f). 2. In Acts xiii, 14, 15, we are told that Paul and Barnabas went into the synagogue at Antioch, and, after the reading of the Law and the Prophets, Paul, on the invitation of the rulers, stood up to make an exhortation. 3. In Acts xiii, 27, we are told that the Prophets were read every Sabbath day.

It is to be noted that neither of the above lists includes a selection from Haggai; also that Isa. lxi, 1f. is not found in either.

DISCUSSION OF THE EVIDENCE

In discussing the assumptions of the critics with regard to the historicity and date of the Book of Daniel on the basis of the evidence just given, I shall consider first the relation between the dates of the books of the Old Testament and their position in the present Hebrew Canon. All the critics argue as if the presence of Daniel among the books which by us are called Hagiographa is a sure indication of the lateness of its composition. That this is not the case, I shall proceed to show, (1) by a consideration of the Law; and, (2) by a consideration of the rest of the books of the Old Testament. In the course of this discussion of the main proposition assumed by the critics, I hope to make it plain, that not merely it, but also the other assumptions and conclusions with regard to the date of the Book of Daniel in so far as they are derived from its position in the present Hebrew Bible, are false.

1. The Order of the Books

The Pentateuch. First, let us take the order of the books in the Pentateuch. According to the order in all Hebrew and Greek manuscripts that contain the Pentateuch, the books were arranged in their present order, that is, the order of the historical sequence of the events and of the supposed order of the codes of law contained in them. Genesis gives the history from the creation to the establishment of Israel in Egypt; Exodus and Leviticus, the account of the exodus and of the events and laws connected with Sinai; Numbers, the story of the wanderings; and Deu-

teronomy, a résumé of the history and of the laws enacted up
to the arrival of the children of Israel at Shittim. The oldest
evidence for this order is to be found in the works of Origen
from the middle of the third century A.D. The only list of the
books of the Law antedating this, is that given by Melito, Bishop
of Sardis, from the latter part of the second century A.D.; but
it gives the books in the order Gen., Ex., Nu., Lev., Dt. Since
Melito and Origen, these two earliest witnesses for the order,
number, and names, of all of the books of the Law, thus differ
as to their order, it is manifest that at the time when they wrote
their order had not yet been fixed. The relative position of a
book in the so-called earliest Canon had, therefore, nothing essential to do with its canonicity.

Again, according to the radical critics, the Hebrew Pentateuch
was not finished till after the time when the translation of the
Seventy was made.[64] Dividing the main sources of the five-fold
book of the Law into the Jehovistic, Elohistic, Deuteronomistic,
and Priestly portions, denoted respectively by J, E, D, and P,
they place J somewhere between 850 and 625 B.C.; E, at about
750; D, at or shortly before 621; and P, at 444 B.C.[65] The
canonization of D was made in 621 B.C., and that of P in 444
B.C.[66] The whole work was put together in its present form about
400 B.C., though additions and corrections are alleged by
some to have been made even subsequently to the time of the
Seventy,[67] that is, after 280 B.C. The redactor Rp, who is said
to have put J, E, D, and P, together, excluded from and added to
the original documents whatever he pleased, and put them together
in the order that seemed to him to be best. But this order, while
chronological according to the time at which the books purport
to have been written, is not chronological according to the time
at which the critics say that they were written; for Rp puts the
laws of P before those of D, although according to the modern
critics of the Wellhausen school, D was written about two
hundred years before the writing of P.

[64] Cornill, *Introduction*, p. 474.
[65] *Id.*, p. 91.
[66] *Id.*, p. 472.
[67] *Id.*, p. 474.

It will be noted, also, that even though the five-fold division of the Law cannot be traced back farther than Philo,[68] and even though it may have existed for only a short time before the time when the version of the Seventy was made,[69] this does not affect the fact that in the Pentateuch as far back as we can trace it,[70] the P laws preceded the laws of D in the document as it came from the hand of Rp.

Further, since the critics claim that D was canonized before P, it follows that the position of a book in the Canon, or in a part of the Canon, was not always, or necessarily determined by the time of its canonization, or by the time of its composition. So, then, the position of Daniel in the present Hebrew Bible has not necessarily anything to do with the time of its composition, or of its canonization.

The Rest of the Old Testament. It will be noted that I have written "present Hebrew Bible"; for there is no evidence to show that any old Hebrew manuscript ever contained the books of the Old Testament Canon as they are arranged in our Hebrew Bibles as now printed. Nor did either of the great schools of Hebrew manuscripts, the Spanish, or the German-French, have the books arranged as they are now printed; nor are they printed in the order given in the Talmud. Nor do they follow the order of the earliest printed Hebrew Bibles, such as the Editio Princeps of Bomberg, which put the five Megilloth immediately after the Pentateuch. Our Bibles agree with the Spanish and Massoretic manuscripts in the order of the Prophets, but with the German and French in the Hagiographa. The order of the Talmud differs from that of the early printed Bibles and from that of the editions in use at present. It differs, also, in the order of the books both in the Prophets and the Hagiographa from the Massoretic, Spanish, and German-French manuscripts. The Peshito Syriac version differs in the order of the books both in Prophets and Hagiographa from every one of these Hebrew orders. The

---

[68] *De Abrahamo*, I.
[69] Cornill, p. 28.
[70] The Samaritan Hebrew text and Targum, as well as all the ancient versions, primary and secondary, and all the lists of the books of the Law, early and late, unite in placing D after P.

lists of Melito, Origen, and Jerome, all of whom derived their information from the Hebrew scholars of their respective times, give an order differing from one another and from all the Hebrew manuscripts, lists, and versions. Moreover, no one of the great Greek uncials, Vaticanus, Sinaiticus, Alexandrinus, and Basiliano-Venetus, agrees in order with any other one of them, or with any one of the Hebrew or Syriac sources. And lastly, of the many lists of the Greek and Latin Fathers and Synods, no two are found to agree with each other; nor does anyone of them agree with any other list from any other ancient source.

In short, of more than sixty lists given above, no two present exactly the same order for the books comprising the Old Testament Canon; so that it can be affirmed positively that the order of those books was never fixed by any accepted authority of either the Jewish or Christian church.

2. *Names, Numbers and Divisions*

When we leave the order and come to the names, numbers and divisions, or groupings, of the books of the Old Testament, we find no evidence, except in the case of the Law, that the position of a book had anything to do with its date. The earliest witnesses give the names of the divisions as follows:

1. The Prologue to Ben Sira, (1) The Law, the Prophets and Others that followed after them. (2) The Law and the Prophets and the other books of our fathers. (3) The Law itself and the Prophecies and the rest of the Books.

2. Second Maccabees says that Nehemiah gathered together (1) the books concerning the kings and prophets, (2) those of David, and (3) epistles of kings concerning votive offerings.

3. Philo says that the Therapeutæ received (1) the Law, and (2) the oracles uttered by the prophets, and (3) the hymns and other (writings) by which knowledge and piety are augmented and perfected.

4. Luke xxiv, 44 speaks of (1) the Law, (2) the Prophets, and (3) the Psalms.

5. Josephus divides the books into (1) the Law, (2) the

Prophets, and (3) the remaining four, containing hymns to God and precepts concerning the conduct of human life.

6. Melito gives (1) the Five of Moses, (2) Josh., Jgs., Ruth, Kgs., Chr., (3) Ps., Prov., Eccl., Song, Job, (4) Prophets (Isa., Jer., The Twelve, Dnl., Ezk.) (5) Esdras.

7. Baba Bathra speaks of (1) Moses' "own book," (2) of the Prophets, of whom it names eight, not including Daniel, and (3) of the Hagiographa, of which it names eleven including Daniel.

8. Origen names (1) the five books of the Law, (2) six historical books, Josh., Jgs. w. Ruth, Sam. (two in one), Kgs. (two in one), Chr. (two in one), Esdr. (two in one), (3) Ps., Prov., Eccl. and the Song,[71] (4) Is., Jer. with Lam. and the Ep. as one, Dnl. and Ezk. (the Twelve having been dropped from the list, probably through an error of some copyist), (5) Job, Est., and (6) outside (*hexo*) these is the Maccabees.

9. The four great Greek uncials give only the names of the books, but no names of divisions, except that A heads the names of the Prophets with the phrase "The sixteen Prophets," among which it puts Daniel. If it be allowed to indicate divisions based on the order and character of the books, they would be as follows: (1) For Vaticanus (B) (a) the Law, Gen., Ex., Lev., Nu., Dt. (b) Historical books, Josh., Jgs., Ruth, Kgdms. 4, Chr. 2, Ezra 2. (c) Poetical books, Ps., Prov., Eccl., the Song, Job, Wisd., Sirach. (d) Est., Jth., Tob. (e) The Twelve, Is., Jer., Bar., Lam., Ep., Ezk., Dnl. (2) For Alexandrinus (A), (a) the Law, Gen., Ex., Lev., Nu., Dt. (b) Historical books, Josh., Jgs., Ruth, Kgs. 4, Chr. 2. (c) Prophets 16: the Twelve, Isa., Jer. also Baruch, Lam., Ep., Ezk., Dnl. (d) Est., Tob., Jth., Ezdras a, b, Macc. 4. (e) Poetical books, Ps., Job, Prov., Song, Wisd., Sirach, Ps. of Sol. (3) For Sinaiticus (א), (a) the Law, of which, however, only fragments of Gen. and Nu. remain. (b) Historical books, of which remain Chr., Ezra-Neh., Est., Tob., Jth. and four of Macc. (c) Proph. books, Isa., Jer., Lam., Joel, Obad., Jon., Nah., Hab., Zeph., Hag., Zech., Mal. The other books have been destroyed. (d) Poetical books, Ps., Prov., Eccl., Song of

[71] Probably the four of Josephus' third division of the Canon.

Songs, Wisd., Sirach, Job. (4) For Basiliano-Venetus. (a)
the Law, Lev., Nu., Dt. (all that remain). (b) Josh., Ruth,
Jgs., Kgdms. 4, Chr. 2, Esdr. 2, Est. (lacuna). (c) Poetical
books, (Ps.), Job, Prov., Eccl., Song, Wisd., Sirach. (d)
Prophetical books, the Twelve, Isa., Jer., Bar., Lam., Ezk., Dnl.
(e) Tob., Jth., Macc. 4.

10. The principal Greek, Latin, and Syrian lists make, or imply,
the following divisions: (1) Melito: Law 5, History 5-9, Poetry
5, Prophecy 5, Others 1. (2) Origen: Law 5, History 6-11.
Poetry 4, Prophecy 4, Others 1-2. (3) Athanasius: Law 5, History 6-11, Poetry 5, Prophecy 5, Others 5. (4) Pseudo-Athanasius: Law 5, Histories 7-11, Poetry 5, Prophets 12, Four others
besides—the Major Prophets, Beside these 8 books. (5) Cyril:
Law 5, History 6-12, Poetry 5, Prophecy 5. (6) Epiphanius a:
Law 5, History 3, Poetry 5, History 2-6, Prophecy, 5, Others
2-3, Extra 2. (7) Epiphanius b: Law 5, Poetry 5, Hagiographa
5, Prophecies 5, Others 2, Extra 2. (8) Epiphanius c: Law 5,
History 3, Psalms 1, History 2-6, Solomon's Works, Prophecies
5, Others 2-3. (9) Gregory Nazianzus: History 12, Poetry 5,
Prophecy 5. (10) Amphilochius: Law 5, History 6-11, Poetry 5,
Prophecy 5, Proverbs 2, Extra: Esther. (11) Pseudo-Chryso-
stom: Octateuch, History 2-5, Admonitory 4, Prophecy 16, Extra
2. (12) Lagarde's Synopsis: Octateuch; History 12, Solomon
4, Prophecies 12, Major Prophets 4. Extra: Wisdom of Jesus
ben Sirach. (13) Dialog. Tim. et Aquila: Mosaic Pentateuch,
History 5, Poetry 4, Prophecy 6, Additional 2. Extra 3. (14)
Junilius: Histories 17, Prophecies 17, Proverbs 2, (Additional
2), Dogmatics 1. (15) Leontius: The Historical Books 12, the
Prophetical 5, the Paranetic 4 (5?). (16) John of Damascus:
First Pentateuch, or Nomothesia; Second Pentateuch, or Hagiog-
rapha; Third Pentateuch, or the Poetical Books, Fourth Penta-
teuch, or the Prophetical. Others 2. Extra: Two. (17)
Nicephorus: Law 5, History 6-10, Poetical 5, Prophetical 6.
Antilegomenoi: 8-10. (18) Ebedyesu: Law 5, History 6, Poetical
7, Prophets 16, Others 12. (19) Canons of Laodicea: Law 5,
Historical 7-11, Poetical 5, Prophetical 5. (20) Apostolic Canons:
Five of Moses, Historical 14, Poetical 5, Prophetical 5. Extra:

The Wisdom of the very learned Sirach. (21) List in Cod. Baroc.: Law 5, Historical 4-9, Poetical 5, Esdras, Prophetical 16, . . . Extra 6-9. (22) Hilary: Five books of Moses, Histories 6-9, Poetical 4, Prophets 12. Six other prophets, among which are included Lamentations and Epistle of Jeremiah, Job, and Esther. Extra 2. (23) Ruffinus: Five books of Moses, Historical 6-10, Prophets 5, Poetical 5. Extra: 5-8. (24) Augustine: Histories 16-22, Prophecies 22. (25) Jerome a (List in *Prologus Galeatus*), Law 5, Prophets 8, Hagiographa 9; b (as given by Cassiodorus) Law 5, Prophets 9, Hagiographa 8. (26) Innocent I.: Five books of Moses, Historical 4-7, Prophets 16, Books of Solomon 5, Psalter, Histories 7-10. (27) Pseudo-Gelasius: Books of Moses 5, Historical 4-8, Prophets 16, Chronicles 1-2, Poetical 6. Likewise, Histories 5-6. (28) Cassiodorus: Law 5, Historical 3-7, Poetical 6, Prophets 16, Others 6-8. (29) Isidorus: Five books of Moses, Historical 10-15, Prophets 22 (including the 5 poetical books). (30) Mommsen's List: Heptateuch (?), Historical 15, Major Prophets 4, Prophets 12. (31) Codex Claromontanus: Law 5, Histories 7, Poetry 6, Prophets 16, Additional 8 (including Job and Esther). (32) Liber Sacramentorum: Law 5, Historical 13, Prophetical 16, Davidic 5, Solomonic 3, Esdras— xliii books. (33) Council of Carthage: Law 5, Histories 5-9. Poetry 7, Prophets 16. Others 5-7.

This review of the testimony given above shows that only one witness puts the Book of Daniel under any other heading than that of the Prophets. This witness is the Baba Bathra, a work not written till about A.D. 200, and deemed by the critics as so unreliable that they reject all that it says in the immediately succeeding context about the writers of the various books of the Old Testament. Besides, it simply says that the *Rabbis* had taught the order of succession. They did not follow it in their MSS Bibles. All of the witnesses who derived their information from Jewish sources antedating this time, either expressly or impliedly, place Daniel among the Prophets,—Philo, Matthew, Luke, Josephus, and Melito. Even Origen and apparently Jerome [72] who studied with the Jewish Rabbis of their time, placed Daniel

[72] See above, pp. 24, 29.

among the Prophets. It is proper, therefore to conclude that the fact that the later Jews placed Daniel among the Hagiographa has nothing to do with the questions of its canonicity and date.

3. Subsidiary Questions

Having thus considered the main charge against the early date of the Book of Daniel based upon its position in the present Hebrew Bibles, I shall next devote myself to some subsidiary questions more or less relevant to the main charge, and which the critics bring forward to support it.

Driver says, that "the age and authorship of the books of the Old Testament can be determined (so far as this is possible) only upon the basis of the internal evidence supplied by the books themselves, by methods such as those followed in the present volume: no external evidence worthy of credit exists." [73] If this proposition were true, it might be well to ask why, then, Driver considered it necessary to present eleven pages of historical and philological reasons, alleged to be derived from, or supported by, evidence external to Daniel, in order to show that it could not have been written in the sixth century B.C. The most admirable thing about Doctor Driver, and that which gained for him his exalted position in the scholarly world, was the masterly manner with which he essayed to support his judgments based upon the internal evidence of a book by evidence external to the book itself. What I object to in the case of Doctor Driver and his followers, is that they seem to seek in every possible way to pervert the internal and external evidence as to the Canon in general, and as to the canonicity and date of Daniel in particular, so as to confirm their own preconceived opinion as to what they ought to be. For as to the internal evidence, no one can doubt that the Book of Daniel claims on the face of it to be genuine. It purports to make known to us the deeds of Daniel and his three companions and the visions of the former. It relates itself to the history of the sixth century B.C. That it is full of alleged miracles and of accurate and detailed predictions, is not internal

[73] *L. O. T.*, p. xi.

evidence against its historicity or date; for the histories of the Old and New Testaments, as well as those of Ashurbanipal, Nabunaid, and Alexander, are full, also, of alleged miracles and predictions. The only thing for us to do is to recognize the internal testimony at its face value and to test this testimony by means of all the external evidence that is relevant and available. In the case before us, the specific charge is made, that the Book of Daniel cannot be genuine, because the book itself claims to be, in large part at least, a work from the sixth century B.C., whereas its position in the Canon indicates that it cannot have been written before the second century B.C. To support this charge, it is alleged that the part of the Old Testament which in our present Hebrew Bibles is called the Prophets, embracing only Josh., Jgs., Sam., Kgs., Isa., Jer., Ezk. and the twelve Minor Prophets,—eight books in all according to the reckoning of the ancient authorities—, was canonized and closed at, or before the year 200 B.C.

Now, since all admit that the prophetical books were canonized before 200 B.C. and called the Prophets, the only question at issue is as to the correctness of the use of the word "closed" as applied to the books called Prophets. Is there evidence to prove that the eight books named in Baba Bathra were then canonized, and called Prophets, and that afterwards no book, or part of a book, was ever added to, or taken away from, the eight that were thus canonized and named Prophets? If this can be proven it would have to be admitted that the Book of Daniel cannot have been among them. If, on the other hand, it can be shown by external evidence, that the division of the Old Testament Canon called the Prophets contained at an earlier time than that at which the Baba Bathra was written more books than the eight named in its list, it follows that Daniel may have been one of these books. For some reason, known or unknown to us, it may have been removed from an earlier position among its fellow prophets; but the fact will be patent that its later position among the Hagiographa would not indicate that the book was not in existence before 200 B.C.

THE CANON OF THE PROPHETS

1. *Direct Evidence*

There are six prime witnesses, antedating the time at which the first sketch of the Mishna was written, and they all testify clearly that an eight-booked Canon of the Prophets was not in existence in the time at which they wrote. These witnesses are the Prologue to Ecclesiasticus, Philo, Luke, Matthew, Josephus, and Melito. I shall discuss them in the order, Josephus, Luke, Matthew, Philo, the Prologue to Ecclesiasticus, and Melito.

1. *Josephus.* Josephus is the principal witness, because he states expressly that the Jews had only twenty-two canonical books.

Of his twenty-two books he specifies five as constituting the Law and four as containing "hymns to God and precepts for the conduct of human life." These last were probably the Ps., Prov., Eccl. and the Song of Songs. This would leave Josh., Jgs., Sam., Kgs., Ezra-Neh., Chr., Est., Job, Isa., Jer., Ezk., Dnl. and the Twelve Minor Prophets as the thirteen others,—he having counted Ruth as part of Jgs., Neh. as one with Ezra, and Lam. as belonging to Jer. Job was accounted a prophetical book, as in Ben Sira, xlix. 9.

Now, whatever may be thought about the opinion of Josephus as to the time when the last of the prophetical books was written, seeing that this opinion is expressed about events which happened 500 years before his time, there is no reason to doubt that in telling of the number and divisions of the books held sacred by the Jews of his time, no witness could possibly be better. For he was a priest of the royal Asmonean line, educated in all the wisdom of the innermost circles of Jewish scholarship, possessed of the official Temple copy of the original Hebrew Scriptures, which had been taken from the Temple and presented to him by Titus himself. He certainly would not in a controversial treatise, like that against Apion, where he challenges the world to dispute his statements and constantly appeals to written documents and to the acknowledged current opinions of the contemporary

Jews,—he certainly would not have dared to divide the books of
the Jews as he does, unless that division was the one accepted
by the learned Jerusalem scholars of his day. And in this
division he certainly places Daniel in the second of the three
divisions, which embraced all the books except the Law and the
Poetical books.

2. *Luke xxiv. 44.* The next Jewish testimony is that of Luke
xxiv. 44, where Jesus is represented as saying, "All things must
be fulfilled, which are written in the Law of Moses, and in the
Prophets, and in the Psalms, concerning me." This passage
from Luke's Gospel I am not introducing in evidence as the
infallible statement of an inspired book, nor as having back of it
the authority of an infallible man, nor even as having ever been
said by Jesus at all; but simply as an ordinary statement of the
writer of this book, called the Gospel of Luke. It is admitted by
all the leading critics that this book was written before or about
the year A.D. 70.[74] And no text is better supported than that of
this verse. What, then does this verse prove? It proves that
in the time when Luke wrote, the Jews divided the books of the
Old Testament into three parts, the Law, the Prophets, and the
Psalms. Everyone admits that by Law the five books of Moses
are meant. In view of the statement of his contemporary,
Josephus, it would be most natural to suppose that by Psalms he
means what Josephus includes in his third division, that is, the
books called by us, Pss., Prov., Eccl., and Song of Songs. In
the Prophets, there would be included the other thirteen books
which Josephus embraces in his second division, including, of
course Daniel.

3. *Matthew xxiv. 15.* That the writer of Matthew's Gospel,
also, considered Daniel to be among the prophets is supported by
Mt. xxiv. 15, where we read of "the abomination of desolation,
spoken of by Daniel the prophet."

Doctor Driver, in his discussion of the Canon in the opening
chapter of his *Literature of the Old Testament,* as well as in his
chapter in the same volume on the Book of Daniel, studiously

[74] J. A. McClymont, *The History and Results of New Testament Criticism,* p. 142f.

avoids all reference to this testimony of the New Testament books to the opinions of the Hebrew writers as to the Old Testament Canon. He appeals at length to the Talmud, Josephus, Ben Sira, 2 Maccabees, and 4 Ezra; but passes by in silence the testimony of the New Testament, of Melito, and of all Christian writers! One might understand the motive for this in a Jew, but it is hard to understand what possible motive a Christian can have in thus ignoring the testimony of writings whose date is certainly as determinable as that of 4 Ezra, 2 Maccabees, or the Talmud, and whose veracity as respects the point here at issue can not be questioned.

Cornill, indeed, goes one step farther than Driver; for he says that "Jesus cannot be appealed to as witness for the Old Testament Canon." [75] This is a confusion of the point in discussion. If he means that we have not written testimony by Jesus himself as to the Old Testament Canon, no one has ever claimed as much. But if he means that we have less direct and reliable testimony as to what Jesus thought about the Old Testament Canon than we have in regard to what the Jews of his time thought, Josephus and the New Testament writers alone excepted, why does he not state where this direct and reliable testimony is to be found? I know of none such. He goes on to say, "He, (i.e., Jesus) indeed lived and moved in the holy literature of Israel, toward which He did not take up any different position from that of His Jewish contemporaries, and, in fact, in His days almost the same books were counted as Holy Scripture as are found in our Old Testament." [76] How does he know that Jesus took up the same position as His contemporaries? He can know it only from Josephus, Philo, and the New Testament, as far as contemporary written testimony is concerned; and, as we have seen, Josephus and the New Testament both have three divisions of the Canon and both place Daniel among the Prophets. Jesus, therefore, must have done the same, Cornill himself being witness.

Cornill's statement that "in fact in His (i.e., Jesus') days almost the same books were counted as Holy Scriptures as are

[75] *Introduction*, p. 482.
[76] *Id.*, pp. 482, 483.

found in our Old Testament," will be readily admitted by all, except for the word "almost." The only ground for the insertion of this limiting particle is that the Sanhedrin, said to have been held at Jamnia at some time between A.D. 70 and 100, expressed itself in favour of the canonicity of certain books whose right to a place in the Canon had been disputed. To which it may be said that no contemporary testimony bears witness to any such Sanhedrin or to any such dispute. Any knowledge that such a Sanhedrin was ever held is due to a tradition among the Jews first put in writing about A.D. 200. A writer who ignores the testimony of Melito and Origen and subjects to severe criticism the testimony of the New Testament and Josephus, should not be so ready to accept an unwritten tradition of the Jews!

But even granting that some books were disputed in A.D. 100, or at the time of Rabbi Akiba (A.D. 135), or at any other time, let it be remarked that *Daniel was not one of the books disputed.* Let it be remarked again that Ezekiel was one of the disputed books. If Ezekiel, a book which all the critics say was in the second part of the Canon—a part which they say was canonized by 200 B.C.—could be disputed as late as A.D. 100, three hundred years after it was canonized, and six hundred and fifty years after it was written, how does it follow that the disputing of the canonicity of Esther, Ecclesiastes, and the Song of Songs shows in the opinion of the critics that they were written late? At any rate, how does the disputing of one or all of these books affect the canonicity of Daniel, a book that, so far as we know, was never disputed?

But not only was the book of Daniel not disputed,[77] but Daniel himself was held by Josephus to have had "strange revelations made to him and those as to one of the greatest of the prophets" (*Antiq.* X. x. 1.7). And with the writers of the New Testament, and from all accounts, with the Lord Himself,

[77] This is certainly true of the Hebrew portion of Daniel. In *Yadaim* iv, 5 it is said that the Aramaic passages in Ezra and Daniel defile the hands (*i.e.,* are canonical). These Aramaic passages may have been disputed simply because they were written in Aramaic rather than Hebrew. (See above, pp. 19 f.).

Daniel was among the greatest in his influence, his book being either referred to or cited by them more than a hundred times.

4. *Philo Judæus.* The next Jewish testimony to the Old Testament Canon is to be found in Philo Judæus, who flourished about A.D. 40. In describing the Therapeutæ, he says that "they receive the Law, and the Oracles uttered by the Prophets, and the hymns and the other (writings) by which knowledge and piety are augmented and perfected." [78] In this statement, the "hymns" are evidently the Psalms, and the "other writings," possibly Prov., Eccl., and the Song of Songs, corresponding to the "precepts for conduct of human life" of Josephus. At any rate, it seems certain that the only place for Daniel in this list is among the Prophets.

5. *The Prologue to Ben Sira.* The fifth direct Jewish witness to the threefold division of the Old Testament books is to be found in the Prologue to the Greek translation of Jesus ben Sira, made by his grandson of the same name. This Prologue was most probably written in 132 B.C. He mentions the threefold division three times. First, he says that "many and great things have been delivered unto us by the law, the prophets, and the other (books) which follow after them." Secondly, he says that his grandfather Jesus had given himself to "the reading of the law and the prophets and other ancestral books." Thirdly, he speaks of "the law itself, and the prophets, and the rest of the books." Since he intimates nothing as to the character of the contents of the second and third parts nor as to the number of books in each, it is simply a matter of conjecture as to where he may have put Daniel. It seems likely that he placed it in the second division rather than in the third, in view of the fact that the next witnesses in point of time (that is, Philo, Luke, Josephus, and perhaps the writer of the Ascension of Isaiah), all put it there; and further, in view of the fact that never till the Talmudical period do we find Daniel placed anywhere else. Certainly, at least, no laws of evidence will permit the critics to force Daniel into the third division on the ground of testimony

---

[78] *De Vita Contemplativa,* ii, 475; vd. Budde, *Kanon,* p. 56.

which was written from 200 to 500 years later than the time
when this Prologue was written.

6. *Melito of Sardis.* The sixth first-class witness is Melito,
bishop of Sardis at about A.D. 180. He says that he desired to
make an accurate statement of the ancient books as regards their
number and order and that when he had gone to the East and
come to the place where the things (recorded in them) were
preached and done, he learned accurately the books of the Old
Testament and sent the names of them in a letter to his friend
Onesimus. In the list of these names he gives the Prophets as
consisting of the following: Isaiah, Jeremiah, the Twelve, Daniel,
Ezekiel and Esdras. Some doubt may be felt as to whether he
meant to put Esdras among the Prophets; but there can be none
as to Daniel, because it precedes Ezekiel. Further, it will be noted
that Melito does not put Joshua, Judges, Samuel, and Kings
among the Prophets; but puts them, followed by Chronicles, after
the Pentateuch and before the Psalms of David. It is scarcely
possible, in view of his deliberate and voluntary statement that
he had carefully investigated as to the number and order of the
books, that he would have intentionally made a false list of them,
especially in view of the fact that such a falsehood could so
easily have been exposed. We are justified, therefore, in concluding that at his time there was either no fixed order and
number of books in the division of the Prophets; or that the
order was afterwards changed.

All the direct evidence, then, that precedes the year 200 A.D.,
supports the view that Daniel was in the earliest times among
the Prophets. Further, this conclusion is supported by all the
direct evidence outside the Talmud, which is later than A.D. 200.
Thus Origen, at A.D. 250, and Jerome, at A.D. 400, both of whom
were taught by Jewish Rabbis and claim to have gained their information from Jewish sources, put Daniel among the Prophets
and separate the strictly prophetical books from those which are
more properly called historical. And, lastly, all the Greek uncials
and the Greek and Latin fathers, unite in placing Daniel among
the Prophets and in separating the Prophets from the Historical
Books.

2. Other Evidence to Canon of Prophets

Nor can the view that Daniel was originally among the Prophets be successfully impugned on the ground that other testimony, mostly late and indirect, indicates the contrary.

1. *Council of Jamnia.* Appeal has frequently been made to the Sanhedrin of Rabbis held at Jamnia some time between A.D. 70 and 100, as having first settled authoritatively for the Jews the extent of their Canon. This testimony, however, is rendered less valuable owing to the fact that it is not contemporaneous, i.e., we have no *written* records referring to any such Sanhedrin going back beyond the two tractates of the Mishna called *Yadayim* and *Idayot,* which were written about 200 A.D. However, admitting that the testimony is genuine, what does it prove? Simply that certain books had a right to be held as canonical. These books were Ezk., Prov., Est., Eccl., the Song of Songs, Jon. and Ruth, and the Aramaic portions of Ezra and Dnl. With regard to Jonah no technical phrase is used; with respect to Ezekiel and Proverbs, the question was whether they should be withdrawn (*genaz*); with regard to the Aramaic portions of Daniel and Ezra, it is said that they defile the hands; with regard to the four others the question was whether they *defiled the hands.* With regard to the meanings of these two terms, the following may be said: (1) *Genaz,* in the technical sense in which it is used in the discussion of the Canon, means "to withdraw from use." [79] "The Talmudical view is that canonical books may *not* be 'hidden,' for this is only done in the case of books which are really offensive." [80] "The books which the Rabbins 'hide' (*genaz*) are always books the contents of which were regarded as objectionable, that is, heretical." [81] "The word would be inapplicable if applied to the books of the Hebrew Canon, or to the books of the Apocrypha." [82] (2) With regard to the phrase, "defile the hands," the author accepts the definition of this term given by Robertson Smith and elaborated by Budde in his work

[79] See Oesterley, *The Books of the Apocrypha,* p. 183.
[80] *Id.,* p. 184.
[81] *Id.,* p. 185.
[82] *Id.,* p. 185.

entitled, *Der Kanon des A. T.,* (p. 3-6). Budde first rejects the opinion of Buhl that it was meant by this phrase to guard against the profane use of worn-out (*abgenutzte*) rolls of the Scriptures; and the opinion of Strack and others that by this phrase it was meant that the Holy Scriptures, as unclean, should always be kept apart so as not to be exposed to harm resulting from touching consecrated corn or from eating by mice; and the opinion of Geiger, that holy books written upon the skin of unclean animals were alone to be declared unclean. "All such explanations," says he, "are contradicted by *Yad*. III. 4, where the question especially is decided whether the margins and back sides of the rolls made the hands unclean. In all these explanations, this question is never raised. It deserves to be noticed rather, that to the Holy Scriptures alone tradition ascribes a rendering of the hands unclean,—their touch making necessary a ritual washing of the hands." The Pharisees (under protest from the Sadducees) [83] attributed to the holy books such a high degree of holiness that whoever touched them dared not touch other things before he had observed the same ritual hand-washing as if he had touched something unclean. The correlative term for this kind of uncleanness of the hands is "holiness." "In accordance with this view, the Old Testament books are called in the Mishna 'the holy books'; or 'books of holiness.'" For these two attributes, holiness and uncleanness of the hands, are expressed at the same time and indeed only of a wholly limited number of writings, that is, the canonical." [84]

It is necessary to observe in connection with this phrase (1) that only the Aramaic part of Daniel is spoken of in the Talmud as defiling the hands, it being taken for granted that the Hebrew portion did; (2) that the Aramaic portions of Ezra are said in

---

[83] Cf. *Yadayim,* iv, 6.

[84] Cf. *Yadayim,* iii, 5. See also Oesterley's discussion of this term in *The Books of the Apocrypha,* pp. 175-182, where he says, "Defilement arose from the fact that the canonical books were 'holy', and holy things defiled by touching them. Compare Lev. x. 10, where holy=unclean. According to Lev. xvii. Aaron washed after coming out of the most holy place and taking off his holy garments. So since sacredness was imputed to the canonical books, contact with them necessitated a washing of the hands; and therefore anyone who touched a sacred book was said to be defiled."

the same passage to defile the hands; (3) that Ezekiel, one of the Major Prophets and one cited already as a prophet by Jesus ben Sira, was disputed; (4) that Jonah, one of the Twelve, a portion of the Canon recognized by Jesus ben Sira, was possibly another one thus disputed; (5) that Proverbs, which all authorities acknowledge to have been one of the four books of Josephus' third division, and also to have been used by Ben Sira, is another of them; and (6) that Ruth, the composition of which Cornill puts in the time of Ezra-Nehemiah, is also disputed. So, then, the fact that the right of a book to a place in the Canon was disputed by some Jewish scholars does not prove that it had not been received as canonical before the time even of Ben Sira, the critics themselves being judges; for they all place Ezekiel and nearly all place Jonah, in the second, or prophetical division, which they state to have been "closed" about 200 B.C.[85] And, if this be so of books whose right to be in the Canon was disputed, how much more must it be true of a book like Daniel whose right to be in the Canon was never denied.

2. *First Maccabees.* Again, there is certain evidence in I Maccabees, also, that Daniel existed before the time of the Maccabees. For from the speech given in chap. ii, 51-60,[86] we learn, (1) that the author supposes that the story of Daniel and his three companions was known to the Jews before the rebellion under the Maccabees commenced. (2) That he considered Daniel and his companions to be as historical as Abraham, Joseph, Phinehas, Joshua, Caleb, David, and Elijah. (3) That a writer who was almost certainly a contemporary of most of the events that he narrates would scarcely have treated the information of a book of fiction written in his own age (i.e., if we date Daniel in 164-5 B.C., and I Macc. between 125 and 100 B.C.) as affording a fitting climax for a stirring exhortation such as Mattathias is said to have made to his compatriots. The writer must have believed that the stories of the fiery furnace and the lions' den were known not merely to Mattathias but to those whom he

[85] But Josephus, about 90 A.D., puts Ruth and Lamentations in the second division.
[86] Cf. supra p. 14.

addressed. As this address was made in the year 169 B.C., it is evident that the stories must have been in existence long enough to have been learned by Mattathias and his followers and also to have been accepted by them as true histories of what had occurred. Otherwise, to have placed the reference to them in the climax of his address would have weakened and made ineffective the force of his argument.

To use a phrase of Bevan's "it is marvellous" that no reference to Daniel is to be met with in 1 Macc. Notwithstanding that this first book of Maccabees is supposed by the critics to have been written at this time for the consolation of the Jewish patriots, this exact and sympathetic narrative never so much as alludes, except in the passage cited above, to either the Book of Daniel or its author! The failure to mention the writer of Daniel might be pardoned, inasmuch as he evidently intended that his work should be accepted as a production of the supposititious Daniel, whom he so often represents as speaking in the first person. Whether it was originated in the sixth or in the second century B.C., it is remarkable, however, that the writer of Second Maccabees takes no notice of it, and the writer of First Maccabees cites it but once. It is another remarkable fact that First Maccabees mentions no division of the Old Testament Canon except the Law.

3. *Aristeas.* Next, the Epistle of Aristeas, which was written about 200 B.C., shows no knowledge on the part of the author of any division of the Old Testament except the Law. This bears upon the controversy about Daniel only in so far as it shows that the omission of all references to books of the Old Testament and to persons and events mentioned in them does not prove that the author who fails to mention them was not cognizant of their existence, or that the books did not actually exist.[87]

4. *Ecclesiasticus.* Again, the greatest of Jewish extra-canonical writings known to us, coming from pre-Maccabean times, is the book of Ecclesiasticus by Jesus ben Sira. The prologue to this

---

[87] Cooper, in the *Last of the Mohicans*, says that he examined many European and British accounts of the battle of Braddock and that in no one of them was the presence of Washington mentioned.

work, written by a second Jesus ben Sira, the grandson of the
first, has already been considered. In the original work itself,
we have a direct reference once to the Law of Moses (xxiv, 23),
and many statements which show a knowledge of its contents.
Many of the heroes of Israelitish history whom the author cele-
brates in his song of praise (xliv-l), are those whose merits are
depicted in the Law. As to the prophetical books he shows his
knowledge of the book of Joshua in his account of Joshua and
Caleb (xlvi, 1-10), refers to Judges (xlvi, 11, 12), to Samuel the
prophet (xlvi, 13-20), to Nathan and David (xlvii, 1-11), to
Solomon (xlvii, 12-23), to Rehoboam and Jereboam the son
of Nebat (xlvii, 23), to Elijah (xlviii, 1-12), to Elisha (xlviii,
12-14), to Hezekiah (xlviii, 17-22), to Isaiah (xlviii, 20-25), to
Josiah (xlix, 1-4), to Jeremiah (xlix, 6, 7), to Ezekiel (xlix, 8),
to Job (xlix, 9), to the Twelve (xlix, 10), though he mentions no
one of them by name. Of the books afterwards classed among
the Hagiographa, he mentions Job and Nehemiah and makes
several citations from the parts of Chronicles which are not found
among the parallels in Kings. He probably refers, also, to Ezra
in xlix, 14, and possibly to Daniel in xlix, 10.

Nowhere in Ecclesiasticus do we find any knowledge of a
threefold, or fourfold, division of the Old Testament; nor any
intimation that the division of the Prophets had been closed; nor
any indication, except perhaps in his use of the Law, of his having considered some books more sacred than others. Besides, he
elaborates the praises of Simon the High Priest more than those
of any of the great men of Israel whose records are found in
the books of the Old Testament Canon. It is a remarkable fact
that he does not pay any regard to the great men who had exercised their functions outside the bounds of the land of Israel,
such as Jonah at Nineveh, Daniel in Babylon, and Mordecai in
Persia. In speaking of Abraham, he does not refer to his coming
out of Ur of the Chaldees, nor to his visit to Egypt. In speaking of Jacob, Joseph, and Aaron, he says nothing of the land of
Egypt; nor does he intimate that Moses had ever been in Egypt,
saying simply of the wonderful deeds done by him there, that
"God gave him might in terrible wonders," and that "through the

word of his mouth he caused signs to happen quickly, and caused him to be strong before the king." Of all the foreign kings mentioned in the Old Testament, he refers to but two—once to Pharaoh and once to Sennacherib. As far as Daniel is concerned, therefore, and the foreign kings among whom he laboured, it is entirely in harmony with the plan of the work of Ben Sira, that no one of them should be noticed. This silence does not show that Ben Sira did not know about them. It was simply his determination to ignore them. Whether the books containing mention of one or all of them were among those deemed canonical by the Jews of his time, does not appear in any suggestion of his work. It will be noted especially that Ben Sira calls Job a prophet (xlix, 8), and that he places him between Ezekiel and the twelve Minor Prophets.

5. *Second Maccabees.* Another piece of circumstantial evidence with regard to the Old Testament Canon is to be found in the second chapter of Second Maccabees, where the author quotes a letter written in 124 B.C. as saying that Jeremiah the prophet gave them that were carried away the Law, charging them not to forget the commandments of the Lord, and exhorting them that the Law should not depart from their hearts and speaking of the things that were reported in the writings (or official archives) and commentaries (or memoirs) of Nehemiah; and how he, founding a library, gathered together the books of the Kings and the Prophets (Syr. "those of the Kings and those of the Prophets"), and those of David, and the epistles of the Kings concerning the holy gifts (Gk. *anathemata;* Syr. "offerings and sacrifices") ; and that Judas in like manner gathered together all the things that had escaped (Syr. "had been scattered"), on account of the wars which we had, and they are still with us. Further in chap. xv, 9, Judas Maccabeus is represented as comforting the people out of the Law and the Prophets, and putting them in mind of the battles which they won afore.

This book of 2 Maccabees was probably written sometime in the first century B.C. and professes to be an epitome of an earlier work by Jason of Cyrene, unfortunately lost, but to which the author of the epitome attributes an exact handling in a work of five books of every particular of the wars of the Maccabees. The author of this letter contained in 2 Macc. seems to have divided the Jewish literature of Nehemiah's time into five or six parts, (1) the Law, (2) the books concerning Kings and Prophets, (3) the memoirs of Nehemiah, (4) the epistles of the Kings, and (5) the books of David. The Syriac version separates the Kings (which it renders kingdoms) from the Prophets, thus making six divisions. Of these divisions, three and four were added in the time of Nehemiah, and would be probably the subject-matter of our books of Ezra and Nehemiah. The books of David would be what Luke calls the Psalms. If Daniel were anywhere in any of these divisions, it would be in the second division of the Greek text, and in the second of its two sub-divisions in the Syriac version, that is, in the sub-division which concerned the Prophets.

It is true that the author of 2 Maccabees never mentions Daniel, nor does he refer to any of the events or persons recorded in his book. This, however, is more extraordinary, if the Book of Daniel were written in the second century B.C. than if it had been composed four centuries earlier.

6. *Martyrdom of Isaiah.* The next Jewish witness to the Canon is the Martyrdom of Isaiah embedded in the larger work called the Ascension of Isaiah. According to Charles, this work was probably known to the writer of the Epistle to the Hebrews, who seems to quote from it in Heb. xi, 37. If so, it will have been written before A.D. 70. In Book iv, 21, 22, he speaks of the Psalms, which he makes to include the Parables[88] of David and the Proverbs of Solomon and the words of Korah, Ethan, and Asaph; and proceeds to speak of the words of Am., Hos., Mic., Joel, Nah., Jon., Ob., Hab., Hag., Zeph., Zech. and Mal.,

---

[88] In the Ethopic original, the word for psalms "mazameret" is clearly the equivalent of the Hebrew "mizmor." The words, parables and proverbs, in Charles' version are translations of the same word "mesaleyata" of the original, the equivalent of the Hebrew "meshalim." While more commonly used for the proverbs of Solomon, it is employed also in Psalms xlix, 4 and lxxviii, 2, and in Job xxvii, 1 and xxix, 1 in the sense of "songs," or "poems."

and of the words of Joseph the Just,[89] and of the words of Daniel.

In this list, it will be observed that Daniel comes after the Minor Prophets and not among the Hagiographa; also, that the Twelve are arranged in an order not to be found elsewhere in any source. This unique arrangement shows conclusively that the books of the Old Testament were not fixed as to their positions when the book of the Ascension of Isaiah was written.

7. *Massoretic Notes.* Attention should be called also to three other items of indirect evidence as to the Old Testament Canon. One is that to be derived from the Massoretic notes to be found at the end of most of the books of the Old Testament. Among these notes is usually one telling of the number of Sedarim, or sections, in each book. Thus, Genesis is said to have 43; Exodus, 29; Leviticus, 23; Numbers, 32; Deuteronomy, 27; Joshua, 14; Judges, 14; 1 and 2 Samuel together, 34; 1 and 2 Kings, 35. So, the number of Sedarim is given at the end of Isaiah, Jeremiah, Ezekiel, Daniel, Job, Psalms, and Proverbs. The twelve Minor Prophets, Ezra and Nehemiah, and 1 and 2 Chronicles, have one each between them. Now, of the five Megilloth, only Esther and Ecclesiastes have a statement of their Sedarim. In the case of Ruth and Lamentations, this was doubtless because when the Sedarim were made and counted, the former was still united to Judges and the latter to Jeremiah. As to the Song of Songs, it would seem as if it in like manner had been counted with Ecclesiastes; since the Sedarim are given but once for the two books. The Talmud and all the ancient lists except Augustine and Junilius place Ecclesiastes before the Song. Augustine agrees with the Spanish and Massoretic manuscripts in giving the opposite order. The printed Bibles follow the German and

[89] Charles thinks that this probably refers to an extra-canonical book of antichristian character. In connection with the name of Daniel, it would be more natural to refer them to the well known Patriarch Joseph of Egypt, who like Daniel was a great interpreter of dreams. One is tempted to believe that the Ethiopic text has made the mistake of putting Joseph for Job. In the book of Job, i, 1, Job is called "the just." The letters for s and b are almost exactly alike in Ethiopic. If Job be the true reading, he would be classed among the Prophets, as in Ecclesiasticus xlix, 9, in the Hebrew and Syriac recensions.

French manuscripts in giving the order of their use in the yearly festivals, that is, the Song of Songs, Ruth, Lamentations, Ecclesiastes, Esther. Junilius has a singular division and classification of his own into Historia, Prophetia, Proverbia, and Dogmatica; putting the Law, Ruth, Esther, and Job in the Historia, the Psalms in the Prophetia, the Song of Songs in the Proverbia, and classing Ecclesiastes all by itself as Dogmatica. He attempts apparently to arrange his so-called Prophetia in a chronological order, resulting as follows: Ps., Hos., Isa., Joel., Am., Ob., Mic., Nah., Hab., Zeph., Jer., Ezk., Dnl., Hag., Zech., Mal. Since this arrangement is thus so obviously due to an attempt to give a combined logical and chronological arrangement, his testimony on this point should be ruled out. This will leave Augustine as the only ancient source placing Ecclesiastes after the Song of Songs. But Augustine, like Junilius, has an arrangement all his own; for he divides all the books into Historiae and Prophetae. Among the Historiae, he counts the five of the Law, Joshua, Judges, Ruth, four of Kings, two of Chronicles, Job, Tobias, Esther, Judith, two of Maccabees, and two of Esdras. Among the Prophets, he counts the Psalms, Proverbs, the Song of Songs, Ecclesiastes, Wisdom, Ecclesiasticus, the Twelve (Minor Prophets), and the four Major Prophets in the order, Isa., Jer., Dnl., Ezek. It will be seen that he has invented an order for himself differing from all others, following the freedom of his own will without regard to the authorities that preceded him. Yet, it is noteworthy that the Massoretic and Spanish manuscripts have the same order as that of Augustine; and since the Massoretic manuscripts have transmitted to us the Massoretic notes, including the numbers of the Sedarim, the note giving the number of the Sedarim of the combined book is placed properly in our Bibles after the book of Ecclesiastes.

The testimony of the Massoretic notes on the Sedarim would indicate that these notes were made at a time when the Jews still counted Ruth as a part of Judges and Lamentations as a part of Jeremiah; and also, that when they were made, they counted Ecclesiastes and the Song of Songs as one book. If Ruth and

Lamentations could, after the time when these notes were made, be separated from among the Prophets, so also could Daniel and Esther be thus separated. The evidence goes to prove that the position and divisions of the books as at present constituted has nothing necessarily to do with their age and canonicity.

8. *The Haphtaroth.* A piece of circumstantial evidence bearing upon the date is that suggested by Bevan when he says that the second or prophetical part of the canon cannot have been in use before 200 B.C. because no selection from Daniel appears in the Haphtaroth, or lessons read on Sabbaths and feast days in the Temple and synagogues. It must be admitted that no selection from Daniel is found in these lessons as read at present; but this is no proof that Daniel did not exist, or was not deemed a prophet, when these selections were made.[90]

For, first, no one knows when these selections were first made and used. The earliest mention of their probable use is to be found in Luke iv, 16, where it is said that Jesus read in the synagogue on the Sabbath day the passage of Isaiah beginning with the words; "The Spirit of the Lord God is upon me" (Isa. lxi, 1), but this is in no known Haphtaroth. But, since the Jews of the first century A.D. certainly acknowledged Daniel to be a prophet, they cannot have failed to make a selection from his prophecy because they did not consider him to be a prophet.

If, however, it be said that selections from the Prophets must have been made long before the first century A.D., I admit that they most probably were; but this is no proof that the Book of Daniel did not exist when they were made, or that it was not then placed among the Prophets, or even that selections from it were not at that time read in the synagogue services. For Büchler and others have shown beyond a doubt that three times as many passages were once read as are read to-day, that the limiting of the length to be read was late, and that passages from some of the prophets from which there are at present no selections were once read. The evidence collected above goes to show that only such sections were selected as magnified the Law and the Sab-

[90] See above pp. 32-35.

bath and the nationalistic hopes and aspirations of the Jews. Most of them have some readily visible point of contact with the portion of the Law which was to be read on the day for which the particular Haphtara was selected. Thus at the feast of the passover, such portions of the prophetical books as Josh. v, 2-vi, 27 which recounts the great passover at Gilgal, and 2 Kgs. xxiii, 1-27 which tells of the great passover of Josiah, were read. For Ex. xxv-xxx, 10, which gives the plan of the tabernacle, or Ex. xxxv-xl, which gives an account of the completion of the tabernacle, the portions chosen as Haphtaroth are from 1 Kgs. v, 26 to vii, 51. For the passage, Ex. xxx, 11 f., which tells about the golden calf, the appropriate Haphtara is the account of the controversy between Elijah and Ahab recorded in 1 Kgs. xviii, 1-39. The account of the spies of Jericho is read with Nu. xiii, which tells of the other spies who were sent to spy out the land. The Haphtaroth, then, were selected with a regard to the appropriateness of their contents for the occasion, and for the portion of the Law which they were meant to illustrate. Those who made the selections were the judges of what they deemed to be appropriate. Some of us might differ from these judges as to the aptness of some of their selections. We might even go so far as to contend that some of their principles of selection were wrong. We might have taken one from Haggai, which they apparently did not. We might have retained one, or more, of the portions which once were read from Zephaniah and Nahum, which the modern Hebrews have rejected. We might, possibly, have found some portion in Daniel appropriate to be read, which they apparently did not find. But the fact remains that the selection of the Haphtaroth had nothing to do with the age of the books nor, as far as we know, with the position of a book among the divisions of the Old Testament as they were constituted at the time when these Haphtaroth were chosen. Did Professor Bevan ever attempt to select a few passages from the Book of Daniel which he thinks more appropriate for reading in the services of the synagogue on any given occasion, or along with any particular portion of the Law, than that which as a matter of fact is now employed? I for one think that the Jews have done about the best that was possible in harmony with the principles upon which they acted in the making of their choice.

Further, it seems to me that what we have just learned about the Haphtaroth affords the best explanation possible for the reduction of the number of the books in the prophetical division from its earlier number as given by Josephus to the number as derived from the list of prophetical books as given in the Mishna, that is, from 13 to 8. When once the Haphtaroth had been selected, a reason would at once be apparent why the books in which they were contained should be put and kept together for readiness of use in the services of the synagogue; just as in later times the five Megilloth were put together for the same purpose, or, as in the modern Vienna edition of Adelbert della Torre, we find the Hebrew Torah, the Targum of Onkelos, the Five Megilloth, and various prayers and comments published in one volume, together with the appropriate Haphtaroth.

9. *O.T. Books written on Rolls or Tablets.* Such considerations as this last lead us naturally to the evidence as to the divisions and arrangements of the Old Testament books to be derived from the way in which we know that ancient books were written. In the pre-Christian times books were written upon tablets of clay or stone, or upon rolls of papyrus, or skin; so that instead of one book, the Old Testament contained from 22 to 39 books according to the number of rolls upon which it was written. These books could be arranged in any order that suited the good pleasure of their owner. According to any system of arrangement, logical or chronological, the Law would naturally be put first; but the lists show that even here Melito and Leontius placed Numbers before Leviticus. It is noteworthy that there is no MS with the Pentateuch and Joshua alone; the Hexateuch is a creature of the imagination. The early editions of the printed Bible put the Megilloth immediately after the Law, though all the manuscripts, versions, and ancient lists, either put them all together in the third part of the Canon, or some among the Prophets, and some among the Poetical books. This will account, also, for the fact that no two ancient sources agree as to the order of the books. As the lists have been handed

down to us, it would be impossible for any one to say where certain books might be found. Job, for example, is placed by Cyril and by Epiphanius (in one of his three lists) immediately after the Law; whereas in the Codex Sinaiticus and in many Syriac MSS, it is the last book of all. Ruth, Lamentations, Chronicles, Esther, Psalms,—all shift their positions according to the pleasure of the owner, or the writer of the list. Some books, never acknowledged as canonical by the Jewish church, such as Tobit, Judith, and Wisdom, became mingled in certain collections of private owners of religious literature with the Holy Books, and in this manner probably they at first assumed a semi-canonical character, and were afterwards listed by their undiscriminating possessors among the canonical books. In the case of Daniel, however, it is found in all lists and sources, in all ages, always among the canonical books, and always in the ancient sources among the Prophets, except in the list found in the Baba Bathra.

CONCLUSIONS

The evidence given above and its discussion permit only of the following conclusions:

1. That the position of a book in the Hebrew Canon was not determined by the time at which it was written.

2. That the position of a book in the list of the Mishna, or of the Hebrew manuscripts, versions, and editions, does not determine the time at which it was admitted to the Canon.

3. That all the earlier Hebrew sources, and all the Greek, Latin, Syriac, and Armenian sources put Daniel among the Prophets.

4. That Daniel's genuineness, or its right to be in the Canon, was never disputed by the ancient Jews or Christians except possibly the Aramaic portions.

5. That there is no external evidence, direct or indirect, except the argument from the silence of Ecclesiasticus, that Daniel was not composed till the time of the Maccabees.

6. That the silence of Ecclesiasticus is more than offset by the silence of 1 and 2 Maccabees, and of all other sources, as to the

origination of any such book, or the existence of the author of any such book, at the time of the Maccabees.

7. That there is no direct evidence of the existence of a threefold division earlier than the prologue of Jesus ben Sira, written in 132 B.C.

8. That the absence of any selection from Daniel in the Haphtaroth does not prove that the Book of Daniel was not in existence, or acknowledged as canonical, when the Haphtaroth were chosen.

9. That Daniel was always considered by Josephus, and by the writers of the New Testament, to be a prophet, and that his book was placed by the same authorities among the prophetical books.

10. That all the early Hebrew authorities which place Daniel among the Prophets, agree with the Mishna in holding to a threefold division of the Canon.

11. That the testimony that we possess does not show that the second part of the Canon was closed before the books of the third part were all written.

12. That the assumption that the division of the Hebrew Canon called the Prophets in our present editions of the Hebrew Bible was doubtless formed prior to the Hagiographa, is unfounded, inasmuch as there is no evidence that this division as it is now made was in existence before the second century A.D.

13. That all witnesses agree in putting the Law first; and that Melito and Leontius alone change the order of the books of the Law, in that they put Numbers before Leviticus.

14. That not one of the ancient witnesses puts the five Megilloth together, not even the Talmud.

15. That in nearly all the lists, the five poetical books are placed together.

16. That the only great difference of order between Philo, Luke, and Josephus, representing the earliest Hebrew arrangement, and the early Christian lists, arises from the fact that the former put the poetical books at the end, whereas the latter usually place them before the sixteen books of the Prophets.

17. That the books of the Old Testament Canon were never

authoritatively and fixedly arranged in any specific order, either by the Jews, or by the Christians.

18. That the order has nothing to do with the canonicity, nor necessarily even with the date of a book.

19. That length, supposed authorship, subject-matter, and convenience, as well as the material upon which a book was written, were the potent factors in all the ancient arrangements of the books.

20. That since the modern Jews have changed the position of Ruth, Lamentations, and Esther, to suit their convenience in the public service, there is every reason to believe that their so-called book of the Prophets was collected together into one for the same reason; and that the omission of Daniel from this collection had nothing to do either with its age or canonicity, but simply with the fact that it was not employed in these public services.

20a. That the Haphtaroth and the eight prophetical books never are found in the same MSS.

21. That all the testimony that the ancient Jewish and Christian sources give, bearing upon the time of the composition of the Old Testament books, is consentient in granting the claims of the books themselves as to their historicity, genuineness, and authority.

22. That the determining factor in the canonization of a book was its supposed age and author, its agreement with the Law, and its approval by the prophets.

23. That in accordance with these rules Ecclesiasticus, Tobit, Maccabees, and other apocryphal books on the one hand, and on the other hand the pseudepigraphical books of Adam, Enoch, Noah, Jubilees and the XII Patriarchs, were rejected from the Canon.

24. That those who rely upon documentary evidence, cannot escape the conclusion that the indictment against the Book of Daniel on the ground that it is not among the Prophets is false; and that in so far as the age and canonicity of the Book of Daniel are assailed on the ground of its position in the Canon, the old view stands approved.

CHAPTER II

DANIEL NOT QUOTED

The design of this chapter is to show the absurdity of the claim made by the critics that the Book of Daniel cannot have been composed in the sixth century B.C. based on the fact that it is not quoted until the second century B.C. Following my usual method in discussing objections put forth against the *prima facie* evidence of the books of Scripture, I shall state the claim founded on the absence of citation, as it is made in the words of Professor Bevan of Cambridge, England, one of the most scholarly of the radical commentators on Daniel. Next, I shall give the assumptions involved in this claim, and lastly, I shall endeavour to show the baselessness of these assumptions.

THE CHARGE

"On the supposition that the narrative in Daniel is historical, it is marvellous that it should be passed over in utter silence by all extant Jewish writers down to the latter half of the 2nd century B.C., that it should have left no trace in any of the later prophetical books, in Ezra, Chronicles, or Ecclesiasticus. It is, of course, possible in each particular case to imagine some reason for the omission of the subject, but the cumulative evidence is not so easily set aside. Thus it has often been said that nothing can be concluded from the silence of Ben Sira in Ecclesiasticus xlix. But in order to realize the true state of the case we should consider how easy it would be to refute, from Jewish literature, any one who asserted that the book of Isaiah or that of Jeremiah was composed entirely in the Maccabean period." [1]

THE ASSUMPTIONS

There are in these objections four assumptions:

1. That it is marvellous that the narrative of Daniel if his-

[1] Bevan, *The Book of Daniel*, pp. 12, 13.

65

torical "should be passed over in utter silence by all extant Jewish writers down to the later half of the 2nd century B.C.

2. That it is marvellous, "that it should have left no trace in any of the later prophetical books, in Ezra, Chronicles or Ecclesiasticus."

3. That it is easy to refute from Jewish literature "anyone who asserted that the book of Isaiah or that of Jeremiah was composed entirely in the Maccabean period."

4. That there is cumulative evidence that Daniel did not exist, in the silence of the later prophets and other books with regard to it.

We will now discuss these four assumptions in the order in which they have been stated:

First Assumption

The first of these assumptions has absolutely nothing to support it, inasmuch as there are no Hebrew writings extant from before the Maccabean period, which could justly have been expected to mention Daniel.

Of the extra-biblical works of this period it is to be noted:

1. The fragments of *Aristobulus,* who wrote about 160 B.C. and is first mentioned in 2 Macc. i, 10 (written about 135 B.C.), say nothing about any of the historical persons or events of any book of the Old Testament; but state simply that the complete translation of the whole of the Law was made in the time of the king surnamed Philadelphus.[2]

2. The Aramaic fragments of *Ahikar* from the fifth century B.C. do not quote from any other Old Testament book. Why then should they have quoted Daniel?

3. Whenever the books of *Jubilees* and the *XII Patriarchs* were written, it is obvious that they could not have quoted Daniel or any of the prophets without stultifying themselves; since they claim to have been apocalypses composed before the time of Moses.

4. The *Letter of Aristeas* written in Greek about 200 B.C. "does

[2] Eusebius, *Praep. Evang.* xiii, 12, 2.

not profess to discuss the origin of any part of the Alexandrian Bible except the Pentateuch." A careful reading of it fails to reveal any reference to any of the books or events or persons of the Old Testament except those that belong to the Books of Moses.

5. Aside from the books named in the second assumption, the only Biblical book which claims to have been written in this period is that of Esther. Since this book does not mention any of the other prophets, there is no good reason why it should be expected to mention Daniel. Again, if its failure to mention Daniel shows that Daniel did not exist, it might be argued that its failure to mention the other prophets proved that they also did not exist. This would be absurd. Besides, no one claims this.

It is, therefore, perfectly fair to affirm that the assumption that Daniel might be expected to have been mentioned in these Jewish writings from before the time of the Maccabees is without any foundation whatever.

Second Assumption

In the second assumption, however, it is presumed that Daniel ought to have been mentioned in the later prophetical writings, or in Ezra, Chronicles, or Ecclesiasticus.

The late prophetical writings are Haggai, Zechariah and Malachi; to which some critics would add Jonah and Joel. Since no one of these prophets refers by name to Isaiah, Jeremiah, Ezekiel, or any of the earlier prophets, it can hardly seem *marvellous* that they do not refer to Daniel. As to Chronicles, why should it be considered marvellous that Daniel is never mentioned in it, seeing that with the exception of the last ten verses and the fragments of one or two genealogies, the history contained therein ceases with the destruction of Jerusalem by Nebuchadnezzar? To be sure, we find Isaiah prominent in the part narrating the political history of Hezekiah, and Jeremiah is said to have lamented the untimely end of Josiah and to have prophesied the captivity in Babylon and its end after 70 years; but there was no occasion for naming Daniel, who had nothing directly to do with the political affairs of Jerusalem. Moreover Daniel's history and visions occurred in the time of Nebuchadnezzar, Belshazzar, Darius and Cyrus, at the beginning and near, or after, the end of the captivity, and the history of Chronicles with the exception of the last two verses extends merely till the destruction of Jerusalem. Besides, Chronicles contains no mention of Ezekiel, nor of any of the Minor Prophets.

As to the last two verses of Chronicles where it is said that Jehovah, in order that the word of the Lord by Jeremiah the prophet might be accomplished, stirred up the spirit of Cyrus so that he made the decree to rebuild Jerusalem, can it really seem marvellous to Bevan that Daniel is not mentioned there? Perhaps, he would have had the author throw out *Jehovah* and put Daniel in its place?

Further, why should it seem a marvellous thing, that no trace of Daniel appears in Ezra? It will be just as hard to find in Ezra any trace of Isaiah, Jeremiah, and of any of the Minor Prophets except Haggai and Zechariah,—and Haggai and Zechariah are named because they lived and laboured with Jeshua and Zerubbabel in the building of the second temple, of which Ezra gives the history. Some analogies to Ezekiel may be found in Ezra, because they are both writing largely of matter concerning the Law; but the name of Ezekiel is not found, nor is his book referred to.

The discussion of the silence of Ecclesiasticus, the last of the books appealed to by Bevan, as to Daniel will be reserved for the next chapter. Suffice it to say at this point that Daniel is possibly referred to in chap. xlix, 10; but if this be not admitted, it is possible that Ben Sira did not mention Daniel, either because he was opposed to his doctrines, or because he was not personally acquainted with his book.

It is not so certain, as Bevan would have us suppose, that the LXX translation of Deut. xxxii, 8 was not influenced by the view of angels propounded in Daniel. It certainly looks as if it were, and we need more than the mere *opinion* of a modern scholar to prove that it was not.

In this connection, too, one might ask why Bevan fails to appeal to Nehemiah. For it is certain that his prayer in chap. ix, has a striking resemblance to the prayer of the ninth chapter of Daniel.

One of them almost certainly had the prayer of the other in mind when he made his own. Since Daniel purports to have made his prayer about the middle of the sixth century B.C. and Nehemiah his toward the end of the fifth, the *prima facie* evidence would assuredly be in favour of Daniel.

Lastly, the testimony of Ezekiel as to the existence and character of Daniel is not to be so easily set aside as Bevan and others suppose. Ezekiel mentions him by name together with Noah and Job in xiv, 14, 20 and xxviii, 3. So far as we know, no other Daniel but the one who flourished at Babylon as a contemporary of Ezekiel can have been compared in wisdom with Noah and Job. It would have been senseless for Ezekiel to have appealed to the wisdom of a person unknown to his hearers and readers. It is not fair to say, that he could not have cited the wisdom of a contemporary. Napoleon, even during his lifetime, was frequently compared to Alexander and Cæsar, and to-day some compare Hindenburg to Napoleon. Anyone of us might use Bismarck or Cavour as examples of statesmanship. It was a natural compliment to his great compatriot on the part of Ezekiel and an appeal which those whom he addressed could all understand, since they had doubtless all heard of the wisdom of Daniel and what it had brought to him at the court of Nebuchadnezzar.

Third Assumption

In regard to the third assumption, it cannot be admitted that the cases of Isaiah and Jeremiah on the one hand, and that of Daniel on the other are identical. In the case of the former, we have the books of Kings and Chronicles covering the whole period in which Isaiah lived and a large part of that in which Jeremiah lived. Besides, Isaiah lived more than one hundred and fifty years before Daniel and his work is one of the earliest of the prophetical books, and Jeremiah laboured mostly before the destruction of Jerusalem, and both were intimately bound up with the history of Jerusalem and its kings and prophesied to and for the people of Israel in particular. Whereas Daniel prophesied and wrote after most of the books of the Old Testament had been written. No history covering his time has come down to us. His labours had nothing to do with Jerusalem, or its kings, and his prophecies concerned the world at large rather than the Jewish people in particular.

Moreover, it is not so much easier to prove by external evidence that the prophecy of Isaiah is pre-Maccabean than it is to show that Daniel was. For what is the evidence aside from the book itself for the early date of Isaiah? The Book of 2 Kings? No, for it contains no evidence as to Isaiah except what is found in substantially the same words in chaps. xxxvi-xxxix of Isaiah itself. The Book of 2 Chronicles? No, for it again contains nothing about Isaiah except what is found in Kings and in chaps. xxxvi-xxxix of the Book of Isaiah. In these three books we have, except for slight textual variations, exactly the same account of the reign of Hezekiah and of the person and work of Isaiah. This account does not mention the prophecies contained in Isa. i-xxxv, and xl-lxvi; nor that Isaiah ever wrote such prophecies at all. For direct evidence in favour of the genuineness and authenticity of the prophetical parts of the Book of Isaiah, we are left, therefore, as far as these three books are concerned, to the internal evidence of the prophecies themselves. They stand on exactly the same footing in this respect as the Book of Daniel. If we are not allowed, then, to use the *prima facie* evidence of the Book of Daniel, neither should we use *prima facie* evidence of the Book of Isaiah.

As to other evidence for the Book of Isaiah, what is there? The three verses of chap. ii, 2-4, which are almost the same as iv, 1-3 of Micah? But, if the author of Isaiah quoted Micah, he may have quoted him as well in the 2nd century B.C. as in the 7th or 8th. In 2 Chron. xxvi, 22, we are told that Isaiah, the son of Amos, wrote the acts of Uzziah, first and last. Whatever this work may have been, it is no part of our present Book of Isaiah. Again, in 2 Chron. xxxii, 32, it is said, that "the rest of the acts of Hezekiah and his goodness are written in the vision of Isaiah, the son of Amoz, in the book of the kings of Judah and Israel." This is probably the book from which the historical section of Isaiah, contained in chaps. xxxvi-xxxix, was taken. It cannot be shown to have embraced the other chapters.

Lastly, there is the evidence of the Book of Ecclesiasticus as to Isaiah. Let us cite the evidence in full. It will be found in Ecclesiasticus xlviii, 17-25, and is as follows:

17. Hezekiah fortified his city and brought water into the midst thereof: he digged the hard rock with iron (Heb. bronze) and constructed wells for water (Heb. dammed up mountains for a pool). 18. In his days Sennacherib came up, and sent Rabshakeh and lifted up his hand against Zion, and boasted proudly. 19. Then trembled their hearts and hands, and they were in pain as women in travail. But they called upon the Lord who is merciful (Heb., God Most High) and stretched out their hands toward him: and immediately the Holy One heard them out of heaven (Heb., and he heard the voice of this prayer), and delivered them by the hand of Isaiah. 21. He smote the camp of the Assyrians and his angel destroyed them (Heb., and he discomfited them with a plague. Syr., with a great plague). 22. For Hezekiah had done the thing that pleased the Lord (Heb. omits the Lord) and was strong in the ways of David his father (Heb. omits his father), according as Isaiah the prophet who was great and faithful in his visions had commanded him. 23. Also in his days the sun went backward (Syr., stood) and he lengthened the king's life. 24. He saw by an excellent spirit (Heb. Syr., "strong spirit") what should come to pass at the last, and he comforted them that mourned in Zion. 25. He showed what should come to pass forever, and secret things or ever they came.

This extract gives the only direct evidence to be found in Ecclesiasticus to the existence and labours of Isaiah. And what does this evidence prove? Only that Ben Sira knew that part of Isaiah which is embraced in chapters xxxvi,-xxxix, (the exact portions which are found also in Kings and Chronicles!) and that he was acquainted with the so-called Deutero-Isaiah beginning in Isa. xl, with the words "Comfort ye, comfort ye, my people," or at least with lxi, 2, 3, where we find the words "to comfort them that mourn in Zion," and with their context, where we find the reference to the glorious future of Israel! In other words, the only part of the *prophecies* of Isaiah which Ben Sira proves to have existed before his time is the part which the critics say that Isaiah never wrote at all!

As to other Biblical testimony, Isaiah is worse off than Daniel. For, whereas in the case of Daniel, Bevan would deem it "marvellous" that he is not mentioned in the later Hebrew prophets (i.e., in Haggai, Zechariah, and Malachi), Isaiah is not merely not mentioned in them, but neither is he mentioned in Zephaniah, Nahum, Habakkuk, Jeremiah, or Ezekiel, nor in Ezra, Nehemiah, or Esther,—all of whom were later than he and must have been acquainted with his works. Furthermore, the letter of Aristeas never mentions Isaiah nor does any extra-Biblical source, except Ecclesiasticus, till the time of Maccabees.

Again, the fatuity of the argument against Daniel based on the fact that he is not mentioned in the post-captivity literature can not be more clearly shown than in the following comparisons:

1. Daniel is mentioned by name only in Ezk. xiv, 14, 20 and xxxviii, 3 and is referred to in 1 Macc. ii, 59, 60.

2. But (1) Isaiah is never mentioned by name by any of the prophets who succeeded him; and is referred to in the O.T., aside from a brief reference in 2 Chron. xxvi, 22, only in the passages of 2 Kings and 2 Chronicles which are as we have seen the same as those found in Isaiah xxxvi,-xxxix. He is quoted possibly in Mic. iv, 1-3. Outside the O.T., he is first cited in Jewish literature in Ecclesiasticus xlviii, 22-25, where his name also is mentioned. The passages in 1 Macc. vii, 41 and 2 Macc. xv, 22 which mention the destruction of the army of Sennacherib, may have been derived from 2 Kings or 2 Chronicles as well as from Isaiah xxxvii. Yet the Book of Ecclesiasticus was written 520 years after the admittedly genuine prophecies of Isaiah.

(2) Jeremiah is referred to by name in Dan. ix, 2 and in 2 Kings and 2 Chronicles; but is not mentioned, nor cited, in Haggai, Zechariah, or Malachi, nor in Ezra, except in i, 1, which is the same as 2 Chr. xxxvi, 22. Afterwards, he is not cited nor mentioned till in Ecclus. xlix, 6, 7 and next in the 1st century B.C. in 2 Macc. ii, 1-8 and xv, 14 and in the introduction of the apocryphal Epistle of Jeremiah. It is remarkable that the book of Baruch does not mention him by name. It thus appears that Jeremiah is not mentioned by any Jewish writer from the time of the captivity till 180 B.C., except by the composer of the first two verses of Ezra, which are the same as the last two verses of 2 Chronicles. As the critics hold that these verses were not written till 300 B.C., or later, the external testimony to Jeremiah would

thus be for *them,* at least 250 years after the time of his death.

(3) Ezekiel is not mentioned by any writer of his own time, nor by any succeeding prophet, nor by any canonical book of the Old Testament. He is mentioned only in Ecclesiasticus xlix, 8 of all the Old Testament apocryphal literature. He is not named in the New Testament nor in Philo; but Josephus mentions him by name four times.[3]

(4) Of the Minor Prophets, Jonah, Haggai, and Zechariah alone are mentioned in the historical writings of the Old Testament and no one of them is mentioned by name in any other prophetic work, except Micah in Jer. xxvi, 18. No one of them is mentioned in extra-Biblical literature till New Testament times except Habakkuk in the apocalyptic additions to Daniel. In the New Testament the prophet Joel is named and cited in Acts ii, 16-21; and Jonah is mentioned and cited in Matt. xii, 39 and Lk. xi, 29. The others are not mentioned by name. It is true that Ben Sira in xlix, 10 speaks of the Twelve Prophets; but as he has not given their names, the testimony is so indefinite as to make it questionable whether Jonah was one of them!

The above considerations will be sufficient to show that the line of argument pursued by Bevan would, if valid, prove too much. It shows, also, that later Jewish writers were not in the habit of naming preceding ones, simply because they did not care to do so. If most of our modern critics, instead of citing what they call authorities, would do more investigating of original sources for themselves, it is certain that they would not make so many erroneous statements as now mar the works of some of them. The mania for citing opinions of modern writers instead of testing the evidence in ancient documents, is, like Achilles' wrath to Greece, the direful spring of woes unnumbered in the history of the literary criticism of the Biblical books.

With regard to Jeremiah, it will be readily admitted, that the proof outside the Book of Jeremiah itself that the prophecies were "not entirely written in the Maccabean period" is amply sufficient to satisfy any reasonable mind. But, when we come to the much more important question, and the real one at issue, as to whether

---

[3] *Antiq.* X. v, 1, vi, 3, vii, 2, viii, 2.

the prophecies as a whole are genuine and authentic, the case of Jeremiah is not so much better, or easier, than is that of Daniel. Might we not say that it is "marvellous" that the Book of Kings which narrates at length the events of the reigns of Josiah, Jehoiakim, Jehoiachin and Zedekiah, never mentions Jeremiah by name, nor cites any of his prophecies or deeds? Is it not "marvellous" that Ezekiel never mentions, nor cites him, and that the post-exilic prophets never allude to him? Daniel, indeed, refers to him (ix, 2), but the critics are debarred from citing him except as a writer of the Maccabean times. It is to be feared that Bevan will find evidence in support of the direct historicity of Jeremiah to be confined in the Old Testament only to the much despised Book of Chronicles and the two verses repeated from it at the beginning of Ezra.[4]

Outside of the Old Testament, of the extant Jewish writings, the only ones which are generally acknowledged as having been written before Maccabean times are the letter of Aristeas, Ahikar, parts of Enoch, the Epistle of Jeremy, and Ecclesiasticus. The first three named do not mention Jeremiah. The fourth purports expressly to be by him. The last cites (chap. xlix, 6, 7) from the first chapter of Jeremiah and from the events spoken of in Jer. xxxvii, 8 and xxxix, 6, as follows: "They burnt the holy city and destroyed its ways, according to the prophecy of Jeremiah. But they afflicted him, although he had been formed a prophet from the womb to root out and to pull down and to destroy, and in like manner to build, and to plant, and to restore."

It will be noted, that Bevan does not say that it would be easy to show that Ezekiel was not entirely Maccabean. And yet it is supported outside of its own self-witness by the statement of Ecclus, xlix, 8, 9 alone. Here we read: "It was Ezekiel who saw a glorious vision which was showed him upon the chariot of the cherubin. For he made mention of the enemies (or of Job) under the figure of the rain and directed them that went right." As

---

[4] These verses according to the critics were written also by the Chronicler (Cornill p. 252). Driver puts the composition of Chronicles at about 300 B.C. (*L.O.T.* p. 535) and Cornill, "with absolute certainty" in the Greek period "perhaps the first half of the third century" B.C. (*Introd.* p. 228).

verse 9 probably refers to Job, only the 8th will refer to Ezekiel. To sum up with regard to the third assumption, it will be seen that, outside of the testimony to be derived from the books themselves, Isaiah and Ezekiel are supported by the testimony of Ben Sira alone, Jeremiah by that of Ben Sira and the Chronicler, and Daniel by that of Ezekiel. According to all the laws of evidence, the testimony to Daniel's existence and wisdom, being that of a contemporary, who had opportunity and intelligence to know whereof he wrote and whose honesty cannot be impeached, would be better than the testimony to the others, dating as *the critics say* it does from the 3rd and 2nd centuries B.C., 400 to 500 years after the death of the men of whom they write.

Fourth Assumption

The fourth assumption is that the cumulative argument from silence shows that Daniel did not exist till about the middle of the second century B.C. While admitting that it is possible in each particular case to imagine some good reason for the silence, it is supposed that the cumulative silence is convincing. This is equivalent to saying that although two times nothing is nothing, yet two times nothing plus two times nothing plus two times nothing is something. Besides, it ignores the positive testimony to Daniel's existence and wisdom given by Ezekiel in three passages and the appeal of Mattathias about 168 B.C. to the lions' den and the fiery furnace, as recorded in I Macc. ii, 59, 60. Lastly, it ignores the obvious fact that by similar reasoning we would have a cumulative argument from silence that Ezekiel and most of the Minor Prophets did not exist until the time of Ben Sira. In short, the argument is absurd.

CHAPTER III

THE SILENCE OF ECCLESIASTICUS CONCERNING DANIEL

IF WE can believe the newspaper reports of the answers of Madame Caillaux, wife of the late Finance Minister of the French Republic, to the interrogatories of the magistrate conducting the preliminary examinations into the reasons why she assassinated M. Calmette, the editor of *Figaro,* it was a difficult matter for her to determine why she fired the fatal shot. It is, in fact, a difficult matter for any of us to analyze the various motives which have conduced to any given course of action, or that have converged toward the production of a certain line of thought. Much more difficult is it to unfold the manifold complexities involved in our critical conclusions and in our literary judgments.

Yet, in spite of this recognized difficulty in discovering our own motives, how many there are who think that they can perform the much more difficult task of discovering the motives of a man who lived two thousand, or more, years ago. This is especially true, when we come to consider the reasons why an author is silent with respect to some person, or event, of his own or preceding times. This silence may have resulted from ignorance; but it may just as well have resulted from prejudice, misjudgment, neglect, or contempt. In no case, however, would the silence prove that the person never existed, or that the event did not occur.

For example, it is found that in Ecclesiasticus, Jesus ben Sira makes no mention of Daniel, nor any reference to the book bearing his name. The motive, or reason, for this silence is utterly unknown to us. Nevertheless, this silence has been assumed to be a proof that at the time of Ben Sira the book of Daniel had not been written, and even, that at that time the Jews were in ignorance of the fact that such a man as Daniel had ever existed. This assumption is made, notwithstanding that there is good reason for supposing that Ben Sira intentionally omitted all reference to Daniel, or his book. For the works of Ben Sira show that he was a man of pronounced prejudices and opinions. His views might be characterised at Sadducean and nationalistic. When he gives an account of the great men of his nation, he selects for his encomiums those who had most distinguished themselves according to his ideas of what constituted greatness. We, doubtless, would have added some names that he has omitted from his list. We might have omitted some that he has selected. We certainly would have given more space to the praise of some than he has given, and less to the praise of others. But after all has been said, we will have to admit that there must be granted to him the right and the liberty to praise as he pleases the men whom he wishes to praise. That he has passed by some whom we most highly esteem does not show that he was not aware of their existence. It simply shows that he had reasons of his own, that seemed satisfactory to him, for rejecting them from his list of worthies.

This brief exordium is by way of introduction to the objections made to the early date of the Book of Daniel on the ground that it cannot have existed before Ecclesiasticus was written, because neither Daniel nor his book is mentioned, nor apparently even referred to, by Ben Sira. The objections are stated as follows:

THE CHARGE

"Jesus the son of Sirach (writing *c.* 200 B.C.), in his enumeration of Israelitish worthies, chaps. xliv-l, though he mentions Isaiah, Jeremiah, Ezekiel, and (collectively) the Twelve Minor Prophets, is silent as to Daniel." [1]

"The silence of Jesus Sirach (Ecclesiasticus) concerning Daniel seems to show that the prophet was unknown to that late writer who, in his list of celebrated men (chap. xlix), makes no mention of Daniel, but passes from Jeremiah to Ezekiel and then to the twelve Minor Prophets and Zerubbabel. If Daniel had been known to Jesus Sirach, we would certainly expect to find his name

[1] Driver, *L.O.T.*, p. 498.

in this list, probably between Jeremiah and Ezekiel. Again, the only explanation seems to be that the Book of Daniel was not known to Sirach who lived and wrote between 200 and 180 B.C. Had so celebrated a person as Daniel been known, he could hardly, have escaped mention in such a complete list of Israel's leading spirits. Hengstenberg remarked that Ezra and Mordecai were also left unmentioned, but the case is not parallel. Daniel is represented in the work attributed to him as a great prophet, while Ezra appears in the Book bearing his name as nothing more than a rather prominent priest and scholar." [2]

That Ben Sira knew nothing about Daniel is said to be supported by his statement in chapter xlix, 17, that "no man was born upon earth like unto Joseph, whereas the narratives respecting Daniel represent him much like unto Joseph in regard to both the high distinctions he attained and the faculties he displayed; and further, the very wording of the narratives in the first part of Daniel is modelled after that of the narratives in Genesis concerning Joseph." [3]

ASSUMPTIONS

The assumptions involved in the above objections are as follows:

1. That Ezra and Mordecai did not deserve mention by Ben Sira as well as Daniel did.

2. That the mention of Isaiah, Jeremiah, Ezekiel, and the Twelve, by Ben Sira, while he is silent as to Daniel, proves that Daniel was unknown to him.

3. That the passing from his mention of the Twelve directly to Zerubbabel, implies that Daniel was not known to Ben Sira.

4. That the silence of Ecclesiasticus concerning Daniel, shows that the prophet and his book were unknown to Ben Sira.

5. That the statement of Ben Sira, that there was no man like Joseph, shows an ignorance on his part of the existence of the man Daniel.

[2] Prince, *Commentary on Daniel*, p. 16f.
[3] Driver, *Daniel*, pp. 17 and 64.

First Assumption

The assumption that the omission of the names of Ezra and Mordecai from the list of Ben Sira's worthies is easily to be accounted for on the ground of their relative inferiority to Daniel is a matter of opinion merely. Prince thinks that "Daniel is represented in the work attributed to him as a great prophet, while Ezra appears in the Book bearing his name as nothing more than a rather prominent priest and scholar." As to the part of this statement which refers to Daniel, I would be the last man to deny it; although as I have shown elsewhere, I believe that Daniel's greatness as a prophet was not recognized until after so many of his predictions had been so accurately fulfilled in the time of Antiochus Epiphanes. But even if he had been recognized as a great prophet, we must remember that he had said and done nothing to exalt or save the Law, the Temple, the city of Jerusalem, or the land or people of Israel. Ezra, however, was the greatest protagonist of the Law since the days of Moses and Joshua. The whole critical hypothesis of the formation of the Canon and of the fixation of the vast fabric of the Jewish ceremonies of the Second Temple, is based on the theory that Ezra collected and edited and induced the people to accept formally the so-called first part of the three-fold Canon of the Old Testament Scriptures. In his own time he was the determiner and the champion of orthodoxy, and in all succeeding ages he has been recognized as the organizer of the Temple service and the first of the ready scribes in the Law of Moses.

Now, as to Ezra, Driver says, that "the second section of the book, chaps. vii,-x, dealing with Ezra's own age, there is no reason to doubt, is throughout either written by Ezra or based upon materials left by him"; [4] and Kosters and Cheyne say, that of his "memoirs, written by himself, some portions unaltered and others considerably modified, have come down to us in the books of Ezra and Nehemiah." [5] If the failure of Ben Sira to mention

[4] *L.O.T.*, p. 549.
[5] *Encyc. Bibl*, p. 1473.

Ezra is no evidence against the existence, the works, and the writings of Ezra, or against Ben Sira's knowledge of the same; so, in like manner, his failure to mention Daniel is no evidence against the existence, the work and the writings of Daniel, or against Ben Sira's knowledge of them.

As to Mordecai's being in the same class of great men as Daniel, I am inclined to agree with Professor Prince that he was not. But unfortunately for Prince's argument, neither his opinion nor mine is the determining factor in this discussion, but that of the Jews of the time of Ben Sira; and as to this I am not so certain as Prince seems to be that in their estimation Mordecai may not have been "parallel" to Daniel but even have outranked him in importance. For to them Daniel was a minister of foreign kings and the interpreter of their dreams, the great seer of the fortunes of world empires, and the least nationalistic—perhaps we might even say the least patriotic—of all the prophets; whereas Mordecai was the upholder of the narrowest form of racial exclusiveness, the deliverer of his people from extermination, and the founder of the great national festival of Purim, the only festival which in the belief of the Jews had been decreed between the time of Moses and that of Ben Sira. By all critics, therefore, who like Driver put the book of Esther as early as the third century B.C.,[6] this omission of the name of Mordecai from a list of Israel's heroes must be acknowledged as parallel to that of Daniel. So that it seems impossible to escape the conclusion that Ben Sira's failure to mention Daniel, Ezra, and Mordecai, is no argument against the existence of the works and writings of the persons bearing their names, nor of Ben Sira's knowledge of the same.

Second Assumption

As to the assumption that because Ben Sira mentions Isaiah, Jeremiah, Ezekiel and the Twelve, without mentioning Daniel, he did not know of Daniel, several remarks may be made:

1. Ben Sira does not propose to mention all the prophets of the Old Testament. As a matter of fact, he names only Moses,

---

[6] *L.O.T.*, p. 484.

Samuel, Nathan, Elijah, Elisha, Isaiah, Jeremiah and Ezekiel. All of these were prominent in the political and religious history of the land and people; whereas, Daniel left his land while a boy, and spent his life among the kings and wise men of Babylon.

2. Ben Sira does not propose to mention the books of the Old Testament; nor does he mention a single one of them, nor cite specifically by name from any one of them.

3. In Ben Sira's time, Daniel may have been counted as one of the Twelve, just as Ruth was, then and as late as the time of Josephus and later, counted as part of Judges; and just as Lamentations was often counted as part of Jeremiah. In the time of Ben Sira, Jonah may have been a part of the book of Kings; for as Driver says: "Both in form and contents, the Book of Jonah resembles the biographical narrative of Elijah and Elisha"[7] It must be remembered that Ben Sira does not name anyone of the Twelve Minor Prophets and that all that he says of them is: "Let their bones be flourishing" (chap. xlix, 10b) and, if the rest of the verse refers to them and not to Daniel, that "they comforted Jacob and saved him with the hope of truth."[8]

Third Assumption

The next assumption is that the Book of Daniel was not known to Ben Sira because he passes from Jeremiah to Ezekiel and then to the Twelve Minor Prophets and Zerubbabel without mentioning Daniel. This assumption is based on two false assumptions. First, that Ben Sira is naming the books of the Old Testament; and secondly, that he is naming all of his heroes in a chronological order. In the former case, one might ask where he finds the books of Phinehas and Zerubbabel. In the latter case, attention need only be called to the facts, that the account of Josiah is inserted between the mention of Isaiah and that of Jeremiah, and the description of Job between that of Ezekiel and that of the Twelve, and that of Joseph between that of Nehemiah and that of Simon.

Again, it is remarkable that just as Nathan is connected with

[7] *L.O.T.*, p. 322.
[8] See below p. 82 f.

David, so Isaiah and Jeremiah are mentioned in connection with
Hezekiah and Josiah respectively. Each of the three kings of
Israel had a good prophet to support him. Each of the three good
prophets had a worthy Israelitish king to support.[9] But of what
good king of Israel was Daniel the prophet? Of Nebuchadnezzar,
forsooth?

Furthermore, Prince fails to notice three other points which are
at least as surprising as Ben Sira's failure to mention Daniel and
Ezra and Mordecai. The first is that Ben Sira should have placed
Zerubbabel among the great men he has mentioned. Certainly,
most men in making a list of twenty of the worthies of Israel
would not have included him among them. The same might be
said of Phinehas and Caleb and Nathan and Adam, and Seth and
Shem and perhaps even of Enoch and Noah and Job.

The second is that he should have given eleven verses to Elijah
and only two to Jeremiah and one to Ezekiel; three verses to
Phinehas and none to Ezra; two verses to Caleb and only eight
to Samuel and but one to all the Minor Prophets; and seventeen
verses to Aaron and twenty-one to Simon (a non-biblical hero)
while giving only five to Moses, one to Nehemiah, and none to
Ezra.

The third is that he mentions such men as Caleb and Seth and
Shem, while never mentioning by name Gideon and Deborah and
Jephthah and Samson; nor Jehoshaphat, Jehoiada, Esther and
Ezra; nor any of the twelve Minor Prophets.

Ben Sira certainly did not estimate the Israelitish worthies as
Prince does, nor as any one of us would do. But what are we
going to do about it? Call him an ignoramus, or admit his right
of private judgment?

Fourth Assumption

The fourth assumption is that the silence of Ben Sira concerning Daniel shows that the prophet and his book were unknown
to him. But is Ben Sira actually silent regarding Daniel and his
book?

---

[9] For as Ben Sira says in xlix, 4: Aside from David, Hezekiah, and
Josiah, all of the kings had acted corruptly.

This is admittedly true of the LXX and Peshito versions of Ecclesiasticus, but it is not certain when we look at the original Hebrew text, which has been discovered since Bleek put forth this objection to the early date of Daniel. In chap. xlix, 10 we read: And I will mention "also the Twelve Prophets; let their bones sprout beneath them." Then follow the words: אשר החלימו את יעקב וישעוהו. If we take the first three letters as the relative the sense may well be: "who comforted Jacob and saved him." But if we point the letters as a segholate noun, the verse would read: "Blessed be they who comforted Jacob and saved him" *etc.*, and since the Greek has the verb in the singular we could render: "Blessed be he who comforted Jacob" *etc.* If taken in this later sense, the words would most naturally refer to Daniel. Or, by adopting a different meaning of the verb we might render the words by "Blessed be he who explained dreams to Jacob" *etc.*[10]

But let us waive this conjecture, granting for the sake of argument either that Sira did not mention Daniel or that he shows no acquaintance with the Book of Daniel. What then? There are three possibilities: (1) he may have known the Book of Daniel, but not have seen fit to use it; (2) he may have known about the man Daniel, while not being acquainted with the book; and (3) both the book and the man may have been unknown to Ben Sira.

1. Taking these three possibilities in order, let us suppose that Sira was acquainted with the Book of Daniel, but did not please to use it. Is there any reasonable way of accounting for such a fact?

This is purely a psychological question having to do with the opinions, feelings, and judgment of Ben Sira himself. He may have been of the opinion that Daniel did not measure up to the standard of the "fathers of the aeon" whose praises he was cele-

---

[10] The sense of "comfort" for the hiphil of חלם is supported by Isa. xxxviii, 16, and by the use of the Aramaic and late Hebrew. But the hiphil of this verb may also mean "to cause to dream" (Jer. xxix, 8), or, after the analogy of חזה, "to show or explain visions" (Isa. xxx, 10; Lam. ii, 14). Comp. New Hebrew where חלם means "an interpreter of dreams." As to the construction and use of אשר in the construct before the verbal sentence in the genitive, compare Ecclus, xlviii, 11: "Blessed be he who saw Thee and died." Compare also Ps. lxv, 5, where אשרי is employed in like manner.

brating. For we must remember that what made the Book of Daniel of such supreme importance to the Jews and Christians of later times were its manifest references to Maccabean and New Testament times. To a Jew living at 200 B.C., its message must have been largely closed and sealed. It is hard to see why he should have been specifically mentioned, in view of the failure of Sira to name Samson, Gideon, or Jonah. Besides, with the deliverance from the fiery furnace, the most extraordinary of the miracles mentioned in his book, Daniel personally had nothing to do. As to,the failure of the lions to eat him, when cast into their den, the pages of Herodotus, Livy, and of many other ancient authors, are full of just as astounding statements. As to his ability to explain dreams, the Egyptian, Assyrian, and Babylonian kings, Croesus, Xerxes, and Alexander, and indeed, one might say, almost all men of all classes, believed in the significance of dreams and in the power of correct interpretation; so that Sira may have thought that there was no special reason for mentioning Daniel on' this account. The equivocal position in which Daniel stood in the Babylonian court may not have been thought by Sira to entitle him to be inscribed in the catalogue of the fathers of his people. He was after all but a slave dancing attendance on a tyrant's will. Besides, so far as is recorded, he never did anything for the Jews in general, but only accomplished the promotion of Shadrach, Meshach, and Abednego. Many other Jews must have been known to Sira who had risen high in the courts of heathen kings, and who had done much more for their contemporary Israelites: such for example, as Ezra, Mordecai, Athanaeus, and Joseph the son of Tobias, the last a contemporary of Ben Sira himself. Why should Daniel have been signalised and these not?

Again, a close study of Sira's encomiums on the celebrated men of his nation reveals some noteworthy facts:

(1) From the time preceding Abraham, he names Enoch (perhaps twice),[11] Noah and apparently Adam, Seth, Enosh, and Shem.

---

[11] Enoch is certainly mentioned in Chap. xliv, 16, which reads, according to the Hebrew text: "Enoch walked with God, a sign of knowledge to all generations." The Greek translation reads: "Enoch pleased God and was translated, being an example of repentance to all generations." The Peshito omits the verse.

(2) From Abraham to Joshua, he names Abraham, Isaac, Israel, Moses, Aaron, Phinehas, Caleb, Joshua, and, as it were as an afterthought, Joseph.

(3) From the times succeeding Joshua, he names only Samuel, David, Nathan, Solomon, Elijah, Elisha, Hezekiah, Isaiah, Josiah, Jeremiah, Ezekiel, Nehemiah, and Daniel, and possibly refers to Job and Ezra.

(4) From post-biblical times, he names Simon the High Priest, who served about 280 B.C.

(5) He refers to the twelve patriarchs, the judges and the twelve Minor Prophets without mentioning any one of them by name, except Samuel.

(6) If his estimate of the relative importance of the great men he mentions can be derived from the number of verses written about them, they will stand in the following order: the high priest Simon 21 verses, Aaron 17, Solomon 12, Elijah 11, David 10, Hezekiah 9, Samuel 8, Moses 5, Josiah 4, Abraham 3, Phinehas 3, Elisha 3, Noah 2, Jeremiah 2, Joseph one or two, and Isaac, Israel, Nathan, Ezekiel, Zerubbabel, Jeshua, and Nehemiah, one each. The twelve Minor Prophets are honoured in but one verse, or less; Shem, Seth and Adam, the three together in one verse; Enoch, in one or two; Job, Ezra and Daniel possibly in one or part of one each.

Whether Ezra and Job are referred to depends as in the case of Daniel, which has already been discussed, upon whether we follow the reading of the Hebrew text or the Greek version.

In xlix, 14, the Greek reads: "But upon the earth was no man created like Enoch; for he was taken from the earth." The Peshito has simply: "Few were created upon earth like Enoch." The Hebrew text as amended by Smend is: מעט נוצרו על הארץ כחנוך וגם הוא נלקח פנים. Thus read, the translation would be: "Few have been formed upon earth like Enoch; and he, also, was taken away bodily." But, it is to be noted, that the Hebrew manuscript gives us כחניך, and that the last letter of נוצרו "appears to have been added" (Smend). Following the general principle of the original writing of the vowel letters as propounded by

Cornill,[12] the text of the first part of the verse might be as follows: מעט נוצר ... כהנך. The verse would, then, read: "For a little while thy priest was kept upon the earth; and he, also, was taken away bodily." מעט would be used adverbially as in Ruth ii, 7, Ps. xxxvii, 10; and נלקח would have the same sense as in the probable original of the Ezra-Apoc. viii, 14. Thus rendered, the verse will refer to Ezra, who may justly be looked upon as the greatest of all the priests. For the belief that Ezra was taken away bodily, compare 4 *Ezra* xiv, 9, 49, vi, 26, vii, 28, viii, 19. In xiv, 9, the voice out of the bush says to Ezra: "Thou shalt be taken up from among men." In xiv, 49, it is said: "Then was Ezra caught away and taken up into the place of such as were like him." In viii, 19 is found: "The beginning of the prayer of Ezra, before he was taken up"; and in vi, 26: "The men who have been taken up, who have not tasted death from their birth, shall appear." In favour, also, of this latter text and rendering are two important circumstances: first, Enoch has already been mentioned by Ben Sira in his proper place in chap. xliv, 16; and secondly, Nehemiah has just been referred to in the preceding verse, and we would naturally expect to have Ezra noticed in connection with his great collaborator.

Job is mentioned in the Peshitto text of xlix, 9, which reads: "And also concerning Job he said, that all his ways were right." The Greek here has: "For he made mention of the enemies under the figure of a cloud." The Hebrew original has: "And also I will mention Job *etc.*" The only difference between the two readings is that one has אויב (enemy) whereas the other had איוב (Job).

(7) It will be observed, further, that our author gives 21 verses to the high priest Simon, a non-biblical character, and one who is known elsewhere only in two short notices by Josephus; whereas he gives 17 verses to Aaron and only five to Moses. Samuel is honoured with 8 verses, and all the other judges with but two. Phinehas is granted as long a notice as Abraham. Hezekiah receives almost as much attention as David and Solomon combined. Caleb is treated with the same consideration as

---

[12] *Introd.*, p. 491.

Jeremiah, and receives twice as much notice as Ezekiel and at least twice as much as all the Minor Prophets together.

(8) Many persons notable in the history of Israel are not mentioned at all by Ben Sira. Such are, of priests, Abiathar, Jehoiada, Hilkiah, Eliashib and Jaddua; of judges, Gideon, Jephthah, and Samson; of kings, Saul, Asa, Jehoshaphat, Jehu, and Jeroboam II; of prophets, Hosea, Jonah, Haggai, and Zechariah. Besides, all the women, without any exception, are passed over in silence,—Sarah, Rachel, Miriam, Deborah, Ruth, and even Esther.

(9) Of the 133 verses employed in the encomiums, 42 are given to the priests, 35 to the kings, 32 (or 33, if we count Job as a prophet) to the prophets, 8 or 9 to the patriarchs, 12 to Joshua and the judges, and two to Zerubbabel and Nehemiah.

(10) Further, it will be noted that, with the exception of the doubtful case of Job, all of the "famous men" from Moses onward exercised their activities in Palestine, and had to do with the establishment, defense, or renovation, of the laws, institutions, and polity of the Jews, with the conquest of the land, or with the building, or restoration, of Jerusalem and the temple. In this connection, Jehoiada, Jehoshaphat, Zechariah, Haggai, and Ezra, might have been mentioned; and also, Mordecai, at least had he laboured and lived in Palestine. But Daniel, so far as we know, originated no laws, did not assist in any national movement, did not participate in the return from Babylon, nor in the rebuilding of the walls of Jerusalem, nor in the reëstablishment of the people and of its laws.

(11) No one can maintain that Ben Sira failed to mention Daniel on account of not being acquainted with him, or with his book, without maintaining that he was also ignorant of the existence and labors of Ezra. But Ben Sira's knowledge of Nehemiah would seem to make it certain that he knew also of Ezra.

(12) Ben Sira's judgment as to what rendered men famous, is certainly odd and eccentric. For example, of the 21 verses of encomium upon the high priest Simon, 17 are taken up with a description of the beauty of his person and of the ceremonies connected with the service at the altar, and of the blessing which

the congregation received at his hands. In the case of Aaron, also, a large part is taken up with a description of his garments. If we compare the ideas of Ben Sira with those of the Book of Daniel, we find very substantial reasons why the former may not have deemed Daniel worthy of a place among the famous men of his nation. The greatest things that Daniel ever did were to interpret the dream of Nebuchadnezzar and to explain the writing on the wall of Belshazzar's palace. Now, in the beginning of chapter xxiv, Ben Sira has expressed plainly his opinion of dreams, when he says among other things, that "dreams lift up fools," "whoso regardeth dreams is like him that catcheth at a shadow and followeth after wind," "divination and soothsaying and dreams are vain," "for dreams have deceived many, and they have failed that put their trust in them."

Again, Daniel expresses his belief in a resurrection, whereas Ben Sira never even hints at such a possibility. The only kind of immortality that he expressly teaches, is the immortality of fame, and of nationality, family, and institutions, such as the covenant and the priesthood. Moreover, Ben Sira never refers to the distinction between clean and unclean foods, or to praying toward Jerusalem, or to praying three times daily, to fasting, or to a *post mortem* judgment of the world—all doctrines that distinguish the book of Daniel. With reference to angels, also, Ben Sira never expresses his own belief, merely mentioning them in allusions to the earlier history.

To sum up, it may be said that while it is probable that Ben Sira does not refer to Daniel, nor show any knowledge of his book, yet this is no indication that he was not acquainted with both. For as a matter of fact, he does not purpose to give, nor does he give, a complete list of Israelitish worthies; the ones he does mention being selected and celebrated after a manner peculiar to himself. After the conquest, he praises especially priests, kings, and prophets, to none of which classes did Daniel officially, at least, belong. After the conquest, moreover, he mentions, with the possible exception of Job, none but those whose activities were passed in Palestine. With the exception of Solomon and Isaiah, the writers of the nation are given scant space and praise. And finally, there are special reasons why Daniel should have been passed over by Ben Sira, arising from the fact that the doctrines and practices of Daniel were out of harmony with those approved and taught by Ben Sira.

2. Some writers, while maintaining that the Book of Daniel was not written till the time of Antiochus Epiphanes, maintain that the man Daniel was, in the words of Driver, "a historical person, one of the Jewish exiles in Babylon, who, with his three companions, was noted for his staunch adherence to the principles of his religion, who attained a position of influence at the court of Babylon, who interpreted Nebuchadnezzar's dreams and foretold, as a seer, something of the future fate of the Chaldean and Persian empires. Perhaps, written materials were at the disposal of the author; it is at any rate probable that for the descriptions contained in chaps. ii-vii he availed himself of some work, or works, dealing with the history of Babylon in the 6th century B.C." [13]

In view of the fact that Ben Sira gives his longest encomium to the high priest Simon, a non-biblical character, it is hard to see how he can have failed to mention Daniel, this well known and distinguished man, even though the book that bears his name had not yet been written. Objections that Ben Sira may have reasonably made to doctrines of the Book of Daniel he can not have made in like measure to the historical character of Daniel ii-vi. If we assert that the Book of Daniel was not written before 180 B.C., we can no longer compare the silence of Ben Sira with his mention of the authors of the books of Isaiah, Jeremiah, Ezekiel and the Twelve; but we must compare this silence with his mention of the great men who, so far as we know, were not authors, that is, with his mention of Caleb, Phinehas, Elijah, Elisha, Josiah, Zerubbabel, and Simon. So that, when we deny the existence of the Book of Daniel and admit the knowledge of the man, whether this knowledge had been gained from "written materials," or from oral tradition, we have not escaped the difficulties involved in Ben Sira's silence. We have simply shifted them from the book to the person. For, if this silence disproves

[13] *L.O.T.*, pp. 510, 511.

the existence of the book, it disproves equally the knowledge of the person. In the opinion of the present writer, the silence of Ben Sira with reference to Daniel neither proves nor disproves anything with regard to either the existence of the book, or his knowledge of the person of Daniel. His silence may have been intentional, or unintentional. It may have been through ignorance, or design. But the reason for it is to be sought in the mind of Ben Sira, and this mind is beyond our ken.

3. Much more consistent is the view of Prince and others, who hold that the silence of Ben Sira with regard to Daniel shows that both the book and the man were unknown to him. When, however, Prince says that the only explanation of this silence "seems to be that the Book of Daniel was not known to Sirach," and "had so celebrated a person as Daniel been known, he could hardly have escaped mention in such a complete list of Israel's leading spirits," he is, as has been shown above, going beyond what his premises justify.

(1) For, first, let us suppose that the Book of Daniel was unknown to Ben Sira. What follows? Not necessarily, as Prince concludes, that there was no such book in existence. Here is a fallacy which few writers on Old Testament introduction seem able to avoid. They confound the time of the writing of an Old Testament book with the time of its assumption into the collection of the canon. The New Testament books were presumably all written before the close of the first century A.D. Their acknowledgment as canonical, and their collection into one book, took place many years afterwards. So, the books of the Old Testament may have been written centuries before they were recognized as canonical, or admitted into the collection of the sacred scriptures. Daniel, for example, may have been written in Babylon in the 6th century B.C., and may not have been received officially into the canon of the Palestinian Jews until after its predictions had been so significantly and accurately fulfilled in the events of the reign of Antiochus Epiphanes.

To be sure, according to Josephus, the high priest Jaddua showed the predictions of the book to Alexander the Great in 332 B.C. To be sure, also, the author of First Maccabees represents Mattathias as inciting the Asmoneans to rebellion against Antiochus in 169 B.C., by citing the deliverance of the three children from the flames and of Daniel from the lions' den. But while Jaddua in the fourth century B.C. may have known of the book, and while Mattathias and his hearers may have known about the fiery furnace and the deliverance from the lions in 169 B.C., it may be possible that Ben Sira, who wrote his work about 180 B.C. was, as Prince and others have brought themselves to believe, entirely ignorant of both the book and the person of Daniel. Jaddua may have known the book. Mattathias and his hearers may have known the person, but for some reason unknown to us Ben Sira may have been unacquainted with either the book or the person of Daniel. But all this does not prove that the book did not exist in the time of Ben Sira, or that the facts recorded in the Book of Daniel had not occurred. For the collection of the sacred books to which Ben Sira had access may not have contained the Book of Daniel; or, for reasons deemed sufficiently good by him, may not have been acknowledged by him as canonical. As has been shown above, he may have known the book, but on account of its doctrines, or of the locality in which its deeds were enacted, he may have refused to recognize its authority, or to celebrate its heroes. Or, the book may not have been accessible to him; for it is a mistake to suppose that all of the books recognized as canonical were at that time bound together in a single volume. Dr. Gregory of Leipzig has shown that folios did not come into use till the second century A.D. Before that time, it was the sacred books (*biblia*) that men had, not the holy Bible, or book (*biblion*). The oldest MS of the Hebrew scriptures, whose date is generally accepted, contains only the Prophets. The next oldest has nothing but the Law. Till printing came into vogue, few institutions, or churches, and still fewer individuals, had a complete collection of the books of the Canon. It is not to be imagined that among the scattered and impoverished Jews of the second century B.C. there were many who were fortunate enough to possess copies of all the Old Testament books. Josephus states that a copy of the Law, which had been laid up in the temple, was carried in the triumphal procession of Titus; but he does not say whether by Law he means only the Pentateuch, or the whole Old Testament. In his *Life*, he says that he himself received from Titus as a special mark of his favour, the "holy books" indicating clearly that he considered this gift of the Cæsar as a noteworthy concession.[14] The Prologue to Ecclesiasticus affirms that Ben Sira the elder had given himself much to the reading of the Law, and of the Prophets, and of the other books of the fathers. What and how many books these were, he does not state. It is altogether possible that he had not access to a copy of the Book of Daniel, and that for this reason his language shows no signs of having been influenced by it. If the book of Daniel had been in circulation in Palestine in his time, it is hardly possible, however, to perceive how something of the principal events and persons described in it could have been utterly unknown to Ben Sira. This knowledge must have seemed to him to be of such a character as not to justify him in placing Daniel among his famous men, especially in view of the fact that he thought best to omit from his list so many others that to us seem equally worthy of mention.

(2) Secondly, let us suppose that Ben Sira did not even know that a man called Daniel had ever lived. In answer to this supposition, one might content himself with referring to the fact that Ezekiel twice mentions a Daniel as a wise man of equal standing with Noah and Job. Since Ezekiel wrote in the early half of the sixth century B.C., the Daniel to whom he refers must have lived as early, at least, as that time; and there is no other Daniel known to history, except the Daniel of our book, who can by any possibility have been referred to in such a connection. Josephus, also, treats Daniel as an historical character. This he would not have done, unless it had been the common opinion of the Jews of his time. Moreover, he and his contemporaries had access to many sources of information which have since ceased to exist. These sources covered the period of the Maccabees. But no one of them gives a hint that anyone had ever suspected that Daniel was a fictitious character, or that the account of him given in his book is not historical.

The author of First Maccabees, also, considered Daniel to be an

[14] Sec. 75.

historical person; for he says that Mattathias, the father of Judas Maccabæus, exhorted his adherents in the following words:

"Call to remembrance what acts our fathers did in their time; so shall ye receive great honour and an everlasting name. Was not Abraham found faithful in temptation, and it was imputed unto him for righteousness? Joseph in the time of his distress kept the commandment, and was made lord of Egypt. Phinehas our father in being zealous and fervent obtained the covenant of an everlasting priesthood. Jesus for fulfilling the word was made a judge in Israel. Caleb for bearing witness before the congregation received the heritage of the land. David for being merciful possessed the throne of an everlasting kingdom. Elias for being zealous and fervent for the law was taken up into heaven. Ananias, Azarias, and Misael, by believing were saved out of the flame. Daniel for his innocency was delivered from the mouth of the lions. And thus consider ye throughout all ages, that none that put their trust in him shall be overcome." [15]

First Maccabees records the history of the Jews from 169 to 135 B.C. and is our principal source of information for the events of which it speaks. The speech of Mattathias was, according to the author of First Maccabees, made in 169 B.C. According to the view of those who deny that there ever was a real Daniel, the book named after him was written about June 164 B.C., about five years after the speech was delivered. Is it possible that a reliable author, such as the writer of First Maccabees certainly was, would have put such statements with regard to Daniel and his companions into a speech made five years before the work of fiction containing the supposititious history of them was written?

Again, how can we account for the fact that the author of First Maccabees, if he himself manufactured the speech, should have placed these fictitious characters in the very climax of his heroic appeal? If he had had a suspicion even that they were not real persons, and that there had been no deliverance from the flame and from the lions, would he have finished this magnificent call to patriotism and faith by descending from the thrilling experiences of Abraham, Joseph, Phinehas, Joshua, David, and Elijah, —all bearing directly upon his attempt to stir up his hearer to their noblest endeavours for God and country—by descending, I

[15] I, ii, 51-61.

say, to such bathos as this? Surely, also, the author of this speech must have known that the enthusiasm of the hearers could not be aroused by appealing to the example of men whose names and deeds were unknown to them. If Mattathias made this speech, it shows that he esteemed the traditions about Daniel as being of equal value with those concerning the others to whom he appeals. If the author of First Maccabees composed the speech, and put it into the mouth of Mattathias, he must have thought, at least, that those for whom he wrote his history would acknowledge that Mattathias might have made such a speech, and that his hearers might have understood it. That it is a good speech for the alleged purpose of it, no one can deny. That it accomplished its purpose is equally undeniable. Finally, the author of First Maccabees writes like one who had first hand information of the facts that he records. He probably lived throughout most, if not all, of the stirring times which Daniel predicts and that he describes. Is it not, then, remarkable that if the Book of Daniel were first written in 164 B.C., and had been expressly published with the purpose of exciting the flagging energies of the despondent and faithless Jews, that no mention is made in First Maccabees of any such publication, or even of its author? But no. The references to Daniel and his companions are made in the same way as to Abraham and David, showing clearly, that the author put the sources of Daniel in the same class as the Law and the Prophets.

That the Jews of the first century A.D., also, considered Daniel to be an historical person is abundantly shown, moreover, in the numerous references which the New Testament writers make to the book. It will not do to say that they would have referred to it in the same way and with the same frequency, if they had looked upon it as fiction; for they do not thus refer to Judith, Tobit, and other works of a fictitious character.

4. Now, against this consentient testimony of the New Testament writers, Josephus, and the Maccabees, as to the existence of a knowledge of Daniel and of his book before the time of Antiochus Epiphanes, what have those who deny this knowledge to advance? Nothing but two opinions: first, that these writers, whose honesty they will probably admit, did not have the oppor-

tunity or the intelligence to judge correctly on such subjects; and
secondly, that it is impossible that there can have been predictions
of such a character as those to be found in the Book of Daniel.

(1) As to the first of these opinions, it may be remarked, first,
with reference to the New Testament writers, that, inspiration
aside, they certainly give us the views prevalent among the Jews
of their time. Writers like the apostle Paul must have known the
history of the Jewish people from the time of the High Priest
Simon the Just onward, much better, at least, than any one can
know it to-day. Hostile readers and critics, such as those to whom
the Epistle to the Hebrews was directed, render it incredible that
an educated author, such as he was who wrote this epistle, could
have referred to what he considered to be imaginary events and
persons in the clauses "stopped the mouths of lions," and
"quenched the violence of fire". Whether Paul, or Apollos, or
whoever wrote this epistle, he was certainly acquainted with the
history of Israel, and he undeniably meant to give us a list of the
real heroes of faith, in order to stimulate his readers to follow
their example. Such a stimulus could not have been derived from
the supposititious heroes of romance, any more than it could be
to-day; unless, indeed, both writer and readers believed that they
were historical. Let our belief in the truthfulness of the cherry
tree incident be dissipated, and it will be vain to cite the veracity
of the boy Washington to excite the emulation of the youth of
America. Let our belief in the reality of the miracles and priva-
tions of the saints be destroyed, and these signal events of their
lives will at once cease to be ensamples for our conduct and consolation. Let our belief in the fact of the incarnation, or of the
resurrection, and in the correctness of the records of the words
and deeds of Jesus once be done away, and our appeal to sinners
to accept of Jesus as their Lord and Saviour will inevitably lose
its conviction and its power. These are psychological facts, which
the experience of every one will approve as true.

In like manner, we must agree that the writer of the Epistle
to the Hebrews would not have appealed to imaginary characters
and events to support and strengthen the failing faith of his
readers. He must, then, himself have believed that Daniel and

his companions lived and acted as the Book of Daniel asserts that they did. Living within 250 years of the time when some assume that the Book of Daniel was written, and at a time of great literary activity, it is scarcely possible that a writer of such intelligence as is displayed throughout the Epistle to the Hebrews should not have known whether the heroes that he cites as examples were real or fictitious characters.

Secondly, as to Josephus, we have in him a witness whose honesty and intelligence no one can dispute. His opportunity to learn the facts can alone be controverted. But we have no evidence with regard to what he says about Daniel, to show that he can be effectually controverted. For he lived only about 250 years after the time of the Maccabees, and all of the earlier part of his life was passed in Palestine. He had access to all of the religious literature of the Jews and to all of the profane literature of the Gentiles, and was thoroughly acquainted with all the laws, institutions, and traditions of his people. Of all ancient historians, none but Polybius and Pliny cite as many authorities, and no one as many archives, as he. No one so often appeals to the best sources of information on the different matters of which he treats. Nor does anyone so persistently defy all critics, nor so consistently marshall the testimony of the original sources.

Now, Josephus treats the Book of Daniel as historical, and gives all of the tenth and eleventh chapters of Book X of his *Antiquities of the Jews,* embracing six whole pages of Whiston's translation, to a narration of the principal events of Daniel's career. In language which cannot be surpassed, he says of him:

"It is fit to give an account of what this man did, which is most admirable to hear; for he was so happy as to have strange revelations made to him, . . . , and now that he is dead, he retains a remembrance that will never fail, for the several books that he wrote and left behind him are still read by us till this time; and from them we believe that Daniel conversed with God. . . . He also wrote and left behind him what made manifest the accuracy and undeniable veracity of his predictions. . . . And indeed, it so came to pass that our nation suffered these things under Antiochus Epiphanes, according to Daniel's vision, and what he wrote many years before they came to pass. In the very same manner, also, Daniel wrote concerning the Roman government, and that our country should be made desolate by them. All these things did this man leave in writing, as God had showed them to him, insomuch that such as read his prophecies and see how they have been fulfilled would wonder at the honour wherewith God honoured Daniel, and may thence discover how the Epicureans are in error, who cast providence out of human life, and do not believe that God takes care of the affairs of the world, nor that the universe is governed and continued in being by that blessed and immortal nature." [16]

From these citations from Josephus it appears clearly that this careful writer, whose great vocation in life it was to defend the institutions and writers of his nation, and to describe the persons and events of its history, never harboured a suspicion that the Book of Daniel was other than historical, or was in any wise different, as a trustworthy source of information, from the other books of the Old Testament, whose records, as Josephus says in his first treatise against Apion, "had been written all along down to his own times with the utmost accuracy." [17] "For we have not," says he, "an innumerable number of books among us, disagreeing from and contradicting one another, but only twenty-two books, which contain the records of all the past times. And of them five belong to Moses, which contain his laws, and the traditions of the origin of mankind till his death. But as to the time from the death of Moses till the reign of Artaxerxes king of Persia, who reigned after Xerxes, the prophets who were after Moses, wrote down what was done in their times in thirteen books. The remaining four books contain hymns to God, and precepts for the conduct of human life." [18] From this last statement of Josephus it is apparent that he classed Daniel among the prophets, and deemed his book of equal authority with the rest.

(2) As to the second opinion mentioned above that it is impossible that there can have been predictions of such a character as those to be found in the Book of Daniel, let it suffice to say here that to one who grants the possibility and the fact of a revelation from God it is unreasonable to lay down the limits and to define the character of that revelation. It is at least probable that God

[16] Book X, xi, 7.
[17] Section 6.
[18] Section 8.

would speak in divers manners through the prophets. No man, be he ever so wise, can say to the All Wise: Thus must Thou have spoken, or not at all. The length, the detailed description, and the literary form of the revelation, may differ as widely as the truth permits; but they do not affect the truth. God alone can be the judge of how, and when, and where, and to whom, He will reveal His thoughts and plans.

Fifth Assumption

The fifth assumption of those who assert that Ben Sira knew nothing about Daniel, is based on the allegation that Ben Sira states that there was no man like Joseph, "whereas the narratives respecting Daniel represent him much like unto Joseph in regard to both the high distinction he attained and the faculties he displayed; and further, the very wording of the narratives in the first part of Daniel is modelled after that of the narratives in Genesis concerning Joseph." [19]

By the method pursued by Driver in this citation, we could establish, or condemn, almost any proposition ever made. By omitting the qualifying clauses of Ben Sira's statement, he has made him appear to say what he does not say at all. Ben Sira does not make the very questionable assertion that no man like Joseph was ever born; but, that no man was born like Joseph in this respect, that his dead body was mustered (i. e., counted in the muster). In the preceding verse, according to Smend's and Strack's texts of the Hebrew original, he had just said that "few were formed upon earth like Enoch, in that he was taken away bodily." In the 16th verse, he says that no man was born like Joseph in that his body was mustered. The two verses are of the same construction. In each case, the comparison is limited by the second clause of the verse; and the statements of the first clauses, when thus limited, are in both cases perfectly true. At least, it is perfectly true concerning Joseph.[20] For of no other man could it be said that his dead body had been preserved as

[19] See Driver, *Daniel,* pp. 17 and 64. (*Vide supra,* p. 78).
[20] In the case of Enoch it might be doubted whether in view of Elijah's ascension it could be said that he alone of all men had been translated bodily.

was that of Joseph in Egypt, and mustered as his was among the embattled hosts of Israel. In this particular, Joseph was and will be forever unlike all other men; and it is in this particular that Ben Sira says that Joseph was unlike all other men. He does not say a word, or give a hint, as to his meaning to suggest or insinuate that no one was like Joseph "as to both the high distinction he attained and the faculties he displayed."

Nor will Driver's assertion derive any support from the Greek version of Ecclesiasticus, which reads: "Neither was there a man born like unto Joseph, a governor of his brethren, a stay of his people, whose bones were regarded of the Lord." Nor will the Syriac Version help him; for it reads: "And no mother has borne a child like Joseph, in that his body was assembled (*i.e.*, gathered to his fathers) in peace."

As to the further part of the citation from Driver, that "the very wording of the narratives in the first part of Daniel is modelled after that of the narratives of Genesis concerning Joseph," it has absolutely nothing to do with the question of the date of the composition of the Book of Daniel. Since, according to Driver himself, the whole history of Joseph belongs to the so-called Jehovistic and Elohistic documents,[21] and since critics agree that both of these documents were certainly finished before 750 B.C.,[22] it is perfectly obvious that a writer of the sixth century B.C. may have imitated the account in Genesis as readily as one who lived in the second century B.C.

Moreover, in only three particulars can the life of Daniel be said to resemble that of Joseph. They were both captives at the court of a mighty foreign monarch; they both rose to positions of preëminence at these respective courts; and they both rose because of their skill in the interpretation of dreams. In all other respects their lives differ as much as it is possible for human lives, especially of men in somewhat similar circumstances, to differ. But finally and chiefly, it is to be noted that it is not to one of these resemblances, but to one of the differences, between Joseph and Daniel, that Ben Sira calls our attention; that is, that

[21] *L.O.T.*, p. 17.
[22] *L.O.T.*, p. 122.

something was done with the body of Joseph such as never happened in the case of any other man. For when Joseph was about to die, he gave commandment concerning his bones, saying to the children of Israel: "God will surely visit you, and ye shall carry up my bones from hence" (Gen. l, 25). In Ex. xiii, 19, we are told that Moses took the bones of Joseph with him, when he went out of the land of Egypt; and in Josh. xxiv, 32, it is said that the children of Israel buried these bones, which they had brought all the way from Egypt, in a parcel of ground in Shechem which became the inheritance of the children of Joseph.

This was the unique, the unparalleled, event in the history of Joseph. It was recognised as such by Ben Sira in his day, and by the writer of the Epistle to the Hebrews in his. And it must be recognized by us to-day. In this one respect there was no one like him among all the children of Israel, nor ever has been, nor ever can be among all the sons of men.

CONCLUSION

Having thus considered fully all the objections to the early date of the Book of Daniel made on the ground of the silence of Ben Sira with respect to it, there seems to be no sufficient reason for doubting the conclusion that notwithstanding this silence the Book of Daniel may have been in existence before 180 B.C.

CHAPTER IV

APOCALYPSES AND THE DATE OF DANIEL

APOCALYPSE means revelation. In Biblical literature and the literature connected with it, there is a large number of books either in part or in whole of an apocalyptic character, either real or assumed, in which there purports to be unveiled before us the secrets of the past, the present, or the future, which could not have been learned by mere human insight or foresight. The preliminary question, and perhaps the more important question, to be answered before we consider the specific case of Daniel, is therefore, whether such a thing as a revelation has taken place, or at least whether it is possible. Every one who believes that Jesus is the Son of God and also every one who believes in the claims of the prophets of the Old Testament, must believe both in the possibility and the fact of such a thing as revelation by God to man. It is to such, and such only, that the discussion in this article is addressed, and we shall discuss in their proper place whether there is anything in the revelations contained in Daniel either in form or in character and content which renders it impossible to believe in the possibility or in the actuality of their having been made in the 6th century B.C.

THE CHARGE

The necessity of entering upon this discussion arises, not from the fact that their predictive character is denied by those who reject the theistic system, but because in its most essential features it is impugned by many who profess their belief that "God who at sundry times and in divers manners spoke in times past unto the fathers by the prophets hath in these last days spoken unto us by his Son." The objections to Daniel to which attention is called will be stated, then, in the words of Professor Charles, and in those of Professor Prince. They are as follows:

"Apocalyptic arose at a time when Israel had been subject for centuries to the sway of one or another of the great world powers. Hence, in order to harmonize such difficulties with God's righteousness, it had to take account of the *rôle* of such empires in the counsels of God; to recount the sway and downfall of each in turn, till, finally, the lordship of the world passed into the hands of Israel, or the final judgment arrived. The chief part of these events belonged, it is true, to the past; but the Apocalyptic writer represented them as still in the future, arranged under certain artificial categories of time, and as definitely determined from the beginning in the counsels of God and revealed by Him to His servants the prophets." [1]

"It should be noticed that the Book of Daniel differs materially from all the prophetic writings of the Old Testament in the general style of its prophecies. Other prophets confine themselves to vague and general predictions, but the author of Daniel gives a detailed account of the historical events," etc. [2]

It is asserted, also, that the apocalypse of Daniel resembles the apocalyptic literature of the period from 200 B.C. onward to 135 A.D. rather than the visions of the earlier centuries.

ASSUMPTIONS

These objections involve the following assumptions:

I. That the form in which the supposed predictive elements of Daniel are clothed is such as could not have been employed in the 6th century B.C.

II. That Daniel's apocalypse resembles those from the 2nd century B.C. to 135 A.D. rather than those of the Biblical writers of earlier times.

III. That the character of the predictive elements is such as to render it in the highest degree improbable, to say the least, that they could have been written before the events which they so accurately describe had actually occurred.

[1] Charles, Art. "Apocalyptic Literature." Hasting's *Dict. of the Bible*, Vol. I, p. 110a.
[2] Prince: *Commentary on Daniel*, p. 21.

IV. That since apocalyptic writers represent past as future, Daniel is false simply because it is or contains apocalypses.

First Assumption

As to the form of the Book of Daniel, it will be noted that only a part can be called apocalyptic. The first six chapters, with the exception of a part of chapter two, contain a narrative of some of the events in the life of Daniel and of his three companions. The form of this narration is not dissimilar from that followed in the case of Joseph, Samuel, David, Jeremiah, and Ahikar, so that no one perhaps would deny that so far as its literary form is concerned, aside from its linguistic characteristics, it might have been written as early as the 6th century B.C.; were it not that, since Daniel is usually considered to be a unit, it is thought necessary to bring this historical part down to a time when the apocalyptic parts, if *post-eventum,* must have been written.

Since, then, it is to the form of the apocalyptic portion that exception is made, we shall confine ourselves strictly to it. It may be said in the first place that the apocalyptic material of Daniel is not an apocalypse but a number of apocalypses occurring under five subsidiary forms. And it is to be observed that each one of these forms occurs in sacred and secular literature of the sixth century B.C. and earlier.

(1) There is a dream and its interpretation (chaps. iv, vii.).

(2) There is a prayer and its answer (chap. ix).

(3) There are two or three visions each consisting of a symbol, or sign, and its explanation; these are to be found in chaps. viii, x, and xii.

(4) There is in chaps. xi-xii, 4 a direct address to the prophet without telling the manner of the coming of the information.

(5) God, or his angel, speaks directly to someone.

1. As to the first of these, the dream apocalypses, we have abundant parallels in the literature preceding the time of Daniel (*cir.* 535 B.C.), both profane and sacred. In the Scriptures, we have among others the dreams of Joseph, of the chief butler and chief baker, and of Pharaoh, recorded in Gen. xxxvii, xl, and xli, and the dream of the Midianite mentioned in Jgs. vii, 13, 14: in

which the Lord revealed his will through dreams. In all these cases, as in that of Nebuchadnezzar, the dreams are such as the persons dreaming them would naturally have had and the interpretations are in harmony with the person and circumstances concerned. The narratives differ in length but not in essential characteristics from those of Daniel.

In profane literature, I shall cite parallels only in the case of five kings, one of Lydia, one of Assyria, one of Babylonia, one of Persia, and one of Greece. Gyges, king of Lydia, is reported by Ashurbanipal to have seen a dream in which Ashur revealed the name Ashurbanipal to Gyges and said: "Grasp the feet of Ashurbanipal, king of Assyria, and thou shall through his name conquer thy enemies." [3]

Again, Ashurbanipal says [4] that he slew Teumman, king of Elam, in the power of Ashur and Marduk the great gods his lords who had encouraged him by means of a sign, an oracular dream, the message of a priest, and again [5] that the goddess Ishtar had caused his troops to see a dream toward the end of night in which she said to them: "I am going before Ashurbanipal the king whom my hands have made"; and that "relying upon this dream, his troops crossed the Idide river in good spirits." He tells, moreover, of a seer of dreams (*shabru*) who lay down toward the end of night and saw in a dream that upon the sickle of the moon stood written: "Whoever plans evil and undertakes war against Ashurbanipal, King of Assyria, him will I cause an evil death to overtake; through the quick iron sword, the firebrand, hunger, the plague of Gira, will I put an end to his life." When the king heard this dream he relied upon the word of Sin his Lord; for as he says [6] the gods had announced to him continually joyous messages concerning the conquest of his enemies and had made his dreams upon his bed favourable.

So Nabunaid was caused to see the following dream:

[3] Schrader, *Keilinschriftliche Bibliothek,* II, 172, 173.
[4] *Id.* II, 253.
[5] *Id.* II, 201.
[6] *Id.* II, 233.

"In the beginning of my enduring reign they caused me to see a dream; Marduk, the great Lord, and Sin, the light of heaven and earth stood beside me. Marduk spoke to me: Nabunaid king of Babylon, with thy horses and wagons bring bricks, build Ehulhul and let Sin, the great Lord make his dwelling therein. Fearfully spake I to Marduk the Lord of the Gods: That temple which thou hast ordered me to make, the Umman-Manda have surrounded it and great is their might. Then spake Marduk to me: The Umman-Manda whereof thou speakest, their land and the kings who stood by their sides to help them exist no more." [7]

Herodotus tells us that Xerxes was not at first inclined to make war against Greece but was driven thereto by a couple of dreams.

"The first night he imagined that a tall and handsome man stood before him and said: Do you, then, change your mind, O Persian, and resolve not to lead an army against Greece, after having ordered the Persians to assemble their forces? You do not well to change your resolution, nor is there any man who will agree with you; therefore pursue that course which you resolved upon in the day. The second night, after that Xerxes had paid no attention to the first dream, the same dream came to him again and said: Son of Darius, you have, then, openly renounced, in the presence of the Persians, the intended expedition, and make no account of my words, as if you had not heard them from anyone. Be well assured, however, of this, that unless you immediately undertake this expedition, this will be the consequence to you: As you have become great and powerful in a short time, so you shall become low again in an equally short time." [8]

Josephus [9] says that Alexander the Great told Jaddua the high priest that while he was at Dios in Macedonia he had seen him in a dream in the very habit in which he came to meet Alexander when on his way to Jerusalem; and that in this dream Jaddua had exhorted him boldly to pass over the sea, for that he would conduct his army and give him the dominion over the Persians.

2. As a parallel to the prayer of Daniel in chapter ix, and its answer we have in the Scriptures the instance where Hezekiah laid the letter of Sennacherib before the Lord and prayed and the answer came to him through Isaiah the prophet assuring him that

[7] *Id.* III, II, p. 99.
[8] Book VII, 12, 14.
[9] *Antiq,* xi, viii, 5.

Sennacherib should return to Assyria without capturing Jerusalem (Isa. xxxvii, 10-35). In like manner Ashurbanipal says that on account of the wickedness which Teumman king of Elam had spoken he went to the exalted Ishtar, stood before her, and bowed down to her, his tears aflowing, and said:

"O Mistress of Arbela! I am Ashurbanipal, king of Assyria, the creature of thy hands . . . of the father thy begetter. For the renovation of the temples of Assyria and the completion of the great cities of Accad, I have sought thy holy places and have gone to worship. . . . But as to Teumman, king of Elam, who honours not the gods, do Thou, O Mistress of Mistresses, goddess of battle, mistress of conflict, queen of the gods, who speakest favourably before Ashur thy father, thy begetter; do thou (destroy) him who has set his army in motion, and made war and taken up arms, to go against Assyria. Do Thou, the warrior of the gods, like a *bitte* in the midst of the battle put him in disarray and smite him with a storm and an evil wind." Ishtar heard my soughing sighs and said, "Fear not" and encouraged my heart. She said: "On account of the raising of thy hands, which thou has raised, and of thy eyes which are filled with tears, I will show thee favour."

Toward the end of that night in which I had turned myself to her, a seer laid himself down and saw a dream-vision, a vision of the night Ishtar caused him to see, and he told it to me, as follows: "Ishtar who dwells in Arbela entered and to right and left she hung quivers. She had her bow in her hand and drew from its sheath a sharp warlike sword. Before her didst thou enter. She, like the mother who bore thee, spake with thee. Ishtar, the exalted of the gods, spake to thee and issued the command to thee: "See that thou givest battle (?); wherever thy person (*panuki*) dwells, I shall go." Thou spakest to her: "To the place where thou goest, will I go, O Mistress of Mistresses." She told thee: " Thou mayest abide here in the place of the habitation of Nebo, eat food, drink wine, make music, honour my godhead, till I go and do that work and fulfill the wish of thy heart; thy face shall not blanch and thy feet shall not turn (*inarridu*), nor shalt thou put thy *kurget* in the midst of the battle; in her good bosom shall she cover thee (*tahsinka*) and protect all thy form (?). Before her, a flame will flare up and for the conquest of thy foes she will cause it to burst forth. Against Teumman, king of Elam, with whom she is enraged, her face is fixed." [10]

3. As to the vision consisting of a symbol and an explanation, we find it to be the favourite method of the prophets just as it was

[10] Dream of Nabunaid.

in the case of Daniel. Thus Amos has the visions of the plumb-line (vii) and of the basket of summer fruit (viii). Isaiah has the vision of the Lord in His temple (vi), and that of Mahar-shalal-hash-baz (viii). Jeremiah has the vision of the two baskets of figs (xxiv). Ezekiel has the visions of the cherubim (i & x), of the fire (viii), of the dry bones (xxxvii), and of the temple (xl-xlviii). Zechariah has those of the red horse, of the four carpenters (i), of Joshua and Satan (iii), of the golden candlestick and the two olive trees (iv), of the flying roll, and of the woman sitting in the ephah (v), and of the four chariots (vi). Compare also the vision of the burning bush (Ex. iii), Elijah at Horeb (1 Kgs. xix), and Micaiah before Ahab (1 Kgs. xxii).

So in profane literature, an Assyrian writer [11] tells the story of how a fox made its way into the royal park of the city of Assur and took refuge in the lake but was afterwards caught and killed.[12] This was interpreted by the astrologers as a sign.

Nabunaid [13] says that on account of the conjunction of a great star with the moon he was thoughtful in his heart, etc.

4. Fourthly, the prophet predicts without telling in what manner he got his information (xi). Compare Dt. xxxii, 33; Gen. xlix and numerous tablets in Thompson's *Reports*.

5. A fifth kind of prediction is frequently found in the prophets of the Old Testament wherein God or his angel is represented as speaking to the prophet without the intervention of a dream or vision, *e.g.*, Dan. ix, 22-27.

So, also, Ashurbanipal says that the goddess Nannai foretold saying: Ashurbanipal shall bring me out of wicked Elam and shall bring me in to Eanna.[14]

Second Assumption

But not only is the form in which the visions and dreams of Daniel are presented to us permissible in the 6th century B.C.

---

[11] K 551.

[12] R. C. Thompson, *The Reports of the Magicians and Astrologers of Assyria and Babylonia*, p. xvii.

[13] In *Deutsche Orientalistische Literaturzeitung*, Num. 8, Col. vii, 4.

[14] *Keilinschriftliche Bibliothek*, II, 211.

We can go further and say that it was not a common form in use in the 2nd century B.C. Of all the apocalyptic literature of the Hebrews, the only ones of which the whole or parts are thought to have been written in the 2nd century B.C. are Jubilees, the XII Patriarchs, and parts of Enoch, of the Sibylline Oracles, and of Baruch.

1. As to *Jubilees,* the form is not at all that found in Daniel. This book gives citations from the historical portions of the Pentateuch and then gives a sort of commentary upon them, in which the author attempts to show that the principal laws of the Pentateuch were in existence in the time of the men whose history is recorded in Genesis, and that in many cases God had revealed these laws to the fathers long before the time of Moses. Long passages of Genesis are cited almost verbatim and certain laws which were afterwards clearly enunciated by Moses are inferred as having been not merely implied in these narratives, but as having been expressly declared at the time when the history was enacted. The form is not that of dreams and visions which are interpreted, with the prayers and the answers of Moses, such as we find in Daniel; but it resembles rather the admixture of history and law which is found in Numbers, or Chronicles.

2. As to *The XII Patriarchs,* the twelve so-called visions of it are fashioned after the prototype of the blessings of Jacob recorded in Gen. xlix, and those of Moses found in Deut. xxxiii. Each one of the patriarchs before his death calls his sons together and makes predictions as to their future, just as Jacob and Moses are said to have done, except that their sons are not mentioned by name nor their blessings divided. The age of each of the patriarchs at the time of his death is usually given at the beginning of his blessing and at the end it is said that the bones of each one of them, except Joseph, were carried up and buried in Hebron. One patriarch discusses the harmful effects of lust, another of theft, another of murder, etc. In the case of others, such as Joseph, the virtues of continence and mercy are exalted. The form is the same in all the twelve and in no one of them is there any resemblance to any one of the visions or dreams of Daniel.

3. The form of that part of the apocryphal book of *Baruch* which is usually put in the 2nd century B.C.[15] is like the narrative in the Book of Jeremiah and has no resemblance whatever to that of the Book of Daniel. The confessions of the people are mostly taken apparently from Neh. ix, and Dan. ix, but are not followed by a vision as in Daniel.

4. The parts of the *Sibylline Oracles* which are thought to have been written before 100 B.C. comprise most of Book III. They are all written in the metre of Homer's *Iliad*. No author is mentioned, nor is any date given. They are admitted to have been formed after the analogy of the heathen oracles of the Sibyl, and nothing like them was, so far as we know, ever composed in Hebrew, and certainly nothing like them is to be found in Daniel.

5. There remain only the portions of *Enoch* which are said to have been written before 100 B.C. These are the only apocalyptic writings of this period which in form may be said to resemble Daniel. The principal argument is that both authors assert that they have received the subject-matter (?) of their narratives by a revelation and this commonly from an angel. But as we have seen above, nearly all of the prophets say that they had visions; and angels are said to have spoken to Abraham, Jacob, Moses, Joshua, Gideon, and especially to Zechariah. The differences however between Daniel and Enoch are very great and should not be overlooked. For example, Daniel always gives a definite time and place for his visions, Enoch never. Daniel confines himself to earthly localities for his revelations. Enoch is snatched off to the heavens for his. Daniel speaks of well known potentates of earth, such as Nebuchadnezzar and Cyrus; whereas Enoch mentions no man by name, but confines his personal designations to archangels, good and bad. Daniel confines himself to dreams and visions such as would naturally be suggested by his earthly surroundings, situated as he is said to have been in the courts of the kings of Babylon and Persia; but Enoch hies away like a witch on a broomstick to sweep the cobwebs from the sky. Daniel confines himself to prose, or the

---

[15] See Churton, on Baruch in *Com. on O. T.*

higher style of prophetic discourse; whereas Enoch slips off into poetry, in which more than half of his material is composed. Daniel is so definite and clear in his allusions and statements that in some parts (as chap. xi) what he writes might well be taken as an outline of the history of the times of which he speaks and all commentators are agreed as to the events to which the larger part of his apocalypse refers; whereas Enoch is so indefinite, that it is only with great difficulty that any two commentators can agree as to the events to which he refers. Daniel by his frankness boldly challenges the world to investigate the truth of his statements; whereas Enoch hides himself behind a mass of dark figures and recondite allusions and veiled and dubious utterances, as if he feared that his meaning should be revealed to those whom he addressed.

Nor is it correct to say that the form of the visions of Daniel was a common form of the apocalypse after 100 B.C. For:

1. The books of *Enoch* and the *Sibylline Oracles* are just as different from Daniel in their later as in their earlier portions.

2. The seven portions of the *Apocalypse of Baruch,* which Professor Charles dates from shortly before 70 A.D. to between 130 and 180 A.D., when a redactor is said to have put them together, have an artistic form that is utterly foreign to Daniel. According to the scheme of the final editor, the seven parts are divided from each other by fasts. Thus in v, 2, ix, 2, xii, 5, xxi, 1, xlvii, 2, there are fasts,—the last four being each of seven days.[16] In each part the fast is generally followed by "a prayer; then a divine message or revelation, then an announcement of this either to an individual or to the people, followed occasionally by a lamentation." [17] In some of the parts we find indications of the form of vision given to Daniel (*e.g.,* xxii, 1, liii, 1, lv, 3); but in general it is copied rather after the style of Jeremiah.

3. The *Assumption of Moses* is in the form of a dying charge from Moses to Joshua, similar to the blessings of Jacob in Gen. xlix, and that of Moses in Deut. xxxiii, only that it gives the fortune of the people of Israel rather than the fortune of the in-

---

[16] These may be compared to the fasts mentioned in Dan. ix, 3, 20-21.

[17] Charles, *Apocalypse of Baruch,* p. 9.

dividual tribes. In parts, such as the ninth verse of chapter vi, it resembles, it is true, in its detailed statement of events, the eleventh chapter of Daniel. But, in chap. x, 1-10 it is more similar in form to the Sibylline Oracles, or to the poetical parts of Enoch, which have no parallel in Daniel; and in chapters vii-ix, it seems to be in imitation of Deut. xxviii. It nowhere purports to contain a vision, or a dream, or an interpretation of a dream; but like the blessings of Isaac, Jacob, and Moses, gives a lengthy prediction of the history of Israel from the standpoint of the time of the supposed speaker. The rest of the book is an expansion of the last scenes and words between Moses and Joshua as recorded in the last chapter of Deuteronomy.

4. The so-called *Ascension of Isaiah* is divided by Professor Charles into three parts—of these, the first, called the "Martyrdom," purports to be and is written as if it were historical, after the manner of the Books of Kings. The second part, the "Testament of Hezekiah," is a professedly predictive description of the coming forth of the Beloved (the Messiah) from the seventh heaven and of his life on earth, of his crucifixion, and the sending forth of the twelve desciples, etc. It is derived apparently from the records of the *Gospels* and of the *Acts of the Apostles*. It appears from iii, 13 that it was meant to represent the contents of a vision of Isaiah. Parts of it may be compared to Daniel xi; though it is much more definite and explicit than anything in Daniel. Parts of it, however, are more like the predictions in the letters of Paul and in the Revelation of St. John and in the discourses of Jesus recorded in Matt. xxiv, Mk. xiii, and Lk. xxi, and to those in Jer. l, Deut. xxviii. and elsewhere in the Old Testament.

The third part of the *Ascension of Isaiah,* called by Professor Charles the "Vision of Isaiah," is based partly on the vision of the sixth chapter of Isaiah and resembles in part the visions of the Revelation of St. John. In form it is like nothing in Daniel, resembling rather the Babylonian poem of the Descent of Ishtar with the seven heavens put in place of the seven departments of Hades.

5. *Fourth Ezra* is divided by its latest editor, Doctor Box, into six parts. (1) The Salathiel Apocalypse, (2) an Ezra Apocalypse, (3) the Eagle Vision, (4) the Son of Man Vision, (5) an Ezra-piece, and (6) the parts added by the Redactor. The *Salathiel Apocalypse* consists of four visions. Each of these is preceded by a fast, followed by a prayer in answer to which the angel Uriel reveals the contents of the Vision. The contents are in the form of a debate relieved by many poetic passages of great beauty. The *Ezra-Apocalypse* has also alternating selections from a poem inserted by the Redactor in the midst of the first three visions of Salathiel. The *Eagle Vision* of chaps. xi-xii, which Doctor Box thinks to have been excerpted from a book of dream visions, is more like the visions of Daniel than any other apocalypse, consisting of a dream, a prayer and an interpretation, and followed by a command to write what he had seen in a book to be put in a secret place. The *Son of Man Vision,* also, is after the same form except that it omits the seal of the vision. The Ezra-piece, the so-called *Seventh Vision* or *Ezra Legend,* is modelled partly on the account of Moses at the burning bush, partly on that of Elijah under the juniper tree, but has nothing specifically like anything in Daniel, except in its reference to the esoteric nature of its disclosures. A large part of it, also, is poetic in form.

6. In the *New Testament,* also, most of the apocalyptic portions differ largely in form from that used in Daniel.

(1) In the apocalypse contained in Matt. xxiv, and in the parallel passages in Mk. xiii, and Lk. xxi, Jesus as usual speaks on his own authority and without the intervention of dreams, visions, or angels, avoiding, also, the form of debate characteristic of Daniel and of others of the apocalypses.

(2) In the apocalyptic parts of the *Epistles,* also, the form is different from that found in Daniel. In the short apocalypse recorded in 1 Tim. iv, 1-3, and in that in 2 Tim. iii, the Spirit is represented as the speaker, no dream vision, or angel being mentioned. The apocalyptic portions of 1 Cor. and of 1 and 2 Thess. describe the coming day of Christ; but they are cast in a form different from that of the ordinary apocalypses. In 2

Peter iii, the apostle bases his apocalypse on the words which were spoken before by the holy prophets and on the commandments of the apostles.

(3) The *Revelation of St. John*, also, cannot be said to be an imitation in form of the Book of Daniel, though in many minor points it resembles it. It has no definite dates like the visions of Daniel, nor any dreams or prayers; nor does it mention the kings by name, nor concern itself preëminently with the kingdoms of this world as Daniel does. In one great particular, however, they are alike: for they both alike make the culmination and consummation of every vision to be the time when the kingdoms of this world shall become the kingdom of our Lord and of his Christ.

From the above review of the forms of the Apocalyptic literature from the time of Isaiah to 135 A.D., it is evident that there was never any time during this period when as far as form is concerned Daniel might not have been written. During this whole time, with the exception of the years from Zechariah to the 2nd century, we have apocalypses resembling these in Daniel in some particular and differing from them in others. No two apocalypses are exactly alike in form. Some of those that are most unlike came from the same period; for example, the Sibylline Oracles, and Jubilees and Enoch and the Testimony of the XII Patriarchs from the 2nd century B.C.; and Baruch, the Testimony of Hezekiah and the Revelation of St. John from the 1st century A.D. In respect to the form of Daniel, then, it seems clear that the critics of Daniel have been drawing on their imagination for their facts, both when they have asserted that judged by the criterion of form it could not have been written in the 6th century B.C. and when they have asserted that judged by the same criterion it must have been written in the 2nd century B.C.

Third Assumption

With regard to the third assertion, that Daniel must have been written after the events which are so accurately described in it actually occurred, we claim that this is not a specific indictment of the Book of Daniel but of the whole system of Christianity which is based upon the possibility and the fact of a supernatural revelation. If we put Daniel at a late date simply because of the fact that otherwise we would be compelled to admit that it accurately predicts events occurring after the 6th century B.C., we must for the same reason put Luke xxi, after 70 A.D.

If Christ were a mere man, his claim to predict events might be cast aside. Were Daniel not a prophet of the Lord, so his also might be cast aside. But if holy men of old spake as they were moved by the Holy Spirit and if God at sundry times and in divers manners spake unto men by the prophets and in the latter times through his Son by whom He made the worlds, then they spake for God who knows the end from the beginning. If God spake by the prophets, and Jesus acknowledged Daniel as a prophet, what man can put a limit to the extent and accuracy of that which God spake? "O fools and slow of heart to believe all that the prophets hath spoken," your *musts* are not the musts of the prophets,—your musts are not the musts of God who hath showed the things that are to come hereafter that they may know that He is God.

Fourth Assumption

But, finally, the critics intimate or assert that the Book of Daniel is false simply because it is, or contains, apocalypses. This is based upon the presumption that all apocalypses are false. Of course, if we define an apocalypse as an account written after certain events have happened and purporting to have been written before they happened, than all apocalypses would be false. But certainly no one would claim that the Revelation of St. John is such an apocalypse; nor do we think that anyone could show that large parts of the books of Enoch, or the 4th Ezra, would come under such a definition of an apocalypse. Nor can the parts at least of any of the pre-Christian apocalypses which speak of a judgment, or a resurrection, or a Messianic kingdom, be put under that definition.

The fact is, however, that an apocalypse claims to be a revelation of events yet future from the standpoint of the writer, or the speaker of the vision. The question for us to determine is, whether this claim to be an apocalypse is true or false. All apocalypses might be false; all might possibly be true. Each must be investigated and judged according to the laws of evidence proper to such predictions. A priori, no man can dogmatically assert that all such predictions are false either in intention or fact; because no man is omniscient. Nor can any man lay down rules for the possibility or character of a divine revelation.

To all who admit the possibility of a revelation from God to man, the truth or falsity of any apparent apocalypse will depend upon its claim and the evidence in support of that claim. Thus, in the case of Matt. xxiv, Mk. xiii, and Lk. xxi, the direct claim is that it is an apocalyptic discourse of the Lord with reference especially to the destruction of Jerusalem. The text of these chapters is supported by the same direct evidence as that which we have for the remaining parts of the books in which they occur. The ability of Jesus to make such a revelation of future events will not be disputed by anyone who believes that He was the Son of God. The fact of the revelation and the trustworthiness of it, were never disputed by the early writers, so far as anyone knows. So far, in fact, as the account in Luke is concerned, the evidence for the rest of the book is so overwhelming that Harnack can reject the 21st chapter only on the ground that it is apocalyptic.

So, also, in regard to the apocalyptic parts of Daniel. The text of the apocalyptic parts is supported by exactly the same evidence as that for the rest of the book. The unity of the book is so generally admitted on reasonable grounds by critics of all schools that it scarcely needs to be defended. In fact, it would probably never have been assailed, were it not for the difficulty of the problem suggested by the apocalyptic parts of the book. To Christians the truth of the claim of Daniel to be a true narrative of the life and apocalypses of the man Daniel would seem to be confirmed by the treatment accorded to it by Christ and the New Testament writers in general.

Again it cannot be said that any Jews of the early ages ever denied the canonicity or authenticity of Daniel on any ground whatever, nor especially on the ground that it was, or contained, an apocalypse. In *Yadayim*, iv, 5, it is expressly stated that "the Aramaic passages in Ezra and Daniel defile the hands," i.e., are canonical. No reference, or allusion is to be found either in the Talmud, or Josephus, or any other source, suggesting that any rabbi, or Jew, of ancient times ever questioned the genuineness, authenticity, or canonicity, of the Hebrew portions of Daniel. The canonicity of Esther is said to have been questioned on the ground that it was not dictated by the Holy Spirit.[18] Ezekiel was in danger of being suppressed, because its contents were alleged to be contradictory to the words of the Law.[19] Some desired to withdraw the Book of Proverbs from use because it contained internal contradictions.[20] Some are said to have withdrawn Proverbs, the Song of Songs, and Ecclesiastes, from public use, because they spoke in proverbs.[21] Some would have withdrawn Ecclesiastes, because it is self-contradictory, contradicts the words of David, and favours heresy.[22]

These instances from the Talmud teach us that the canonicity of certain books was questioned because of the language in which they were written, on the ground of their proverbial character, of their self-contradictions, or of their disagreement with the Psalter or the Law; or, because they were thought not to have been dictated by the Holy Spirit. No one ever disputed a book on the ground of its apocalyptic character. It remained for the heathen, Neo-Platonic philosopher Porphyry, at the end of the third century, A.D., to enunciate and elaborate this objection to the Book of Daniel. It is a heathenish objection, resting simply on the philosophical assumption that there is no such thing as predictive prophecy.

---

[18] *Megilla*, fol. 7d.
[19] *Moed Katan*, 5a.
[20] *Sabbath*, 30b.
[21] *Aboth di Rabbi Nathan.*
[22] *Sabbath*, 30a, *Midrash Vayyikra Rabba*, c. 28.

CHAPTER V

THE ORIGIN OF THE IDEAS OF DANIEL

BEFORE entering upon the discussion of the origin of the ideas of Daniel, several fallacies must first be considered.

Thus it is claimed that it is possible to determine the time of a revelation from its ideas in the same manner as we would determine that of a mere human production. But, for those who believe in a thinking God who has made the universe, including man, it is impossible to deny the possibility of a revelation to His creatures of Himself and of His plans up to the capacity of those creatures to receive such a revelation. How and why He makes such a revelation it may be impossible for the objects of it to determine or to understand: but that He can reveal what He desires to reveal must be admitted.

Further, to all who believe that God has begun to make such a revelation it is clear that no limits as to the time and manner and order and emphasis, extent and subject-matter, of such a revelation can be set by the creatures who receive it. These are matters for the Revealer to determine and not for the persons to whom the revelation is made.

To those who accept these premises (and we take it that all Christians must accept them), all objections against the Book of Daniel on the ground of the character of the revelation that it contains may safely be looked upon as beyond the legitimate realm of discussion. Whether God saw fit to reveal these truths in the sixth or in the second century B.C. must be a matter of comparatively little importance. What is of importance for us is, that He has revealed them.

To object to the fact of a certain alleged revelation that it is too detailed, or that it is written in veiled language, or in an unusual rhetorical style, or in a novel literary manner, is fatuous and unreasonable. At sundry times and in divers manners, God spake unto man through the prophets.

Further, though we admit that there is a development in the fullness and clearness of God's revelation of certain truths to man, there is no reason for contending that no revelation of an entirely new truth should ever be made, nor for attempting to fix the time at which the revelation of the new truth should be made. These points, again, are fixed by the Revealer.

It is to be observed further that the laws of the evolution of ideas which may be justly applied to a purely human production do not necessarily apply to a document which is said to be, or contain, a revelation from God. This may be observed in the case of the idea of a Messiah. In the sense in which this idea is put forth in the Scriptures it is unique and can be, if it be true, naught but a matter of revelation as over against a result of mere human longing and development. Most of what any prophet did, or could, say with regard to such a person would be necessarily dependent upon what God pleased to reveal to him. The time and place at which the lineaments of character and work should be made known to man would be subject to the divine will and pleasure. What Isaiah, Micah, Zechariah, or any prophet said with regard to Him, or what any prophet might have said, is not for us to judge, nor for any man to judge.

Sometimes, it is true, it may be possible to determine the date of a document by the ideas that are found to be expressed in it for the first time, especially where we have a vast mass of literature revealing a natural intellectual development for a long period of time, or where the idea has been declared by the author or acknowledged by contemporaries or successors to have originated with him. But where these ideas are religious or philosophical, and above all where they are contained in what claims to be a revelation from God, the time when the ideas are first stated or promulgated depends on the mind of the Thinker and the will of the Revealer rather than upon the general condition of mankind. This general condition may indeed suggest the thought of the Thinker and may occasion the form of the revelation; but it can not be said to have originated it. For example, there were many times before that of the Maccabees, when the Israelites had been grievously oppressed by foreign foes—by Egyptians, Philistines, Assyrians, Babylonians, Persians, and Greeks—and when Israel's heroes had performed deeds of valour in their own defence. It would seem absurd to attempt to determine the date of a psalm or prophecy from a general reference to persecution or destitution or from words of comfort contained in it. It would seem equally absurd to attempt to fix the date of a literary production from the fact that it contains words, or references, which would suit many known or unknown eventualities; as, for example, when a distinguished scholar attempts to place the composition of parts of Nahum in the time of the Maccabees, because in chap. ii, 2 the prophet speaks of him who dashes in pieces (מפיץ). This word might just as well indicate the time of Deborah because she says that Jael "took a hammer" (המקבת) and "smote" (תקע) the head of Sisera.

Another absurdity is to assert that the fact that a book alleged to have been written by a certain author is not quoted or used by a later author proves either that the apparently earlier one did not exist, or that his work was unknown to the later writer. Take in illustration of this the Book of Esther. Here we find no mention of God, nor of the prophets, nor even of the Law. Nor does the writer quote from any of the Psalms, nor from any of the historical books. Does this silence on his part disprove his knowledge of any of these books, or show that they did not exist? Everyone will say, Certainly not! How then has the failure of the post-captivity authors to mention Daniel, or to cite from him, or to refer to the ideas which he first promulgated, proved that Daniel did not exist at the time when Esther was written?

It is equally absurd to suppose that it is always possible to determine from a comparison of similar, or the same words, phrases, or ideas, occurring in two writings which of them has borrowed from the other. For in most cases it is obvious that both may have had before them the same original from which they have both cited, or that they may both unconsciously have happened to use the same words or to express the same thought in the same or in like language. Thus the verses in Mic. iv, 1-4 are the same as ii,

2-5 of Isaiah. Does this show that Isaiah borrowed from Micah or that Micah borrowed from Isaiah or that both derived from a common original? Again, Deut. xiv, is almost the same as Lev. xi. Does this show that D is later than P or that P is later than D, or may the same writer have expressed the same thought at different times in slightly different phraseology? The accounts of the Sermon on the Mount as given by Matthew and Luke differ in many particulars from one another. Did one of them derive the discourse from the other, or did they both derive it from the same source, or from different accounts given by hearers of the original discourse?

A multitude of such questions confronts us in the literary study of almost every book of the Bible and of the apocryphal and apocalyptic literature; and as we might expect, we find a number of them awaiting us when we enter upon the literary discussions centering around the Book of Daniel. From a comparison of the prayer in Daniel ix, with that in Neh. ix, it has been attempted to prove that Daniel is later than Nehemiah or *vice versa*. In the opinion of the present writer such attempts taken by themselves are almost sure to be in all cases devoid of convincing results; especially when, as in this instance, the similar phrases may have been derived from a common source found in the literature of the Jews written long before the time either of Nehemiah or of Daniel, or, where not thus found, may well have been the natural and appropriate language of prayer when made by men situated in like circumstances, reared in the same traditions, experiencing the same needs, and desiring help from the same God. Numerous prayers of the Egyptian, Assyrian, and Babylonian kings have in them many words and phrases that are the same and many more that are similar; but it would be impossible in most cases to determine from these words and phrases the relative dates of the prayers. There are certain phrases that for centuries were the same, that had been stereotyped, so to speak, and that consequently can determine nothing definite as to the date of the document in which they occur.

Lastly, it is ridiculous for a Christian to be always running to heathen sources for the origin of the religious ideas which are contained in the Scriptures, and especially for their confirmation.

If Daniel speaking of himself says that there will be a resurrection of those who sleep in the dust, then, it may be an interesting question as to whether he is the first human being that ever put this thought in writing. It would, however, be merely his opinion and no better than any other man's; unless this other could prove by experiment, or scientific proof, that a resurrection will certainly take place. But if Daniel, speaking by revelation from God, says there will be a resurrection, this statement is no longer a man's opinion merely, but the truth of God to which all men must attend.

OBJECTIONS OF THE CRITICS

According to Driver: "It is undeniable that the doctrines of the Messiah, of angels, of the resurrection, and of a judgment on the world, are taught with greater distinctness, and in a more developed form [in Daniel] than elsewhere in the Old Testament, and with features approximating to (though not identical with) those met with in the earlier parts of the Book of Enoch, c. 100 B.C." [1]

Cornill says: "At the present time the view which sees in Daniel a work of the Maccabean period is the all-prevailing one." Among the "objective reasons of the utmost weight, which render the view of its non-genuineness necessary" is the presence in it of a "developed angelology" and of a "twofold individual resurrection of the dead to bliss and to damnation." [2]

Prince tells us: "It is now very generally admitted that this doctrine [of the resurrection] also originated among the Persians and could only have become engrafted on the Jewish mind after a long period of intercourse with the Zoroastrian religion. . . . The investigations of Persian scholars, especially of Haug, Spiegel, and Windischmann, show that this is a real Zoroastrian doctrine. . . . It is clearly impossible, therefore, that the author of passages showing such beliefs could have lived as early as the time of Nebuchadnezzar." The angelology of Daniel, there can be little doubt, "is an indication of prolonged Persian influence." [3]

[1] *L.O.T.*, p. 508.
[2] *Introduction*, pp. 384-386.
[3] *Commentary on Daniel*, p. 21.

ASSUMPTIONS

I. It is assumed in the above statements that the doctrine of Daniel on the resurrection, angels, Messiah, and judgment is shown by comparison with other biblical documents to be too highly developed for the sixth century B.C., and especially that the doctrines of the resurrection and of angels as stated in Daniel originated among the Persians, that they were derived by the Jews from the Zoroastrians, and that, hence, they could not have been known to a Jewish author living as early as the time of Nebuchadnezzar.

II. It is assumed that the features of these doctrines as found in Daniel approximate those met with in parts of Enoch to such an extent as to justify the conclusion that the Book of Daniel and these parts of Enoch are from the same time.

ANSWERS TO ASSUMPTIONS

Taking up these assumptions in order we shall endeavor to show that all of the four doctrines mentioned by Driver as indications of the late date of Daniel may have been treated of in the sixth century B.C. as well as in the second. To one who believes that the Bible contains a revelation or a series of revelations from God to man, the question of the origin of the ideas peculiar to any individual writer of the Old Testament is interesting principally from the standpoint of the Biblical theologian who desires to trace the manner and order of those revelations, or of the historian who would give us an account of the gradual preparation of the world for the coming of Christ. A study of the history of Israel seems to teach that an acknowledgment of a need of light from above upon some question insoluble by unaided human intellect, or the expression of a desire for such light, has usually preceded in point of time the revelation which supplies the light needed and meets the want expressed. Hence, such questions as those that concern the origin of the ideas of angels, resurrection, judgment and a Messiah are proper for us to consider even apart from the fact of whether God has seen fit to give us any light upon this subject and when and how He has given this light. That man has recognized that he is a sinner against God, and has need of redemption is one thing; that God has supplied a redemption to meet the need is another thing. That man is mortal and desires immortality is one thing; that God should declare that he is, or may become, immortal is another thing. So also, that men should think that there are angels and hope or fear that there may be a resurrection, or judgment and a Messiah, is one thing; whereas the questions of whether God has said that angels do exist, and as to whether there will be a resurrection and a judgment and a Messiah are an entirely different thing.

Recognizing, then, these distinctions, it will be understood that in the following pages we are not going to consider whether God could have made revelations with regard to angels, resurrection, judgment and the Messianic kingdom as early as the sixth century B.C.; but merely whether we have any evidence that men had thought about these questions as early as that time and as to what they had thought about them. If we can show that they had already thought about these things, then the statements of Daniel might be looked upon as the answers which God gave to their natural queries upon these matters for which the human mind could find no solution. If we find that they did not express any thoughts upon these subjects, we may still suppose that they had thought upon them or that possibly there first arose in the great mind of Daniel or Isaiah the questions concerning these important matters affecting the future of humanity to which God saw fit to vouchsafe the answers. In no case will it be necessary to suppose that such questions must have arisen or that the unaided human intellect could have found an answer to such questions more readily in the second century B.C. than in the sixth. Nor, in any case, can it be thought for a moment, that God knew the answers to such questions better in the second than in the sixth century B.C.

THE ANTIQUITY OF THE IDEAS OF DANIEL

Resurrection

1. First, then, let us consider where and when the idea of a resurrection is first met.

a. According to Professor Breasted [4] the early Egyptians (about 4000 B.C.) believed in a life hereafter, subject to wants of the same nature as those of the present life. The most obvious explanation of the origin of embalming is that it was expected that the soul which had departed would after a time return again to its former body.[5]

b. Among the Babylonians the phrase "giver of life to the dead" (*muballiṭ mituti.*) which is found frequently of Marduk "who loves to make the dead alive" and of others of the gods, certainly shows at least that the Babylonians had a conception of revivification of the dead. The argument seems to be, "O Marduk, who can raise the dead to life, restore this sick person to health once more." The sentence in King's *Babylonian Magic* (No. ii, 21) expresses the idea more clearly; for it says: "The body of the man who has been brought down to Arallu (their place of the dead), thou dost (or canst) bring back" (*ša ana aralli šurudu pagaršu tutira*). These texts show that the Assyrians and Babylonians in the times of Ashurbanipal and Nebuchadnezzar had at least the idea of and the longing for, a restoration or continuation, of life after death and a belief that the gods could, if they would, give life unto the dead and bring back their bodies from the place of the dead.

c. Among the old Iranians the doctrine of the resurrection of the body seems to be clearly taught in the nineteenth, or Zamyâd, Yasht.[6] The three passages in the Yashts are almost exactly the

---

[4] *A History of the Ancient Egyptians,* p. 36.

[5] That the ancient Egyptians of the pyramid dynasties believed in the resurrection of the body is demonstrated from numerous texts by Professor Erman of Berlin in his *Handbook of Egyptian Religion,* pp. 85-114.

[6] §§ 11, 12; 19, 20; 89, 90. See the *Zend-Avesta* in the *Sacred Books of the East,* Vol. XXIII, translated by J. Darmesteter, and a fragment translated by L. H. Mills in the *Zend-Avesta,* Part 3 in the *Sacred Books of the East,* Vol. XXXI, p. 390.

same. In the first, it is said that the creatures of Ahura-Mazda, in the second, that the Amesha-Spentas, in the third, that the victorious Saosyant and his helpers, "shall restore the world, which will (thenceforth) never grow old and never die, never decaying and never rotting, ever living and ever increasing, and master of its wish, when *the dead will rise*, when life and immortality will come, and the world will be restored at its wish," etc. In the fragment translated by Mills we read, "Let the dead arise unhindered by these foes [i.e., Angra Manyu and the Dævas] and let bodily life be sustained in these lifeless bodies."

This evidence shows us that the Avesta manuscripts teach clearly a resurrection of the dead. It is to be noted, however, that the oldest of these manuscripts is dated in the year 1323 A.D.[7] Besides, as expert a critic as de Harlez maintains that this resurrection is spiritual and that the Pahlavi theology first introduced the notion of a *resurrectio carnis*. Still after having read the testimony of such experts as Windischmann, Spiegel, Haug, West, Moulton, Jackson, Mills, Geldner, Darmesteter, de Harlez, and Soderblom, and also the testimony of the Greek and other sources of information as to the religion of the ancient Persians,[8] one is driven to accept the opinion that the doctrine of the resurrection spoken of in these passages refers to a literal resurrection of the body and that the sixth Yasht at least was most probably written before the time of Alexander the Great. Moulton suggests that the doctrine itself was probably much older than these records, or even than the time of Zoroaster.[9] While accepting this suggestion, it is fair to say that by analogy it is also probable that the doctrine of the resurrection as propounded by Isaiah, Job, and Daniel, is much older than any one of these books.

Since the latest authorities on the Avesta [10] do not place Yasht xix among the Gathas, it may be well to quote part of what Moulton says on the *Saosyant*.[11] "The 'Consummation' of the

---

[7] Haug in West's edition of the *Language, Writings and Religion of the Parsis* in the chapter on the "Extant Pahlavi Literature," pp. 93-115.

[8] *Ibid.*, pp. 3-54.

[9] *Early Zoroastrianism*, p. 260.

[10] *Ibid.*, 343 f.

[11] *Ibid.*, 158 f.

Gathas involves a 'Renovation of the World,' a divine event towards which the whole creation is moving. It is accomplished by the present labours of 'those that will deliver,' the *saosyants*. In the Gathas these are simply Zarathushtra himself and his fellow-workers." [12] Saosyant comes from a root *sav* meaning "to benefit." [13] A Persian word corresponding to the Messiah (the anointed) of Daniel is not found in the Avesta, nor is "the Benefactor" called a prince or a prince of princes.

d. In the Old Testament outside of Daniel, a resurrection is referred to:

(1) In Isa. xxvi, 19, which reads: "Thy dead shall live, with my dead body shall they arise. Awake and sing, ye that dwell in dust; for thy dew is as the dew in the herbs, and the earth shall cast out the dead."

(2) In Ezek. xxxvii, the idea of a resurrection of the dead is clearly expressed in the vision of the dry bones.

(3) In Isa. liii, 10 it is said that when the Lord shall have made the soul of his servant an offering for sin, he shall see his seed, he shall prolong his days and the pleasure of the Lord shall prosper in his hands.

(4) In Job xvi, 13 ff. and xix, 25 the author "rises to the thought and throws out the wish that there may be release from sheol, and later on is assured that his redeemer (*gō'ēl*) lives, and that his flesh will see God. All this implies literal death, and then restoration of life after death, i.e., resurrection in the proper sense of the word."

(5) Finally, the actual raisings to life by Elijah and Elisha recorded in 1 Kings xvii, and 2 Kings iv, express a belief in the possibility, and in these cases in the fact, of a revivification of the dead.[14] The assumptions of Enoch and Elijah show that the Hebrews believed in a future life in a physical body, and

[13] Thus in *Yasna* 49.9 the helper (*saosyant*) who was created to bring deliverance is said by Moulton to have been Jamaspa the son-in-law of Vishtaspa.

[13] *Ibid.,* p. 145.

[14] For any further information as to the O.T. teaching on this subject, see the article by E. R. Bernard in Hastings' *Dict. of the Bible,* Vol. IV, p. 232.

the raising of Samuel that some at least thought that there was a life after death and that there could be a resumption of the well known physical body.

Judgment to Come

2. As to the origin of the idea of a judgment to come, we find that it also was prevalent among the Egyptians and Babylonians as well as among the Persians.

a. The Egyptians taught that there would be an "ethical test at the close of life, making life hereafter depend upon the character of the life lived on earth." [15] Erman cites the *Pyramid Texts* as follows: "Around thee stand the gods and call to thee 'rise, stand up' and thou awakest." [15a] This reminds us of Daniel. And, "Thou eatest the food of the gods. He (Re) places thee as the morning star in the midst of the field of Eavu." [16] "Those that failed to pass the judgment must lie hungry and thirsty in their graves and can not behold the sun." [17]

b. The Babylonians, also, believed in some kind of a judgment after death involving a separation and a determination of death or life to the departed.[18]

c. According to the Avesta,[19] Ahura Mazda will conduct a judgment after death in which he will be assisted by Zoroaster as advocate for the good.[20]

d. In the books of the Bible written before 550 B.C., we find frequent references to a judgment.[21]

Angelology

3. Regarding the Angelology:

a. There is no proof that the Hebrews derived their ideas con-

---

[15] Breasted, *History of Egypt,* p. 67 and Budge, *The Book of the Dead* I, xciii-cix.

[15a] *Op. cit. supra.*

[16] See also Naville, *The Old Egyptian Faith,* pp. 193-207.

[17] *Ibid.,* p. 105.

[18] See Zimmern, *Keilinschriften und das A. T.,* p. 637.

[19] Gatha, *Yasna* 46.

[20] *Early Zoroastrianism,* pp. 166, 374 f. See Tisdall, *Christianity and Other Faiths,* p. 133.

[21] See especially Isaiah, chapter two.

cerning angels from the Persians. The earliest portions of the Avesta, as we have it, were collected and edited in the time of the Sassanians (226 A.D.-637 A.D.). Parts of the collection, called the Gathas, most probably date back to about the year 600 B.C., or possibly even earlier. The word Amashaspand which is said to be equivalent to archangel does not occur in the Gathas, nor indeed in any of the earliest texts.[22] *Vohu Manu* "Good Thought" and other terms which came to be used in later Mazda-ism to denote the beings or ideas called Amashaspands are never used in the Gathas to denote persons, though at times they are personified, like the Hebrew wisdom in Proverbs. In the memoric stanza (*Yasna*, 47. 1) the names of all the future Amashaspands are found. The stanza as translated by Moul-ton [23] reads as follows: "By his Holy Spirit and by Best Thought, and Word, in accordance with Right, Mazda Ahura with Domin-ion and Piety shall give us Welfare and Immortality." It is absurd to suppose that Daniel's ideas of angels were derived from such abstractions or personifications as the Best Thought, Right, Dominion, Piety, Welfare, and Immortality of this passage. The verse sounds like, "I, Wisdom dwell with Prudence" of Prov-erbs. In Daniel, Michael, Gabriel and all the angels are real persons, the messengers of God and mediators between God and man, whereas in the Gathas Mills says that he can recall no passage in which the so-called angels "are not felt to mean exactly what they signify as words," i.e., Right, Piety, etc.[24]

The *Yashts*, the next oldest portions of the Avesta, (except the small prose portion called *Haptanghaite*) seem to have been composed in their original form about 400 B.C.,[25] or as Mills says, "in the third or fourth century before Christ." Here the attributes of God such as Right, Might, etc., have not merely been personified but are treated as objects of worship, just like the gods Ahura Mazda, Mithra, and Anahita. The only example of any one's being sent is in *Yasht* V, 8, 5, where Ahura Mazda

[22] It occurs first in the Haptanghaite. See Mills in *Sacred Books of the East*, xxxi, 281; Moulton, in *Early Zoroastrianism*, p. 121.
[23] *Early Zoroastrianism*, p. 376.
[24] *Sacred Books of the East*, Vol. XXXI, p. xxiv.
[25] *Early Zoroastrianism*, p. 78.

orders Anahita to come down from the stars to earth. Anahita was a god and not an Amashaspand. Zeus in Homer also sends his messengers and in the Babylonion Nabu is called the messenger of Bel. A word for messenger, or angel, never occurs in the Gathas or Yashts. Except for the compound word Ahura Mazda, no name compounded with the name for god and hence corresponding to Gabri-El and Micha-El, is found in the early Parsi literature. Daniel's angels are not numbered, nor worshipped, like the Amashaspands of the Yashts, Yasnas, and other literature of the Parsis. The general charge made by Prince of the dependence of Daniel's ideas on those of the Persians is so devoid of all direct evidence and even of probable inference, that one is filled with amazement that he could have made it. In support of this amazement, appeal is made to the works of Moulton,[26] and Darmesteter.[27]

b. The Assyrio-Babylonians believed in messengers of the gods and in good and evil spirits. Many of these had names. A man had his guardian angel, dwelling within him or going beside him. In a letter from the time of Hammurabi we find the phrase: "Thy guardian god hold thy head for good." A letter to the mother of Esarhaddon says: "A messenger of grace from Bel and Nebo goes at the side of the king." Nabopolassar says: Marduk "caused a good demon (*šedu damḳu*) to go at my side; in all that I do he causes my work to prosper." Further, the assembly of the Igigi and Anunnaki was a great council in which the destiny of the earth and of men was determined, as in the host of heaven in the vision of Micaiah recorded in 1 Ki. xxii, 19 and in the sons of God of Ps. xxix, 1 and elsewhere, and in the council of the holy ones of Ps. lxix, 6-8. The evil spirits among the Babylonians have distinctive class names such as *ekimmu, šedu* and *lilîtu.* Judging from the magical texts, the number of these spirits is incalculable. In the Creation Story (III, 67-71) Gaga is the messenger of his father Ansar; in the story of Nergal and Eriškigal a messenger (*mar šipri*) is sent by the gods to

---

[26] *Early Zoroastrianism,* especially the translation of the Gathas, pages 343-390.
[27] *The Zend-Avesta,* Part II, in the *Sacred Books of the East,* Vol. xxiii.

Eriškigal (1, 3). On the Reverse I, 5f the messenger of the gods (Nergal) is accompanied by fourteen others whose *names are given*. In Ishtar's *Descent to Hell*, Namtar is called the messenger (*sukallu*) of Eriškigal. See other examples in the story of Adapa.[28]

c. With regard to angels, *Daniel* gives the following information:

(1) The ordinary word for angel (מַלְאָךְ) occurs only in iii, 28 and vi, 22, both in the Aramaic part.[29] In the former passage it is used by Nebuchadnezzar; in the latter, by Daniel.

(2) In the dream of Nebuchadnezzar recorded in chapter iv, he says that he saw "a watchful one and a holy" (vss. 13, 23) coming down from heaven.[30] This messenger from heaven speaks of the decree of "the watchful ones" and the word of "the holy ones" (vs. 17).

(3) In vii, 10, speaking of the judgment by the Ancient of Days, Daniel says that he beheld "a thousand thousand ministering unto him and ten thousand times ten thousand standing before him." Whether these multitudes are angels or men, or angels and men, is not certain. Since, according to verses 1, 2 it was in a dream-vision by night that Daniel saw this judgment scene of the Most High, it may be looked upon as an enlargement of what he was accustomed to see at the court of Nebuchadnezzar, the greatest of earthly potentates. Or he may have been attempting to enumerate "all the

---

[28] *Keilinschriften und das Alte Testament*, VI, i.

[29] The root of this word does not occur in Hebrew or Aramaic, or Assyrian. It is common in Ethiopic in the sense "to send." It appears to have been used in Arabic also.

[30] עִיר is commonly derived from the verb עוּר "to be awake," found in Syriac also in this sense. Some would connect it with the Hebrew צִיר *messenger*, thus making it a synonym of מַלְאָךְ, the usual word in Hebrew, Aramaic, and Arabic for messenger, or angel. Thus in Obad. 1, "a messenger has been sent among the nations," (cf. Jer. xlix, 14). In Isa. xviii, 1, 2, "Ethiopia that sendeth צִירִים by the sea . . . Go ye swift מַלְאָכִים" etc., and in Prov. xiii, 17, the two words are in the parallel sentences. (Compare also Isa. lvii, 9 and Prov. xxv, 13). Philologically, it would be equally possible to connect עִיר with the Babylonian *siru* "exalted." Since Nebuchadnezzar is the one using this word, it would be entirely in harmony with Babylonian usage for him to speak of the person seen in his vision as "an exalted and illustrious one," i.e., *siru u kuddušu*.

host of heaven" of which Micaiah speaks in the vision of Jehovah's judgment recorded in I Kings xxii, 19, which even the critics
would scarcely put later than the sixth century B.C., and which the
writer of Kings places in the ninth.

(4) An angel named Gabriel is commissioned to explain a
vision to Daniel while the latter is in a deep sleep (viii, 16-18).
This same angel in the form of a man explains another vision in
ix, 21ff.

(5) A man clothed in fine linen and certain other nameless
angels are mentioned here and there, e.g., x, 5, xii, 6. So, also
the "saint" (קדוש) of viii, 13.

(6) Michael, "one of the chief princes," is said to have come to
help Daniel (x, 13). He is called Michael your (i.e. Israel's)
prince (x, 21) and "the great prince which standeth for the children of your people" (xii, 1), and it is said that he shall stand up
at the time of the end.

d. Of the Old Testament as a whole it may be said that the idea
of angels pervades the literature from the oldest to the latest. Of
evil angels Satan is mentioned as the name of one in Zech. iii, 1,
Job i, 6, and I Chr. xxi, 1; Lilith is found in Isa. xxxiv, 14 and
Shed in Deut. xxxii, 17 and Ps. cvi, 37. Of the good angels
Gabriel and Michael alone are mentioned by name and that in
Daniel only.[31]

It seems evident from the above facts that the ideas of Daniel
about angels can be accounted for *on their human side* by the preceding literature of the Old Testament reinforced by the Babylonian without recourse being had to Persian analogies.

Messiah

4. With regard to the idea of a Messiah,

a. It seems certain that no Egyptian or Babylonian text has as
yet revealed any hope or belief that any one of the gods was going
to intervene in the affairs of men for their redemption from sin

[31] These angels are mentioned by name in the New Testament also,
Michael in Jude 9 and again in Rev. xii, 7, and Gabriel in Luke i, 26. See
Article "Angel" in Hastings' *Dictionary* by A. B. Davidson and the chapter
on "Angels and Demons" in *The Religion of Israel* by Barton.

and suffering and death.   The only ancient records,—from any nation at least that came into contact with the Jews—which give any such idea are those of the Zoroastrians.   It is said in *Yasht* xix §§ 88, 89 that the prophet Saosyant the Victorious and his assistant will make a new world and that at his will the dead will rise again and immortal life will come.[32]

b. The Old Testament, however, is full of the idea of redemption from sin and its consequences.   Daniel and Psalm ii, are the only parts in which the agent in this redemption is called Messiah and Daniel the only one in which he is called the Prince; but the idea of a redeemer from sin and of God's appearing at the end of the world for judgment and to establish a kingdom is found all through the Old Testament.

DANIEL AND ENOCH

The assumption is groundless, that Daniel and the earlier part of Enoch approximate so closely in their treatment of the four subjects under discussion as to make certain the conclusion that they are from the same time.   This will appear from a comparison of the teachings of Daniel on angels, resurrection, judgment, and the Messiah with what we find in other Old Testament works, in Enoch and in the other works of the second and first centuries B.C. and in the New Testament and other works of the first century A.D.   In making these comparisons we shall follow the divisions and dates of the Book of Enoch as given by Charles.[33] We shall give the teachings on these four subjects of (a) Daniel, (b) the rest of the Old Testament, (c) Enoch and other extra-canonical works of the second and first centuries B.C., and (d) the New Testament and other works of the first century A.D.

Resurrection

a. Daniel refers to the resurrection but once, that is, in xii, 2: "And many of them that sleep in the dust of the earth shall awake, some to everlasting life, and some to shame and everlasting contempt."

---

[32] Tisdall p. 110. See above under "Resurrection" (pp. 125 f.).
[33] In the *Apocrypha and Pseudepigrapha of the Old Testament* II, 170.

b. Of the rest of the *Old Testament*, the fifty-seven psalms which Reuss, Cheyne, or other critics assign to the second century B.C., do not once mention a resurrection, nor does Ecclesiastes, nor the Song, nor any other portion of Scripture which is placed in this period by the critics. The references to the resurrection have been discussed above.

c. The Book of Enoch, etc.

(1) Of the four parts of the Book of Enoch thought to have been written in the second century B.C.:

(a) The *Book of Noah*, containing all or parts of sixteen chapters, says nothing about a resurrection.

(b) The only reference to a resurrection in the First Section of *Enoch* is in the passage (xxv), where it is said that the fruit of a fragrant tree shall after the great judgment be given to the righteous and holy elect and they shall live a long life on earth.

(c) The Second Section of *Enoch* (lxxxiii-xc) contains only a "veiled reference to the resurrection." In xc, 33, it is said that all that had been destroyed and dispersed assembled in the Lord's house, and that the Lord rejoiced because they were all good.

(d) The Third Section of *Enoch* (lxxii-lxxxii) does not mention a resurrection.

(2) The *Testaments of the XII Patriarchs* (written, according to Charles, between 137 and 107 B.C.) speak of the resurrection oftener than any other pre-Christian book. Thus in Benjamin x, 6-8, we read: "Ye shall see Enoch, Noah, and Shem, Abraham, Isaac, and Jacob, rising on the right hand in gladness. Then shall we also rise, each over our own tribe, and we shall worship the heavenly king. Then shall we all be changed, some into glory, and some into shame." In Simeon x, 2, the patriarch says: "Then shall I arise." In Zebulon x, 2, he says: "Then shall I arise again in the world." In Judah xxv, 1, 4 we read: "And after these things, shall Abraham and Isaac and Jacob arise unto life" and "those who have died in grief shall arise in joy and they who are put to death for the Lord's sake shall arise."

(3) The *Book of Jubilees* has given up all hope of a resurrection. According to Charles this book was written between 153 and 105 B.C.

(4) The parts of the *Sibylline Oracles* supposed to have been written in the second century B.C., do not mention a resurrection.

(5) The so-called *Addenda to the Book of Esther*, the *Book of Baruch*, the *Epistle of Jeremiah*, the *Story of Zerubbabel*, the *Additions to the Book of Daniel, Tobit, Judith* and *1 Maccabees* make no reference to a resurrection.

(6) The *Wisdom of Solomon* may make a negative reference to it in ii, 1, where it represents the ungodly as reasoning within themselves but not rightly: "Our life is short and tedious, and in the death of a man there is no remedy; neither was there any man known to have returned from the grave."

(7) *Ecclesiasticus* makes no reference to a general resurrection.

(8) *Second Maccabees* shows a highly developed view of a resurrection. Thus in vii, 9 the second of the seven brethren who were slain by Antiochus for not eating swine's flesh says at his last gasp: "The king of the world shall raise us up, who have died for his laws, unto everlasting life." In verse 14, the third brother says: "It is good, being put to death by men, to look for help from God to be raised up again by him; as for thee [meaning king Antiochus], thou shalt have no resurrection to life." In vs. 23, the mother exhorts her last child saying: "Doubtless the Creator of the world will give you breath and life again." In xii, 43-45 Judas is said to have been mindful of the resurrection, "for if he had not hoped that they that were slain should have risen again, it had been superfluous and vain to pray for the dead." And also, "he perceived that there was great favour laid up for those that did godly." Lastly, in xiv, 46 Razis "plucked out his bowels, calling upon the Lord of life and spirit to restore them to him again."

(9) The Fifth Section of *Enoch* says merely that "the righteous sleep a long sleep and have nought to fear" (c. 5.).

(10) The Sixth Section of *Enoch* says in li, 1 that "the earth shall give back that which has been entrusted to it"; and in lxi, 5 that the righteous and the elect "shall return and stay themselves on the day of the Elect One."

(11) The Third and Fourth Books of *Maccabees*, the Fourth

Section of *Enoch,* and the *Psalms of Solomon,* do not mention the resurrection.

d. The Literature from the First Century A.D.

(1) At least seventeen of the *New Testament* books speak of a resurrection. Two of them, 1 Cor. xv, and Rev. xx, enlarge upon the nature of it.

(2) The *Testimony of Hezekiah* speaks of the resurrection of the beloved, (iii, 18).

(3) The *Vision of Isaiah* mentions the resurrection of the righteous, (ix, 17).

(4) The *Salathiel Section* of Fourth Ezra written about 100 A.D., implies a resurrection, (v, 37, 45).

(5) The *Zadokite Fragments* (written about 40 A.D.), the *Ezra Apocalypse,* the *Son of Man Vision,* the *Ezra Piece,* the *Eagle Vision,* the *Martyrdom of Isaiah,* the *Assumption of Moses* and apparently *Fourth Maccabees* do not refer to a resurrection.

Judgment

a. Daniel speaks of a judgment only in vii, 10, 22, 26. In verse 10 we read: "The judgment was set and the books were opened"; in vs. 22, "The Ancient of days came, and judgment was given to the saints of the Most High," and in vs. 26, "the judgment shall sit," etc.

b. The only references to a judgment in the other parts of the *Old Testament* are:

(1) Isa. xlii, 1-4 where it is said that Jehovah's servant "shall bring forth judgment to the gentiles," "shall bring forth judgment unto truth," and "shall set judgment on the earth."

(2) Ps. ix, 7, 8 where we read that Jehovah "hath prepared his throne for judgment and he shall judge the world in righteousness, he shall minister judgment to the people in uprightness."

(3) Ps. i, 5, "the wicked shall not stand in the judgment."

(4) Joel iii, 9-17, Ps. lxxvi, 9, lxviii, 14, speak of a judgment on the nations.

(5) Of the fifty-seven psalms assigned by one or another critic to the second century B.C., only Ps. lxxvi, 9 refers to a judgment.

(6) Ecclesiastes refers to it (iii, 17) in the words, "I had said

in my heart that God will judge the righteous and the wicked";
and in xii, 14, that he will bring every work into judgment and
every secret thing whether it be good or whether it be evil.
In iii, 20 he says that men shall return to dust and in xii, 7
that the dust shall return to the earth as it was and the spirit to
God who gave it.

c. The *Book of Enoch*, etc.

(1) In the *Book of Noah* we read of "the day of the great
judgment" (x, 6) when Azazel "shall be cast into the fire"; and
in x, 11, 12 that Semjaza and his associate angels are to be
bound fast till the day of their judgment, the judgment that is
for ever and ever.

(2) In the First Section of *Enoch* it is said (xvi, 1) that the
giants shall destroy until the day of the consummation, the great
judgment over the Watchers and the godless; in xxv, 4, that no
judgment, when the Holy Great One, the Lord of Glory, the
mortal is permitted to touch the fragrant tree of life until the great
Eternal King shall sit on his throne and take vengeance on all
and bring everything to its consummation for ever; and in xxvii,
2, there is mention of an accursed valley which shall be the place
of judgment (or habitation).

(3) In Section Two of *Enoch* we are told (xc, 20-27) that
"a throne was erected in the pleasant land and the Lord of the
sheep sat himself thereon and one took all the sealed books and
opened those books before the Lord of the sheep." "And the
judgment was held first over the stars and they were judged
and found guilty and likewise the seventy shepherds to whom the
sheep had been delivered were judged and found guilty and last
of all the blinded sheep were judged and found guilty and all were
cast into a fiery abyss and burned."

(4) The Third Section of *Enoch* does not mention the judgment.

(5) The *Testaments of the XII Patriarchs* mention the judgment three times. Benj. x, 8, 9 reads: "For the Lord judges
Israel first for the unrighteousness which they have committed
and then so shall he judge all the gentiles"; and Levi. iii, 3 says
that "in the second (or third?) heaven are the hosts of the armies

which are ordained for the day of judgment," and in iv, 1 it is said that "the Lord shall execute judgment upon the sons of men."

(6) The *Book of Jubilees* speaks of "the day of the great judgment" (xxiii, 11); and apparently it is on this day that the righteous "shall see all their judgments and all their curses on their enemies," (xxiii, 30).

(7) The *Sibylline Books* speak of "the judgment of the great king, the deathless God" (iii, 56).

(8) The *Addenda to Esther,* the *Book of Baruch,* the *Epistle of Jeremiah,* the *Story of Zerubbabel,* the *Additions to the Book of Daniel, Tobit* and *1 Maccabees* do not refer to the judgment.

(9) *Judith* says: "Woe to the nations that rise up against my kindred! The Lord Almighty will take vengeance of them in the day of judgment" (xvi, 17).

(10) The *Wisdom of Solomon* says that the souls of the righteous "shall judge the nations" (iv, 8).

(11) *Second Maccabees* mentions a judgment (vii, 35, 36), but it is doubtful whether the passage refers to a judgment in the present life or hereafter.

(12) The Fourth Section of *Enoch* speaks of the day of judgment (lxxxi, 4).

(13) The Fifth Section of *Enoch* speaks of a final judgment with the destruction of the present heavens and earth and the creation of new ones (xci, 14-16).

(14) The Sixth Section of *Enoch* says there will be a judgment of the righteous and the wicked, on angels and on men (xcvi, 2-4, xlviii, 2).

(15) *Third and Fourth Maccabees* are silent on the subject.

d. In the literature of the First Century, A.D.

(1) All of the *Gospels,* the *Acts,* the *Revelation,* and most of the *Epistles* speak of a judgment.

(2) The *Testament of Hezekiah* speaks of the judgment once in iv, 18.

(3) The *Vision of Isaiah* mentions it in x, 12.

(4) The *Assumption of Moses* describes how the Heavenly One will arise from his royal throne and amid the disturbance

of earth and sea and sun and stars will punish the gentiles and Israel shall be exalted (x, 3-10).

(5) The *Son of Man Vision* tells how God's Son is to judge and to destroy the nations of the earth and to defend the people of Israel (xiii, 37, 49).

(6) The *Eagle Vision* speaks of the Messiah's making the kings of Rome alive for judgment and then destroying them (xii, 12).

(7) The *Salathiel Section* speaks of the judgment and of punishment and salvation after death (vii, 67, 70, 73, 102-105, viii, 38, 61, x, 16).

(8) The *Martyrdom of Isaiah,* the *Ezra Apocalypse,* and the *Ezra Piece,* do not mention a judgment.

(9) In *Second Baruch,* there is a long and detailed account of the judgment extending from xxiv, 1 to xxx, 1.

(10) In the *Zadokite Fragments* the judgment is probably referred to in ii, 4, where it says that with God are "power and might and great fury with flames of fire wherein are all the angels of destruction." (Compare i, 2 and ix, 12.)

(11) *Philo* and *Josephus* are silent on the subject.

Messiah

a. Daniel ix, 25, 26 is one of the two Old Testament passages where the expected Saviour of Israel is called *Messiah.* The verses read: "Know therefore and understand that from the going forth of the commandment to restore and to build Jerusalem unto the Messiah the Prince shall be seven weeks, and three score and two weeks: the street shall be built again, and the wall, even in troublous times. And after three score and two weeks shall Messiah be cut off, but not for himself . . . " In viii, 25 the king of fierce countenance is represented as standing up "against the Prince of princes." In ii, 34, 45, the deliverer is likened to a stone cut out without hands that smote and broke in pieces the image of iron and clay. In iii, 25, he may possibly be the Son of God thus spoken of. In vii, 13, he is likened to a son of man and comes to the Ancient of days and is given dominion and glory and a kingdom which shall not pass away. It is possible, also, that Michael the prince of x, 21 and the Michael of xii, 1 is none other than the Messiah himself.

b. The Rest of the *Old Testament.*

(1) Ps. ii, (which Driver thinks to be pre-exilic and which neither Reuss, Cheyne nor W. Robertson Smith places as late as the Maccabean times) agrees with Daniel in calling the Son of God the *Messiah.*

(2) Already in the seed of the woman of Gen. iii, 15 and in the Shiloh of xlix, 10 we have intimations of the coming king who should bruise the head of the serpent. These passages are both assigned to J.

(3) In Num. xxiv, which is assigned to JE, the Messiah is prefigured in the star which was to come out of Jacob, and the sceptre which should arise out of Israel.

(4) The Prince of Peace of Isa. ix, 6, 7 and the root that should come forth out of the stem of Jesse and the branch out of his roots of Isa. xi, 1, also refer to him. Both of these passages are assigned by the critics to the genuine Isaiah.

(5) The ruler in Israel who, according to Mi. v, 2, should come forth from Bethlehem of Judah must refer to the Messiah, as must also the "Lord" of Ps. cx, 1.

(6) In the writers contemporary with Daniel, the Branch of Jer. xxiii, 5, 6 and xxxiii, 15-17 and the Shepherd of Ezek. xxxiv, 23-31 clearly indicate the Saviour to come.

(7) Zechariah, who wrote but a few years after the time of Daniel, speaks of him as the Branch (iii, 8, vi, 12), the Shepherd (xi, 16, xiii, 7), the fountain opened for sin (xiii, 1), the one from the house of David who was to be pierced (xii, 10) and the King who was to come to Zion (ix, 9) and the one whose price was thirty pieces of silver (xi, 12).

(8) Of the fifty-seven psalms assigned by one or more of the critics to the Maccabean period only cx, 1, and cxviii, 22 refer to a Messiah. Driver [34] thought that Ps. cx, "may be presumed to be pre-exilic." Reuss, Cheyne and W. Robertson Smith class Ps. cxviii, as Maccabean, to which date Cheyne assigns Ps. cx, also. The verse "The Lord said unto my Lord," etc. is

[34] *L.O.T.,* p. 384.

attributed expressly by the New Testament writers and by the Lord himself to David. See Matt. xxii, 49, Mk. xii, 36, Lk. xx, 42, Acts ii, 34.

  c. The *Book of Enoch,* etc.

  (1) The *Book of Noah* and the First and Third Sections of the *Book of Enoch* are silent as to a Messiah.

  (2) The Second Section of *Enoch* speaks of a white bull with large horns whom all the beasts of the field and all the birds of the air feared and to whom they made petitions all the time (xc, 37).

  (3) The *Testaments of the XII Patriarchs* says in Judah xxiv, 5, 6: "Then shall the sceptre of my kingdom shine forth, and from your root shall arise a stem, and from it shall grow a rod of righteousness to the gentiles, to judge and save all that call upon the Lord." In Judah xxiv, 1-3, we read: "And after these things shall a star arise to you from Jacob in peace and a man shall arise like the sun of righteousness, walking with the sons of men in meekness and righteousness and no sin shall be found in him," etc. In Levi viii, 14 we read that "a king shall arise in Judah and shall be beloved as a prophet of the Most High," etc. Dan v, 10, says that the salvation of the Lord shall arise from Levi. Joseph xix, 11 says: "Honour Levi and Judah, for from them shall arise unto you one who saveth Israel." Zebulun ix, 8 reads: "After these things shall arise unto you the Lord Himself, the light of righteousness." In Levi xviii, 1-14 there is a long and beautiful description of the new priest to whom all the words of the Lord shall be revealed.

  (4) One place only in *Jubilees* refers to the Messiah. In xxxi, 18, 19, in a passage recording an alleged blessing of Levi and Judah, by Isaac, it is said of Judah in evident imitation of Gen. xlix, 10 that one of his sons should be a prince over the sons of Jacob and that in him should be the help of Jacob and the salvation of Israel.

  (5) The *Sibylline Books* have a long passage (Book III, 652-818) containing an account of a king sent by God from the sunrise who shall give every land relief from the bane of war in obedience to the good ordinances of the mighty God.

(6) *Ecclesiasticus, Wisdom, Tobit, Judith,* and *1 Maccabees,* do not mention a Messiah.

(7) The Fifth Section of *Enoch* speaks of a kingdom where God and his Son will be united for ever with the children of earth (cv, 2).

(8) In the Sixth Section of *Enoch* the Messiah is called:

(a) The Son of Man (xlvi, 2-4, xlviii, 2, 9, xlix, 2, 4, li, 5, 6, lii, 6, 9, liii, 6, lv, 4, lxi, 5, 8, lxii, 1).

(b) God's Anointed (xlviii, 10).

(c) The Elect One (xlv, 4).

(d) He will have universal dominion, sit on the throne of his glory, and judge angels and men.

(9) The *Psalms of Solomon* call the Messiah, the king, the son of David and the servant of God (Ps. xviii, 6).

(10) The Second, Third, and Fourth Books of *Maccabees* and the Fourth Section of *Enoch* are silent on this subject.

d. The Literature of the First Century A.D.

(1) The Messiah is mentioned in every book of the *New Testament.*

(2) The *Testament of Hezekiah* speaks of "Jesus the Lord" (x, 4, 13) and of the "Beloved" (iii, 17, 18, iv, 3, 6, 9, 13).

(3) The *Vision of Isaiah* mentions "the Messiah" (vii, 8, 12), "the Beloved" (vii, 17, 23), "His Beloved the Christ" (viii, 18), "His Beloved the Son" (viii, 15), "the Only Begotten" (vii, 37), "the Elect One" (viii, 7), "Lord God the Lord Christ who will be called Jesus" (ix, 5), "Lord who will be called Christ" (ix, 13), "Lord Christ" (ix, 17, 32), "That One" (ix, 26, 38), "This One" (ix, 31), "a Certain One" (ix, 27).

(4) The *Son of Man Vision* of Fourth Ezra calls the Messiah "God's Son" (xiii, 32, 37) and says he is to judge and to destroy the earth (xiii, 37, 49) and to defend the people of Israel (xiii, 49).

(5) The *Ezra Piece* speaks of Ezra's translation to be with God's Son, but otherwise does not refer to the Son.

(6) The *Eagle Vision* mentions a Messiah who is to spring from the seed of David and make the kings of Rome alive for judgment and destruction (xii, 32).

(7) The *Martyrdom of Isaiah,* the *Assumption of Moses,* the *Ezra Apocalypse,* and the *Salathiel Section* do not mention a personal Messiah.

(8) The *Zadokite Fragments* say that God through his Messiah will make known his Holy Spirit (ii, 10). Also, ix, 3 (in Text B) quotes Zech. xiii, 7 where the shepherd refers to the Messiah; and in ix, 8 the scepter of Gen. 49, 10 "appears to denote the Messiah." In ix, 10 (B), 29 (B), the sword of the Messiah is spoken of.

Angels

a. The *Book of Daniel.*

(1) In iii, 25, Nebuchadnezzar says that he saw four *men* in the midst of the fire and that the form of the fourth was like to a "son of gods" (*cp.* Gen. vi, 3). In iii, 28, this fourth man is called an angel.

(2) In iv, 17 we read of "the decree of the watchers and the demand by the word of the holy ones"; and in iv, 23 it speaks of "a watcher and a holy one coming down from heaven" and announcing the decree.

(3) In vi, 22 God is said to have "sent his angel who shut the mouths of the lions."

(4) In vii, 10, "a thousand thousands minister unto Him (the Ancient of days) and ten thousand times ten thousand stand before Him."

(5) In x, 5, Daniel saw "one man" clothed in linen, etc. So, also, xii, 6, 7.

(6) In x, 16, one like the similitude of the sons of a man (Adam) touched his lips, etc.

(7) In x, 18, one like the appearance of a man (Adam) came and strengthened him.

(8) In viii, 13, Daniel heard "one holy one" speaking to "another holy one."

(9) In viii, 16, Gabriel is mentioned. In ix, 21, he is called the *man* Gabriel (*cp.* Gen. xxxii, 24).

(10) In x, 13, 21, xii, 1, Michael the prince or "the great prince" or "one of the chief princes" is mentioned.

b. In the other Books of the *Old Testament* we find:

(1) The angel of Jehovah, (Gen. xvi, 7, 9, 10, 11, xxii, 11, 15, Ex. iii, 2, Num. xxii, 22, 23, 24, 25, 26, 27, 31, 32, 34, 35, Jud. ii, 1, 4, v, 23, vi, 11, 12, 21*bis*, 22*bis*, xiii, 3, 13, 15, 16*bis*, 17, 18, 20, 21*bis*, 2 Sam. xxiv, 16, 1 Ki. xix, 7, 2 Ki. i, 3, 15, xix, 35, 1 Chr. xxi, 12, 15, 16, 18, 30, Ps. xxxiv, 8, xxxv, 5, 6, Isa, xxxvii, 36, Zech. i, 11, 12, iii, 1, 5, 6, xii, 8, Mal. ii, 7.)

(2) The angel of (the) God, (Gen. xxi, 17, xxxi, 11, Ex. xiv, 19, Jud. vi, 20, xiii, 6, 9, 1 Sam. xxi, 9, 2 Sam. xiv, 17, 20, xix, 27).

(3) The (an) angel (Gen. xlviii, 16, Ex. xxiii, 20, xxxiii, 2, Nu. xx, 16, 2 Sam. xxiv, 16*bis*, 17, 1 Kgs. xiii, 18, xix, 5, 1 Chr. xxi, 15*bis*, xv, 20-27, 2 Chr. xxxii, 21, Hos. xii, 4, Zech. i, 9, 13, 14, ii, 2, 7, iii, 3, iv, 1, 4, 5, v, 5, 10, vi, 4, 5).

(4) His (mine) angel (Gen. xxiv, 17, 40, Ex. xxiii, 23, xxxii, 34, Mal. iii, 1.)

(5) Angels (of God), (Gen. xix, 1, 15, xxviii, 12, xxxii, 2.

(6) His angels (Ps. xci, 11, ciii, 20, civ, 4, cxlviii, 2).

(7) Evil angels (Ps. lxxviii, 49).

(8) Angel of his presence (Isa. lxiii, 9).

(9) Angel of the Covenant (Mal. iii, 1).

(10) Angel of the Lord of hosts (Mal. ii, 7).

(11) Cherubim (Gen. iii, 24, Ps. xviii, 10, Ez. ix, 3, x, 1, (*et passim*), xi, 22, xxviii, 14, 16).

(12) Seraphim (Isa. vi, 2, 6).

(13) A man clothed with linen (Ez. ix, 2, 3, 11, x, 2, 6, 7).

(14) Sons of God (Gen. vi, 3 (?), Deut. xxxii, 19, Job i, 6, ii, 1).

(15) Gods (Ps. viii, 6).

(16) Twenty thousand thousands of angels (שנאן), Ps. lxviii, 18).

(17) Mighty (angels?) (Ps. lxxviii, 25, Joel iii, 11).

(18) Holy ones, (Deut. xxxiii, 3 (?), Job v. 1, xv, 15, Zech. xiv, 5, Ps. lxxxix, 6, 8).

(19) Sons of the Mighty (Ps. xxix, 1, lxxxix, 6).

(20) Watchmen (Isa. lxii, 6).

(21) The host of the high ones (Isa. xxiv, 21).

(22) Morning stars (Job xxxviii, 7).

(23) Members of God's council (Job i, Ps. lxxxix, 7, 1 Ki. xxii).

(24) Guardian angels (Ps. xxxiv, 8, xci, 11).

(25) Intercessors (Job. v, 1).

(26) Punishers of the wicked (Ps. lxxviii, 49).

(27) (The) Satan (Zech. iii, 1, 2*bis*, Job, i-ii (*passim*), Ps. cix, 6, 1 Chr. xxi, 1).

(28) Demons (*shedim*, Ps. cvi, 37).

(29) Satyr (?*sa'ir*, Isa. xxxiv, 14).

(30) Night Monster (*Lilith*, Isa. xxxiv, 14).

(31) Deep (?*Tehom* Deut. xxxiii, 13, Ps. cxlviii, 7).

(32) Rahab (Isa. li, 9, Ps. lxxxix, 10, Job ix, 13, xxvi, 12).

(33) Leviathan (Job iii, 8, Ps. lxxiv, 14).

(34) Azazel (Lev. xvi, 8, 10*bis*, 26).

(35) Princes of God (LXX version of Deut. xxxii, 8).

(36) Ecclesiastes and the Song of Songs do not speak of angels and in all the fifty-seven psalms assigned by one or more critics to the second century, B.C., we find angels referred to only in Psalm cxlviii, 2.

c. The *Book of Enoch*, etc.

(1) The *Testaments of the XII Patriarchs* mention Satan and Beliar by name. They speak, also, of the angel of God, of angels of the presence, of watchers, and archangels.

(2) The *Book of Jubilees* mentions by name Mastema (Satan) and Beliar. It speaks, also, of angels of the presence, and of guardian angels and of angels of the wood, fire, clouds, etc. It describes the creation and circumstances of the fallen angels, their marrying the daughters of men, their judgment and punishment.

(3) The *Sibylline Books* mention the angel Beliar.

(4) The *Book of Noah* is almost entirely an imaginative explanation of the "sons of God" of Gen. vi, 2, giving their names, duties, teachings, sins, judgment, and punishment.

(a) vi, 7, 8 gives the names of the eighteen chiefs of tens, and lxix, 2, 3, the names of twenty-one chiefs over hundreds and over fifties and over tens. In alphabetical order the eighteen are

Ananel, Armaros, Arakiba, Asael, Baraqijal, Batarel, Danel, Ezeqeel, Jomjael, Kokabiel, Rameel, Samiazaz, Samsapeel, Sariel, Satarel, Tamiel, Turel, Zaqiel. Over all these Semjaza was chief. In lxvi, 2, 3 the names are given as, Armaros, Armen, Artaqifa, Azazel (two of this name), Baraqiel, Batarjal, Busasejal, Danjal, Hananel Jetrel, Kokabel, Neqael, Rumael, Rumjal, Samjaza, Simapesiel, Tumael, Turael, Turel (two of this name). To these are added in verses 4-12 the names Asbeel, Gadreel, Jeqon, Kasdja, and Penemue. Allowing for differences of spelling we have here the names of thirty-seven fallen angels.

(b) In ix, 1 four good angels are named (Michael, Raphael, Uriel, and Gabriel), who are called "holy ones" (ix, 3, lx, 4). These intercede with the Lord of the Ages for the souls of men (ix, 3, 4). Another good angel, Phanuel, is named in liv, 6.

(c) The "angel of peace," (liv, 4, lx, 24).

(d) An "angel of punishment," (lxvi, 1).

(e) An angel without name, (lx. 4, 9, 11, lxviii, 5).

(f) Spirits of the hoar-frost, hail, and snow are called angels, (lx, 17); also, spirits of the mist, the rain, and the dew, (18-21).

(g) Angels without names, (x, 7, cvi, 6, lxvii, 4, 7, 11, 12, lxviii, 2).

(h) Watchers, (x, 7, 9, 15).

(i) "Angels, children of the heaven," (vi, 2). These are said to have been two hundred in number (vi, 6).

(j) The angels are a thousand thousands and a thousand times ten thousand (lx, 1).

(k) "Satans" are mentioned in lxv, 6 where they seem to be distinguished from the angels.

(l) The duties, or functions, of the bad angels are mentioned at length in viii, 3, and of angels in xx.

(m) The duties of the good angels are mentioned in ix, 1, 4, x, 1, lx, 2, 21, 23, lxvi, 2, lxvii, 2, lxix, 4f.

(5) In the First Section of the *Book of Enoch*.

(a) Of the evil angels, Azazel only is mentioned (xiii, 1).

(b) There are some holy angels "who watch" (xx, 2-8), and whose names are Michael, Raphael, Uriel, and Raguel, Saraqiel,

Gabriel and Remiel. See also xxiv, 6, xx, 3, 6, xxxii, 6, xix, 1, xxiii, 4, xxxiii, 4, xxvii, 2, xxi, 5, 9.

(c) Watchers are mentioned (xvi, 1), who are called holy (xv, 9), eternal (xiv, 1), heavenly (xii, 4), children of heaven (xiv, 3, xii, 2, 3, 4, 10, 15²).

(d) Holy one (xiv, 25), the most holy ones (xiv, 23), seven holy angels (xx, 2-8).

(e) Seven stars of heaven (xxi, 6).

(f) Angels (alone) (xxxvi, 4) prisons of angels (xxi, 10, xiv, 21).

(g) Giants (=evil spirits) (xv, 8).

(h) "Ten thousand times ten thousand" angels (xxi, 24).

(6) The Second Section of *Enoch* calls Azazel a star (lxxxvi, 1), speaks of the angels of heaven (lxxxiv, 4) and calls the angels "white men" (lxxxvii, 2). Probably, also, the "seventy shepherds" of lxxxix, 59 are angels.

(7) In the Third Section of *Enoch* angels are mentioned once (xci, 15) and holy angels once (xciii, 2).

(8) The *Song of the Three Children* speaks twice of the angel of the Lord (vss. 26, 37).

(9) *Susannah* mentions the angel of the Lord (vs. 45) and the angel of God (vss. 55, 59).

(10) *Bel and the Dragon* mentions the angel of the Lord in vss. 36, 39.

(11) *Tobit* mentions:

(a) Raphael by name (iii, 17, xii, 15).

(b) Guardian angels (v. 17, 22).

(c) Holy angels (xi, 14).

(d) Seven angels (xii, 15).

(e) Asmodeus, an evil demon (iii, 8, and elsewhere).

(12) *Ecclesiasticus* refers to angels in xxxix, 28, xli, 2, 45, xlviii, 1, but only in passages cited from the canonical books of the Old Testament.

(13) The *Addenda to Esther* represent Esther as saying that the king of Persia appeared to her as an angel of God, (xv, 13).

(14) The *Epistle of Jeremiah* mentions an angel in vs. 7.

(15) The *Book of Baruch* mentions devils (iv, 7).

(16) The *Book of Wisdom* mentions the devil (ii, 24) and speaks of angels' food (xvi, 20).

(17) *Judith*, *1 Maccabees*, the *Prayer of Manasseh*, and the *Story of Zerubbabel* are silent as to angels.

(18) The Sixth Section of *Enoch* (xxxvii-lxxi) speaks of:

(a) A righteous angel (xxxix, 5).

(b) Four angels of the presence (Michael, Raphael, Sahiel, and Phanuel) (xl, 9).

(c) Thousands of thousands and ten thousand times ten thousand (xl, 1).

(d) The angel of peace (xliii, 3, lii, 3, liv, 4).

(e) Angels of punishment (liii, 3, lvi, 1).

(f) Satan (liii, 3, 6).

(g) Azazel (liii, 5, lv, 4).

(h) The host of God, Cherubim, Seraphim, and Ophannim (lxi, 10).

(i) The holy ones (lxi, 10).

(19) *Fourth Maccabees,* and the *Psalms of Solomon* are silent on the subject of angels.

(20) In *Second Maccabees* "the terrible rider" and the two men notable in strength who smote at and scourged Heliodorus were probably angels (iii, 25, 26), as were also "the five comely men upon horses" of x, 29, and "the one in white clothing" of xi, 8. Judas, in xv, 22 refers to the angel who smote the host of Sennacherib and prays for God to "send a good angel" to go before the Jewish army.

(21) *Third Maccabees* speaks of two angels glorious and terrible who appeared to Eleazar the high priest.

(22) The Fourth Section of *Enoch* speaks of seven holy ones (lxxxi, 5) and gives the names of the four leaders who divide the four parts of the year and their three followers. These seven are named Milkiel, Hel'emmelek, Mel'ejal, Narel, Adnar'el, Ijasusa'el, 'Elome'el. The leaders under them are called Birka'el, Zelebs'el, Hilujaseph, Gida'yal, Ke'el, He'el, and Asfa'el (lxxxi, 13-20). Uriel also is mentioned in lxxiv, 2, lxxv, 3, 4, and is the one who shows things to Enoch.

(23) The Fifth Section of *Enoch* (xci-civ) mentions the holy

angels (xci, 2) and the wicked (xci, 15). Angels are said to place the prayers of the righteous for a memorial before the Most High (xcix, 3, c, 1) to gather the works for judgment (c. 4) and to be guardians over the righteous (c. 5).

d. The Literature of the First Century A.D.

(1) The *Martyrdom of Isaiah* speaks of the angel Sammael (i, 11, ii, 1) Sammael Malchira (1, 8), Beliar (i, 8, 9, ii, 4, iii, 11, 51), and Satan (ii, 2, 7) and of Satan's angels (ii, 2).

(2) The *Testament of Hezekiah* mentions Sammael (iii, 13) Beliar (iii, 13, iv, 2, 16), Beliar and his armies (iv, 14) and the angels and armies of the holy ones (iv, 14).

(3) The *Vision of Isaiah* mentions:

(a) By name, Sammael (vii, 9) and Satan (xi, 43, vii, 9).

(b) An angel who was sent to make the prophet see (vi, 3, vii, 11, 21, 25).

(c) A glorious angel (vii, 2).

(d) Angel of death (ix, 16, x, 14).

(e) Angels about the throne (vii, 14-16, 19).

(f) Angels of fire and Sheol (x, 10).

(g) Angels of the air (x, 30).

(h) Angels of Satan (vii, 9).

(i) Sammael and his hosts (vii, 9).

(j) Angel of the Holy Spirit (vii, 23, ix, 36, 39, 40, x, 4, xi, 4, 33).

(k) Princes, angels, and powers of the world (x, 12).

(l) Princes and powers of this world (x, 15).

(m) Angels (alone) (vii, 22, 27, 37, ix, 6, 28, 29, 42, viii, 2, 15, 19, x, 19).

(4) The *Zadokite Fragments* mention the angels of destruction (ii, 4).[35] Belial, also, is named in vi, 9, 10, vii, 19, ix, 12.

(5) The *Assumption of Moses* mentions Satan and an angel (x, 2).

(6) The *Ezra Apocalypse* mentions only the angel who came to speak to him.

(7) The *Son of Man Vision,* the *Ezra Piece,* and the *Eagle Vision* and the parts added by the Redactor do not mention angels.

[35] Said by Charles to be an interpolation.

(8) The *Salathiel Section* mentions:
(a) The angel who had been sent unto him (v. 31, vii, 10, 29).
(b) Armies of angels (vi, 3).
(c) Angels who guard the souls of the righteous (vii, 85, 95).
(d) By name Jeramiel (iv, 36) and Uriel (v, 20, x, 28).

(9) The *Apocalypse of Baruch* speaks of the creation of the angels (xxi, 6), of their fall (lvi, 11-13), of armies of them (xlviii, 10, li, 11, lix, 10), of the angel of death (xxi, 6), and names Ramiel (lv, 3, lxiii, 6).

(10) The *New Testament* books mention Michael, Gabriel, Satan, and Beelzebub.[36]

SPECIAL CONCLUSIONS

In view of the evidence given above it will be obvious to the attentive reader who makes a résumé and a comparison of the documents,

1. That of the books put by the critics themselves in the second century B.C., only three out of the seventy-nine[37] make any kind of reference to a *resurrection*.

a. The *Testaments of the XII Patriarchs* is the only one which distinctly mentions a resurrection. It has four such references, of which only that in Benjamin x, 6-8 refers to the resurrection of some to shame. Since the critics place the composition of this work between 137 and 105 B.C., it cannot have influenced the author of *Daniel*, even if he wrote as late as 164 B.C. On the other hand, the author of the *Testaments* may have been influenced by *Daniel*, whether the latter was written in 164 or 535 B.C.

b. As to the testimony to a resurrection in the parts of *Enoch*, assigned by Charles to the second century B.C., it will be observed that the Third Section contains only a veiled reference to it, and that the First Section says of it only that the

---

[36] For further information, see Bernard in Hastings' *Dict. of the Bible*, Vol. IV, p. 233 f.
[37] In this total the 57 O.T. Psalms assigned by one or more of the critics to this period and the three additions to Daniel, *Susannah, Bel and the Dragon*, and the *Prayer of the Three Children* each count as one.

righteous shall after the judgment live a long life on earth, the implication being that they shall live this life in the resurrected body.

c. That the statement of *Daniel* is nearest in form and sense to that of Isa. xxvi, 19, which even the critics do not place later than the fourth century B.C.

2. That *Daniel* and *Enoch* are not the only books which refer to the *judgment,* and that their statements are not identical.

a. That there will be a judgment is stated not merely in *Daniel* and the *Book of Enoch* but also in Isa xlii, 1-4, Joel iii, 9-17, and in Pss. ix, 7, 8, i, 5, lxxvi, 9, and lxviii, 14.

b. That it will be set is stated not merely in *Daniel* and *Enoch* but also in Isa. xlii, 4 and Ps. x, 7.

c. That the books will be opened is stated only in *Daniel* and in Section Two of *Enoch* which is assigned to the first century B.C.

d. That the Ancient of days will come is stated in *Daniel,* but not in *Enoch.*

e. That judgment will be given to the saints of the Most High is stated in *Daniel,* but not in *Enoch.*

f. In *Daniel* the kings and nations of earth will be condemned, whereas in *Enoch* it is the evil angels and the godless.

3. That, with regard to the *Messiah* the ideas of Daniel are distinctive:

a. The name "Messiah" as applied to the future redeemer of Israel, is found in the literature up to the year 100 B.C., only in *Daniel* and Ps. ii, 2.

b. The phrase "Messiah the Prince" is found nowhere except in *Daniel.*

c. The phrase "Prince of princes" is found nowhere else, though Prince of Peace occurs in Isa. ix, 6. The word "prince" in Ezekiel xxxiv, 24 renders a Hebrew word differing from that found in Daniel.

d. The title "stone" is found outside of *Daniel* only in Isa. xxviii, 16 and Ps. cxviii, 22.

e. The title "son of gods" occurs nowhere else, but the Messiah is called God's son in Ps. ii, 7, Isa. ix, 6.

f. "Son of man" as a title of the Messiah does not occur outside of Daniel till the first century B.C. In Ezekiel it is appropriated to the prophet himself.

g. If Michael the prince be the Messiah, he is so named elsewhere only in the Revelation of St. John.

h. That Messiah was to be "cut off" is stated also in Isa. liii, 8, but nowhere else except in Mk. ix, 12, Lk. xxiv, 26.

i. The statement and figure of the breaking of the image is found nowhere except in *Daniel.*

j. The glory and the kingdom find their best analogy in Zech. ix, 10.

k. Of the early parts of *Enoch,* the fragments of the Book of Adam, and the First and Third Sections are absolutely silent with regard to a Messiah. The Second Section (from the first century B.C.) refers to him but once and that under the figure of a *white bull* whom all the beasts of the field and all the birds of the air feared and to whom they made petitions all the time! This is the only "approximation" of Enoch to Daniel concerning the doctrine of the Messiah. It will be seen that Daniel approximates to Isaiah four times, to Zechariah once, and to the Second Psalm twice. The other phrases and titles used of the Messiah by Daniel are all peculiar to himself.

4. With regard to *Angels* it will be noted:

a. In the books of the Old Testament outside Daniel.

(1) They are mentioned in Gen., Ex., Lev., (?), Num., Deut., Josh., Jgs., Sam., Kgs., Chr., Isa., Joel, Zech., Mal., Pss., and Job.

(2) That, if we take demons, or evil spirits, to be angels we have Lilith, Sa'ir, and Rahab mentioned by name in Isaiah; Shedu in Deut. and Ps. cxlviii; Leviathan in Job and Ps. lxxiv; Rahab in Isa., Ps. lxxxix, and Job; Azazel in Lev. (H); Satan in 1 Chron., Zech., Job, Ps. cix.

(3) That classes of angels seem to be denoted by the Seraphim, Cherubim, Shedim and by the Princes of God.

(4) That angels are distinguished as holy, guardian, mighty, watchers, intercessors, sons of God, punishers of the wicked, members of God's council, and as evil and tempters of mankind,

and that they are practically innumerable, being a host and thousands of thousands.

b. That the *New Testament* agrees with *Daniel* in almost every particular. It speaks of the angels as mighty and strong, as guardians, as mediators, as punishers of the wicked, as surrounding the throne of God, of evil angels, of the Devil as a tempter, of ten thousand times ten thousand, and thousands of thousands, and it names Michael, Gabriel, Satan or Diabolos, Beelzebub and Abaddon or Apollyon.

c. That the treatment of angels differs in the four sections of the *Book of Enoch* and that in no one of the sections can it be fairly said that there is an "approximation" of the treatment of angels with that of *Daniel*. Thus,

(1) In the Third Section of *Enoch* the angels are mentioned but twice, once with the epithet "holy."

(2) In the Second Section of *Enoch,* angels are mentioned only three times certainly and possibly four times. They are called "angels of heaven," "white men," one of them "Azazel," and "seventy shepherds" are spoken of. Not one of these phrases, nor the name Azazel, occurs in Daniel.

(3) The First Section of *Enoch* and the *Book of Noah* both agree with *Daniel* and other books of the *Old Testament,*

(a) In expressing a belief in angels.

(b) In giving names to some of them.

(c) In arranging them in classes, or ranks.

(d) In mentioning "watchers." This designation of angels is found also in Isa. lxii, 6.

(e) Further, *Daniel* agrees with the *Book of Noah* alone, in speaking of angels as a thousand thousand and ten thousand times ten thousand. A similar phrase is found also in Rev. v. 11. The First Section of *Enoch* has the latter part of this phrase "ten thousand times ten thousand" (*cp.* Ps. lxviii, 18).

(f) Daniel agrees with the First Section alone of *Enoch* in designating angels as "holy." This designation is found, also, in Job v. 1, xv, 15, Zech. xiv, 5, Ps. lxxxix, 6, 8, and Deut. xxxiii, 3 (?).

(4) The First Section of *Enoch* and the *Book of Noah* disagree with *Daniel* in the following particulars:

(a) *Daniel* introduces angels merely incidentally, whether as messengers to communicate the will of God or as agents for the deliverance or strengthening of His servants; whereas in both the *Book of Noah* and the First Section of *Enoch,* the angels are the subject of the discourse and the whole narration is taken up with the story of the "sons of God" of Gen. vi, 2, 3.

(b) *Daniel* mentions good angels only, whereas the *Book of Noah* and the First Section of *Enoch* are concerned almost entirely with the angels who fell.

(c) *Daniel* names two good angels alone, whereas the *Book of Noah* mentions four good angels and thirty-seven wicked angels, and the First Section of *Enoch* mentions by name one bad angel and seven holy ones.

(d) The *Book of Noah* speaks of two hundred "angels, children of heaven," of spirits of hoar-frost, hail, snow, mist, rain and dew, of an angel of peace and of an angel of punishment, and of Satans. *Daniel* never refers to any of these.

(e) The First Section of *Enoch* calls angels "stars" and "giants." *Daniel* never does this.

(f) The duties, or functions, of the angels both good and bad are given at length and specifically both in the *Book of Noah* and the First Section of *Enoch.* Daniel never refers to their duties as such and leaves us to infer them from the words which they spake and the actions they performed.

GENERAL CONCLUSIONS

The following general conclusions may be drawn from the above discussion and special conclusions.

1. That of the four doctrines cited by Doctor Driver it cannot be fairly said that the teachings of Daniel approximate to those of the early parts of the Book of Enoch, seeing that no one of these parts expressly mentions all of the doctrines.

2. That on the doctrine of the resurrection, Daniel approximates most nearly the teachings of Isa. xxvi; on that of the

judgment, he makes a slight advance on the teachings of Joel,
Isaiah and certain of the psalms, but agrees in only one particular
with any one of the Sections of Enoch alone; that on the matter
of the Messiah, his closest approximations are to Isaiah,
Zechariah and certain of the psalms; and that on the doctrine of
angels he is unique as far as the pre-Christian literature is concerned and is approximated only by the Book of the Revelation
of St. John.

3. It is asserted by Driver that whether or not, in one or two
instances, the development of the four doctrines of the resurrection, judgment, Messiah, and angels "may have been *partially*
moulded by foreign influences, they undoubtedly mark a later
phase of revelation than that which is set before us in [most of
the] other books of the Old Testament." [38]

If by "revelation," Driver had meant what the New Testament
and the Christian Church have always meant by it (that is, a
making known to man by God of certain ideas in accordance
with his good pleasure), we cannot see why God could not
have revealed the ideas of Daniel in the sixth century B.C., as
well as in the second. If the old view of the dates of the books
is taken, Daniel would still represent a comparatively late view
of these four doctrines. Moreover there is no doubt that the
doctrine of angels is more fully developed in Daniel than in
any other book of the Old Testament, the nearest approximation being in Zechariah, another prophecy of the sixth
century. As to the resurrection, Isaiah xxvi, 29, and, as to
the judgment, Joel iii, are as fully developed as Daniel; and
as to the Messiah, the teachings of the other books of the Old
Testament such as Isaiah, Zechariah, and certain of the psalms,
though different in some respects from Daniel, are in the view
of the New Testament writers, (and we think of any fair
minded critic) more explicit, and just as important and highly
developed as anything in Daniel. Driver, and those who agree
with him, think and say that God *must* have revealed his ideas
in a certain order of time and in the midst of certain circumstances and temporal conditions. Having assumed this order

[38] *L.O.T.*, p. 508.

and these conditions, it seems "undoubtedly" true, that this or that prophecy must have been written or spoken at a certain place and time. "Undoubtedly," if the doctrines could all be proven to be late, the books containing them would be late. "Undoubtedly," if the books, or parts of books, containing the doctrines could be proven to be late, the doctrines also would be late. But *undoubtedly,* also, it is not fair to say without positive proof that the doctrines are late because they are in certain books or parts of books, and that the books or parts of books are late because they contain the doctrines. This, however, is exactly what the critics do. One of their principal reasons for putting Isa. xxiv,-xxvi, and Job late is the fact that the doctrine of the resurrection is taught in them. Joel is said to be late because of its prophecy on the judgment and the kingdom.

Lastly, might I be pardoned for asking a question to which I would like to have an answer? If the absence of any reference to these doctrines is a proof that the earlier prophets and psalmists did not know anything about them, how about the fifty-seven psalms, Ecclesiastes, and other parts of the Old Testament which the critics put in the time of the Greek domination and many of them as late even as the Maccabean times? Why is First Maccabees altogether silent on all of them and Ecclesiasticus substantially so? If the absence of all reference to a resurrection in Zechariah, Haggai, Malachi and Chronicles proves that Daniel was written later than they were, why does the silence of the Third and Fourth Sections of the Book of Enoch, of Jubilees, of the Sibylline Oracles, of the Addenda to Esther and Daniel, of Tobit, Judith, First, Third and Fourth Maccabees, the Book of Baruch, the Book of Wisdom, and the Psalms of Solomon not show that Daniel was not written till after they were? Finally, since Haggai, Malachi, Chronicles, and Ezra-Nehemiah, are absolutely silent on most, or all, of these four doctrines, how do the critics know what were the views of the authors of these books upon these doctrines? Or, if we hold that the doctrines as expounded in Daniel are not his own opinions on these doctrines, but are really revelations from God, do the critics mean to insinuate that God could not have revealed them to the authors of these books, if He had thought it well so to do? Is it necessary to suppose that every author of a book must have told all he knew on every subject, or that God must have given the same message to every writer of the same period, no matter what may have been the purpose of his writing, or the work he had to do?

CHAPTER VI

THE INFLUENCE OF DANIEL

A LARGE part of the difficulty which confronts us when we consider the origin of a writer's ideas meets us also when we try to trace the influence of these ideas upon succeeding literary productions. The seeming traces may have come from some other source than the one supposed, or they may be original in the mind of the later writer without any real, or at least conscious, knowledge of the work of the preceding author. If the two works be from approximately the same period of time, or if the circumstances of the two periods of time were substantially the same, the same or similar *Zeitgeist,* or spirit of the times, would naturally produce the same or similar thoughts and expressions of thought. For example, the ennui, the *Weltschmerz,* the disgust with the world and its gifts, and the despairing flight of the soul to its refuge in God, which are manifest in the Book of Ecclesiastes, may have been equally characteristic of any period of outward natural prosperity, coincident with moral and spiritual decay. The moralists of the old Egyptians of the Fifth Dynasty, such as Ptahhotep and Imhotep, as well as the Roman satirists, such as Juvenal and Seneca, bear witness to the fact that the soul of man can not be satisfied with mere earthly grandeur and material success. The Aramaic fragments of Achikar as well as the Jewish proverbs of Solomon, Hezekiah, Ben Sira, and Wisdom, exhibit in like manner the vanity of earthly greatness and the transitoriness of human friendship, wealth and happiness. How much, if anything, the Greek philosophers may have derived from the Egyptians, Babylonians, Hindoos, and Hebrews, we may never be able to determine. The Greeks assert that Pythagoras, Plato, and Æsop, were all influenced by oriental savants. In the case of Æsop, this assertion is confirmed by the recent find of

157

the Aramaic fragments of Achikar. In view of the fact that Herodotus, Xenophon, and many other Greek historians, made known to the Greeks much of the history of the oriental nations and that this knowledge was increased by contributions to national history such as those of Berossus, Manetho, Nicolaus of Damascus, Dius of Tyre, Menander and Josephus, it is most probable that the philosophical ideas combined with the proverbs and the wisdom literature of the Hebrews, Arameans, Egyptians and others would also have been communicated to the Greeks by hearsay if not by writing. Since scarcely one in a thousand of the writings of the Greeks and hardly any of those of the orientals have come down to our day, it is impossible for us to judge of all the literary influences which may have shaped the thoughts and forms of expression of the few writers who are known to us.

So, in like manner, to attempt to show the influence exerted by a given writer upon his successors from the scanty literary material which we possess is futile. It is doomed to failure because of the paucity of the material at our disposal. And the failure is more sure in the case of the literature of the Egyptians, Persians, Arameans, Phoenicians and Hebrews than it is in the case of the Greeks and Romans, because in the case of the former, the content and extent of the literature known to us is much less and in some instances almost nil.

When we come to investigate the influence of Daniel upon succeeding generations we must remember, then, that there are in our possession from the period between 550 and 150 B.C. but a very few Hebrew works at most which could possibly have been subjected to this influence and that for a long period of time there is not known to us a single literary production of any kind in which such influence could possibly be found, or at least, be justly expected to be found. Before going further into the discussion of this subject, let us first state the objections made to the early date of the Book of Daniel on the ground that the influence of its ideas cannot be traced in the literature of the Hebrews which precedes the time of the Maccabees.

OBJECTIONS OF THE CRITICS

Cornill says: "If Daniel had been composed by a contemporary of Cyrus, we should necessarily have expected that so peculiar and highly important a work would have shown some evidence of its being known and used. When one sees how echoes and reminiscences of Deuteronomy, Jeremiah, Ezekiel, Deutero-Isaiah are traceable in all the literary productions that were written after them, the same results would be looked for from Daniel. But nothing of this is to be discovered." [1]

Bevan holds that, "On the supposition that the narrative of Daniel is historical, it is marvellous that it should be passed over in utter silence by all extant Jewish writers down to the latter half of the second century B.C., that it should leave no trace in any of the later prophetical books, in Ezra, Chronicles, or Ecclesiasticus." [2] And he adds, "In order to realize the true state of the case we should consider how easy it would be to refute, from Jewish literature, anyone who asserted that the book of Isaiah or that of Jeremiah was composed entirely in the Maccabean period." [3]

According to Driver, ". . . it is undeniable that the doctrines of the Messiah, of angels, of the resurrection, and of a judgment on the world, are taught with greater distinctness, and in a more developed form, than elsewhere in the Old Testament, and with features approximating to (though not identical with) those met with in the early parts of the Book of Enoch, c. 100 B.C." [4]

It was the view of Farrar that, "Admitting that this pinnacle of eminence, [assigned to Daniel of which the Dean has just spoken in the preceding context] may have been due to the peculiar splendour of Daniel's career, it becomes the less easy to account for the total silence respecting him in the other books of the Old Testament, in the Prophets who were contemporary with

[1] *Introduction*, p. 386f.
[2] *The Book of Daniel*, p. 12.
[3] *Ibid.*, p. 13.
[4] *L.O.T.*, p. 508.

the Exile and its close, like Haggai, Zechariah, and Malachi; and in the Books of Ezra and Nehemiah, which give us the details of the Return." [5]

ASSUMPTIONS

These objections are all based upon the following *assumptions*:

I. That if there were no traces of the influence of Daniel found in pre-Christian literature till 165 B.C., the Book of Daniel could not have been writen till then.

II. That, as a matter of fact, there is no trace of the influence of Daniel in pre-Christian literature till 165 B.C., the implication being that after that date the influence is marked.

III. That this literature is of such a character that we would have expected to find traces of this influence, provided that Daniel had written as early as the latter part of the sixth century B.C.

IV. That the same measure of influence would be expected from Daniel as from other books, especially Deuteronomy, Jeremiah, Ezekiel and Deutero-Isaiah.

V. That because the ideas of Daniel and those of the First Section of Enoch approximate, they must have been from the same time.

ANSWERS TO ASSUMPTIONS

We will discuss these assumptions under the following heads: (1) the alleged silence of the pre-Maccabean literature; (2) the traces of the influence of Daniel up to 200 B.C.; (3) the traces of the influence of Daniel from 200 B.C. to 135 A.D.; (4) a comparative study of Daniel's influence; (5) the approximation of Daniel and Enoch.

I. THE ARGUMENT FROM SILENCE

In answer to the first of these assumptions, let it be said that it would not be necessary to admit that Daniel could not have been written in the sixth century B.C., even if no trace of it were to be found in the pre-Christian literature before 165 B.C. No one knows enough about the history and literature of that time to

[5] *The Book of Daniel* (Expositors' Bible), p. 11.

be able to make any such assertion upon the basis of evidence. We can gather from the contents of the book itself that it was most probably written at or near Babylon. This conclusion is rendered almost certainly conclusive by the character of the language in which the book is written.[6] What convincing reason have we, then, for supposing that a book written at Babylon about 535 B.C. *must* have been known to Zechariah and Haggai writing at Jerusalem about 520 B.C. in the second year of Darius Hystaspis (Hag. i, 1, Zech. i, 1)? It was not the age of printing presses, nor of the rapid multiplying of copies. Besides, we can see good reasons why Daniel, the trusted servant of Cyrus, might not have desired to publish a work which predicted—in unmistakable terms—the eventual overthrow of the kingdom of Persia. Such a publication would certainly have done no good, either to Daniel or to the people of Israel.

Further, Daniel was commanded by the angel to shut up and seal the book until the time of the end (Dan. xii, 4, 9). Whatever these words mean, they would certainly indicate that the Book of Daniel was not intended so much to meet the immediate religious needs of the Israelites, as to serve the wants of future generations. According to the book itself (ix, 24, 25) the vision and prophecy were to be sealed until Messiah-Prince should come. It is possible therefore that the book was preserved in secret until the time of the Maccabees when it was thought that in some prince of the Asmonean line the predicted Messiah had at last come unto his own. If it be said in reply to this, that we have no record of any such publication in the time of the Maccabees, a sufficient answer is, Neither have we any record of the existence of the pseudo-Daniel of the critics nor of the publication of his work at that time.

It will be seen from the above that we are not prepared to admit that the Book of Daniel was not written in the sixth century B.C., even though it may not have been known to the Jewish Palestinian writers of the time from 535 down to 165 B.C. But, we go further and affirm that it is not necessary to suppose that

---

[6] See article on "The Aramaic of Daniel" in *Biblical and Theological Studies*, by the Faculty of Princeton Theological Seminary, 1912.

they were not acquainted with the work because they have not cited from it, nor shown any traceable influence of it. There are few citations in any of these works from any of the works preceding them. There are few traces of previous authors to be found in any of the literature of these times, Ecclesiasticus alone excepted. They were too full of the important matter which they were describing and of the messages from God which they had to deliver, to be pre-occupied with the thoughts and messages of the prophets and holy men that had preceded them.

II. TRACES OF DANIEL'S INFLUENCE ON HEBREW LITERATURE UP TO 200 B.C.

Having thus repudiated at the start any presupposition of the critics with regard to the date of Daniel based upon the possible absence of traces of Daniel's influence on the pre-Christian writings, let us now examine whether after all there are traces of the influence of the ideas of Daniel in any part of this pre-Christian literature; and if in some parts of it there are no traces, how we are to account for this fact.

And first, let us ask what are these pre-Christian books to which the critics appeal? It will be admitted by all that they embrace the books of Zechariah, Haggai, Malachi, Esther, Ezra-Nehemiah, and Chronicles. To these, some of the critics would add Ecclesiastes, the Song of Songs, and some of the Psalms; while others would also add Joel, Jeremiah, and many parts of other books, such as the priestly part of the Pentateuch, commonly denoted by P, the larger part of the Book of Proverbs, parts of Isaiah and Nahum, the larger part of the Psalter, and even Job.

1. Taking up first of all the works which are admittedly from the period between 538 and 200 B.C., let us inquire whether any trace of the ideas of Daniel can be found in them; and if not, why not. In treating of this subject we shall confine ourselves to the four marks of influence the lack of which is said by Driver to show that Daniel was not written till the middle of the second century B.C., i.e., angels, resurrection, judgment, and the Messiah.

a. Beginning with Haggai, we observe that this short book of two chapters is taken up entirely with the affairs connected with the rebuilding of the temple, and that it contains several messages from Jehovah directed to Zerubbabel, the governor of Judah, to Joshua the High Priest, and to the rest of the people urging them to build the house of the Lord. Yet even here we find in chapter ii, 7, 9, 22, 23 statements concerning the overthrow of the kingdoms of the nations and the establishment of the peace of Jehovah in his temple at Jerusalem. This overthrow of the kingdoms of the nations may be compared with Dan. ii, 44 where it says that the Lord God shall set up a kingdom which shall break in pieces and consume all the kingdoms of the earth. Since Haggai does not speak of the resurrection, nor of angels, no one can tell what his ideas on these subjects may have been. Certainly it is not fair to say that they must have been different from those of Daniel. Haggai says that the word of the Lord came unto him and that he had a message (*mal'ekhuth*) from Him. He calls himself also, an angel or messenger (*mal'ak*) of Jehovah, a phrase peculiar to himself, putting us in mind of the *mar shipri* of the Babylonians just as the word for message recalls the *shipru* with which the gods of Babylonia communicated their will to men.[7]

b. In Zechariah, however, we find the use of the vision method which characterizes Daniel (as in i, 8, 18, ii, 1, iii, 1, iv, 1, v, 1, 6, vi, 1) ; but he says that the word of Jehovah came unto him (as in i, 1, vii, 1, 4, 8, viii, 1, 18) and speaks of the burden (*massa'*) of Jehovah (ix, 1, xii, 1). He makes frequent mention of the Messiah and of his kingdom, (vi, 12, ix, 9, xiii, 1) and speaks of the angel who was talking with him and of another angel who went out to meet him (ii, 3). He speaks also of Satan and of the angel of Jehovah (iii, 1), and of the holy ones (xiv, 5). He speaks of a judgment of Jehovah and his saints upon the nations and of the establishment of the kingdom of God over all the earth. Of the specific doctrines of Daniel of which Driver speaks, all but the resurrection are mentioned in Zechariah. On

---

[7] Haggai mentions no proverbs; does this prove that there were no proverbs before Haggai?

angels and the Messiah the statements of Zechariah are even more explicit than those of Daniel. Of the doctrines mentioned by both Zechariah and Daniel the latter is more explicit on the judgment alone.

c. Malachi does not mention the resurrection; nor does he speak of angels, unless Malachi itself means "my angel." He does speak, however, of the Messiah as the messenger or angel (*mal'ak*) of the covenant (iii, 1) and as the Sun of righteousness who should arise with healing in his wings (iii, 20 AV, iv, 2 in the MT); and of the judgment (iii, 5).

d. The Books of Ezra and Nehemiah are taken up with geneological and historical matter connected with the building of the wall of Jerusalem and with the reforms of religion in Israel. Being filled with the accounts of such earthly matters, they say nothing about resurrection, angels, judgment, or Messiah. What the author, or authors, may have thought on these subjects, is not even hinted at. This does not imply that they had no thoughts on these subjects, nor, if they had thoughts, that they did not agree with Daniel. Nor does the fact that they do not mention Daniel imply that they did not know about him any more than the fact that they do not mention Isaiah, Hosea, and the other prophets, implies that they did not know about them.

e. The Books of Chronicles, however late they may have been written, do not, except in the last four verses, bring down the history of Israel later than the time of the conquest of Jerusalem by Nebuchadnezzar. In a history such as this there was never any occasion for the author's speaking of the resurrection, nor of the judgment, nor of the Messiah. Incidentally, he mentions Satan as having stood up against Israel and tempted David to number Israel (1 Chr. xxi, 1).

f. Esther treats of but one subject, the origin of the feast of Purim. The writer of this book never mentions the name of God. We might as well infer from this omission that he did not know about God as to infer from his omission of all reference to the resurrection, angels, etc. that he had no opinion on these matters. It seems wonderful, that if the author of Daniel lived in Palestine, as the critics say, at about the same time that the author of Esther did, he should have been so influenced by the Persian religion as to adopt from them his ideas about resurrection, judgment, angels, and Messiah; whereas a writer that knows so much about Persia, as it is admitted that the author of Esther did,[8] should never have referred to any of those ideas at all. In view of the frequency with which the Behistun and other Persian inscriptions mention the name of God, it is remarkable also that this Jewish writer should never refer to Him. Evidently, the influence of the Persian conquerors upon the religion of their subjects was not so great as some would have us imagine.

It thus appears that of the books (Chron. Ezra-Neh., Esther, Zech., Haggai, and Mal.) which according to the traditional view were written after 538 B.C., Chronicles, Zechariah, and Malachi, mention angels; Zechariah, Haggai and Malachi refer to the Messianic times, and to the judgment.

2. According to the critics, Joel, Jonah, Lamentations, Ecclesiastes, Canticles, the document P, most of the Psalms, Job, parts of Isaiah, Hosea, Amos, Micah, Obadiah, Habakkuk, Zephaniah, Nahum, and Proverbs, were also written in post-exilic times. Of these the following mention one or more of the four subjects under discussion:

(1) Messiah, or his Kingdom—Joel, Psalms, Micah.
(2) The Judgment—Joel, Psalms, Obadiah, Isaiah.
(3) The Resurrection—Job, Psalms, Isaiah.
(4) Angels—Psalms, Job, Isaiah, Ecclesiastes, Proverbs.

The following mention none of the four subjects:

(1) The passages, or parts, of Nahum, Hosea, Amos and Zephaniah alleged to be post-exilic.
(2) The books alleged to be entirely post-exilic, such as Jonah, Joel, Canticles and P.

It is obvious, that if the failure of these documents to mention any one of these four subjects proves that Daniel did not exist, it proves also that JE and Isaiah did not exist; for both JE and Isaiah mention angels and Isaiah certainly refers to the Messiah. That a document says nothing about certain subjects proves noth-

[8] Hastings, *Dict. of the Bible*, Vol. I, 774.

ing as to the ideas of the author of the document upon the subjects not spoken of by him. An author cannot say all he knows in every book he writes.

a. Taking up these books and parts of books which some critics claim to have been written between 538 and 200 B.C., the general remarks may be made with regard to them that: (1) As respects angels, it is true that no influence of Daniel can be discerned in them. For they never mention them at all. But if this failure to mention angels proves that they did not know about the Book of Daniel (i.e., supposing it could be shown that they were written in the period between 538 and 200 B.C.), it would prove also that their authors were ignorant of J and E, of the first part of Isaiah and Ezekiel and Zechariah, all of which mention angels. In other words, it would prove too much, the critics themselves being judges. For none of them would place J and E and Zechariah and Isaiah vi, after their alleged dates for Jonah, Joel and Isaiah xxiv-xxvii. It would be remarkable, also, that the Persian doctrine of angels should be accepted in the second century under Greek rule rather than under Cyrus. (2) As to the resurrection, neither Jonah nor Joel alludes to it. What they may have thought about it or whether they thought of it at all, they do not state and we cannot possibly know. Consequently, it is evident, that we cannot make a comparison between their view of the resurrection and that of Daniel. All we can say is that in the small fragments of their works that have come down to us, they do not talk upon this subject. A large part of the literature written about the Old Testament would never have been written, if the critics had only remembered, that we have no way of judging from the few chapters which most of the Old Testament writers have handed down to us, what their views were upon the countless subjects which they never treat. But let us examine the subject more in detail.

b. If we place, as many of the critics (e. g. Budde) do, the Book of Jonah in this period we find that Jonah makes no reference to any of the four doctrines which Driver propounds as characteristic of Daniel. Neither resurrection, angels, general judgment, nor the Messiah, is even remotely referred to in the whole work. The only judgment hinted at is an earthly cne, consisting of a threatened destruction of Nineveh. Sheol is mentioned (ii, 2), but only figuratively in describing the descent of Jonah into the depths of the sea. If it could be proven that Jonah was not written till post-captivity times, his silence with regard to Daniel might possibly have some significance. But that remains to be proven. Moreover, even if it could be proven that Jonah was later than 500 b.c., an argument as to whether Daniel was earlier or later than Jonah could not be made on the basis of these four doctrines, since Jonah has made no allusions to them.

c. In Isaiah xxiv,-xxvii, we find an apocalypse which Driver refers to the early post-exilic period: [9] (1) because, he says, modern critics are generally agreed that it lacks a suitable occasion in Isaiah's age, (2) because in literary treatment it is in many respects unlike Isaiah and (3) because the thoughts are different from Isaiah.

Before calling attention to the teachings of this passage on the four subjects which, Driver says, were developed by Daniel, I cannot refrain from remarking upon the kind of evidence put forth by the critics and accepted by Driver as sufficient to form their conclusions. "*Modern* critics are agreed" forsooth! But on what grounds are they agreed? Does anyone of them know enough about the age of Isaiah to say that this passage was not suitable to his times? Where do they get their information? There is none, except what is contained in the Old Testament itself and in the few references to the Jewish history of that period that are contained in the Assyrian and Egyptian documents.

According to Cheyne and Duhm, the genuine verses of Isaiah, 269 to 307½ in number,[10] cover the period from 740 to 701 b.c.

---

[9] *L.O.T.*, p. 221.

[10] Duhm limits the genuine prophecies of Isaiah to i, 2-26, 29, 31, ii, 2-4, 6-19, 21, iii, 1-9, 12-15, iv, 1, v, 1-14, 17-29, vi, 1-13, vii, 2, 8a, 9-14, 16, 18-20, viii, 1-18, 21, 22, ix, 2-7, 8-14, 17, x, 4, 5-9, 13, 14, xi, 1-8, xiv, 24, 25a, 26, 27, xvii, 1-6, 9-14, xviii, 1-6, xx, 1, 3-6, xxi, 16, 17, xxii, 1-9a, 11b-14, 15a, 16-18, xxviii, 1-4, 7-29, xxix, 1-4a, 5-7, 9-10, 13-15, xxx, 1-7a, 8-17, 27-32, xxxi, 1-4, 5, 8a, 9b, xxxii, 1-5, 9-18, 20. Cheyne limits the genuine parts of

From the earlier part of this period, we have the prophecies of Hosea, 746-734 B.C., several passages of which are held by certain critics to be later additions, partly on the ground that in their opinion they express thoughts alien to Hosea's position, partly because they are supposed to interrupt the connection of thought. From the later years of Isaiah we have the prophecies of Micah. Here, again, the critics find that much material has been interpolated, such as part, or all, of chaps. iv and v. These interpolations, or additions, are alleged on the ground that to the critics they seem to be "inconsistent," "not to harmonize," or "difficult to reconcile" with the portions they admit to be genuine. 2 Kings xv-xx treat, also, of the times of Isaiah. But, since large portions of these chapters are supposed to be "the work of a prophet writing in the subsequent generation," [11] it is left to the judgment of each critic to determine how much of them is reliable history. The Books of Chronicles, so far as they contain matter additional to that of Kings, need not, in the opinion of the critics, be considered, inasmuch as it does not seem possible to treat them "as strictly and literally historical." [12]

Having thus rejected more than half of the records attributed by the sources to the period from 740 to 700 B.C., because it does not seem to them to be consistent with what they think to be genuine, the critics proceed to give us their view of what Isaiah and his contemporaries thought. The amusing thing about this method of procedure is, that those using it do not seem to

---

Isaiah to i, 5-26, 29-31, ii, 6-21, iii, 1-4, 5, 8, 9, 12-17, 24, 41, v, 1-14, 17-25b, vi, 1-13, vii, 2-8a, 9-14, 16, 18-20, viii, 1-18, 20b-22, ix, 8-13, 16, x, 4, 5-9, 13, 14, 27-32, xiv, 24, 25a, 26, 27, 29-32, xvi, 14 (from *within*), xvii, 1-6, 9-14, xviii, 1-6, xx, 1, 3-6, xxi, 16, 17, xxii, 1-9a, 11b-14, 15a, 16-18, xxiii, 1, 2, 3, 4, 6-12, 14, xxviii, 1-4, 7-19, 21, 22, xxix, 1-4, 6, 9, 10, 13-15; xxx, 1-7a, 8-17; xxxi, 1-5a (to *birds*) : all that remains consist of editors' additions or post-exilic insertions. That is, out of the 1295 verses attributed to Isaiah by the Massoretes, Duhm accounts 307½ and Cheyne 269 to be genuine. They deliberately throw out from three-quarters to four-fifths of the entire book without any documentary or even circumstantial evidence except that which is to be derived from their own precarious theories or opinions of what Isaiah ought to, or might have, written.

[11] *L.O.T.*, 197.
[12] *Ibid*, 532.

see how absurd it is. The serious thing about it is, that they do not see how wicked it is. To change a document for a purpose is not permissible in the ordinary transactions of life, nor in the editing of letters and other literary documents. In legal phraseology, it is called falsification, that is, "the intentional alteration of a record, or of any document so as to render it untrue," or different from what the original writers wrote.

In all this, I am not intending to cast a slur upon any well directed attempt to arrive by means of manuscripts and versions, or even by means of established principles of textual criticism, at the correct original of the Scriptures, nor to reflect upon any sincere endeavour to get at the right meaning of them; but I do intend to protest against the tacit claim on the part of some, without any superhuman knowledge, who pretend to be able to interpret the Mene-mene-tekel-upharsins of ancient history. Befor any one has the right to deny that Isaiah xxiv-xxvii had a "suitable occasion" in the age of Hezekiah, he must know thoroughly the history of the period in which Isaiah lived. No one knows thoroughly that history. Therefore, no one has the right to deny that these chapters may have been written by Isaiah.

Again, it is said, that the literary treatment is unlike that of Isaiah. Of course, the critics mean by this statement, that the literary treatment of chapters xxiv-xxvii is unlike that of the parts of Isaiah which they recognize as genuine. Here, once more, a caveat must be made. For even at the risk of appearing to reflect on the literary judgment of the eminent critics who make this assertion, I am constrained to express the opinion, that they do not know enough of the literary possibilities of a writer of the imagination and versatility of Isaiah to affirm that he could not have employed styles differing as much as are claimed to appear in various parts of the works bearing his name. Of the style of Ezekiel, or of Jeremiah, we might form a correct judgment because of general sameness. But a gifted genius like Isaiah transcends all ordinary canons. He must be compared, not to Johnson, or Macaulay, with their stereotyped and stilted style; but rather with him "whose soul was like a star, and dwelt apart" who had "a voice whose sound was like the sea," now moving in majestic numbers as he narrates the speech of Satan to his marshalled hosts of embattled angels, now swelling in joyful pæans to the heaven-born Redeemer, now sounding in reverberating denunciations the doom of Waldensian persecutors, now booming in the grandiloquent prose of the Areopagitica in praise of that liberty that he loved so well; but, again, moving along in his *History of England* with scarcely a break to the monotony, or sinking to the almost frozen stiffness of the Common Place Book. Milton's Note Book shows that he wrote some of his lines five times before he published them. Macaulay says that he put three whole years upon the production of his *Lays of Ancient* Rome, writing and re-writing until they had reached the highest degree of perfection to which he could bring them. May not Isaiah have elaborated some of his works with more assiduity than others? May he not have cultivated, as we know that Robert Louis Stevenson did, a variety of styles sufficient to express most appropriately his varied ideas? May he not intentionally have put into the sections including chapters xxiv-xxvii the "synonymous clauses," "the alliterations and word-plays" the "many unusual expressions" and all the other features, "which though they may be found occasionally [elsewhere] in Isaiah, are never aggregated in his writings as they are here?" Who knows? The critics think they do. How do they know? How can they know? Have they sufficient evidence to show that they know? We think not.

Lastly, the critics assert that the thought of chapters xxiv-xxvii is different from Isaiah's. There are "points of contact" which show that the author of these chapters "was familiar with Isaiah's writings"; but there are features "which seem to spring out of a different (and later) vein of thought from Isaiah's." [13] "Veins of thought" forsooth! and "different veins of thought"! and "later veins of thought"! Beautiful phrases! Empty phrases! Unjustifiable phrases! For by what method of psychological analysis, or historical investigation, have the critics arrived at the conclusion, that Isaiah may not have had different veins of thought at different periods of his life? Who of us has not had

[13] *L.O.T.*, 220.

in the course of forty years, or less, many new veins of thought, a new philosophy of life, perhaps an altered view of the universe and God? Who of us does not know of many men, who in a score of years or less, have apparently changed their whole attitude toward the scheme of things? That these changes have taken place, we know; but whence and how they came, we cannot always tell. We do not know all the influences that shape and change our own lives, much less the lives of others. But, as to those who have long since been dead, and of whose outer and inner life little information has come down to us, it is, and must be, impossible for us to determine the number, variety, and causes, of their changes of thought, and of the frequency and extent of these changes. How, then, when we go back twenty-five hundred years to the time of Isaiah, can we expect to tell what veins of thought he may have had, and whence and how they may have originated? How can we measure the periphery of the circle of his ideas? How can we sound the depths of his researches, or soar to the heights of his imagination? How can we determine, that he may have discovered certain "veins of thought," but that certain others must have been unknown to him?

And yet, this is just what the critics of Isaiah claim the capacity for doing. They claim to have the ability to distinguish from the thoughts expressed the parts of the present Book of Isaiah that were composed about 700 B.C., the parts that are alleged to have been written from 550 to 500 B.C., and the parts that, they say, must have been written as late as 400, or even 175 B.C. On the face of it, this claim has the appearance of a hypersensitized egoism.

For, says Driver, "it is true," that in these chapters, "the author follows Isaiah more than other prophets"; but, at the same time, "his prophecy contains similarly reminiscences from other prophets," such as Hosea, Amos, Micah, Nahum, and Jeremiah.[14] But Driver fails to inform us, how he knows that Nahum and Jeremiah were not influenced by the writer of these chapters, rather than the opposite, or that all three may not have

[14] *L.O.T.*, 220.

been influenced by some earlier unknown prophet whose works have been lost. In the case of Nah. ii, 11, and Isa. xxiv, 1-4, the reminiscence (*sic!*) seems to have been confined to the use of the one root "to be empty" (*buq,* or *baqaq*),—a very slender support for a literary reminiscence, especially since Hosea and Jeremiah, also, use the same word. Must every one who speaks of the sound of a voice have a reminiscence of Wordsworth's sonnet to Milton, or of Tennyson's *In Memoriam?*

Again, Driver says that "the absence of *distinct* historical allusions" makes the question as to what period the prophecy is to be assigned a difficult one to answer.[15] "The unnamed city is, most probably, Babylon." Yet he adds, "it is doubtful, however, whether the literal Babylon is intended by the author. The lineaments of the city which he depicts are so indistinct and unsubstantial that the picture seems rather to be an ideal one: Babylon becomes a type of the powers of heathenism, which the prophet imagines as entrenched behind the walls of a great city, strongly fortified, indeed, but destined in God's good time to be overthrown." And yet, on the ground of this imaginary picture, the critics attempt to fix the date of these chapters; some placing it as late as about 334 B.C. This could be, says Driver, because Babylon "remained an important city till the close of the Persian empire. . . ." While this is true, yet it was even more true in the times of Hammurabi, of Merodach-Baladan (during whose reign Isaiah the son of Amos prophesied) and of Nebuchadnezzar. Always, from the time of Hammurabi to that of Alexander, Babylon the Great was the centre of Semitic heathenism. To Isaiah and his contemporaries, it was not merely a type; it was the real, living, Jehovah-defying, centralized and radiating, power of this world. According to the prophecies expressly assigned to Isaiah in the book that bears his name, a large part of his thoughts and predictions were taken up with the future relations of Israel with this crowning city of heathendom. In chap xxxix, he predicts that Hezekiah's descendents should be taken captive thither; in xl-lxvi, he comforts the people with the assurance of the faithfulness and power of Jehovah and of their eventual

[15] *L.O.T.,* 221.

return from exile; in xiii-xiv, the ultimate complete destruction of Babylon is predicted. If we believe in predictive prophecy, the whole of the Book of Isaiah may confidently be attributed to him. But, granting for the sake of argument all that the critics claim as to the date of Isa. xxiv-xxvii, what effect would this have upon the theory of the absence of the influence of ideas of Daniel on post-exilic literature? If with Driver, we were to refer these chapters "most plausibly to the early post-exilic period," we might mark the influence of Daniel in regard to angels, the judgment, and the Messianic kingdom. For in xxiv, 21-23, we read that "It shall come to pass in that day, that the Lord shall punish the host of the high ones that are on high [i.e., the angels] and the kings of the earth upon the earth. And they shall be gathered together, as prisoners are gathered in the pit, and shall be put in the prison, and after many days shall they be visited.[16] Then the moon shall be confounded, and the sun ashamed, when the LORD of hosts shall reign in mount Zion, and in Jerusalem, and before his ancients gloriously." [17] Again touching the resurrection, we read in xxvi, 19: "Thy dead men shall live, together with my dead body shall they arise. Awake and sing, ye that dwell in dust: for thy dew is as the dew of herbs, and the earth shall cast out the dead." Surely if we were to place the composition of Daniel at about 535 B.C., and that of Isa. xxiv-xxvii at 525, or after, it would be difficult to escape the conclusion that the latter was influenced by the former.

d. As to the *Priests' Codex* (P) which is put by the critics from 400 to 300 B.C., it will be admitted by all that it contains no intimation of a resurrection, of angels, of a judgment following death, nor even of a Messiah. It is noteworthy, however, if the author of this part of the Pentateuch wrote at so late a date (for he is put in the Persian times), that he should have said nothing about a Messiah or about angels, even if he be silent as to a resurrection and an after judgment. The critics may satisfy themselves as to the absence of reference to the latter by supposing that they were first suggested by a Daniel living in

[16] i.e., in judgment. See also xxvi, 21, xxvii, 1.
[17] i.e., in the Messianic kingdom. See also xxvii, 6.

the second century B.C., but how on their own principle that the influence of the ideas of preceding authors should be traceable in later ones, will they explain the absence of all reference to the Messiah, and to angels in this great P document? If the absence of all reference to two of the doctrines proves that Daniel did not exist before P was written, the absence of all of them would prove that Isaiah and Zechariah did not exist.

e. The Proverbs of Solomon mention no future judgment, no Messiah, no kingdom, and no resurrection. The word for angel occurs in xvi, 14 where the wrath of a king is said to be as angels of death, and in xvii, 11, "An evil man seeketh only rebellion: therefore a cruel angel shall be sent against him."

f. With regard to Joel, the case is different. It makes no mention of the resurrection or of angels. The Messianic times, however, are described in ii, 28-30 and iii, 18-20, though the Messiah himself is not referred to. The great day of Jehovah (ii, 2) is the main theme of the book. On this day, the Lord will bring the nations down to the valley of Jehoshaphat and will judge them there. Thither, also, according to iii, 12, the nations, having been awakened, shall come up, when Jehovah shall sit there to judge all the nations round about.

g. At whatever date the critics place the composition of the Song of Songs, it would be preposterous to expect to find in a poetical work of its character, any reference to any one of the four subjects that are said to characterize the Book of Daniel. Whatever its symbolical interpretation may be, its strict adherence to the theme of an earthly love that is stronger than death, excludes the expectation of finding any allusion in it, to any of the higher matters which are the theme of Daniel's discourse. This is not a matter of date and influence, but one of subject matter and literary consistency.[18]

3. The Apocryphal and other Extra-Canonical Writings of the Hebrews probably antedating the alleged date of Daniel in 164 B.C., are, Tobit, Ecclesiasticus, Achikar, the Aramaic Egyp-

[18] For a discussion of the Psalms assigned by critics to this period, see below.

tian papyri, and the Letter of Aristeas. As to the four subjects under discussion, the following traces are to be found in them:

a. Tobit[19] says nothing about resurrection, judgment, Messiah or kingdom; but has a great deal to say about angels. Thus in iii, 17 he names *Raphael* who is the *deus ex machina* sent by God to direct the whole plan of God's providence with reference to Tobit and Sara. The belief in guardian angels is expressed in v, 17, 22 and in holy angels in xi, 14. Raphael (xii, 15) is called one of the seven holy angels who stand and enter before the glory of the Lord. *Asmodeus*, an evil demon, is mentioned by name (iii, 8 and elsewhere).

b. Ecclesiasticus mentions (1) angels (xxix, 28, xli, 2, xlviii, 21, and (2) resurrection (xlvi, 12, 20, xlviii, 5, xlix, 10).

c. Achikar (500-400 B.C.) is silent on all four subjects and displays no knowledge of the law or of the prophets, nor even of the history of Israel.

d. The other *Aramaic Documents* from Elephantine are equally silent on these four subjects.

e. Aristeas (200 B.C.) is silent on all four subjects.

III. TRACES OF DANIEL'S INFLUENCE FROM 200 B.C. TO 135 A.D.

For convenience of discussion we shall sub-divide this long period into three divisions: the period from 200-100 B.C., that that from 100 B.C. to 1 A.D., and the third from 1-135 A.D.

Second Century B.C. Taking up the Post-Captivity Literature that was, or is thought to have been, written between 200 and 100 B.C., let us see whether the ideas which characterize Daniel are to be found, also, in them.

a. And first, let us consider the Canonical Books or parts of books, that are said by certain critics to have been composed in the second century B.C.

(1) Fifty-seven of the Psalms are alleged by either Driver, or Cheyne, or Reuss, or Robertson Smith, to have been written in the time of the Maccabees. In these psalms, there is no mention

---

[19] Dating from 350 to 170 B.C. according to Simpson in *Apocrypha and Pseudepigrapha of the O. T.*, ed. by Charles. Vol. I, p. 183.

of the resurrection, nor of the final judgment. Psalm cxlviii, 2 alone speaks of angels; and only cx, 1 and cxviii, 26 refer clearly to the Messiah. In the three psalms (xliv, lxxiv, and lxxix) which Driver puts in these times, there is no reference to any one of the four subjects that, in discussing Daniel, he alleges to be indicative of the Maccabean period, the distinguishing mark of its *Zeitgeist*. Strange, indeed, is it that those who make so much of the spirit of the times, of Persian ideas and Grecian philosophy, in the consideration of Ecclesiastes and Daniel, should be blind to the absence of Persian and Greek influences from the psalms! Think of it! In none of these fifty-seven psalms is Persia, or Greece once mentioned. No king of Persia, or Greece, is named. No Persian, or Greek, word is employed. The phalanx and the elephant, those mighty and almost invincible weapons of Seleucid warfare, are passed over in silence.

But, the absence of all direct and indisputable evidence of the Maccabean origin of these psalms might in a measure be considered negligible, if the critics were unanimous in their conclusions as to what were Maccabean. But, we find that in their conclusions, no two of them are agreed. Cheyne assigns 30 psalms to this period and Reuss 31; but they agree only as to eight of them. Perowne and Delitzsch put Pss. xliv, lxxiv, and lxxix, in Maccabean times; but Cheyne agrees with them only as to Ps. xliv, assigning Ps. lxxiv and lxxix to the time of Artaxerxes Ochus, while Reuss assigns no one of the three to the time of the Maccabees. In the midst of such glaring, and, if we follow the subjective methods of their sponsors, such inevitable disagreements, as to the dates of these poetic compositions, one may be pardoned for judging that their methods are inconclusive and their opinions unreliable.

(2) Ecclesiastes, the date of whose composition is placed by Plumptre, Cornill, and Driver, at about 200 B.C., mentions neither the Messiah nor the Messianic kingdom, nor angels, nor the resurrection. With regard to judgment, it represents the author as saying in his heart that God will judge the righteous and the wicked (iii, 17) and as stating that God will bring every work into judgment with every secret thing whether it be good, or

whether it be evil (xii, 14) ; and that the dead know not anything, neither have they any more a reward (ix, 5).[20]

(3) Up to the present time, Professor Haupt of Johns Hopkins seems to be the only critic who has had the presumption to place any part of the Book of Nahum in the Maccabean period. Yet, among the many equivocal grounds which he gives in favour of the late date of parts of this prophecy, he does not even suggest that there is the slightest hint in any verse of Nahum at

[20] It will be known to most of my readers, that the three great criteria used by the critics for determining the approximate dates of literary documents are the agreements, or disagreements, in reference to history, doctrine and language. One may perceive from the above statement that Daniel and Ecclesiastes both treat of but one doctrine in common, and that they differ considerably even in the treatment of this one. As to history, they never touch on the same subjects. Daniel, indeed, speaks expressly of certain events in the lives of Nebuchadnezzar, Belshazzar, Darius the Mede, and Cyrus; but Ecclesiastes makes no direct or definite allusion to anyone, save Solomon. When we come to the third criterion, that of language, to which Driver in his *L.O.T.* has appealed so frequently and with such an assumption of cocksureness, we find that the disagreements are sufficient to make us doubt entirely the manner in which this criterion is used by the critics. If the prima facie and traditional view of the dates of the Old Testament books be correct we would expect the linguistic characteristics of Daniel to agree in large measure with those of Chronicles, Ezra-Nehemiah, and Esther. If the views of the critics were correct, we would expect to find a still closer resemblance between the language of Daniel and that of Ecclesiastes, the so-called Maccabean psalms, and Ecclesiasticus. Now, of the thirty-two words marshalled on pp. 506-507 of *L.O.T.* to show that the Hebrew of Daniel resembles in all distinctive features the Hebrew of the age subsequent to Nehemiah, we find that twenty-five are found also in other books of the Old Testament. It will be seen, also, that fourteen of the words and seven of the phrases, that is, all but four, occur in Chronicles. Of the remaining four, one occurs in Nehemiah and two in Esther. Of the whole thirty-two, only one word and one phrase are met with in Ecclesiastes and only one word in the fifty-seven so-called Maccabean psalms. On the other hand, of the fifteen words and phrases cited on page 475 of *L.O.T.* as proof of the late date of Ecclesiastes, not one occurs in Daniel and only one in any of the supposedly Maccabean psalms.

All that is needed to test these almost unbelievable statements is to read and compare the collections of words and references on pp. 475, 506-7, and 387-9 of *L.O.T.* And while the gentle reader of these lines is testing these statements, let him read also what Driver has to say on pages 484-5, 535-540, and 545-547, about the expressions characteristic of Esther, Chronicles and Ezra-Nehemiah, and he will observe that they agree with Daniel in

any one of these four doctrines which are said to characterize the Book of Daniel and to be indicative of the second century B.C., and for this good and sufficient reason, that as a matter of fact, not one of them is so much as hinted at in the whole book.[21]

---

employing a goodly number of Persian words; whereas, the fifty-seven psalms have not one; and only one, and that of doubtful origin, is alleged to be found in Ecclesiastes.

Furthermore, of the four great peculiarities of the language of Ecclesiastes—the frequent use of nouns ending in -*uth* and -*on,* the employment of the relative *she,* and of the *waw* conjunctive with the perfect—not one is found in the Hebrew of Daniel. So that in the words of Driver himself (*L.O.T.,* 473), we may say, that "linguistically, Qohéleth stands by itself in the O.T." And since it stands by itself, it shows the futility of attempting, by such methods as those employed by the critics, to determine the date and composition of the documents on the ground of peculiar expressions found in them.

[21] One of the fanciful reasons that are given by Haupt for the late date of a part of Nahum is the word *mephets* occurring in ii, 2. This word means "he that dashes in pieces," and it is supposed by Haupt that it refers to Judas Maccabæus. The plural of the word is found in Jer. xxiii, 1, where it is translated in the English version by "scatter." A noun of the same form is found in Prov. xxv, 18, in the sense of "maul," or "hammer." This verse is among those that were copied out by the men of Hezekiah from the proverbs of Solomon. If the author of Nahum ii, 2 had employed some derivative of *nakab* "to hammer," there would have been the appearance at least of an argument in favour of Professor Haupt's view arising from the fact that Judas was called the *Makkabi.* This appearance, however, would not be significant of a late date, first, because the words *makkabah* and *makkebeth* "hammer" occur in Isaiah, Jeremiah, and 1 Kings, and also in Judges iv, 21, which many of the critics consider to be about the earliest part of the Old Testament. Now, since a hammer implies a hammerer, it is obvious that *makkabi* might have been used as early as Judges iv. Surely, Jael was a great hammerer!

Secondly, no argument for the late date of a document can be made on the basis of this word, seeing that not merely is it absent from the Old Testament literature of the late period—even from the so-called Maccabean portions—but the word, except possibly as a proper noun, is not found in the New Hebrew and Aramaic of the Targums and Talmud, nor in the Syriac.

Since this fancied reference of this one word to Judas Maccabæus is the nearest approach to objective evidence for the late date of a part of Nahum to be found in the whole of Professor Haupt's work, our readers cannot imagine with what far-fetched conjectures and might-have-beens, with what flashes of "phosporescent punk and nothingness" the writer attempts to enlighten us with his subjective lucubrations. Brilliant they often are, but they lack the first principles of science, logic, and evidential value.

(4) As to the ninety-two, or more of the Psalms of David said by the critics to have been written between 539 and 100 B.C., the following references to the four subjects under discussion occur in them, to wit:

(a) Angels are said in ciii, 20, 21, to be strong heroes that do Jehovah's word and his ministers that do his will. In xci, 11, they are said to keep us in all our ways; and in xxxiv, 8, to encamp around those that fear Him and to deliver them. In lxviii, 17, they are said to be many thousands in number.

(b) As to the resurrection, these psalms have nothing to say, except possibly Ps. xxx, 4.

(c) As to the judgment, there are probable intimations in ix, 7, 8, and l, 1ff.

(d) The Messiah is expressly named in ii, 2, and is called God's Son in ii, 5, and is referred to in lxxii, 7, 8, cxxxii, 11, and in xxi, xxiv, xxvii, xxx, xxxiv, xxxv, xli, lxviii, lxix and cix.

In the Hebrew text, three of these psalms (i, ii, xci) are without headings; the fiftieth is ascribed to Asaph, the seventieth, to Solomon, the eighty-ninth to Ethan, and all the rest, except possibly the one hundred and thirty-second to David.[22]

(5) Isaiah xxiv-xxvii, which some critics allege to have been written in the Maccabean period has already been sufficiently discussed.

b. In the second place, in the Apocryphal and Pseudepigraphical Books written from 200 to 100 B.C. the following situation with regard to these four doctrines is to be found:

(1) *Ecclesiasticus* mentions angels, but only in references to

[22] In *L.O.T.*, pp. 384-386, Driver gives the dates of the psalms as follows: In Books I and II, psalms ii, xviii, xx, xxi, xxviii, xlv, lxi, lxiii, and lxxii, will presumably be pre-exilic; of the rest, many, it it probable, spring from different parts of the Persian period. In Book III (psalms lxxiii-lxxxix), he supposes lxxvii, lxxviii, lxxx, lxxxi, lxxxv, lxxxvi, lxxxvii, to be post-exilic; lxxiv, lxxix, and perhaps lxxxiii, to be Maccabean; and lxxiii, lxxv, lxxxii, and lxxxiv, not earlier than Jeremiah. In Books IV and V, he makes ci and cx to be presumably from before the exile, xc and xci possibly so, and cii, exilic; xciii, xcvi-xcix, are either from the latter part of the exile, or soon after.

the narratives in the canonical books. The other three subjects are not even hinted at.

(2) The *Book of Wisdom* calls the manna "angels' food" (xvi, 20), says that the righteous shall receive a glorious kingdom (v, 15, 16), rebukes the ungodly for saying that no man was known to have returned from the grave (ii, 1), says that the souls of the righteous shall judge the nation (iii, 1, 8), and the unrighteous "shall have no hope, nor comfort, on the day of trial" (iii, 18).

(3) *First Maccabees* is silent on all four subjects; but emphasizes the importance of keeping the sabbath, as to which Daniel says nothing.

(4) The *Addenda to Daniel* show no trace of the influence of the canonical Daniel, as far as it affects these four doctrines.

(5) The *Addenda to Esther* represent Esther as saying to the king of Persia, that he appeared to her as an angel of God. (xv, 13).

(6) The Book of *Baruch* mentions none of the four subjects, unless by devils (iv, 7) evil angels are meant.

(7) *Judith* is silent on all four subjects.

(8) Fragments of the *Book of Noah* are said to be embedded in the *Book of Enoch*. These fragments are supposed by Charles to be parts of a work that was written about 170 B.C., though the grounds upon which this early date is assigned to it are not absolutely convincing. They consist mostly of a commentary on the life of Noah as recorded in Genesis, and especially upon chapter vi, 1-4, which treats of the fallen angels, or "sons of God." Chaps. liv, lv, lx, and lxv-lxix give an account of the flood and of the judgment on the fallen angels; and cvi, cvii of the birth of Noah. The book names nineteen leaders of the rebellious sons of God and four others as leaders of the holy ones of heaven; and mentions Satan and even Satans (vi, 7, ix, 1, liv, 6, lxv, 6, lxix, 2-11). An angel of peace is spoken of in liii, 4, liv, 4, and lx, 24, and angels of punishment in v, 33, lxvi, 1. An angel went with Enoch (Noah?) and angels built the ark (lx, 11, lxvii, 2). There were

a thousand thousand and ten thousand times ten thousand of angels, some of whom were called watchers (lx, 1; x, 7, 9, 15).

The day of the great judgment is referred to in x, 6, lx, 6, 25, after which the bad angels will be led off to the abyss of fire (x, 15, lxvii, 12, lxviii, 2), and the Messianic times of righteousness and truth and peace will be established (x, 16, xi, 2). Nothing is said in this book about a resurrection.

(9) The so-called First Section of the *Book of Enoch,* containing chaps. vi-xxxvi, names Raphael, Michael, Uriel, Raguel, and Azazel (xxii, 3, 6, xxiv, 2, xix, 1, xxi, 5, 9, xxvii, 2, xxiii, 4, xiii, 1) and seven holy angels who watch (xx, 2-8). It mentions the watchers of heaven (xii, 2, 3, 4, xiii, 10, xv, 21), watchers (xvi, 1), holy watchers (xv, 9), and the seven stars of heaven (xxi, 6). It speaks of holy ones (xiv, 25), and of most holy ones (xiv, 23), and calls them eternal (xiv, 1), children of heaven (xiv, 3) and says that they see the glory of God (xxxvi, 4). Evil spirits are called giants (xv, 8), for whom a prison is reserved (xxi, 10). The duties of angels are declared in xx. The spirit of Abel lives on after death (xxii, 7), and compartments of Sheol exist for the spirits of the dead (xxii, 5, 8-13). In number there are ten thousand times ten thousand angels (xiv, 22).

The judgment is referred to in xiv, 4, xix, 1, xxv, 4, xxvii, 11, and a resurrection is implied in xxv, 6. No Messiah is mentioned.

(10) The Second Section of the *Book of Enoch* embraces lxxxiii-xc. Except in a veiled reference in xc, 33, it does not mention the resurrection; nor, since xc, 37 may refer to John Hyrcanus, does it mention in express terms a Messiah. Angels may be meant by the seventy shepherds. A judgment on the stars and shepherds and blinded sheep is spoken of in xc, 24-27.

(11) *The Testaments of the Twelve Patriarchs,* written according to Charles about 107 B.C., never name Gabriel or Michael, but speak of Satan and Beliar. They speak, also, of the angel of God, of angels of the presence, and of archangels and watchers. In Benjamin x, 8, 9, it speaks of the judgment and says: The Lord judges Israel first for the unrighteousness which they have committed, and then so shall they judge the gentiles [compare

Levi iii, 3]. In Benj. x, 6-8, it speaks of a resurrection of the wicked as well as of the righteous, saying: Ye shall see Enoch, Noah, and Shem, Abraham, and Isaac and Jacob, rising on the right hand of gladness; then, shall we also rise, each over our own tribe, and we shall worship the heavenly king. Then, shall we all be changed, some into glory and some into shame; for the Lord shall judge Israel first for the unrighteousness which they have committed and then shall he judge also the gentiles. In Sim. x, 2, the patriarch says: Then shall I arise; and in Zeb. x, 2, we read: Then shall I arise again in the world. Judah xxv, 1, 3, 4, reads: And after these things shall Abraham, Isaac, and Jacob, arise unto life, and I and my brethren shall be the chiefs of the tribes of Israel . . . and ye shall be the people of the Lord and have one tongue; and there shall be no spirit of deceit, for he shall be cast into the fire forever and they who have died in grief shall arise in joy and they who are put to death for the Lord's sake shall awake. Of the Messiah, the book says in two places that he will be from Judah, and in six, that he will be from Levi. It says, also, that he will war against Beliar and deliver his captives, that he will be free from sin, will walk in meekness and righteousness and open Paradise to the righteous.

(12) The *Book of Jubilees*, written according to Charles at about 107 B.C., has given up all hope in a resurrection. It mentions by name Mastema and Beliar and speaks of the creation and circumstances of angels, of guardian angels, of angels of the presence, of the duty of angels to instruct mankind, and of angels of wood, clouds, fire, etc.; as also, of their marrying the daughters of men, of their punishment, and of their children. It speaks, also, of the final judgment of the fallen angels and of their sons, and of a great judgment, apparently for all men (xxiii, 11, 30). Of the Messiah, it speaks in but one ambiguous passage (xxxi, 18, 19), where it says to Judah: A prince shalt thou be, thou and one of thy sons, over the sons of Jacob: in thee shall be the help of Jacob and in thee be found the salvation of Israel. This reference to the Messiah is based on Gen. xlix, 10.

(13) The *Sibylline Books* are composed of material of such uncertain date, that it is impossible to determine exactly when the

different parts were written. Parts of Book Three are generally supposed to have been written in the latter part of the second century B.C. In line 775 of this book the Messiah is called the son of the great God, and in lines 49, 50, a holy king ruling all the lands of earth. In line 56 the sibyl speaks of the judgment of the great king, the deathless God; and in line 63, of the angel Beliar.

First Century B.C. In the Jewish Literature of the First Century B.C., we find the following testimony about the four subjects.

a. Second Maccabees is silent as to the Messiah and the kingdom. It refers to a good angel sent to save Israel (xi, 6, xv, 21), shows a belief in the resurrection of the righteous (vii, 29) and in a judgment.

b. Third Maccabees speaks of two angels, glorious and terrible, who appear to Eleazar the high-priest; it has nothing to say of the other subjects.

c. The writer of *Fourth Maccabees* does not believe in a resurrection of the body, but "in the immortality of all souls." He is silent on the other doctrines.

d. The *Epistle of Jeremiah* mentions an angel in verse 7, but is silent on the other subjects.

e. The *Psalms of Solomon* speak of the Messiah and of the king, the son of David and God's servant (xviii, 6). They do not mention the other three doctrines.

f. The *Story of Zerubbabel* says nothing about any of these doctrines.

g. The *Song of the Three Children* mentions neither resurrection, judgment, nor Messiah. In verse 26, it speaks of the angel of the Lord as coming into the furnace with Azariah and his fellows; and in verse 37, calls upon the angel of the Lord to bless him.

h. In the *History of Susanna,* the angel of the Lord is mentioned in vs. 45, and the angel of God in vss. 55, 59; but the other subjects are not mentioned.

i. In the story of *Bel and the Dragon,* the angel of the Lord is said to have brought Habbakkuk from Judah to Babylon and to have carried him back again (vss. 36, 39) ; but no reference is made to the other subjects.

j. In the Third Section of *Enoch,* angels are mentioned in xci, 15, and holy angels in xciii, 2; the righteous judgment in xci, 14, and the eternal judgment in xci, 15. Resurrection and Messiah are not referred to.

k. The Fourth Section of *Enoch* in certain passages, where according to Professor Charles the redactor tries to bring the subject-matter of this section into harmony with the rest of the book, mentions the son of man, the day of judgment, seven holy ones, and the names of the leaders of the stars, one for each season and one for each of the twelve months. Uriel is named as leader and shows things to Enoch.

l. The Fifth Section of *Enoch,* written between 95 and 64 B.C., mentions clearly all four subjects. There will be a judgment and a resurrection of the righteous dead (c, 5), a final judgment with the destruction of the former heavens and earth and the creation of a new heaven (xci, 14-16), and a Messianic kingdom, where God and His Son will be united with the children of the earth forever (cv, 2). The holy angels are spoken of in xci, 2 and the wicked in xci, 15. Angels are said to place the prayers of the righteous for a memorial before the Most High (xcix, 3), and to gather the world for judgment (c, 4) and to be guarding over the righteous (c, 5).

m. The Sixth Section of *Enoch,* written between 94 and 79 B.C., speaks of a resurrection of all Israel (li, 1, lxi, 5) and of a judgment on the righteous and the wicked, on angels and on men (xlvi, 2-4, xlviii, 2). The Messiah is called the elect one (xlv, 4, xlviii, 8, xlix, 2, 4, li, 5, 6, lii, 6, 9, liii, 6, lv, 4, lxi, 5, 8, lxii, 1), God's anointed (xlviii, 10), the son of man (xlvi, 2, 3, 4, xlviii, 2), who will possess universal dominion, sit on the throne of his glory, and judge all angels and men, slaying the wicked by the word of his mouth (lxii, 7, 9, 14, lxix, 26, 28, 29). There are righteous angels and the five angels of the presence, Raphael and Michael among them (xxxix, 5, xl, 9), and the angel of peace who went with Enoch (xliii, 3, lii, 3, liv, 4, lv, 2), and angels of punishment (liii, 3, lvi, 1), and thou-

sands of thousands and ten thousand times ten thousand (xl, 1).
Of bad angels, Satan and Azazel are named (liii, 3, 5, 6, lv, 4),
and five Satans (lxix, 4), and twenty leaders of the evil angels
(lxviii, 2). He speaks, also, of the host of God, of Cherubim,
Seraphim, and Ophanim, and all the angels of power (lxi, 10).

1-135 A.D. In the Jewish and Judæo-Christian Literature
from the year 1 A.D. to the year 135 A.D., or thereabouts, we find
the following testimony on these subjects.

a. Apocalyptic and Pseudepigraphical Literature:

(1) The *Martyrdom of Isaiah* mentions several bad angels
Sammael, Malchira, Beliar, and Satan; but it is silent with respect
to the other three subjects, except that by the beloved of i, 13 the
Messiah is probably meant.

(2) The *Assumption of Moses* contains ostensibly a revelation
of Moses, which mentions an angel (x, 2), the judgment (x, 3-8),
and the kingdom (x, 1); but no resurrection, nor Messiah.

(3) The *Apocalypse of Baruch* speaks of angels as created on
the first day (xxi, 6), of the existence of armies of them (xlviii,
10, li, 11, lix, 10), of the fall of them (lvi, 11-13), of the angel
of death (xxi, 6), and names one of them Ramiel, who presides
over true visions (lv, 3, lxiii, 6). It speaks in xxx, 1 of the time
of the advent of the Messiah "when all who have fallen asleep in
hope in him shall rise again"; and in chaps. l and li, the resurrection is described at length. It speaks, also, of the revelation of
the Messiah (xxix, 3), of his correcting the leader of the wicked
and all his impieties (xl, 1), and of his summoning all the nations,
some of whom he will save and some of whom he will slay (lxxii,
2). The Messiah is called a judge (xlviii, 39) and there will be a
day of judgment (lix, 8).

(4) The *Testament of Hezekiah* mentions Sammael, Beliar, and
the armies of Beliar, the angels and armies of the beloved one. It
speaks of the beloved (iii, 17, 18, iv, 3, 6, 9, 13), and of Jesus the
Lord Christ (iv, 13). In iii, 18, the resurrection of the beloved
is mentioned and in iv, 18 the judgment.

(5) The *Vision of Isaiah* speaks frequently of angels (vii,
22, 27, 37, ix, 6, 28, 29, 42, viii, 2, 15, 19, x, 19), and of the angels

of the glory of this world (vi, 13, vii, 2, viii, 4, 23, 25, ix, 11, 21, 25, 31, 32, 37, 39, x, 6, 18, 28, xi, 1, 34), and of angels about the throne (vii, 14-16, 19, 24, 30, 31, 33, viii, 16), and of the angel of the Holy Spirit (vii, 23, ix, 36, 39, 40, x, 4, xi, 4, 33). It also speaks of an angel who was sent to make him see (vi, 13, vii, 11, 21, 25), of a glorious angel (vii, 2), of an angel of death (ix, 16, x, 14), of an angel of Sheol (x, 8), of angels of the firmament and of Sheol (x, 10), and of angels of the air (x, 30). It names Satan and Sammael (xi, 41, 43), and Sammael and his hosts (vii, 9), and speaks of princes, angels, and gods of the world (x, 12), and of princes and powers of that world (x, 15). The Messiah is named (vii, 8, 12), and has many titles, such as beloved (vii, 17, 23, ix, 12), his beloved the Christ (viii, 18), his beloved the Son (viii, 25), the Son crucified (ix, 14), the only begotten (vii, 37), the elect one (viii, 7), one (ix, 26, 38), this one (ix, 33), a certain one (ix, 27), Lord (viii, 26), Lord Christ (x, 17, 32), the Lord who will be called Christ (ix, 13). The Lord, the Lord Christ, who will be called Jesus (ix, 5), is said to have ascended from the grave (ix, 1). The resurrection of the righteous is spoken of in ix, 17, and the judgment in x, 12.

(6) The *Ascension of Isaiah* contains two visions which are said to have been revealed to Isaiah just before he was put to death by Manasseh king of Judah. In form, these visions, especially the one recorded in vii, 1f, are more like those in Daniel than any other thus far noticed, in that they give the details of the history of the times of Jesus in much the same way that Daniel presents the details of the history of the Seleucid kings.

(7) Following for the sake of convenience the divisions suggested by Box, the book of *Fourth Ezra* will be considered under six sections.

(a) The *Ezra Apocalypse* refers only to Messianic woes and tells of an angel who came to speak with Ezra.

(b) The *Son of Man Vision* calls the Messiah God's Son (xiii, 32, 37), and says that he is to judge and to destroy the nations of the earth (xiii, 37, 49), and to defend the people of Israel (xii-xiii, 49).

(c) The *Ezra-Piece* speaks of Ezra's translation to be with God's Son (xiv, 9).

(d) The *Eagle Vision* tells of the Messiah (xii, 32), who shall spring from the seed of David, who shall make the people alive for judgment and then destroy them.

(e) *The Salathiel Section* mentions armies of angels (vi, 3), and angels who guard the souls of the righteous (vii, 85, 95); also, the angel that was sent unto him (v, 31, vii, 7, x, 29). Jeramiel (iv, 36), and Uriel alone are named. Immortality is spoken of in viii, 54 and the resurrection in v, 37, 45. There is to be a judgment (vii, 102-115, viii, 38, 61, x, 16); and punishment and salvation after death (vii, 66, xiv, 34, 35). No personal Messiah is spoken of; but the Messianic times are referred to in vii, 75.

(f) In the passages which Box assigns to the redactor, it is said that God's son, the Messiah, shall be revealed (vii, 28), and after his death, the earth shall restore those who sleep in her (vii, 32) and the dust of those that are at rest therein. The Most High shall be revealed upon his throne of judgment and judge the nations that have been raised (vii, 33-44).

(8) The Book of the *Secrets of Enoch* gives the names of seven individual angels and of at least eight classes of angels. It speaks, also, of the prince of the watchmen and of the rulers of Tartarus. There are elders and rulers of the stellar orders, and terrible angels guarding the snows and clouds and dews. There are angels guarding night and day and sun and paradise and the keys of hell. These angels are myriads in number and will all be brought into judgment. There are at least three archangels, Michael, Gabriel and Praviel (or Vretil), and Sataniel is called the prince of the watchmen. Men also will be judged. There appears to be no reference to a resurrection or to a Messiah.

(9) The *Zadokite Fragments* mention the angels of destruction, the angel of the Mastema, Belial, and the watchers of heaven. A Messiah is spoken of in ii, 10, ix, 10 (B) and a Messiah from Aaron and from Israel in ix, 29 and xv, 4. There is no reference to a resurrection, nor to a judgment to come.

(10) *Philo* discusses angels a number of times,[23] but he does

* See Bohn's Translation, i, 332, ii, 237, 341, 418-420, iv, 252, 334.

not assign names to them, nor give their number. He gives no hint of a Messiah, nor of a resurrection, though he does imply a judgment (iv, 243).

(11) *Josephus,* in discussing Genesis (vi, 1-6), speaks of the angels. If the passage is genuine, he refers to Jesus as the Christ in *Ant.* XVIII, iii, 3. In *Ant.* XVIII, 1, 3; and in *The Wars of the Jews,* VI, v, 4, he tells of a prediction that about the time of the fall of Jerusalem "one from their own country should become governor of the habitable earth."

b. The New Testament:

(1) In the New Testament, angels are mentioned in every book, except Philippians, 1 Thes., 2 Tim., Tit., Philemon, James, and 1, 2 and 3 John. They are given names in Mat., Mark, Luke, John, Acts, Jude, Rev., Rom., 1 Cor., 2 Cor., 1 Thes., 2 Thes., 1 Tim. In Matthew, there are said to be legions of them; and in Hebrews, an innumerable company. Paul denotes their relations to mankind by such words as principalities, authorities, powers, lordships and thrones. They are good or evil. Michael is the archangel of the good and Beelzebub, or Satan, is the prince of this world, of the demons, and of the powers of the air.[24]

(2) The resurrection is mentioned in all the Gospels and in Acts, Rom., 1 Cor., Eph., Phil., 1 Thes., 2 Tim., Heb., 1 Pet., and Rev.; and described at length in 1 Cor. xv.

(3) The judgment is referred to in all the Gospels and in Acts, Rom., 1 Cor., 1 Tim., 2 Tim., Heb., James, 1 Pet., 2 Pet., 1 John, Jude, and Rev.

(4) The Messiah, or Christ, is named in every book of the New Testament. Since the whole New Testament is concerned with Him, it is impossible and unnecessary to give any particular items of evidence upon this subject.

IV. A COMPARATIVE STUDY OF DANIEL'S INFLUENCE

From the survey which has just been given of the literature of the Jews and Christians from the time of Cyrus to 135 A.D., as far as this literature is concerned with the four subjects (angels,

---

[24] See further in any concordance of the Bible.

resurrection, judgment and Messiah) mentioned by Driver as tests of the influence of Daniel on later literature,[25] it is evident that the absence of all apparent reference to these subjects in a given work does not prove that the Book of Daniel was not known to any given author of a later book, much less that the Book of Daniel did not exist before the time of the composition of the later one.

Angels

For, first, with regard to the argument from angels, five points may be considered, covering the statements of the Jewish and Christian writers up to 135 A.D., respecting the existence of angels and their number, classes, ranks, names and duties.

a. As to the existence of angels, no book of the Scriptures denies that there are angels, and most of them, from the earliest to the latest, state expressly that there are angels. Thus, according to J (Gen. xvii; xviii) angels appeared to Abraham; and according to E, Jacob saw angels ascending and descending the ladder (Gen. xxviii). According to JE, an angel appeared to Joshua (Josh. v, 15) and according to Judges to Gideon, Manoah and the wife of Manoah (Jud. vi, 11-24, xiii, 3, 13-21). In 2 Sam. xxiv, 16, it is said that an angel smote Israel with a pest. This evidence is sufficient to show that the idea of the existence of angels was known in Israel long before the time of Cyrus.

b. As to the number of the angels, J speaks of cherubim (Gen. iii, 24) and of sons of God (Gen. vi, 2); and Isaiah vi of seraphim. Michaiah saw the Lord sitting on his throne and all the host of heaven standing by him (1 Kings xxii, 19). It is not necessary to give more examples to prove that Daniel is in agreement with the older Old Testament writers as to the number of the angels.

c. As to the classes, or ranks, of angels, Daniel mentions princes, watchers, and angels. Elsewhere in the Old Testament cherubim and seraphim are spoken of (Gen. iii, 24 and Isa. vi). In Joshua v, 15, the prince of the host of Jehovah addresses Joshua in a JE passage. No writer of the Old Testament, however, had a de-

---

[25] See above pp. 159 f., 175 f.

veloped system of ranks and classes such as we find in Enoch. It follows, therefore, that no argument for the date of Daniel can be made on the basis of what he teaches as to the ranks and classes of angels, nor on the ground of the absence of the influence of what little he says upon these subjects upon later literature. If what he says is a reason for putting his book late, we should also put Isaiah and JE late.

d. As to names of angels, Daniel gives only two, Michael and Gabriel, neither of which is found elsewhere in the Old Testament. Satan, however, is found in 1 Chron. xxi, 1 and in Ps. cix, 6, and with the article (*the* Satan) in Job i, 6, ii, 1 and Zech. iii, 1. Cherubim are mentioned in Gen. iii, 24 and Ezek. x; and seraphim in Isa. vi.

(1) *Tobit,* written probably in the fourth century B.C., names Raphael.

(2) Of works from the second century B.C., the *Sibylline Books* name Beliar; the *Testaments of the Twelve Patriarchs,* Beliar and Satan; and the *Book of Jubilees,* Beliar and Mastema. Of all the other literature of this century the *Book of Enoch* alone mentions the name of any of the angels. Thus, the first part, called the *Book of Noah,* gives the names of nineteen angels and five satans who were leaders of the rebellious sons of God and of four others who were leaders of the holy ones, among whom are Gabriel and Michael; and the so-called First Section mentions the bad angel Azazel and seven holy angels, among whom, also, are Gabriel and Michael.

(3) Of the large number of works from the first century B.C. the Sixth Section of Enoch alone mentions angels by name.

(4) Of works from the year 1 A.D. up to 135 A.D., the *Apocalypse of Baruch* names Ramiel; the *Testament of Hezekiah* Beliar and Sammael; the *Vision of Isaiah,* Sammael and Satan; and the Book of *Fourth Ezra,* Uriel and Jeramiel.

(5) In the New Testament books, Satan is named in Mat. iv, 10 and Rev. xii, 9; Beelzebub in Mat. x, 25, xii, 24, 27, Mark iii, 22; Belial in 2 Cor. vi, 15; Abaddon, or Apollyon, in Rev. ix, 11; "the prince of the demons" in Mat. ix, 34; Gabriel in Luke i, 19, 26; and Michael, in Jude 9, Rev. xii, 7.

e. As to the duties, or functions, of the angels of Daniel, they are three in number, (1) to reveal the will of God; (2) to protect and deliver his people; (3) to preside over the nations.

(1) That it was a function of angels to reveal the will of God is clearly shown in the earliest records of the Old Testament. Angels delivered God's messages to Abraham, Joshua, Gideon, and Manoah; and the Angel of Jehovah spake to Moses, Isaiah and Zechariah. In New Testament times, also, angels spake to Zacharias and Mary and to the shepherds at Bethlehem. That the angels of Daniel performed this function is therefore, no indication of date.

(2) That another function of angels was to protect the people is clearly shown, also, throughout all the history of Israel. They kept the way to the tree of life. They destroyed the armies of Sennacherib. They protected Joshua. They delivered Peter. That an angel should have delivered Daniel from the lions is, therefore, no indication of the date of Daniel v.

(3) That each nation has an angelic prince presiding over its destinies is a doctrine peculiar to Daniel and, hence, is no indication of its date. It is barely possible that there is some ground for such a doctrine in Deut. xxxii, 8, where the Greek translation says, that God set the boundaries of the nations according to the number of the angels of God.[26] The best and closest analogy to this teaching of Daniel is to be found, however, in the view of the Babylonian astrologers, that every nation had a particular star and a particular god presiding over it and representing it in the calculations of the seers. Versed in the literature and customs of the Babylonian wise-men, Daniel has substituted for the stars and gods of their heathen superstition the archangels of the one true God. This affords another proof that Daniel was written at Babylon.

The conclusions which can be drawn from the testimony regarding Angels are as follows:

a. The New Testament recognizes, not merely the existence of

---

[26] This translation involves the change of ישראל into שריאל. Every student of Hebrew palaeography and textual criticism must admit that the Greek reading may be correct.

angels, but that these angels have names. The only good angels mentioned in the New Testament are designated by the very names used by Daniel. No Christian, therefore, who accepts the authority of the New Testament, can logically deny that these names may have been employed as early as the sixth century B.C. Jude says that an archangel named Michael had contended with the devil for the body of Moses. In his vision of the war in heaven, St. John sees this same Michael casting down the Devil and Satan. Luke states Gabriel to have been the name of the angel who brought messages from heaven to Zacharias and Mary, the mother of our Lord. These New Testament writers, therefore, agree in representing the two angels of Daniel as real persons, and not as merely creatures of the imagination. If they are real persons with real names, why may the persons and the names not have been made known at 600 B.C. as well as at 200 B.C.?

b. In the Old Testament outside of Daniel, no good angel is ever named. It is doubtful, also, if in the Old Testament any evil spirit, or angel, is ever designated by a proper name.[27] The good angels are described simply as spirits, or messengers of Jehovah, or of God; and the bad as evil spirits or adversaries. How, then, does it come that Daniel alone among biblical writers designates two of the good angels by proper names? (1) The simplest answer to this question is to say that it pleased God to have his messengers reveal their names to Daniel alone of the Old Testament prophets. (2) Another answer might be, that a revelation of the names of angels at an earlier time might have enticed the people to the worship of the messengers. (3) A third answer is that the idea of naming angels was derived from the Persians, who designated the Amashpands, or attributes of the Deity, by the terms that denote them. But, as we have already shown,[28]

---

[27] The Hebrew word *satan*, employed in 1 Chron. xxi, 1 and Psalm cix, 6, is probably to be translated simply as adversary. In Job i, 6, ii, 1, and Zech. iii, 1, 2, where it has the definite article, the rendering "the adversary" should almost certainly be given. In Gen. iii, 1, this adversary is called the serpent. Hence, in Rev. xii, 9, we are told, that "the great dragon was cast out, that old serpent, called the Devil, and Satan, which deceiveth the whole world."

[28] See chapter V.

these names are names of attributes and not of persons and they are never used to designate the messengers of God. If, however, the Jews derived the idea of naming angels from the Persians, how are we to account for the fact that of Old Testament writers Daniel alone gives names to angels? The critics assign about half of the literature of the Old Testament to Persian and Greek times; and of this literature, Daniel alone names angels, though it was written they tell us among the very latest of them all. Long after the Persian empire had ceased to exist, after the greatest of Alexander's successors had been crushed at Pydna and Magnesia, when the ashes of Corinth were lifting their grey bosom to the unheeding sun and the Roman legates were dictating peace to the rival monarchs of Syria and Egypt, this Persian idea, like a long lost seed, is supposed to have suddenly sprung up in Palestine, a thousand miles from the place of its birth and four hundred years after the time that Babylon fell before the arms of Cyrus. Believe it who can and will!

(4) The fourth and most probable answer to the question as to why the names of the angels of God were first revealed to Daniel is, that he was the first and only writer of an Old Testament book that lived in Babylon and was conversant with the literature and language of the Babylonians. From the earliest times, the Babylonians had been in the habit of giving names to the messengers of the gods. In the Creation Tablets, Gaga is the messenger of Anshar. In the story of Erishkigal, Nergal and fourteen others who accompany him are mentioned by name. In Ishtar's Descent to Hades, Namtar is called the messenger of Erishkigal. When, therefore, a messenger came from the true God to a Jew who had been educated in all these old Babylonian legends which assigned names to the messengers of their false gods, it was perfectly natural that his name should be announced. The fact that Daniel names his angels and that the writers who lived in Palestine do not name them is a strong proof of the genuineness of Daniel's book, and that it was really written in Babylon.

c. The main theme of the *Book of Noah* is the fall of the angels, as recorded in Gen. vi, 1-8. In large measure, the fallen angels are the theme, also, of the First Section of *Enoch*. It was natural, therefore, that those writing on such a subject should have given names to the sons of God that they were describing. None of the other five Sections of *Enoch*, however, nor any other of the numerous works whose teaching on angels is cited above, covering a period of nearly seven centuries, gives the names of more than two or three angels; many of them name one only. The Revelation of St. John alone names three, and most of the New Testament books name none. As against twelve different names for good and bad angels together in all the other literature of these seven centuries, the three Sections of *Enoch* give the names of about thirty.

The penchant for naming angels seems, therefore, to have been confined to the writers of the parts of *Enoch* which deal expressly with angels and their history. To argue from such documents as to the usage of books that only mention angels incidentally is, to say the least, a hazardous and inconclusive method of procedure. Judging from the numerous names of the messengers of the gods and of the evil spirits that are found in the Babylonian legends and magical works the Book of Enoch and Daniel and all the other works naming angels, may have been written at any time after the children of Israel were carried captive and brought into contact with the demon worshippers of Babylon.

We conclude, therefore, that there is nothing in the teachings of Daniel with regard to angels, that necessitates the placing of the composition of the book at a date later than the sixth century B.C.; and that, on the contrary, there is much that indicates Babylon as the place where it was written.

Resurrection

With regard to the Resurrection:

a. Daniel makes but one statement. In xii, 2, he says that "many of them that sleep in the dust of the earth shall awake, some to everlasting life, and some to shame and everlasting contempt." A resurrection is taught, also, in Isaiah xxvi, 19, where we read: "Thy dead men shall live, together with my dead body shall they arise. Awake and sing, ye that dwell in dust: for thy dew is as the dew of herbs, and the earth shall cast out the dead."

In Job xix, 25, 26 a belief in a resurrection is expressed by the patriarch in the words: "I know that my Redeemer liveth, and that he shall stand at the latter day upon the earth: and though, after my skin, (worms) destroy this body, yet in my flesh shall I see God." Moreover, the thought of a possible resurrection was present in his mind, when he asked, "If a man die, shall he live (again)?" (xiv, 14). In Matthew xxii, 31, Jesus seems to assert that the fact of a resurrection was involved in the statement, "I am the God of Abraham, and the God of Isaac, and the God of Jacob." In Acts ii, 27-32, Peter declares that David had taught the doctrine of the resurrection in Ps. xvi, 10, where he says: "Thou wilt not leave my soul in hell; neither wilt thou suffer thy Holy One to see corruption." In 1 Cor. xv, 54, Paul discerns a reference to a resurrection in the words of Isaiah xxv, 8: "He will swallow up death in victory."

b. Further, that the ancient Israelites believed in the possibility at least of a resurrection is shown by the story of the raising of Samuel by the witch of Endor (1 Sam. xxviii, 11-20), by the story of the man who was revived by touching the bones of Elisha (2 Kings xiii, 21), and by Ezekiel's vision of the dry bones (Ezek. xxxvii, 1-10). Moreover, Elijah and Elisha each raised the dead to life (1 Kings xvii, 17-24, 2 Kings iv, 32-35); and Enoch and Elijah were both translated that they should not see death, thus teaching that the soul and the body could be united in the other world.

c. Of uncanonical works from before the year 100 B.C., the only ones that refer to a resurrection are the First Section of *Enoch* which says in xxv, 3-6 that the righteous and holy shall eat of a tree, whose fragrance shall be in their bones, and they shall live a long life on the earth; and the *Testaments of the XII Patri-archs,* which speak of a resurrection of the wicked as well as of the righteous (Benj. x, 6-8).

d. Of works from the first century B.C., *Second Maccabees,* the Fourth Section of *Enoch* (c, 5), the Fifth Section of *Enoch* (li, 1, lxi, 5), and the *Psalms of Solomon* (ii, 35, xiv, 2), teach a resurrection of the righteous dead; but not one of them teaches clearly the resurrection of the wicked, though the writer of *4 Enoch* may possibly mean that they shall be raised for judgment.

e. Of non-biblical works from the first century A.D., the *Apocalypse of Baruch* (l, 2) states that all that have fallen asleep in hope in God shall rise again, and that the earth will assuredly restore the dead (xxx, 1, 1, 2). In a passage from 4 Ezra, which is said by Box to have been added about 120 A.D., it is said that those that sleep in the earth shall be restored to life in order to be judged (vii, 52). Josephus, also, affirms his belief in a resurrection. The *Testament of Hezekiah* refers to the resurrection of the beloved (iii, 18), and the *Vision of Isaiah,* to the resurrection of the righteous (ix, 17).

f. All of the New Testament writers, with the exception of James and Jude, who say nothing about it, teach a resurrection of both good and bad.

From this testimony, it is evident, that, outside the New Testament, of the vast body of literature cited above only the *XII Patriarchs, 2 Maccabees,* the Fourth and Fifth and possibly the First Section of *Enoch,* the *Psalms of Solomon,* the *Apocalypse of Baruch,* and *4 Ezra,* and *Josephus,* refer to a resurrection and that of these, the *XII Patriarchs* alone teaches that both righteous and wicked shall be raised. Since the last mentioned work was written, according to Professor Charles, about 107 B.C., it is evident that, even if the author got his idea of a resurrection from Daniel, this will not determine whether Daniel was written in the sixth, or in the second century B.C.

Judgment

As to the Judgment:

a. Daniel says that the judgment was set, the Ancient of Days presiding, and that the books were opened and the beast slain (vii, 10-14, 26) ; and that judgment was given to the saints of the Most High and they possessed the kingdom (vii, 22). There are involved in these statements the following facts:

(1) There will be a judgment. (2) There will be a judge. (3) Certain titles of the judge. (4) Books will be opened. (5) The beast will be slain. (6) Judgment will be given to the saints

of the Most High. Taking these facts up one after the other, it will be seen from the testimony that they do not support the view that Daniel was composed in the second century B.C.

(1) The fact of a judgment is mentioned in Isa. xxviii, 17, xlii, 1, Zeph. iii, 8, Hag. ii, 7, 9, 22, 23, Zech. vii-xiv, Mal. iii, Ps. i, 5, lviii, 11, xcvi, 14, xcviii, 9. Most of these texts concern the judgment of the nations, just as those in Daniel do.

(2) In all of the texts cited under (1) the person of the judge is God, just as in Daniel.

(3) The titles of the judge are "the Ancient of Days" and "the most High." The first of these is found nowhere except in Daniel. The second phrase, the most High, occurs as early as Num. xxiv, 16 and 2 Sam, xxii, 14.

(4) The idea of a book of life being kept by the Lord appears already in Ex. xxxii, 32, 33 (ascribed by the critics to E), in Isa. iv, 3, and in Ps. lxix, 28. In Mal. iii, 16 (cf. Ps. xl, 8, lvi, 8) these books are called books of remembrance in which good deeds were recorded, and in Isa. lxv, 6, books where evil deeds are recorded. It is obvious, therefore, that the idea is earlier than the sixth century B.C.

(5) The statement that the beast was slain is merely a detail of the vision of the four beasts. As this whole vision is peculiar to Daniel, so also is this feature of the description of the fourth beast. It is worthy of note, however, in this connection, that no vision of any of the apocalyptic books names the same animals as those mentioned here by Daniel. Daniel mentions the lion *(aryeh)*, a word familiar from its use in Judges xiv, 8, 1 Kings xiii, 24, and elsewhere. The word for bear *(dov)* is found in 1 Sam. xvii, 34; the word for leopard *(nemer)* in Hos. xiii, 7, Is. xi, 6—all early passages. It will be noted, also, that Daniel's lion has eagle's wings, like the winged lions of Assyria and Babylonia,—a very appropriate figure in a vision at Babylon in the time of Belshazzar; but scarcely fitting to one seen, or imagined, by a Jew in Palestine in the time of the anti-foreign revival under the Maccabees. This winged lion may be compared to the living creatures of Ezekiel and to the seraphim of Isaiah. The apocalyptic literature of the post-Babylonian times dropped this symbolism of wings as a fea-

ture of animals that did not naturally have them. In 4 Ezra x, 1, the wings are wings of eagles.

(6) That the judgment was given to the saints of the Most High is ambiguous, since it is not clear whether it means that the saints were judged, or that they issued judgment. That by saints the holy people is meant seems certain from vii, 27, where it is said, that the kingdom shall be given to the people of the saints of the Most High. That God will judge his people is taught in Deut. xxxii, 36, Mal. iii, 5, Ps. l, 4, cxxxv, 14, and in the *XII Patriarchs* (Benj. x, 8). In the Fifth Section of *Enoch* (xlvii, 2) written about 95 B.C., this idea of Daniel may be referred to when it says that the holy angels pray on behalf of the righteous that judgment may be done unto them. It is clear, then, that according to this interpretation the Book of Daniel may have been written either in the sixth, or in the second century B.C. The other interpretation, which makes the holy people participate in the judgment, is taught by Mat. xix, 28, Luke xxii, 30, and 1 Cor. vi, 3. Since it is not found in the early apocalyptical literature, it can have no bearing upon the date of Daniel.

As far, then, as the teaching of Daniel on the judgment is concerned, there is no reason for supposing that it may not have been written as early as 535 B.C.

Messiah

The teachings of Daniel with regard to the Messiah may be considered under the four heads of (a) the idea of a Messiah, (b) the names and titles of the Messiah, (c) his character, and (d) his functions.

a. As to the Idea of a Messiah:

(1) In the literature of the Old Testament preceding the time of Daniel, it is found expressed with more or less clearness and certainty in the "seed" of Gen. iii, 15 (J), in the "Shiloh" of Gen. xlix, 10 (J), in the "star" of Num. xxiv, 17, (JE), in the "prophet" of Deut. xviii, 15 (D), in the "prince of peace" of Is. ix, 6, 7, in the "rod of the stem of Jesse and the branch out of his roots" of Is. xi, 1, in the "righteous branch" of Jer. xxiii, 5, 6, and xxxiii, 11-17, in the "shepherd and prince (*nasi'*)" of

Ezek. xxxiv, 23-31, and in the "ruler in Israel" of Mi. v, 2. From these passages, it is evident that the idea of a Messiah antedated the time of Cyrus, and hence that the presence of this idea in Daniel does not require us to place its date as late as the second century B.C.

(2) The idea of a Messiah is found, also, in the literature between Cyrus and 200 B.C. Thus, the "branch" is spoken of in Zech. iii, 8, vi, 12, the "king" in ix, 9; while Mal. iii, 1 speaks of the coming of the "messenger of the covenant."

That the idea of a Messiah should be absent from Esther and certain other post-captivity books is no more an argument against the early date of Daniel than it is an argument against the early date of J, E, D, Isaiah, Jeremiah, and Ezekiel. On the contrary, according to the critics' way of arguing, the presence of the idea in Zechariah and Malachi should argue for the earlier date of Daniel.

Again, if the absence of the idea of a Messiah from Esther, Ezra, Nehemiah, P, and other alleged post-captivity works proves that Daniel was not known to the authors of these works, by parity of reasoning its absence from the four books of Maccabees, from the additions to Daniel and Esther, from the Martyrdom of Isaiah, the Ascension of Moses, and other late works would prove that their authors, also, knew nothing of Daniel. Besides, since most of them show no knowledge of J, D, Isaiah, Jeremiah, Ezekiel, and many other Old Testament books, are we to presume that they, also, were unknown to them? It is absurd to suppose that every writer should express all his ideas on every subject in every book that he writes. No one does do it. No one can do it. No one should be expected to do it. Nor should anyone be accused of ignorance, because he says nothing about a subject concerning which he may have had an opinion, but did not think best to express it. How can Bevan or Cornill know what the author of Esther knew about the idea of a Messiah? It would be interesting to all historians and searchers after truth, if they would reveal the sources of their information. The author of Esther is dead. He has said not a word about the Messiah, nor about why he said not a word. Neither intellect, nor imagination, can possibly discover what he might have written, had he written, nor why he did not write what he did not write.

b. Nor do the Names and Titles of the Messiah give us information from which we may determine the date of Daniel. We shall demonstrate this by giving these names and titles as they appear in the literature of Jews and Christians up to the year 135 A.D. And here we shall give, not merely those that have been universally acknowledged as designating the Messiah, but those also that were in later times interpreted as referring to him.

I. NAMES AND TITLES OF THE MESSIAH IN THE OLD TESTAMENT

1. The seed of Eve, Gen. iii, 15.
2. The seed of Abraham, Gen. xxii, 18.
3. Shiloh, Gen. xlix, 10 (Targum of Onkelos: Messiah whose is the kingdom).
4. A prophet like Moses, Deut. xviii, 18.
5. A star, Num. xxiv, 17.
6. A sceptre, Num. xxiv, 17 (Onkelos translates by "Messiah").
7. A Son of God, Ps. ii, 7, Isa. ix, 6 (?).
8. The prince of peace, Isa. ix, 6 (Targum: Messiah who shall multiply peace, etc.).
9. Wonderful, Isa. ix, 6.
10. Counsellor, Isa. ix, 6.
11. Mighty God, Isa. ix, 6.
12. The everlasting Father, Isa. ix, 6.
13. Jehovah, our righteousness, Jer. xxiii, 6.
14. God's messenger, Isa. xlii, 19.
15. God's servant, Isa. xlix, 3 (Targum to xlii, 1, lii, 13, liii, 10, calls this servant "Messiah").
16. God's righteous servant, Isa. liii, 11.
17. The man of sorrows, Isa. liii, 3.
18. The shepherd of Israel, Ezek. xxxiv, 23.
19. The root of Jesse, Isa. xi, 10.
20. A rod out of the stem of Jesse, and a branch (Heb. נצר, Targum משיחא) from his roots, Isa. xi, 1.
21. The branch of Jehovah, Isa. iv, 2 (Targum: The Messiah of Jehovah).
22. The branch of righteousness, Jer., xxxiii, 15 (Targum: A Messiah of righteousness).
23. The righteous branch, Jer. xxiii, 5 (Targum: A Messiah of the righteous).

24. A plant of renown, Ezek. xxxiv, 29.
25. A great light, Isa. ix, 2.
26. The rock of ages, Isa. xxvi, 4.
27. A stone, Isa. xxviii, 16.
28. A tried stone, Isa. xxviii, 16.
29. A precious corner stone, Isa. xxviii, 16.
30. The head of the corner, Ps. cxviii, 22.
31. A sure foundation, Isa. xxviii, 16.
32. God's elect, Isa. xlii, 1.
33. The redeemer (*goel*), Isa. lix, 20.
34. The witness, Isa. lv, 4.
35. The holy one of Israel, Isa. xlix, 7.
36. A leader (*nagid*), Isa. lv, 4.
37. A commander, Isa. lv, 4, A ruler, Mi. v, 2.
38. David their king, Jer. xxx, 9 (Targum: Messiah the son of David their king).
39. Messiah, Ps. ii, 2.
40. The man of (Jehovah's) fellowship, Zech. xiii, 7.
41. My (Jehovah's) Shepherd, Zech. xiii, 7.
42. My servant, the branch, Zech. iii, 8 (Targum: My servant, the Messiah).
43. The branch, Zech. vi, 12 (Targum: Messiah).
44. The king, Zech. xiv, 16, Jer. xxx, 9.
45. The King, just and having salvation, Zech. ix, 9.
46. A fountain for sin and for uncleanness, Zech. xiii, 1.
47. The one whom they have pierced, Zech. xii, 10.
48. The angel of the covenant, Mal. iii, 1.
49. The sun of righteousness, Mal. iii, 20.
50. (David's) Lord. Ps. cx, 1.
51. The salvation of Israel, Ps. xiv, 7, liii, 7.

II. Names and Titles from the Extra-Biblical Literature before Christ

1. King, Sib. Oracles iii, 652, Pss. Sol. xvii, 23.
2. Righteous king, Pss. Sol. xvii, 35.
3. King, son of David, Pss. Sol. xvii, 23.
4. King Christ the Lord, Pss. Sol. xvii, 36.
5. His King is Lord, Pss. Sol. xvii, 38 (?).
6. God's anointed, or Messiah, Enoch xlviii, 10, lii, 4. [29]

[29] This and the following titles up to 11 inclusive are from the Fifth Section of Enoch, which was written, according to Professor Charles, between 94 and 64 B.C. In Enoch, the Ethiopic word is *Mahih* the exact equivalent of the Hebrew Mashiah.

7. The elect one, Enoch xlv, 3, 4, xlix, 2, 4, li, 5bis, lii, 6, 9, lv, 4, lxi, 5, 8, 10, lxii, 1.
8. The elect one of righteousness and faith, Enoch xxxix, 6.
9. The righteous one, Enoch xxxviii, 2.
10. The righteous and elect one, Enoch liii, 6.
11. The son of man, Enoch xlvi, 2, 3, 4, xlviii, 2, lxii, 5, 7, 9, 14, lxiii, 11, lxix, 26, 27, 29, lxx, 1, lxxi, 14, 17.
12. The white bull, Enoch xc, 37.
13. God's son, Enoch cv, 2.
14. A prince, Jubilees xxxi, 18.
15. The help of Jacob, Jub. xxxi, 19.
16. The salvation of Israel, Jub. xxxi, 19.
17. God's servant, Pss. Sol. xviii, 6.
18. The king, the son of David, Pss. Sol. xviii, 6.
19. King, the anointed of the Lord, Pss. Sol. xvii, 6, xviii, 8.
20. His (God's) anointed, Pss. Sol. xviii, 6.
21. The Messiah, 2 Bar. xxix, 3, xxx, 1, xxxix, 7, xl, 1, lxxii, 2.
22. The rod of righteousness, XII, Pat. Jud. xxiv, 6.
23. The star of peace, XII, Pat. Jud. xxiv, 1a.
24. The salvation of the Lord, XII. Pat. Dan v. 10.
25. A lamb, XII. Pat. Jos. xix, 8, Enoch xc, 38 (?).

III. Names and Titles in the Extra-Biblical Literature from 1 to 135 a.d.

1. The beloved, Vision of Isaiah vii, 17, 23, ix, 12, Mart. Isa. i, 13, Test. Hez. iii, 17, 18, iv, 3, 6, 9, 13.
2. His beloved the Christ, Vis. Isa. viii, 18.
3. His beloved son, Vis. Isa. viii, 25.
4. Jesus, the Lord Christ, Test. Hez. iv, 13.
5. The only begotten, Vis. Isa. vii, 37.
6. The elect one, Vis. Isa. viii, 7.
7. The Lord, Vis. Isa. viii, 26.
8. The Lord God, the Lord Christ, who is called Jesus, Vis. Isa. ix, 5.
9. The Lord who will be called Christ, Vis. Isa. ix, 13.
10. (God's) son, Vis. Isa. ix, 14, 16, Son of Man Vis. xiii, 32, 37, 4 Ezra xiii, 52, xiv, 9.
11. The Lord Christ, Vis. Isa. ix, 5, 17, 32, Test. Hez. iv, 13, Odes. Sol. xvii, 15, xxxix, 10.
12. That one, Vis. Isa. ix, 26, 27, 31, 38.
13. Messiah, Odes Sol. xxiv, 1, xli, 16, Eagle Vis. xii, 32, Redactor Ezra vii, 28, Zad. Frag. ii, 10, ix, 10b, 29, xv, 4.
14. The loving one, Odes Sol. iii, 8.
15. The pleroma, Odes Sol. vii, 14.

16. The word, Odes Sol. xii, 8, 9, 11, xli, 11.
17. The Son of God, Odes Sol. xxxvi, 3, xlii, 21.
18. The son of the Most High, Odes Sol. xli, 14.
19. Jesus, Test. Hez. iv, 13, Vis. Isa. ix, 5, Josephus Antiq. xviii, iii, 3.
20. Christ, Josephus Ant. xviii, iii, 3, Tacitus: Annals. xv, 44, Odes Sol. ix, 2, xxix, 6, xli, 3, Vis. Isa. viii, 18, ix, 13.
21. Jesus who was called Christ, Jos. Ant. xx, ix, 1.
22. (God's) Son the Messiah, 4 Ezra vii, 27, 29.
23. The lion, the Messiah from the seed of David, 4 Ezra xii, 32.

IV. NAMES AND TITLES OF THE MESSIAH IN THE DIFFERENT BOOKS OF THE NEW TESTAMENT

A. NAMES AND TITLES IN MATTHEW

1. Son (i.e., of God or of the Lord) ii, 15, xi, 27 *ter*, xxviii, 19.
2. Young child, ii, 8, 9, 11, 13, 14, 20, 21.
3. Son of man, 32 times.
4. The son of the carpenter, xiii, 55.
5. Son of God, iv, 3, xiv, 33, xxvii, 40, 43, 54.
6. Jesus, son of God, viii, 29.
7. Christ, son of God, xxvi, 63.
8. Christ, the son of the living God, xvi, 16.
9. Beloved Son, iii, 17.
10. The (my, his) son, xxi, 37, 38, xxii, 2.
11. Son of David, ix, 27, xii, 23, xxi, 9, 15, cf. xxii, 42.
12. Lord, son of David, xv, 22, xx, 30, 31.
13. Jesus, 131 times.
14. Christ 11 times.
15. Jesus Christ, i, 1, 18.
16. Jesus, the Christ, xvi, 20.
17. Jesus which is called Christ, xxvii, 17, 22.
18. Jesus Christ, the son of David, the son of Abraham, i. 1.
19. Lord (of Christ), 33 times.
20. King, xxi, 5, xxv, 34, 40.
21. King of Israel, xxvii, 42.
22. King of the Jews, ii, 2, xxvii, 11, 37.
23. Great King, v, 35.
24. Governor (*hegoumenos*), ii, 6.
25. Master (*rabbi*), xxiii, 7, 8, xxvi, 25, 49.
26. Master (*didaskalos*), viii, 19, ix, 11, xii, 38, xvii, 24, xix, 16, xxii, 16, 24, 36, xxvi, 18.
27. Master (*kathegetes*), xxiii, 10.
28. Nazarene, ii, 23.
29. Jesus, the Nazarene, xxvi, 71.

30. Jesus, the prophet of Nazareth of Galilee, xxi, 11.
31. One of the prophets, xvi, 14.
32. John the Baptist, xvi, 14.
33. Elijah, xvi, 14.
34. Jeremiah, xvi, 14.
35. He that should come, xi, 3.
36. One greater than the temple, xii, 6.
37. One greater than Jonah, xii, 41.
38. One greater than Solomon, xii, 42.
39. My (i.e., God's) servant, xii, 18.
40. My (i.e., God's) beloved, xii, 18.
41. Just (man), xxvii, 19, 24.
42. This (man, or fellow), xii, 24, xxvi, 61.
43. That deceiver, xxvii, 63.
44. Beelzebub, x, 25.
45. Stone, xxi, 42.

B. NAMES AND TITLES IN MARK AND PETER

MARK

1. Son (i.e., of God), xiii, 32.
2. Son of man, 14 times.
3. Son of Mary, vi, 3.
4. Son of God, iii, 11, xv, 39.
5. Beloved Son (i.e., of God), i, 11, ix, 7.
6. Jesus, son of the Most High God, v, 7.
7. Jesus Christ, the son of God, i, 1.
8. Christ, the son of the Blessed, xiv, 61.
9. Son of David, x, 48, xii, 35.
10. Jesus, son of David, x, 47.
11. Jesus, 93 times.
12. Jesus of Nazareth (or the Nazarene), i, 24, xiv, 67
13. Christ, viii, 29, ix, 41, xii, 35, xiii, 21.
14. Jesus Christ, i, 1.
15. Christ, the king of Israel, xv, 32.
16. Lord (of Christ), 8 times.
17. Lord of the sabbath, ii, 28.
18. Holy One of God, i, 24.
19. The king of the Jews, xv, 2, 9, 12, 18, 26.
20. Master (rabbi), ix, 5, xi, 21, xiv, 45 bis.
21. Master (rabboni), x, 51.
22. Master (didaskalos), 12 times.
23. Good master (didaskalos), x, 17.
24. A prophet, vi, 15, viii, 28.

25. John, vi, 16.
26. John the Baptist, vi, 14, viii, 28.
27. Elijah, vi, 15, viii, 28.
28. Stone, xii, 10.

FIRST PETER

1. Christ, 8 times.
2. Christ Jesus, v, 10 (?), 14 (?).
3. Jesus Christ, 8 times.
4. Lord (i.e., of Christ), ii, 3, 13, iii, 12*bis*.
5. Lord Jesus, iii, 15 (Syr. Pesh: Lord Messiah).
6. Lord Jesus Christ, i, 3.
7. Shepherd and bishop of souls, ii, 25.
8. Chief Shepherd, v, 4.
9. Stone, ii, 7.
10. Precious corner stone, ii, 6.

SECOND PETER

1. Our God and our Saviour, Jesus Christ, i, 1.
2. My beloved Son, i, 17.
3. Lord, (i.e., of Christ), ii, 9, 11, iii, 9, 10, 15.
4. Jesus Christ, i, 1.
5. Jesus our Lord, i, 2.
6. Lord Jesus Christ, i, 8, 14, 16.
7. Lord and Saviour, iii, 2.
8. Master (*despotes*), ii, 1.

PETER'S SPEECHES IN ACTS

1. Seed, iii, 25.
2. (God's) son, (Jesus), iii, 13, 26.
3. Holy child Jesus, iv, 27, 30.
4. Jesus, i, 16, ii, 32, 36.
5. Jesus of Nazareth (or the Nazarene), ii, 22, x, 38.
6. Christ, ii, 31, 36, iii, 18, iv, 26.
7. Jesus Christ, ii, 38, iii, 20, ix, 34, x, 36, 48 (?).
8. Jesus Christ, the Nazarene, iii, 6, iv, 10.
9. Lord, i, 24 (?), ii, 21 (?), 25 (?), 34, 36, iii, 19, iv, 29, xii, 11, 17.
10. Lord Jesus, i, 21.
11. Lord of all, x, 36.
12. Lord Jesus Christ, xi, 17, xv, 11 (?).
13. Holy One, ii, 27, iii, 14.
14. The Just, iii, 14.
15. Prince of life, iii, 15.
16. A prophet, iii, 22.

C. NAMES AND TITLES IN LUKE AND ACTS

LUKE

1. Son, x, 22 *ter*.
2. Son of man, 26 times.
3. Son of Joseph, iii, 23, iv, 22 (?).
4. Son of God, i, 35, iv, 3, 9, xxii, 70.
5. Son of the Highest, i, 32.
6. Jesus, son of God Most high, viii, 28.
7. Christ, the son of God, iv, 41 (?).
8. Beloved Son, iii, 22, ix, 35.
9. Son of David, xviii, 39, xx, 41 (?).
10. Jesus, son of David, xviii, 38.
11. Christ, the son of David, xx, 41 (?).
12. Jesus, 98 times.
13. Christ, ii, 11, iv, 41, xxii, 67, xxiii, 2, 39, xxiv, 26, 46.
14. Jesus, Master (*epistates*), ix, 33.
15. Jesus, the Nazarene, iv, 34, xviii, 37, xxiv, 19.
16. Jesus, Lord, xxiii, 42.
17. Lord (*despotes*), xxiii, 42.
18. Lord Jesus, xxiv, 3.
19. Lord's Christ, ii, 26.
20. Christ, the Lord, ii, 11.
21. Christ of God, ix, 20.
22. Holy One of God, iv, 34.
23. Holy thing that shall be born, i, 35.
24. Christ, the chosen of God, xxiii, 35.
25. King, xix, 38.
26. King of the Jews, xxiii, 3, 37, 38.
27. Master (*epistates*), v, 5, viii, 24*bis*, 45, ix, 33, 49, xvii, 13.
28. Master (*didaskalos*), 14 times.
29. Good Master (*didaskalos*), xviii, 18.
30. A prophet, ix, 19.
31. Great prophet, vii, 16.
32. One of the old prophets, ix, 19.
33. He that should come, vii, 19.
34. John the Baptist, ix, 19.
35. Elijah, ix, 19.
36. Christ, a king, xxiii, 2.
37. Salvation, ii, 30.
38. A man eating and drinking, a friend of publicans and sinners, vii, 34.
39. Stone, xx, 17.

Acts

1. Son (i.e., of God), xiii, 33.
2. Son of man, vii, 56.
3. Son of God, viii, 37 (?), ix, 20.
4. Lord (*despotes*), iv, 24 (?).
5. Lord Jesus, 12 times.
6. Lord Jesus Christ, 6 times.
7. His (God's) child (Jesus), iii, 13, 26.
8. Thy (God's) holy child, Jesus, iv, 27, 30.
9. Jesus, 26 times.
10. Christ, iv, 26, xviii, 5 (?).
11. Jesus Christ, 9 times.
12. Christ Jesus, xix, 4 (?).
13. Jesus of Nazareth, or the Nazarene, ii, 22, vi, 14, x, 38, xxii, 8, xxvi, 9.
14. Jesus Christ, the Nazarene, iii, 6, iv, 10.
15. Saviour, Jesus, xiii, 23.
16. Prince and Saviour, v, 31.
17. Holy One, ii, 27.
18. The holy One and just, iii, 14.
19. Just One, vii, 52, xxii, 14.
20. A prophet, iii, 22, 23, vii, 37.
21. Judge of quick and dead, x, 42.
22. Prince of life, iii, 15.
23. Lord of all, x, 36.
24. Stone, iv, 11.

D. NAMES AND TITLES IN JOHN'S WRITINGS [30]

1. Son (i.e., of God), 16 times, 1 John, 9 times, 2 John, vs. 9.
2. Son of man, 11 times.
3. Son of God, 7 times, 1 John, 8 times.
4. (God's) son, Jesus Christ, 1 John i, 3, iii, 23, v, 20.
5. Jesus (Christ ?), His Son, 1 John i, 7.
6. Christ, the son of God, xi, 27, xx, 31.
7. Christ, the son of the living God, vi, 69 (A.V.); the Holy One of God (ARV).
8. Only begotten Son, iii, 16, 1 John iv, 9.
9. The only begotten Son which is in the bosom of the Father, i, 18.
10. The only begotten of the Father, i, 14.
11. The only begotten Son of God, iii, 18.

[30] Unless specially noted the references will be to the *Gospel* of John.

12. The Son of the Father, 2 John 3.
13. The Lord Jesus Christ, the Son of the Father, 2 John, 3.
14. Jesus, 252 times, 1 John ii, 22, iv, 15, v, 1, 5, Rev. xiv, 12, xvii, 6, xix, 10*bis*, xx, 4, xxii, 16.
15. Jesus, the son of Joseph, vi, 42.
16. Jesus, the Nazarene, xviii, 5, 7.
17. Jesus of Nazareth, the son of Joseph, i, 45.
18. Christ 14 times, 1 John ii, 22, v, 1; 2 John 9*bis*; Rev. xi, 15, xii, 10, xx, 4, 6.
19. Jesus Christ, i, 17, xvii, 3; 1 John iv, 2, 3, v, 6; 2 John 7; Rev. i, 1, 2, 5, 9*bis*, xii, 17.
20. Jesus Christ, the righteous, 1 John ii, 1.
21. Jesus Christ, the faithful witness, the firstborn from the dead, the ruler of the kings of the earth, Rev. i, 5.
22. Lamb, Rev., 23 times.
23. The lamb of God, i, 29, 36.
24. Lord, 37 times, Rev., 7 times.
25. Lord Jesus, Rev. xxii, 20.
26. Lord Jesus Christ, Rev. xxii, 21 (A. V.; A. R. V., Lord Jesus).
27. Lord of lords and king of kings, Rev. xvii, 14.
28. Lord God of the spirits of the prophets, Rev. xxii, 6.
29. Lord and God, xx, 28.
30. The Logos, (or Word), i, 1*ter*, 14, 1 John v, 7 (?).
31. The Word of God, Rev. xix, 13.
32. The Word of life, 1 John, i, 1.
33. Holy One, 1 John ii, 20 (?).
34. The holy, the true, who has the key of David *et cet.* Rev. iii, 7.
35. Rabbi, i, 38, 49, iii, 2, vi, 25, ix, 2, xi, 8.
36. Rabboni, xx, 16.
37. Master (*didaskalos*), 8 times.
38. Master, or Lord (*despotes*), Rev. vi, 10.
39. Sir (*kurios*), 17 times.
40. A prophet, vi, 14, ix, 17.
41. The prophet, vii, 40.
42. The door, x, 9.
43. The door of the sheep, x, 7.
44. The vine, xv, 5.
45. The true vine, xv, 1.
46. The bread of life, vi, 35.
47. The light, xii, 46.
48. The light of the world, viii, 12, ix, 5.
49. The comforter, xiv, 16.
50. Messias, i, 41, iv, 25.
51. King, xii, 15.

52. King of Israel, i, 49, xii, 13.
53. King of the Jews, xviii, 39, xix, 3, 19, 21.
54. Jesus of Nazareth, the king of the Jews, xix, 19.
55. King of saints, Rev. xv, 3.
56. King of kings and Lord of lords, Rev. xix, 16.
57. Saviour of the world, iv, 42.
58. The good shepherd, x, 11, 14.
59. The Amen, the faithful and true witness, the beginning of the creation of God, Rev. iii, 14.
60. Alpha and Omega, Rev. i, 8, 11, xxi, 6, xxii, 13.
61. The beginning and the end, Rev. xxi, 6.
62. The first and the last, Rev. 1, 17.
63. The living One, Rev. 1, 18.
64. The lion of the tribe of Judah, the root of David, Rev. v, 5.
65. The root and offspring of David, the bright and morning star, Rev. xxii, 16.
66. Faithful and true, Rev. xix, 11.

E. NAMES AND TITLES IN PAUL'S WRITINGS

1. Son (i.e., of God), Rom. v, 10, viii, 3, 29, 32; 1 Cor. xv, 28, Gal. i, 16, iv, 4; 1 Thes. i, 10; Acts. xiii, 33 cit.
2. Son of God, Rom. i, 4; Gal. ii, 20; Eph. iv, 13.
3. Son of God, Jesus Christ, 2 Cor. i, 19.
4. His (God's) son, Jesus Christ our Lord, Rom. i, 3; 1 Cor. i, 9.
5. Jesus, Rom. iii, 26, viii, 11; 1 Cor. xii, 3*bis;* 2 Cor. iv, 10, 11*bis,* xi, 4; Eph. iv. 21; Phil. ii, 10; 1 Thes. i, 10, iv, 14*bis;* Acts xiii, 33, xxii, 8, xxvi, 15, xxviii, 23.
6. (God's) dear son, Col. i, 13.
7. Christ, Romans, 35 times; 1 Cor., 47; 2 Cor., 38; Gal., 25; Eph., 28; Phil., 18; Col., 19; 1 Thes., 3; 2 Thes., 2; 1 Tim., 2; 2 Tim., 1; Philemon, 2; Acts (in Paul's speeches), 3.
8. Christ Jesus, Rom. iii, 24, viii, 1, 2, xv, 5, xvi, 3; Gal. ii, 4, iii, 26, 28, iv, 14; Eph. i, 1, ii, 6, 7, 10, 13, iii, 21; Phil. i, 1, ii, 5, iii, 3, 12, 14, iv, 7, 19, 21; Col. i, 4, 28; 1 Thes. ii, 14, v. 18; 1 Tim. i, 14, 15, iii, 13, vi, 13; 2 Tim. i, 1, 9, 13, ii, 1, 3, 10, iii, 12, 15; Philemon 1, 9.
9. Christ Jesus, our Lord, Rom. viii, 39; 1 Cor. xv, 31; 2 Cor. iv, 5 (?); Eph. iii, 11; Phil. iii, 8; Col. ii, 6; 1 Tim. i, 12; 2 Tim. i, 2.
10. Christ who is over all, blessed for ever, Rom. ix, 5.
11. Jesus Christ, Rom., 13 times; 1 Cor., 2; 2 Cor., 4; Gal., 8; Eph., 5; Phil., 7; Col., 1; 1 Tim., 3; 2 Tim., 3; Ti., 1; Acts xvi, 18.
12. Jesus (Christ) our Lord, Rom. iv, 24; 1 Cor. i, 9, ix, 1; 1 Tim. i, 2.
13. Jesus Christ, our Saviour, Titus iii, 6.

14. Lord, Rom., 14 times; 1 Cor., 43; 2 Cor., 21; Gal., i, 19; Eph.,
    17; Phil., 9; Col., 9; 1 Thes., 12; 2 Thes., 9; 1 Tim. i, 14; 2 Tim.,
    14; Philemon 16, 20bis (?); Acts xiii, 10, 11, xvi, 32, xx, 19, xxii,
    10, 16.
15. Lord Jesus, Rom. x, 9, xiv, 14, xvi, 18; 1 Cor., v, 4bis, 5 (?), vi, 11
    (?), xi, 23; 2 Cor. i, 14, iv, 10, 14; Gal. vi, 17; Eph. i, 15; Phil. ii,
    19; Col. iii, 17; 1 Thes. ii, 15, iv, 1, 2; 2 Thes. i, 7; Philemon 5;
    Acts xx, 24, 35.
16. Lord Christ, Rom. xvi, 18 (?); Col. iii, 24.
17. Lord Jesus Christ, Rom., 9 times; 1 Cor., 12; 2 Cor., 5; Gal. 3;
    Eph., 7; Phil., 2; Col., 2; 1 Thes., 9; 2 Thes., 11; 1 Tim., 4; 2
    Tim., 2; Philemon, 2; Acts xvi, 31, xx, 21, xxi, 13, xxviii, 31.
18. Lord Jesus Christ, Saviour, Titus i, 4.
19. Lord of glory, 1 Cor. ii, 8.
20. Lord of peace, 2 Thes. iii, 16.
21. Master (kurios), Eph. vi, 9, Col. iv, 1.
22. Saviour, Jesus Christ, 2 Tim. i, 10.
23. Saviour, Lord Jesus Christ, Phil. iii, 20.
24. Jesus our deliverer, 1 Thes. i, 10.
25. The man, Acts. xvii, 31.
26. This man, Acts xiii, 38.
27. The second man, the Lord from heaven, 1 Cor. xv, 47.
28. The man Christ Jesus, 1 Tim. ii, 5.
29. God (?) manifest in the flesh, 1 Tim. iii, 16.
30. Great God and our Saviour, Jesus Christ, Titus ii, 13.
31. Holy One, Acts xiii, 35.
32. Just One, Acts xxii, 14.
33. God, Acts xx, 28.
34. Jesus, the Nazarene, Acts xxii, 8, xxvi, 9.
35. The light of the gentiles, Acts xiii, 47.
36. The seed of Abraham, Gal. iii, 16.

F. NAMES AND TITLES IN HEBREWS

1. Son, i, 2, 5bis, 8, ii, 6, v, 5, 8, vii, 28.
2. Son of God, vi, 6, vii, 3, x, 29.
3. Jesus, the son of God, iv, 14.
4. Only begotten, xi, 17.
5. Jesus, ii, 9, vi, 20, vii, 22, x, 19, xii, 2, 24, xiii, 12.
6. Christ, iii, 6, 14, v, 5, vi, 1, ix, 11, 14, 24, 28, xi, 26
7. Lord, ii, 3, vii, 14.
8. Jesus Christ, x, 10, xiii, 8, 21.
9. Lord Jesus, xiii, 20.
10. Priest, vii, 17, 21.

11. High Priest, x, 21.
12. Apostle and High Priest of our profession Christ Jesus, iii, 1.
13. Great High Priest, Jesus the Son of God, iv, 14.
14. Mediator, viii, 6, ix, 15.
15. Jesus, the Mediator of the new covenant, xii, 24.
16. Forerunner, vi, 20.
17. Captain of salvation, ii, 10.
18. He that shall come, x, 37.
19. Author and finisher of our faith, x, 2.
20. Lord Jesus Christ, the great shepherd of the sheep, xiii, 20.

G. NAMES AND TITLES IN JAMES

1. Lord, 10 times.
2. Lord Jesus Christ, i, 1, ii, 1.
3. Lord Jesus Christ, the Lord of glory, ii, 1.

H. NAMES AND TITLES IN JUDE

1. Jesus Christ, 1bis.
2. Lord Jesus Christ, 17, 21.
3. Lord, 5, 9, 14 (?).
4. Our only Lord and Master (*despoten kai kurion*) Jesus Christ, 4.

I. NAMES AND TITLES IN STEPHEN'S SPEECH

1. Son of man, Acts vii, 56.
2. Lord, vii, 60.
3. Lord Jesus, vii, 59.
4. A prophet, vii, 37.
5. Just One, vii, 52.

V. THE TITLES OF THE MESSIAH IN DANIEL

1. The Messiah, ix, 26.
2. Messiah prince (*nagid*), ix, 25.
3. The prince of princes, viii, 25.
4. The stone, ii, 34, 35.
5. One like a son of gods, iii, 25.
6. One like a son of man, vii, 13.

Our conclusions based on the testimony regarding the Messiah
are:

   a. It cannot be argued from the titles of the Messiah that

Daniel was written in the second century B.C.; for the titles given in Daniel are not significant of that period of time, as will be seen from the evidence collected from the above lists.

(1) Messiah, as a title of the expected redeemer of Israel, occurs already in Ps. ii, which Driver [31] admits to be presumably pre-exilic. Then, outside of Dan. ix, 26, it does not occur again till in the Second Section of *Enoch* (xlviii, 10, lii, 4), and the *Pss. of Solomon* (xvii, 6, xviii, 6, 8), both from the first century B.C. In the later literature, outside the New Testament, it is found in the Odes of Solomon, Fourth Ezra, the Vision of Isaiah, the Testament of Hezekiah, the Zadokite Fragments, Josephus, and Tacitus, mostly written under Christian influences; and in the Targums and Talmud.

(2) Messiah the Prince is found only in Daniel ix, 25, and hence, cannot be indicative of date. Besides, the term *nagid* used by Daniel for prince, is found elsewhere as a title of the Messiah only in Is. lv, 4.

(3) The title "Prince of princes" occurs nowhere else as a designation of the Messiah, not even in the New Testament; though *sar*, the word used in Dan. viii, 25 for prince, is found in Is. ix, 6 in the phrase "the prince of peace."

(4) The title "stone" of Dan. ii, 34, 35, is used besides in the Old Testament only in Is. xxviii, 16 and Ps. cxviii, 22, and the phrase "rock of ages" only in Is. xxvi, 4. In the New Testament, this "stone" is used of Christ in Mat. xxi, 42, Mark xii, 10, 1 Pet. ii, 6, 7. It occurs also, in Barnabas vi, 4.

(5) The phrase "one who is like a son of gods" occurs in Dan. iii, 25 alone. "Sons of God" [32] is used in Gen. vi, 2 to denote the angels. If the word *bar* [33] in Ps. ii, 12 means son,

---

[31] *L.O.T.*, p. 385.

[32] In the later literature outside the New Testament, the phrase occurs only in the *Vision of Isaiah* (ix, 14, 16) and in Fourth Ezra (xiii, 32, 37). If the plural here means God, it is the only example of the plural of majesty found in Aramaic. Since it is Nebuchadnezzar who employs the phrase, he probably meant by it a godlike person.

[33] The occurrence of the word *bar* on a lately discovered Phenician document from about 850 B.C. does away with any supposed necessity for ascribing the use of *bar* to Aramaic influence.

it must mean the son of God and designate the Messiah of verse 2. The phrase is not met with again till in Enoch cv, 2, according to Charles "a passage of uncertain date and origin." [34]

(6) Whatever the origin and meaning of the phrase "son of man," it is used outside of Daniel as a title of the Messiah only in the New Testament and in the Fifth Section of Enoch (which was probably written in the early part of the first century B.C.), in the Traditions of Matthias (once), in Justin twice, in Ignatius once, and in Celsus once. "The likeness of a man" in 4 Ezra xiii, 3 probably refers to the same person.

We have no right, therefore, to presume that Daniel cannot have been written before 200 B.C. because the designations of the Messiah found in it are absent from the post-captivity literature composed before that date, unless we are prepared, also, to maintain that Isaiah, Jeremiah, Ezekiel, and Zechariah, are later than 200 B.C. For Isaiah's designations "stone," "rock of ages," "prince" (both *nagid* and *sar*), "prince of peace," "servant," and "righteous servant" are all absent from the literature from 500 to 200 B.C.; so also, are Jeremiah's designations "David the king," "branch," "righteous branch," and "branch of righteousness," and the "king" and "shepherd" of Zechariah and Ezekiel. So that, it is evident that, if this method of reasoning from the silence of one document as to doctrines taught in another is valid, Isaiah, Jeremiah, Ezekiel, and Zechariah, must also be later than 200 B.C.

b. No argument for the late date of Daniel can be made from the use of its designations of the Messiah in the literature written after 200 B.C., that will not for the same reason make a stronger argument for putting the composition of Isaiah and Zechariah after 200 B.C. For Isaiah's designations, "the elect one," "a child," "servant," and Zechariah's designations, "king" and "one that was pierced" are found in the literature from 200 B.C. to 135 A.D.; whereas, no designation peculiar to Daniel, except possibly the phrase "son of man," occurs in this period. "Son of God"

---

[34] The one hundred and fifth chapter of the Book of Enoch follows the so-called Fifth Section of Enoch and constitutes a sort of appendix to the whole book. It will probably have been written, therefore, not earlier than about 50 B.C.

may just as well come from Ps. ii, 12, or Is. ix, 6, as from Nebuchadnezzar's phrase "one like a son of gods" in Dan. iii, 25. Messiah may be due to Ps. ii, 2, as well as to Dan. ix, 26. "The stone" is derived from Isa. xxviii, 16, or Ps. cxviii, 22, rather than from Dan. ii, 34, 35.

c. As to the character of the Messiah, it is said in Daniel that he would be an anointed leader, a prince of princes, and that he would be cut off, but not for himself. The idea of the anointed leader is found in the Second Psalm's anointed king. He is called a leader (*nagid*) in Isa. lv, 4 and with the synonym *nasi'* in Ezek. xxxiv, 24. The phrase nearest to "prince of princes" is found in the prince of peace of Isa. ix, 6, *sar* being used for prince in both phrases. The idea that the Messiah should suffer, involved in the cutting off of ix, 26, is expressed most fully in Isa. liii, and in Ps. xxii, both placed by the critics during, or a little after, the captivity.[35]

The only one of Daniel's characteristics of the Messiah that is found in the literature of the second century is "prince," which occurs in Jubilees xxxi, 18. Since Jubilees, even if written originally in Hebrew, is now known only in a translation, it is impossible to determine whether its word prince stands for one of the words for prince used in Daniel, or whether it represents some other word, such as the *nasi'* of Ezekiel. The only one of the characteristics found in the literature of the first century B.C. is "anointed," appearing in Enoch lii, 4. It thus appears that the usage of Daniel agrees with that of captivity rather than of Maccabean times, even if we accept the dates assigned by the critics to Isaiah and the Psalms.

d. As to the functions of the Messiah, Daniel states simply that his dominion shall be everlasting and that all nations shall serve him. In order to show that these ideas with regard to the length and extent of the dominion of the Messiah were held by the people of Israel before, or about the sixth century B.C., I shall cite first what Daniel says and next, what we find in other early works.

(1) In Dan. vii, 14, we read that there was given to him who was like a son of man dominion and glory and a kingdom that

[35] *L.O.T.*, p. 245, 386.

all peoples, nations, and languages shall serve him: his dominion is an everlasting dominion which shall not pass away, and his kingdom that which shall not be destroyed.

(2) In Isa. ix, 6, 7,[86] it is said of the prince of peace that "of the increase of his government and peace there shall be no end, upon the throne of David, and upon his kingdom to order it, and to establish it, with judgment and with justice from henceforth even for evermore."

(3) In Ps. lxxii, which Driver says to be presumably pre-exilic,[87] it is said in vs. 11 that all kings shall fall down before the king whom Solomon typified; and in vs. 17, that his name should endure forever, and all nations shall call him blessed.

The two points of everlastingness and universality of the kingdom of the Messiah are thus shown to have been taught long before the time of Cyrus.

CONCLUSIONS

From the above testimony and discussions it will be seen that the four subjects to which Driver appeals as evidence proving the late date of Daniel are all mentioned in Isaiah as well as in Daniel, that three of them are mentioned in Zechariah, and that not more than one, or at most two of them, are mentioned in that vast mass of canonical literature which the critics assign to post-captivity times. That some works written between 500 and 200 B.C. do not refer to any one of these four subjects, no more proves that Daniel did not exist, or was not known, than it proves that Isaiah and Zechariah did not exist, or were unknown to the authors of these works. Many books written after 150 B.C. do not show any knowledge of any of these doctrines. This does not prove that Isaiah, Daniel, and Zechariah were not known before the birth of Christ. The Martyrdom of Isaiah, the Ezra-Apocalypse, and the Ezra-piece, are silent as to all but one of these doctrines. This does not prove that Isaiah, Daniel, and Zechariah, were not composed until after 135 A.D.

---

[86] Dating according to L.O.T. from 735-734 B.C.
[87] L.O.T., p. 385.

In short, this argument from silence has been much over-emphasized by the critics; and besides, it proves too much.

That more indications of the existence of Daniel are not found in post-captivity writers may be accounted for on the ground that it was a sealed book, or that the Palestinian writers were not acquainted with a work that had been composed at Babylon, or that they had not yet admitted its canonicity, or simply on the ground that the subjects of which they were treating gave no opportunity of expressing their views on these doctrines; just as, for similar reasons, many writers after 150 B.C., have failed to mention either him, or his doctrines.

Having seen that the doctrines of Daniel agree more nearly with those of Isaiah and Zechariah than with those of any other books of the Israelites up to 135 A.D., let us, before closing this chapter, and by way of summarizing the argument for the early date, give in short compass the results gathered from all of our investigations. The critics in their attack on Daniel appeal to the evidence of history, literature, language, and doctrine. It was shown in volume one of *Studies in the Book of Daniel,* that there is no sufficient reason for denying the historical statements of Daniel. Belshazzar was certainly in some sense a king of Babylon; and Darius the Mede may have been a sub-king under Cyrus. In the discussion of *Apocalypses and the Book of Daniel* in the present volume we have seen that the literary forms of Daniel were known in the sixth century B.C. and that these forms differ from those found in Enoch. We have also showed[38] that the foreign words in Daniel, especially the Persian, support the traditional view that Daniel was written in the Persian period, which produced, also, the books of Zechariah, Haggai, Esther, Chronicles, Ezra and Nehemiah; for these books are characterized by Persian words and no other books of the Old Testament are. Not one of the numerous psalms assigned by the critics to the post-captivity period has a single Persian word, nor has Ecclesiasticus, Ecclesiastes, the Song of Songs,[39] Jonah, Joel,

---

[38] "The Aramaic of Daniel," in *Biblical and Theological Studies,* 1912.

[39] The so-called Persian words in the Ecclesiastes and the Song of Songs are more probably Hittite.

Nahum, the so-called Priestly Document of the Pentateuch, nor
any of the parts of Isaiah, Hosea, Amos, Proverbs, nor any
other possible excerpts from any other Old Testament composition. In short, Persian words occur where one would expect
them to occur,—in works from Persian times—and Daniel is
one of these works. Nor, as we shall show in the next chapter,
if Daniel were written in the second century B.C., is it easy to account for the absence in it of any mention of elephants and
phalanxes, the main strength of the Grecian army of the
Seleucids.

Taken, therefore, either separately, or collectively, the form,
language, and contents, of Daniel point to the sixth century B.C.,
rather than to the second, as the time of its composition. The
only grounds left for impugning the historicity of the Book of
Daniel are the character of the miracles and predictions recorded
in it. On these grounds alone, no Christian, or theist, can
logically or consistently reject the evidence in its favour.

It is assumed by the critics that, had the Book of Daniel been
written in the sixth century B.C., the biblical literature written
after that time would show larger traces of its influence, than it
does show.

This assumption has been partly answered in the discussion of
the second assumption. It may be said further, that the Book
of Daniel was composed at Babylon; and, hence, may not have
been known in Palestine until after the other books were written.
It was sealed. This implies that it was inscribed on clay tablets.
These tablets may not have been unsealed until long after Daniel
was dead. They may even have been written in Babylonian
cuneiform, and perhaps even in the Babylonian language.

Besides, the Book of Daniel was not meant so much for immediate effect as for the time of the end. It is doubtful whether
it would have been safe, or prudent, to have published it—full,
as it is, of predictions of the fall of Babylon and Persia—while
the threatened world-powers were still flourishing. When the
Maccabean heroes had smashed the power of the last of these,
and when the star of Judah was once more in the ascendent, its
contents could be revealed without endangering the people of

Israel. The record of the constancy of Daniel and his three companions, and of their extraordinary deliverance from their oppressors, and especially, the marvellous and exact fulfilment of the predictions contained in the book, would then serve to arm the despondent nation against the sea of troubles that seemed about to overwhelm it. The broad view which Daniel held of the purposes of God, that he unfolds for us in his vast panorama of world-history—relegating the Jews to their proper place in the movements of the current of human progress—would naturally make his book unpopular among a people, and particularly among leaders like Zerubbabel, Ezra, and Nehemiah, who were intensely narrow and nationalistic in their conception of God's mercy and of the extent and ultimate purpose of his call of Israel and of his government of the nations.

But, even granting that the Book of Daniel was published about 535 B.C., the above assumption cannot be admitted, whether we accept the conservative or radical view of the dates of the other books of the Old Testament.

For, first, according to the opinion of both conservative and radical scholars, Haggai, Esther, Ezra, Nehemiah, Chronicles, and the first part of Zechariah, were composed after the return from captivity.

Haggai, having been written about 520 B.C., can hardly be expected to show many traces of Daniel's influence. It has only thirty-eight verses, and the subject of his prophecy is the rebuilding of the temple. Mere silence, therefore, about the matters treated of in Daniel proves nothing as to what Haggai's views on these matters may have been.

Zechariah, both in form and subject-matter, shows more likeness to the Book of Daniel than can be found in any other work of the Old Testament.

Esther presents few traces of any earlier literature, and as the events narrated by its writer have no connection, historically or doctrinally, with the events and teachings of Daniel, it is hard to see that they are of such a character as that traces of Daniel should certainly be found in them.

Malachi exhibits as many possible traces of Daniel as it does of Isaiah, Jeremiah, Ezekiel, and the other prophetic works.

Chronicles purports to give the history of Israel down to the captivity alone. It would be an evident anachronism for its writer to have shown traces of the influence of a book written fifty years after the destruction of Jerusalem.

Ezra and Nehemiah are largely personal memoirs, genealogies, and narratives concerning the building of the wall of Jerusalem and the reëstablishment of the Law. They show slight traces of any of the prophets and none of most of them; why then should we expect to find large traces of Daniel in them? None but a critic's eye "in a fine frenzy rolling" could have expected to trace the marks of Daniel's teachings on the great things of the kingdom amid the intricacies of the laws on intermarriage with heathen wives, amid the descriptions of the building of the wall, among the special injunctions for the observance of the Sabbath, or even in the account of the keeping of the feast of Tabernacles and of the renewal of the covenant. The prayer of Nehemiah, recorded in chapter nine of the book named after him, certainly has some resemblances to chapter nine of Daniel; but in the chapters themselves there is no evidence to show which of them copied from the other.

Secondly, as to the various books and parts of books that the critics assign to the period from 535 to 165 B.C., such as Joel, Jonah, the Priestly Narrative, Isaiah xxiv-xxvii, the Song of Songs, etc., it may be remarked in general, that here, as frequently, the critics are resorting to the fallacy of attempting to prove one assumption by another equally inadmissible. For, we do not admit that it has been proven, nor that it can be proven, that these assumedly post-captivity productions were really so. But, even granting that some of these works were written in post-captivity times, what reason have we for expecting that they must in that case have exhibited large traces of the influence of Daniel? Take Jonah, for example. Suppose its author had been acquainted with the history of Daniel and his three companions, how can he have been expected to show his acquaintanceship in a narrative about his mission to Nineveh, or in his description of his experiences in the belly of the fish, or under the shadow of the gourd? The same is true of Ruth and of the Song of Songs. Only a perverted imagination and a literary acumen possessed only by "all eminent scholars" would have looked for traces of the fiery furnace and the lions' den in the field of Boaz or the paradise of Solomon.

It cannot be denied by the critics who date Isa. xxiv-xxvii about 400 B.C. that the doctrine of the resurrection taught in xxvi, 19, might have been derived from Daniel xii, 2, provided the latter was written in the sixth century B.C.

The critics assert that most of the psalms were written in post-captivity times. It is, indeed, surprising that so little is said in them about these four doctrines which are characteristic of Daniel; but is it not even more surprising that still less is said about them in the fifty-seven psalms which are assigned by these same critics to Maccabean times? Does it not seem as if there were a conflict here between the literary critics' doctrine of the *Zeitgeist*, or spirit of the times, and that of the traceability of the influence of ideas in successive stages of literary development? If the *Zeitgeist* theory be appealed to, in order to put Daniel and Enoch in the same age, how about these fifty-seven psalms; and how about Ecclesiastes, Ecclesiasticus, Jubilees, Judith, Wisdom, and First Maccabees, most of which make no reference to any of the doctrines characteristic of Daniel? If large traces of the influence of a document of a pre-existent period must be found in all succeeding literature of the same people, how comes it that the great work of Isaiah (except the historical part occurring in chapters xxxvi-xxxix) is never referred to during all the period from 700 to 200 B.C., nor Ezekiel from 550 to 200 B.C.? Further, if Daniel were written in 164 B.C., why is there no trace of his influence on a large part of the Jewish literature that was composed after that time?

Of course, the obvious and only sensible answer to this last question is, that traces of the influence of the ideas of Daniel upon First Maccabees, the Zadokite Fragments, and other works, can only be expected to be found, where and when the author of the later works were treating of the same subjects as those about which Daniel writes. So also, we have the right to presume that the sensible way of accounting for the absence of large traces of the influence of Daniel upon Haggai, Ezra, Nehemiah, and the authors of other post-captivity works, is the recognition of the fact that they treated of different subjects from those of which Daniel speaks. Galen, writing about medicine, can not be dated by the traces of the Roman laws and jurisprudence that might possibly be looked for in his works. The code of Justinian would not be expected to say much about medicine. Ezra, Nehemiah, and Chronicles, are long on genealogies and short on angels and the resurrection. Daniel is short on genealogies and long on angels and the doctrines of the Messiah, the resurrection, and the judgment. Do men gather grapes of thorns, or figs of thistles?

While, on account of the reasons just given, I think that we should not expect to find traces of the ideas of Daniel in such works as Haggai, Esther, and Ezra, I cannot see how there should be so few traces of these ideas in the Psalms, if, as the critics assert, nearly all of them were composed for the service of the second temple, and more than fifty of them in Maccabean times. For example, is it not remarkable that angels are so seldom mentioned in the psalms, and that neither Gabriel, nor Michael, is named? Why do so few of these numerous poems refer to the Messiah, and why is the glorious and comforting doctrine of the resurrection scarcely hinted at? The theories of *Zeitgeist* and of traces of influence must not be used by the critics only when they seem to support their assumptions. In the case of the psalms, the theories are both dead against the critics.

It is assumed that the same measure of influence on post-captivity literature would be expected from Daniel, as from other early books, especially such as from Deuteronomy, Jeremiah, Ezekiel, and Deutero-Isaiah.

This assumption expresses the opinion and expectation of Professor Cornill, its author; but we doubt, if many other critics will agree with him. It gives too much honour and relative importance to Daniel in comparison with these four great masterpieces of Hebrew literature. Since Professor Cornill gives no

222 Studies In the Book of Daniel

reasons for his expectation, it becomes incumbent upon us to state both side of the questions raised by his assertion.

Suppose we admit that these four great books exerted a larger measure of influence upon post-captivity literature than Daniel did, why should they not have done so? They are larger works. They are earlier works. They were ascribed to four of the greatest and most conspicuous of the prophets. Deuteronomy was universally ascribed to their accredited lawgiver, the supposed founder of their nation. "Deutero-Isaiah" was accepted as a production of the most prominent and influential of the prophet-counsellors of the kings of Judah and certainly possessed all the brilliancy and convincingness of his "genuine" works. Jeremiah stood in a unique relationship to the Jews of the captivity, as the one who had predicted its beginning and its end, and had thus demonstrated that he was truly a prophet of God in a distinguished degree. Ezekiel was himself one of the captives and lived and prophesied among his fellow exiles; and if the radical view of the origin of the Priestly-code be correct, he was the originator of many of its peculiar ordinances.

Besides, all these works are distinctively nationalistic. They are specifically addressed to the Israelites and speak of the other nations only in their connection with the children of Abraham. Whereas, Daniel is a book full of the history of foreign kings and their Hebrew subjects. It is one of the least nationalistic and one of the most catholic and world-embracing of all the Old Testament books. It supplies not a single Haphtara, or reading lesson, to be read by the Jews on the Sabbath day. It arrived at its proper influence only when the gospel, as the means of salvation for all the world, had been proclaimed.

Again, distinctions in books as well as among individuals are invidious. The question in dispute about Daniel is one of existence and not one of relative influence. A book may exist without having any perceptible influence, or any great number of readers. Some books only can be the best sellers of the year. Some of Paul's epistles have exerted tenfold the influence that others have and are read ten times as much. Some of Milton's works are read by all pupils in the high schools; others are read by all cultivated people; others are scarcely read at all. That Daniel cannot have existed unless we can show traces of his having influenced his contemporaries and successors as much as Jeremiah and others did is simply an assertion made thoughtlessly, hastily, or in the heat of argument. It is utterly without proof and is beyond the reach of proof. It is unworthy of the learned man that made it. May the day soon be past when the dictum of a professor will be considered to outweigh the evidence of common sense, analogy, and documents. Homer sometimes nods; and so also does the most eminent of scholars.

V. The Approximation of Daniel and Enoch

It is assumed that the ideas of Daniel and those of the first part of Enoch approximate and that, because the ideas approximate, the books must have been written at about the same time.[40] There are here two assertions: first, that the ideas approximate, and second, that this approximation shows that the two works must have been composed at about the same time.

The first of these assertions will have credence only with those who have not read the first section of Enoch; for both in the subjects treated and in the manner of their treatment, the two works differ materially. The First Part of Enoch is concerned with the fall and punishment of the angels who kept not their first estate, but took wives from the daughters of men. It is a kind of commentary, or sermon, on the first part of the sixth chapter of Genesis, and gives numerous details about the fallen sons of God. It tells the number of the angels and the names of the leaders and describes the unpardonable nature of their sin and the kind and place of their judgment. It mentions, also, by name the seven good archangels among whom appear Michael and Gabriel. These two names are the only particular in which this section of Enoch can be said to show any approximate connection with Daniel .

It is probable, however, that Doctor Driver referred to the section of Enoch which is embraced in chapters lxxxiii-xc, which

[40] See above p. 160.

is denominated by Professor Charles as the Third Section. This section contains two dream-visions, the first on the deluge, and the second on the history of the world from the fall of the angels to the founding of the Messianic kingdom. Chapter xc, gives a figurative résumé of the history from Alexander the Great to the coming of the white bull, which may possibly represent the Messiah. In order that our readers may be able to judge for themselves as to the approximation of this chapter to the Book of Daniel, I shall cite it, beginning with the preceding context (lxxxix, 68), where it begins to treat of the period following the destruction of Jerusalem.

And the shepherds and their associates delivered over those sheep to all the wild beasts, to devour them, and each one of them received in his time a definite number: it was written by the other in a book how many each one of them destroyed of them. And each one slew and destroyed many more than was prescribed; and I began to weep and lament on account of those sheep. And thus in the vision I saw that one who wrote, how he wrote down every one that was destroyed by those shepherds, day by day, and carried up and laid down and showed actually the whole book to the Lord of the sheep—everything that they had done, and all that each one of them had made away with, and all that they had given over to destruction. And the book was read before the Lord of the sheep, and He took the book from his hand and read it and sealed it and laid it down.

And forthwith I saw how the shepherds pastured for twelve hours, and behold three of those sheep turned back and came and entered and began to build up all that had fallen down of that house; but the wild boars tried to hinder them, but they were not able. And they began again to build as before, and they reared up that tower, and it was named the high tower; and they began again to place a table before the tower, but all the bread on it was polluted and not pure. And as touching all this the eyes of those sheep were blinded so that they saw not, and (the eyes of) their shepherds likewise; and they delivered them in large numbers to their shepherds for destruction, and they trampled the sheep with their feet and devoured them. And the Lord of the sheep remained unmoved till all the sheep were dispersed over the field and mingled with them (i.e., the beasts), and they (i.e., the shepherds) did not save them out of the hand of the beasts. And this one who wrote the book carried it up, and showed it and read it before the Lord of the sheep, and implored Him on their account, and besought Him on their account as he showed Him all the doings of the shepherds, and gave testimony before Him against all the shepherds. And he took the actual book and laid it down beside Him and departed.

xc. And I saw till that in this manner thirty-five shepherds undertook the pasturing (of the sheep), and they severally completed their periods as did the first; and others received them into their hands, to pasture them for their period, each shepherd in his own period. And after that I saw in my vision all the birds of heaven coming, the eagles, the vultures, the kites, the ravens; but the eagles led all the birds; and they began to devour those sheep, and to pick out their eyes and to devour their flesh. And the sheep cried out because their flesh was being devoured by the birds, and as for me I looked and lamented in my sleep over that shepherd who pastured the sheep. And I saw until those sheep were devoured by the dogs and eagles and kites, and they left neither flesh nor skin nor sinew remaining on them till only their bones stood there: and their bones too fell to the earth and the sheep became few. And I saw until that twenty-three had undertaken the pasturing and completed in their several periods fifty-eight times.

But behold lambs were borne by those white sheep, and they began to open their eyes and to see, and to cry to the sheep. Yea, they cried to them, but they did not hearken to what they said to them, but were exceedingly deaf, and their eyes were very exceedingly blinded. And I saw in the vision how the ravens flew upon those lambs and took one of those lambs, and dashed the sheep in pieces and devoured them. And I saw till horns grew upon those lambs, and the ravens cast down their horns; and I saw till there sprouted a great horn of one of those sheep, and their eyes were opened. And it looked at them (and their eyes opened), and it cried to the sheep, and the rams saw it and all ran to it. And notwithstanding all this those eagles and vultures and ravens and kites still kept tearing the sheep and swooping down upon them and devouring them: still the sheep remained silent, but the rams lamented and cried out. And those ravens fought and battled with it, and sought to lay low its horn, but they had no power over it.

All the eagles and vultures and ravens and kites were gathered together, and there came with them all the sheep of the field, yea, they all came together, and helped each other to break that horn of the ram. And I saw till a great sword was given to the sheep, and the sheep proceeded against all the beasts of the field to slay them, and all the beasts and the birds of the heaven fled before their face. And I saw that man who wrote the book according to the command of the Lord, till he opened that book concerning the destruction which those twelve last shepherds had wrought, and showed that they had destroyed much more than their predecessors, before the Lord of the sheep. And I saw till the Lord of the sheep came unto them and took in His hand the staff of His wrath, and smote the earth, and the earth clave asunder, and all the beasts and all the birds of the heaven fell from among those sheep, and were swallowed up in the earth and it covered them.[41]

And I saw till a throne was erected in the pleasant land, and the Lord of the sheep sat Himself thereon, and the other took the sealed books and opened those books before the Lord of the sheep. And the Lord called those men the seven first white ones, and commanded that they should bring before Him, beginning with the first star which led the way, all the stars whose privy members were like those of horses, and they brought them all before Him. And He said to that man who wrote before Him, being one of those seven white ones, and said unto him: "Take those seventy shepherds to whom I delivered the sheep, and who taking them on their own authority slew more than I commanded them." And behold they were all bound, I saw, and they all stood before Him. And the judgment was held first over the stars, and they were judged and found guilty, and went to the place of condemnation, and they were cast into an abyss, full of fire and flaming, and full of pillars of fire. And those seventy shepherds were judged and found guilty, and they were cast into that fiery abyss. And I saw at that time how a like abyss was opened in the midst of the earth, full of fire, and they brought those blinded sheep, and they were all judged and found guilty and cast into this fiery abyss, and they burned; now this abyss was to the right of that house. And I saw those sheep burning and their bones burning.[42]

In this whole passage Professor Charles finds but one verse showing verbal coincidences with Daniel; whereas, he cites five verses using ideas and phrases similar to those found in ten different places in Isaiah, two verses probably referring to three places in Zechariah, two referring to two in Micah, and four verses referring respectively to a passage in Ezekiel, Haggai, Malachi, or Tobit. The verse showing resemblances to Daniel is the twentieth verse in chapter xc. This verse speaks of "the pleasant land," of a "throne being erected" upon which "the judge sat," and of "sealed books" that were opened before the judge. Each of these statements is fully paralleled in Daniel; but it does not follow from this, that Daniel and Enoch were composed at about the same time, nor that one of them borrowed from the other. As to the phrase "pleasant land," a closer exami-

---

[41] I have omitted the duplicate verses from 13 to 15 inclusive.

[42] See *The Apocrypha and Pseudepigrapha of the Old Testament*, vol. ii, 256-260.

nation of the original Hebrew seems to show that the English word "pleasant" is the correct translation in Jer. iii, 19, Zech. vii, 14, Ps. cvi, 24; but in Daniel xi, 16, 41, 45, the "glorious land" of the Revised Version is better. Unfortunately, the Hebrew, or Aramaic original of Enoch has utterly disappeared; and not a single fragment of this section is preserved in any version except the Ethiopic. In the Ethiopic, the word rendered by "pleasant" is *chawwaz*, derived from a root corresponding to the Hebrew and Arabic *chamad* or *chamada*. In the verses cited above from Jeremiah, Zechariah, and Ps. cvi, a derivative of this verb is rightly rendered by "pleasant" in both Ethiopic and English.[42a]

Now, it is generally admitted that the Ethiopic version was made from the Greek, though it may afterwards have been revised in parts on the basis of the Hebrew. But, the Greek translators, Theodotion as well as the Seventy, give us little light on the meaning of this word as employed in Daniel. In Dan. viii, 9, the Seventy render it north (βόρραν) and Theodotion probably by power (δύναμις).[43]

In Dan. xi, 16, 41, and 45, Theodotion transliterates and the Seventy omit except in the forty-fifth verse, where they render by "wish," having doubtless read *ṣebu* (צבו) which in Syriac means wish, or will.

The Syriac Peshitto gives us even less light than the Greek versions. In viii, 9, it gives no translation; in xi, 16 and 41, it

---

[42a] The verb *patawa* is commonly used in Ethiopic to render *chamad*, as also *'awah* to desire, or covet. The Ethiopic verb *chawaz* and its derivatives are used to render at least eight different Hebrew words for sweet, or pleasant. The idea of glory, however, is expressed by seven, or more roots, all different from those used to render the idea of pleasant. The distinction between pleasant and glorious is thus closely observed all through the Ethiopic version. Now, it is a singular fact that no one of these fifteen Hebrew roots thus clearly distinguished is the one found in Daniel; but a sixteenth root occurs in the derivative *ṣebi*.

[43] Theodotion renders the last part of the ninth verse by "towards the south and towards the power," thus omitting the second direction "towards the east." He has evidently read צבא instead of צבי, or else has given the same meaning to the two words; for *dunamis* is the usual rendering of the former, being employed by the LXX more than one hundred and forty times as the translation of צבא .

renders by the phrase "land of Israel"; and in xi, 45, by a form of the verb "to be."

Jerome is the only one of the ancient first-hand translators to be consistent and correct in the rendering. In xi, 41, he renders by "gloriosam," and in xi, 16, 45, by "inclyta" and "inclytum." In viii, 9, he has probably read *ṣaba* (צבא), as Theodotion did, and has rendered by "fortitudinem."

From the evidence just given it appears that the Ethiopic version always distinguishes between the ideas of glorious and pleasant; that the idea of a pleasant land is found in Jeremiah, Zechariah, and Ps. cvi, and may easily have been derived by the author of Enoch from one or another of these places; and that Daniel never speaks of a pleasant land, but always of a glorious one. There is in this phrase, therefore, no evidence that proves that Enoch and Daniel were from the same age, or derived one from the other.

But even if *ṣebi* meant glory, there would be in this no certain proof that the writer of Enoch derived his idea from Daniel; for Ezekiel uses the same word twice to describe the land of Palestine (xx, 6, 15), once of Moab (xxv, 9), and once of Tyre (xxvi, 20); while Isaiah uses a similar phrase of Babylon (xiii, 19).

As to the second phrase in Enoch xc, 20, saying that "a throne was erected," it is scarcely possible to imagine that any writer of antiquity can have been so ignorant as not to know that gods, kings, and all kinds of judges sat upon thrones when they were hearing cases brought before them. In the Egyptian judgment scenes, Osiris and the other gods sit as judges.[44] Among the Assyrians, the judge was said to have a throne of judgment.[45] One of the inscriptions of Ashurbanipal[46] uses the phrase *dinu ishakan,* which is almost identical with the *dina yethib* of Daniel. The third clause of xc, 20, stating that books were opened, is the same as one found in Daniel vii, 10. This does not prove, however, that Daniel derived the idea from Enoch, or Enoch from

---

[44] See Budge; *Osiris and the Egyptian Resurrection,* vol. i, 318.

[45] A *kussu daianuti.* See Johns; *Babylonian and Assyrian Laws,* etc., p. 81.

[46] IV Rawlinson xlviii, 10.

Daniel. For, that a book of life was kept by the Lord appears already in Ex. xxxii, 32, 33 (ascribed by the critics to E), in Is. iv, 3, and Ps. lxix, 28. In Mal. iii, 16, (cf Ps. lvi, 8) these books are called books of remembrance in which good deeds were recorded; and in Is. lxv, 6, records of evil deeds are said to be written. Among the Egyptians, also, as early as the fourth millennium B.C., Osiris was able to be a just judge, because all the words and deeds of men had been written down carefully by the two scribe-gods, Thoth and Sesheta, and his verdict was according to the evidence written.[47] Among the Babylonians, we have two documents dictated by Hammurabi in which he tells of cases that had been brought before him which were determined on the evidence of tablets that were examined before him. We know that most of these tablets were covered with an envelope of clay. When wanted to be read in a court, these tablets are said to have been opened.[48] In Muss-Arnolt (page 850) we find the phrase *sha unqu ipattani* "whosoever opens the seal, or tablet." "Opening a letter" is also a phrase in use. (*id.*) In short, it stands to reason, that tablets which were written, sealed, covered, sealed again, and indorsed, in order to be kept as evidence of certain transactions, would be opened in case of need in order to get at the very evidence on account of which they were written and preserved.

It is noteworthy that the verb *pitu* used in Babylonian for the opening of tablets, is the same as the verb for the opening of letters found in Dan. vii, 10 and Neh. viii, 5. The word translated "book" in Dan. vii, 10 is the one commonly employed in Hebrew as an equivalent of the various words used for tablets of record in Babylonian for documents of different kinds. Moreover, these books of the Hebrews were sealed "according to law and custom." (Is. xxix, 11, Jer. xxxii, 10), apparently in a way similar to that employed among the Babylonians.[49]

It seems evident, therefore, that from Abraham downwards

[47] See Budge: *Osiris* i, 309.
[48] See King; *The Letters and Inscriptions of Hammurabi*, pp. 23-28.
[49] See Schorr; *Urkunden des altbabylonischen Zivil- und Prozessrechts*, p. xxxvii.

there were sealed books in the libraries of Babylon that would be opened whenever a case came for adjudication before a judge. It is further evident that the phrases used by Daniel describe accurately what may have been observed every day in the law courts of Babylon, in one of which Daniel himself may have sat as judge. In fact, these phrases afford one of the best undesigned coincidences in favour of the veracity and the Babylonian provenance of Daniel.

Further, an argument for a close connection between Daniel and Enoch might seem to be found in the frequent use in both of the word for horn. Enoch employs it a number of times in xc, 9, 12, 16, 37, and Daniel in the Hebrew of viii, 3, 5, 6, 8, 9, 20, 21, and in the Aramaic of vii, 7, 8, 11 20 21, 22. But that there is no real force in this argument may be seen from the fact that horns are mentioned also in Amos vi, 13, Mi. iv, 13, Deut. xxxiii, 17, 1 Sam. ii, 1, 10; 2 Sam. xxii, 3, Jer. xlviii, 25, Ezek. xxix, 21, xxxiv, 21; Lam. ii, 3, 17, Job. xvi, 1-5, Pss. lxxv, 4, 5, 10, lxxxix, 17, 24, xcii, 10, cxxxii, 17, cxlviii, 14. In the symbolic use of the word these passages show that in all ages and kinds of Hebrew literature horn was employed exactly as in Enoch and Daniel.

Nor can the fact that both Daniel and Enoch see animals in their visions prove approximation, imitation, or contemporaneity. For, animals are characteristic of the dreams and visions of Jacob, Pharaoh, and Zechariah.

Nor can the fact that both mention stars prove approximation. For stars are mentioned among other places in the vision of Abraham (Gen. xv, 5) in the dream of Joseph (Gen. xxxvii, 9) and in the prophecy of Balaam (Num. xxiv, 17). Besides, Daniel says that the righteous shall shine like stars; but, Enoch that judgment was held over the stars (xc, 24). Enoch, moreover, employs "star" to denote living beings, but Daniel never.

Nor can the fact that Enoch, like Daniel, is said to have seen in a vision all these things that he records, be interpreted as implying any special approximation to Daniel. For visions had been a common means of the communication of divine thoughts from the time of Abraham onwards. The Egyptians, Assyrians, and Babylonians, also, believed in visions from the earliest times and all through their history.[50]

Again, the visions of Daniel are distinguished from those of Enoch in that they give definite dates, and mention the names of the kings in whose reigns they occurred. In fact, the main objection made to the reality of Daniel's visions is that they are too definite and so closely in harmony with what we know from other sources to have happened. It has been argued from this very harmony, that the records of Daniel's visions are historical rather than predictive, and the events narrated in them are actually employed in constructing the history of the period of the successors of Alexander.

Contrast with this exactness of description the indefiniteness of Enoch. It gives no dates, mentions no names of kings, and counts the number of the shepherds, or rulers, in vs. 1, as thirty-five, in vs. 5, as fifty-eight, in vs. 22, as seventy, without giving any clear intimation of whom they mean.[51]

The only possible reference to the Messiah found in Enoch is xc, 37, 38, where a white bull is said to have been born which afterwards became a lamb. No angel is mentioned by name in this passage, nor is there any reference to a resurrection. Some interpreters make the "new house" of verse 29 to be the New Jerusalem, but it may, so far as the context indicates, refer to a rebuilding of the temple.

But, even if it could be shown that this ninetieth chapter of Enoch, or any other chapter, or section, approximates in form or content to Daniel, it does not follow that such an approxi-

[50] See above Chapter IV.

[51] Charles, indeed, says (p. 257), that this number 35 is found by counting twenty-three kings of Egypt from 330 to 200 B.C. and twelve Seleucid kings from 200 to 130 B.C. If, as he further says on p. 171, this section of Enoch must have been written before the death of Judas Maccabaeus in 161 B.C., it follows that the writer must have been able to predict the exact number of the kings of Syria between 161 and 131 B.C., an exceedingly difficult performance in view of the fact that kings of Syria were rising and falling at that time at the rate of about one every five years. In his endeavour to give to his beloved Enoch the gift of predictive prophecy, Charles fails to note the inconsistency of denying the same power to Daniel. In fleeing from Daniel's bear he rushes into the jaws of Enoch's lion.

mation would prove that Daniel and Enoch are from the same time. Enoch may be an imitation of Daniel. No one would affirm that the Revelation of St. John is from the same time as Daniel, and yet it resembles Daniel much more closely than Enoch does. Macauley says that he imitated Thucydides. Many a man has attempted to imitate the Latin of Cicero. Robert Louis Stevenson says that he studied to make his style suit the particular subject which he treated. The sonnet which was taken over into English from the Italian of Petrarch was brought to perfection by Shakespeare and Milton. Yet, equal perfection of form and wealth of idea and expression can scarcely be denied to Landor, Wordsworth, and Keats. Do these "approximations" prove that all these poets were from the same age? Such examples convince us that no trustworthy argument as to the time of the composition of a document can be based upon form, or style, or subject alone.

CHAPTER VII

THE BACKGROUND OF DANIEL

THE critics are in the habit of making one or more unfounded assumptions and then basing upon these unproved and unprovable assumptions still others equally baseless. In the case of Daniel they have assumed that the book is unhistorical, that its miracles are impossible, and that its presumedly predictive prophecies are dim recollections of long past events. They even assume that there was no man called Daniel living in the time of Nebuchadnezzar and Cyrus,[1] and that the customs, objects, and events mentioned or not mentioned in the book, as well as the language in which they are mentioned, indicate the age of Judas Maccabeus. That there is no ground for denying the existence and the deeds of Daniel as recorded in the book named after him has been shown in *Studies in Daniel,* Series One, where the harmony between the life of the man and his surroundings has been maintained. The existence of such a Daniel is upheld by the testimony of his great contemporary Ezekiel who mentions him three times as a model of wisdom and righteousness (xiv, 14, 20, xxviii, 3). No other man worthy of being placed alongside of Noah and Job, as is done by Ezekiel, is known to history, or would, so far as we know, have been known to the Jews whom Ezekiel addressed. The critics, in their endeavours to account for this singular prominence given by their favourite author to an otherwise unknown person, are reduced to the most absurd conjectures. Hitzig supposed that Daniel was another name for Melchizedek.[2] Prince conjectures that he was "really a well known character under the disguise of another name," probably "some celebrated ancient prophet," but which one "cannot possibly be known, as there is not a single trace

[1] Prince, *Commentary on Daniel,* p. 28.
[2] *Id.,* p. viii.

233

to guide research as to his origin and date." Bevan says it is "impossible to decide who the Daniel was to whom reference" is made by Ezekiel,[3] but he qualifies this statement with the remark: "Presumably Ezekiel believed him to be, like Noah and Job, a person of the remote past." Bevan here assumes that Ezekiel believed Job to be a person from the remote past.

This is an example of a kind of assumption frequently indulged in by certain critics, that is, that they can tell exactly what an ancient prophet *believed*. Cornill maintains that the Book of Job was written after Jeremiah, Ezekiel, Proverbs and P.[4] If this be so, then we would have Ezekiel citing as models two men not known to have existed before his time, and of whom his readers could have known merely the names and an indefinite number of traditions, as the works describing them had not yet been written. We could understand this concerning Job, since the book gives no indication of time; but we cannot see why a writer later than Ezekiel would have taken traditions current among the people before the time of Ezekiel and have centered these traditions about a contemporary of Ezekiel. According to the critics, the writer of Daniel knew the prophets. According to some of them he got the name of Daniel from these very passages in Ezekiel. Why then did he not place Daniel at the court of some Pharaoh, or of some Assyrian or Elamite king, instead of making him a younger contemporary of Ezekiel? We leave the critics to conjecture why, and returning to our subject, we sum up by saying that we have two first class witnesses to the fact that Daniel lived at the time of Nebuchadnezzar; first, the Book of Daniel itself, and secondly, the Book of Ezekiel. They both testify also that he was a man of wisdom and righteousness. Further, another first class witness, the First Book of the Maccabees, testifies that the two most notable events recorded in Daniel (the fiery furnace and the den of lions) were known to the Jews in 169 B.C., when they were cited by Mattathias in the climax of his great speech in which he stirred up his compatriots to rebellion. This speech is reported to have been delivered five years before the date at which the critics assign the

---

[3] *Commentary*, p. 12.
[4] *Introduction*, p. 433.

composition of the Book of Daniel. Josephus, also, testifies that the Book of Daniel was shown to Alexander the Great in 336 B.C. Dare we ignore the testimony of such a scholar?

Now compared with this direct evidence in favour of the existence of Daniel in the sixth century B.C., and of a knowledge of some of the contents of his book before the time of the Maccabees, what direct evidence have the critics to offer in favour of the year 164 B.C. as the time of the composition of the book? Absolutely none. Not a single word, or intimation, or opinion, can be produced from any source before the third century A.D. in favour of the view that Daniel was written in Maccabean times. The New Testament in its references to Daniel the prophet and to the fiery furnace and the den of lions implies at least that Daniel is what it appears to be, a record of historic facts enacted in the sixth century B.C. Josephus treats the book as reliable and the author as the Daniel of the book, and one of the greatest of the prophets. It is not till the third century A.D in the writings of a heathen assailant of Christianity that we find the first expression of the *opinion* that the book may have been a fabrication, full of pseudo-predictions written *post eventum*. This opinion was never accepted by Origen or any of the scholars claiming to be of the Jewish or Christian faith, till the beginning of the nineteenth century. Bertholdt and Gesenius were the proponents of the view that Daniel was neither authentic nor genuine, that its historical parts were a pure fabrication, and that its alleged predictions were written *post eventum*. These professors were both German rationalists of the most pronounced type. They based their opinion of Daniel upon the assumption that miracles and predictive prophecies are impossible, that the historical statements are largely false, and that the language, customs, and ideas are those of the age of Antiochus Epiphanes. Like Bevan and other living members of their school, they preferred the opinion of the neo-Platonist Porphyry in his virulent and prejudiced assault on Christianity, and especially on the Book of Daniel, to the opinions of Eusebius of Cæsarea, Origen, and Jerome in their answers to Porphyry; although these three are justly esteemed the greatest scholars and critics of the early church and had before them all the sources of information and all the evidence possessed by the heathen Porphyry; neither is there any proof that they were more prejudiced in favour of Christianity than he was against it. Besides, in Josephus, that great Jewish scholar of the first century A.D., we have a better judge of the reliability of Daniel than any of these third and fourth century critics.

JOSEPHUS

In the first place, Josephus lived two hundred years earlier than Porphyry and Origen.   Secondly, he had access to many more and much better sources of information as to Seleucidian times than the later writers give evidence of.   Of the sources which Jerome says to have been used by Porphyry, Josephus names Polybius, Posidonius, and Hieronymus.   Of Polybius, Josephus speaks in high praise in general,[5] but differs modestly with him in regard to the death of Antiochus Epiphanes.[6]   Posidonius, who lived about 300 B.C., he accuses of telling lies about the Jews and of "framing absurd and reproachful stories about our temple," [7] and cites against him the testimony of Polybius, Strabo, Nicolaus of Damascus, Timagenes, Castor the chronologer, and Apollodorus.[8]   Of Hieronymus he asserts that he "never mentions us in his history, although he was bred up very near to the places where we live." [9]   The other sources of Porphyry mentioned by Jerome are not named by Josephus; and since the works of most of them have been lost, we can form no correct opinion as to their merits.   Callinicus, we know, lived about 300 B.C., and consequently can have testified only as to matters concerning Alexander and his sons and his generals who immediately followed him.

[5] As in *Antiquities,* XII, III, 3, XII, IX, I, and *Contra Apion,* II, 7.
[6] *Antiquities,* XII, IX, I.
[7] *Contra Apion,* II, 7.
[8] *Id.*
[9] *Contra Apion* I, 23.   The question naturally arises, whether Jerome was wrong in saying that Hieronymus was one of the authorities of Porphyry.   Even if he was an authority, it could have been only for the time of Alexander's immediate successors, since he was a friend of Antigonus and a contemporary of Hecateus.

Diodorus flourished in the reign of Augustus and can only have written at second hand. Having access to the same sources, Josephus may have thought it unnecessary to allude to him. As to Claudius, Theon, and Andronicus, not only are their works lost, but nothing is known of their age or histories.

On the other hand, Josephus had the use of many sources that are not mentioned as having been known to Porphyry. Aside from official documents from Jerusalem, Tyre, Sparta, Rome, and from the kings of Egypt and Syria, he cites among others Hecatæus of Abdera, Nicolaus of Damascus, Menander of Tyre, Berosus for Babylon, Manetho for Egypt, Epistles of Alexander, Ptolemy Soter and the succeeding kings, Agatharcides, Posidonius, Lysimachus, Aristeus, Theopompus, Theodotus, Apollodorus, Apollonius, Molo, Timagenes, Strabo, Polybius, Hieronymus, Castor, Theophilus, Mnasias, Aristophanes, Hermogenes, Euhemerus, Conon, Zopyrion, Eupolemus, Demetrius Phalereus, the elder Philo, and others. In addition to these, he would know, of course, the Books of the Maccabees, and a large number of the apocryphal and pseudepigraphical works of the Jews. His mention of the elder Philo implies his knowledge of the younger.

In the third place, Josephus was not an aspiring publicist seeking to gain a livelihood, nor an ambitious writer hoping to win an Olympian crown by his rhetoric and patriotic utterances, regardless of truth and reckless of consequences; but as the learned Scaliger justly says, "he was the greatest lover of truth of all writers and it is safer to believe him, not only as to the affairs of the Jews, but also as to those that are foreign to them, than all the Greek and Latin writers; and this because his fidelity and compass of learning are everywhere conspicuous." Besides, his writings were a challenge and an affirmation. He defied the world to deny or refute his statements and he affirmed the incontestable truth of his history. Nor was he an unknown author hiding in a corner, unrecognised by his contemporaries or unworthy of their acceptance as an opponent. Educated as a priest in all the learning of his people, versed in Hebrew, Aramaic, Greek and Latin, and in a measure in Babylonian, Egyptian, and Phenician, he cites his authorities at first hand, and uses them with a skill that betrays on every page the hand of the master. The laws and literature of all the preceding ages seem to have been at his command, mostly in the original languages in which they were written. Homer and Hesiod, Herodotus and Thucydides, Plato and Pythagoras, Berosus, Menander, Nicolaus, Manetho, and Polybius were known to him. He compares the laws of Moses with those of Draco, Lycurgus, and Solon. He discusses the histories and the historians of the different states of Greece and condemns forgeries and lies in the most unsparing terms. His purpose in all his writings was to vindicate the truth and to correct and instruct the ignorant.

The accuracy and truthfulness with which Josephus wrote his histories was attested in his own time by the emperors Vespasian and Titus and by king Agrippa. Titus subscribed the *Wars* with his own hand and ordered them to be published. Agrippa wrote a letter to Josephus in which he said: "I have read over thy book with great pleasure, and it appears to me that thou hast done it much more accurately and with greater care, than the other writers." [10] Besides, the accuracy of the transmission and the truthfulness of the subject matter of his writings are attested by an almost unbroken succession of the most brilliant scholars from his own time up to the present. Tacitus and Justin Martyr seem to have used his statements and certainly Origen, Eusebius, Ambrose, Jerome, Isodorus, Sozomen, Cassiodorus, Syncellus, Photius, and Suidas cite him and attest his works as reliable. [11] According to the ordinary laws of evidence, these giants of old were better able to testify as to the text and veracity of Josephus than any scholars of to-day. For they lived nearer to the time of Josephus by a thousand to fifteen hundred years. They were the brightest men and the most accomplished scholars of their respective generations. They did not read laboriously a musty manuscript, or a classical author, with the aid of grammar and dictionary; but were to the language born. They had not merely fragments and desultory references and short descriptions concerning the events to which Josephus alludes, but possessed many complete works

---

[10] *Life of Flavius Josephus,* 65.
[11] See Dissertation I, in Whiston's *Josephus.*

which since have perished. We may safely conclude, therefore, that Josephus knew what he was writing about and that he told the truth.

Knowing, then, all the sources of information that we have to-day and a great many more than either we or Porphyry can claim, and animated by the highest principles of veracity and the strongest desire for accuracy, Josephus agrees with both Porphyry and his opponents as to the exactness with which the narratives in Daniel harmonize with the events that occurred in the time of the Maccabees. But he does not on that account consider that Daniel was a forgery written *post eventum*. On the contrary, he narrates at length the history of Daniel at the courts of Nebuchadnezzar, Belshazzar, and Darius the Mede, following herein the Book of Daniel. He says that Daniel was one of the greatest of the prophets; that the several books that he wrote were still read in his time; that Daniel conversed with God; that he did not only prophesy of future events, as did the other prophets, but that he determined also the time of their accomplishment, and that by their accomplishment he secured belief in the truth of his predictions. He emphasises especially the vision of Daniel at Susa, recorded in the 8th chapter, and says expressly that the Jews suffered in the days of Antiochus Epiphanes the things predicted there so many years before they came to pass.[12] He says, further, that the Book of Daniel was shown to Alexander who supposed that himself was the person intended to destroy the empire of the Persians, as Daniel had predicted in chapter xi, 3.[13] And again he states that in the same manner Daniel wrote also concerning the Roman government and that his country should be made desolate by it.[14] "All these things," he says, "did this man leave in writing, as God had showed them to him, insomuch that such as read his prophecies, and see how they have been fulfilled, would wonder at the honour with which God honoured Daniel; and would thence discover how the Epicureans are in error, who cast providence out of human life, and do not believe that God takes care of the affairs of the

[12] Bk. X, xi, 7.
[13] Bk. XI, viii, 5. Prince, p. 14.
[14] Bk. X, xi, 7.

world." [15] Finally, Josephus says that the desolation of the temple by the Macedonians had been predicted by Daniel four hundred and eight years before it was accomplished.[16] It is possible, also, that when Josephus [17] calls Jesus *Christ* he derived the title Christ from Daniel; for we have shown elsewhere,[18] that, contrary to the common opinion, the title Messiah or Christ, as applied to the Saviour was a very unusual one, being found in the Old Testament only in Ps. ii, 2, and Dnl. ix, 25, 26, and in the other pre-Christian literature of the Jews in Enoch xliii, 10, lii, 4, Ps. of Sol. xviii, 6, 8, alone.[19]

It is evident, then, that Josephus must have thought that the background of Daniel was that of the times of Nebuchadnezzar and Cyrus and not that of the Maccabees. If there had been any indication of the later time, surely one of his knowledge and opportunities and methods and love of veracity would have detected it, whether it was in the sphere of history, customs, or language. Surely, also, he, if anyone, was in a position to know that it was written in the second century B.C., if that had been the age of its composition. But neither he, nor any of his sources, nor any source possibly unknown to him, gives any intimation that anyone even thought that it was written then. More than 500 years after the death of Antiochus Epiphanes, a heathen philosopher antagonistic to Christianity startles the world with his opinion that it was composed shortly before the death of Epiphanes, and lo! the German critic puts this forth as *evidence* that it was written then. Let him follow Porphyry who will, but let him cease to say that he does so on the ground of evidence. Let him be honest enough to say that he does so because like Porphyry he does not believe in the possibility of miracles, nor in predictive prophecy,—at least in that kind of predictive prophecy which is found in Daniel.

[15] *Id.*
[16] Bk. XII, vii, 6.
[17] Bk. XVIII, iii, 3.
[18] *Vide supra*, pp. 132, 138, 212.
[19] Since Josephus never elsewhere pays any attention to this apocryphal literature it is possible at least that he derived the title *Christ* from Daniel directly, as the people of New Testament times seem to have done.

ALLEGED EVIDENCE OF LATE DATE

Daniel's Praying

But, since Josephus was not infallible, let us look at some of the other alleged evidence that the background of Daniel is that of the second century B.C. Professor Cornill reasserts [20] the old opinion that the fact that Daniel is said to have *prayed three times a day with his face turned to Jerusalem* shows that Daniel was written in the second century B.C. rather than in the sixth. He gives no evidence in support of this assertion and for the very good reason that there is none to give. He says only that "all this would have been unintelligible at the time of the Babylonian exile," a statement of the kind frequently indulged in by special pleaders of Professor Cornill's school, but which has absolutely no value as evidence. How can we know that it was unintelligible? To pray three times a day is a very simple act. To pray with one's face toward Jerusalem, the place of Jehovah's residence, is another very simple act. Why could either of these acts be more intelligible in the second century B.C. than in the sixth? What is unintelligible is, that a German professor of the twentieth century A.D. should make such an unfounded statement.

For, in fact, no better illustration of the falseness of the critical method can be found than this very case. As to praying *toward Jerusalem*, the practice is referred to three times in the prayer of Solomon (1 Kings viii).[21] That this prayer of Solomon was

[20] *Introduction*, p. 388.

[21] The three places are 1 Kings viii, 30, 38, and 48, which read as follows:

> And hearken thou to the supplication of thy servant, and of thy people Israel, when they shall pray toward this place: yea hear thou in heaven thy dwelling-place; and when thou hearest, forgive. . . .
>
> What prayer and supplication soever be made by any man, or by all thy people Israel, who shall know every man the plague of his own heart, and spread forth his hands toward this house. . . .
>
> If they return unto thee with all their heart and all their soul in the land of their enemies, who carried them captive, and pray unto thee toward their land, which thou gavest unto their fathers, the city which thou hast chosen, and the house which I have built for thy name.

known to Daniel seems evident from the fact that in his own prayer he uses such significant phrases of Solomon's as "prayer and supplication," "we have sinned, we have done iniquity, we have transgressed," and "keeping the covenant and the mercy." [22] It is immaterial as far as Daniel's use of the direction is concerned, whether this prayer was really made by Solomon, as the Book of Kings affirms, or was written during the captivity as the critics assert.[23] Since, according to Driver, the compiler of Kings was "a man like-minded with Jeremiah, and almost certainly a contemporary," [24] the prayer of Solomon, even according to the higher critics themselves, was written before the reign of Cyrus when Daniel's prayer was made. After a hundred years of diligent search, no other trace of this custom has been found by the critics, till we come to the Mohammedan times in the 7th century A.D., unless with Hitzig we find an allusion to the custom in Tobit iii, 7, where Sarah is said to have "stretched forth her hands toward the window and prayed." However we may attempt to account for this failure of the immense Jewish literature to mention the fact that the direction in Solomon's prayer had become a custom, certain it is that no argument for the late date of Daniel can be based upon the fact that he alone of all men in the long period from 550 B.C. to 600 A.D. is recorded to have followed the direction of Solomon.

As for the statement that Daniel prayed *three times a day*, the case for the critics is not much better. In Psalm lv, 18 the Psalmist says: "Evening and morning and at noon will I pray and cry aloud." In the heading this Psalm is ascribed to David; but the critics regard it as probably from the time of Jeremiah.[25] The next reference to the custom is found in the Acts of the Apostles (x, 9) a work written about 70 A.D.; so that if we suppose that Jeremiah died about 550 B.C. there were at least 620 years between these two solitary allusions to the custom that the critics can find outside of Daniel. As far as this custom is concerned it is evident, therefore,

---

[22] Daniel ix, 3, 4, 5 compared with 1 Kings viii, 28, 47, and 23.
[23] Thus Hitzig, *Com. on Daniel*, p. 94; Bevan, *The Book of Daniel*, p. 111.
[24] *L.O.T.*, p. 199.
[25] Prince, *Com.*, p. 126.

that Daniel may have been written at any time between 550 B.C. and 70 A.D. In other words the custom proves nothing as to the date of the book.

Fasting

Cornill makes the importance placed upon *fasting* in Daniel another evidence of its late date. In favour of this importance he cites ix, 3 and x, 3. The former reads: "And I set my face unto the Lord God, to seek by prayer and supplications, with fasting and sackcloth and ashes." The latter reads, beginning with verse two, "In those days I Daniel was mourning three full weeks. I ate no pleasant bread, neither came flesh nor wine in my mouth," etc. Cornill might have added vi, 18, where we read: "Then the king went to his palace and passed the night fasting: neither were instruments of music brought before him." In the first of these passages the Hebrew word for fasting is *ṣôm* from a root found in Hebrew, Aramaic, and Arabic. The verb is found twenty-one times in the Old Testament Hebrew, and the noun twenty-six times. Neither of them is found in the Hexateuch; but one or the other occurs in thirteen of the other books of the Old Testament (Jgs. *1*, Sam. *8*, Kgs. *3*, Chr. *2*, Ezra *2*, Neh. *2*, Est. *4*, Isa. *7*, Jer. *3*, Joel. *3*, Jon. *1*, Zech. *7*, Ps. *3*, and Dnl. *1*. In Isaiah it occurs only in chap. lviii, 3, 4, 5, and 6, where we find the verb three times and the noun four times. In Zechariah the verb occurs three times in chap. vii and the noun four times in chap. viii. In 2 Sam. xii, the verb is found four times and the noun once. In the literature classed by the critics as late, the verb is found once in Chronicles and that in a passage found also in Samuel, once in Ezra, once in Nehemiah, and twice in Esther; while the noun occurs once in Chronicles, once in Ezra, once in Nehemiah, twice in Esther, three times in Joel, once in Jonah, and three times in the Psalms. Altogether, therefore, even granting the claims of the critics as to the dates of the books, the verb occurs in the late literature five times as compared with sixteen in the earlier and the noun twelve as compared with fourteen times. According to the traditional view of the dates, the verb occurs in the early literature sixteen times and five times in the later literature, and the noun eighteen or nineteen times in the one and eight or seven times in the other. It should be noticed that verb and noun occur eight times in Samuel, seven times in Zechariah vii-viii, seven times in Isaiah lviii. Wherein any special importance can be found in Daniel's single and appropriate act of fasting from which to determine the late date of the book named after him, the superman professor of Koenigsberg has not made known to us. Presumably, he has willed it thus to be and so it must be! When the lion roars, let all the beasts of the forest keep silence.

Our German professor has discovered another important act of fasting in chap. x, 3, where Daniel says that because he was mourning he ate no pleasant bread nor partook of meat or wine for three weeks. Surely no one but an eminent professor in the school of Kant could have the penetration into the evolution of nature and history to perceive that a man depressed with mourning might have abstained from his ordinary diet 2100 years ago but could not or would not have done so 2500 years ago. Nor is it clear to the writer how the phrase "I ate not, I drank not" could have been used by the Sumerian author of the Nimrod Epic[26] hundreds of years before the time of Darius the Mede and still could be an important factor in determining the late date of the Book of Daniel. Is it not probable that in all the ages since man has lived upon the earth deep grief has taken away the desire for the ordinary pleasures of the palate? Real mourning does not express itself in champagne suppers and pâtés de fois gras, and disgust with life has driven many a hermit to a lonely cave and a beggar's fare.

The third instance of fasting mentioned in Daniel (to which Cornill has failed to allude) is found in vi, 18, where Darius is said to have passed the night fasting because of the predicament of Daniel who had just been cast into the den of lions. Since this chapter is in Aramaic, the word for fasting is in Aramaic also, and is not found in Biblical Hebrew.[27] While the word is

[26] See Haupt, *Nimrod-Epos, in loco.*
[27] The root occurs in Arabic, where it means "to be hungry." In Syriac the verb means to "roast," but the noun has the sense of fasting. The usual word for fast in both Aramaic and Arabic is the same as the Hebrew *ṣum.*

not found in Babylonian, a parallel to the whole passage occurs in an inscription of Ashurbanipal where it says that Ishtar of Arbila said to him: "Where the place of Nebo is, eat food and drink wine, let music be made, and honour my divinity." [28] Numerous parallels can be found, also, in the *Arabian Nights,* which show clearly that to oriental kings eating and drinking and music were the ordinary means of distraction and dissipation. Abstention from them was a sign of low spirits. Haroun ar Rashid is represented as frequently refusing these common enjoyments and as demanding some extraordinary means of relieving the gloom and ennui of life. That Darius should have been sorely grieved because of his friend Daniel was natural and commendable and that he should have abstained from the nightly routine of pleasures was to have been expected, because he was a man as well as a disgruntled king made helpless by his own thoughtless decree; but to assert that his fasting was an important event or an indication of the date of the book that records it, would be preposterous. It was simply human. Had he done otherwise, he would have been a monster.

The phrase "to afflict one's soul" which is employed in the so-called Holiness and Priestly codes as an equivalent of the words for fasting, is not found in Daniel; but even if it were, it would not indicate the late date of Daniel, inasmuch as the Holiness code at least is usually assigned by the critics to the time of the captivity.[29]

The conclusion from the review of fasting, as far as it is mentioned in the Old Testament, can only be that the writer of Daniel does not attach an importance to it superior to that to be found in Samuel, Isaiah and Zechariah, and that no indication of date can be derived from the reference to it in Daniel. In works antedating the New Testament writings the only sure evidence (aside from the special "affliction of the soul" that characterized the services of the Day of Atonement) of any particular importance imputed to the act of fasting is to be found in the

[28] *Keilinschriftliche Bibliothek,* II, p. 252.
[29] See Lev. xvi. 31, xxiii, 27, 29, 32, Num. xxix, 7. Compare Cornill, *Introduction* p. 132-36.

Testaments of the Twelve Patriarchs. This book according to Charles was written between 109 and 107 B.C.[30] According to this document "Reuben practices abstinence for seven years (i, 10), Simeon for two (iii, 4), and Judah till old age (xv, 4, xix, 2), in expiation of their sins. Joseph fasts seven years to preserve his chastity (iii, 4). Issachar in his righteousness and self-control abstains from wine all his life (vii, 3). The righteous man combines fasting with chastity (ix, 2), the double-hearted man superstitiously combines fasting and adultery, (ii, 8, iv, 3)."[31] None of the other pre-Christian writings even so much as mention fasting. To be sure, Charles finds in the second chapter of Tobit a fasting that had "not reached the culmination of its development." To show how far this fasting of Tobit's was from a culmination it is only necessary to quote the passage in full:

"When Esarhaddon was king I came home again, and my wife Anna was restored unto me, and my son Tobias. And at our feast of the Pentecost, which is the holy feast of the Weeks, there was a good dinner prepared for me; and I laid me down to dine. And the table was set for me, and abundant victuals were set for me, and I said unto Tobias my son, Go, my boy, and what poor man soever thou shalt find of our brethren of the Ninevite captives, who is mindful of God with his whole heart, bring him and he shall eat together with me; and lo, I tarry for thee, my boy, until thou come.

"And Tobias went to seek some poor man of our brethren and returned and said, Father. And I said to him, Here am I, my child. And he answered and said, Father, behold, one of our nation hath been murdered and cast out in the marketplace, and he hath but now been strangled. And I sprang up and left my dinner before I had tasted it, and took him up from the street and put him in one of the chambers until the sun was set, to bury him. Therefore I returned and washed myself, and ate food with mourning, and remembered the word of the prophet which Amos spake against Bethel, saying: Your feasts shall be turned into mourning, and all your ways into lamentation."[32]

The Oxford professor who can discern the undeveloped custom of fasting in this story of Tobit is evidently not the editor

---

[30] *The Apocrypha and Pseudepigrapha of the Old Testament*, II, p. 290.
[31] *Id.*, p. 296, note to vs. 10.
[32] Tobit, 1-6.

of *Punch* nor a lecturer on the humour of Dickens and Jerome K. Jerome. One can imagine him sitting down to an abundant repast in honour of the king of England's birthday, while a captive in Broussa or Iconium, and sending out a messenger to invite to his dinner some stranded countryman. The messenger returns with the terrifying announcement that while going out at the front gate he stumbled over the dead body of an Englishman just slain by the Bashi Bazouks. The nice fresh corpse is brought in. But the professor says in sang froid: On with the dinner. Let joy be unconfined. And so he gorges himself with soupe a la reine, and ros-bif and chilton cheese and plum pudding and gooseberry tart and a cup of Mocha with a glass of Benedictine and a Sumatra cigar (or a half dozen Memnon cigarettes), while the company drink their port and raise the rafters with the chorus: Britannia Rules the Waves. According to him Harpagus would have sent up his plate for some more little boy soup after he had been informed that the soup had been made from his own little boy; and Hannibal would have celebrated the unexpected arrival of the head of Asdrubal. As for your humble servant, he would have done as Tobit did. When Tobit saw the dead body of his countryman, he simply did not eat. Reader, what would you have done? And is it not absurd to express a belief that in this natural loss of appetite on the part of Tobit one can see the undeveloped germs of a custom of religious fasting for the good of one's soul?

Almsgiving

Another late custom which Cornill discerns as proving the late date of Daniel is that of Almsgiving. The only statement that can possibly support his view is the clause in iv, 24 (27) where Daniel advises Nebuchadnezzar to "break off his sins in righteousness and his iniquities by showing mercy to the poor." He follows the Septuagint, Peshitto, and Talmud by rendering the Aramaic word usually translated "righteousness" by "almsgiving," and then argues that this use of the word is later than the sixth century. In view of the use of this word in the Teima Aramaic inscription from the fifth century, it is doubtful if a good case could be made against the early date of Daniel, even if it were admitted that the word meant almsgiving here in Daniel.[33] This, however, would not prove that it was used in this sense in Daniel, nor does the fact that the early translators into Greek and Aramaic interpreted it as meaning alms. No one disputes that when these translations were made the word had acquired this meaning. In fact, in Aramaic the common word for sin denoted originally "debt," and so the word for righteousness came to mean the means of getting rid of the debt by payment. It was a *quid pro quo* system of redemption; so much sin, so much righteousness, a system of indulgences on a universal scale. But that it is not so used in Dan. iv, 24 appears from the following reasons. First, righteousness or right conduct suits the connection. Secondly, a king would more naturally be asked to be righteous than to give alms. Thirdly, the parallel clause "showing mercy" favours the judicial rather than the beneficiary interpretation. Fourthly, many of the radical critics hold to the sense of righteousness.[34] Fifthly, in ix, 7, 16, 18, the only other places where Daniel employs the word, it is admitted by all to be used in the sense of righteousness, or righteous deeds.

Abstinence

The last custom which Cornill cites as indicating a late origin for Daniel is that of abstaining from flesh and wine in intercourse with the heathen.[35] In regard to this abstention Prince says that it is a "distinctly Maccabean touch." [36] "We have," he adds,

[33] Compare Bevan (*Commentary*, p. 94) who says that its use on the Teima inscription shows that the Aramaic word had acquired the sense of a "payment for religious purposes" long before the second century.

[34] So, Von Lengerke, *Das Buch Daniel*, p. 185; Prince, in his *Commentary*, p. 88, makes it mean "kind acts."

[35] *Introduction*, p. 288: Objection must be made to Cornill's translation of *patbag* by "flesh." In none of the derivations for this word suggested by the eminent Persian scholars and by the translators and lexicographers who have attempted to give its meaning is the sense confined to flesh. Prince's "dainties" is better but his "food" is better still, since the writer of Daniel defines it in verse 12 by *ma'ᵃkal*, a term which means "anything that is eaten." The good old word "victuals" is, perhaps, as correct an equivalent as the English language affords.

[36] *Commentary on Daniel*, p. 61.

"only to refer to 1 Macc. i, 62-63 to see how such a defilement [as that of eating unclean food] was regarded by the pious Jews of that period. The persecuting Syrian king was particularly importunate against the ritualistic requirements of the Jewish Law and especially against the regulation forbidding the Jews to touch a strange food (see *l.c.* i, 60). The author of Daniel, therefore, in emphasizing this act of piety on the part of his hero, is plainly touching on a point of vital importance to his readers." [37]

Since this passage in First Maccabees is the only one in pre-Christian literature outside the Bible bearing upon uncleanness of food, we shall give it in full before proceeding to comment on the subject. We shall quote the passage from the 54th verse to the 64th, inclusive:

"And on the fifteenth day of Chislev in the one hundred and forty-fifth year [i.e., 168 b.c.] they set up upon the altar an abomination of desolation, and in the cities of Judah on every side they established high places; and they offered sacrifices at the doors of the houses and in the streets. And the books of the, Law which they found they rent in pieces and burned them in the fire. And with whomsoever was found a book of the covenant, and if he was consenting unto the Law, such an one was, according to the king's sentence, condemned to death. Thus did they in their might to the Israelites who were found month by month in their cities. And on the twenty-fifth day of the month they sacrificed upon the altar which was upon the altar of burnt-offering. And, according to the decree, they put to death the women who had circumcised their children, hanging their babes round their (mothers') necks, and they put to death their (entire) families, together with those who had circumcised them. Nevertheless, many in Israel stood firm and determined in their hearts that they would not eat unclean things, and chose rather to die so that they might not be defiled with meats, thereby profaning the holy covenant; and they did die."

Upon this passage from Maccabees it may be remarked:

1. It is the only place in the book in which unclean foods are mentioned.

2. Abstention from wine is not expressed in it.

3. It was the law as a whole and in all its parts that Antiochus

[37] *Id.*, p. 61, 62.

was attempting to destroy, the laws against eating certain meats being only a part of it.

4. The laws about clean and unclean animals occur in Deut. xiv, as well as in Lev. xi. They were in existence, therefore, according to the critics, before the sixth century B.C., so that they would be as binding on Jews in Babylon in the time of Nebuchadnezzar as on those in Palestine in the time of Antiochus Epiphanes.

5. A strange inconsistency is latent in this assumption of the anti-biblical critics with regard to the alleged emphasis placed upon unclean foods in the second century B.C. It is a fundamental assumption of those who believe in the natural evolution of religion that fetichism and totemism, with their involved distinctions of holy and unholy, clean and unclean, are to be found in the first stages of religious development, and yet these critics of Daniel would have us believe that the importance attached to it arose in the second century B.C! To carry one point they argue that the distinction is among the earliest of all customs. To carry another point, they argue that it is among the latest.

6. There was no more reason for a pious Jew's abstention from unclean meats in the second century B.C. than there was in the sixth. The Law of God was just as binding at the earlier as at the later period. And this Law, according to the critics themselves, contained the injunctions and regulations with regard to clean and unclean animals and with regard to the eating of blood. According to these same critics the man Daniel is represented in the book named after him as a pious Jew living in Babylon in the sixth century B.C., but the ignorant author makes him in fact live like a pious Jew of the time of the Maccabees. No proof of this opinion can be found either in the law or the custom of abstention from unclean animals. Besides, the inscriptions of Nebuchadnezzar clearly show that no man was ever a more ardent and faithful and munificent worshipper of the gods than he and hence would be more likely than he to require conformity to the religious customs prevailing in his palace. The numerous temples which he built or renovated and the bountiful gifts with which he endowed them are the theme of his tireless boastings and

the ground of his repeated prayers. In some cases he has enumerated his donations toward the support of the temple service. Thus in the Grotefend Cylinder [38] he says that he had increased his fat offerings and clean freewill offerings to Marduk, among which he names "for every day one fat ox, a perfect ox, . . . fish, birds, various kinds of vegetables, honey, butter, milk, the best oil and a dozen different kinds of wine and strong drink," which he made to abound "upon the table of Marduk and Zarpinat my (his) Lords." In the same inscription, he is said to have offered substantially the same things to Nebo and Nana. Now, from what we know of all ancient nations and their religions we are certain that they all had rules as to what was a proper offering to make to the gods and how it should be offered. Their offerings were usually the best of what they allowed themselves. Reasoning from analogy, it is certain that the Babylonian court would have its etiquette and the priests their observances, and that every courtier and servant of the king would be compelled to submit to them, especially if he had an order of the king to that effect. Daniel and his three companions at court were therefore in an apparently inescapable dilemma. They must either obey the law of their God or obey the king. By a permissable subterfuge they circumvented the king. By confining themselves to a diet of cereals and, possibly, fruits and herbs, they escaped the danger of eating blood, eels, swans, and other unclean things, and of drinking strong or mixed drinks, perhaps mixed with blood; and especially they avoided the outward appearance of honouring the gods to whom possibly all of the meats and drinks on the king's table had first been offered.[39] In short, so true to what the life of a pious Jew at the court of Nebuchadnezzar in Daniel's circumstances must have been is this first chapter, that the author of it, if he really lived in the second century, must have had the genius of an historical novelist of the first order. The injunction about clean and unclean foods

[38] *Keilinschriftliche Bibliothek*, III, II, 32 f.
[39] So, at least, thinks Hitzig: "Sie wollten keine Speise geniessen, von der möglicher Weise den Götzen geopfert werden, oder die vielleicht noch obendrein von einem unreinen Thier herrührte" (*Das Buch Daniel*, p. 10.)

had been given long before the sixth century. The observance of the injunction by a pious Jew of the sixth century was to be presupposed. Daniel is represented as such a pious Jew. Therefore he must have observed the injunction. And consequently, to use the statement that Daniel observed this injunction as an argument for the late date of the book is absurd.

POSITIVE EVIDENCE OF EARLY DATE

Thus far we have been on the defensive with regard to the customs referred to in Daniel which are said to have been emphasized, also, in the time of the Maccabees and thus to indicate an origin of Daniel at that time. Now, before concluding this matter, a few offensive, or offensive-defensive, counter charges along this line of customs must be made.

The Law

Take, for example, the custom of magnifying the importance of the Law which is the outstanding feature of First Maccabees and Jubilees, and compare it with the fact that the Law is never mentioned in Daniel except in ix, 11 and 13.[40] Jubilees is really a sort of commentary on the laws of Moses, and First Maccabees again and again represents the great war of liberation as a revolt against the attempt of Antiochus Epiphanes and his successors to suppress the Law and to Grecize the Jews. Thus in I Macc. i, 42, Epiphanes writes to his whole kingdom that everyone should give up his usages, and letters from the king were sent to Judea to the effect that they should practice foreign customs, cease the offerings in the sanctuary, profane the Sabbaths, feasts, and sanctuary, build high-places, sacred groves, shrines for idols, sacrifice swine and other unclean animals, and leave their sons uncircumcised, *so that they might forget the Law.* In accordance with this decree, high places were established in the cities, sacrifices were offered at the doors of the houses and in the streets, the books of the Law were rent in pieces and burnt, whoever had a copy of the Law was put to death, and the women

[40] In verse 10 the laws of the prophets are spoken of.

who had circumcised their children were put to death with their families.[41] In ii, 21, Mattathias proclaimed the principle of the rebels when he said with a loud voice: Heaven forbid that we should forsake the Law and the ordinances. He showed his zeal for the Law by killing the king's officer who had come to Modin to enforce the king's decree and fled to the mountains after he had cried: Let everyone that is zealous for the Law and that would maintain the covenant come forth after me.[42] Afterwards there were gathered unto him the mighty men who willingly offered themselves for the Law,[43] and they went round about and pulled down altars and circumcised children by force and rescued the Law out of the hand of the Gentiles.[44] In his great speech delivered just before his death he says among other things: "My children, be zealous for the Law and give your lives for the covenant of your fathers, be strong and show yourselfs men on behalf of the Law, take all who observe the Law and avenge the wrong of your people, and render a recompense to the Gentiles and take heed to the commandments of the Law." [45] After the death of Epiphanes, when his commander Lysias wanted to make peace with the Jews, he said: "Let us settle with them that they be permitted to walk after their own laws as aforetime; for because of their laws which we abolished were they angered and did all these things." [46] In comparing the references to the Law and laws in Daniel with what is said in Maccabees, it must be noticed, also, that in the former it is the wilful transgressions of them by the fathers that are always in mind; whereas in Maccabees, it is the attempted annulment of them by an alien, and an enforced transgression of them by the living Israelites to which allusion is made.

Circumcision and Sabbath

What is true of the Law in general is true of circumcision and the Sabbath in particular. First Maccabees contains numerous and scattered references to the Sabbath and one to the sabbatic

[41] i, 44-61. [43] ii, 19-28. [45] ii, 42.
[42] ii, 45-48. [44] ii, 49-68.
[46] vi, 55-60. For other references to the Law and the laws, see iii, 29, 48, 56; iv, 42, 47, 53; x, 14; xi, 21; xiii, 3; xiv, 14, 29.

year, and the first two chapters describe at length the endeavours to suppress the usage of circumcision and on the part of apostate Jews to conceal even its traces; whereas Daniel never mentions either Sabbath or circumcision. If Daniel were a fiction with Maccabean background, it certainly seems a great defect that the author failed to show how his heroes refused to work on the Sabbath day or that they were tempted to hide their circumcision.

Elephants and Phalanx

One other feature that is conspicuous in the background of the Maccabees is utterly ignored in Daniel, that is the use of the phalanx and of elephants in war. The Egyptian, Assyrian, Babylonian, and Persian armies never employed the elephant; and in harmony with this fact, the books of the Old Testament never mention it. Alexander the Great was the first of the Greeks to come in contact with the elephant as an instrument of warfare. This was in his battle with Porus in the Punjaub. Seleucus Nicator introduced it first in the battles of Western Asia. Pyrrhus and the Carthaginians used it in their wars with Rome and it continued to be a much dreaded arm of service until at the command of Scipio Africanus the Romans at the battle of Zama which sealed the fate of Carthage discomfited his great rival Hannibal by opening up the legions so that the elephants would pass between the serried ranks. In the wars against Antiochus the Romans triumphed by using the same tactics, and we hear nothing of their use in battle after the fall of Carthage and of the Seleucid kingdom. In the wars of Antiochus Epiphanes and his successors against the Jews, however, they were still the main arm of the service and at first they struck terror into their rebellious adversaries. Eleazar, one of the brothers of Judas Maccabeus, was crushed by the falling on him of an elephant which he had stabbed from underneath in an endeavour to kill the king. [47] They are mentioned, also, elsewhere [48] as constituent and important parts of the Syrian armies.

The phalanx, that great Greek rival of the Roman legion, was

[47] I Macc. vi, 36-46.
[48] In i, 17, iii, 34; viii, 6; and xi, 56.

the ordinary formation of the heavy armed troops of the Syrian as well as the Macedonian armies, and the word is found in I Macc. vi, 35, 38, 45; ix, 12; and x, 82. In Daniel, however, neither elephant nor phalanx is mentioned, but simply the old time horses and chariots of the Persian and pre-Persian period. It seems to be incumbent on the critics to explain how an artist of the ability of the writer of Daniel could be so correct in some parts of his background and so defective in others,—that is, if this artist really lived in the second century, and painted the background of his fiction with the colours of his time. This wonderful accuracy of his in describing what existed in the sixth century confirms us in our belief that the author of the book really lived in that period. For we cannot see how one who was so ignorant of the history of Babylon, Persia, and Greece, as the critics assert that this author was, could have known that the elephants and phalanxes were not in existence in the time of which he feigned the history. He is supposed (?) to err on such important and easily ascertained matters as who was the last king of Babylon, who was Darius the Mede, and how many were the kings of Persia, and yet he knows enough about their times to steer clear of any mention of elephants in his description of the great army of the king of the north referred to in xi, 40. He describes so accurately the history of the wars between the Ptolemies and Seleucids that the critics say that the account must have been written *post eventum*, and yet he knows so little of their armies as to speak of their chariots, and horsemen, and fleet and never mention their phalanxes and their elephants.

Sealing Documents

One other custom is mentioned in Daniel which seems eminently fitted to a Babylonian background in the sixth century B.C., but for which we will look in vain in the Palestine of the second century. This is the custom of closing and sealing documents. As is well known, the Babylonian clay tablet or brick was first prepared and inscribed and then was covered with an envelope of clay upon which a docket or endorsement was written, and the whole was stamped with a seal.[49] The statements of Dan. viii, 26 and xii, 4, 9 would then be clear. Daniel's visions were to be written on tablets, closed up, and sealed, until the time of the end.[50] The endorsement on the envelope may have directed when the tablet was to be uncovered. Two tablets of the size of the Creation Tablets would contain the whole of Daniel. The first tablet may have contained the part in Aramaic and the second that in Hebrew (i.e., chapters viii-xii) or there may have been nine or ten tablets. The injunction of the prophetic writer to keep the vision secret would then be not a "mere literary device to explain to the readers of Daniel why the book was not known before their time"; but it would be a real part of the vision, repeated on the endorsement, and designed as it says to preserve the contents of the vision from the prying eyes of the curious. That the keeping of the contents of a document "hidden from immediate posterity" was not a difficulty in the view of "the oriental mind" is apparent from the fact that the contents of their contract tablets were concealed by their envelopes from all prying eyes, until the time of breaking off the envelope arrived. That time would be determined either by the instructions on the envelope or by the decision of the custodians or judges. The Assyrian and Babylonian tablets were preserved in the archives of the temples, palaces, and banks. Daniel's tablets would naturally be entrusted to the care of the proper Jewish custodians, to be opened according to the instruction given in the endorsement, or docket, which was inscribed on the envelope. If in chap. xii, 11 we read *daleth* instead of *resh* giving us *husad* instead of *husar,* the endorsement may have read that the tablet

[49] It is possible that the Babylonian word *šatam,* used to denote an official of the temples, may be derived from the root "to close, or shut up." The man who closed up the inside tablet and endorsed and sealed it would be a more important individual than the scribe who wrote the document. Hommel's translation "secretary" would be a very good equivalent. One *šatam* might have a dozen tablet-writers under him, it being his business to read over, and close up, endorse, and seal the letters and contracts.

[50] One is tempted to take the word *ḳeṣ,* usually meaning *end,* as an infinitive from *ḳaṣaṣ* meaning "to break off," and to translate "until the time of breaking off," i.e., of taking off the clay envelope which contained the tablet on which the vision was written.

was to be opened 1290 years after the daily offering had been instituted at Sinai. If Daniel and the custodians dated this institution at Sinai at 1460 B.C., the time for the opening would be 170 B.C. If the text as it stands is preferred and the 1290 days be interpreted as literal days, it might mean, as Bevan suggests,[51] 1290 days after the desecration of the temple and the taking away of the daily offerings. In 2 Macc. ii, 14, Judas is said to have collected all the writings which had been scattered owing to the outbreak of the war. Among these writings the Book of Daniel may have been found with the tablets still in their original envelopes which may then have been broken, and the book translated, and published. Whatever may be said of this conjecture, it is certainly as sensible as many of those put forward by commentators. It would eliminate all objections made to the early date of Daniel, in so far as they are based upon the character of the language in which the book is written.

[51] *Commentary*, p. 207.

CHAPTER VIII

THE PROPHECIES OF DANIEL

THE FOURTH KINGDOM

It is assumed by the critics that the fourth kingdom of Daniel is the Greek instead of the Roman empire.[1] This involves the further assumption that not merely xi, 20-45 but also ii, 31-34, 40-43, vii, 9, 19-27, viii, 9-14, 23-26 refer to Antiochus Epiphanes.

The assumption that Alexander and his successors, especially the kingdom of the Seleucids, represent the fourth kingdom of Daniel, depends on the further assumption that the second kingdom was Median, an assumption that has no foundation in the Book of Daniel.[2] To be sure Darius is called a Mede (vi, 1), and is said to have received the kingdom of Belshazzar; and the two horns of the ram spoken of in viii, 20 are said to denote the kings of Media and Persia. But since Belshazzar was not king of Media but of Babylon and probably of Accad and Chaldea, it is to be presumed that Darius the Mede received the kingship over that comparatively small part of the empire of Cyrus that had been ruled over by Belshazzar the Chaldean. There is absolutely no foundation for the assertion of the critics that Daniel makes Darius the Mede to have ruled over Babylon before the accession of Cyrus.[3] He is said in vi, 1 to have "received" (*kabbel*) the kingdom and from whom could he have received it except from Cyrus?[4]

[1] Prince, *Commentary on Daniel*, p. 71.

[2] For a full discussion of the assumption that the second kingdom was Median the reader is referred to the writer's *Studies in the Book of Daniel*, Series One, pp. 128-238.

[3] So Bevan, *Commentary on Daniel*, p. 20.

[4] The verb *kabbel* means "receive," not "take by force." Brockelmann in his Syriac Dictionary renders it by *accepit*, that is *annehmen*, not *einnehmen*. In the Targum of Onkelos, it always has the sense of "receive," the sense of "taking by force" being expressed by *kevash* and *'eḥad*.

In ix, 1, it is said that Darius was *made* king (*homlak*) over the realm of the Chaldeans. Who could have made him king but Cyrus? Hitzig, indeed, says that this does not mean merely that he was made king by God, but that he must by human action have been made king of Babylon and that this action was taken by the army led by Cyrus.[5] It seems convenient for Bevan and Prince to ignore these two passages in their discussions of Darius the Mede, an admirable way for a special pleader to escape the necessary conclusion to be derived from indisputable evidence against his side of the case![6] They confuse the issue by making long dissertations on irrelevant matters connected with the Median kingdom of Deioces and his successors down to Astyages whom Cyrus overthrew. For example, Prince affirms, that "Babylon was captured by Cyrus the Persian, who, sometime previously, had obtained possession of Media and its king Astyages."[7] He then discusses the theory formerly advanced by some that Darius the Mede was "identical with Cyaxares, son of Astyages, mentioned in Xenophon's Cyropædia."[8] He then compares "the data of Xenophon regarding the last Median kings with those of Herodotus on the same subject," and notices in passing that "neither Berosus nor any other ancient author knows of a Median ruler after the fall of Babylon."[9] He next states that the Annals of Nabonidus and the Cyrus Cylinder make no mention "of any ruler of Media between Astyages and Cyrus nor of any king of Babylon intervening between Nabonidus and Cyrus."[10] He then continues to discourse at length on the Cyaxares of Xenophon, the Darius of Eusebius, and the coin *darik*, and gives a résumé of the history of Media from Deioces to Cyaxares and finally gives his views as to the probable origin of the conception of Darius the Mede as given in Daniel.[11] He concludes by saying

[5] *Commentary on Daniel*, p. 145.
[6] Bevan assumes that *ḳabbel* means "take possession," (*Comm.*, p. 109), but he does not attempt to prove it.
[7] *Commentary on Daniel*, p. 44.
[8] *id.* pp. 45, 46.
[9] *id.* p. 47.
[10] *id.* p. 48.
[11] *id.* pp. 48-55.

that Darius the Mede "appears therefore to have been a product of a mixture of traditions" of the "destruction of Nineveh by the Medes" and of the "capture of Babylon by Darius Hystaspis," [12] and thinks that "it seems apparent that the interpolation of Darius the Mede must be regarded as the most glaring inaccuracy in the Book of Daniel." [13]

THE SECOND KINGDOM NOT MEDIAN

We readily give Professor Prince the credit of having produced the most scholarly and up to date presentation of the case of the critics *versus* Daniel that has so far been published. We think that most of his statements as to facts are undeniable, that Cyrus did conquer Babylon, that Xenophon and Herodotus differ as he says, that Berosus and the other ancient authors know nothing of a Median ruler after the fall of Babylon, that the Annals of Nabonidus and the Cyrus Cylinder make no mention of a Median king of Babylon, that there is doubt as to who the Cyaxares of Xenophon was and as to the Darius of Eusebius; but he will pardon us for the inability to perceive that his views and conclusions are justified by the facts and the evidence that he has produced. Our reasons for differing from his conclusions are the following:

1. All authorities are agreed that Cyrus took Babylon. Herodotus and Xenophon say so expressly. Isaiah implies it. The Cyrus Cylinder confirms it, but adds that his general Gubaru took it for him and that Cyrus himself did not enter the city till four months later. Gubaru, according to the Cylinder, was made "governor" (in Aramaic *malka* "king") of the city by Cyrus, a position which he seems to have held for at least twelve years.[14]

2. Whether there was a Cyaxares the son of Astyages and what his relationship to Cyrus may have been, are interesting

---

[12] *id.* p. 55.
[13] *id.* p. 56.
[14] See tablet published by Pinches in *The Expository Times* for 1915.

questions; but the Book of Daniel says nothing bearing directly on either question.[15]

3. Since Daniel does not say that a Median king independent of Cyrus ruled over Babylon after the Chaldean empire was destroyed, the silence of Berosus and other ancient authors on this subject agrees with the silence of Daniel. The statement that Darius was a Mede no more proves that he was king of Media than does the statement that Napoleon was a Corsican prove that he was king of Corsica. Besides he may have been a king of Media and still have been subordinate to Cyrus king of Persia. Murat was a Frenchman who was made king of Naples and was subordinate to a Corsican Italian who had become emperor of the French.[16]

4. Prince points out that the Annals of Nabonidus and the Cyrus Cylinder make no mention of a ruler of Media between Astyages and Cyrus. In this they agree with Daniel.

5. The Annals of Nabonidus and the Cyrus Cylinder are said to make no mention of any king of Babylon intervening between Nabonidus and Cyrus. To this statement we take exception because of the ambiguity of both terms of the phrase "king of Babylon," and because of the use of the word "intervening." As

[15] Since the *Ku* of the Greek Kuaxares corresponds to *Eva* in the Persian cuneiform of the Behistun inscription, it might be possible that the Hebrew and Aramaic Ahasuerus represents the *axares* of Cyaxares. In this case, Darius the Mede would be the son of Cyaxares, the son of Astyages, the son of Cyaxares; or he might be descended from the father of Astyages. In the Behistun Inscription the Median claimants to the throne call themselves the sons of Cyaxares. If Darius the Mede were the son of Cyaxares the son of Astyages, he could be called "of the seed of Media," that is, of the royal family of Media, without his father or himself having really been king of Media.

[16] Again Darius the Mede may have been the son of Cyaxares, predecessor of Astyages, king of Media. Since he was sixty-two years old when he was made king of Babylon (by Cyrus?), he would have been born in 600 B.C. If Sayce is right in supposing that Astyages was a Scythian who conquered Media, Darius the Mede may have been the heir of Cyaxares. The defection of the Medes under Harpagus during the battle between Astyages and Cyrus would be accounted for if we could be certain that Astyages was a Scythian conqueror of the Medes. The Medes in this case were simply going over to their kinsmen the Persians and throwing off the yoke of the foreign despot who had subdued them.

has been shown elsewhere,[17] the Aramaic word for king may denote the son of a king, the ruler of a city, of a province, or of an empire. Babylon, also, may mean the city of Babylon, or the lower region of the Euphrates-Tigris valley, or the whole Babylonian empire. Now, it is true that the records of Nabonidus and Cyrus do not mention a king of the empire as intervening between Nabonidus and Cyrus; but the records of Nabonidus and Cyrus do speak of many kings as reigning in subordination to them. Thus, in the Abu-Habba Cylinder (I, 45), Nabonidus refers to the kings, princes, and governors which the gods had made subject to him, and in I, 27, speaks of Astyages and the kings who helped him; and Cyrus in his Cylinder Inscription says that all the kings from the upper to the lower sea came to Babylon and kissed his feet. In the Chronicle, also, the kings of the sea-land (i.e. Phenicia) who were subject to Nabonidus are mentioned.[18]   In the Abu-Habba Cylinder, (I, 29), Cyrus king of the land of Anzan is called the "little servant of Astyages." In the Chronicle (lines 15-17), Cyrus king of Persia is said to have crossed the Tigris below Arbela and to have killed a king who must have been a sub-king to Nabonidus, king of Babylon. Neriglissar in the Cambridge Cylinder (I, 14) calls himself the son of Belshumishkun king of Babylon. This Belshumishkun must have been king of the city of Babylon at some time when Nabopolassar or Nebuchadnezzar was king of the empire; for the Chaldean empire began in 626 B.C., and the reign of Neriglissar began in 559 B.C.[19] It is probable that a son of Nabonidus of the same name and title as his father was king of Harran while his father and overlord was still reigning as king of the empire of Babylon.[20] Belshazzar is treated as king when his name is used in an oath along with that of his father. Besides, his father invokes

[17] *Studies in the Book of Daniel*, Series One, pp. 90-94.
[18] Reverse 3.
[19] Of course if he were sixty-seven or over when he began to reign, his father may have been king of Babylon before Nabopolassar. In this case he must have been sub-king to Shamashshumukin or to Ashurbanipal king of Assyria; for the latter was overlord of Babylon till his death in 626 B.C.
[20] See the Eshki-Harran Inscription edited by Pognon.

the gods to bless him just as he invokes them to bless himself. Antiochus in like manner joins his son Seleucus with him and expressly calls his son king.[21] The "son of the king" who commanded Nabonidus' armies in Accad was probably Belshazzar and in the 10th year of Nabonidus this son seems to have been made governor (Aramaic, *malka* "king") of Erech.[22] He would be the natural successor in the kingship over Babylon as soon as his father was made prisoner by Cyrus at Sippar. Gubaru the governor (*piḫu*) of the land of Gutium took Babylon for Cyrus and was then made governor (*piḫu*) of the city of Babylon, a position which he seems to have been occupying as late as the 4th year of Cambyses.[23] Finally Cyrus and Cambyses were both kings of Babylon at once.[24]

The above evidence proves that Nabonidus, Astyages, and Cyrus were all kings of kings, and that in the two accredited instances of Belshumishkun and Cambyses these sub-kings were called on the Babylonian monuments and in the Babylonian language king (*sharru*) of Babylon. Gubaru, also, although he is not called *sharru* is called *shaknu* of Babylon and this would in Aramaic be equivalent to *malka* "king" of Babylon. "Out of the mouth of two or three witnesses shall every word be established." The necessity for supposing that, if Daniel is true, there must have been a king *intervening* between Nabonidus and Cyrus does not exist. Like many other objections to the statements of the Bible, it is not merely unsupported by the evidence we possess, but is absolutely contrary to it.

6. Who the Cyaxares of Xenophon may have been, or whether he existed at all, is a question of importance for students of Xenophon, or historians of Media or Cyrus; but we agree with Professor Prince that there is not sufficient evidence to justify us in supposing that he was the same as Darius the Mede of Daniel. The same may be said of the Darius of Eusebius.

7. As to the word *darik*, it is now generally agreed that it has

---

[21] *Keilinschriftliche Bibliothek*, III, 11, 139.
[22] *Id.*, 133.
[23] cf. Footnote 14 *supra*.
[24] See, *Studies in the Book of Daniel*, Vol. 1. 132f.

probably no connection with the name Darius; since it occurs in a contract tablet from the reign of Nabonidus.[25]

The conclusion, then, to be derived from this long discussion of Darius and the Medes is that Darius the Mede is one of the hundreds of sub-kings who reigned over parts of the great empires of the Assyrians, Babylonians, Medes, and Persians, whose name has been rescued from oblivion because of his connection with the prophet Daniel. Who he was and what he was we may never definitely determine. Most probably, he was either the same as Gubaru to whom Cyrus entrusted the government of Babylon immediately after its capture, or a greater sub-king who ruled over Media as well as Assyria and Babylonia and Chaldea, or a subordinate of Gubaru who we know was governor of Gutium before he was given the government of Babylon. But, whoever he was and whatever the extent of his government, there is no intimation in Daniel, or elsewhere, that he ever ruled over an independent kingdom, or that he ever was king of the Medes, or that his kingdom intervened between that of Nabonidus and Cyrus. Consequently, that the second empire of Daniel was that of the Medes is a figment of the critics' imagination. With no evidence in support of its existence, it should be dropped from all serious discussion of the meaning of the predictions of Daniel.

Having thus ruled out the supposititious Median empire, the four kingdoms of Daniel's visions will be the Babylonian, the Persian, the Greek, and the Roman, as has been held by most of the ablest Christians interpreters from the earliest times to the present.[26]

DARKNESS AND LIGHT IN DANIEL'S PREDICTIONS

It is assumed by the critics, (1) that the part of Daniel which treats of the Ptolemies and Seleucids down to the year of the

[25] Strassmaier: *Inschriften von Nabonidus*, 1013, 26.

[26] It seems, also, to have been the view of our Lord; for he speaks of "the abomination of desolation spoken of by the prophet Daniel" as being about to be fulfilled in its true import in the time future to his own (Matt. xxiv, 15). No new evidence has appeared since the old commentaries were written that could cause us to change the traditional interpretation. On the contrary, the new evidence is preponderatingly in favour not merely of the historicity of Daniel, but of the old view of the meaning of his predictions.

death of Antiochus Epiphanes is substantially correct, and (2) that all before and after this is enveloped in darkness.[27]

1. With the first statement, all conservative scholars will agree. The part of Daniel concerned with Antiochus Epiphanes is correct as far as we can judge, but it is frequently enveloped in the same kind of darkness that is supposed to characterize the rest of the book. In their commentaries, the radical critics admit this "darkness." In their attempts at interpretation of the passages referred to Epiphanes, they indulge in such words as "probable," "incorrect," author's "ignorance of facts," and obscurity "owing to our ignorance regarding the history of Israel at this period."[28] They disagree among themselves and resort to many violent changes of the text in order to make it suit their conception of what it ought to be. The most damning evidence of their inability to make the account of Antiochus Epiphanes harmonize with their view of the date of Daniel occurs in xi, 40-45. DeWette-Schrader put the time of writing Daniel at between 167 and 164.[29] Driver at sometime about 168 B.C.;[30] and Cornill asserts that it must have been written between the end of December 165 and June 164, thus probably in January 164.[31] But the commentators of the radical school say that the campaign against Egypt spoken of in verses 40-43 never occurred.[32] Yet we are expected to believe that the people of Israel were such a lot of innocents (?) and ignoramuses as to accept shortly after it was written this book as a genuine and authentic work of a great prophet living 400 years before! It was, says Cornill, "the work of a pious Jew, loyal to the Law, of the time of Antiochus Epiphanes, who was animated with the desire to encourage and support his persecuted and suffering comrades."[33] Bevan asserts that "everything combines to show that the Book of Daniel is, from beginning to end, an exhortation addressed to the pious Israelites in the days of the great religious

[27] Bevan, *Comm.* p. 162; Cornill, *Introduction*, p. 384.
[28] See Prince, *Commentary*, pp. 171-188.
[29] *Einleitung*, p. 507.
[30] *L.O.T.*, p. 497.
[31] *id.*, p. 390.
[32] Prince, p. 186; Bevan, p. 198.
[33] *Introduction*, p. 388.

struggle under Antiochus Epiphanes." [34] Prince makes it a "consolation to God's people in their dire distress at the time of Antiochus Epiphanes." [35] Bevan asserts that it was "read aloud in public." [36] All are agreed that it was known in the Maccabean times, for the author of First Maccabees cites from it.[37]

And yet, we are asked to believe, that those men who had lived through the whole reign of Epiphanes and must have known all about his various campaigns accepted a work as historical and its predictions as having been fulfilled, when it speaks of a whirlwind conquest of Egypt which never took place at all! Why, it is fifty-three years since the American war of secession, and there are tens of thousands of us now living who were boys in 1865 and thousands of veterans of the blue and of the grey who would laugh to scorn a historian who attempted to palm off on us a third Bull Run, or to add to the campaign of Antietam and Gettysburg a third great invasion of the Northern States under the command of General Lee! But if the historian camouflaged himself as a prophet of the Lord and sought to encourage us in these troublous times by stating that in his third campaign, Lee had captured Washington, Baltimore, and Philadelphia, but had suddenly turned back across the Potomac because of rumours which he had heard from the west and from the south, we would peremptorily reject his whole series of stories and visions as a tissue of lies and would refuse to be comforted by all his exhortations and consolations. We would inevitably conclude that a book claiming to have been written four hundred years ago and narrating the marvellous interventions of God in behalf of his people in the days of old and predicting the persecutions and triumphs of the nation in our own times for our encouragement and support was an impudent and baseless forgery, provided that we saw clearly that the author was incontrovertibly wrong in his alleged prognostications with regard to the events which were transpiring before our very eyes.

[34] *Comm.* p. 23.
[35] *Comm.* p. 24.
[36] *Comm.* p. 25.
[37] I Macc. ii, 59, 60.

But, one can hear the supermen of Germany and their English and American scholars cry out in amazement, "You must not suppose that the Jews of Maccabean times were men of intelligence like us of to-day. Our people have *die Kultur, la civilisation,* the university professor, to guard them from the acceptance of such forgeries; but the Jews of Maccabean times were ignorant peasants, knowing nothing of criticism and sources." In such an opinion there is some measure of truth. The average man of to-day has doubtless more both of learning and scientific knowledge than the average man then possessed. But this is not a matter of education but of memory and common sense, and in these two particulars there is no evidence to show that the men of to-day are superior to what they were two thousand years ago. At that time, when there were fewer books, the memories of men were most highly cultivated. Besides, there never was a man not an idiot who did not remember the great events of his own life time.

Further, Daniel was not received by the common man alone, but by the leaders of the nation, by men like the Maccabees who had fought the armies of this same Antiochus Epiphanes and with zealous care had watched all his wicked machinations against their people from the beginning of his tyrannical conduct unto the end of his career. This was a time also when the Greek learning was spread all over the countries that had been conquered by Alexander. Most of the Old Testament books had already been translated into Greek by Jewish scholars who were competent for their task. It was the age when Jewish writers of ability like Aristobulus, and Jason of Cyrene, and the Ben Siras, and the writers of First and perhaps of Second Maccabees, and Wisdom and Judith and parts of Enoch flourished. The Jews of Egypt, Cyrene, Syria, Cyprus, and other parts of the Diaspora had adopted Greek as their language. A hellenizing party had arisen even in Palestine itself which was ready to accept the innovations imposed by the Syrian king and prided itself on its Greek citizenship and customs. Alexandria and Antioch with their teeming Jewish populations were already the rivals of Athens and the centres of Greek learning. The critics of Alexandria were discussing the text of Homer and the works of Plato and Aristotle, and some at least of their Jewish scholars would be acquainted with their methods. Polybius, that great historian of Rome, was writing his unsurpassed discussion of how history should be written and condemning in unsparing terms the false statements of Timæus, Calisthenes and the others of their kind. In order to prevent interpolations, the works of Æschylus, Sophocles, and Euripides had been collected at Athens in a standard edition which later was secured through fraud by Ptolemy Philadelphus for his library at Alexandria. As to the sacred writings of the Jews, they were most certainly looked upon with the deepest veneration long before the time of Antiochus Epiphanes. This is attested, not merely by the fact that most of them at least had been translated into Greek before this time, but also by the fact that the astute tyrant saw the necessity of destroying the books if he would destroy the religion based upon them, and by the further fact that the Jews preferred death to the giving up of their sacred writings.

Now, the radical critics, without any direct evidence to support them, profess to believe that, into the midst of these sacred writings for which men readily died, a forged document of unknown authorship and (according to the critics) full of easily detected errors and of doctrines unrecognized in the Law and the other books of the Prophets was quietly admitted as a genuine and authentic writing of a prophet hitherto unknown to history. They would have us believe that this fictitious volume became immediately the model of a vast amount of similar literature and they admit that in the New Testament its influence is apparent almost everywhere and that "no writing of the Old Testament had so great a share in the development of Christianity." [38] They admit, also, that in early times its canonicity and truthfulness were never seriously disputed by Jews or Christians. Truly, the credulity of these critics is pitiable in its eccentricities! They cannot believe in miracles and predictive prophecy which involve nothing but a simple faith in a wise and mighty and merciful God intervening in behalf of his people for his own glory and

[38] Bevan, *Comm.*, p. 15, quoting Westcott.

their salvation; but they can believe that a lot of obstreperous and cantankerous Jews who through all their history from Jacob and Esau down to the present time have disagreed and quarrelled about almost everything, or nothing, could have accepted, unanimously and without a murmur, in an age when they were enlightened by the brilliant light of Plato's philosophy, and Aristole's logic, and the criticism of the schools of Alexandria, a forged and fictitious document, untrue to the well remembered facts of their own experience and to the easily ascertained facts concerning their own past history and the history of the Babylonians, Medes, Persians, and Greeks of whom the author writes. Such a psychological improbability, devoid of any direct evidence in its support, let the critic believe if he can. Your unsophisticated servant prefers his belief in predictive prophecy to any such quixotic and sciolistic attempts to belittle and besmirch a book simply because we cannot understand the why and the how of all the extraordinary deeds and doctrines that are recorded there.

2. As to the second part of the assumption of the critics, to wit, that all the records of Daniel before the time of the Seleucids and after June 164 B.C., is "enveloped in darkness," the whole of the first volume of *Studies in the Book of Daniel* is intended to show that this is not true of the historical part which treats of the reigns of Nebuchadnezzar, Belshazzar, Darius the Mede, and Cyrus. As to the predictions which touch matters subsequent to June 164 B.C., the visions and interpretations of Daniel were no more veiled in darkness to those who lived in the sixth century B.C., than were those of Jacob, Moses, Balaam, Nathan, David, Isaiah, and Zechariah to those of their time, or than the predictions of Jesus, Peter, Paul, and John to the men of the first century A.D. The prophets, we are told on the highest authority, foretold many things which they themselves did not fully understand, let alone their hearers, but which they "desired to look into." [39] To the question of the disciples as to when the things of which Jesus spoke should be, the Lord replied: No man knoweth these things but the Father. [40]

[39] 1 Peter i, 10, 11.
[40] Mat. xxiv, 3, 36.

The predictions of Daniel in regard to the resurrection, the judgment, the world kingdoms, and the Messiah, are no more obscure or difficult of interpretation than are some of those in the Gospels, the Epistles, and the Book of the Revelation of St. John. Of course, those who do not believe in God, nor in a revelation from God to man, nor in any superhuman prediction of future events, will reject alike the predictions of Daniel, Jesus, Paul, and John. But for those who call themselves Christians to deny the resurrection, the judgment, the second coming, and other predicted events, is absurd enough to make all the logicians in Hades laugh and all the angels weep. To reject a book from the sacred writings because it contains such statements with regard to the future, is to reject that in the book which most of all makes it sacred. For the distinguishing characteristic of sacred as contrasted with profane writings is this very fact, that they do contain, or are related to, such predictions. The most precious promises of the gospel from the protevangelium to the last verses of the Book of the Revelation of St. John all refer to that blessed future which now we see through a glass darkly, but where we are assured sorrow and sin and death shall be no more. To the true Christian those things to come are the brightest things in all the universe, the anchor of the soul sure and steadfast; but the god of this world has blinded the eyes of the children of disobedience, lest seeing with their eyes they should believe and be converted. Woe to the so-called Christian who under the pretence of a science falsely so-called denies the reality of revelation. Like Esau, he has sold his birthright of the hope of eternal glory for a mess of pottage, the beggarly elements of worldly wisdom and pride.[41]

THE IMPORTANCE OF ANTIOCHUS EPIPHANES

The time has now arrived to grapple with the most insidious and treacherous attack that has been made upon the Book of Daniel. It is insidious because it claims to be philosophical and scientific. It is treacherous in so far as it is made by professing

[41] For a thorough discussion of this subject, see Pusey's *Lectures on Daniel*, pp. 60-233.

Christians. A philosopher who believes that God wound up the universe, like a clock, and then let it run its course without any interference, must refuse to accept the Book of Daniel as true. So, also, must one who thinks that nothing contrary to the ordinary course of human or natural events can be proved by testimony. A scientist (or shall we say sciolist?) who thinks he knows that the laws of nature are binding on their Creator and that a modern chemist or psychologist or animal trainer can manipulate the elements, or the minds of men, or of lions, better than the Almighty, will not hesitate to reject Daniel because of the extraordinary events recorded there as having been wrought by God. But a Christian who necessarily accepts the principles of theism, and who consequently believes in God's intervention in the affairs of men, and in predictive prophecy as well as miracle, cannot refuse to accept the Book of Daniel as historical and reliable, as authentic, genuine, and veracious, simply because of the *character* of its predictions. Now, in works already published [42] and elsewhere in this volume we have endeavoured to show, that the objections against Daniel based upon the alleged inaccuracy of its statements about the age of Nebuchadnezzar and Cyrus are unfounded, that the argument from silence as illustrated in Ecclesiasticus and other cases is fallacious, that the argument from Daniel's place in the present Hebrew Bible has no basis to rest on, and that the origin and influence of its ideas and its background including its language are in harmony with its claims to have been written in the sixth century B.C in a Babylonian environment. [43] There remains but one important obstacle standing in the way of the Christian who desires to follow Christ and the apostles in their apparent acceptance of the Book of Daniel as being what it purports to be. It is the fact that Antiochus Epiphanes looms so high in the mind of the prophet. It is difficult to account for the prominence given to this "contemptible" monarch in the midst of a narrative that opens with an account of Nebuchadnezzar the king of great Babylon that he had built, that thinks Cyrus the founder of the Persian empire to be worthy of the merest reference, and that

[42] Especially in *Studies in the Book of Daniel*, Series One (1916).
[43] See above, Introduction p. 5f.

alludes to Alexander the Great in the most cursory fashion. Why should Epiphanes be selected from all the successors of Alexander, the Ptolemies, the Seleucids, Perdiccas, Eumenes, Antigonus, Demetrius Poliorcetes, and the rest? Why should he be given forty verses, or more, of a book which barely squints at the Persian kings, and never gives but a glimmering intimation that the Roman fleets and legions were to become in his time the masters of the world? Why should a vision predicting with such accuracy and detail the campaigns of the kings of the North and the South never allude to that unequalled family of heroes who were to begin at Modin the liberation of God's people and scatter like the leaves of Vallombrosa the numerous and frequent hosts of deadly enemies who were to desolate the homes and attempt to suppress the religion of that Jehovah in whose name the prophet spoke? Why above all was his detailed vision to cease with the renovation of the temple and fade off into dim outlines when it passed beyond that time into the more distant vistas but the more glorious hopes of the Messianic kingdom? Why especially should he describe the true course of events in Epiphanes' expedition against Egypt till the year 169 and then picture another campaign which according to the critics never occurred at all?

These and similar questions have vexed the righteous souls of many who would like to believe in the real Daniel and who have no prejudices against the possibility of the kind of predictive prophecy alleged to be found in the book. They can accept the first six chapters which record the striking occurrences in the lives of Daniel and his companions. They can accept the principle of the possibility and the fact of divine revelation of future events. But they hesitate at accepting the whole, at least, of Daniel, because they see no good and sufficient reason why he should have narrated with such length and clearness the history of the Seleucids up to the death of Epiphanes and have given so much emphasis to the deeds of this tyrant while barely mentioning such superlatively and relatively important events as the resurrection, the judgment, and the kingdom of the Messiah.

Now, in order to remove this hesitation, it may seem to some sufficient to affirm our belief that these predictions might have been made by God through Daniel, even though we could perceive no good reason for them. We think, however, that we can perceive a good and sufficient reason for them, one at least that justifies them in our estimation, and we shall proceed to state it, in order that if possible we may make the ways of God appear just to the men of little faith.

It appears to us, then, that the persecution of Antiochus Epiphanes was one of the most important events in the history of the church. It can be rivalled only by the call of Abraham, the giving of the Law, the Captivity, and the Incarnation. Among all the crises to which the people of God have been subjected, it can be compared only with the dispersion in the time of Nebuchadnezzar. The return of the exiles had been definitely foretold by Jeremiah, and Jeremiah's prediction was known and pondered by Daniel.[44] He was not needed, nor was it given to him, to supplement the work of his great predecessor. But he performed a greater and more lasting service for the church. He showed clearly that all the tyrants of the earth were under the control of the God of heaven, that the kingdoms of this world were foreordained by Him and should at last be superseded by the Kingdom of the Messiah and his saints, and he encouraged the people not merely of his own time but of all time to be steadfast in the midst of fiery trials and deadly perils of all kinds in view of the certainty that God could and would eventually circumvent or crush the tyrants and deliver the innocent for time and for eternity.

Now, the deadliest peril that the church has ever confronted was the attempt of Antiochus Epiphanes to suppress it utterly. For reasons of state, and perhaps also of religion, he determined to enforce conformity of worship throughout his dominions. His plan of operations was the most astute that has ever been devised. He ordered the cessation of circumcision, the sign of the covenant between the people and their God and that which held them together as a race. He stopped the services in the temple and instituted in their stead the worship of Jupiter. He set up idol altars in every city and demanded that every Jew should sacrifice according to the heathen ritual which he had introduced. He commanded that the

[44] See Dan. ix, 2.

holy writings should be destroyed so that the laws and customs and institutions might be gradually but surely forgotten and eliminated. And for all who refused to accept these severe and stringent regulations and requirements he pronounced the penalty of death; whereas he crowned with honours and emoluments all who apostatized and renounced the God of their fathers. The result of his well calculated machinations was almost complete enough to equal the most sanguine expectations. Most of the Jewish people seem to have cast away without any apparent qualm the hereditary claims of race and country and religion, and to have grasped with eagerness the proffered hand of the subtle enemy of their faith. The blood-thirsty tyrant executed his threats of death upon all who opposed his will. Men, women, and children were ruthlessly slaughtered. Whole families were extirpated for the guilt of one of their number. The chosen people were on the point of being annihilated and the promises and the hopes of the covenant of being annulled for ever.

There never was, before or since, such a period of desperation and despondency in the history of the church. Pharaoh's aim had been to destroy the race, but the promise to Abraham had been fulfilled through Moses and Joshua. Nebuchadnezzar had carried the people captive and destroyed Jerusalem and the temple; but the sacred books had been preserved, apostasy was rare, and through God's servants, the kings of Persia, the people and the temple were at length restored to their former worship, as it had been foretold by the prophets. But, now, under Epiphanes, was attempted what had never been proposed by Babylonian conqueror or Persian friends, the entire destruction of people and religion at one fell blow. Prophecy had ceased. The tribes of Israel were scattered over the earth, some foreign cities like Alexandria and Antioch having more Jewish inhabitants than Jerusalem. The Holy Land was largely in possession of the Gentiles. The Jews themselves had become indifferent to the Law. The High Priests were murdering each other and one of them when deposed at Jerusalem built a rival temple in Egypt. The whole polity of the Jews was disintegrated, all their fortresses and cities were in the hands of the enemy, they had no army and no leaders, and all seemed lost.

Then it was that one man stood up and defied the haughty king. His name was Mattathias. He lived at a village named Modin. The heathen had constructed an altar. The priest was ready to sacrifice the victim, when Mattathias slew him and made a fiery appeal to his fellow citizens to take arms against the tyrant. To hearten them, he called to mind the great deeds of their fathers and the faith that had inspired them. In the climax of his speech he referred to the fiery furnace and to Daniel in the den of lions. This recalled to them that their God could and would save those who put their trust in Him. They rallied round Mattathias and his five noble sons, the most valiant and able of them all. The pious sprang to arms and after many a hard fought fight the Syrians were overcome and the kingdom of the Jews was reëstablished under the Asmonean rulers. Had the attempt of Antiochus succeeded, the preparation for the coming of the Messiah could not have been completed. A people waiting for his appearing would not have been existent. A Diaspora eager to receive and disseminate the gospel would not have been ready. In short, the continuity of the church would have been destroyed, the records of the Old Testament might have disappeared as utterly as the archives of Tyre and the memoirs of Hannibal, the New Testament could not have been written, the life of Jesus would have been entirely different, the method of the early propagation of the gospel must have been altered and the whole plan of salvation changed.

But, it will be said, how did the time when these alleged predictions of Daniel were written affect all this? Only in this respect, that it affords sufficient reason for their having been made so many years before. Just as the deliverance of the three children from the fiery furnace and of Daniel from the lions' den on account of their faith in Israel's God gave Mattathias a fitting climax in his speech inciting the people to steadfastness in their trials, so the knowledge that their evil condition had been foretold nearly four hundred years before would strengthen the hearers' confidence that the rest of the prediction would be fulfilled in the overthrow of the oppressor and in the ultimate triumph of the kingdom of God. The stupendous crisis justified the prediction; the prediction justified the expectation of deliverance. Because the hearers of Mattathias knew about the three children and Daniel, they were incited by Mattathias' speech to emulate their conduct and to imitate their faith. Because the learned leaders of the Jews believed that the visions were really those of Daniel, they accepted the book as true and received it as canonical. Had the history been fictitious, Mattathias would not have cited from it and the people would not have been roused by it. Had the visions not been considered genuine, the educated church of that day would not have acknowledged the book as holy and its teachings as divine. Had the book not been deemed authentic, it would have been condemned as a forgery and would have failed in that purpose of consolation and encouragement to which all critics ascribe the reason of its existence. Because both people and rulers and literati esteemed the book to be authentic, genuine, and veracious, they placed it among those holy writing for whose preservation they willingly gave up their lives.

No other satisfactory explanation of the canonization and influence of Daniel has ever been given. The theories that the Jews received into their canon all of their national literature, or all that was written in their own language, or all that was religious in character, all break down in view of the Book of Ecclesiasticus alone; for it was written in Hebrew and is exceedingly religious and nationalistic. It is impossible also to see why First Maccabees and Tobit and the first and third sections of Enoch should have been rejected on the ground of not possessing these qualifications. Moreover, Jubilees, Judith, and the Testimony of the Twelve Patriarchs are religious and nationalistic in an eminent degree. We are shut up, therefore, to the conclusion that the sharp-witted and intensely conscientious Jews of the second century B.C., who determined the limits of the canon, investigated thoroughly the origin, purpose, and contents, of the books which they accepted as authoritative as a rule of faith and practice, and that Daniel, if a forgery, could not have escaped detection and rejection when subjected to their intelligent and searching scrutiny.

It is utterly irrelevant to assert that there were many "pious frauds" that were put forth during the second century B.C. and later, and that consequently Daniel must have been a fraud. There are three inadmissible assumptions in this proposition.

1. It is assumed that the proof that one document is a forgery, or fraud, or fiction, shows that another is of the same character. You might as well assume that all coins are counterfeit because some are. You might as well assume that Polybius was a liar as he asserts that Ephorus and Timæus were; that Cicero's and Pliny's letters were not authentic, because the epistles of Phalaris have been demonstrated by Bentley to have been written 500 years after Phalaris was dead; that all the tragedies of Euripides were falsely ascribed to him, because some are acknowledged to have been written by other and unknown authors; that the four canonical gospels were identical in origin with the gospel of Peter and those of the Infancy; that the lives of Augustine and Jerome were of the same character as those of St. Anthony and St. Christopher; that the decrees of Constantine, Theodosius, and Charlemagne in favour of the papacy were forged because the decretals of Isodore are false; that all parts of Ashurbanipal's Annals are unreliable because some parts certainly are; that Cæsar's Commentaries on the Gallic War are spurious because his Commentaries on the Civil War may be. In short the argument is absurd. For counterfeits involve the existence of the genuine; forgeries presuppose similar documents that are authentic; fictions are but the shadows of verisimilitude. The Jewish religious authorities accepted the Book of Daniel because they believed it to be authentic, genuine, and true. They rejected Tobit, Judith, Enoch, Jubilees, The Testaments of the Twelve Patriarchs, and the other apocryphal and pseudepigraphical writings, because in their judgment they were lacking in one or more of these features.

It may be attempted to escape this judgment by affirming that the Jews who accepted Daniel as canonical were deceived, or befooled, so that they decided wrongly with reference to this particular book. But this affirmation cannot be established as true. For the Jews who made the decision were living and present at the very time when the critics allege that Daniel was written and when the events described in the eleventh chapter, upon which the allegation is based, were enacted. Many of them had taken part in the glorious conflict for freedom and religion, and could no more be deceived as to what had happened than could the common soldiers of the Grand Army of the Republic who participated in the campaigns of Meade or Grant be deceived about the results of Gettysburg and Appomattox. As to the customs, they certainly would recognize anachronisms, incongruities, and inconsistencies better than we can do to-day after two thousand years have passed. As to the languages also, it is passing strange, if they contain so many marks of Hebrew and Aramaic of Maccabean times as the critics claim, that the Hebrew purists did not recognize the anachronisms; and, on the other hand, if the book were designed for a stimulus to the common people, how does it come to contain so many uncommon words and so many difficult constructions as to have rendered it largely "unintelligible" (to use Bevan's word) to the Hebrews who, shortly after it was written (if we accept the critics' date), translated it into Greek. It must have been hard to fool a people as to what was good Hebrew in the age that produced the Ben Siras, for the grandfather certainly knew how to write good Hebrew, unadulterated with foreign words and clear in its rhetoric and grammar; and the grandson knew both Hebrew and Greek well enough to make a magnificent version of his grandfather's work. As to the Aramaic portions of the book, if they were, as Bevan suggests to be probable, a version of the original Hebrew by the author himself, the decision as to the date of the original would be made regardless of the peculiarities of the Aramaic version. If, however, the Aramaic was the original, it seems hard to account for the use, in a work designed to comfort the people, of so many words that must have been unintelligible to them; for there is no proof in favour of, and the analogies are all against, the probability of the presence of so many Babylonian and Persian words in an Aramaic composition of the second century B.C.[45] To say that the author, like

---

[45] See the writer's article on "Babylon and Israel" in the *Presbyterian and Reformed Review* for April 1903, pp. 239 f.

another Chatterton, had dived into the records of the past and drawn from them a number of antique expressions in order to give credence to his forgery and to deceive his readers, breaks down because of three considerations: (1) a scholar with learning enough to investigate such ancient documents in order to give an antique colouring to his writings would certainly have used the antique spelling and pronouns, whose absence from Daniel is the strongest objective argument against its early date; (2) he would have used the eastern forms of the verb, if, as the critics affirm, those eastern forms were different from those of Palestine; and (3) he could hardly have known so much of the character of the ancient documents without having more knowledge of the times in which they were written than the critics ascribe to him.

3. There remains, then, only the hypothesis that the writer of the book and those who accepted it as true were united in an endeavour to impose upon the common people. The chief objection to this hypothesis is that there is not a single item of evidence in its favour. It is absurd to suppose that men who were willingly giving up their lives for the preservation of their holy writings from destruction would have been participants in a fraud to perpetuate the Book of Daniel as one of their holy writings. But since such general charges of fraud without specifications and proofs are beneath the notice of a sober, scientific, historian, we leave the consideration of the charge of fraud until such time as the critics advance a specific charge with alleged proofs in its behalf. The investigation and arraignment of unexpressed motives and plausible possibilities are hereby relegated to the speculative philosopher and the examiner of psychological phenomena; the undeniable fact is that history knows nothing of the alleged composition and publication and canonization of the Book of Daniel in the Maccabean age. When it first emerged into historic view, it was already stamped with the same authority as the other books of the Old Testament. Its authenticity, genuineness, and veracity, have never been denied except by those who have disbelieved in miracle and predictive prophecy and by some weak-kneed Jews and Christians of these later de-

cades who have thought that they were scientific when they were merely blind followers of the blind. Scientific? This word implies knowledge. And where did they get their knowledge? Let the critics produce it. Where are their facts in evidence? The great jury of Christendom demand that they be produced. History and philology and archæology, have been searched for centuries and they have failed to present a single fact of direct evidence in support of the critics' positions. The time is past when a German professor can pound his desk and overawe his submissive students with the shout, "Meine Herren, es ist unmöglich," or "Es ist ganz selbstverständlich."

We Christians demand some facts to prove that the Book of Daniel is false before we will admit the charge from any man. We still believe that Christ and the Apostles and the Maccabean and Rabbinical Jews knew more about the origin and veracity and authority of Daniel than the critics do or can know. The vociferous and continuous cry of "all scholars agree" has weight only with those who are ignorant of what these scholars really know. As a fact, they know very little about Daniel, or any other Old Testament book, except what the book testifies as to itself. Against this first hand and direct testimony they put forth a host of conjectures and opinions and ask the world to accept them as the testimony of science and scholarship. They set up their golden calves of what they call history and criticism and cry out: These be thy gods, O Israel, which brought thee out of the land of Egypt, out of the house of bondage. They make a golden image of their own reason and imagination and command that all men shall bow down and do homage, in pain of being cast into the fiery furnace of their professional contempt and branded as bigots and ignoramuses. But the church of Christ will never bow down to this image, and God will deliver it from all evil and in the fiery furnace of the world's criticism there will always be one like unto the Son of God to save it from all its foes. In the case of Daniel, Daniel is with us and Christ is with us. *Caveat criticus!*

INDICES

GENERAL

Abstinence of Daniel, 248-252
Ahura Mazda, 125, 127
Alexander the Great, 90, 105
Alexandrinus, Codex, see "Greek MSS"
Almsgiving, 247-248
Amashaspand, 128
Amesha Spenta, 125
Amphilochius on Canon, 26; on Divisions of O.T., 40
Angelology among Persians, 127ff.; Assyrio-Babylonians, 129; Daniel, 130; Daniel Compared w. other literature, 142; Conclusions regarding, 151, 154, 166, 189, 191
Antiochus Epiphanes, 90, 270-276
Apocalypses, of Jubilees, 108; of Twelve Patriarchs, 108; of Baruch, 109f.; of Sibylline Oracles, 109f.; of Enoch, 109; of Assumption of Moses, 110; of Ascension of Isaiah, 111; of iv. Esdras, 112; of New Testament, 112; of Revelation, 113
Apocalypses and Date of Daniel, 101; found in Daniel, 103; in profane literature, 104; Daniel's form not common in second century B.C., 108; nor after 100 B.C., 110
Apostolic Canons, on O.T. Canon, 28; on Divisions of O.T., 40
Arabian Nights, 245
Aramaic Documents of Elephantine, 175
Aristobulus, 66
Armenian Version, evidence on Canon, 23
Ashurbanipal, 104, 106
Assyrio-Babylonian belief in heavenly messengers, 107, 129; doctrine of Resurrection, 124; of Judgment, 127
Astyages, 260
Athanasius on Canon, 24; on Divisions of O.T., 40
Augustine on Canon, 29; on Divisions of O.T., 41; also 57-58
Avesta MSS on Resurrection, 125

Baba Bathra, 39, 41
Barhebraeus on Canon, 31
Basiliano-Venetus, Codex, see "Greek MSS"
Belshazzar, 262
Belshumishkun, 262
Ben Sira the Elder, Silence on Daniel, 76; Silence on Ezra and Mordecai, 79; Possible reference to Daniel, 82; Reasons for silence on Daniel, 83; Judgment as to fame, 87; opinions of dreams, 88
Bertholdt, 235
Bevan, A. A., on Daniel, 10, 59, 65, 68, 73; on Silence regarding Daniel, 159; on Ezekiel, 234; cf., 265
Book of Life, 229
Breasted, J. H., on Resurrection, 124
Büchler on Haphtaroth, 34, 59
Budde, K., on meaning of "defile the hands," 50f.

Callinicus, 236
Cambyses, 263
Canon of O.T., Evidence on Divisions, Number and Order of Books, 14-32; Evidence on use of Books, 32-35
Canon of Prophets, 44f.
Canons of Laodicea, on Canon, 27f.; on Divisions of O.T., 40
Carthage, Council of, on Canon, 31; on Divisions of O. T., 41
Cassiodorus on Canon, 30; on Divisions of O.T., 41; on Jerome in Institutio, 29, 41.
Charles, R. H., on Apocalypses of Daniel, 162; on Fasting of Daniel, 246
Circumcision, 253f.
Claromontanus, Codex, on Canon, 31; on Divisions of O.T., 41
Cod. Barocc. on Canon, 28; on Divisions of O.T., 41

Cornill, C. H., on Date of Daniel, 11; on Testimony of N.T., 46; on Doctrines of Daniel, 121; on Silence regarding Daniel, 159; on Job, 234; on Daniel, 265

Cyaxares, 259, 263

Cyril of Jerusalem, on Canon, 25; on Divisions of O.T., 40

Cyrus Cylinder, 259

Daniel the man, referred to by Mattathias, 14, 91, 93; Josephus on, 16f., 96; Silence of Ben Sira, 92; References to in N.T., 94f.; Compared to Joseph, 98f.; Praying of, 241; Fasting of, 243

Daniel, Prayer of, paralleled by Hezekiah's, 105; paralleled in profane literature, 105

Darius the Mede, 258, 264

"Defile the hands," meaning of, 50

Diodorus, 237

Driver, S. R., on Daniel, 9, 10; on internal evidence, 42; on Testimony of N.T., 45f., 48; on Silence of Ecclus., 77f.; on Daniel the man, 89; on Daniel and Joseph, 98; on Doctrines of Daniel, 121, 154, 159; on Genuineness of Isaiah, 171f.

Ebedyesu on Canon, 28; on Divisions of Canon, 40

Egyptian idea of Resurrection, 124; of judgment, 127

Elephants, 254

Epiphanius on Canon, 25; on Divisions of O.T., 40

Ethiopic Bible, on Order of books, 32

Farrar, F. W., on Silence concerning Daniel, 159

Fasting of Daniel, 243

Gabriel, 131

Gathas, 128

"Genaz," meaning of, 50

Gesenius, W., 235

Greek MSS, Evidence on Canon, 22f.; on Divisions of O.T., 39

Gregory of Nazianzus on Canon, 25f.; on Divisions of O.T., 40

Gubaru, 260, 263

Gyges, 104

Haphtaroth, Evidence on Canon, 21; Blessings before and after, 32; Selections now in use, 33; used by Karaites, etc., 34; indicated in N.T., 34; on Daniel, 59

Harclensian Syriac on Canon, 23

Haupt, P., on Nahum, 177

Herodotus, 105

Hexaplaric Syriac on Canon, 23

Hilary on Canon, 28; on Divisions of O.T., 41

Innocent I., on Canon, 30; on Divisions of O.T., 41

Institutio of Cassiodorus, on Jerome and O.T., 29, 41

Iranian, Old, Idea of Resurrection, 124; of Judgment, 127; Angelology, 128

Ishtar, 104, 106; Descent of, 130

Isidorus on Canon, 30; on Divisions of O.T., 41

Itala, Evidence on Canon, 24

Jaddua, High Priest, 90, 105

Jamnia, Council of, 47, 50

Jerome on Canon, 29; on Divisions of O.T., 41; on Daniel among the prophets, 49

John of Damascus on Canon, 27; on Divisions of O.T., 40

Joseph, Compared with Daniel, 98

Josephus on Canon, 16; on Daniel the man, 16f., 90f., 96; on Divisions of O.T., 38f.; on Canon of Prophets, 44f.; on Judgment, 138; on Resurrection, 196; importance as historian, 236ff.

Judgment to come, Idea of, 127; References to in ancient literature, 135; Conclusions regarding, 150, 154, 196

Junilius on Canon, 26; on Divisions of O.T., 40, 58

Laodicea, Canons of, see "Canons of L."

Leontius on Canon, 27; on Divisions of O.T., 40

Law, the, in Maccabees and Daniel, 252

Liber Sacramentorum on Canon, 31; on Divisions of O.T., 41

Marduk, 105, 124

Index

283

Massoretic notes, evidence on Canon, 57

Mattathias on O.T. heroes, 14, 52, 93, 275

Mazdaism, 128

Melito on Canon, 17f.; on order of Pentateuch, 36; on Divisions of O.T., 39, 40; on Canon of Prophets, 49

Messiah, Idea of, 131ff.; Not found among Babylonians or Iranians, 131; Zoroastrian, 132; in Daniel and other literature, 138; conclusions regarding, 150, 154, 198, 211f.

Messiah, Names and Titles of in O.T., 200; in Apoc. literature, 201; in N.T., 203

Method of investigation, 10

Michael, 131

Milton, 169

Minor Prophets, citations of compared with Daniel, 73

Mishna on Canon, 20

Mommsen, T., on Canon, 30; on Divisions of O.T., 41

Monophysites on Canon of O.T., 31

Mordecai not mentioned by Ben Sira, 79f.

Nabopolassar, 129

Nabunaid, 105, 107, 261, 262

Nebuchadnezzar, 251

Nergal and Erishkigal, 129

Neriglissar, 262

Nestorians on Canon, 31

New Testament on Canon, 15; Haphtara indicated in, 34; Apocalypses of, 112; on Resurrection, 135; on Judgment, 137; on Messiah, 141; on Angels, 149, 188, 190

Nicephorus on Canon, 27; on Divisions of O.T., 40

Old Testament, Order of Books in, 37; Doctrine of Judgment, 127; References to judgment, 135; on Messiah, 139, 198; on Angels, 143, 192; Traces of Daniel's influence, 163f.; on Resurrection, 133, 195; on Judgment, 197

Origen on Canon, 24; on Divisions of O.T., 39, 40, 49

Palimpsesta Vaticana, Fragmenta, see "Itala"

Pentateuch, order of books in, 35f.; critical reconstruction of, 36

Peshito on order of Books, 31

Phalanx, 254

Philo on Therapeutae and Canon, 15; on Divisions of O.T., 38; on Canon of prophets, 46; on Judgment, 138, 187

"Pleasant Land," meaning of phrase in Enoch and Daniel, 226

Polybius, 268

Porphyry, 9, 116, 235

Praying of Daniel, 241f.

"Priest's Codex" (P) and influence of Daniel, 173

Prince, J. D., on Daniel, 11, 79, 82, 266; on Silence of Ecclus. regarding Daniel, 77; on Apocalypses, 102; on Doctrines of Daniel, 121, 129

Prologus Galeatus on Canon, 29

Prophets, Canon of, 44ff.

Pseudo-Athanasius on Canon, 24; on Divisions of O.T., 40

Pseudo-Chrysostom on Canon, 26; on Divisions of O.T., 40

Pseudo-Gelasius on Canon, 30; on Divisions of O.T., 41

Pyramid Texts, 127

Resurrection, Idea of, 124; among ancient Egyptians, 124; among ancient Babylonians, 124; among ancient Iranians, 124; in O.T., 126f.; Daniel compared w. other literature, 132f.; conclusions regarding, 149, 152, 194

Rolls, O.T. written on, 61

Rufinus on Canon, 29; on Divisions of O.T., 41

Sabbath, 253f.

Saosyant, 125f.

Sealing of Documents, 255

Simon, mentioned by Ben Sira, 86

Sinaiticus, Codex, see "Greek MSS"

Stutgardiana, Fragmenta, see "Itala"

Synopsis of Lagarde on Canon, 26; on Divisions of O.T., 40

Talmud on Canon, 18

Theodore of Mopsuestia, on Books of O.T., 31
Therapeutae on Canon, 15; on Divisions of O.T., 38, 48

Vaticanus, Codex, *see* "Greek MSS"
Visions, use of by prophets, 105f.

Weingartensia, Fragmenta, *see* "Itala"
Wellhausen School, theory on Pentateuch, 36

Wirceburgensia, Fragmenta, *see* "Itala"

Xerxes, 105

Yashts, 128

Zoroaster, 127
Zoroastrianism, Early, on Resurrection, 124-125; on Judgment to come, 127; on Angels, 128-129; on Messiah, 132

BIBLICAL

Deuteronomy xxxii. 8; 68, 191

Ruth, Book of, disputed at Jamnia, 52

Chronicles, Book of, Silence regarding Daniel, 67f.; and influence of Daniel, 164

Ezra, Book of, Silence on Daniel, 68; not mentioned by Ben Sira, 79; Possible reference to in Ben Sira, 85; and influence of Daniel, 164

Nehemiah, Book of, and influence of Daniel, 164
Nehemiah ix., 68, 120

Esther, Book of, Silence on Daniel, 67; and influence of Daniel, 164

Job, Book of, Possible reference to in Ben Sira, 86
Job xvi. 13 and xix. 25; 126

Psalms, Book of, and Ideas of Daniel, 175

Proverbs, Book of, disputed at Jamnia, 52; and influence of Daniel, 174

Ecclesiastes, Book of, and Ideas of Daniel, 176

Song of Songs, and influence of Daniel, 174

Isaiah, Book of, Citations of, 70; Citations of, analyzed, 72; and influence of Daniel, 167; critic's treatment of, 167ff.

Isaiah xxiv.-xxvii., 167ff.; lxi. 1; 35; lxi. 2, 3; 71

Jeremiah, Book of, Citations compared with Daniel's, 72; Value of citations, 73

Ezekiel, Book of, disputed at Jamnia, 52; and Daniel, 69; citations of compared with Daniel, 73; Testimony to Daniel, 233
Ezekiel xiv. 14, 20 and xxviii. 3; 69

Daniel, Book of, and the Canon, 9-64; Charge stated, 65; Assumptions of critics, 12; Admissions of critics, 12f.; Evidence presented, 13ff.; Evidence discussed, 35ff.; and the Canon of the prophets, 44-62; Conclusions, 62-64
——, Not Quoted, 65-75; Charge stated, 65; Assumptions of critics, 65; Discussion of Assumptions, 66ff.; Comparison with citations of prophets, 72
——, Silence of Ecclesiasticus concerning, 76-100; Charge stated, 77; Assumptions of critics, 78; Discussion of Assumptions, 79ff.; Conclusions, 100
——, Apocalypses and, 101-116; Charge stated, 101; Assumptions of critics, 102; Discussion of Assumptions, 103ff.
——, Origin of Ideas of, 117-156; Erroneous claims discussed, 117; Objections of critics, 121; Assumptions of critics, 122; Regarding antiquity of ideas, 124; re-

garding Daniel and Enoch, 132; Special conclusions, 149; General conclusions, 153
——, Influence of, 157-232; Objections of Critics, 159; Assumptions of Critics, 160; Answers to Assumptions, 160; Argument from Silence, 160; Influence before 200 B.C., 162; up to 135 A.D., 175; Comparative study of influence, 188; Conclusions, 215; Approximation of Daniel and Enoch, 223
——, The Background of, 233-257; Testimony of Josephus, 236; Alleged evidence of late date, 241; Positive evidence of early date, 252ff.
——, The Prophecies of, 258-280; The Fourth Kingdom, 258; Second Kingdom not Median, 260; Darkness and Light in Daniel's predictions, 264; Importance of Antiochus Epiphanes, 270

Daniel, Book of, Not disputed at Jamnia, 47; Aramaic part defiles hands, 51; Possible reference in Ben Sira, 82f.; on Angels, 142
Daniel vi., 1; 258; ix., 1; 259; ix., 24, 25; 161; xi., 16, 41, 45; 227; xii., 4, 9; 161
Joel, Book of, and Influence of Daniel, 174
Jonah, Book of, Disputed at Jamnia, 52; and influence of Daniel, 166

Nahum, Book of, and Ideas of Daniel, 177

Haggai, Book of, Possible traces of Daniel's influence, 163

Zechariah, Book of, Possible traces of Daniel's influence, 163

Malachi, Book of, Traces of Daniel's Influence, 164
Matthew xxiv., 15; 15, 45

Luke iv., 17; 34; xxiv., 27; 15; xxiv., 44; 38, 45

John xv., 25; 15

Acts xiii., 14, 15, 27; 35

Hebrews, Epistle to, on Daniel, 95
Hebrews xi., 37; 56

Revelation of St. John, Apocalypse of, 113

APOCRYPHA AND PSEUDEPIGRAPHA

Ahikar, Aramaic fragments of, 66, 74, 157f., 175
Apocalypse of Baruch, on Angels, 149, 185, 190; on Resurrection, 196
Aristeas, Epistle of, 53, 66, 72, 74, 175
Ascension of Isaiah, on Canon, 17, 56; Apocalypse of, 111; Cf., 186
Assumption of Moses, Apocalypse of, 110; on Resurrection, 135; on Judgment, 137; on Messiah, 142; on Angels, 148, 185

Baruch, Book of, Apocalyptic not like Daniel, 109; Apocalypse of, 110; on Resurrection, 134; on Judgment, 137; on Angels, 146, 180
II. Baruch on Judgment, 138
Bel and the Dragon, on Angels, 146, 183

Ben Sira the Elder, on Canon, 14; on Divisions of O.T., 53ff.; on Isaiah, 71; References to Prophets, 81; References to Israelite Heroes, 84; on Daniel the man, 89; on the Resurrection, 134; on Messiah, 141; on Angels, 146, 175, 179 (Cf. also in General Index)
Ben Sira the Younger, on Canon, 14; on Divisions of O.T., 38, 48; on Ben Sira and the Prophets, 92

Daniel, Additions to Book of, on Resurrection, 134; on Judgment, 137, 180

Eagle Vision, Form of, 112; on Resurrection, 135; on Judgment, 138; on Messiah, 141; on Angels, 148, 187

Ecclesiasticus, *see* "Ben Sira the Elder"

Enoch, Book of, 74; Alleged resemblance to Daniel, 109; Apocalypses of, 110; on Resurrection, 132f., 195; on Judgment, 136f., 198; on Messiah, 140; on Angels, 145f., 180, 184, 190; Ideas of compared with Daniel, 223

IV. Esdras on Canon, 17; Apocalypse of, 112, 186; on Angels, 190; on Resurrection, 196

Esther, Addenda to Book of, on Resurrection, 134; on Judgment, 137; on Angels, 146, 180

Ezra Apocalypse, 112; on Resurrection, 135; on Judgment, 138; on Messiah, 142; on Angels, 148, 186

Ezra Legend, 112

Ezra Piece on Resurrection, 135; on Judgment, 138; on Messiah, 141; on Angels, 148, 187

Isaiah, Martyrdom of, on Canon, 56; on Resurrection, 135; on Judgment, 138; on Messiah, 142; on Angels, 148, 185

Jeremiah, Epistle of, 74; on Resurrection, 134; on Judgment, 137; on Angels, 146, 183

Jubilees, Book of, 66; visions of, 108; Apocalypse of, 108; on Resurrection, 133; on Judgment, 137; on Messiah, 140; on Angels, 144, 182, 190

Judith, Book of, on Resurrection, 134; on Judgment, 137; on Messiah, 141; on Angels, 147, 180

I. Maccabees on Canon, 14, 52, 93; on Resurrection, 134; on Judgment, 137; on Messiah, 141; on Angels, 147, 180; on Unclean foods, 249

II. Maccabees on Canon, 15, 55; on Divisions of O.T., 38; on Resurrection, 134; on Judgment, 137; on Messiah, 141; on Angels, 147, 183

III. Maccabees on Resurrection, 134f.; on Judgment, 137; on Messiah, 141; on Angels, 147

IV. Maccabees on Resurrection, 134; on Judgment, 137; on Messiah, 141; on Angels, 147, 183

Noah, Book of, on Resurrection, 133; on Judgment, 136; on Messiah, 140; on Angels, 144, 180, 190

Prayer of Manasseh on Angels, 147

Psalms of Solomon, on Resurrection, 135; on Messiah, 141; on Angels, 147, 183

Salathiel Apocalypse, 112; on Resurrection, 135; on Judgment, 138; on Messiah, 142; on Angels, 149, 187

Sibylline Oracles not like Daniel, 109; Apocalypse of 110; on Resurrection, 134; on Judgment, 137; on Messiah, 140; on Angels, 144, 182

Son of Man Vision, 112; on Resurrection, 135; on Judgment, 138; on Messiah, 141; on Angels, 148, 186

Song of the Three Children, on Angels, 146, 183

Susannah on Angels, 146, 183

Testament of Hezekiah, form of, 111; on Resurrection, 135; on Judgment, 137; on Messiah, 141; on Angels, 148, 190

Timothy and Aquila, Dialogue of, on Canon, 26; on Divisions of O.T., 40

Tobit, Book of, on Resurrection, 134; on Judgment, 137; on Messiah, 141; on Angels, 146, 190; on Ideas of Daniel, 175; Fasting of, 246

Twelve Patriarchs, Testaments of, 66; visions of, 108; on Resurrection, 133, 196; on Judgment, 198; on Messiah, 140; on Angels, 144, 181, 190, 246

Vision of Isaiah, form of, 111; on Resurrection, 135, 196; on Judgment, 137; on Messiah, 141; on Angels, 148, 185, 190

Wisdom of Solomon, on Resurrection, 134; on Judgment, 137; on Messiah, 141; on Angels, 147, 180

Zadokite Fragments, on Resurrection, 135; on Judgment, 138; on Messiah, 142; on Angels, 148, 187

Zerubbabel, Story of, on Resurrection, 134; on Judgment, 137; on Angels, 147, 183